Daniel

Understanding the Bible Commentary Series

GENERAL EDITORS

W. Ward Gasque
Robert L. Hubbard Jr.
Robert K. Johnston

Daniel

William B. Nelson

a division of Baker Publishing Group
Grand Rapids, Michigan

To my wonderful daughters, Jennifer and Amanda,
who were patient and understanding
when I had to be away in the library
writing this commentary

Ps. 19:7–11, 3 Jn. 4

© 2012 by William B. Nelson

Published by Baker Books
a division of Baker Publishing Group
P.O. Box 6287, Grand Rapids, MI 49516-6287
www.bakerbooks.com

All rights reserved. No part of this publication may be reproduced, stored in a retrieval system, or transmitted in any form or by any means—for example, electronic, photocopy, recording—without the prior written permission of the publisher. The only exception is brief quotations in printed reviews.

Library of Congress Cataloging-in-Publication Data
Nelson, William (William B.)
    Daniel / William Nelson.
        p. cm. — (Understanding the Bible commentary series)
    Includes bibliographical references and indexes.
    ISBN 978-0-8010-4834-0 (pbk.)
    1. Bible. O.T. Daniel—Commentaries. I. Title.
BS1555.53.N45 2013
224'.507—dc23   2012028376

Unless otherwise indicated, Scripture quotations are from the Holy Bible, New International Version®. NIV®. Copyright © 1973, 1978, 1984 by Biblica, Inc.™ Used by permission of Zondervan. All rights reserved worldwide. www.zondervan.com

Scripture quotations labeled NRSV are from the New Revised Standard Version of the Bible, copyright © 1989, by the Division of Christian Education of the National Council of the Churches of Christ in the United States of America. Used by permission. All rights reserved.

Scripture quotations labeled RSV are from the Revised Standard Version of the Bible, copyright 1952 [2nd edition, 1971] by the Division of Christian Education of the National Council of the Churches of Christ in the United States of America. Used by permission. All rights reserved.

12 13 14 15 16 17 18   7 6 5 4 3 2 1

Table of Contents

Foreword vii

Abbreviations ix

Introduction 1

§1 Daniel and His Three Friends Avoid Defilement
    (Dan. 1:1–21) 53
§2 Daniel Interprets Nebuchadnezzar's Dream
    (Dan. 2:1–49) 76
§3 The Gold Image and the Blazing Furnace
    (Dan. 3:1–30) 103
§4 The King Becomes a Beast-Man and Then Recovers
    (Dan. 4:1–37) 121
§5 The Writing on the Wall (Dan. 5:1–31) 145
§6 The Lions' Pit (Dan. 6:1–28) 161
§7 The Four Beastly Kingdoms and God's Kingdom
    (Dan. 7:1–28) 178
§8 The Vision of the Ram and the Male Goat
    (Dan. 8:1–27) 197
§9 Daniel's Prayer and the Seventy Weeks
    (Dan. 9:1–27) 220
§10 The Final Revelation: Prologue (Dan. 10:1–11:2a) 246
§11 The Final Revelation: The Body (Dan. 11:2b–12:4) 269
§12 The Final Revelation: Epilogue (Dan. 12:5–13) 309

For Further Reading 317

Subject Index 322

Scripture Index 329

Foreword

As an ancient document, the Old Testament often seems something quite foreign to modern men and women. Opening its pages may feel, to the modern reader, like traversing a kind of literary time warp into a whole other world. In that world sisters and brothers marry, long hair mysteriously makes men superhuman, and temple altars daily smell of savory burning flesh and sweet incense. There, desert bushes burn but leave no ashes, water gushes from rocks, and cities fall because people march around them. A different world, indeed!

Even God, the Old Testament's main character, seems a stranger compared to his more familiar New Testament counterpart. Sometimes the divine is portrayed as a loving father and faithful friend, someone who rescues people from their greatest dangers or generously rewards them for heroic deeds. At other times, however, God resembles more a cruel despot, one furious at human failures, raving against enemies, and bloodthirsty for revenge. Thus, skittish about the Old Testament's diverse portrayal of God, some readers carefully select which portions of the text to study, or they avoid the Old Testament altogether.

The purpose of this commentary series is to help readers navigate this strange and sometimes forbidding literary and spiritual terrain. Its goal is to break down the barriers between the ancient and modern worlds so that the power and meaning of these biblical texts become transparent to contemporary readers. How is this to be done? And what sets this series apart from others currently on the market?

This commentary series will bypass several popular approaches to biblical interpretation. It will not follow a *precritical* approach that interprets the text without reference to recent scholarly conversations. Such a commentary contents itself with offering little more than a paraphrase of the text with occasional supplements from archaeology, word studies, and classical theology. It mistakenly believes that there have been few insights into the Bible since Calvin or Luther. Nor will this series pursue an *anticritical* approach whose preoccupation is to defend the Bible against its detractors, especially scholarly ones. Such a commentary has little space left to move beyond showing why the Bible's critics are wrong to explaining what the biblical text means. The result is a paucity of vibrant biblical theology. Again, this series finds inadequate a *critical* approach that seeks to understand the text apart from belief in the meaning it conveys. Though modern readers have been taught to be discerning, they do not want to live in the "desert of criticism" either.

Instead, as its editors, we have sought to align this series with what has been labeled *believing criticism*. This approach marries probing, reflective interpretation of the text to loyal biblical devotion and warm Christian affection. Our contributors tackle the task of interpretation using the full range of critical methodologies and practices. Yet they do so as people of faith who hold the text in the highest regard. The commentators in this series use criticism to bring the message of the biblical texts vividly to life so the minds of modern readers may be illumined and their faith deepened.

The authors in this series combine a firm commitment to modern scholarship with a similar commitment to the Bible's full authority for Christians. They bring to the task the highest technical skills, warm theological commitment, and rich insight from their various communities. In so doing, they hope to enrich the life of the academy as well as the life of the church.

Part of the richness of this commentary series derives from its authors' breadth of experience and ecclesial background. As editors, we have consciously brought together a diverse group of scholars in terms of age, gender, denominational affiliation, and race. We make no claim that they represent the full expression of the people of God, but they do bring fresh, broad perspectives to the interpretive task. But though this series has sought out diversity among its contributors, they also reflect a commitment to a common center. These commentators write as "believing critics"—scholars who desire to speak for church and academy, for academy and church. As editors, we offer this series in devotion to God and for the enrichment of God's people.

ROBERT L. HUBBARD JR.
ROBERT K. JOHNSTON
Editors

Abbreviations

AB	Anchor Bible
'Abod. Zar.	'Abodah Zarah
A.D.	anno Domini
ANEP	*The Ancient Near East in Pictures Relating to the Old Testament*. Edited by J. B. Pritchard. Princeton, 1954
ANET	*Ancient Near Eastern Texts Relating to the Old Testament*. Edited by J. B. Pritchard. Princeton, 1969
Ant.	Josephus, *Jewish Antiquities*
AOTC	Abingdon Old Testament Commentaries
Aram.	Aramaic
BASOR	*Bulletin of the American Schools of Oriental Research*
B.C.	before Christ
BDB	Brown, F., S. R. Driver, and C. A. Briggs, *A Hebrew and English Lexicon of the Old Testament*. Oxford, 1907
BHS	*Biblia Hebraica Stuttgartensia*. Edited by K. Elliger and W. Rudolph. Stuttgart, 1983
ca.	circa
CBQ	*Catholic Biblical Quarterly*
cent.	century
cf.	*confer*, compare
ch(s).	chapter(s)
col.	column
CTA	*Corpus des tablettes en cunéiformes alphabétiques découvertes à Ras Shamra-Ugarit de 1929 à 1939*. Edited by A. Herdner. Mission de Ras Shamra 10. Paris, 1963
DSS	Dead Sea Scrolls
e.g.	*exempli gratia,* for example
1 En.	1 Enoch
2 Esd.	2 Esdras
EvQ	*Evangelical Quarterly*
ExpTim	*Expository Times*
GBS	Grove Biblical Series
Gk.	Greek

GKC	*Gesenius' Hebrew Grammar.* Edited by E. Kautzsch. Translated by A. E. Cowley, 2nd ed. Oxford, 1910
HC	Hammurabi's Code
Heb.	Hebrew
hiph.	*hiphil*
Hist.	Herodotus, *Histories*; Polybius, *Histories*
HSM	Harvard Semitic Monographs
ICC	International Critical Commentary
i.e.	*id est,* that is
Interp	Interpretation
ITC	International Theological Commentary
JB	Jerusalem Bible
JBL	*Journal of Biblical Literature*
Jdt.	Judith
JETS	*Journal of the Evangelical Theological Society*
JNES	*Journal of Near Eastern Studies*
JSJSup	*Journal for the Study of Judaism*, Supplements
JTS	*Journal of Theological Studies*
J.W.	Josephus, *Jewish Wars*
KJV	King James Version
LCL	Loeb Classical Library
Lib.	Diodorus Siculus, *Library of History*
lit.	literally
LXX	Septuagint
MT	Masoretic Text
n.	note
NAB	New American Bible
NAC	New American Commentary
NEB	New English Bible
NIV	New International Version
NIVAC	NIV Application Commentary
no(s).	number(s)
NRSV	New Revised Standard Version
NT	New Testament
OT	Old Testament
OTL	Old Testament Library
p(p).	page(s)
pl.	plural
Pr. Azar.	Prayer of Azariah
4QPrNab	*Prayer of Nabonidus*
11QMelch	*Melchizedek*

RSV	Revised Standard Version
SBLDS	Society of Biblical Literature Dissertation Series
SBM	Stuttgarter biblische Monographien
sg.	singular
Sg. Three	Song of the Three Young Men
Sus.	Susanna
TDNT	*Theological Dictionary of the New Testament.* Edited by G. Kittel and G. Friedrich. Translated by G. W. Bromiley. 10 vols. Grand Rapids, 1964–1976
TDOT	*Theological Dictionary of the Old Testament.* Edited by G. J. Botterweck and H. Ringgren. Translated by J. T. Willis, G. W. Bromiley, and D. E. Green. 16 vols. Grand Rapids, 1974–
Them	*Themelios*
v(v).	verse(s)
vol(s).	volume(s)
VT	*Vetus Testamentum*
WBC	Word Biblical Commentary
Wis.	Wisdom of Solomon
ZA	*Zeitschrift für Assyriologie*
ZAW	*Zeitschrift für die alttestamentliche Wissenschaft*

Introduction

Traditionally, the book of Daniel has been understood to be both history and prophecy. Chapters 1–6 tell the story of Daniel and his friends, who were exiled to Babylon. Because the stories sound like history, the reader may assume that the information is historical fact and intended to be read as such. Chapters 7–12 (and to a certain extent chapter 2), on the other hand, have typically been read as prophecy. In light of modern scholarship, however, many commentators now consider the book—especially the second half (chs. 7–12)—to be a different kind of literature, a different genre, known as apocalyptic. Apocalyptic literature often includes historical details, and it is related to prophecy, but it has a different purpose: to emphasize in the midst of oppression that God is in control (see "Genre," below). Understanding the genre of Daniel and reading it as apocalyptic literature rather than as strictly history or prophecy will help the reader to understand the text better.

In addition to recognizing the genre of the book, the reader of Daniel needs to be familiar with the historical period covered by the book: the history of Israel from the exile in the sixth century B.C. to the Maccabean revolt in the second century B.C.[1] Ostensibly, the book is about one Daniel who was carried to Babylon in the time of the Babylonian king Nebuchadnezzar (1:1) and who remained there through the reign of Cyrus, king of Persia (1:21). To understand the book of Daniel, it is therefore essential to study the Babylonian and Persian periods. However, the book speaks of the later Greek (Hellenistic) period as well (8:5–8, 21–22). In fact, many scholars now date the book in its final form to the Hellenistic era, sometime between 167 and 164 B.C. Yet even if Daniel was written earlier (in the sixth century), it speaks of second-century B.C. events. Therefore, we must explore that time frame also.

Jews have some acquaintance with the Hellenistic period from the festival of Hanukkah, which occurred during the Maccabean revolt. Some Christians read the books of Maccabees, which cover that Jewish revolt against the Seleucids in the second century B.C. Those who wish to comprehend Daniel would benefit from reading 1 and 2 Maccabees, even though they are part of the Apocrypha rather than part of the Protestant canon, because they provide important historical background information for this time period.

The book of Daniel also includes a number of historical problems, details that may present a challenge to our interpretation of the book. The best approach to these difficulties is to allow the text to speak on its own terms, while trusting that it is inspired and authoritative. We should remember, first of all, that both synagogue and church agree that Daniel is part of sacred Scripture. After that, we should be open to what modern scholarship uncovers through careful investigation of the text and of the ancient world. This approach may require us to resist the inclination to make the text agree with our preconceived notions and may therefore lead to some changes in our interpretation of the text. We should conform our interpretations to the text and to history instead of making them conform to our expectations. Listening to the text through ears of faith means courageously following the evidence wherever it leads. The commentary that follows adopts this approach—allowing the text to speak on its own terms—and invites the reader to do likewise, to build understanding on a foundation of faith.

Historical Background

In the seventh century B.C., the Assyrian Empire—the empire that had conquered and exiled the kingdom of Israel—declined and fell to the Neo-Babylonians. The first Neo-Babylonian king, Nabopolassar, was of Chaldean stock. His initial task was to extricate Babylon from Assyrian hegemony, which he accomplished in 626. Next he set out to displace the Assyrians. With the help of the Medes, he sacked Nineveh, the Assyrian capital, in 612. The Assyrians, gasping out their last breaths, retreated westward to Haran to make a stand against their pursuing enemies. In 610, the Babylonians and Medes took Haran. A year later the Assyrians, along with their Egyptian allies, attempted to regroup and assail Haran. They failed miserably, and the Assyrian Empire expired in 609. The Medes and Babylonians divided up the former Assyrian Empire. Media dominated the area to the north and east of Mesopotamia, while Babylon inherited central Mesopotamia and points west. The western regions, however, were contested by Egypt. For a brief time the Egyptians were able to assume control over Syria, Israel, and Judah, until in 605 they were routed by the Babylonian army at Carchemish. At that time, Israel passed into the hands of the Babylonians.

Leading the Babylonian forces against Egypt was Nabopolassar's son, the crown prince Nebuchadnezzar II. While he was pressing his advantage against the Egyptians, news reached him of his father's death. Nebuchadnezzar quickly returned to Babylon to claim the throne, which he held for forty-three years (605–562). His reign included several campaigns in the west. During one campaign, King Jehoiakim of Judah (609–598) made a show of submission; but then three years later, around 602, he foolishly rebelled against his Babylonian overlord (2 Kgs. 24:1). Though it took some time before Nebuchadnezzar could deal with Jehoiakim, he eventually dispatched troops to the region in 598. Jehoiakim, however, did not live to see the consequences of his actions. When he died in 598, his son, Jehoiachin, had to bear the brunt of the Babylonian attack after ruling for only a few months. Following a brief siege, Jerusalem capitulated, leading to the first deportation in 597. Nebuchadnezzar took to Babylon most of the leaders of Judah—King Jehoiachin, his mother, his chief officials, his army, and the craftsmen—leaving behind mainly poor farmers (2 Kgs. 24:12, 14–15). Nebuchadnezzar also captured the wealth of Judah, including the temple treasures, such as the gold vessels used in the service of Yahweh (2 Kgs. 24:13). The next king, Zedekiah, who was the last Judean king, did not learn from Jehoiakim's mistake. He also rebelled against Babylon, leading to another invasion, a second deportation, the loss of the temple, and the destruction of Jerusalem, in 587. A third deportation occurred in 582 after the governor, Gedaliah, was assassinated.

When Nebuchadnezzar died in 562, his son Amel-Marduk (Evil-Merodach of 2 Kgs. 25:27) inherited the throne. He ruled for only two years (562–560) before he was replaced by his brother-in-law Neriglissar (560–556). When Neriglissar died four years later, his son Labashi-Marduk briefly wore the crown until he was deposed by Nabonidus (556–539), the last king of Babylon. Nabonidus was a usurper from Haran, a cult center of the moon god Sin. His mother was a priestess of Sin there. By favoring the moon god, he angered the priests and worshipers of the other Babylonian gods, especially the followers of Marduk. Nabonidus later abandoned Babylon for Teima, an oasis in the Arabian desert, where he lived for ten years. During that time he delegated the administration of Babylon to his son Belshazzar. While the king was in Teima, the New Year Festival could not be celebrated, because this important religious holiday required the king's presence and participation. This further alienated him from his people, who were deeply offended and outraged by his egregious religious failure. He also brought gods (images) from particular cult centers to Babylon, infuriating their devotees. This was a final act of desperation by a beleaguered monarch. Threatened by Persia, he hoped that surrounding himself with the nations' gods would ensure deliverance from his enemy. Sadly for him, it did not work.

As mentioned above, the Medes and Babylonians had carved out separate empires, with Media holding sway over the territory north and east of Babylonia. The Median and Babylonian Empires were therefore contemporaneous. To the south and east of both lay Persia, which had been subservient to Media in the time of the Median king Astyages (585–550). However, that power relationship did not last. Astyages gave his daughter Mandane in marriage to Cambyses I, king of Persia. She gave birth to Cyrus II, who became king of Persia in 559. Though Cyrus began as a vassal to Astyages, he rebelled and defeated the Medes in 550. Then, in 539, Cyrus captured Babylon with little resistance. Nabonidus, the last king of Babylon, was so despised that Cyrus was welcomed as a liberator. In these two moves Cyrus added to his own Persian kingdom the vast empires of Media and Babylonia (Dan. 8:1–4, 20).

In 538, Cyrus issued a decree allowing the Jews to return to their land to rebuild Yahweh's temple in Jerusalem and to do so with Persian funds (Ezra 1:1–4; 6:3–5). It is no wonder, then, that the Jews viewed Cyrus as a kind of "messiah," or anointed one (Isa. 45:1). Cyrus was succeeded by his oldest son, Cambyses (530–522). He in turn was followed by Darius I Hystaspes (522–486). Darius divided his empire into twenty satrapies, or provinces, each headed by a satrap, or provincial governor. During this period the second Jewish temple was completed (in 515). Although Darius accomplished many things, he failed in his bid to append Greece to his empire, suffering a painful defeat by the Greeks at the famous battle of Marathon in 490. Similarly, the next Persian king, Xerxes (486–465; known as Ahasuerus in the Bible [Ezra 4:6; Dan. 9:1; and twenty-eight times in Esther]), was rebuffed by the Greeks at Salamis and Samos (480–479). Following Xerxes was Artaxerxes I Longimanus (465–424), during whose long reign two significant biblical events occurred: Ezra returned to Judah with the Torah (458), and Nehemiah, the king's cupbearer, came back to rebuild the walls of Jerusalem (445). Passing over six more kings, we come at last to the final Persian monarch, Darius III Codomannus (336–331), who succumbed to the invasion of Alexander the Great.

Alexander had become king of Macedon in 336 when his father, Philip II, died. After establishing his control over Greece to the south and subduing some barbarians to the north, Alexander set out to take over the Persian Empire (Dan. 8:5–7). In 334 he flowed into Asia Minor (modern Turkey) like a flood, overwhelming everything in his path. After dealing crushing defeats to the Persians at Issus (333) and Gaugamela (331), Alexander went south, adding all the territory from Syria to Egypt (including Judah) to his possessions. Then he went north and east to claim all of Mesopotamia and Persia. After advancing to the Indus River Valley (modern Pakistan and western India), he returned to Babylon, where he died of a fever at the age of 33 (in 323; see Dan. 8:8). Since Alexander left no male heir, his empire was divided among his generals, known as the Diadochi, or successors. These squabbled among themselves in efforts to win more territory and power. Some survived the power struggles while others did not; boundaries frequently changed. The battle of Ipsus in Phrygia (in 301) was a turning point. Four of the Diadochi formed an alliance in order to bring down the most powerful general, Antigonus Monophthalmus. This resulted in four kingdoms: Macedonia and Greece, ruled by Cassander; Thrace and Asia Minor, ruled by Lysimachus; Syria, Babylonia, and Persia, ruled by Seleucus; and Israel and Egypt, ruled by Ptolemy (see Dan. 8:8, 22).

For the study of Daniel, the two most important kings of these four are Seleucus and Ptolemy, as well as their dynasties, because the Jews came under the hegemony of first the Ptolemies and later the Seleucids. In Daniel 11 "the king of the North" refers to a Seleucid and "the king of the South" to a Ptolemy (e.g., see Dan. 11:6). The Seleucid kings were named Seleucus or Antiochus (Seleucus I, Antiochus I, Antiochus II, Seleucus II, etc.); the Ptolemies were all named Ptolemy (I, II, III, etc.). Ptolemaic control of the land of Israel continued until the reign of the Seleucid king Antiochus III, the Great (223–187). He reclaimed much territory in Asia Minor and in the eastern provinces that had been lost during the reigns of his predecessors. In 198, he also wrested control of the land of Israel from Ptolemy V Epiphanes (203–181; for more historical detail on the period from Seleucus I to Antiochus III as it relates to Daniel, see the commentary on Dan. 11). However, Antiochus III made a colossal error by invading Greece. Rome was on the rise at this time and would not allow Antiochus to expand any further to the west. The Roman army pushed the Syrians back into Asia Minor and vanquished them there, forcing them to accept onerous peace terms. These included paying huge reparations, which seriously weakened the Seleucid kingdom. In addition, one of the king's sons, Antiochus IV, was sent to Rome as a hostage to ensure that annual payments were made.

When Antiochus III died in 187, another son, Seleucus IV Philopator, succeeded him. In 175, Antiochus IV was allowed to leave Rome, because Demetrius, son of Seleucus IV, was taking his place as hostage. However, Seleucus IV was assassinated at about the same time, so that Antiochus IV gained not only his freedom but the Seleucid throne as well. This turned out to be a disaster for the religious Jews living in his realm. Trouble began with the king's meddling with the office of high priest. Although Onias III was the legitimate high priest in Jerusalem, his brother Jason offered the new king a large bribe in order to steal the position. Accepting the gift, Antiochus replaced Onias with Jason. This led to further conflict as Jason, who was of the Hellenizing party, sought to advance Greek culture, which was offensive to pious Jews. For example, Jason encouraged Greek athletic contests, which were not religiously neutral, as sporting events are today, but were closely associated with the pagan gods. Young men, for instance, wore a special broad-brimmed hat connected to the cult of Hermes (2 Macc. 4:12), and sacrifices were offered to the Greek deities. Furthermore, the athletes exercised in the nude, which put pressure on some Jews, marked as they were by circumcision, to try to assimilate; they sought through surgery to hide their circumcision so that they would look like the Greek men (1 Macc. 1:15).

In 172, the office of high priest changed hands again. A man named Menelaus was appointed to the office when he promised the crown a sum of money larger than Jason's. He was even willing to sell gold temple vessels to pay Antiochus. Onias denounced this corruption and paid for it with his life when Menelaus had him murdered in 171 (2 Macc. 4:30–34; Dan. 9:26; 11:22). In 169, Antiochus began using the title Epiphanes, meaning "God manifest." In that year, he also campaigned with some success in Egypt. When an untrue rumor circulated that Antiochus had died in Egypt, Jason made an attempt to reclaim his office; he gathered a force of supporters and marched on Jerusalem. Antiochus understood this action to be a revolt and quelled it mercilessly. He massacred many Jews, drove out Jason, restored Menelaus, and plundered Yahweh's holy temple (2 Macc. 5:5–16).

In 168, the Seleucid king invaded Egypt again. However, this time it was different, because Rome intervened (see Dan. 11:29–30a). The Roman legate Popilius Laenas traveled to Egypt by ship with a force to stop the advance of Antiochus Epiphanes. When the two men met on the battlefield, Popilius Laenas drew a circle around Antiochus in the sand and instructed him to decide before leaving that circle whether he would withdraw his army. Antiochus had no alternative but to retreat, which put him in a foul mood, having been humiliated by the Romans in front of his own army. Meanwhile, in Jerusalem there was more unrest as faithful Jews resisted the policy of Hellenization. In 167, Epiphanes took his wrath out on the Jewish people (see Dan. 11:30b–31), sending Apollonius, one of his military commanders, to do his dirty work. Apollonius pretended to come in peace when he entered Jerusalem with his troops. He waited until the Sabbath, when the Jews would be most vulnerable, because they would be less likely to resist on their holy day. Then he ruthlessly attacked. He killed many, sold women and children into slavery, plundered and burned the city, and pulled down the outer walls (1 Macc. 1:29–35; 2 Macc. 5:23–26). The practice of the Jewish religion now became illegal: sacrifices to Yahweh ceased, circumcision was forbidden, the keeping of Sabbath and feast days was outlawed, and copies of Scripture were ripped and burned (1 Macc. 1:41–61). Syrian troops went through Jewish towns, offering pigs in sacrifice to Greek deities and forcing the Jews to eat the unclean meat (1 Macc. 6:18–31). The climax of these sacrileges was the setting up of a pagan altar on the altar of burnt offering in the Jewish temple. There, nonkosher animals were offered up to Zeus Olympios (1 Macc. 1:54, 59; 2 Macc. 6:2, 4–5). This was known as "the abomination that causes desolation" (Dan. 9:27; 11:31; 12:11; 1 Macc. 1:54); it led to the Maccabean revolt (probably the "little help" referred to in Dan. 11:34), during which the Jews successfully drove out the Syrian forces and recaptured Jerusalem. They entered the temple and reconsecrated Yahweh's altar in 164. The relighting of the menorah (the lampstand in the temple) at that time is commemorated in the Jewish festival of Hanukkah.

Historical Problems

The book of Daniel exhibits a number of historical problems that are noted often in the commentaries. The first problem occurs in the very first verse, where the text recounts an invasion of Judah and deportation by Nebuchadnezzar in 606, the third year of Jehoiakim (1:1). This is in conflict with Kings and Chronicles as well as Babylonian records (see the commentary on 1:1), which report the first deportation as taking place in 597.

A second problem is the tension between chapter 1, in which Daniel and his friends spend three years in training (1:5, 18), and chapter 2, in which they are promoted after two years (2:1, 48–49).

Another difficulty is that Belshazzar is presented as the son of Nebuchadnezzar (5:2, 11, 13, 18) and the last king of Babylon (5:1, 2, 3, 30–31). However, we know that Nabonidus rather than Nebuchadnezzar was the father of Belshazzar. Nor is there any evidence that Belshazzar was a descendant of Nebuchadnezzar, because Nabonidus was a usurper. It is also clear from Babylonian records that Belshazzar was not crowned king. He may have exercised some royal functions while his father was away, but Nabonidus was the last king of Babylon.

The author of Daniel also seems confused about the Persian monarchy. Apparently he only knows of four kings of Persia (11:2), whereas there were actually eleven from Cyrus to Darius III Codomannus (336–331).

Daniel 4 reports that Nebuchadnezzar went insane for a time and was driven out from court. There is no support for this from Babylonian records. However, there is mention in a text from Qumran (*Prayer of Nabonidus* [4Q242]) that Nabonidus was healed of an illness by God through a Jewish exile. The details are different, but the story in Daniel 4 would fit Nabonidus much better, especially since we know that Nabonidus left Babylon for a time to reside in the Arabian oasis of Teima. Furthermore, Daniel records that this event happened to the father of Belshazzar, who was, in fact, Nabonidus.

One of the biggest puzzles concerns the place of the Median kingdom in general and the mention of Darius the Mede in particular (5:31; 6:1; 9:1; 11:1). Daniel presents a succession of four kingdoms (Dan. 2; 7). From evidence within the book of Daniel it is clear that those kingdoms are Babylonia, Media, Persia, and Greece (see the commentary on Dan. 2 and 7). According to Daniel, the Babylonian kingdom fell to Darius the Mede (5:30–31), who was in turn succeeded by Cyrus the Persian (6:28). But the Median Empire was contemporaneous with the Babylonian Empire. Persia conquered first Media and then Babylon. So, the picture of Media taking over Babylon and then falling to Persia seems to be inaccurate. Furthermore, apart from Daniel, Darius the Mede is unknown from history. Indeed the evidence is in conflict with this figure. He is said to be the son of Ahasuerus (Xerxes; 9:1) and the one who took over Babylon after Belshazzar died (5:31); in addition, he divided his kingdom into 120 satrapies (6:1). However, we know that Cyrus the Persian conquered Babylon, taking the crown from Nabonidus, the last Babylonian monarch. Later there were several kings named Darius, but they do not fit the description in Daniel. It might be possible to see Darius the Mede as a creative development from traditions about Darius I (522–486). Although Darius I did not take over the kingdom from Belshazzar (5:31), he did quell two revolts in Babylon during his reign. Furthermore, he divided his empire into satrapies, though it was 20 rather than 120. Perhaps these events gave rise to the confusion. But Darius I was Persian (Ezra 4:5, 24; 6:14; Neh. 12:22), not Median, and he was the father of Ahasuerus (Xerxes), not his son. Attempts have been made to identify Darius the Mede with other historical figures, such as Cyrus, Astyages (a Median king), Ugbaru (a Gutian governor who actually did the work of capturing Babylon for Cyrus), and Gubaru (a governor of Babylon). However, there is no evidence that any one of these was the son of Ahasuerus (Xerxes) or was called Darius, and the latter two were not kings.

Daniel seems to predict the end of evil kingdoms and the arrival of the kingdom of God in the time of Antiochus IV. Daniel 2 is less specific, pointing to the Hellenistic era. But chapter 7 clearly fingers Antiochus IV as the "horn" who persecutes the "saints" (7:21, 25). When he is destroyed, dominion will pass to "the people of the holy ones of the Most High" (7:27 NRSV; NIV "the saints, the people of the Most High"). This spells the end of "beastly" kingdoms (7:3–7) but ushers in the fullness of God's eternal reign (7:27). Chapters 8 and 11 make it even more transparent that Antiochus IV is in view. These visions culminate in the resurrection of the dead (12:1–4). Yet, history has continued since the second century B.C. Many more kingdoms have arisen and fallen; the resurrection is still future.

In chapter 9, we meet another conundrum: the seventy weeks of years (9:24). There would be a period of seventy sevens, or 490 years total. This first period of seven sevens, or forty-nine years, begins with a word to rebuild Jerusalem and ends with the arrival of an anointed prince (9:25). That would be followed by a period of sixty-two sevens, or 434 years. During that time Jerusalem would be restored, but the end of that period would be marked by the cutting off of an anointed one (9:25–26). Leading up to the last week of seven years would be war and destruction. The first half of the week would be characterized by cessation of the sacrifice and an abomination of desolation. After that, the end would come (9:27). It seems fairly transparent what events are in view: the first anointed one is Joshua the high priest (or perhaps Zerubbabel) in the time of the rebuilding of the temple after the exile in Babylonia; the anointed one who is cut off is Onias III in 171; the first half of the last week points to the abominations of Antiochus IV. Unfortunately, the numbers defy a solution; it is not possible to fit them exactly into history as we know it.

Finally, there is the death of Antiochus IV. Daniel 11:21–39 preserves a detailed summary of this king's career. Historical sources from the period corroborate this account, showing it to be remarkably accurate. However, after that point in the narrative there is a shift. Daniel 11:40–45 anticipates a further battle with Egypt and the demise of this wicked king in the land of Israel "between the seas at the beautiful holy mountain" (11:45). In sharp contrast to this, ancient records inform us that Antiochus IV did not attack Egypt again. Rather, he campaigned in the eastern portion of his empire, losing his life in Persia in 164.

How should people of faith respond to these textual difficulties? The answer to this question is affected by how one interprets the genre of the book. When those who understand the genre of the text to be history are confronted with these historical problems, they might feel the historicity of the Bible is being questioned and so try to demonstrate how to preserve Daniel's version of history. For example, some people argue that maybe there was an invasion of Judah in 606 that was not recorded elsewhere. Perhaps, they say, Belshazzar was a descendant of Nebuchadnezzar through his mother's line and the title "king" really only indicates governing authority. Some suggest that the "horn" of Daniel 7 is not Antiochus and that the fourth kingdom is not that of the Seleucids. They conjecture that possibly Cyrus, Ugbaru, or Gubaru was known by the alternate title "Darius the Mede." In this view, the inspiration of the text is dependent on the events happening exactly as recorded in Daniel; if the events did not happen literally in this way, then the book's authority is compromised.

Likewise, those who understand the genre of Daniel to be prophecy may be concerned that unfulfilled predictions from Daniel would discredit the book or its author. Therefore, they argue that Daniel 7 is not predicting the coming of the kingdom of God in the second century B.C., even though some commentators see this as the plain sense of the passage. Similarly, such readers might contend that Daniel 11 does not predict the death of Antiochus IV because the details cannot be substantiated from history (Dan. 11:40–45).

There is another approach to the text, however: understanding the genre of Daniel to be apocalyptic literature. This genre follows rules different from those of historical or prophetic writing and uses different literary devices (see "Genre," below). For people of faith, this approach allows us to focus on the authority and inspiration of the text as being based on its identity as sacred Scripture, independent from its historical details. If Daniel is not a work of history, then historical problems in the text are not a challenge to the Bible's integrity. A better understanding of the genre will allow us to see how the historical information in Daniel serves the author's purpose.

Genre

Most modern commentators consider the genre of the book of Daniel to be apocalyptic. Apocalyptic literature in the ancient Near East grew out of a social situation of oppression. The purpose of this literature was to comfort those being persecuted. To do this the author might use history, but the intention is not so much to rehearse the facts of the past as to give hope to a suffering community. It is a bold and imaginative literature. The author therefore might play with the historical events and use them creatively. The main message of apocalyptic literature is that all the temporal, tyrannical regimes of this world will one day be displaced by the eternal, equitable kingdom of God. Because of this future orientation, this genre looks a little like prophecy. In fact, the genre of apocalyptic literature grows out of prophetic literature, but once again, it is imaginative literature. It expresses a belief that God is still in control even when evil is triumphing, and it engenders hope that God will soon intervene and reverse the state of affairs. To do this, the apocalyptist might write about the past as if it were future (e.g., 11:1–39) and might convey hope in the form of a prediction (11:40–45).

By form Daniel can be separated into two sections: chapters 1–6 are stories about Daniel and his friends, told in the third person by an anonymous author; chapters 7–12 are Daniel's visions recounted mostly in the first person (for exceptions, see 7:1; 10:1). In the former section, Daniel does not receive revelations (except in 2:19, which is a revelation about the king's dream), but he functions as an interpreter: he explains the dreams of Nebuchadnezzar (chs. 2 and 4) and the writing on the wall (ch. 5). In the latter section, he has his own visions, which he cannot interpret by himself: he needs an angel to explain the meanings to him. There is not a huge difference here between chapters 1–6 and 7–12, for Daniel gets his interpretations from God in chapters 1–6 as well (2:19; 4:8; 5:11), but in chapters 7–12 they are mediated by an angel.

Further evidence for a division between chapter 6 and 7 can be found in the chronological headers to the chapters (or to the section, as in the case of chs. 10–12). Each introduction mentions an ancient king, but there are two series. The first includes chapters 1 through 6, and the second, chapters 7 through 12. Chapters 1–4 are situated in the era of Nebuchadnezzar. Chapter 5 comes from the time of Belshazzar. Chapter 6 is dated to the reign of Darius the Mede. While there are kings who come between Nebuchadnezzar and Belshazzar, and Darius the Mede is unknown from history, it is nevertheless clear that the author of Daniel is putting them in chronological order. Nebuchadnezzar is an early Neo-Babylonian king; Belshazzar is the last in the dynasty; Darius is said to take the empire from Belshazzar. However, a new progression begins in chapter 7. The time marker is pushed back to the end of the Neo-Babylonian period. Chapters 7 and 8 spring from the reign of Belshazzar. Chapter 9 is from the first year of Darius. Chapters 10–12 are located in the third year of Cyrus. Therefore, we have another set of kings, ordered from earlier to later, in chapters 7–12. The second series of kings starts later than does the first, with Belshazzar rather than Nebuchadnezzar, and also runs later, to Cyrus rather than Darius, into the Persian period. It can be diagrammed as follows:

Nebuchadnezzar	Belshazzar	Darius	Cyrus
Chs. 1–4	Ch. 5	Ch. 6	
	Chs. 7–8	Ch. 9	Chs. 10–12

Commentators often say that chapters 1–6 are court tales, whereas only chapters 7–12 are apocalyptic. However, this observation is complicated by the fact that chapter 2 also has apocalyptic elements. Because it projects four kingdoms followed by the coming kingdom of God, chapter 2 is a close parallel to chapter 7. Commentators also often claim that the kings who figure in the narratives of chapters 1–6 are kinder, or at least somewhat more reasonable, than the thoroughly evil king featured in the visions of chapters 7–11, who "was waging war against the saints and defeating them" (7:21) and who sought to attack heaven itself (8:10–12, 25). To be sure, Daniel and his friends rise to the top in the first half of the book because of their wisdom and because of Daniel's skill at dream interpretation. However, there is still hostility in the environment. Chapter 1 implies a mild threat should the Jews not manifest a healthy appearance (although the expressed threat is to the Babylonian official [1:10]). In chapter 2, the lives of the Jews are at risk if they cannot describe and interpret the dream. In chapter 3, Nebuchadnezzar is quite willing to throw the three Jews into the furnace for not worshiping the image. Although Belshazzar does not persecute the Jews, he is profane, for he desecrates their sacred temple vessels by using them at a feast in which he praises "the gods of gold and silver, of bronze, iron, wood and stone" (5:4). In chapter 6, Darius cares for Daniel and hopes that his God is able to deliver him from the lions, while the other administrators plot to have him destroyed. Finally, chapter 2 implies that the kingdoms of this world are wicked, because they come under the judgment of God. Even though the description is not as graphic as that found in chapter 7, where the empires are ravenous beasts, the fourth beast/empire is destructive enough. It is compared to iron, which "breaks and smashes everything" (2:40). As in chapter 7, these world powers are slated for destruction in order to make way for God's eternal kingdom. So, this notion of a contrast between benevolent kings and kingdoms in chapters 1–6 and malevolent ones in chapters 7–12 needs to be qualified.

Chapters 1–6

The stories in chapters 1–6 show how Jews should live under foreign domination. They hold out the hope that Jews may thrive in such a situation. In fact, because God may endow his people with wisdom, it is even possible to rise to the top to serve the king in positions of prominence as do Daniel and his three friends. These stories may be further subdivided. Chapters 3 and 6 are stories of miraculous deliverance. Both episodes have similarly dangerous settings, for the Jews are threatened with death if they remain faithful to their God. In chapter 3, Daniel's friends Shadrach, Meshach, and Abednego (also known by their Hebrew names: Hananiah, Mishael, and Azariah) are commanded to worship an image or be cast into the fire. In chapter 6, Daniel is expected to refrain from praying or be thrown to the lions. Apart from the supernatural elements, these accounts are somewhat parallel to the book of Esther, where Haman wants to kill Mordecai for not bowing down before him. When Mordecai is spared, Haman is executed on the gallows he built to execute Mordecai. In the same way in Daniel, after God delivers his servants, the men who threw them into the furnace are burned up (Dan. 3:22; although they are not personally seeking to harm the Jews, as Haman plots against Mordecai and as the men in Daniel 6 conspire against Daniel). Likewise, after Daniel is rescued, the men who sought to trap and eliminate him are themselves thrown into the lions' den with their families (Dan. 6:24).

Chapters 1, 2, 4, and 5 contain the recurring motif of the successful courtier who wins a contest against the other court counselors. In chapter 1, Daniel and his three friends prove to be healthier by following their religious dietary rules (1:15) and are judged by the king to be "ten times better than all the magicians and enchanters in his whole kingdom" (1:20). In chapter 2, when all the other wise men fail, Daniel is able to recount the king's dream and interpret it. In chapter 4, he also shows up the other advisers, this time by only interpreting the king's dream. In chapter 5, Daniel manifests superiority over the Babylonian sages and shows that he is endowed with the spirit of God by interpreting the handwriting on the wall. These stories are parallel to the story of Joseph. Like Daniel, Joseph rose to prominence in the court of a foreign king because of his wisdom and skill in interpreting dreams (Gen. 40–41).

Chapters 7–12

While other OT books or sections of books, such as Isaiah 24–27; 56–66; Ezekiel; Joel; and Zechariah 9–14, have apocalyptic elements in them, they are more appropriately called proto-apocalyptic, because they stand in between classical prophecy and fully developed apocalyptic. Daniel in the OT and Revelation in the NT are the only apocalypses in the Bible, and in Daniel, the designation applies more to the second half of the book, because these chapters have more apocalyptic elements in them than chapters 1–6. The following are some of the typical characteristics of the apocalyptic genre.

1. *Revelations.* The term "apocalypse" comes from the Greek noun *apokalypsis*, meaning "revelation," "uncovering," "unveiling," or "disclosure." God's hidden plans are made known to a human being, often in visions (Dan. 7–12) or dreams (Dan. 2). These revelations are then recounted in narrative form.

2. *Symbolism.* The images in the visions and the words in the revelations are often mysterious or fantastic and may be drawn from mythological material. Examples in Daniel include the beasts coming out of the sea (Dan. 7:2–7) and designations such as "time, times and half a time" (Dan. 7:25; 12:7; see also Rev. 12:14) and "seventy 'sevens'" (Dan. 9:24; compare the number 666 in Rev. 13:18).

3. *Angels.* Heavenly beings appear in order to explain the vision or to give revelation (e.g., Dan. 7:16; 8:15–19; 9:21–22; 10:4–11; 12:5–13).

4. *Pseudonymity.* The narration of the visions is attributed to a revered figure of an earlier time. Many scholars consider the book of Daniel to be typical in this regard, arguing that chapters 7–12 were written in the second century B.C. and credited to one Daniel—an exilic person of the sixth century. Other readers of Daniel reject pseudonymity and consider the book to have been written in the sixth century by the one after whom the book is named. To support this argument, they often point to Revelation in the NT, which was writen by the apostle John. But it should be kept in mind that Revelation is a Christian work, whereas all pre-Christian, Jewish apocalypses are pseudonymous (for example 1 Enoch, 2 Enoch, 2 Baruch, 3 Baruch, 4 Ezra).

5. *Prophecy after the event.* To those who accept pseudonymous authorship, it appears that the second-century author recounts the events of history in the form of predictions from Daniel of the sixth century. This is a typical literary device of apocalyptic that seems to be most transparent in Daniel 7 and especially in Daniel 11:1–39. The author of Daniel is not attempting to deceive his audience. They most likely would recognize the traits of the genre and, therefore, understand what he is doing, that is, simply trying to show that history has a *telos*—an end, a goal.

6. *Periodization of history.* In this case history is divided into five epochs. The visions depict a series of empires that will rule in succession. The first four are the kingdoms of Babylonia, Media, Persia, and Greece. These are followed by the kingdom of God (Dan. 2; 7).

7. *Eschatology.* The word "eschatology" comes from the Greek word *eschaton*, meaning "end." Daniel is concerned with the "time of the end" (8:17, 19; 11:35, 40; 12:4, 9; cf. 12:13). The kingdom of God

would not come from below, by human means (2:45; 8:25; 11:34), but from above, "with the clouds of heaven" (7:13). The book envisions a judgment and resurrection of the dead (7:9–14; 12:1–2).

8. *Hope.* The visions of Daniel 7–12 were recorded to engender hope among the Jews, most likely the Jews being persecuted by Antiochus IV in the second century B.C. First, they were encouraged to believe that God would deliver them soon from their enemies. He would destroy the oppressive kingdoms of this world and usher in his eternal kingdom of justice and righteousness. Second, in the meantime they were encouraged to be faithful to God, even unto death, so that they might experience a resurrection to everlasting life.

Date

Traditionally the entire book of Daniel has been dated to the sixth century B.C., the time period of the person Daniel and of the exile in Babylonia that is the setting for the narrative. However, a number of commentators locate the book in its final form, and especially chapters 7–12, in the second century B.C. This conclusion was reached partly by studying apocalyptic literature, which is characterized by pseudonymous authorship and prediction after the event, and partly by following the clues in the text of Daniel itself.

As noted above, there are several historical problems in the book. The history from the Babylonian period to the Greek period is sketchy and somewhat distorted. The author interjects an invasion of Judah and deportation by Nebuchadnezzar in 606 B.C. (1:1), when the first deportation was actually in 597 B.C. He seems to be acquainted with only two Babylonian kings: Nebuchadnezzar (Dan. 1–4) and Belshazzar (Dan. 5), when there were more. He thinks Belshazzar is Nebuchadnezzar's son (Dan. 5), which is doubtful. He knows of only four Persian kings (11:2), even though there were eleven. He imagines a Median Empire that comes between the Babylonian and Persian Empires (Dan. 2 and 7). It appears that he invents King Darius the Mede (5:30–31; 6:1; 9:1).

But then there is a shift; events come into sharper focus in the Hellenistic period. We see Alexander the Great displace Persia (8:1–7; 11:2–3). We learn of his death "at the height of his power" (8:8). We follow the division of his empire into the four kingdoms of the Diadochi (8:8; 11:4). We even learn of the ten Seleucid kings between Alexander and Antiochus IV (7:7). Then there is a further development. The writer becomes extremely precise about the Seleucid and Ptolemaic kings (Dan. 11). He is an expert on this period, recounting in detail the alliances, murders, and battles (11:5–20). Yet in this material there is also a distinction between earlier and later. Almost 150 years are covered in 20 verses (Dan. 11:1–20), from the last Persian king to Antiochus III the Great. But the finer brush strokes are reserved for Antiochus IV, who is depicted in the 19 verses of Daniel 11:21–39 (he is also central to the visions in Dan. 7 and 8). The author knows how this king persecuted the Jews and how he desecrated the temple with "the abomination that causes desolation" (Dan. 9:27; 11:31; 12:11; see also Dan. 8:13; 1 Macc. 1:54; 2 Macc. 6:2). It is also evident from chapters 7–9 that the author of Daniel expected the kingdom of God to come in the time of Antiochus IV Epiphanes. In addition, he knows about the beginning of the Maccabean revolt, which he refers to as "a little help" (Dan. 11:34) because he looks for the real deliverance to come from God (7:13–14), not from human hands (2:34, 45; 8:25). There is no mention of the cleansing of the temple by the Maccabees in 164. This historical survey up to and including the reign of Antiochus IV (Dan. 11:39) dovetails nicely with external evidence. But then comes a surprise: the account of Antiochus's death (11:40–45) cannot be corroborated with historical records.

To sum up, the book of Daniel appears to be fuzzy about events in the sixth century; crystal clear about the Hellenistic era, with special emphasis on Antiochus IV; and then out of focus again about his death. It stands to reason that the details would be sharpest for the period in which the book was written. To many commentators, then, this suggests that the bulk of the book was composed after 167, when the persecution began, but before the purification of the temple and the king's demise in 164 B.C. Further evidence for a second-century date can be seen in the command to "close up and seal the words of the scroll until the time of the end" (Dan. 12:4). If the book is really about some future end-time period, it should still be sealed, because the end has not happened yet. In other words, we should not know about the book of Daniel now. It is supposed to be discovered and unsealed just before the end. However, this is really a literary device of the second-century B.C. apocalyptic author. He wrote under the name of Daniel, who lived in the exilic period. He presents the book as having been composed and sealed in the sixth-century B.C., but uncovered in the Hellenistic period just before the eschatological events recorded in it were to occur. The author did this because he believed and hoped that God would intervene in history to deliver the Jews from Antiochus's persecution and to bring the kingdom of God.

Even if the final composition of the book took place in the second century, however, this does not mean that the entire book comes from that time. On the one hand, the stories of Daniel and his friends (chs. 2–6) seem to be earlier, because they were written in Aramaic and because they reflect a time when there were better relations between the Jews and the foreign king—there was still hope of attaining positions of prominence in the king's service. Commentators often date these chapters to the Persian or early Hellenistic period. However, as will be shown later, it appears these may have been selected and shaped by the second-century author according to his concerns. On the other end, the final verses of Daniel might come from a later hand. When the end does not come after 1,150 days (8:14), it is pushed later to 1,290 days (12:11). The heavenly kingdom still does not arrive, so it is revised to 1,335 days (12:12). When that day passes uneventfully, the book closes with the general assurance that the end will eventually come (12:13).

The Person Daniel

Traditionally the book is attributed to a Jew named Daniel who was taken into exile by Nebuchadnezzar in the sixth century B.C. (1:1–6). Chapters 1–6 are anonymous stories written in the third person about Daniel and his three friends. Chapters 7–12 are mostly presented as first-person accounts written by Daniel himself. Nevertheless, as already noted, many scholars think the actual author of the book of Daniel was someone living in the Maccabean era who took on the guise of a legendary individual of the exile especially known for wisdom and skill in interpreting dreams and visions. ("Legendary" does not preclude the possibility of a historical Daniel on whom the stories are based.) In the book, Daniel and his three friends show themselves to be far superior in wisdom to all the other Babylonian sages (1:20), but Daniel clearly outshines the other three (2:48; 4:9; 5:11–12). Although he is limited to the role of interpreter in the first half of the book, he has his own visions in the second half.

In considering how the tradition of Daniel developed, it is interesting to note that there are other Daniels in the Bible: David's son (1 Chron. 3:1), from the pre-exilic period before the time of the prophet Daniel; and a priest who returned to Judah in the postexilic period (Ezra 8:2; Neh. 10:6) and lived after the prophet's time (ca. 458). However, there is no apparent connection between these passages and the exilic hero of the Babylonian court.

Ezekiel mentions a figure along with Noah and Job whose name is Daniel (the consonantal Hebrew text has "Danel," but the name is vocalized as "Daniel"; Ezek. 14:14, 20). These three are esteemed for their righteousness. It is unlikely, though, that this reference is to the Daniel of the exile, because Ezekiel himself was also deported to Babylon. He seems to be alluding to well-known heroes from the past, not to his contemporaries.

Since Noah and Job were figures known from antiquity, it would be unusual for Ezekiel to single out someone of his own day along with the other two. In fact there is a Daniel from before the flood who was related to Enoch, recorded in *Jubilees* 4:20. Perhaps Ezekiel was thinking of him. While Ezekiel 14 focuses on Daniel's righteousness, a later passage highlights his wisdom. God tells the king of Tyre: "You are indeed wiser than Daniel; no secret is hidden from you" (Ezek. 28:3 NRSV). Once again, Ezekiel is probably recalling a worthy from the distant past, yet this is precisely the reputation of the prophet Daniel: wise and adept at revealing secret things. Therefore, these passages may have influenced the author of the book of Daniel.

Some have also wondered if there is a connection in Ezekiel or Daniel with the Ugaritic figure Danel, renowned for being a just king who defends the widow and orphan (in the Aqhat story from ancient Ugarit). Likewise, in the story of Susanna (from the Apocrypha), the biblical Daniel brings justice to Susanna when through careful examination he shows her accusers to be false. This motif of judgment or justice is related to the meaning of the name Danel or Daniel: "my judge is El" or "El judges." El was the high god depicted in Canaanite texts from the second millennium B.C. as the ancient one with white hair who sits in judgment on his throne, much as God is presented in Daniel 7:9–10, 13. There are also similarities between the El of Canaanite myth and God, known as "El" or "Elohim," in the patriarchal narratives. Both reveal themselves through dreams and visions (for biblical examples, see Gen. 15:1; 20:3, 6; 28:12; 31:10, 11, 24). This also characterizes God in the book of Daniel, who gives revelations to pagan kings (e.g., to Nebuchadnezzar in Dan. 2) as well as to his servant Daniel (e.g., in Dan. 7).

There emerges from this discussion a set of themes: Daniel is righteous, wise, and endowed with good judgment, while God is a hoary-headed judge who sits on a throne and reveals himself and his plans in dreams and visions. Apparently the author of the book of Daniel drew on these traditions to imbue the character Daniel with admirable traits and to describe his God. In addition, there may have been an actual Daniel among the exiles who already had this reputation for being exceptionally wise and an interpreter of dreams and visions. This would then be the basis for the stories of Daniel 1–6, the historical kernel from which the court tales grew.

Canon

In Protestant English Bibles, Daniel is located among the prophets, between Ezekiel and the twelve Minor Prophets. The Hebrew arrangement is different. In the Masoretic Text (MT), Daniel is placed not in the second section, the Prophets (the first section being the Torah, or Law), but in the third section, the Writings. It is not clear why this is so. If Daniel is a sixth-century work, it may have been canonized late because of its controversial content—apocalyptic literature was frowned upon by some rabbis. However, if it was written in the second century, it is likely that the prophetic canon was already closed, while the Writings were still fluid. That is to say, the Jewish community was still editing certain books and discussing whether they should be considered authoritative. Daniel ultimately found acceptance, while other books, such as Maccabees, did not.

Because Daniel is not in the Prophets section of the Hebrew Bible, one might question whether Daniel was indeed a prophet. The book is certainly quite different from the other prophetic books. For example, it is not a collection of oracles like the others. Nor does it begin with the typical introduction of the prophet and his father (see, e.g., Isa. 1:1; Jer. 1:1; Ezek. 1:1–3; Hos. 1:1). Rather, Daniel is unique in being a collection of court narratives and end-time visions. Over time, however, Daniel came to be understood as a prophet. There is a text from Qumran (4Q174) that says, "This is the [time of whic]h it is written in the book of Daniel the prophet."[2] Josephus also called Daniel a "prophet" and the book, "prophecies" (*Ant.* 10.268–269). Similarly, by the time of Jesus, Daniel was understood to be a prophet (Matt. 24:15).

In the Hebrew Bible, the book of Daniel is situated after Esther and before Ezra. Daniel may have been placed there because of its subject matter and historical setting. In terms of subject matter, Esther is a narrative about Jews who succeed in the court of a foreign (in this case Persian) king. Perhaps Daniel was located after Esther, then, because the first six chapters of Daniel center on four Jews who succeed in the Babylonian court. In terms of historical setting, since Daniel is ostensibly exilic, it would come before Ezra chronologically, which is set in the postexilic period.

In Catholic and Orthodox Bibles, the text of Daniel is longer because it includes some additional stories that are not part of the Hebrew Bible. These pieces of literature were appended to the Greek manuscripts of Daniel. The first is the Prayer of Azariah and the Song of the Three Young Men; in Catholic Bibles they are verses 24–90 of chapter 3. The Catholic canon also adds the story of Susanna to the end of Daniel as chapter 13 and the stories of Bel and the Dragon as chapter 14. In Protestant and ecumenical versions of the Bible, when these are included, they are usually found separately in the Apocrypha. Since Protestants follow the Jewish canon and do not consider these stories inspired or authoritative, this commentary will be limited to the material in the Hebrew Bible.

Language Problem and Literary Development

In the MT, Daniel is recorded in two languages. Daniel 1:1–2:4a and chapters 8–12 are in Hebrew, while Daniel 2:4b through the end of chapter 7 (7:28) is in Aramaic. This is one of the biggest puzzles in Daniel because the language divisions are not where one might expect. As noted earlier (see "Genre"), the natural division is between chapters 6 and 7, because chapters 1–6 are stories about Daniel and his friends told in the third person; chapters 7–12 are Daniel's visions, mostly in the first person. Based on literary analysis, then, one would anticipate that if two languages were to be used, the first six chapters would be in one language and the last six chapters in another. However, it is not that way. Surprisingly, the first story is in Hebrew but the rest are in Aramaic. Likewise, the first of Daniel's visions is in Aramaic but the rest are in Hebrew.

The above discussion raises some important questions. Why is the book bilingual? Why do the language divisions not match up with the literary division? And, how do our answers to those questions inform our understanding of the literary development of the book? Various proposals have been made. One scenario is that the book was originally written in Hebrew. Somehow the central Hebrew section of the book was lost (Dan. 2:4b–7:28) but subsequently restored from an Aramaic translation. However, it is not clear why the middle of the book would drop out.

A second possibility is that the whole was composed in Aramaic. It is conjectured that the Jewish community would not consider an Aramaic book to be authoritative, so someone translated the beginning (1:1–2:4a) and end (chs. 8–12) into Hebrew. But why would the translator change the first chapter and the last five? Why not translate the whole into Hebrew or the first and last chapters? Or, why not translate all the visions into Hebrew (chs. 7–12) instead of just the last five chapters?

A third suggestion is that the stories (chs. 1–6) at first were in Aramaic, while the visions (chs. 7–12) were in Hebrew. At a later stage, the first of the stories (1:1–2:4a) was translated into Hebrew and the first of the visions (ch. 7) was translated into Aramaic in order to weave the two parts of the book together. This is a little strange, for while it does tie the first vision in chapter 7 to the stories in chapters 2–6 by putting them in the same language, it also unnecessarily puts a division between the first story and the rest of the stories and between the first vision and the rest of the visions.

A fourth interpretation is that the author purposely composed the book in two languages, using an A-B-A pattern. Hammurabi's Code and Job are offered as supporting examples. In the former case, the laws, composing the middle section, are sandwiched between a prologue and an epilogue, which are statements by Hammurabi: Hammurabi's introduction (A), the laws (B), and Hammurabi's conclusion (A). In the case of Job, the prologue (Job 1:1–2:13) and epilogue (42:7–17) tell the basic story in prose narrative; these frame the poetic center (3:1–42:6), which consists mostly of dialogues between Job and his friends: prose prologue (A), poetic dialogues (B), prose epilogue (A). Unfortunately, Daniel does not follow those examples exactly. Unlike Daniel, in those two examples there is a unity of language. Also, in Hammurabi and Job, the A-B-A pattern is based on literary analysis. Literary analysis of Daniel instead yields a two-part division: court stories (chs. 1–6) and apocalyptic visions (chs. 7–12). If the author deliberately composed the book in two languages, why did he not do so in such a way that the literary division matches the language divisions?

Based on the evidence in the book, it seems that a more complex description of literary development in stages is required. During the first stage, a number of traditions arose about the sixth-century figure Daniel that coalesced into a collection now preserved as Daniel 4–6. In the second stage, copying and transmission of that collection produced two variant forms of it in Aramaic, one that stands behind the Old Greek translation and the other behind the MT version. In the third stage, the author of Daniel added more stories to this collection (Dan. 2, 3, and 7) and composed additional material (Dan. 1; 8–12) to create the book of Daniel. During the fourth stage, the final three verses of the book were added. The canonical form of the book, as it appears in our Bibles, represents the product of all four stages.

Stage One

By the second century B.C., there must have been a rich variety of traditions about Daniel and his three friends. Evidence for this can be seen in the additions to the book of Daniel found in the Apocrypha: the Prayer of Azariah and the Song of the Three Young Men, Susanna, and Bel and the Dragon (see "Canon," above). While not original to the book, they may well be as old as the stories in Daniel 2–7 and may come from some of the same sources used by the author of the final form of Daniel.

Evidence for multiple traditions regarding Daniel can also be seen in the Dead Sea Scrolls. There are at least seven Qumran manuscripts that are relevant to the study of Daniel. All are fragmentary and all are in Aramaic. The first (4Q242 [*Prayer of Nabonidus*]) tells how the Babylonian king Nabonidus was healed of a disease and forgiven of his sins during an encounter with a Jewish exile; most scholars see some connection between this account and Daniel 4. The next three texts (4Q243–245, or 4QPseudo-Daniel[a–c]) apparently preserve a vision of Daniel (not all scholars agree that 4Q245 goes with the other two) that partly outlines Israel's history. The fifth (4Q246) predicts a coming tribulation with nations trampling one another until the kingdom of God comes, bringing an end to war. The sixth and seventh (4Q552–553) use imagery of four trees for kingdoms, reminiscent of Daniel 2 and 7.

Since only a small percentage of writings from antiquity has survived, the above sources suggest that there were probably many stories about Daniel and other Jews such as Hananiah, Mishael, and Azariah. There were probably also many other visions of the end, similar to the ones preserved in the biblical book of Daniel, circulating in the second century B.C. That some of these traditions were originally independent and unconnected can still be seen in the final form of the book. Daniel 3 is about Hananiah, Mishael, and Azariah; there is no mention of Daniel or other Jews who might have stood with the three, refusing to worship the image. Likewise, chapter 6 focuses exclusively on Daniel; whoever first told this story of the lions' den apparently knew nothing of the three friends.

Stage Two

The first collection of stories likely comprised chapters 4–6. It is interesting to note that these chapters exhibit the greatest differences between the Old Greek text and the MT. This suggests that the Aramaic text that stands behind the Greek for these chapters is different from the Aramaic text preserved in the MT. One way to account for this is to posit that chapters 4–6 circulated separately before the rest of the book was added in. This would explain why the Aramaic and Greek versions are so divergent in chapters 4–6 while being more harmonious in the rest of the book. They had time to grow apart before the full development of the book. In the process of copying and transmission, changes were introduced, resulting in at least two textual traditions. One version found its way into the MT while another version was absorbed into the text that was translated into Greek.[3]

Besides the textual evidence, the form of the text supports seeing chapters 4–6 as a unit. They are delimited by similar royal decrees (though by different kings) at the beginning and end. This envelope construction, or A-B-A pattern, defines the block of material. The opening decree is addressed "to the peoples, nations and men of every language, who live in all the world" (4:1). In the same way, the closing one is sent "to all the peoples, nations and men of every language throughout the land" (6:25). In both cases, the king expresses the same wish: "May you prosper greatly!" (4:1; 6:25). Both decrees mention signs and wonders (4:2, 3; 6:27) and testify to the everlasting nature of God's kingdom (4:3; 6:26).[4]

It is difficult to say exactly what the form of the stories was at this point. For example, the king in Daniel 4 may have been Nabonidus rather than Nebuchadnezzar, as it is now. When chapters 2 and 3, which are about Nebuchadnezzar—the more famous king—were added in, the name may have been changed. Also, it may be that Darius in chapter 6 was understood to be the Persian king of that name, rather than Darius the Mede of the final form of the text. One reason for thinking so is that the writing on the wall included the symbolic word "Peres," which suggests the coming of the Persians, even though the text says that the kingdom would be given to "the Medes and the Persians" (5:28). Also, the phrase "the law/laws of the Medes and the Persians" (6:8, 12, 15) suggests a time after Persia absorbed Media into its empire. When chapters 2 and 7 became incorporated into the growing book, the four-kingdom scheme was imposed on the composition. The first kingdom was Babylonia and the last two kingdoms were Persia and Greece. Perhaps this was the impetus for inserting the kingdom of the Medes in between Babylonia and Persia. If so, that, in turn, may have led to the transformation of Darius the Persian into Darius the Mede (5:31).

Stage Three

The next stage saw the book grow to its penultimate form. The author of the final form of the book took chapters 4–6 and added a substantial amount of material. First, he gathered some more Aramaic stories similar to chapters 4–6. These he edited together as Daniel 2:4b–7:28. Then he composed Daniel 1:1–2:4a and chapters 8–12 in Hebrew. Presumably, his motivation was to work the Danielic material into a message of encouragement for his people.

The Aramaic Section: Daniel 2:4b–7:28. Although the traditions in Daniel 2–7 were likely once independent, they have been shaped into a literary whole. For one thing, they are united by language: the book shifts to Aramaic in Daniel 2:4b and remains in Aramaic through the end of chapter 7. More important, it is obvious that these chapters were intentionally placed in a *chiastic* order: A B C : C′ B′ A′.

    A Ch. 2: Dream of four kingdoms (metals) followed by the kingdom of God
      B Ch. 3: Miraculous deliverance (from the fiery furnace)
        C Ch. 4: Judgment on a king (Nebuchadnezzar)
        C' Ch. 5: Judgment on a king (Belshazzar)
      B' Ch. 6: Miraculous deliverance (from the lions' den)
    A' Ch. 7: Vision of four kingdoms (beasts) followed by the kingdom of God

    Chapter 2 corresponds to chapter 7 because both present a dream or vision involving a four-kingdom scheme culminating in the coming of the kingdom of God. In chapter 2, the dream is of a human image with body parts consisting of different metals representing the four kingdoms; in chapter 7, the kingdoms are beasts rising out of the sea. Chapter 3 corresponds to chapter 6 because both tell stories of miraculous deliverance. In chapter 3, Hananiah, Mishael, and Azariah (Shadrach, Meshach, and Abednego) are saved from the fiery furnace; in chapter 6, Daniel is rescued from the lions' den. Chapters 4 and 5 have in common the theme of judgment on a Babylonian king. In chapter 4, Daniel interprets Nebuchadnezzar's dream, which predicts he will be forced to live like a beast for a time; in chapter 5, Daniel interprets the handwriting on the wall, which declares the end of Belshazzar's kingdom.

    Many downplay the similarities between Daniel 2 and 7 and emphasize the differences instead. Chapter 2 records a dream of the Babylonian king that Daniel both reveals and interprets. Chapter 7 is one of Daniel's own visions, which is interpreted by a heavenly visitor. Chapter 2 makes no reference to Antiochus IV, but predicts the arrival of God's kingdom more generally in the period of Alexander's successors. Chapter 7 condemns Antiochus IV, represented by the little horn (7:8, 20b–22, 24b–25), and anticipates the end more specifically during his reign. This leads to the claim that chapter 7 is later than chapter 2. Since chapter 2 does not mention Antiochus Epiphanes, it is argued that this chapter was written before Antiochus persecuted the Jews. It is further argued that chapter 7 fits better with chapters 8–12. In chapters 2–6, Daniel does not have visions. He interprets the revelations of Nebuchadnezzar (chs. 2 and 4) and the handwriting on the wall (ch. 5). But chapters 7–12 record the visions of Daniel himself. Often the conclusion reached is that chapters 7–12 are a block and that only they are apocalyptic.

    However, because chapters 2–7 are bound together by the Aramaic language and because of the chiastic arrangement, I think the definition of Daniel 2–7 as a block is primary while the grouping of Daniel 7–12 is secondary. Chapter 2 is very similar to chapter 7 in being an apocalyptic vision, and these two visions of the coming of God's kingdom frame the other narratives in chapters 3–6. The strong division between chapters 2–6 and 7–12 is only apparent in the final form of the book. As noted earlier, there were probably many disparate Aramaic traditions about Daniel and other Jews circulating in the second century B.C. It is quite believable that some represented Daniel as being a prophet who had his own visions, as in chapter 7, while others fashioned Daniel as a wise man who interpreted dreams and visions, as in chapters 2 and 4. This would explain why chapter 7 is in Aramaic: it is traditional material just like the other narratives in chapters 2 through 6. As for the mention of Antiochus IV in Daniel 7, that may be accounted for in one of two ways. If it is original to the unit, then the Aramaic block of material in Daniel 2 through 7 may have been designed to show progression from the evil of the Hellenistic kings (ch. 2) to the greater evil of one particular Seleucid king (ch. 7). Alternatively, the part about the horn may have been added in by the author of chapters 8–12 (who must have been able to compose in both Hebrew and Aramaic); this second option seems more likely.

It is not possible to reconstruct earlier forms of the Aramaic stories with confidence. We cannot be sure how much of what is in the book of Daniel now is original (meaning earlier Aramaic tradition handed on to the second-century B.C. author) and how much was part of the author's shaping. However, it may be that the three friends did not appear in the earliest version of chapter 2; if so, verses 13–23, which include Hananiah, Mishael, and Azariah, are secondary. At the other end of the Aramaic block, it seems quite likely that Daniel 7 originally looked more like Daniel 2 in pronouncing judgment on the Seleucid kingdom without specifically focusing on Antiochus IV. The parts of chapter 7 about the little horn may have been inserted to connect chapter 7 to the vision of the little horn in chapter 8. In these ways the author cleverly smoothed over the transition from his own material written in Hebrew (1:1–2:4a) to the Aramaic traditions (2:4b) and then back again to his Hebrew composition (Dan. 8–12).

The Hebrew Sections: Daniel 1:1–2:4a and Daniel 8–12. Besides compiling more Aramaic material and arranging it, the author, at this stage, also composed Daniel 1:1–2:4a and Daniel 8–12 in Hebrew and added these chapters in. Chapter 1 serves as an introduction to the Aramaic stories in chapters 2–7. Since chapter 3 mentions Shadrach, Meshach, and Abednego, but not Daniel, and since chapter 6 tells of Daniel but not his friends, chapter 1 helps to unify these disconnected traditions. It tells how all four Jews were taken into exile and how they went through their training program together. The contest theme links chapter 1 with chapters 2, 4, and 5. In the opening chapter Daniel and his friends show themselves to be ten times wiser than the other magicians and enchanters (Dan. 1:20). This is similar to chapter 2, where the other wise men are stymied and only Daniel is able to recount and interpret the dream. In chapter 4, Daniel once again succeeds in interpreting the king's dream where the others fail. In chapter 5, no one can make sense of the handwriting except Daniel. The threat motif of chapters 3 (the blazing furnace) and 6 (the lions' den) can also be found in the danger to the supervisor: if the four Jews do not appear to be as healthy as the other students, the king might have his head (1:10). Furthermore, mention of the temple vessels (1:2) anticipates Belshazzar's feast in chapter 5 (5:2–4). Finally, the author replaced the original heading of chapter 2 with one of his own in Hebrew (2:1–4a). He introduced the Aramaic material by having the Babylonian sages speak: "Then the astrologers answered the king in Aramaic." What follows is in Aramaic. However, it is obvious that this is merely a literary device, because the text stays in Aramaic after the astrologers finish speaking.

Not only does chapter 1 set the stage for chapters 2–7; it also serves as a fitting introduction to the whole book because it focuses on the wisdom of Daniel and his friends (1:4 ["showing aptitude"], 17 ["understanding"]) using the Hebrew root *skl*, "to be prudent, wise, clever, or skillful." This root recurs later in the book (9:13 ["giving attention"], 22 ["to give you insight"], 25 ["understand"]) and is especially prominent toward the end, where the author shows his esteem for the wise who will instruct others in righteousness (11:33 ["those who are wise"]), face martyrdom (11:35 ["some of the wise"]), shine like the stars and lead others to righteousness (12:3 ["those who are wise"]), and understand (12:10 ["those who are wise"]). Therefore, the use of the *skl* motif acts as a unifying factor binding chapter 1 to the other Hebrew section at the end of the book (chs. 8–12).

Although the author, who was bilingual, composed Daniel 1:1–2:4a as an introduction, he also edited the Aramaic material to bring greater unity to the whole and to improve the transitions between the Aramaic center and the Hebrew ends. Daniel 2:13–23 was probably added in (see the Additional Note on 2:13–23). In the original account, Daniel probably was not one of the royal sages in chapter 2. When he hears of the impending execution of the king's advisers, he presents himself to Arioch and is brought before the king, who apparently does not know him yet; then Daniel supplies the dream and its interpretation. In the later version (including 2:13–23) Daniel is one of the wise men and is threatened by the king's decree. He goes to his friends for prayer support, after which God reveals to Daniel the dream and its meaning. These verses were inserted to agree with chapter 1, where Daniel and his friends had been trained, had entered the service of the king as his advisers, and had met the king (1:18–20). So, the author of Daniel changed chapter 2 to make Daniel a member of the threatened group of sages. But he also added the friends into chapter 2, which was originally only about Daniel. Hananiah, Mishael, and Azariah link chapter 2 to chapter 1, which mentions all four Jews. They also link chapter 2 to chapter 3, which mentions only the three friends and excludes Daniel.

The author also had to deal with the seam between chapters 7 and 8. He likely composed, in Aramaic, and inserted in chapter 7 the verse concerning the little horn (7:8, 20b–22, 24b–25) in order to link chapter 7 to chapter 8. The result is that both Daniel 7 and 8 point to a wicked king, represented as a little horn. In chapter 7, he is arrogant (7:8, 20b) and wages war against the holy ones (probably understood to be angels [7:21]). In chapter 8, the little horn becomes very powerful, attacks the host of heaven, puts a stop to the temple sacrifices, and commits a desolating transgression (8:9–13). At this time also, the date formulas were put in as headings to each chapter to shape the two halves of the book. As noted earlier (see "Genre"), there are two progressions of dates. The first runs from chapter 1 to chapter 6: Nebuchadnezzar (chs. 1–4), Belshazzar (ch. 5), and Darius (ch. 6). The second runs from chapter 7 to chapter 12 as the time marker steps back one king to Belshazzar in chapter 7 before moving forward again and ending later than the first progression: Belshazzar (chs. 7–8), Darius (ch. 9), and Cyrus (chs. 10–12). These time indicators make clear the identity of the four kingdoms. The first three must be Babylonia, Media, and Persia. The fourth, Greece, is specified within the chapters. The male goat of chapter 8 (8:5–8) is identified as Greece (8:21). In chapter 10, the angel predicts that the kingdom to come after Persia will be Greece (10:20).

Daniel's Unity. If this analysis is correct, the problem of the tension between the formal division (stories in chs. 1–6; visions in chs. 7–12) and the language division (1:1–2:4a and chs. 8–12 in Hebrew; 2:4b–7:28 in Aramaic) is resolved. The formal division is the product of the author. He found various traditions about Daniel and the three Jews and arranged them so that Daniel's vision was last (Dan. 7). He then recorded the visions of chapters 8–12. By placing the other court narratives first (2:4b–6:28) and adding an introductory chapter (Dan. 1), he created a structure that appears to have a major division between chapters 6 and 7. The first half of the book is an anonymous collection of stories about

Daniel and three other Jews who were exiled to Babylon. The second half is a pseudonymous collection of visions attributed to Daniel. The first half is usually dated earlier (from the Persian or early Hellenistic period) and not considered apocalyptic. The second half is often dated to the second century B.C. and designated apocalyptic.

Too much should not be made of the division between chapters 6 and 7. We must remember that Daniel 2 and 7 are linked by predicting that the kingdom of God will displace four earlier kingdoms of this world. Furthermore, we should not overemphasize the earlier date of the Aramaic material, as some scholars do, treating these stories merely as examples of how Jews may succeed in pagan courts. The author selected and shaped the inherited traditions in such a way that they fit his message, probably addressed to the Jews of the second century B.C. By adding in his Hebrew compositions, he then created a unified work of literary art meant to encourage the Jews who were being persecuted by Antiochus IV. The following summary considers the historical and contextual background of each chapter, with special emphasis on how Daniel might have been relevant to a second-century audience.

Chapter 1. The Seleucid soldiers were forcing Jews to eat pork that had been sacrificed to Zeus. The first chapter of Daniel warns the Jews not to defile themselves with the king's meat (1:8).

Chapter 2. Some Jews were afraid of the Greek king and his power. The vision of Daniel 2 offers tremendous hope to those suffering under the hand of the oppressive ruler: human regimes will be smashed, but "not by human hands" (2:34, 45), when God sets up his own everlasting kingdom. (Later the hope is expressed that the tyrant himself "will be destroyed, but not by human power" [8:25].)

Chapter 3. In the second century B.C., the Seleucid king demanded that Jews worship the Greek gods or die. Parallel to this, in Daniel 3, Nebuchadnezzar insists that Shadrach, Meshach, and Abednego bow down before an image. By refusing, they serve as role models to the Jews of later times. Their confession is also significant for the interpretation of the whole book: "If we are thrown into the blazing furnace, the God we serve is able to save us from it, and he will rescue us from your hand, O king. But even if he does not, we want you to know, O king, that we will not serve your gods or worship the image of gold you have set up" (3:17–18). The author of Daniel used this to convey his own faith. He believed that God would intervene in history to rescue the beleaguered Jews and to destroy the kingdom of Antiochus IV. However, if God refrained or delayed, it was better to die a martyr's death than to deny the faith.

Chapter 4. Antiochus IV used the title "Epiphanes" (Greek *epiphanēs*) to convey that he was a manifestation of God. However, he was really *epimanēs,* or "mad." Clearly, the Jews considered him to be a megalomaniac. Therefore, the depiction in Daniel 4 of a proud king whom God drove crazy fits the situation of the second century B.C. Although Nebuchadnezzar did not persecute the Jews, he is represented as becoming beastly. Faithful Jews suffering under the Seleucid persecution would have seen in this story about Nebuchadnezzar an indictment of Antiochus IV, who was deranged and under the judgment of God.

Chapter 5. Jews of the second century B.C. would not have missed the allusion in Daniel 5 to Antiochus IV, who "arrogantly entered the sanctuary and took the golden altar, the lampstand for the light, and all its utensils" as well as "bowls" and "costly vessels" (1 Macc. 1:21–23 NRSV). This was an outrageous sacrilege. In like manner, in Daniel 5, Belshazzar dares to profane the holy temple vessels by using them during a drunken feast while praising "the gods of gold and silver, of bronze, iron, wood and stone" (Dan. 5:4). This triggers God's action to bring about Belshazzar's demise and the termination of his kingdom (Dan. 5:25–28, 30). The Jews of Antiochus's day hoped that God would remove him as God had removed Belshazzar earlier; they hoped that God would end the Seleucid kingdom as he had the Babylonian.

Chapter 6. The Jews in the second century faced martyrdom because the king had declared it a capital offense to practice Judaism. Similarly, Daniel is threatened with death in chapter 6 for continuing his religious practice of prayer, which has been outlawed. No one is allowed to pray "to any god or man" for "thirty days," except to the king (6:7). This specifically rebuked Antiochus IV, whose power encroached upon that of the deity.

Chapter 7. Antiochus Epiphanes waged war on the Jews in his time. In the vision of Daniel 7, an arrogant ruler attacks the holy ones and is successful for a time, until God interrupts the events of history with the advent of his eternal kingdom. This brings an end to the beastly kingdoms of earth as dominion is given to "the people of the holy ones of the Most High" (7:27 NRSV). This was the hope of the author of the book of Daniel: that God would destroy the Seleucid kingdom and give sovereignty to his people.

Chapters 8–12. These apocalyptic visions make more explicit God's judgment on Antiochus IV and God's plan to deliver his people.

No one questions that Daniel 7 is apocalyptic. Most also accept that chapters 8–12 continue with apocalyptic visions tied to the reign of Antiochus IV. But the analysis above shows that chapters 1 through 6 are part and parcel of the whole program of the apocalyptist who wrote and edited the book of Daniel. Even though the Aramaic material originated in an earlier period and may have functioned differently when first composed, it has been brought into the service of a larger vision: the elimination of Seleucid rule and the irruption of the kingdom of God.

Stage Four

In Daniel, the end is expected to come after "a time, times and half a time" (12:7; see also 7:25; 9:27), or three and a half years, which by one reckoning amounts to 1,150 days (8:14). Actually, the Maccabees were able to cleanse the temple and drive out the Seleucids after about three years, but the kingdom of God did not come in its fullness then. When it still did not arrive after the set time of 1,150 days, an editor may have added Daniel 12:11, lengthening it to 1,290 days. After that date passed uneventfully, Daniel 12:12 was added, extending the deadline to 1,335 days. When the new age still did not dawn, the last verse of the book was added: "As for you, go your way till the end. You will rest, and then at the end of the days you will rise to receive your allotted inheritance" (12:13). In other words, there was to be no more setting of dates. The end would eventually come and when it did, Daniel would rise from the dead to participate in the rule of God and his people.

History of Interpretation

When the kingdom of God did not arrive in the time of Antiochus IV, the Jews did not cast the book of Daniel aside as a false prophecy; rather, they reinterpreted it.[5] Originally, the fourth kingdom was Greece in the time of the Diadochi. However, Rome became the next great world empire to take center stage in history, showing that Greece could not have been the last kingdom before the end. In this way, the fourth kingdom came to be identified with Rome. This is clear in the Jewish apocalypse of *4 Ezra*, which is dated to the first century A.D. The seer is told that the eagle in his vision corresponds to Daniel's fourth kingdom, except that there is a new explanation of it, different from the one given to Daniel. In the context, that kingdom has to be Rome (*4 Ezra* 12:1–13).

Josephus also reinterpreted the final kingdom as Rome. When he discussed the stone of Daniel 2, he refused to divulge its meaning, referring the reader to the book of Daniel instead. This is probably because in the vision the stone destroys the statue (2:34–35, 44–45), including the fourth kingdom, understood to be Rome (Josephus, *Ant.* 10.210).

Josephus's reluctance was doubtless due to fear of his Roman patrons; they would not be enthused by a prediction of Rome's demise. Although he allowed that Daniel's prophecy about the persecution of the Jews was partly fulfilled by the evil deeds of Antiochus IV, Josephus also believed that Daniel predicted the Roman conquest of Jerusalem and the destruction of the temple (*Ant.* 10.276; see also *J.W.* 6.310–314). Here he was probably thinking of Daniel 9:26: "The people of the ruler who will come will destroy the city and the sanctuary." Since the Romans at times persecuted the Jews and since they razed the holy city, it was natural to see them as the embodiment of the violent beast of Daniel 7:7.

Christian theology was similar to Jewish teaching in identifying the fourth kingdom with Rome. Daniel predicted the coming of God's kingdom from above after the fourth beastly kingdom from below (Dan. 2:44; 7:14, 27). Since the church associated the arrival of God's kingdom, or at least its dawning, with the advent of Jesus (Matt. 3:2; Mark 1:14–15; Luke 11:20), the fourth kingdom had to be the dominant empire of Jesus's day. This is especially evident in Revelation, where John reinterprets the evil beast of Daniel as Rome (Rev. 13; 17). Paul also understood this era to be significant: God sent forth his Son to be born of a woman in the fullness of time (Gal. 4:4–5), which was the Roman period. Once Rome took the last slot, the second and third kingdoms of Daniel had to be reinterpreted as well. Media and Persia were combined so that the four kingdoms came to be construed as Babylonia, Medo-Persia, Greece, and Rome (instead of Babylonia, Media, Persia, and Greece).

Besides the motifs of the fourth kingdom and the kingdom of God, many other influences from Daniel appear in the NT. Jesus understands himself to be a crushing stone (Luke 20:18), reminiscent of Daniel 2:34–35, 44–45. He frequently calls himself the Son of Man (Mark 2:10–11; 8:31; 9:9), sometimes in clear reference to the transcendent one of Daniel 7:13 (Mark 8:38; 14:61–62). In the context of predicting the leveling of the temple (Matt. 24:1–2), Jesus also announces the coming of other signs of the end (Matt. 24:3–31): wars, persecution of the believers, apostasy, betrayal, the desolating abomination, great suffering, and finally the appearance of the Son of Man in heaven. All of these are allusions to Daniel. In fact, Jesus even mentions Daniel: "So when you see standing in the holy place 'the abomination that causes desolation,' spoken of through the prophet Daniel—let the reader understand—then let those who are in Judea flee to the mountains" (Matt. 24:15–16). Presumably this was fulfilled in A.D. 70 when the temple was destroyed. Paul picks up on the descriptions of Antiochus IV in Daniel to anticipate a future "man of lawlessness" who "will exalt himself over everything that is called God or is worshiped, so that he sets himself up in God's temple, proclaiming himself to be God" (2 Thess. 2:3–4).

As time went on, Christians began to see Jesus in other passages of Daniel. The stone in Nebuchadnezzar's vision was not cut out by human hands (2:34). This came to be read as a witness to the virgin birth of Jesus. The coming of an anointed one (9:25) and the cutting off of an anointed one (9:26) were both interpreted in light of Jesus. The first was thought to predict his coming, and the second, his death. Because of this, some Christians have endeavored to develop schemes so that the sixty-nine weeks of years, or 483 years, of Daniel 9:25–26 exactly lead up to Jesus's crucifixion. These have not proved to be convincing (see the commentary on 9:25–26).

Later still, with the rise of Islam and its threatening armies, some Christians and Jews reinterpreted the fourth kingdom as Islam. During the Reformation it was common for Protestants to see in the Roman Catholic Church a continuation of Rome, the fourth beast; they then designated the pope to be the Antichrist. Some have tried to use the numbers in Daniel to calculate the date of Christ's return. For example, William Miller in the nineteenth century made two unsuccessful predictions that the second coming of Jesus would be in his time, based on his interpretation of Daniel.[6]

How should the book of Daniel be interpreted today? Some Christians continue to read it as a collection of predictions about Jesus. They understand Daniel to have predicted both advents of Jesus: the first advent, including his death, in the verses mentioned above (9:24–27) and the second advent in the vision of one like a human being coming in the heavenly clouds (7:13). Some use the book to predict future events, or they point to current events as fulfillments of prophecies in Daniel. While it is the case that the author of Daniel wrote of events that took place in the second century B.C., his words were later reinterpreted by Jesus and his followers. It seems, then, that we should first read Daniel in its original context. As Christians, we also accept the authority and inspiration of the reinterpretations of Daniel within the NT. But those later reinterpretations were not the original meaning of Daniel, and we need not read them as such.

The notion that Daniel was written in the second century B.C. and addressed people and events in that era was not unknown in the early Christian centuries. Porphyry, in the third century A.D., took this position, but his view was discredited because he was a pagan philosopher writing against Christianity. However, since the rise of modern scientific methods of biblical interpretation in the seventeenth century A.D., most scholars have conceded that Porphyry was correct about the date of Daniel (though Christian scholars would say he was wrong about their faith). Our interest in the book of Daniel need not be merely antiquarian, however. The truths of this apocalypse are for all believers in all ages.

Theology

The message of Daniel is not so narrow that it only had relevance for the Jews living under Antiochus IV. On the contrary, the teaching of Daniel is very rich and has much to say to us today as well.

The Problem of Evil

The book of Daniel grew out of a social situation where Jews were being persecuted for their faith, causing them to wrestle with the problem of evil. Earlier Jewish texts had focused on sin as the cause of suffering. In Deuteronomy 28 we find long lists of blessings and curses: keeping the law brings blessings; breaking the law brings curses. The history books following Deuteronomy, known to scholars as the Deuteronomistic History (Joshua, Judges, 1 and 2 Samuel, and 1 and 2 Kings), were written from that perspective and provide numerous illustrations. For example, in the book of Judges, when the Israelites go astray, God allows enemies to oppress them; but when they repent, he raises up judges to deliver them. Second Kings portrays the fall of the northern kingdom of Israel (2 Kgs. 17) and the later fall of the southern kingdom of Judah (2 Kgs. 24–25) as judgments resulting from disobedience. Prophets generally held the same theology. Jeremiah and Ezekiel, for instance, agree that Jerusalem fell because of the Jews' iniquity.

In strong contrast to that, Daniel largely places the blame for Jewish suffering on the wicked oppressors. The only exception is in chapter 9, where Daniel fasts while confessing his sins and the sins of his people (9:1–20). There he acknowledges that the destruction of Jerusalem was a punishment for transgression. However, the deuteronomistic language in his prayer is traditional, and the whole prayer may be secondary to the passage. Alternatively, it is possible that the author of Daniel accepted the theology of retribution for the destruction of Jerusalem in 587 B.C. but not for the persecution of the Jews in 167 B.C. Elsewhere in Daniel, God does punish sin. He causes Nebuchadnezzar to suffer for his hubris in chapter 4, and he pronounces judgment on Belshazzar in chapter 5, but these are foreigners. Other than chapter 9, the one case where God judges his people is in chapter 12. He raises from the dead some of the wicked, who probably are Hellenistic Jews who apostatized, to experience "shame and everlasting contempt" (12:2). But the book does not teach a cause-and-effect relationship between the sins of the Jews and the sufferings they have endured.

Rather, wicked people cause suffering. The king tries to have the Jews killed in the fiery furnace (Dan. 3). Conspirators try to do away with Daniel (Dan. 6). And, of course, Antiochus IV is the major villain; much of the book is devoted to describing his wickedness. He "spoke boastfully" (7:8, 20). He "was waging war against the saints and defeating them" (7:21; see also v. 25). The Aramaic word translated "saints" is better translated "holy ones," because it probably does not refer to the earthly saints but to the holy ones in heaven, or angels. To be sure, Antiochus Epiphanes was oppressing the Jews on earth, yet the narrator describes him as storming heaven. In the apocalyptist's theology, if Antiochus IV was successful in persecuting the Jews, heaven itself must be under siege. This is confirmed in the next chapter: the horn (Antiochus IV) "grew until it reached the host of the heavens, and it threw some of the starry host down to the earth and trampled on them. It set itself up to be as great as the Prince of the host.... Because of rebellion, the host of the saints and the daily sacrifice were given over to it" (8:10–12). This evil king "will destroy the mighty and the holy people" (8:24). "He will destroy many and take his stand against the Prince of princes" (8:25). The individual designated "Prince of the host" (8:11) and "Prince of princes" (8:25) is probably Michael (12:1); "the host" and "the host of the saints" (8:10–12) probably refer to the other heavenly beings. Persecuting the Jews is tantamount to attacking heaven and the angels.

It is difficult for us even to conceive of the possibility of a human king attacking God's angels, much less that he would actually succeed in bringing some of them down. The author of Daniel had a different problem. How could heaven stand by and allow the Jews to be persecuted? For him this was inconceivable. Therefore, in the mind of the apocalyptist, the heavenly host were unable to respond immediately to the crisis because of the serious warfare being waged against them. The Jews were suffering at the hands of an evil king, which prompted the author of Daniel to compose this book in response. It explained the situation not as a result of the disobedience of the people but as the result of a cosmic battle. The Jewish people were not guilty sinners but innocent victims. Yet the book did not stop with this analysis, which by itself might lead to despair. Daniel was written to give the Jews hope. Heaven might be delayed, as in Daniel 10, where the heavenly being (probably Gabriel) was prevented from getting through for three weeks by the prince of Persia until Michael assisted him (10:13). But God was still on his throne and would eventually prevail, destroying the wicked Antiochus IV and his kingdom and ushering in God's glorious, eternal kingdom. The appeal of this apocalyptic sermon, then, was for the Jews to look to God for deliverance.

Names for God

It is interesting that "Yahweh" (*YHWH*, usually rendered Lord in the English translations), the proper name for Israel's God, is rarely used in Daniel; it is found only in chapter 9: twice in the narrative (9:2, 20) and the other times in the body of the prayer (9:4, 8, 10, 13, 14). "God" (*'elohim*; Aramaic *'elah*) is most common, occurring fifty times in forty-five verses (e.g., 1:2, 9, 17; 2:20; 3:17; 5:26). One explanation is that if the book was composed when the Jews were living in a pagan Greek realm, they would have been accustomed to using the generic term for God, rather than the more particular name, "Yahweh," which would have been foreign to their Gentile neighbors. Nevertheless, the writer particularizes God by associating him with the Jewish people: "God of my fathers" (2:23); "the God of Shadrach, Meshach and Abednego" (3:28, 29); "the God of Daniel" (6:26; also "his God," "your God," or "my God" in reference to Daniel [see 6:10, 16, 20, 22]); "our God" (9:9, 10, 13, 14, 15, 17). In the lions' den episode, the king twice uses the epithet "the living God" (6:20; 26), while also highlighting the fact that this is Daniel's God. God is described as "living" because he and his kingdom will endure forever (6:26; see also 4:34 and 12:7, which say that God "lives forever"). That he is living is also evident from his power: he "performs signs and wonders" (6:27) and "rescued Daniel from the power of the lions" (6:26–27; see also v. 20).

Four times we find "the Most High God" (3:26; 4:2; 5:18, 21), although "the Most High" by itself is more common (4:17, 24, 25, 32, 34; 7:18, 22, 25, 27). These terms seem to emphasize the sovereignty of God: "the Most High is sovereign" (4:17, 25, 32; 5:21); the Most High gives sovereignty to Nebuchadnezzar (5:18); the Most High will share his kingdom with his holy ones (7:18, 22) and with the people of his holy ones (7:27),[7] and this kingdom will last forever (7:27); and the Most High makes binding decrees—a royal function (4:24).

Once, God is indicated by the word "Heaven." Here also, sovereignty is in view: Nebuchadnezzar's kingdom will not be restored until he acknowledges that "Heaven rules" (4:26). Similarly, God is "the Lord of heaven" (5:23) and "the King of heaven" (4:37), as well as "the God of heaven" (2:18, 19, 37, 44) and "God in heaven" (2:28). Daniel's God is "the God of gods" and "the Lord of kings" (a confession of the pagan king Nebuchadnezzar in 2:47; see also 11:36 for another occurrence of "the God of gods"), showing that the God of Israel rules over heaven and earth. We can see from the above discussion of names and epithets that a major emphasis in the book of Daniel is the kingship of God.

The Kingship of God

While the Jews were being persecuted, it may not have been obvious to them that God was in control. That is why the author of Daniel had to sound this note so strongly: God is still on his throne. This was not a new theme for the Jews. One of the reasons traditional Yahwists resisted the establishment of an earthly monarch was that Yahweh was the sole king and allowed no other (Judg. 8:23; 1 Sam. 8:6–7). The kingship of Yahweh was important in Israel's worship as expressed in the enthronement psalms (for example, Pss. 93; 95; 96; and 97). But this theme obtained greater prominence in Daniel than in many other books.

First of all, God rules over the kingdom of heaven. Israel's neighbors believed there were many gods who had power, but the Jews believed that their God was vastly superior to the other gods and would triumph over them. From time to time the Bible presents contests between Yahweh and the gods of the nations. There was a contest between Yahweh and the gods of Egypt in the story of the Exodus (Exod. 12:12); between Yahweh and Dagon in Israel's struggle with the Philistines (1 Sam. 5); and between Yahweh and Baal on Mount Carmel in the conflict with the Canaanites (1 Kgs. 18). Daniel presents a contest between Israel's God and the Babylonian gods. On one level it is a contest between the Jews (Daniel and his friends) and the Babylonians (diviners and wise men) as Daniel and his friends excel in wisdom beyond all the others. But on another level, it is really a contest between the God of the Jews and the gods of the Babylonians; the outcome is that the God of the Jews rules.

His kingship is manifested in his superiority to the other divinities. The gods of the Babylonians cannot reveal secrets or interpret dreams or visions, but the Jews' deity can (2:19, 27–28, 47; 4:7–9). Therefore he is the "God of gods" (2:47; 11:36), meaning that he is the greatest of the gods and rules over the other gods. The God of the Jews delivers from the fiery furnace those who refuse to worship the pagan image (Dan. 3). King Nebuchadnezzar is so amazed at this that he declares, "no other god can save in this way" (3:29). King Darius is similarly impressed when Daniel survives a night with hungry lions (Dan. 6). His question of Daniel the next morning implies that other gods could not do this: "Daniel, servant of the living God, has your God, whom you serve continually, been able to rescue you from the lions?" (6:20). The king then issues a decree that everyone in his dominion "must fear and reverence the God of Daniel" (6:26), because he "rescues and he saves; he performs signs and wonders" (6:27; see also 3:28–29) and "he has rescued Daniel from the power of the lions" (6:27). Evidently the king does not think other gods are capable of such acts. Furthermore, Darius connects God's superiority with kingship, for he speaks in his decree of God's "kingdom" and "dominion" (6:26). Also, in Babylonian religion, the gods "do not live among men" (2:11), but Daniel's God comes to him in a night vision (2:19) and is present with the three Jews in the furnace in the form of his angel (3:25).

While the author of Daniel confidently affirms God's rule in heaven, he is not naive concerning evil. He knows that wicked elements contrive to harm God's people. Daniel and his friends are threatened with death (2:13). Daniel's friends willingly risk death (3:18, 28) as the king angrily commands them to be cast into the furnace (3:13, 19–20). Daniel's colleagues conspire to destroy him (6:4–9, 12–13). Sometimes God's people will be rescued immediately, as in the stories of the fiery furnace and the lions' den. But the author is also aware that sometimes "for a time they will fall by the sword or be burned or captured or plundered" (11:33). This seems to follow from the agency of more nefarious forces in the universe. As mentioned earlier, there is spiritual warfare in heaven between evil spirits and the angels (10:13), and there is warfare between Antiochus IV and the host of heaven (7:21, 25; 8:10–12, 25). However, God's side will eventually triumph (7:22, 27); deliverance will come (12:1). The apocalyptic writer believed that even though initially evil seemed to prevail, its success would be fleeting. The divine king would ultimately subdue the dark powers to reign supreme in heaven over all.

Secondly, God rules over the kings of earth. The book of Daniel is very concerned about kings. It opens with King Jehoiakim of Judah being subjugated by King Nebuchadnezzar of Babylon. While chapters 2 and 7 present the sweep of history as a succession of kingdoms, they also accentuate certain kings such as Nebuchadnezzar (2:36–38) and Antiochus IV (though he is not actually named; 7:8, 20–22, 24–26). Besides Nebuchadnezzar (Dan. 1–4) and Antiochus IV (Dan. 7–12), two other kings are focused on in the book: Belshazzar (Dan. 5) and Darius the Mede (5:31; 6; 9:1). The book also throws passing glances at Cyrus (1:21; 6:28; 10:1) and Alexander the Great (8:5–8, 21). Yet throughout the narrative the real emphasis is on the heavenly king. Daniel's God is the "Lord of kings" (2:47). Earthly kings cannot rule without the divine king's permission, because "he sets up kings and deposes them" (2:21); he "is sovereign over the kingdoms of men and gives them to anyone he wishes" (4:17, 25, 32; see also 5:21).

One should not be impressed with earthly kings. Even Nebuchadnezzar, who is addressed by Daniel as "the king of kings" (2:37) and who has "dominion and power and might and glory" (2:37; see also 5:18), can only boast of these things because God gave them to him (2:37; 5:18). Furthermore, God's choices are not always obvious. He does not always choose the strongest or most powerful. On the contrary, "he sets over [the kingdoms] the lowliest of men" (4:17). This anticipates the intervention of the heavenly king in the affairs of the earthly kings and the giving of the kingdom to the people of the saints of the Most High in chapter 7 (7:27). The Jews, as a persecuted people, would have felt like the lowliest of human beings in that time. The book of Daniel gave them hope that God would bring his reign to earth in a more visible way and that he would share governance with them.

The Kingdom of God

A king must have a kingdom. The notion of the kingdom of God is bound up with the notion of his kingship. In the period of the tribal league (described in Judges), the Israelites did not have an earthly king, yet they were a kingdom ruled by God, the heavenly king (Judg. 8:23; 1 Sam. 8:6–7). Even after they established an earthly monarchy, God was still understood to be their real king; the earthly kingdom was an extension of the heavenly. In the covenant God made with David, a father-son relationship was established (2 Sam. 7:14; Ps. 89:26). On the day of his coronation, the Davidic descendant was adopted as son of God, a sort of vice-regent (Ps. 2:7). To that covenant were attached promises of dominion over Israel's enemies (Ps. 110:1) and indeed over "the ends of the earth" (Ps. 2:8). The theological expectation was that God's kingdom would grow on earth until it eventually took over the world.

As time went on, this image of an anointed king, a conquering hero, became ever more lofty and idealized. In the time of Isaiah, the people looked for a Davidic ruler who would bring a kingdom of righteousness and peace (Isa. 9; 11) and a return to paradise (Isa. 11). However, the history of the monarchy in Israel was a history of failure. None of the earthly kings fulfilled the hopes and promises; none brought the hoped-for righteous, eternal kingdom. This came to a climax in the Babylonian exile in the sixth century B.C., when the Judean kingdom actually came to an end. During that period of suffering, Isaiah 40–55 (sometimes referred to as Second Isaiah) picked up the theme of the Davidic covenant and democratized it, offering it to all the Jews. In plural terms, addressed to the community, God said through the prophet: "Give ear and come to me; hear me, that your soul may live. I will make an everlasting covenant with you, my faithful love promised to David. . . . Surely, you will summon nations you know not, and nations that do not know you will hasten to you, because of the LORD your God, the Holy One of Israel, for he has endowed you with splendor" (Isa. 55:3, 5). In effect, the Jewish community becomes the Messiah. The influence of God's kingdom spreads through his word and through his people, not through the sword. It involves a summoning of human hearts to submit to God, not the conquest of territory. This kingdom is more spiritual than geographical.

The theme of the kingdom of God comes to greater maturity of expression in Daniel, during the postexilic period. The sovereign God will eventually destroy the kingdoms of this world (Dan. 2; 7). When he does, he will bring his own eternal kingdom to earth. The apocalyptist did not expect deliverance to come from below, from a human descendant of David, as was thought earlier. In his view, God's people might get a little help from the human side, that is, from the Maccabees (11:34), but deliverance would not come from that quarter. Rather, it would come from above, from heaven, from the transcendent one who looks like a human being (NIV "son of man" [7:13]). At first this appears to be an individual, perhaps an angel such as Michael. And yet, as in Second Isaiah, it is actually a community. The interpretation clearly shows that the kingdom is given to the holy ones (NIV "saints") of the Most High (probably angels) (Dan. 7:18, 22). But later on, it refers to the "people of the saints of the Most High" (NIV "the saints, the people of the Most High" [Dan. 7:27]). In contrast to human kingdoms, God's kingdom will never end. Earthly realms are ephemeral, but God's "dominion is an eternal dominion" that endures forever (Dan. 4:34; see also 2:44; 7:14, 18, 27). While of some importance in the OT, this motif becomes central in the teachings of John the Baptist (Matt. 3:1–2 [kingdom of heaven]) and of Jesus (Matt. 4:17 [kingdom of heaven]; Mark 1:14–15 and Luke 4:43 [kingdom of God]) in the NT.

Humility

Because God is the exalted heavenly king, whose kingdom extends to earth, it is appropriate for mortals to display humility before him. Nebuchadnezzar failed to do this. When he lifts himself up in pride, God acts to humble him by making him live as a beast for a time (4:17, 25, 28–30, 32, 34–35, esp. v. 37; 5:20–23). Belshazzar should learn from Nebuchadnezzar's mistake, but he does not. On the contrary, he exalts himself against the Lord of heaven by drinking from the temple vessels (5:20–23). Therefore, God will bring Belshazzar's kingdom to an end (5:26, 30). Antiochus IV, presumably the person represented by the little horn, "spoke boastfully" (7:8; cf. v. 11) "against the Most High" (7:25). Furthermore, this horn "grew until it reached the host of the heavens" (8:10), and "it set itself up to be as great as the Prince of the host" (8:11). "He will consider himself superior" (8:25). "He will exalt himself above every god and will say unheard-of things against the God of gods" (11:36; see also vv. 37–39). Scripture teaches that those who humble themselves will be exalted, but "those who walk in pride [God] is able to humble" (Dan. 4:37; see also Prov. 11:2; 16:18; 29:23; Matt. 23:12; Luke 14:11; 18:14; James 4:10; 1 Pet. 5:6). Antiochus IV may get by with his evil deeds for a brief time, but he is destined to fall (Dan. 8:25).

Humility is a theme that unites the court narratives with the visions. The kings of Daniel 1–6 may be less malevolent than the wicked king at the center of Daniel 7–12, but the narratives in the first half of the book apparently have still been shaped by the events of the second century B.C. It is hard not to see the arrogance of Antiochus IV in the hubris of Nebuchadnezzar and Belshazzar. One important message of the book of Daniel is that all should humble themselves before the king of heaven. This leads to a kind of evangelistic or gospel thrust.

Evangelism

A sense of witness permeates the book of Daniel. It seems the author was influenced by the vision of Isaiah 40–55 (Second Isaiah). God, speaking through the author of Second Isaiah (thought to be an anonymous prophet of the exile), called the Jews to be witnesses to the oneness of God (Isa. 43:10–13; 44:8). They were called to be a light to the Gentiles, proclaiming God the creator and savior and denouncing idolatry (Isa. 42:5–8; 49:6). One day foreigners, and even rulers, would bow down to the Jews, acknowledging their God (Isa. 45:14; 49:7, 22–23). God himself appeals to the nations directly, inviting them to turn to him and be saved (Isa. 45:22). This theme is also found earlier in Isaiah 1–39 (First Isaiah; see Isa. 2:1–4) and later in Isaiah 56–66 (Third Isaiah; see Isa. 60:1–12).

Daniel and his friends bear witness to their supervisors by being faithful to their dietary rules (Dan. 1). Daniel is so successful in his testimony that Nebuchadnezzar apparently converts. In a fulfillment of Second Isaiah's prophecy (Isa. 49:7, 23), Nebuchadnezzar bows down before Daniel (Dan. 2:46) and acknowledges his God: "Surely your God is the God of gods and the Lord of kings and a revealer of mysteries, for you were able to reveal this mystery" (Dan. 2:47). Shadrach, Meshach, and Abednego bear witness to a God who is able to do miracles. Because God delivers them from the blazing furnace, Nebuchadnezzar praises them for faithfulness and decrees a severe judgment on anyone who should speak against their

God (3:28–29). The king himself confesses, "No other god can save in this way" (3:29). Nebuchadnezzar continues his praise of God in chapter 4: God is the "Most High"; he performs miracles; his kingdom will endure forever; he is just and righteous (4:2–3, 34–35, 37). By way of contrast, Belshazzar does not repent at Daniel's preaching but rather falls under the judgment of God (Dan. 5). Darius offers an ascription of praise similar to that of Nebuchadnezzar: "he is the living God"; he and his kingdom are eternal; "he rescues and saves"; he performs miracles (6:26–27). However, in one respect Darius surpasses even Nebuchadnezzar in his response to Daniel's faithful testimony (Dan. 6). Whereas Nebuchadnezzar acts negatively to protect the Jews' God from slander (3:28–29), Darius acts positively, demanding that his subjects "fear and reverence the God of Daniel" (6:26).

In the second half of the book (Dan. 7–12), Daniel does not interact with kings or other Gentiles. He has his own visions, which he keeps to himself (7:28). However, in two places the author makes clear what he expects of the faithful Jews during persecution, such as that of Antiochus IV: "Those who are wise will instruct many, though for a time they will fall by the sword or be burned or captured or plundered" (11:33); "Those who are wise will shine like the brightness of the heavens, and those who lead many to righteousness, like the stars for ever and ever" (12:3). This last verse may also have been influenced by Second Isaiah, since the expression "lead many to righteousness" (Dan. 12:3) is reminiscent of "justify many" (Isa. 53:11).

The author of Daniel expected the Jews to be faithful unto death and to witness to others. They were to teach others and lead them to righteousness. Primarily, this mission was to the Jews who had assimilated to the Hellenistic culture. The faithful Jews were to restore the unfaithful ones (cf. Isa. 49:5–6). But there was also the secondary mission of being a light to the Gentiles. The Jewish witness to the Gentiles continued down to the time of Jesus. Jesus pointed to missionary activity by the Jews in his time (Matt. 23:15). The book of Acts mentions Gentiles who worshiped or feared God (Acts 13:16, 26). The court of the Gentiles in the Jerusalem temple was for these non-Jewish God fearers. They had not gone all the way and converted to Judaism. According to the rabbis, it was enough that they gave up their idols, worshiped the one true God, and kept those commandments pertaining to all people.

All of this prepares the way for the Great Commission. Jesus instructed his followers to bear witness of him and to bring the good news of salvation in him to all people (Matt. 28:18–20; Mark 16:15; Acts 1:8). The mission of Isaiah 40–55 and of Daniel was to announce that the God of the Jews is the only true God and that all should worship him. To this Daniel adds that God will one day bring his kingdom to earth in a visible way. In Jesus's first advent we see the inauguration of the kingdom of God (Matt. 12:28; Mark 1:14–15) and the promise of Jesus's return, when that kingdom will be manifested in all its fullness (1 Cor. 15:22–26). At that time, every eye will see him (Rev. 1:7) and every tongue will confess that he is Lord (Phil. 2:9–11). Those who have believed in Jesus, the Messiah, will rejoice at their redemption (Luke 21:28), for they will have a part in God's kingdom, reigning with Christ (2 Tim. 2:12; Rev. 5:10; 20:6). Those who have denied him will shrink in fear (Rev. 1:7; 6:16–17). We are commanded to disseminate this message of salvation in Christ and of the coming kingdom of God so that others will believe in Jesus and be saved. We should be concerned not only about getting into heaven but also about bringing others with us. It is clear, then, that a drama is unfolding on the stage that is this world. There is a struggle for human souls. While humans are the main players, heavenly beings also play important roles.

Angels

Angels figure prominently in the book of Daniel. There is a heavenly being in the fiery furnace to protect Shadrach, Meshach, and Abednego (3:25). An angel rescues Daniel by shutting the mouths of the lions (6:22). Heavenly beings interpret Daniel's visions for him (7:15–16; 8:15–17; 9:21–22; 10:5, 10, 13–14, 16, 18, 21; 12:8–9). Two angels are named: Gabriel (8:16; 9:21) and Michael (10:13; 12:1). A hierarchy is indicated because Michael is called "one of the chief princes" (10:13) and "the great prince" (12:1). There is conflict in the heavenly realm between God's angels and the spiritual princes of Persia and Greece (10:13, 20–21).

Continuity exists here between the OT and the NT. Gabriel figures in the birth narratives of Jesus (Luke 1:19, 26). The hierarchy and conflict aspects of Daniel's vision can be found in Paul's description of spiritual battle against an army of evil spirits organized into ranks: "rulers," "authorities," "powers of this dark world," and "spiritual forces of evil in the heavenly realms" (Eph. 6:12). Also, the other archangel of Daniel appears in Revelation, as John depicts war in heaven between Michael and his angels on one side and Satan and his angels on the other (Rev. 12:7). However, heaven prevails, casting the devil and his demons to earth (Rev. 12:8–9). Ultimately, the enemies are thrown into the lake of fire (Rev. 20:10) at the end of time.

Eschatology

A nascent prophetic eschatology is present in Amos and Hosea. They anticipated an end coming upon Israel, brought about by Assyria. The end would take place in history, followed by a new move of God in the future when God would restore his people and heal them. Similarly, Isaiah, Jeremiah, and Ezekiel looked for an end to come upon Judah, brought on by the Babylonians. They also looked to a future restoration within time.

Daniel exhibits a more developed apocalyptic eschatology. The end will come upon all the kingdoms of this world. History will continue, but there will be a more radical break between what went before and what is to follow after. God's kingdom will come, and it will be an everlasting kingdom. Preceding the arrival of God's kingdom will be the appearance of a wicked ruler who is arrogant and exalts himself above God (7:8, 11, 20; 8:9–12, 23; 11:36), the persecution of the saints (7:21, 25; 8:24), an abomination that makes desolate (8:13; 9:27; 11:31; 12:11), and a period of great distress unlike any previous one (12:1). After that will be a series of events listed in Daniel 7 and 12. It is difficult to know how to order these chronologically; one possibility is as follows. God and his heavenly court will judge the wicked king and his kingdom (7:9–10, 26). Michael, the great prince, will arise to bring deliverance to the Jews (12:1) by destroying the wicked king and his kingdom (7:11, 26). There will be a resurrection of the dead and final judgment (12:2). The kingdom of God will be given to the heavenly being who looks like a human (7:13–14), to all the heavenly beings (7:22), and finally to the people of the heavenly beings (7:27).

The book of Daniel influenced NT eschatology considerably. Before the return of Jesus, a lawless ruler will arise who will exalt himself above God (2 Thess. 2:3–4). The saints will be persecuted (Matt. 24:9). There will be another abomination that causes desolation—and here Daniel is actually cited (Matt. 24:15). There will be a period of great distress, unlike any before or afterward (Matt. 24:21). The beast of Revelation is reminiscent of the beasts of Daniel 7. It rises out of the sea (Rev. 13:1; Dan. 7:3). It resembles a leopard, a bear, and a lion (Rev. 13:2; Dan. 7:4–6). It utters "proud words and blasphemies" (Rev. 13:5–6; cf. Dan. 7:8, 11) and is in power for "forty-two months," or three and a half years (Rev. 13:5; cf. Dan. 7:25; 8:14; 9:27; 12:7, 11, 12). It makes "war against the saints" and conquers them (Rev. 13:7; Dan. 7:21; see also Rev. 13:12–15; 17).

The Wicked Ruler

As mentioned above under "Eschatology," the end is preceded by the appearance of a wicked ruler. This gives rise to the motif of the Antichrist in the New Testament. False messiahs will arise who will do great works (Matt. 24:5, 23–24; see also the parallel passage in Mark 13:22). Paul advances this theme further in 2 Thessalonians 2:3–10. The coming of the Lord will be preceded by the manifestation of "a man of lawlessness" (v. 3), who "will exalt himself" and proclaim "himself to be God" (v. 4). But

Jesus will destroy him when he comes (v. 8). For John there are "many antichrists" (1 John 2:18). Antichrists deny "that Jesus is the Christ" and deny "the Father and the Son" (1 John 2:22). They do not "acknowledge Jesus" (1 John 4:3) or confess "Jesus Christ as coming in the flesh" (2 John 7).

Son of Man

The term "son of man" means "human being." It is clearly used thus in the book of Ezekiel, where the prophet is often addressed that way (e.g., Ezek. 2:1, 3, 6, 8). In Ezekiel, the NIV renders this literally with "son of man," which is confusing to the English reader who may not be familiar with the idiom; the NRSV's "mortal" better communicates the meaning. The contrast is between God and heavenly beings on the one hand and the prophet, who is a mortal or human, on the other. In fact, Ezekiel's usage is even found once in Daniel. A heavenly being addresses Daniel: "'Son of man,' he said to me, 'understand that the vision concerns the time of the end'" (Dan. 8:17; NRSV "Understand, O mortal . . ."). In a similar usage of the idiom the psalmist asks, "What is man that you are mindful of him, the son of man that you care for him?" (Ps. 8:4). The parallelism is transparent: "man" is equivalent to "son of man" or "mortal." In other words, the term "son of man" is not a title for a heavenly being or Messiah or for anything at all. It is simply a designation for a mortal human being.

So, the vision in Daniel 7:13 is of one who looks like a human being. Of course, he is not a human being, but a heavenly being who appears to be human. The biblical writers often describe angels as looking like men (e.g., Gen. 18:2, 16, 22). An excellent illustration of this in Daniel is in chapter 8, where a heavenly being is portrayed as "one who looked like a man" (Dan. 8:15). Therefore, the NRSV's "I saw one like a human being coming with the clouds of heaven" is preferable to the NIV's "I looked, and there before me was one like a son of man, coming with the clouds of heaven" (Dan. 7:13). We should not translate, as the NIV, "one like a son of man," because readers tend to think "son of man" is a title. It is used that way in the NT for Jesus, but we should be cautious about reading the NT meaning back into the OT. When we do this, we distort the meaning of the OT. The NT writers reinterpret Daniel 7:13 in the light of Jesus Christ. This is valid for the NT writers, but in the era when the book of Daniel was composed, this person was probably understood to be the archangel Michael (Dan. 12:1–4).[8]

It is natural to think of NT usage, where Jesus frequently referred to himself as "the Son of Man" (e.g., Matt. 8:20; 9:6; 11:19). Those passages especially come to mind where Jesus alludes to Daniel 7:13.

> Jesus said to them, "I tell you the truth, at the renewal of all things, when the Son of Man sits on his glorious throne . . ." (Matt. 19:28).

> For as lightning that comes from the east is visible even in the west, so will be the coming of the Son of Man. (Matt. 24:27)

> At that time the sign of the Son of Man will appear in the sky, and all the nations of the earth will mourn. They will see the Son of Man coming on the clouds of the sky, with power and great glory. (Matt. 24:30)

> But I say to all of you: In the future you will see the Son of Man sitting at the right hand of the Mighty One and coming on the clouds of heaven. (Matt. 26:64)

John also makes such allusions in his apocalypse.

> Look, he is coming with the clouds, and every eye will see him, even those who pierced him; and all the peoples of the earth will mourn because of him. So shall it be! Amen. (Rev. 1:7)

> And among the lampstands was someone "like a son of man," dressed in a robe reaching down to his feet and with a golden sash around his chest. (Rev. 1:13)

> I looked, and there before me was a white cloud, and seated on the cloud was one "like a son of man" with a crown of gold on his head and a sharp sickle in his hand. (Rev. 14:14)

The NT writers clearly understood Jesus to be the fulfillment of the vision in Daniel 7:13. He partially fulfilled it in his first coming, because he came down from above (John 3:13; 6:62). But he will fulfill it completely and more visibly when he returns. According to the NT, another event that will accompany the second coming of Jesus and the arrival of God's kingdom is the resurrection of the dead (1 Cor. 15:22–26; 1 Thess. 4:14–17).

The Resurrection

The dominant view throughout most of the OT period was that after death one went to Sheol, the grave. All were thought to go there: animals as well as humans (Eccl. 3:10–21), the righteous as well as the wicked (Eccl. 9:2–3). In Sheol there is no reward, memory, love, hate, envy, work, thought, knowledge, or wisdom (Eccl. 9:5–6, 10). The dead do not remember God or praise him (Pss. 6:5; 30:9; 88:10–12; 115:17). Some passages in the Psalms are occasionally cited as teaching resurrection (Pss. 16:10; 18:4–6; 30:3; 86:13). However, when they speak of rescue from Sheol, they probably mean recovery from a life-threatening illness. Similarly, people who are restored to health today might recall their time of distress by saying that they were so sick that they had one foot in the grave. It is true that Enoch (Gen. 5:24) and Elijah (2 Kgs. 2:11) did not die, but they were extraordinary men; others could not hope to follow them. Even Psalm 73:23–26, which seems to express hope for immortality, might be understood as an expression of confidence in God for this life. The psalmist says, "I am always with you" (Ps. 73:23) and "God is the strength of my heart and my portion forever" (Ps. 73:26). Yet "always" and "forever" may mean "as long as I live." (Alternatively, Psalm 73 might be a late psalm.) Ezekiel's vision of the skeletons coming to life probably refers to the restoration of the Jews to their land after the exile, not to bodily resurrection of individuals (Ezek. 37). Likewise, some take Isaiah 26:19 ("But your dead will live; their bodies will rise") in a national sense. Others allow it indicates resurrection but date it, like Daniel, to the postexilic period. Undisputed teaching about the resurrection from the dead, therefore, apparently dates to that era. This is another argument for dating Daniel to the second century B.C.: Daniel unambiguously affirms a resurrection. What is surprising, though, is that it is a partial resurrection. "Many" (NIV "multitudes"), but not all, "who sleep in the dust of the earth will awake" (Dan. 12:2). Daniel's theology, then, is more developed than most of the OT, but not as developed as later Judaism, segments of which taught a general resurrection of the dead. Christianity inherited the Jewish doctrine of a general resurrection. This doctrine is implied in Matthew 25, where all people, righteous and wicked, saved and lost, appear before God's judgment. It is made explicit in John 5:28–29. In this passage, clearly echoing Daniel 12:2, Jesus teaches the resurrection of the good to life and the resurrection of the evil to condemnation. The rest of the NT concurs (e.g., Acts 24:15; Rev. 20:12–15). After the resurrection will come the final judgment.

Judgment

Daniel 2 does not use the language of the courtroom, but judgment is implied. The kingdoms of this world are destroyed (2:35, 44–45) by the rock "cut out, but not by human hands" (2:34; see also v. 45). This rock represents the kingdom of God, which "will never be destroyed" (2:44).

Judgment is also a key theme in Daniel 4–5. Because King Nebuchadnezzar lifts himself up in pride (4:30; 5:20), heaven sentences him to live like a beast for a time in order to humble him until he would acknowledge the sovereignty of God (4:31–32; 5:21). The climax of Daniel 5 occurs when Belshazzar is condemned because he refuses to humble himself (5:22); he uses the sacred temple vessels and worships idols (5:2–4, 23). Judgment comes in the form of a mysterious hand that writes an enigmatic inscription on the wall (5:5, 24).

In Daniel 7, God appears with his heavenly entourage of many thousands of attendants: "Thrones were set in place" (7:9); "the court was seated, and the books were opened" (7:10). This is a picture of judgment, a description of a divine trial of the fourth beast, which is "terrifying and frightening" and very violent (7:7). This last beast represents a kingdom, which is eventually ruled by a tyrant, who is pictured as a little horn (7:8, 20, 24). The little horn was able to persecute the holy ones "until the Ancient of Days came and pronounced judgment in favor of the saints of the Most High, and the time came when they possessed the kingdom" (7:22). The fourth beast is found guilty and punished with destruction (7:11, 26). Similarly, judgment falls on the oppressive horn (ruler) of Daniel 8 (8:9–12, 24–25). Judgment figures in Daniel 9 as well. The "one who causes desolation" and who sets up "abomination[s]" will only continue "until the end that is decreed is poured out on him" (9:27; cf. NIV's footnote).

Daniel concludes with a final courtroom drama. Michael, the great prince, arises. A book is consulted that contains the names of the faithful, who "will be delivered" (12:1). Apparently there is a judgment of those raised from the dead, because some are rewarded with "everlasting life" whereas others are punished with "shame and everlasting contempt" (12:2). The final verse includes a promise to Daniel: "at the end of the days you will rise to receive your allotted inheritance" (12:13).

The notion of a final judgment is probably rooted in the enthronement psalms, which speak of the kingship of Yahweh, who comes to judge the earth in righteousness (Pss. 96:13; 98:9). It underwent further development in Daniel and other late Jewish works of the Second Temple period (*1 Enoch*, *4 Ezra*, Baruch, *Testament of Benjamin*, and Judith). It became an important part of Judaism, as we see in the teaching of Jesus and the writings of the NT.

Jesus was probably alluding to Daniel 7 when he taught that the Son of Man would sit "on his glorious throne" next to the twelve disciples on their thrones "judging the twelve tribes of Israel" (Matt. 19:28; see also Luke 22:30). Similarly, Daniel 12:1–3 as well as Daniel 7 must have been on Jesus's mind when he articulated a vision for the last judgment in Matthew 25:31–46. The Son of Man will come with all the angels and "will sit on his throne in heavenly glory" (Matt. 25:31). All people will be assembled and will be divided as sheep from goats (Matt. 25:32–33), depending on their compassionate action (Matt. 25:34–36, 41–43) toward the least of his brothers (Matt. 25:40). Jesus's concluding statement ("Then they will go away to eternal punishment, but the righteous to eternal life" [Matt. 25:46]) is reminiscent of "some to everlasting life, others to shame and everlasting contempt" (Dan. 12:2). According to John's gospel, Jesus proclaimed a judgment following the resurrection: "those who have done good will rise to live, and those who have done evil will rise to be condemned" (John 5:28–29).

Daniel's influence can also be seen in Revelation, the NT apocalypse. The author, John, saw thrones set out with judges seated on them (Rev. 20:4, 11–15; cf. Dan. 7:9–10). Then all the dead stood before "a great white throne" to be judged by their works "as recorded in the books" that were opened (Rev. 20:11–12; cf. Dan. 7:10). "The book of life" was also opened; it contained the names of those who were to be saved (Rev. 20:12, 15; cf. Dan. 12:1). Other NT passages also proclaim a final judgment (Acts 17:30–31; 1 Cor. 3:12–15; 2 Cor. 5:10).

Setting Dates

It seems likely that the author of the final form of Daniel expected that the end would come in the time of Antiochus IV. His oppression would last for "a time, times and half a time" (7:25; 12:7), usually understood to be three and a half years, and then the kingdom of God would "be given to the people of the holy ones of the Most High; their kingdom shall be an everlasting kingdom, and all dominions shall serve and obey them" (7:27 NRSV). This agrees with the reckoning of chapter 9, which speaks of half of a week of years (9:27), in other words, half of seven or three and a half. Daniel 8 measures it in days: "2,300 evenings and mornings" (8:14), which equals 1,150 days. Although this is less than three and a half years, it may be close enough if the author was counting from a later starting point. Daniel 8 focuses on the defilement of the sanctuary, but the persecution began before that. Therefore, passages that predict three and a half years are including the whole period of tribulation, while Daniel 8:13–14 is delimiting a shorter period, starting with the desecration of the temple. When the end did not come after the 1,150 days, the author or an editor added the following verse to the book: "From the time that the daily sacrifice is abolished and the abomination that causes desolation is set up, there will be 1,290 days" (12:11). When that deadline passed, another update was added:

"Blessed is the one who waits for and reaches the end of the 1,335 days" (12:12). When the kingdom of God still did not arrive, the final ending was penned: "As for you, go your way till the end. You will rest, and then at the end of the days you will rise to receive your allotted inheritance" (12:13).

From this it can be seen that there are actually two problems with the timetable of Daniel. One is that the tribulation under Antiochus IV was only about three years, rather than three and a half. The other is that the kingdom of God did not come in the second century B.C. But the last verse smooths things over by telling us not to worry about the specifics. The final version of the book, therefore, teaches us not to set dates for end-time events but to be patient. Though we cannot figure out the exact date, the book affirms that the end will eventually come, and when it does, Daniel will be raised from the dead in order to receive his reward.

Humans are curious. We want to know when the end is going to come. Daniel embodies this curiosity: "How long will it be before these astonishing things are fulfilled?" (Dan. 12:6; NRSV "How long shall it be until the end of these wonders?"). Similarly, Jesus's disciples wanted to know the timetable for the *eschaton*. In Matthew 24, they ask, "when will this happen, and what will be the sign of your coming and of the end of the age?" (Matt. 24:3). Jesus then proceeds to give them some signs: false messiahs, wars, persecutions, apostasy, the abomination of desolation, and a time of great distress (Matt. 24:4–21). However, later in the chapter Jesus says, "No one knows about that day or hour, not even the angels in heaven, nor the Son, but only the Father" (Matt. 24:36). Also, just before his ascension, Jesus announces the coming of the Holy Spirit. His followers ask, "Lord, are you at this time going to restore the kingdom to Israel?" He says in reply, "It is not for you to know the times or dates the Father has set by his own authority" (Acts 1:6–7). These verses, along with the ending of Daniel, discourage the setting of dates. Yet, throughout the ages people have tried to predict the coming of Jesus.

William Miller, an American, was mentioned briefly earlier (see "History of Interpretation," above). In the 1830s he predicted that the second coming of Jesus would be in 1843. He took the number 2,300 from Daniel 8:14 and decided it referred to years. He then put that together with Daniel 9:25, which mentions a "decree to restore and rebuild Jerusalem." He associated that decree with Ezra's mission, which he dated to 457 B.C. Subtracting 457 from 2,300 leaves 1,843, the number of years he thought there would be from Christ's birth until the end. Of course, the end did not come in 1843, so he pushed it back to 1844. When Jesus still did not return, many of Miller's followers gave up and abandoned his movement; other Millerites formed denominations, one of which became the Seventh-Day

Adventist Church. More recently (in the 1980s), Edgar Whisenant also made failed predictions of the "rapture": First he predicted that it would occur on Rosh Hashanah (the Jewish New Year), 1988. Then, after the date passed, he postponed it to 1989. In the early 1990s, about 20,000 Christians in Seoul, South Korea, as well as other followers in Los Angeles and New York, were misled by the pastor of the Dami Mission, Lee Jang Rim, and the child prophet Bang-Ik Ha, who announced that Jesus would return in October of 1992. Some burned their furniture; a number died fasting; about four committed suicide; several wrote directions for the distribution of their possessions should they disappear. Thousands were distraught and angry when the rapture did not occur. More recently, Harold Camping predicted from his reading of the Bible that the rapture would occur May 21, 2011, and that the world would end four months later.

We have to think of Daniel not as a hard-and-fast prediction that the end would come in that day, although the author may have believed that it would. We have to see Daniel as a hope for the destruction of a tyrant (Antiochus IV) and his kingdom. More than a hope, it is a call for the destruction of the oppressive kingdom (the Seleucid Empire). It is pronouncing a curse on it, as in the Psalms (Pss. 58:6–11; 59:4–5; 69:22–29; 70:1–3; 75:7–8; 109:6–31). It is a prayer for the coming of the kingdom of God, as in the Lord's Prayer (Matt. 6:10). If we look at Daniel as prediction, we either have to say it is failed prophecy, with the implication that Daniel was a false prophet (and we then have to consider taking it out of the canon); or, we have to project it into the future and say that parts have not been fulfilled but will be when Jesus returns and the final Antichrist and his kingdom are destroyed. Since the NT picks up on that, we as Christians are bound to follow that line to a certain extent. But we should refrain from predictions ourselves. People have been embarrassed by this too many times. We should leave our eschatology somewhat general. It is enough to say that Jesus will come again and bring his glorious kingdom. There will be a resurrection of the dead and a last judgment.

The author of Daniel may have believed that the kingdom of God would come in his own generation, but he left himself a sort of escape clause in chapter 3. The message there is that God may choose not to save immediately. The apocalyptist is saying that God will save, but even if he does not, his people prefer death to worshiping idols (3:17–18). So it was with the early Christians, who believed Jesus would return in their lifetime. When he did not, they were willing to suffer martyrdom. The book of Daniel calls us to decision as well. We must not live for ourselves or for this world; rather, we must be faithful to God in all circumstances, even when threatened with persecution or death.

Notes

1. The following works are very helpful for exploring the historical background in more detail: J. Bright, *A History of Israel* (3d ed.; Philadelphia: Westminster, 1981); W. W. Hallo and W. K. Simpson, *The Ancient Near East: A History* (2d ed.; Belmont, Calif.: Wadsworth/Thomson, 1998); J. H. Hayes and J. M. Miller, eds., *Israelite and Judaean History* (London: SCM, 1977); S. Herrmann, *A History of Israel in Old Testament Times* (Philadelphia: Fortress, 1981); H. Koester, *History, Culture, and Religion of the Hellenistic Age* (vol. 1 of *Introduction to the New Testament*; Philadelphia: Fortress, 1982); S. J. Schwantes, *A Short History of the Ancient Near East* (Grand Rapids: Baker, 1965); V. Tcherikover, *Hellenistic Civilization and the Jews* (New York: Atheneum, 1975); M. Van De Mieroop, *A History of the Ancient Near East, ca. 3000–323 BC* (2d ed.; Malden, Mass.: Blackwell, 2007).

2. M. Wise, et al., *The Dead Sea Scrolls: A New Translation* (New York: HarperCollins, 1996), p. 228. The text goes on to quote Dan. 12:10.

3. J. J. Collins, *Daniel: A Commentary on the Book of Daniel* (Hermeneia; Minneapolis: Fortress, 1993), p. 37.

4. Collins, *Daniel*, p. 37.

5. For more detailed surveys see Collins, *Daniel*, pp. 72–123, and J. E. Goldingay, *Daniel* (WBC 30; Dallas: Word, 1989), pp. xxi–xl.

6. This was based on his reading of Dan. 8:14 and 9:25. For further details and for more examples, see below, "Setting Dates."

7. See the NRSV, "the people of the holy ones of the Most High," which is superior to NIV's "the saints, the people of the Most High."

8. Collins, *Daniel*, pp. 308–10.

§1 Daniel and His Three Friends Avoid Defilement (Dan. 1:1–21)

Chronological notations frame the opening chapter. It begins with the third year of King Jehoiakim of Judah, at which time the Babylonian king Nebuchadnezzar besieged Jerusalem (1:1). It ends with the first year of King Cyrus of Persia (1:21). These are roughly the parameters of the exile; apparently they are also the bookends for Daniel's career. Nebuchadnezzar deported to Babylon the Jewish leaders, including Daniel and his friends; Cyrus conquered Babylon and later released the Jews, allowing them to return to Judah. Remarkably, the book of Daniel does not mention the return from exile. But it does record that Daniel remained in Babylon until the Persian period. Although chapter 1 mentions the first year of Cyrus (1:21), Daniel later has a vision in Cyrus's third year (10:1).

Daniel 1 sets the stage for the rest of the book, especially for events in chapters 1–6. Daniel 1:2, which notes that the temple vessels were taken to Babylon, prepares us for chapter 5, where King Belshazzar profanes them, bringing judgment on himself. Daniel 1:17, which mentions Daniel's skill in dream interpretation, anticipates chapters 2 and 4, where he displays that skill (and also chapter 5, where he interprets the handwriting on the wall). There are also ties between Daniel 1 and later parts of the book. "The Lord delivered Jehoiakim king of Judah into" the hand of King Nebuchadnezzar, presumably because of sin (1:2). Later, Daniel confesses his sin and the sin of his people (9:4–19). In that passage, he clearly indicates that disobedience brought about the exile. Daniel is one of the wise (1:4; NIV "showing aptitude") to whom God gave "understanding" (1:17). The final vision of the book elevates those who are "wise" (11:33, 35; 12:3, 10), using words from the same Hebrew root.

Daniel 1 also serves to unify separate stories that at one time probably circulated independently. The traditions about Daniel (Belteshazzar) apparently were originally independent of the traditions about the other three heroes: Hananiah (Shadrach), Mishael (Meshach), and Azariah (Abednego). This is evident in Daniel 3, where Shadrach, Meshach, and Abednego refuse to worship the statue and are thrown into the fiery furnace but there is no notice of Daniel. Likewise, the original author of chapter 6, where Daniel is thrown into the lions' den, seems to be unaware of the other three Jews, as there is no mention of them. Daniel 1 brings Daniel together with the other three men, recounting how they were exiled to Babylon and were enrolled in King Nebuchadnezzar's training program. In this way, the first chapter helps to overcome the sense that these are disparate accounts.

Daniel is presented in chapter 1 as a new Joseph. Joseph was taken as a captive to Egypt (Gen. 39:1); Daniel was carried to exile in Babylon (Dan. 1:1–7). Both served in the court of a foreign king: Joseph under Pharaoh (Gen. 41:39–41), Daniel under Nebuchadnezzar (Dan. 1:5, 19). Joseph was "well-built and handsome" (Gen. 39:6); Daniel and his friends were "without any physical defect" and "handsome" (Dan. 1:4). Joseph was given the foreign name "Zaphenath-Paneah" (Gen. 41:45); Daniel was renamed "Belteshazzar" (Dan. 1:7; his friends were also given Babylonian names). Concerning Joseph, God "showed him kindness and granted him favor in the eyes of the prison warden" (Gen. 39:21). Similarly, "God had caused the official to show favor and sympathy to Daniel" (Dan. 1:9). In Genesis, the Egyptian magicians (Gen. 41:8, 24) and wise men (Gen. 41:8) could not interpret Pharaoh's dream, while Joseph could (Gen. 41:25–32), which showed Joseph to be wiser than everyone else (Gen. 41:39). Parallel to this, "in every matter of wisdom and understanding" Daniel and his friends, upon examination, were found to be "ten times better than all the magicians and enchanters in his whole kingdom" (Dan. 1:20). The parallels continue in the following chapters as Daniel bests the pagan wise men and magicians by interpreting dreams (chs. 2 and 4) and the writing on the wall (ch. 5). Furthermore, just as Joseph was given a position second only to Pharaoh (Gen. 41:40–41) and was given gifts, including a gold chain (Gen. 41:42), so Daniel was promoted over everyone else (Dan. 2:48–49; 5:29) and given a gold chain (Dan. 5:29).

1:1–2 / The book of Daniel is famous for its historical problems (see the Introduction). We encounter the first one right away. Daniel 1:1 asserts that **in the third year of the reign of Jehoiakim king of Judah, Nebuchadnezzar king of Babylon came to Jerusalem and besieged it.** Since Jehoiakim came to the throne in 609 B.C., that would seem to locate this siege of Jerusalem in 606 B.C. (or possibly 605 B.C., depending on whether one uses the accession or nonaccession method of counting the years of a king's reign; see below). However, based on internal evidence from Scripture and external evidence from historical sources outside the Bible, a Babylonian invasion of Judah that early is unlikely (see the Additional Note on 1:1).

To summarize the evidence, the author of Kings seems to know about a military campaign by Nebuchadnezzar to Philistia in 604 B.C. He tells us that Jehoiakim became Nebuchadnezzar's vassal for three years and then rebelled (in 601 B.C. or so; 2 Kgs. 24:1). He also knows about the invasion and siege of Jerusalem in 597 B.C., but he does not show awareness of a siege of Jerusalem in 606 or 605 B.C., as recorded in Daniel. Furthermore, since Babylonian texts do not record an attack on Jerusalem at that time either, they cannot be used to corroborate such an event. Finally, 2 Chronicles 36:5–7 seems to militate against an invasion as early as 606/605 B.C. There we learn that Jehoiakim ruled a total of eleven years and then was succeeded by his son, Jehoiachin, in 597. According to 2 Kings 24:6, that succession took place after Jehoiakim died. However, the Chronicler appears to record that Jehoiakim was bound and taken to Babylon (2 Chron. 36:6). It makes sense that this would precipitate the accession of Jehoiachin, but Jehoiachin himself was taken into exile three months after inheriting the reins of power. Therefore, the capturing of Jehoiakim and Jehoiachin can be seen as two parts of one invasion or deportation by Nebuchadnezzar in 597 B.C. This apparent discrepancy between Daniel, on the one hand, and Kings, Chronicles, and extrabiblical historical sources, on the other, is a real problem that resists harmonization. It may be that when the author of Daniel read in Kings about Jehoiakim's three years of submission to Nebuchadnezzar, he simply assumed those were the first three years of Jehoiakim's reign.

Another historical difficulty is that Daniel 1:1 considers Nebuchadnezzar to be king already in the third year of Jehoiakim, or 606 B.C., when he was not crowned until 605 B.C. It seems that Daniel also contradicts Jeremiah 25:1, which says that the first year of Nebuchadnezzar's reign was the fourth year of Jehoiakim, rather than the third as Daniel would imply. Some scholars harmonize Jeremiah and Daniel by noting that in ancient times there were different methods of counting the first year of a king's reign. This solution argues that perhaps Jeremiah was using the nonaccession-year method, whereby the time from the accession to the next New Year's day was counted as one full year and the first official year of the king's reign. This method increases the count by one because the first partial year is reckoned as a complete year. On the other hand, maybe Daniel was using the accession-year method, that is, counting the months between accession and the next New Year's day as a special accession year. Then the first official year of the king's reign would not have begun until the first New Year's day. This method does not count the first months of the reign, resulting in a number smaller by one than the number arrived at by the other method. This analysis would then explain why Jeremiah counts four years to Daniel's three. In other words, Jeremiah would call 605 the fourth year of Jehoiakim, whereas Daniel would count it the third. So, when Daniel 1:1 says, "in the third year of the reign of Jehoiakim," it means 605 B.C. rather than 606 B.C., and if it intends the later part of 605, Nebuchadnezzar really was king and there is no discrepancy.

The above harmonization is possible, but it remains speculative, because we do not know what methods of counting Daniel and Jeremiah were using. Also, Jeremiah 46:2 is similar to Jeremiah 25:1 in designating Nebuchadnezzar as king, and in having the date given as the fourth year of Jehoiakim. Yet Jeremiah 46:2 is referring to the battle of Carchemish, which occurred before Nebuchadnezzar ascended the throne. Apparently, Jeremiah is calling him king proleptically, that is, in anticipation of his coronation. Another way to look at it is that he was writing after the coronation took place, so it was natural for him to refer to Nebuchadnezzar as king, even though it is anachronistic in this context. The author of Daniel may be doing something similar. Therefore, it is unnecessary to invoke accession- versus nonaccession-year dating for Daniel.

In verse 2, the author makes an important theological point: Nebuchadnezzar did not take Judah on his own. Rather, **the Lord delivered Jehoiakim king of Judah into his hand** (1:2). This indicates that the sovereign God of Israel caused the Babylonian king to triumph over the Jewish people. The notion that God acted in history by bringing in the Babylonians as an instrument of punishment is also found in Kings, Chronicles, Jeremiah, Ezekiel, and Lamentations, among other books. Daniel makes the same point in his lengthy prayer in chapter 9 (9:4–19). The word translated "delivered" in Daniel 1:2 is from the common Hebrew root meaning "to give." This verb is used three times in chapter 1 with God as the subject. The Lord *gave* Jehoiakim into Nebuchadnezzar's hand (1:2). God *gave* Daniel favor and sympathy before the chief official (1:9). God *gave* to the four young men knowledge and understanding (1:17). By repeating this theme, the author highlights the fact that God is in control. One might think that Nebuchadnezzar was responsible for the deportation of the Jews to Babylon. One might conclude that Daniel was lucky to be allowed his special diet (1:8–16). One might surmise that Daniel and his friends succeeded in school because of their natural ability or because of the excellence of the training (1:5, 19–20). In each case, one would be dead wrong. It was God who caused the exile, who gave Daniel favor so that he could avoid defilement, and who gave the four Jewish youths wisdom with the result that they outshone all the other sages of Babylon. This would have been a very encouraging message to

Jews living under oppressive kings, such as the Seleucids in the second century B.C. It also gives strength to Christians living in a secular society today. God is still in charge and able to protect and prosper his people. He is also the ultimate source for wisdom and knowledge.

In the ancient Near East, when kings and armies clashed, they believed their gods were also fighting each other. Whichever side won claimed that their god was greater. This explains why Nebuchadnezzar wanted to present Jehoiakim and **some of the articles from the temple of God** in the temple of his god in Babylonia: it was to honor and thank his deity for the victory and to show him the spoils of war that that god had presumably won. Nebuchadnezzar then placed the articles from the Jerusalem temple **in the treasure house of his god** (1:2). These were trophies of a successful battle. In Nebuchadnezzar's view they displayed Marduk's defeat of Yahweh; but Scripture corrects this faulty thinking. As noted above, it was the God of Israel who caused Babylon to be victorious against Jerusalem. Similarly, the Philistines placed the captured ark in their shrine to Dagon, thinking that Dagon had triumphed over Yahweh (1 Sam. 5:1–2). They were disabused of that notion when Yahweh struck them with a plague and caused "Dagon" (the idol) to fall off his perch in order to bow down in worship before Yahweh at the ark (1 Sam. 5:3–7). The Israelites also used worship centers to house war trophies. David took the head of Goliath to Jerusalem and placed the giant's armor in his tent (1 Sam. 17:54). (Since David had not yet conquered Jerusalem at that point in the story, this may be an anachronism. It may mean that later he put these things in his tent shrine to Yahweh after he had become king and made Jerusalem his capital [2 Sam. 6:17]). David also deposited the sword of Goliath with the priests at Nob (1 Sam. 21:9).

The rare Hebrew word "Shinar" is rendered "Babylonia" in verse 2, as it is explained in the NIV footnote. One significant place where the name occurs is in the tower of Babel story (Gen. 11). "Babel" means "gate of god" and refers to Babylon, which is located on "a plain in Shinar" (Gen. 11:2). There God shows his judgment on the Babylonians' religion by changing their language and scattering them (Gen. 11:8–10). They think that their temple towers, known as ziggurats, are gateways to the gods; in fact they are only places of confusion (Gen. 11:9). "Shinar" also occurs in Zechariah 5, again in a very negative context. The prophet sees a vision of a basket with a woman inside signifying wickedness. The basket is being carried to Shinar, where a house will be built for it. Since "house" suggests temple, the woman in the basket may then indicate some foreign cult object or idol. The writer of Daniel probably uses "Shinar" to connote the uncleanness of Babylon and the abominable character of its religion.

The NIV translation obscures the meaning of verse 2 by omitting "the articles" in the last clause. The NIV records that "Jehoiakim" was handed over to Nebuchadnezzar "along with some of the articles from the temple of God." Then it says, "These he carried off to the temple of his god in Babylonia and put in the treasure house of his god." One might think that Jehoiakim was put in the treasure house with the articles. But the Hebrew text is clear that only the temple artifacts were placed in the treasury and not King Jehoiakim: "The articles he brought to the treasure house of his god."

Another historical question arises: Was Jehoiakim exiled to Babylon? Once again, it is important to review the earlier biblical texts. According to 2 Kings 24:5, Jehoiakim died in Judah and was buried with his ancestors. Instead, it was Jehoiachin, not Jehoiakim, whom Nebuchadnezzar took to Babylon along with the temple articles (2 Kgs. 24:10–15). However, Chronicles paints a different picture. On the one hand, it disagrees with Kings about Jehoiakim: Nebuchadnezzar captured Jehoiakim to take him to Babylon along with the temple articles (2 Chron. 36:6–7). On the other hand, it agrees with Kings about Jehoiachin, because it also relates that he was taken to Babylon with temple articles (2 Chron. 36:9–10). Daniel seems to be following the Chronicler on this point regarding Jehoiakim, although Daniel dates the event to the third year of Jehoiakim, which the Chronicler does not do. On the contrary, as mentioned above, based on Chronicles it seems best to date the deportation of Jehoiakim to the end of his eleven-year reign, or 597 B.C.

How do we account for Daniel's idiosyncratic history? It seems to result from the creative way the author read his sources. Apparently he preferred the Chronicler's account of what happened to Jehoiakim: he was exiled to Babylon. But, as mentioned earlier, the author of Daniel may have gotten "the third year of the reign of Jehoiakim" (Dan. 1:1) from Kings. Second Kings 24:1 says that "Jehoiakim became" Nebuchadnezzar's "vassal for three years." After that, he rebelled. While that period of servitude and subsequent rebellion was probably in the middle or near the end of Jehoiakim's reign, the author of Daniel understood it to be at the beginning.

Jehoiakim paid tribute to Nebuchadnezzar for three years and then rebelled. Before Nebuchadnezzar was able to deal with this rebellion, Jehoiakim died in 597 and was buried in Jerusalem. His son Jehoiachin succeeded in ruling for only a few months before the invasion. He had to bear the punishment for his father's rebellion. He was carried away captive to Babylon in the first deportation of 597 B.C. The Chronicler follows another tradition, which has Jehoiakim being taken to Babylon at the end of his eleven-year reign instead of dying in Judah. Daniel seems to create a third tradition (unless he is following a tradition no longer preserved elsewhere) by moving Jehoiakim's exile to the third year of his reign.

One reason for the creativity of chapter 1 might be the author's desire to show how Scripture had been fulfilled. Jeremiah predicted that the exile would last seventy years (Jer. 25:11–12; 29:10). According to the Chronicler, the period of the exile began with the destruction of the temple in 587/586 B.C. and ended with the return to the land under Cyrus in 538 B.C. (2 Chron. 36:19–23). This spans a period of only forty-nine years or so. If we start with 597, the date of the first deportation, we can stretch the time to fifty-nine years. It is possible that the author of Daniel wanted to move the beginning of the exile back to an even earlier year so that the exile would extend to seventy years, or something closer to it. The third year of Jehoiakim would be 606 B.C. From that point down to Cyrus's decree in 538 to release the Jews would be 68 years. Since the author of Daniel may not have had a precise grasp of those dates, he might have thought it worked out to seventy years. Although the book of Daniel does not mention the return to the land, it does record the dates for Daniel's ministry. By one account, he continues until the first year of King Cyrus in 539 B.C. (Dan. 1:21). But Daniel has a revelation in Cyrus's third year (Dan. 10:1), which might be 537 or 536. It is interesting to note that there are seventy years between 606 and 536 B.C.

1:3–5 / The purpose of the first paragraph (1:1–2) is to set the stage historically by introducing the reader to the deportation. King Nebuchadnezzar conquered Jerusalem and brought King Jehoiakim and temple articles to Babylon. But the book of Daniel is not concerned with King Jehoiakim as much as it is with Daniel and his three friends who were carried into exile at the same time. The second paragraph (1:3–5) introduces them and also prepares for the conflict later in the chapter by mentioning the king's food.

King Nebuchadnezzar **ordered Ashpenaz** (1:3) to select a small, elite group of young men from among the Jewish exiles. Although "Ashpenaz" may have been a title for the administrator in charge of accommodations, it is attested as a proper name and is usually treated that way by the translations, ancient and modern. This administrator was **chief of** the king's **court officials**. The term for "court officials" used to be rendered "eunuchs," as in the KJV. However, the Hebrew *sarisim* (pl.) probably derives from Akkadian *sha reshi*, "the one of the head," so called because he was in close proximity to the king and attended him. Such officials were not necessarily eunuchs, although the ones appointed to guard the king's harem would have been.

Ashpenaz was to choose his men from among the **Israelites from the royal family and the nobility** (1:3). The NIV indicates two groups: Israelite royalty and Israelite nobility. However, the Hebrew text could be read as listing three groups—Israelites, royal family, and nobility—because of the way the three terms are connected by the conjunction *waw*. In other words, it may be that the last two were not Israelite. It does appear likely that lads from other people groups entered the training (1:6). They might have been Babylonian princes and nobles, or they might have been captives from other nations. It would be odd if there were other Israelites in Daniel's class, besides Hananiah, Mishael, and Azariah, because they are never mentioned. Are we to assume that only these four kept the Jewish dietary laws while the other Jews defiled themselves with the king's food (1:8–16)? In spite of that, most recent commentators agree with the NIV that there were only two groups—members of the royal family and aristocrats—both of which were Israelites. If this is correct, perhaps the writer of Daniel was thinking of 2 Kings 24:12, 14–15, which list all the elite of Judah who were taken to Babylon. Of course, as already mentioned, Kings is referring to a deportation in 597 B.C., in the time of Jehoiachin, not in 606 B.C., during the reign of Jehoiakim. Nevertheless, the author of Daniel may have used that information for his retelling of the story.

These leaders were special. They were to be **young men without any physical defect** (1:4). As already noted, it therefore seems unlikely that they were eunuchs. The Bible gives the same requirement for priests (Lev. 21:17–23) and for sacrificial animals (Lev. 22:18–25). The fact that they were to be **handsome** shows a perceived relationship between beauty and divine favor. This way of thinking was not exclusive to Babylon. Even though 1 Samuel 16:7 warns against looking on the outward appearance as a sign of God's election, a few verses later David is described as having "a fine appearance and handsome features" (1 Sam. 16:12; see also 17:42), and this is in the context of his being anointed king and being filled with the Spirit (1 Sam. 16:13). Appearance was only one descriptive element. Since these elite men were going to become the king's wise men, the most important qualifications were intellectual ones. They must show **aptitude for every kind of learning** and be **well informed** and **quick to understand**. The terms used here occur frequently in Proverbs. Wisdom was an international phenomenon valued at court in Egypt and Mesopotamia as well as in Israel.

The new captives were enrolled in school so that they would be **qualified to serve in the king's palace** (1:4). The curriculum included more than the study of proverbs. The youths were trained in **the language and literature of the Babylonians** (1:4). The word for "Babylonians" is actually "Chaldeans," as the NIV footnote acknowledges (see also NRSV). Originally, this word referred to a people who lived in southern Mesopotamia. Over time they expanded northward and eventually came to dominate Babylonia. The book of Daniel retains this meaning in 5:30 and 9:1, where "Chaldean" (NIV "Babylonian[s]") denotes a people group (see also "Chaldean" in Ezra 5:12). However, by the time the book of Daniel was put in its final form, the meaning had shifted. Here in Daniel 1:4, as well as in 2:2–5, 10; 3:8; 4:7; 5:7, 11, the term denotes magicians, astrologers, fortune-tellers, diviners, soothsayers, and prognosticators. This later usage had become common by the Hellenistic era. When the shift took place is not known, but the usage in Daniel points to a postexilic date for the book.

The literature of the Chaldeans would have included various myths, legends, and texts explaining how to interpret dreams and omens. Presumably the students would have been trained in the Babylonian rituals, magical practices, and methods of divination, such as hepatoscopy (reading the livers of animals). Daniel and his friends objected to the food, but interestingly, they raised no objections concerning the curriculum. Rather Daniel, Hananiah, Mishael, and Azariah demonstrated a grasp of that material superior to all the others (1:20). When the time arrived for their final examination given orally by the king, they graduated at the top of their class. That being said, when Daniel excelled in his role as sage and counselor, he did not do so through human wisdom, much less through the media of Babylonian divination. Rather, the one true God of Israel gave him revelation (1:17).

Although the language of the Chaldeans is sometimes understood to be Aramaic because Aramaic became the *lingua franca* of the Babylonian Empire, the language of the Chaldeans actually was Akkadian. Besides learning to speak Akkadian, the language of the Babylonians, Daniel and his companions would have studied the cuneiform script. In English, our writing system is composed of letters that represent individual sounds. Virtually all the sounds we need can be reduced to twenty-six characters. But cuneiform is syllabic rather than alphabetic. Each group of wedges and lines represents a combination of either a consonant plus a vowel (an open syllable, such as "ba") or a consonant plus a vowel plus a consonant (a closed syllable, such as "bat"). Since there are hundreds of such possible combinations, literacy was a very difficult thing to achieve.

Because these were special students destined **to enter the king's service** (1:5), they were treated to royal fare. **The king assigned them a daily** amount of food and wine from the king's table. The author of Daniel may have been thinking of 2 Kings 25:29–30 and Jeremiah 52:33–34, where it is recorded that the Babylonian king Evil-Merodach (Amel-Marduk) released King Jehoiachin from prison and allowed him to eat daily at the royal table. (Kings and Jeremiah use a different word for "food" [NIV "allowance"], but they use the same expression for "daily" [NIV "regular/regularly"].) Of course, Daniel and his friends did not eat at the king's table, but they did eat from his cuisine. The word "food" in Daniel 1:5 is from Persian and means "royal fare," or "the king's rations"; it also occurs in Daniel 1:8, 13, 15, 16; and 11:26.

1:6–7 / In verse 6, the main character of the book is introduced along with his three friends who figure in the first six chapters. No genealogy is supplied, nor any historical background except to say that they were **among** those who came **from Judah**. It is not clear whether that means the others were Gentiles or Israelites (that is, members of Israelite tribes other than Judah; see the commentary on 1:3). The only captives mentioned by name are **Daniel, Hananiah, Mishael and Azariah.**

Like most OT names, all three are theophoric. In other words, each has a divine element in it: either "El" (-el), which means "God," or "Yah" (-iah), which is an abbreviated form of "Yahweh," the proper name of Israel's deity. Daniel means "El is my judge"; Hananiah, "Yahweh is gracious"; Mishael, "Who is what El is?"; and Azariah, "Yahweh has helped." The **chief official** changed their names to Babylonian ones (1:7) since they were now servants of the Babylonian king. Daniel became **Belteshazzar**, which probably means "protect his life." The Akkadian forms and meanings of **Shadrach** and **Meshach** are not clear. Perhaps they were deliberately obscured by the biblical writer because they contained the names of pagan gods. **Abednego** may be a corruption of *abed-nabu*, meaning "servant of [the god] Nabu." Just as there is no struggle recorded over the curriculum, so there is no objection raised about their names, even though they may be pagan.

If the names themselves are not transparent, the significance of the naming is. It shows the dominance of the Babylonians over the Jews. Only one in power may rename another. Adam gave names to the animals, demonstrating that he had dominion over them (Gen. 2:20). God, the divine sovereign, sometimes changed the names of people: Abram to Abraham (Gen. 17:5), Sarai to Sarah (Gen. 17:15), and Jacob to Israel (Gen. 32:28). Also, human kings show their sovereignty in this way. Pharaoh Neco not only decided to replace King Jehoahaz with Eliakim, but he also changed his name to Jehoiakim (2 Kgs. 23:34). Similarly, Nebuchadnezzar put

Mattaniah on the Judean throne when he took Jehoiachin into exile, and he changed Mattaniah's name to Zedekiah (2 Kgs. 24:17). A closer parallel to Daniel is Joseph, whose name was changed by Pharaoh to Zaphenath-Paneah when he came into royal service (Gen. 41:45).

In Daniel 2:17, the narrator uses the Hebrew names for the three friends. At some points in the book we find explanations: "Daniel (also called Belteshazzar)" (Dan. 2:26); "Daniel . . . (He is called Belteshazzar . . .)" (Dan. 4:8; see also 10:1). In Daniel 3, "Shadrach," "Meshach," and "Abednego" are used, probably because it is a story of conflict between those three and the Babylonians. The king and his lords would call the Jewish subjects not by their Hebrew names but by their new Babylonian ones. Likewise, in Daniel 4, Nebuchadnezzar naturally addresses Daniel as Belteshazzar (Dan. 4:9). In Daniel 7–12, however, the hero is usually called "Daniel" (the only exception is Dan. 10:1), perhaps because he speaks of the visions in the first person. In other words, in the narratives of the first half of the book (Daniel 1–6), the emphasis is on the contacts and conflicts with the Babylonians, so it is natural to use the Babylonian names more. By way of contrast, in the second half of the book (Daniel 7–12), the prophet is represented as having visions, which he recounts. Naturally he would prefer his Hebrew name, Daniel.

Apparently it was not unusual for Jews to take Babylonian names in the exile. The two prime examples are the governors Sheshbazzar (Ezra 1:11) and Zerubbabel (Ezra 3:2). In Persia, a faithful Jew, Mordecai, had a name related to the Babylonian god Marduk (Esth. 2:5). His cousin's Hebrew name, "Hadassah," is preserved (Esth. 2:7), although she is better known as Esther, a name related to the Babylonian goddess of love, Ishtar. Later in the Hellenistic period, Joshua, the brother of Onias III, changed his name to the Greek form, Jason (2 Macc. 4:7).

1:8–10 / The next section of chapter 1 lays out the conflict. So far, things have progressed rather smoothly. Nebuchadnezzar brought the youths to pagan Babylon and enrolled them in school to study Babylonian forms of divination. There was no protest. Then the chief officer even changed their names to Babylonian ones, eliminating the names of their God (El or Yahweh). Again there was no objection. And the three years of training they were facing were to prepare them to serve the polytheistic Babylonian king. Even that did not generate a crisis of faith. But the diet does: **Daniel resolved not to defile himself with the royal food and wine, and he asked the chief official for permission not to defile himself this way** (1:8). The word for "resolved" is the same word rendered "gave" in the previous verse. The root meaning is "place" or "put." The chief official *put* names to them (1:7). In contrast, Daniel *put* upon his heart that he would not defile himself (1:8). It may be that the author is intentionally communicating a distinction here between the will of the chief official and the will of faithful Daniel (Seow, *Daniel*, p. 25). The former can choose names for the Jewish captives without resistance, but Daniel can choose to refuse the king's food and drink. Daniel will accept the imposition of a foreign name but will not acquiesce to defiling fare.

Only Daniel objected to the royal food; Hananiah, Mishael, and Azariah did not. They did become part of the experiment later, but the fact that only Daniel is mentioned here calls to mind Daniel 6, where Daniel is the only character, and Daniel 3, where only the three friends are included. Perhaps this was once an independent story that originally involved only Daniel. At some later stage when this chapter was shaped into an introduction, which was meant to give unity to the court stories in chapters 1–6, the other three Jewish lads were added here. It is interesting to note that Daniel was not added to chapter 3, and the other three were not added to chapter 6.

Many commentators have puzzled over this passage. If the text only mentioned food and not wine, one might think of the rules in the Pentateuch regarding clean and unclean food (Lev. 11:1–47). Perhaps the royal food consisted of pork, shellfish, or other things forbidden to pious Jews. Another related possibility is that the meat had blood in it, for this would also violate the covenant (Gen. 9:4; Lev. 17:10–13; Deut. 12:23–24). Isaiah 59:3 and 63:3 associate blood with defilement, using words from the same root as the word "defile" in Daniel 1:8. These and several other passages suggest that ritual impurity is in view (Mal. 1:7; Ezra 2:62; Neh. 7:64). But the problem with these suggestions is the wine. Why would they refuse wine, since wine is neither unclean, nor does it have blood in it? Some have wondered whether the problem for Daniel was that the meat and drink would have been offered to the Babylonian gods in sacrifice first. He wanted to eat vegetables and drink water to avoid this (Exod. 34:15; Deut. 32:38; Acts 15:29; 21:25; 1 Cor. 8–10). However, the Babylonians may have offered the vegetables to the gods as well, so a vegetarian diet would not necessarily have helped.

Some believe that Daniel refused the fine food in order to maintain his independence, in effect saying his allegiance was to God, not the king. This is not very convincing. While in one passage he did seem to reject promotions and gifts (5:17), it turns out that he later accepted them (5:29; see also 2:48). Furthermore, he did not seem to object to being in the service of the king. In fact, one point of the stories in Daniel 1–6 is that faithful Jews can prosper in the service of earthly kings. Plus,

Daniel did not make his diet public, so he was not making any statement of loyalty. Nor did Daniel seem to be of such a weak character that he would be corrupted by richer food. Besides, Daniel was still indebted to the king for his sustenance, even if he only received vegetables. Finally, this explanation does not fit the term "defile." If he was concerned only with loyalty, why does it say he "resolved not to defile himself" (1:8)? The same objection could be raised against the suggestion that Daniel wanted to eat a simpler diet as an expression of grief and sorrow because of the exile. If his only concern was to fast as a way of grieving, why does the text use the term "defile"? He would be full instead of hungry, but he would not be *defiled* by eating the royal provisions.

Although this story may go back at least to the Persian period, we must consider that evidence points to the final form of the book being from the second century B.C., in which case the book is addressed to the Jews suffering under Antiochus IV. It may not be clear what Daniel 1:8 meant in its original context, but the message it would convey to the Jews just before the Maccabean revolt is very clear. They were forced to eat pork and other unclean meat that had been sacrificed to idols, or they would die (1 Macc. 1:41–64): "But many in Israel stood firm and were resolved in their hearts not to eat unclean food. They chose to die rather than to be defiled by food or to profane the holy covenant; and they did die" (1 Macc. 1:62–63 NRSV). The similarity of language between these verses and Daniel 1:8 is striking. The author of 1 Maccabees lionizes those who chose death over sacrilege, who refused to defile themselves with the food of the king (that is, Antiochus).

What about the wine? There is a passage in the Mishnah that proscribes Gentile wine (*'Abod. Zar.* 2.3; 4.8–12; 5.1–12), but this prohibition may have originated later than the second century B.C. Closer in time is the book of Judith, which some scholars date to the latter half of the second century B.C. Judith refused both the food and wine of Holofernes (Jdt. 12:1–2). Unfortunately, Maccabees does not say the Jews were forced to drink wine offered to idols, too, but it does record that during a feast of Dionysus, Jews were forced to participate in some aspects of the celebration, such as wearing ivy wreaths and walking in the god's procession (2 Macc. 6:7). Since Dionysus was the god of wine and revelry, perhaps this led to the refusal to drink wine.

An objection often raised to this interpretation is that Nebuchadnezzar is not represented as an evil tyrant in chapter 1, as he is in the later parts of the book, and is therefore a poor substitute for Antiochus Epiphanes. However, the author of Daniel is using stories from an earlier time to preach to the people of his day. He does not need to refashion the whole tradition, for if he did, it would no longer carry the verisimilitude of the earlier time. But he shapes it to apply the message to the later context. Alternatively, it is possible that chapter 1 comes from a time in the second century before the intense persecution by Antiochus. During the earlier period, there was tension between the pious Jews, who would not assimilate to the pagan Greek culture, and the more worldly Jews, who would. Perhaps the author is warning Jews not to defile themselves by eating food that the Torah forbids. In the period before Antiochus, it was not because they were forced to do so but because they were merely tempted to do so. This fits the story better because Daniel was not forced to eat the king's food; pressure was applied, but ultimately he was allowed to choose.

Another puzzling thing about Daniel 1:8 is that Daniel's vegetarian diet is not a lifelong regimen. He later enters into a three-week fast from meat and wine (10:3), indicating that before and after that particular fast he partakes of such things. Either the author of the book wanted to communicate that Daniel's simple diet was only for his period of training, or it may be that chapter 1 and chapter 10 contain competing traditions.

As the story develops, we see divine providence at work. In spite of the fact that Daniel was brought low by being taken to Babylon, God promotes him. The text notes that **God had caused the official to show favor and sympathy to Daniel** (1:9). In this Daniel is parallel to Joseph, who was taken to Egypt as a slave but whom God gave favor with his owner (Gen. 39:1–4). Solomon's prayer of dedication for the temple also comes to mind. It includes a request for his people in case they should be carried into exile: ". . . and cause their conquerors to show them mercy" (1 Kgs. 8:50).

Even though the overseer likes Daniel, he is reluctant to grant his request. Ashpenaz is **afraid of his lord the king.** If Daniel refused the royal menu and ended up **looking worse than the other young men . . . the king** would **then have his head** (1:10). The dramatic tension intensifies as the narrator recounts how much is at stake. What if Ashpenaz is put to death on account of Daniel's piety? The threat of death is a recurring dramatic feature in court narratives in Daniel. In chapter 2, all the wise men face execution, including the four heroes, unless they can tell the dream and its interpretation (2:5, 12–13), and of course, there are the terrors of the fiery furnace in chapter 3 and the lions in chapter 6.

1:11–14 / Rather than press the issue with the chief official, Daniel approaches his more immediate supervisor, **the guard whom the chief official . . . appointed over** the youths. Daniel requests an experiment in which the guard will test them **for ten days** with a diet of only **vegetables and water. Then he will compare their appearances with those of the young men who eat the royal food**. After this he will act accordingly. Presumably, if they look healthy they can continue with their diet, but if not they will agree to eat the same food as the others. Fortunately, the guard agrees to this and tests them **for ten days.**

1:15–16 / The youths succeed in proving that their diet is superior: **At the end of the ten days they looked healthier and better nourished than any of the young men who ate the royal food** (1:15). It is possible that the narrator has in mind a miracle—that God supernaturally has caused the Jewish youths to be healthier in spite of their meager diet. However, since there is no indication of a miracle, it seems more plausible that the narrator thinks that what they ate really is healthier. To be sure, God has been at work blessing them, giving them favor, and promoting them, but in this case God works through the food in a more natural way. Consuming the unclean Babylonian food and drink is defiling and unhealthy; eating that which God allows leads to better health. The Hebrew phrase rendered by the NIV "better nourished" actually means "fatter of flesh." A similar phrase is used in the Joseph story for the seven "fat" cows in Pharaoh's dream (Gen. 41:2).

While their healthy appearance does not win others over to their side to try their diet, it does win them the right to continue with it: **the guard took away their choice food and the wine they were to drink and gave them vegetables instead** (1:16). This is a triumph for the Jews and for their religion. They are vindicated and protected for being faithful to their dietary rules, and they continue to serve as role models to those who read these stories. God blesses those who obey him.

1:17 / Not only do the youths succeed in looking fit, but they succeed in school as well: **To these four young men God gave knowledge and understanding of all kinds of literature and learning. And Daniel could understand visions and dreams of all kinds** (1:17). The text indicates two kinds of wisdom. The first has to do with book learning. All four are good students, excelling in their studies. As he was with the diet, God is involved, but not in an outwardly dramatic or miraculous manner. Rather it is more hidden and ordinary, as someone today who graduates *summa cum laude* might be called gifted. Even nonreligious people use such language, but those who are religious would go further and say more explicitly that God has endowed that person with intellectual powers. Nevertheless, they do not usually intend to suggest something miraculous. However, there is another kind of wisdom that is special to Daniel. This second kind, the ability to "understand visions and dreams," is a supernatural gift. All four are able to study and master the Babylonian curriculum for sages, demonstrating the ability to understand the language, literature, wisdom, and lore of their captors. But verse 17 anticipates chapter 2, where Daniel not only can interpret the king's dream but can tell the king what the dream itself was. No one could do this on one's own, no matter how intelligent that person is. Both kinds of wisdom come from God, but the latter is more obviously supernatural. The former involves study, but the latter only comes by divine revelation. Daniel's ability in dream interpretation is reminiscent of Joseph, who interpreted Pharaoh's dream concerning the coming seven fat years followed by seven lean years. On account of this, Pharaoh recognized that "the spirit of God" resided in Joseph (Gen. 41:38; cf. Dan. 4:8, 9, 18; 5:11, 14).

The term "understanding" has relevance for the second half of the book, which talks about the wise who will instruct others during the time of persecution (11:33), who will lead others to righteousness, and who will shine like the stars (12:3). The author of this book apparently thought of himself as one of those wise ones; through this literary work he hoped to save others. Those who resisted oppressive leaders, such as the Seleucids, by refusing to eat their food (ch. 1) and refusing to worship their idols (ch. 3) would be given understanding and would have a part in the resurrection (12:2).

The expression "understanding of all kinds of literature and learning" may be a clue to the method of the author. He was writing the book of Daniel with various books as his sources, such as Kings, Chronicles, Isaiah, and Jeremiah. We have already seen how he used Kings, Chronicles, and possibly Jeremiah to reconstruct the events of the exile. His understanding of a Median empire coming between the Babylonians and the Persians, which figures later in the book (chs. 2 and 7), was perhaps based on his reading of Isaiah and Jeremiah (Dan. 5:30–31; see Isa. 13:17; 21:2; Jer. 51:11, 28). Later he reinterpreted the seventy years of Jeremiah in a creative way (Dan. 9). The author saw himself as gifted with this wisdom that allowed him to understand and interpret Israelite literature.

1:18–20 / Verse 18 (**At the end of the time set by the king to bring them in, the chief official presented them to Nebuchadnezzar**) introduces another historical problem. The set time for their training was three years (1:5), which presumably began in the first year of Nebuchadnezzar's reign (1:1). However, there seems to be a discrepancy with Daniel 2:1, which dates the events of that chapter to the second year of Nebuchadnezzar.

In Daniel 2 the king promotes Daniel over the other wise men for telling and interpreting his dream (2:48). In other words, according to chapter 1, Daniel finishes his three years of training and enters the king's service. According to chapter 2, he is promoted over all the others in his second year of training. (For further discussion and possible harmonizations, see the commentary on 2:1.)

As noted in the commentary on verse 17, Daniel and his friends excel in learning. The king himself examines them, and the outcome is that in **every matter of wisdom and understanding, they are found to be ten times better than all the magicians and enchanters in his whole kingdom** (1:20). We are reminded again of Joseph, who was superior in wisdom to the Egyptian magicians, because he could interpret Pharaoh's dream when the others failed (Gen. 41:8, 15, 24). "No one" was "so discerning and wise as" Joseph (Gen. 41:39). In addition, we are reminded of Jesus, who impresses everyone in the temple with his wisdom at an early age (Luke 2:46–47). Moreover, Jesus is wiser than Solomon (Matt. 12:42; Luke 11:31), the wisest man who ever lived (1 Kgs. 3:12).

Although the motif is stronger in Daniel 2, chapter 1 can also be understood as a contest between Israel's God and foreign gods. The other students training to become sages are presumably devotees of pagan gods. Clearly the "magicians and enchanters" are. The Jewish youths come out on top, because the one true God is the source of their wisdom. The other gods, being inferior and impotent, or nonexistent, cannot supply their servants with understanding or with the supernatural gift of dream interpretation. The contest theme is found elsewhere in the Bible. In Exodus 1–13, Yahweh shows himself to be greater than the gods of Egypt by putting a series of plagues on the Egyptians (Exod. 12:12). Pharaoh's magicians are humiliated: they can only duplicate the first two plagues of water to blood (Exod. 7:22) and frogs (Exod. 8:7); they fail to produce gnats (Exod. 8:18); eventually, they cannot even show up, because they are so afflicted by the plague of boils (Exod. 9:11). By contrast, God exalts Moses as a miracle worker. In similar contests, Yahweh shows that he is greater than Dagon as the Philistine god bows before the ark of the covenant (1 Sam. 5), and he proves his superiority to Baal when Elijah faces Baal's prophets in calling fire down from heaven (1 Kgs. 18:1–40).

1:21 / Chapter 1 begins with the mention of two kings: Jehoiakim of Judah and Nebuchadnezzar of Babylon; it ends with the mention of King Cyrus of Persia. This envelope construction not only delimits the chapter but gives the parameters of Daniel's career or possibly his life. Daniel was taken into exile in Babylon in 606 B.C. (according to the author of the book of Daniel the first deportation occurred this early; see the commentary on 1:1) and **remained there until the first year of King Cyrus** (539 B.C.). The reign of Cyrus is significant because he is the one who, after conquering Babylon, released the Jews from captivity (although it was in his second year, 538, not his first). He let them return to Jerusalem, rebuild the temple, and do so with Persian financial assistance (Ezra 1:2–4). This means that the beginning and ending of this chapter also frame the exile. However, the chapter and indeed the book, except for Daniel 9:25, are strangely silent about the return from exile. The author's interest is not in the return to the land but in a return to paradise. The book of Daniel is not about the Jews coming back to Judah but about the kingdom of God coming to earth.

If the author of chapter 1 intended to communicate that the last year of Daniel's career, or of his life, was in the first year of Cyrus, then there is a discrepancy between chapter 1 and chapter 10. God gives Daniel a revelatory vision in the third year of Cyrus, according to Daniel 10:1. One could harmonize by saying that Daniel retired from the royal service in the first year of Cyrus yet continued to receive visions, but the text does not say this. It is better to see this as evidence of the book's complex compositional history. Perhaps there were competing traditions regarding the end of Daniel's career.

To sum up, Daniel 1 leads off with a strong depiction of the sovereignty of God. Nebuchadnezzar may sack Jerusalem, but only because God gives it to him. The chief official tries to fix the fare of Daniel and his friends, but because of God's favor and Daniel's determination, the Jewish lads maintain their diet, resulting in a healthier appearance. Many youths study for the king's service, but Daniel and his friends outshine them all. This is not accidental. Rather, it is because God grants them wisdom and knowledge.

In our day, living as we do with fears of terrorism, of the proliferation of nuclear weapons, of global warming, of a worldwide energy and economic crisis when fossil fuels are depleted, and of disease epidemics, we need to remember that God is still on his throne. He may not intervene as often as we like in human history, but we know that nothing happens without his allowing it, and we know he is bringing this world to its consummation according to his plan, in his time.

We need to trust that just as God provided for Daniel and his friends, keeping them healthy with their simple vegetarian diet, God will take care of us. God may not place us in a palace, but Jesus promises that God will clothe us just as he "clothes" the lilies of the field (Matt. 6:28–30). If we seek God's kingdom and his righteousness, all the things we need will be given to us (Matt. 6:33). God may not promote us over everyone else. Paul reminds us that "not many" followers of Christ are "wise by human standards"; "not many" are "influential"; "not many" are "of noble birth" (1 Cor. 1:26). Yet God turns things upside down by using the weak and foolish of this world to shame the wise and powerful (1 Cor. 1:27–28). Furthermore, we can be like the Jewish youths in receiving God's wisdom. It is not the world's human wisdom but God's secret, hidden wisdom, so that we have the very mind of Christ (1 Cor. 2:7–16).

Finally, we should ask ourselves what it means to avoid the defilements of this world. For Daniel and his companions that means abstaining from certain foods. The NT, however, discourages being overly concerned about diet (Acts 11:5–9; Rom. 14:17; Col. 2:20–23). John warns us not to love the world, which is characterized by "the lust of the flesh, and the lust of the eyes, and the pride of life" (1 John 2:16 KJV). Sometimes the church has made rules about hairstyles and clothing fashion. There are Christian communities that refrain from wearing jewelry and forbid their women from wearing makeup or from cutting or braiding their hair (1 Tim. 2:9–10). Other Christians leave it open to the individual conscience to determine what it means to be pure and holy, separate from the world, not touching unclean things (2 Cor. 6:14–7:1). Our Lord taught that defilement does not come from external things, such as what we eat, or from failure to observe ritual washings, as in Judaism, but from the sins of the heart: "But what comes out of the mouth proceeds from the heart, and this is what defiles. For out of the heart come evil intentions, murder, adultery, fornication, theft, false witness, slander. These are what defile a person, but to eat with unwashed hands does not defile" (Matt. 15:18–20 NRSV).

Additional Notes §1

1:1 / Both internal, biblical evidence and evidence external to the Bible seem to suggest that a Babylonian invasion of Judah did not happen as early as 606/605 B.C., "in the third year of the reign of Jehoiakim." 2 Kgs. 24:10 records a Babylonian invasion of Judah in 597 B.C. Some say that corroborating evidence for an earlier invasion in line with Dan. 1:1 can be found in 2 Kgs. 24:1. However, that verse only says "Nebuchadnezzar, King of Babylon, came up," meaning that he carried out a campaign. It does not say where; it certainly does not say that he invaded Judah or attacked Jerusalem. The NIV, therefore, goes beyond the text by saying that he "invaded the land," which gives that misleading impression. Furthermore, 2 Kgs. 24:1 does not say when this took place. While it indicates that Jehoiakim became Nebuchadnezzar's vassal for three years, it does not say that these were the first three years of his reign. To which of Nebuchadnezzar's campaigns, then, does 2 Kgs. 24:1 refer?

According to the Babylonian Chronicles, in 605 B.C. Nebuchadnezzar, who was not yet king, met the Egyptians at Carchemish in Syria and defeated them (D. J. Wiseman, *Chronicles of Chaldaean Kings [626–556 B.C.] in the British Museum* [London: Trustees of the British Museum, 1956], pp. 23–28, 67–69). While it is possible that the campaign of 2 Kgs. 24:1 refers to the battle of Carchemish (Jer. 46:2), it seems unlikely because Nebuchadnezzar did not come close to Judah at that time. The same could probably be said for Nebuchadnezzar's expedition to Hatti land later in 605 B.C. However, in 604 B.C. he came as far south as Philistia, along Israel's coast, and sacked Ashkelon. That is close enough to Jerusalem have posed a serious threat to Jehoiakim. It is best to date his submission to that time and his rebellion to around 601 B.C. But since Nebuchadnezzar was occupied elsewhere, he probably did not get around to punishing Judah until 597 B.C. (J. Bright, *A History of Israel* [3rd ed.; Philadelphia: Westminster, 1981], p. 326).

There are variant spellings for the name of King **Nebuchadnezzar.** In this verse it is spelled *nebukadne'tsar* (long u; with *'aleph*). However, in 1:18; 2:1; 3:14; 5:11, it is *nebukadnetsar* (short u; no *'aleph*); in 2:28, 46 and twenty-six other verses, it is *nebukadnetsar* (long u; no *'aleph*). While some have tried to defend the form "Nebuchadnezzar" with "n," which is found in Kings, Chronicles, Ezra, Nehemiah, Daniel, and a few times in Jeremiah (J. G. Baldwin, *Daniel: An Introduction and Commentary* [Downers Grove, Ill.: InterVarsity, 1978], p. 78 n. 1, citing P.-R. Berger, "Der Kyros-Zylinder mit den Zusatzfragment BIN II Nr. 32 und die akkadischen Personennamen im Danielbuch," *ZA* 64 [1975], pp. 227–30), most scholars prefer the form "Nebuchadrezzar." In Babylonian texts the name is *nabu-kudurri-utsur*. Therefore, "Nebuchadrezzar" with an "r" (Jer. 21:2, 7; 22:25 plus thirty other times in Jer. and Ezek.; see NRSV) seems to be the more accurate transliteration. J. J. Collins explains, "The Danielic form arises by dissimilation of the two *r*'s. The name, formerly explained as 'O Nabû, protect the boundary,' is now interpreted as 'O Nabû, protect the offspring'" (J. J. Collins, *Daniel: A Commentary on the Book of Daniel* [Hermeneia; Minneapolis: Fortress, 1993], p. 133). Nabû was a Babylonian deity.

1:2 / **The Lord** translates the Hebrew word *'adonay*, not the proper name for Israel's God, which is "Yahweh" ("LORD"). "Yahweh" only occurs in ch. 9.

Most translations have "vessels" instead of **articles.** The Hebrew word is quite general, but since these "articles" are used for drinking wine in 5:2–4, perhaps "vessels" is a better choice.

The Hebrew word behind **Babylonia,** transliterated "Shinar," is used infrequently in the Bible (Gen. 10:10; 11:2; 14:1, 9; Josh. 7:21; Isa. 11:11; Zech. 5:11). It is not clear what this term comes from; some think it is related to *Shumer*, the name for Southern Babylonia (S. R. Driver, *The Book of Daniel* [Cambridge: Cambridge University Press, 1936], p. 3).

How is **the treasure house of his god** (lit. "house of the treasury of his god") different from **the temple of his god** (lit. "the house of his god")? From the NIV one might get the impression that two places are indicated. However, the second one might be a gloss to explain the first, or it might be a duplication, the result of a copy error. S. R. Driver argues against the latter: since "the author's Hebrew is often far from elegant, . . . the anomalous wording of the verse is possibly original" (Driver, *Daniel*, p. 4). In any case, there is only one place in view: the temple, which is also the treasury. The placement of the gods of conquered peoples under the victors' gods was a great ancient propaganda tool. But the Jews had no such images, so the temple vessels from Jerusalem served the same purpose (D. L. Smith-Christopher, "The Book of Daniel," *The New Interpreter's Bible*, vol. 7 [ed. L. Keck; Nashville: Abingdon, 1996], p. 38).

1:3 / The word **Ashpenaz** comes from an Old Persian word meaning "guest" (L. F. Hartman and A. Di Lella, *The Book of Daniel* [AB 23; Garden City, N.Y.: Doubleday, 1978], p. 129) or "lodging" (Collins, *Daniel*, p. 134), suggesting the title "innkeeper" (Collins, *Daniel*, p. 134) or "keeper of the court" (Smith-Christopher, "Book of Daniel," p. 42). Collins translates "major-domo" (*Daniel*, p. 134). The term has been found on an Aramaic incantation bowl dating from about A.D. 600. There it is not a title but a proper name. See D. W. Myhrman, "An Aramaic Incantation Text," in *Hilprecht Anniversary Volume* (Leipzig: J. C. Hinrichs, 1909), p. 345, line 1; and C. D. Isbell, *Corpus of the Aramaic Incantation Bowls* (SBLDS 17; Missoula, Mont.: Scholars Press, 1975), pp. 24–25.

In the Bible, the evidence for the translation "eunuch" (Heb. *sarisim*; NIV **court officials**) is mixed. The term *saris* (sg.) is used of Potiphar (Gen. 39:1), who was not a eunuch, since he was married (Gen. 39:7–20). In a less obvious context, Isaiah predicts that some of Hezekiah's descendants will be taken to Babylon and be made *sarisim* (Isa. 39:7; NIV "eunuchs"). In Isa. 56:4–5, the context clearly indicates that the *sarisim* are eunuchs. Those two passages in Isaiah gave rise to the view that the Babylonians frequently castrated their captives; therefore, some believe that not only Ashpenaz but Daniel and his three friends were eunuchs. Since the text says that they were "without any physical defect" (Dan. 1:4), however, they could not have been castrated. So, although there is some ambiguity, it is best to understand these as "court officials" along with the NIV. Ancient sources seem to suggest that the Persians more commonly practiced castrating captives and using eunuchs as court officials than the Babylonians. If the stories in Dan. 1–6 were composed in the Persian period, as some scholars think, then it would be more likely that the author intended *sarisim* to be understood as "eunuchs" (see Collins, *Daniel*, p. 135).

Partemim (**nobility**) is a Persian word used only here and in Esth. 1:3 and 6:9. It may indicate a Persian date for the stories in Dan. 1–6 (see Hartman and Di Lella, *Daniel*, p. 129).

1:4 / The phrase translated **showing aptitude** is *maskilim*, which becomes an important term in the last two chapters of the book of Daniel. When the term is used as a noun, *maskilim* means "the wise ones," who "will shine like the brightness of the heavens" (12:3; see also 11:35). These are the ones who will be knowledgeable about the apocalyptic events and will instruct others.

The term translated **Babylonians** here is *kasdim*. As explained above, originally it referred to a people living in southern Mesopotamia, but it later shifted to mean magicians, astrologers, and the like. When did the shift occur? In the first century B.C., Diodorus Siculus described the *kasdim* as using astrology, soothsaying, and divination (Diodorus Siculus, *Lib.* 2.29). Since Daniel uses the term this way, this might be evidence for a late, or Hellenistic, date of Daniel. However, the shift may have occurred earlier. *Kasdim* is found in Herodotus, *Hist.* 1.181–182 in the fifth century B.C., referring to the priests of Bel, the Babylonian deity, but it is a very brief notice that does not mention magic or astrology. Collins wants to leave open the possibility that Herodotus was using the term with the later meaning, which would push the shift in meaning back to the fifth century B.C. (Collins, *Daniel*, pp. 137–38).

1:5 / The Hebrew word for **food** here is *pat-bag*. It comes from Persian *patibaga*, meaning a royal "allotment of food," and is found only in Daniel. In this verse and in 11:26, the Hebrew separates the *pat* and *bag*, probably because an ancient editor construed the first part to come from the Hebrew word *pat*, which means "fragment," "bit," or "morsel." In the other three instances, it is written more correctly as one word (1:8, 13, 15).

1:7 / **Belteshazzar** is a Hebraized or corrupt form of Akkadian *balat-su-utsur*, meaning "protect his life" (Collins, *Daniel*, p. 141). There is no divine element to the name, although "Marduk" may be the understood subject, as El was probably the understood subject of the name Jacob in Hebrew (i.e., "El grasps the heel"). However, by popular etymology it was thought that the name Belteshazzar began with "Bel," another name for Marduk, the chief Babylonian deity. This is evident from the way the Hebrew word is vocalized and also from 4:8: "He is called Belteshazzar, after the name of my god." Baldwin seeks to remove the discrepancy by construing Belteshazzar to be from *Belet-shar-utsur*, "lady, protect the king," referring to Bel's consort (Baldwin, *Daniel*, p. 81, following A. R. Millard, "Daniel 1–6 and History," *EvQ* 49 [1977], p. 72, and Berger, "Kyros-Zylinder," pp. 224–34). While this might be possible, that interpretation would still differ from 4:8, which uses the masculine "god," not "goddess." It could be argued that the Aramaic word for "god" means "goddess" as the corresponding masculine Hebrew noun for "god" does in 1 Kgs. 11:5 and 33 (in reference to the goddess Ashtoreth). However, such a meaning is unusual, and there is no "r" in the middle of Belteshazzar, making *shar* "king" less likely. Therefore, it seems more plausible that Belteshazzar exhibits a popular etymology—people thought it had the divine name "Bel" in it.

The name **Meshach** might have the element *Misha* in it, which is another form of Mithras, a Persian deity (Collins, *Daniel*, p. 141). If so, this might indicate a Persian date for the first half of the book, or at least for chapter 1.

1:8 / Smith-Christopher supports an idea that was suggested (though rejected) by J. E. Goldingay, that the **royal food and wine** symbolize feasting, whereas in the exile they should be mourning. Furthermore, this fare represents the food of the wealthy, whereas Daniel preferred the humble diet of the poor. Finally, the wealth came at the expense of conquered and oppressed people from whom it was plundered (Smith-Christopher, "Book of Daniel," p. 40). But the text says nothing about fasting, identifying with peasants by eating their simple diet, or eating vegetables to protest Babylonian conquests. Rather, the express concern is to avoid defilement. Smith-Christopher's interpretation does not explain Daniel's concern **not to defile himself** (J. E. Goldingay, *Daniel* [WBC 30; Dallas: Word, 1989], p. 19). Baldwin argues that the king's food and wine represent a covenant meal that Daniel wanted to avoid so that he would not be bound to the king through such fellowship. He wanted to express his loyalty to God rather than to the earthly king, and he wanted to avoid being co-opted by the king's largess. Baldwin thinks Daniel is concerned about being defiled morally rather than ritually (Baldwin, *Daniel*, p. 83). But Collins considers this a rationalization to avoid the idea of ritual purity, which was part of OT faith (Collins, *Daniel*, p. 142). Collins is correct that the Hebrew word for "defile" seems to mean ritual impurity (Mal. 1:7; see also Ezra 2:62; Neh. 7:64; Isa. 59:3; 63:3). Furthermore, as argued above, Daniel does become a servant of Nebuchadnezzar, and he later accepts other royal gifts.

1:9 / The **favor and sympathy** shown **to Daniel** in this verse display the friendly relationship between the Jews and the Gentiles in the Persian and early Hellenistic eras. For this reason, Collins is strongly opposed to dating chs. 1–6 to the second century B.C. (Collins, *Daniel*, p. 143). As I have argued in the text, the friendliness shows the Persian origin, but the stories have been shaped by the author of the Hellenistic era to instruct the Jews of his day, as can be seen in the exhortation to avoid defilement by eating the king's food. Other examples of Jews who enjoyed good relationships with Persians can be seen in the stories of Esther, Zerubbabel, Ezra, and Nehemiah.

1:10 / As stated in the introduction to this chapter, there are a number of parallels between the Joseph story and that of Daniel. The word translated **worse** here is used of the butler and baker in the Joseph narrative. They look sad and "dejected" because they are disturbed about their dreams (Gen. 40:6). In Daniel, though, the idea is that the Jewish youths would exhibit an inferior appearance not because of psychological distress but because of a deficient diet.

J. A. Montgomery questions whether to take literally the official's statement, **The king would then have my head.** It may mean merely that Ashpenaz would be held accountable for Daniel's health (J. A. Montgomery, *The Book of Daniel* [Edinburgh: T&T Clark, 1927], p. 131). But considering how often death is a threat, as in chs. 2, 3, and 6, it is more reasonable to take this expression literally.

1:20 / The Hebrew word for **magicians**, *khartummim*, is the same word used in the Joseph narrative in Gen. 41:8 (*khartumme mitsrayim*, "magicians of Egypt") and 41:24 (*hakhartummim*, "the magicians") and in the exodus story in Exod. 8:3, 14, 15; 9:11. See also Dan. 2:2.

§2 Daniel Interprets Nebuchadnezzar's Dream (Dan. 2:1–49)

The stories in Daniel 2–7 probably did not all circulate together originally. As mentioned earlier, evidence for this can be seen especially in chapters 3 and 6. The original author of chapter 3 focuses on Hananiah, Mishael, and Azariah, seemingly unaware of Daniel, while the original author of chapter 6 highlights Daniel, seemingly oblivious to his three friends. These independent traditions have been brought together and shaped into a literary whole. (For a more complete discussion of the literary development, see the Introduction.) They are united by language—the book shifts to Aramaic in 2:4 and remains in Aramaic through the end of chapter 7—and also by a *chiastic* literary structure: A B C : C' B' A'.

- A Daniel 2: Dream of four kingdoms (metals) followed by the kingdom of God
  - B Daniel 3: Miraculous deliverance (from the fiery furnace)
    - C Daniel 4: Judgment on a king (Nebuchadnezzar)
    - C' Daniel 5: Judgment on a king (Belshazzar)
  - B' Daniel 6: Miraculous deliverance (from the lions' den)
- A' Daniel 7: Vision of four kingdoms (beasts) followed by the kingdom of God

According to the above analysis, which describes the main structure, Daniel 2 is paired with Daniel 7. However, chapter 2 is also similar to chapters 4 and 5 because all three contain contests between Daniel on the one hand and the Babylonian wise men and diviners on the other. In Daniel 2, the king's pagan sages cannot tell the dream or its meaning, but Daniel, the Jew, can. In chapter 4, likewise, the Babylonians fail to interpret Nebuchadnezzar's vision, whereas Daniel succeeds. In chapter 5, a cryptic inscription baffles the Babylonian magicians, while Daniel is able to explain the mystery. Daniel 1 also contains an element of the contest motif; when Daniel and his friends are examined, they prove to be "ten times better than all" the rest of the royal counselors (1:20).

Daniel 2 appears to have been modeled after the Joseph story in Genesis, especially chapter 41. Both use the same key Hebrew words. Both show that it is possible to be successful while living as a faithful Jew in the court of a foreign king. Both Joseph and Daniel are adept at interpreting dreams. In both cases the king has a dream that troubles him (Gen. 41:8; Dan. 2:1). In both, the king summons the magicians (Gen. 41:8; 41:24; Dan. 2:2) and wise men (Gen. 41:8; Dan. 2:12), but they fail to interpret the dream. Both mention the "captain of the guard" or "chief executioner" (Gen. 37:36; 39:1; 41:10, 12; Dan. 2:14). Both use the word "interpret." While that may not seem surprising given that both stories deal with dream interpretation, the Hebrew verb meaning "to interpret" and the related noun "interpretation" are used in the Hebrew Bible only in Genesis 40 and 41 (e.g., Gen. 40:8, 16; 41:8, 12). Daniel 2 uses the Aramaic cognate term (primarily as a noun, "interpretation," although the NIV sometimes translates it as a verb; see, e.g., Dan. 2:4, 5, 6). Both stories have a young Jewish captive give the interpretation when the pagan magicians and wise men fail. Both declare that it is not the human (Joseph or Daniel) but God who gives the interpretation (Gen. 41:16; Dan. 2:28, 30). Both indicate that God has shown the king (Pharaoh or Nebuchadnezzar) the future (Gen. 41:25, 28; Dan. 2:28). Both have the hero promoted as a reward for his service (Gen. 41:40–42; Dan. 2:48; also note the gold chain of Gen. 41:42, paralleled later in Dan. 5:29, and the notion that the Spirit of God dwells within Joseph [Gen. 41:38], paralleled in Dan. 4:8, 9, 18; 5:11, 14).

There are differences as well as similarities. Daniel might be considered to be greater than Joseph, because he not only interprets the dream but is able to reveal the content of the dream. Also, Nebuchadnezzar is a more frightening king than Pharaoh, because he terrorizes the wise men with the threat of execution if they cannot recount as well as interpret the dream. Finally, the dream is more significant, predicting not merely a temporal famine but the end of the age when all the kingdoms of the world will fall before the eternal kingdom of God.

It appears that two traditions have been woven together into one story in chapter 2. In the earlier version, Daniel is not a member of the wise men and there is no mention of his three companions. He is just one of the exiles of Judah who has been discovered (2:25). He cannot approach the king directly but must go through Arioch (2:24). In the later, alternate version (especially vv. 13–23), Daniel and his friends are among the wise men slated for execution (2:13). When he discovers this, Daniel asks Arioch why (2:15). After Arioch explains the situation, Daniel goes directly to the king to ask for time to come up with an interpretation

(2:16). It seems that the three friends were imported to connect chapter 2 with the mention of them in chapter 1 and also to anticipate chapter 3 where they are the main characters. Both versions are somewhat in tension with chapter 1 where Daniel and his friends are considered wiser than all the others (1:20), because in chapter 2 they are apparently not even important enough to be consulted about the dream (2:2, 15–16). (For more on the literary development, see "Language Problem and Literary Development" in the Introduction.)

The main message of chapter 2 is the announcement of the coming kingdom of God. The main purpose is to comfort and encourage Jews living under foreign domination. Since chapter 2 does not describe the persecution of the Jews as in the similar chapter 7, chapter 2 may date from an earlier time: after Alexander's empire split into several kingdoms, including those of the Seleucids and Ptolemies, but before the Seleucid king Antiochus IV initiated his attacks on the Jews. Alternatively, it is possible that chapters 2–7 all come from the same period (perhaps the Persian era) but the parts of chapter 7 that emphasize Antiochus's oppression were added after the persecutions began.

2:1 / Nebuchadnezzar's dream is dated to **the second year of his reign.** But this is at odds with chapter 1, which states that Nebuchadnezzar was already king when Daniel was taken to Babylon (1:1), that Daniel was in training for three years (1:5), and that he completed his course of study (1:18). That means that at the beginning of chapter 2, it should be the third year of Nebuchadnezzar's reign. Attempts have been made to harmonize this discrepancy. For example, we could suppose chapter 2 is a flashback. The events of chapter 2 take place in Nebuchadnezzar's second year, after which Daniel and his friends go back to school to finish their program, the graduation of which is already recounted at the end of chapter 1. This might explain why Daniel and his friends are not summoned with the other wise men in chapter 2, because they have not entered the ranks of trained advisers yet. This is an unlikely interpretation, though, because chapter 2 seems to follow chapter 1 with no indication that the narrative is jumping back in time. Another suggestion is that the chronology of chapter 2 is based on the accession-year method of counting, which reckons the first year of the king from the first New Year's day of his reign, ignoring the previous months as an accession year. If we choose to count those months of the accession year as a first year, then the first year becomes the second, and therefore, when the text says "the second year of his reign," it really could be considered the third. The trouble is, Daniel 2:1 does not say when in the second year it is. If early, then the training period might be two years or less (a few months for the accession year, one full regnal year, and another few months for the "second" year of reign). This is difficult to square with the three years of chapter 1, unless one counts partial years as whole years, which seems forced. Also, the author does not indicate what method of counting years he is using. Another way to harmonize is to say that Nebuchadnezzar is called king proleptically in chapter 1. This would mean that Daniel was carried to Babylon and began his training during the year before Nebuchadnezzar's coronation. The second year of the king would then be the third year of school. Unfortunately, there is no indication in chapter 1 that Nebuchadnezzar is not already king. Finally, one could argue for a copy error, because one Greek papyrus has "twelfth" year instead of "second." However, it is more likely that an ancient scribe attempted to correct the text by changing it to "twelfth," than that "twelfth" is the original reading.

While the above harmonizations may be possible, they are not convincing. Furthermore, it is important to mention that the date is not the only point of tension between the two chapters. As already noted, even though according to chapter 1 Daniel and his friends are ten times greater than the other students (1:20), they are strangely not even consulted regarding the king's dream in chapter 2 (2:2–11). If the four youths had distinguished themselves by graduating at the top of their class, one would expect that the king would specifically seek them out to see if they could tell the dream and its interpretation; but he does not (Collins, *Daniel*, p. 155). The only harmonization that addresses this problem is the first, but as already noted, there is no hint of a flashback in the text. Therefore, it is best to let the tensions between chapters 1 and 2 stand; we should not try to harmonize them. When chapter 1 was added as an introductory chapter, the author either did not notice the discrepancies or did not think them important enough to smooth over.

2:2 / The first word in the series of wise men, **magicians**, is the same term used in Exodus for the Egyptian magicians who could duplicate some of the plagues and miracles of Moses (Exod. 8:3, 14, 15; 9:11). It is also used for those called upon by Pharaoh to interpret his dream in the Joseph cycle (Gen. 41:8, 24). Its use here may be influenced by that. A similar word in Akkadian means "dream interpreter." **Enchanters** were religious figures who recited incantations and interpreted omens. **Sorcerers** practiced magic, sorcery, witchcraft—strictly proscribed in Israel (Exod. 22:18; Deut. 18:10; Isa. 47:9; Mal. 3:5). The term rendered **astrologers** is actually "Chaldeans." It initially referred to a group of people in southern Babylonia but came to designate a group of wise men or counselors (see the commentary on 1:4). Eventually, the term came to mean "astrologer," but it is questionable whether the Hebrew word should be translated that way here, as in the NIV. Most modern versions have "Chaldeans."

2:3 / The Hebrew text has the king say, "I dreamed a dream; now my spirit has become troubled to know the dream." The expression "to know the dream" is ambiguous. It is unclear whether the king merely wants to know what the dream was or whether he wants to know, that is, understand the dream—in other words, its meaning or interpretation. The NIV goes beyond translation by removing the ambiguity: **I have had a dream that troubles me and I want to know what it means.** Since knowing the dream would be useless without the interpretation, the NIV may be correct, but it is not a precise translation. Moreover, in the next verse the advisers ask the king to tell them the dream so that they can supply the interpretation, and subsequently the king asks for both the dream and the interpretation. Therefore, it is more likely that he is simply asking them to tell him the dream here (see the NIV footnote).

It is also unclear whether the king remembered the dream but wanted to test his wise men, or whether he forgot the dream and needed them to remind him of its content, in which case he must have been confident that he would recognize the dream if they told it to him. Perhaps he remembered fragments of it that would allow him to confirm the authenticity of the advisers' words if they got those elements right. If he could recollect the dream, then he is not troubled to know the dream, but only its interpretation, which supports the NIV's reading above. Indeed, it seems from verse 9, where he accuses them of lying, that he does know the dream and is merely testing them. It would be easy for them to make up an interpretation if he recounts the dream, but if they really have supernatural abilities, they should be able to communicate both the dream and its meaning. Furthermore, if they succeed in doing so, he can be certain that the interpretation comes from the gods as well. Nevertheless, it is still possible that he could not recall the dream itself. In fact, that position is supported by an ancient text that says, "If a man cannot remember the dream he saw (it means): his (personal) god is angry with him" (Babylonian omen text VAT 7525 in the Berlin Museum, cited in Oppenheim, *Interpretation of Dreams*, p. 232). Maybe the king is especially troubled, then, because he cannot remember the dream and consequently fears divine wrath. Further support for this comes from an ancient belief that an untold and uninterpreted dream is dangerous to the dreamer. If the king remembered it, he would be motivated to verbalize it, because telling a dream was thought to have a cleansing, healing effect that would remove its negative consequences (Oppenheim, *Interpretation of Dreams*, pp. 217–19). Therefore, one might conclude that he could not remember it, or he would surely tell it, but of this we cannot be certain.

2:4 / Although there is a list of different classes of wise men in verse 2, the text that follows mentions only the **astrologers** (Chaldeans) dialoguing with the king (vv. 4–11). The term is probably inclusive, however, encompassing all of the advisers.

It is here in verse 4 that the text shifts to Aramaic with the speech of the Chaldeans. The phrase **in Aramaic** is curious. Why would the narrator inform us of the language of the Chaldeans, as if Nebuchadnezzar incredibly had been speaking in Hebrew up to this point? Why make a point of shifting to Aramaic for the speech of the Chaldeans, when the book actually stays in Aramaic until the end of chapter 7 whether anyone is speaking or not? This is probably a scribal insertion. Ancient scribes used to put notes in the margins of manuscripts to explain things. In this case the word was added to show where the text shifts to Aramaic (not to show what language the Chaldeans spoke). But scribes also sometimes used the margins to correct faulty manuscripts, inserting words that had been left out. In subsequent copying, sometimes marginal words were inserted into the text. In cases of corrections, that would be appropriate (although words were not always inserted in the proper places), but in this case, it appears an explanatory word was inserted that was not originally part of the text. This interpretation is supported by the Dead Sea Scroll 1QDan^a. In this manuscript of Daniel, there is a space before the speech of the Chaldeans begins, with no trace of "in Aramaic" there. However, this fact is not conclusive, because the end of the previous line is missing and "in Aramaic" would fit there.

2:5–9 / The king lays out his punishments and rewards, threats and promises. If they fail to **tell him what the dream was and interpret it, he will have them cut into pieces and their houses turned into piles of rubble**. On the other hand, if they succeed, he will give them **gifts and rewards and great honor** (2:5–6). Again, they implore the king to **tell his servants the dream**. They are confident that they can **interpret it** once they know it (2:7). Of course, they have books and traditions that will tell them how to interpret various dream images. The king accuses them of **trying to gain time,** meaning they are stalling for time so that they can delay their execution. They are **hoping the situation will change,** meaning that it will become more favorable to them (2:8–9).

He also accuses them of conspiring **to tell** him **misleading and wicked things** (2:9). Ancient kings were sometimes aware that their advisers might confer together to work out an interpretation favorable to the king; they tended to tell the king what he wanted to hear. It might therefore be merely a human contrivance and not a true interpretation. To that extent it would be "misleading and wicked." A good biblical example of this is when the four hundred prophets of King Ahab of Israel all agree that he will succeed in battle. But King Jehoshaphat of Judah is skeptical and asks for another opinion, so they summon the independent prophet Micaiah. When he arrives, the leader of the royal prophets tries to pressure Micaiah to say the same thing as the others; but he alone brings a negative word, and his is the true word of God, as confirmed by history (1 Kgs. 22). An extrabiblical example can be found in the Assyrian king Sennacherib. In one instance he shows his suspicious attitude toward his omen interpreters by dividing them into separate units to prevent their collaboration (Oppenheim, *Interpretation of Dreams*, p. 227, citing Tadmor, "Sin of Sargon," pp. 150–63).

When King Nebuchadnezzar therefore insists, **"tell me the dream, and I will know that you can interpret it for me"** (2:9), it is possible that he is testing them because he does not trust them. As mentioned above, it is not clear whether the king remembers the dream. However, the test is the same whether he recalls it or not. If they successfully tell him the dream, which they can only learn supernaturally, that will verify that they have been in touch with the gods and can give the correct interpretation. If they cannot recount the dream, their powers are in doubt and their interpretations suspect.

2:10–12 / Although it is not important to know whether the king recollects his dream, it is very important to the author that the Chaldeans are not able to discover the dream or interpret it. They complain to the king that no one **on earth . . . can do what the king asks** or **can reveal it to the king except the gods, and they do not live among men** (2:10–11). The point of the story is that the gods of the Babylonians are impotent, while the God of Daniel is able to do what the king asks. He can reveal the dream, and he does dwell with men. Compare also verses 27–28, where Daniel points out the same thing: the wise men and magicians cannot convey the mystery, but the God of heaven can. The negative response of the Chaldeans provokes the king. He becomes **so angry and furious that he** orders **the execution of all the wise men** (2:12).

2:13–23 / These verses appear to be either a later addition meant to smooth over differences with chapter 1 or a variant tradition. We would expect that, in the original story, if Daniel was one of the wise men, he would have been summoned with them (2:2). Though Daniel is not presented as a member of this group, he is interested in saving them (2:24). He himself is merely "a man among the exiles" (2:25). He therefore must go through Arioch to see the king (2:24–25). By contrast, in verses 13–23, **men were sent to look for Daniel and his friends to put them to death** (2:13), which indicates that they must have been among the royal counselors. Daniel then endeavors to save himself **and his friends** so that they **might not be executed with the rest of the wise men of Babylon** (2:18). Also, Daniel does not need to be introduced to the king, as in verse 25. Instead he goes **in to the king and** asks **for time, so that he might interpret the dream for him** (2:16). This makes sense if the king already knows Daniel, as in chapter 1.

Finally, the story is really about Daniel; the original account probably did not mention his companions. However, since Hananiah, Mishael, and Azariah were introduced in chapter 1, they are brought into the story of the dream at this point as prayer partners. Compare also verse 49, where they figure in the conclusion of the account as an editorial link to chapter 3, which mainly concerns them. Here in verse 17 they are called by their Hebrew names, which is reminiscent of chapter 1, but in verse 49 they are called by their Babylonian names in anticipation of chapter 3, where those names are used throughout.

These additional verses (2:13–23) do not remove all tensions: they do not explain why Daniel does not even know what is going on until he is about to be executed (2:15). Another interesting contrast is in verse 16, where Daniel is not rebuked by the king when he asks "for time," whereas the other wise men are accused of stalling for time (2:8).

Following his audience with the king, Daniel enlists his friends to join him in prayer. Together they **plead for mercy from the God of heaven,** who they hope will supply the needed revelation **concerning this mystery** (2:18). This verse presents Daniel and his companions as pious men of prayer. They serve as role models for anyone facing persecution or unjust royal decrees, such as the Jews faced under Antiochus IV. But of course, they also bear witness to the importance of prayer for all believers in all times who are facing distressing circumstances. God is gracious and delights to supply our needs (Phil. 4:19). Paul testifies to God's rescue from deadly peril and looks to God for future deliverance through the prayers of other believers (2 Cor. 1:8–11).

God answers the prayers of the youths: **During the night the mystery was revealed to Daniel in a vision** (2:19). That Daniel receives a vision here is significant. Commentators often make a big distinction between Daniel 1–6, where Daniel interprets the visions of others, and Daniel 7–12, where he has his own visions. While that discontinuity is not without merit, there is more continuity between Daniel 2–6 and 7 than is often acknowledged. It is true that Daniel's vision here is for the purpose of interpreting Nebuchadnezzar's dream, but it is a vision nevertheless. This lends support for reading Daniel 7 with the other Aramaic chapters (Dan. 2–6) that precede, rather than seeing it as connected only to what follows (Dan. 8–12). Daniel has a vision here in chapter 2 as well as in chapter 7. In both cases the revelations are supernatural, for mysteries cannot be discerned through effort, investigation, divination, or natural endowments of wisdom. Rather, they are revealed by God to his chosen instruments, in this case Daniel ("mystery" occurs also in 2:19, 27, 28, 29, 30, 47; 4:9). They are mysteries about the future (2:29) and about the end of days (2:28). The term "mystery" is frequently used in similar ways in the Dead Sea Scrolls (see Additional Note on 2:18).

Daniel responds appropriately to God's revelation with a psalm of thanksgiving. Thus Daniel is not only a man of prayer but a man of praise. He knows how to petition God; he also knows how to give thanks and offer worship. He is not like the nine healed lepers who failed to express gratitude but like the one Samaritan who returned to praise God with a loud voice and to thank Jesus (Luke 17:12–19). Daniel praises God for his **wisdom and power** (2:20), which corresponds to the **wisdom and power** (2:23) God imparts to his servant. Mentioning that God **changes times and seasons** (2:21) looks back to verse 9, where the powerless sages are accused of trying to delay until the time changes. It also anticipates chapter 7: the beasts/kingdoms continue for "a period of time," literally "a season and a time" (7:12), and the little horn (Antiochus IV) will "try to change the set times and the laws" (7:25). But in contrast to these, the sovereign God of Israel is in control of times and seasons, and of historical events, changing them as he will (see also Acts 1:7; 1 Thess. 5:1). Specifically, **he sets up kings and deposes them** (Dan. 2:21). This anticipates the content of the dream, which presents the rise and fall of kings and kingdoms. More to the point of Daniel's situation, God is praised because he **made known** to them **the dream of the king** (2:23), which could not be discovered naturally. God **reveals deep and hidden things,** which lie **in darkness** (2:22). Perhaps the author of Daniel was thinking of God's promise to the exiles: "I will give you the treasures of darkness, riches stored in secret places" (Isa. 45:3). Other doxologies in Daniel complement this one in chapter 2. Unlike Daniel's doxology, Nebuchadnezzar's (Dan. 4:3, 34–35, 37) and Darius's (Dan. 6:26–27) both emphasize the eternal nature of God's kingdom. All three share the theme of God's power, but each doxology is particular to its situation. Daniel's highlights God's wisdom and knowledge, because he received a revelation. Nebuchadnezzar praises God for his "signs" and "wonders" (4:3), for doing "as he pleases with . . . the peoples of the earth" (4:35), and for humbling the proud (4:37), because he was driven insane and then restored. Darius exalts the Lord as savior, because he "rescued Daniel from the power of the lions" (6:27).

2:24–28 / As mentioned before, in this earlier version of the story, Daniel is not counted among the wise men, though he is interested in saving them (see the commentary on 2:13–23). In contrast to verse 16, Daniel has no access to the king. Therefore he must go to Arioch first, entreating him **not to execute the wise men** but to **take** him **to the king** so that he can **interpret his dream for him** (2:24). Arioch does indeed bring **Daniel to the king,** introducing him as someone he **found from among the exiles of Judah who can tell the king what his dream means** (2:25). This calls to mind the story of Joseph, who is simply one of the Hebrews; he is brought before Pharaoh because he can interpret dreams. It also brings to mind the Qumran text *Prayer of Nabonidus*. In that text, the ailing Babylonian king discovers a Jewish diviner who helps him to acknowledge God and find healing (4QPrNab [4Q242]). The word for "diviner" in the scroll is from the same root as the word "diviner" in Daniel 2:27. In that verse, Daniel agrees with the Chaldeans (see vv. 10–11) that what the king asks is humanly impossible. He also agrees that heaven can reveal the mystery (2:11, 28). However, there is a strong contrast between the two religions at this point. Daniel worships the one, true **God in heaven** (2:28), who not only can but will communicate to his chosen servants, whereas the Babylonian wise men and magicians worship worthless gods who "do not live among men" (2:11). How different is the God of Daniel, who lived in the middle of the Israelites in tabernacle and temple and who initiated and sustained conversation with them through the centuries. This present scene is a contest between Israel's God and the Babylonian gods, between Daniel and the Babylonian diviners (this theme is also found in Dan. 1, 4, and 5; see the commentary on 1:18–20 for other references to this motif in the Bible). However, there is really no contest, because Yahweh wins handily.

The revelation that God gives concerns **what will happen in days to come** (2:28). The Aramaic expression for "in days to come" (and its equivalent in Hebrew) can refer generally to the future. That is why the NIV renders it so. However, the expression can also mean "in the end of the days" or "in the latter days," which makes more sense here. In the context, it is hard to avoid this eschatological meaning, since in the vision all the kingdoms are destroyed by the final kingdom of God, which will have no end. Here and in 10:14 (NIV "in the future"), it should be understood as pointing to the consummation of the ages.

2:29–30 / These verses are a doublet of verses 27–28. One would expect the dream account to follow immediately after verse 28: **Your dream and the visions that passed through your mind as you lay on your bed are these.** Instead, verse 29 interrupts the flow of the passage, coming between that statement and the dream narrative, which begins in verse 31. Furthermore, verses 29–30 repeat elements of verses 27–28.

2:27–28	2:29–30
as you lay on your bed	as you were lying there
what will happen in days to come	things to come . . . what is going to happen
who reveals mysteries	the revealer of mysteries
he has shown King Nebuchadnezzar	showed you
there is a God in heaven who reveals mysteries	this mystery has been revealed to me
no wise man, enchanter, magician or diviner can explain to the king the mystery he has asked about	not because I have greater wisdom than other living men
your dream and the visions	that you may understand
that passed through your mind	what went through your mind

Both verses 27–28 and 29–30 mention that the king was lying down and that the dream concerns the future. In both, God reveals mysteries and shows the king. Each communicates that God is the source of revelation, not humans. This last example portrays Daniel as humble: even though he showed up the king's other counselors, Daniel does not claim credit but gives the glory to God. Finally, both versions note that the dream went through the king's mind. The humility motif in this section is also parallel to the story of Joseph. When Pharaoh mentions that Joseph is reputed to be able to interpret dreams, Joseph replies, "I cannot do it . . . but God will give Pharaoh the answer he desires" (Gen. 41:16). So, Daniel is a man of prayer; a man of praise, thanksgiving, and worship; and a man of exemplary humility who, like Joseph, acknowledges God to be the source of his wisdom.

2:31–35 / In his dream, Nebuchadnezzar saw **a large statue— an enormous, dazzling statue, awesome in appearance** (3:31). Colossal statues were common in the ancient Near East; those of Rhodes and Egypt are the most famous, but Mesopotamia also had them. For example, according to Herodotus there was a twelve-cubit-high gold statue in Bel's temple in Babylon (*Hist.* 1.183). Such statues would often be composed partially or totally of precious metals such as gold, silver, or bronze. Dream reports of giant figures have also been found (Oppenheim, *Interpretation of Dreams*, p. 189). In addition, some scholars see influence here from literary figures of gigantic men representing the world. However, the closest parallels from ancient writings are related to the list of metals in the next verse of Daniel 2.

The earliest parallel to the description of the statue and its materials (2:32–33) comes from Hesiod, a Greek writer of the eighth century B.C., which predates Daniel. He divides history into five periods of descending value: gold, silver, bronze, a time of demi-gods (not associated with any substance), and iron (*Works and Days* 1.109–201). The Latin poet Ovid, from a much later period (late first century B.C.–early first century A.D.), has a similar scheme: gold, silver, brass, and iron (*Metamorphoses* 1.89–150). There is also a Persian text in which a tree has four branches, of gold, silver, steel, and mixed iron, representing historical periods identified with the reigns of certain kings (*Bahman Yasht*, ch. 1). Although the Persian text is from the ninth century A.D., it may contain material from the beginning of the Hellenistic era. The author of Daniel may not have been directly aware of Hesiod or the Persian material, but he was likely aware of similar ideas from other sources. In other words, there was a diffusion of these motifs in the ancient world.

The image in Daniel 2:32–33 has five parts with the materials diminishing in value: the **head (pure gold), chest and arms (silver), belly and thighs (bronze), legs (iron),** and **feet (iron** and **baked clay)**. The feet of iron and clay are variously understood. Statues were sometimes formed of clay or pottery and overlaid with metal, but that is probably not what is meant here by "partly of iron and partly of baked clay," because then the clay would not be visible. It is better to visualize pieces of iron set in pottery or bits of pottery set on iron, perhaps as decoration. The feet, which should be the strongest part in order to support the large, heavy statue, are ironically the weakest. When the **rock ... struck the statue on its feet** (2:34), the whole colossus disintegrated. Since the feet are struck first, the elements are listed in reverse order as the image collapses: **the iron, the clay, the bronze, the silver and the gold** (2:35).

Statues are crafted by humans. In contrast to this, the rock **was cut out, but not by human hands** (2:34). At the least, this highlights the difference between the human and the divine, but it also may be a veiled attack on idolatry. We are not told that the image is an idol, but it certainly looks like one. In the context, the pagan magicians have been exposed as frauds; perhaps the destruction of the statue is also pointing to the failure of idolatry. The Jews do not worship gods made by hands; God is their rock (Pss. 94:22; 95:1; 144:1–2). Something else may be intended as well. The apocalyptic message of the book of Daniel is that deliverance will not come from below, from human hands, but from above, directly from God. This is the message of Daniel 11:34: the Jews will get only "a little help" from below, that is, from the Maccabees. Finally, we are reminded of Daniel 8:25, which indicates that Antiochus IV, the evil king represented by the horn, "will be destroyed, but not by human power." God will bring about the demise of the one who persecutes God's people.

After the statue is atomized and **swept . . . away without leaving a trace, . . . the rock that struck the statue** becomes **a huge mountain and fills the whole earth** (2:35). Here Daniel is probably drawing on Isaianic tradition, found especially in Isaiah 2 and the parallel text in Micah:

> In the last days the mountain of the LORD's temple will be established as chief among the mountains; it will be raised above the hills, and all nations will stream to it. Many peoples will come and say, "Come, let us go up to the mountain of the LORD, to the house of the God of Jacob. He will teach us his ways, so that we may walk in his paths." The law will go out from Zion, the word of the LORD from Jerusalem. (Isa. 2:2–3; cf. Mic. 4:1–2)

This same tradition is found in Isaiah 11:9 ("for the earth will be full of the knowledge of the LORD as the waters cover the sea") and 6:3 ("the whole earth is full of his glory"). Similar teachings appear in Zechariah 4:7; 14:10; and Ezekiel 17:23; 20:40; 40:2. In this tradition, Mount Zion will become the center of the earth, the holy mountain from which Yahweh rules. The fact that in Daniel 2:35 the mountain will fill the whole earth indicates that it is an earthly, not a heavenly, kingdom (see the commentary on 2:44).

2:36–38 / This section presents the interpretation of the dream. Since Daniel begins in the first person singular (2:30), it is surprising that he shifts to the plural: **now we will interpret it to the king** (2:36). Perhaps he includes his companions. Although they were not present with the king and did not receive the revelation, they were partners in prayer with Daniel. Another possibility is that the author is portraying Daniel's humility, as "I" might sound boastful. Against that, however, are verse 24, where Daniel states, "I will interpret his dream for him," and verse

30, where he announces, "As for me, this mystery has been revealed to me, not because I have greater wisdom . . ." On the other hand, verses 29–30 may be secondary to the text, since they are a doublet of verses 27–28 (as already noted).

Daniel begins by praising the king: **You, O king, are the king of kings** (v. 37). The NIV does not do the best job of capturing the Aramaic syntax here. The title "king of kings" is not in the predicate but is in apposition to "O king." There follows a series of subordinate parenthetical clauses concluding with a resumptive "you" in verse 38. The NRSV rendering is preferable:

> You, O king, the king of kings—to whom the God of heaven has given the kingdom, the power, the might, and the glory, into whose hand he has given human beings, wherever they live, the wild animals of the field, and the birds of the air, and whom he has established as ruler over them all—you are the head of gold. (2:37 NRSV)

The main clause is "You, O king . . . **you are that head of gold**" (2:37–38). The second "you" resumes the sentence, which was interrupted by all the material between the first "you," which is the subject, and the second "you," which leads into the predicate. The title "king of kings" itself is attested in Akkadian, but it is normally used in the third person, not in the second person, to address a king (Montgomery, *Daniel*, p. 171). It is used of Nebuchadnezzar also in Ezekiel 26:7. Persian kings claimed the title, and the Bible uses it for Artaxerxes in Ezra 7:12. In the NT it is a title for God (1 Tim. 6:15) and Jesus (Rev. 17:14; 19:16).

It is interesting that the king who destroyed Jerusalem and took the Jews into exile should be praised so highly. God has given him **dominion and power and might and glory** (2:37). These are divine attributes (see also 4:25, 32; 5:21), which God may choose to give to humans. God is praised in these terms in various places in Scripture. A number of similar terms are piled up in praise of God in 1 Chronicles 29:11–12: "greatness," "power," "glory," "majesty," "splendor," "strength," and "power." The idea that human political power comes from God is also affirmed in the NT (John 19:10; Rom. 13:1–5).

The king is given dominion not only over **mankind** but also over **the beasts of the field and the birds of the air** (2:38). Jeremiah also mentions Nebuchadnezzar's rule over humans and animals (Jer. 27:6; 28:14). This is reminiscent of humans in the beginning of time, who were given dominion over everything on earth (Gen. 1:26, 28; Ps. 8:6–8). To show his authority, God put his image (*tselem*) there, namely humanity (Gen.

1:26–27); the word for "statue" in Daniel 2:31 is from the same root (*tslm*). Verse 38 also may allude to the hunting practices of Mesopotamian kings. In reliefs they are pictured hunting lions, and they sometimes kept wild animals in captivity as a symbol of their power. Daniel 2:38 also anticipates 4:10–12, 20–22, where King Nebuchadnezzar is represented as a tree that provides nesting space for the birds, shelter for the beasts of the field, and food for all animals. Daniel tells the king that it symbolizes his strength and greatness and his dominion, which "extends to distant parts of the earth" (4:22). Because of his power and wealth, gold is a fitting material to represent King Nebuchadnezzar and his Neo-Babylonian Empire. Babylon truly was a head of gold.

2:39 / After Babylon would come **another kingdom,** which would be **inferior,** just as silver (see 2:31) is not as precious as gold (2:39). Though the text does not repeat every time that each kingdom is inferior to the previous one, it is implied in the decreasing value of the substances: gold, silver, **bronze, iron,** and **iron mixed with baked clay** (2:39–43). Too much should not be made of this, however, because the third kingdom, which probably represents Persia, was actually superior to Media, which preceded it. Also, iron, while not as precious, is in one way superior to gold, silver, and bronze in that it is stronger. The text even indicates this, for the iron kingdom is fierce and destructive (2:40). Nevertheless, the succession of kingdoms represents a decline in glory. Perhaps the fourth kingdom is less glorious partly because of its violence. Does its destructive behavior necessarily make it evil? Considering that the kingdom that God sets up also destroys its predecessors, destruction is not by itself evil. But as will be seen from the identification of the fourth kingdom in history and from the further elaboration of the four-kingdoms motif in chapter 7, this kingdom is in fact very evil, at least in its second phase. When God destroys, he does so with justice; not so with the fourth kingdom, which unjustly oppresses God's holy ones (7:22, 25, 27).

One important question in this chapter (and in the similar chapter 7) is the identity of the four kingdoms. The text identifies the first kingdom as Babylon (2:38). The second and third kingdoms are not obvious, because they are so nondescript (2:39), but careful study suggests that the author understood the fourth kingdom to be Greece. This is apparent from the way he divides the fourth kingdom into two phases: iron and iron mixed with fired clay (2:33, 40–42). In the first phase, under Alexander, the Greek Empire was united and strong as iron. However, after he died, it was divided among his generals known as the Diadochi, or successors; verse 41 even states that it will be a "divided kingdom." In this second, divided phase, it was weaker, just as iron mixed with clay is weaker than iron. In addition, the reference to the mixture of people in verse 43 corresponds to later references in Daniel to intermarriage between the Seleucids and Ptolemies, two of the successor dynasties (11:6, 17): Antiochus II married Berenice, daughter of Ptolemy II Philadelphus, in 252 B.C., and Ptolemy V Epiphanes married Cleopatra I, daughter of Antiochus III, in 193/192 B.C.

Beyond chapter 2, the rest of the book further supports this identification of Greece as the fourth in the series. In chapter 7, there is a similar four-kingdom scheme, with beasts instead of metals representing the dominions. It seems clear that in chapter 7 the fourth kingdom is Greece and that the oppressive king represented by the little horn (7:8, 11, 20–22, 24–25) is Antiochus IV Epiphanes, a Seleucid monarch who persecuted the Jews. Subsequent chapters also suggest that Greece, particularly during the time of Antiochus IV, was the focus of the author. Chapter 8 apparently alludes to Alexander's (the goat's) defeat of the Persians (the ram; 8:7), to the subsequent death of Alexander (8:8), to the division of his empire into the kingdoms of the Diadochi (8:8), and to the rise of Antiochus IV (8:9–12). Chapter 11 appears to recount the battles between the Seleucids (king of the North) and the Ptolemies (king of the South), emphasizing Antiochus IV (11:29–37). Working backward, if the fourth kingdom is Greece, then the second and third must be Media and Persia, respectively.

For Jews living in the second century B.C. (who were possibly the original audience of the book of Daniel), several things would have influenced them to think of history up to their day as a succession of the four kingdoms: Babylonia, Media, Persia, and Greece. First, in ancient times, it was common to list the successive kingdoms thus: Assyria, Media, Persia (e.g., Herodotus, *Hist.* 1.95, 130). Babylonia was probably left out of the sequence because it was in a sense an extension of Assyria. However, the biblical writer substituted Babylonia for Assyria, because the period he was writing about was long after the fall of the Assyrians and because the fall of the temple, the destruction of Jerusalem, and the exile of the Jews under the Babylonians were such momentous events. The biblical writer also added Greece, likely because it was the period in which he lived and the period of the new crisis of faith for the Jews. So, the common scheme of Assyria, Media, Persia became Babylonia, Media, Persia, Greece. Secondly, the Median kingdom did come between Babylonia and Persia, although it did not conquer Babylon. Thirdly, the author of Daniel was probably influenced by Scriptures that predicted that Media would conquer Babylon (Isa. 13:17; 21:2; Jer. 51:11, 27–29).

These passages pose one historical difficulty worthy of comment. As far as we know, the Medians helped to overthrow Assyria but not Babylonia. Persia defeated and incorporated Media into its own empire in 550 B.C. and then took over Babylonia in 539 B.C. Perhaps we are to understand the above passages to say that the Medians, who were a prominent part of the Persian army, had a part in the conquest of Babylon. However, the texts from Isaiah and Jeremiah give the impression that Media would act alone. Indeed, the book of Daniel seems to project a Babylonian kingdom followed by a Median kingdom, for "Darius the Mede took over the kingdom" of Babylonia (5:31). Following Darius the Mede was Cyrus the Persian (6:28). And of course, Greece followed Persia (10:20). In short, the question of how the above prophetic texts relate to history remains unanswered.

Finally, Daniel 2 and 7 indicate that the author of Daniel expected the coming of God's kingdom in his day. Yet the kingdom of God did not appear in the time of Antiochus IV. In fact another kingdom displaced Greece: Rome. This led the Jews (Josephus, *Ant.* 10.10.4 §209) and later the Christians to reinterpret the four kingdoms as Babylonia, Medo-Persia, Greece, and Rome. Some commentators assert that this is the original meaning of the four empires, arguing that the book points to a combined Medo-Persian kingdom. For example, Daniel 6:8, 12, and 15 use the expression "the laws of the Medes and Persians." Yet, this is in tension with the rest of the chapter, where Darius the Mede rules before Cyrus the Persian (Dan. 6:28; see also 5:31). Perhaps the writer understood the laws of the two kingdoms to be intertwined before Cyrus, or perhaps it is an anachronism. Another verse, Daniel 5:28, says that the Babylonian kingdom would be "divided and given to the Medes and Persians." In the context, though, Darius the Mede takes over the kingdom (5:31), so the writer must intend two successive kingdoms—first Media and then Persia. This is supported by another passage that presents one Medo-Persian kingdom in the figure of the ram with two horns (8:3–7): close reading, however, shows that they are sequential, because the longer (Persian) horn "grew up later" (8:3). Therefore, it is clear that the Babylonia-Media-Persia-Greece scheme dominates the book of Daniel. Most scholars today agree that these are the kingdoms intended by the biblical writer.

2:40–43 / Attention now moves from the third to the fourth kingdom. Immediately, the question arises as to how the fourth kingdom can **crush and break all the others** (2:40). The notion of the feet smashing the rest of the statue is odd, and logically, if each kingdom destroys its predecessor, the fourth kingdom can only demolish the third. Also, there is some tension between verse 40, which has the *fourth* kingdom demolishing all the previous ones, and verse 44, which has the *stone* destroying all the preceding kingdoms. How can the stone obliterate all the dominions if the fourth one has already accomplished this? One possible solution is to take the phrase "all the others" with what precedes instead of with what follows, so in place of "**and as iron breaks things to pieces, so it will** crush and break all the others" (v. 40 NIV), we should read "and as iron breaks to pieces all the others [that is, iron can break all the other materials], so it [the kingdom] will crush and break" (similarly Collins, *Daniel*, p. 151). Then the fourth kingdom is not said to crush the other kingdoms. However, it is not essential to expect such tight logic from ancient texts, especially when this is supposed to be a dream. If the author describes the fourth kingdom as destroying the others, he is not necessarily thinking of the feet of the statue destroying the other parts; nor is he arguing that the other empires are still standing. He is simply reflecting on the fact that the fourth kingdom does conquer the world. And to the extent that the subjugated lands contain remnants of the peoples of the earlier realms, it can truly be said that the fourth kingdom conquers the others. So it is with the stone: vestiges of the previous dominions survive, and the later rulers incorporate much of what they subdue. Therefore, it can be said that the stone destroys them all.

Although there are five materials, there are only four kingdoms. This is clear in verse 40, which says, **finally, there will be a fourth kingdom,** and in verse 41, which says that the mixture of iron and clay indicates a **divided kingdom.** It is actually one kingdom in two phases (see above). The first phase is formidable, like iron, because it is united. The second phase is weaker, like iron mixed with pottery. Just as pottery can be broken, the kingdom in its second phase is more **brittle** (2:42). It will be weaker because it is divided into parts.

Since the vision only mentions feet of iron and clay (2:33), it is a bit surprising to find "toes" in the interpretation: the king saw **feet and toes** that **were partly of baked clay and partly of iron** (2:41); and **toes** that **were partly iron and partly clay** (2:42). Similarly, the dream has nothing about a mountain from which the rock comes (2:34), while the interpretation does (2:45). Also, verses 41–43 are repetitious, mentioning the iron mixed with clay three times. Furthermore, verse 43 seems to give a different reason from verse 41 for the weakness. Verse 41 says it is because the kingdom is divided, while verse 43 says it is because **the people will be a mixture.** For these reasons some scholars see these verses as the result of editing or the mixture of sources. In other words, some things were added to the original text over time by later redactors. While this is plausible, it is not possible to reconstruct an earlier form of the story with confidence. In addition, the two reasons, while distinct and possibly stemming from different hands, are not contradictory. It is possible for the kingdom both to be divided and to be a mixture.

Regarding the translation itself, NIV's "the people will be a mixture" (2:43) is ambiguous. This is not the most felicitous translation. A more literal rendering would be "they will be mixed with the seed of man," meaning mixed families, mixed marriages, mixed offspring. As already mentioned, this probably refers to intermarriage between two royal families, the Seleucids and the Ptolemies. That is, in the second phase when the kingdom is divided, a marriage alliance will be formed between two of the rival powers, but it will be unsuccessful. These dynasties will not blend any more than iron will mix with pottery. Daniel 11:6 and 17 also give examples of marriages between members of the Seleucid line and members of the Ptolemaic.

2:44–45 / Finally, the interpretation speaks of one last kingdom. The term **kings** is unexpected in verse 44 since kingdoms are in view (2:39, 40, 41, 42). But kings and kingdoms are often inseparable, as each stands for the other. After all, we began with an individual king, Nebuchadnezzar, but surely the head of gold represents Babylonia and not just one king. With a slight emendation, however, it is also possible to read "kingdoms" instead of kings. Perhaps that was the original reading.

Whereas earthly kingdoms are built by humans, the ultimate kingdom is represented by a **rock cut out ... but not by human hands** (2:45)—it is built by God. While human kingdoms are transitory, the kingdom of God **will itself endure forever** (2:44). This theme is repeated in chapter 7 (7:14, 18, 27), which goes into more elaborate detail on the evil of the earthly empires. Nevertheless, their corruption and wickedness are implied here in chapter 2, because God's kingdom **will crush all those kingdoms and bring them to an end** (2:44). If they were righteous, there would be no need for God to intervene in judgment. Chapter 7 also develops more the notion that the eternal kingdom will be given to the Jews (7:18, 22, 27). Chapter 2 anticipates that notion with the announcement that when God sets up his kingdom, it will not **be left to another people** (2:44).

Although Daniel envisages the kingdom of God to be everlasting, it is not clear that the book is projecting a cataclysmic end of this world leading up to it. For instance, the book does not describe the destruction of the earth and heavens as do other apocalyptic passages (Isa. 66:22;

2 Pet. 3:10). It seems rather that what is described is the rule of God on this present earth. The writer may have imagined things continuing mostly as before, except that the oppressive human kingdoms would be replaced with the just rule of God. The notion that God will rule from the holy mountain, which probably represents Mount Zion in Jerusalem (Dan. 2:35; Isa. 2:2–3 [cf. Mic. 4:1–2]), supports this understanding, for the stony mountain will fill "the whole earth" (Dan. 2:35; see above). The resurrection of the dead is not incompatible with this view, as the people could be raised to continue their previous lives in this world (Dan. 12:2). It is not clear that death will be abolished, as in other apocalyptic passages (Isa. 25:8; Rev. 21:4).

Although the interpretation of the dream does not make direct reference to a Messiah, the idea that the stone represents the Messiah is found in rabbinic literature (Ginzberg, *Legends of the Jews*, vol. 6, p. 415 n. 80). Likewise, Christians have often seen the stone as a type of Messiah or Christ. The book of Psalms often speaks of the Lord as the rock (e.g., Pss. 18:2, 31, 46; 19:14; 28:1; 31:2–3; 42:9; 62:2, 6–7). Psalm 78 recalls the time when the Lord gave the Israelites water from a rock (Ps. 78:16, 20) and also confesses that God is Israel's rock and redeemer (Ps. 78:35). Paul makes the identification explicit: the rock that provided water for the Israelites in the wilderness was Christ (1 Cor. 10:4; cf. Exod. 17:6; Num. 20:11). In the NT, other OT passages are cited in reference to Christ the stone or rock. Jesus is the precious, tested cornerstone (Rom. 9:33; 1 Pet. 2:6, 8; based on Isa. 8:14; 28:16). He is also the rejected building stone that becomes the capstone (Matt. 21:42; Mark 12:10–11; Luke 20:17; 1 Pet. 2:7; based on Ps. 118:22). Closer to Daniel's judgment imagery, Matthew and Luke add that those who fall on the rock will be broken, and those on whom it falls will be crushed (Matt. 21:44; Luke 20:18).

The great God, as opposed to the gods of the Babylonians who do not communicate to humans (see 2:11), **has shown the king what will take place in the future** (2:45). Israel's God can predict and determine what is to be. By emphasizing God's role, the text holds the phony dream interpreters and their pantheon up to ridicule. Not only is the counsel of the Babylonian sages unreliable; it is "misleading and wicked" (2:9). In contrast, this **dream from God is true** and its **interpretation is trustworthy** (2:45). Similarly, the heavenly being later tells Daniel, "The vision of the evenings and mornings that has been given you is true" (8:26). God's word does not fail. This theme of God's ability to predict the future accurately when the pagan diviners fail predominates in Isaiah 40–55 (Second Isaiah) as well. Israel's God "foils the signs of false prophets and makes fools of diviners" (Isa. 44:25) but "fulfills the predictions of his messengers" (Isa. 44:26). Chaldean diviners are mocked for their failed enchantments, charms, and sorceries, which will not be able to deliver them from disaster (Isa. 47:5–15). The gods are nothing, because they cannot predict the future, whereas Yahweh can (Isa. 41:21–29; 42:9); the idols fail, but the Lord declares in advance what will happen (Isa. 44:6–19; 46:10; 48:3, 5–6).

2:46–49 / **Nebuchadnezzar** at this point worships Daniel: he falls **prostrate before** him and pays **him honor** (meaning worship) and commands that **offering and incense be presented to him** (as to a god) (2:46). If God alone is to receive worship, why does Daniel not object? Jewish interpreters must have been troubled by this, because their folklore embellishes the text by recounting that he actually did refuse the homage (Ginzberg, *Legends of the Jews*, vol. 4, pp. 327–28). Some commentators have argued that Nebuchadnezzar was actually worshiping not Daniel but the God who gave Daniel the revelation, Daniel being the representative. In support of this is Daniel 2:47, where the king confesses, **"Surely your God is the God of gods and the Lord of kings and a revealer of mysteries, for you were able to reveal this mystery."** That is, God is the one who deserves praise, more than Daniel, for making known the mystery. Josephus's account of Alexander falling down before Simon, the high priest, may be cited as well. Alexander explains that he is worshiping not Simon but the God whom Simon serves as priest (*Ant*. 11.8.5). Besides giving glory to God, the biblical writer may also have been trying to present a fulfillment of prophecies. For example, Isaiah 60:14 says, "Sons of your oppressors will come bowing before you; all who despise you will bow down at your feet" (Isa. 60:14; see also Isa. 49:23; 45:14; Zech. 8:23).

Daniel does not balk at Nebuchadnezzar's obeisance, offering, and incense, but in the NT things are different. Because Paul heals a man, the people of Lystra consider Paul and Barnabas gods (Acts 14:8–12) and want to sacrifice to them (Acts 14:13). However, Paul corrects them and refuses the sacrifice (Acts 14:18). The NT is also opposed to the adoration of angels. When John tries to bow down before God's messenger, he is rebuked and instructed to worship God instead (Rev. 22:8–9). It is interesting to note, however, that Daniel is not prevented from bowing before heavenly beings (Dan. 8:17; 10:9). In the OT it is appropriate to prostrate oneself before divine emissaries (Josh. 5:14; Judg. 13:20).

Nebuchadnezzar's confession of the supremacy of Daniel's God is the climax of this chapter. The king does not actually convert to Judaism or monotheism, although he comes close when he acknowledges "the God of gods" (2:47). Likewise, King Cyrus acknowledges Yahweh to be the God of heaven, who commissioned him (Ezra 1:1–4; cf. Isa. 45:1–7, which says Cyrus does not know Yahweh). In a Jewish legend, Antiochus Epiphanes is presented as trying to reform when he is stricken with a fatal disease. He reverses some of his oppressive measures against the Jews and promises to convert to Judaism and to travel around proclaiming "the power of God" (2 Macc. 9:13–17 NRSV). However, it is to no avail; he dies anyway without convincing the Jews of his sincerity.

Not only does Nebuchadnezzar praise God; he promotes Daniel to **a high position and** lavishes **many gifts on him** (2:48). The Babylonian Empire was subdivided into administrative provinces, one of which included the capital city of Babylon. **Over** this **province,** Nebuchadnezzar makes Daniel the ruler. He also places **him in charge of all its wise men.** We already saw in chapter 1 that Daniel and his comrades excel over all the others (1:19–20). Later Daniel is called "chief of the magicians" (4:9). This creates some tension with Israelite religion. If Daniel goes to the head of his class and then becomes the dean of the college and the chief magician, it suggests that he learned the Babylonians' arts and could use them more proficiently than they. At the least he would have allowed them to continue in their arts while he appealed to God in prayer for revelation, for we read of no conversion of the Babylonian school of sages to Jewish practices. The biblical writer is not concerned to address this, however, except perhaps tangentially in projecting a spirit of tolerance, allowing the Babylonians to continue on in their benighted ways. Daniel, unlike Elijah, does not seek to put the others to death (1 Kgs. 18). Like Elijah, Daniel shows the superiority of Yahweh to the pagan gods and the superiority of Yahweh's servant to the other sages; these are the main concerns of the author of Daniel. Regarding Daniel's possible involvement in Babylonian religion, we note that Joseph, whom the character of Daniel resembles in many ways, married the daughter of an Egyptian priest of On (Heliopolis; Gen. 41:45) and was promoted to a position second only to Pharaoh, where he would have had to countenance Egyptian religion. Also, Moses "was educated in all the wisdom of the Egyptians" (Acts 7:22) and married the daughter of the priest of Midian (Exod. 18:1–2). So, there are other precedents for a certain degree of assimilation.

We shall see that the next chapter (Dan. 3) involves only Daniel's three friends, which is puzzling. Why is Daniel not involved in the fiery furnace episode? Some say that the last verse in Daniel 2 is an attempt to explain that. The image in chapter 3 is set up in Dura, not far from the capital. The implication of verse 49 is that the friends are out in **the province** while Daniel is at **the royal court** in the city of **Babylon.**

Therefore, he is not present when everyone is commanded to bow down to the statue. But this does not completely explain things, because Daniel 3:2 says that all important officials are summoned. How could Daniel have been excluded from that list? We have the same problem in chapter 6: Why are Daniel's Jewish colleagues not mentioned there? The way to answer such questions is to pay attention to the history of transmission of the individual stories. As stated earlier, it appears that chapters 2 and 6 were originally about Daniel alone. Chapter 3 concerns only Shadrach, Meshach, and Abednego (Hananiah, Mishael, and Azariah). Chapter 1 was likely composed in order to integrate Daniel and the three friends into one story. The literary effect of this move is twofold: to introduce readers to all the main characters who will appear subsequently, and to present them as contemporaries and allies. Hananiah, Mishael, and Azariah were later woven into chapter 2 (vv. 17–18, 49), though not chapter 6. Daniel was not inserted into chapter 3. Once again, the use of the Hebrew names (Hananiah, Mishael, and Azariah) in Daniel 2:17 looks back to chapter 1, while the use of the Babylonian names here at the end of the chapter (v. 49) looks ahead to chapter 3, where that account uses the names Shadrach, Meshach, and Abednego exclusively.

Additional Notes §2

2:2 / The lists of advisers vary somewhat within the book. Dan. 1:20 has "magicians and enchanters." Later in ch. 2 are two more lists: "any magician or enchanter or astrologer [Chaldean]" (2:10); "no wise man, enchanter, magician or diviner" (2:27). Elsewhere we read "magicians, enchanters, astrologers [Chaldeans] and diviners" (4:7); "enchanters, astrologers [Chaldeans] and diviners" (5:7); "magicians, enchanters, astrologers [Chaldeans] and diviners" (5:11); and "wise men and enchanters" (5:15). "Wise men" is used collectively for all of them in 2:48 and 5:7. "Astrologers [Chaldeans]" is used that way in 2:4–10, and "magicians" in 4:9. (On the Hebrew word for **magicians**, see the Additional Note on 1:20.)

2:4 / The Aramaic root *pshr* (translated **interpret**) occurs here in its noun form, "interpretation" (2:4, 5, 6 [twice], 7, 9, 16, 24, 25, 26, 30, 36, 45; also in Dan. 4 and 5); the verb means "to interpret" (5:12, 16). The equivalent Hebrew root is *ptr*; used as a noun it means "interpretation" (Gen. 40:5, 8, 12, 18; 41:11), and as a verb, "to interpret" (Gen. 40:8, 16, 22; 41:8, 12, 13, 15). In the Bible, these Hebrew terms are found only in the Joseph story. The Aramaic *pesher* was used by the Qumran community for commentaries on the Bible (interpretations), such as *Pesher Habakkuk*, the Dead Sea Scroll commentary on Habakkuk.

2:8 / When Paul tells believers to redeem the time (Eph. 5:16; Col. 4:5), he uses the same Greek expression for **to gain time** found in the LXX of Dan. 2:8. Paul intends for us to redeem the time, that is, to make better use of it for the kingdom of God. By contrast, the Chaldeans are trying to redeem the time, that is, to gain more time by taking control of it and exploiting it for their self-preservation.

2:9 / Literally, **the situation will change** means "until the time changes." A similar idiom is used in v. 21 in Daniel's hymn to God: "he changes times and seasons." Although there is a lot of text between vv. 9 and 21, there may be a deliberate contrast. The diviners are hoping that the situation they are in will change, but they and their gods are powerless to bring it about. However, the one true God is able to change times and seasons (cf. also 7:12 and 25), because he is sovereign and all-powerful.

2:12 / **The wise men of Babylon** (*khakkime babel*) is another parallel with the Joseph story, which uses the same Hebrew root to refer to Egypt's wise men (*khakameha* [Gen. 41:8]).

2:14 / The name **Arioch** occurs in Gen. 14:1, 9 for the king of Ellasar and in Jdt. 1:6 for the king of the Elymeans. It was once thought to have a Sumerian derivation (*eri-aku*), but that is now untenable. It might be related to the Hurrian name *A-ri-wu-uk* found at Mari, or perhaps it is from Old Persian *Ariyauka* (Collins, *Daniel*, p. 158).

The Hebrew for **the commander of the king's guard**, *sar hattabbakhim* (Aram. *rab-tabbakhayya'*), is found in Gen. 37:36; 39:1; 41:10, 12 of an Egyptian; the similar phrase *rab-hattabbakhim* occurs in 2 Kgs. 25:8 and Jer. 39:9; 52:12 of Nebuzaradan, a Babylonian. In Akkadian the root of the word for "the king's guard," *tbkh*, means "to slaughter," "slay," or "execute." Originally, then, it would have referred to the chief executioner. Over time, the title developed a more general meaning. Therefore, NIV's "commander of the king's guard" is not wrong. However, since Arioch is commissioned to slay the king's wise men, NRSV's "the king's chief executioner" is a better translation.

2:18 / The term **God of heaven** and variations on it are used seven times in Daniel: "God of heaven" (2:18, 19, 37, 44); "King of heaven" (4:37); "Heaven" (as a substitute for "God"; 4:26); "Lord of heaven" (5:23). Although "God of heaven" is used in Gen. 24:3, 7, it was otherwise avoided in the preexilic period—probably because of conflict with the Baal cult, which used *Ba'al Shamem*, "Baal of heaven" or "lord of heaven." The term became common in the postexilic period, however; it is often found in Chronicles, Ezra, Nehemiah, Tobit, Judith, and the Aramaic papyri from Elephantine (e.g., 2 Chron. 36:23; Ezra 1:2; 6:9; 7:12, 21; Neh. 1:4, 5; 2:4, 20; Tob. 10:11; Jdt. 5:8; 6:19; 11:17; A. E. Cowley, *Aramaic Papyri of the Fifth Century B.C.* [Oxford: Clarendon, 1923], nos. 30:2, 28; 31:27; 32:4; 38:3, 5; 40:1). Perhaps this enabled the Jews to communicate the nature of their God in a way that the Persians could comprehend, for they too served a heavenly deity. The Persians, though, did not use this epithet

(Collins, *Daniel*, p. 159). The term was eschewed again in the Greek period. Apparently the Jews felt that it was too pagan, being close to the Greek term *Zeus Ouranios*, "Heavenly Zeus."

The Aramaic term *raz*, **mystery**, occurs eight times in Daniel: 2:18, 19, 27, 28, 29, 30, 47; and 4:9 (4:6 MT). It is frequently found in the Qumran scrolls, signifying hidden things that had become known to the Dead Sea community regarding God's plans, biblical prophecies, interpretations of the Jewish law, the order of the cosmos, and the workings and eventual destruction of evil (1QM 3.8–9; 14.14; 1QS 3.20–23; 9.18–19; 11.3–4; 1QpHab 7.1–5, 8, 13–14; 1QH 1.11–12; 11.9–10; 13.13–14; see R. E. Brown, *The Semitic Background of the Term "Mystery" in the New Testament* [Philadelphia: Fortress, 1968], pp. 22–30). Reference is made in certain cases to God as the source of that secret knowledge and to God's holy spirit (e.g., 1QH 12.11–13). It is therefore, at least in some instances, knowledge that comes by revelation and not by human cleverness.

2:28 / The phrase **in days to come** (Aram. *be'akharit yomayya'*; Heb. *be'akharit hayyamim*) occurs fourteen times in the OT. In passages such as Gen. 49:1; Num. 24:14; Deut. 4:30; and 31:29 it is not eschatological but indicates what will happen later, in the future, in coming days. However, over time the idiom evolved into an expression for the end of the ages. In the prophetic books the usage is often eschatological: Isa. 2:2 (cf. Mic. 4:1); Ezek. 38:16; Dan. 10:14; Hos. 3:5 (H. Seebass, "*'acharith*," *TDOT* 1:207–12). So it is in the two occurrences in Daniel.

2:31, 36a / The dream narrative is delimited by standard forms. It is introduced with **You looked, O king,** [and behold] . . . (2:31) and concluded with **This was the dream** (2:36a). (Because "behold" is an archaic term in English, modern versions of the Bible, such as the NIV, often do not translate it. I have chosen to include it here and below, in brackets.) The vision in ch. 4 is similar, beginning with "I looked, and [behold]" (4:10) and ending with "This is the dream that I, King Nebuchadnezzar, had" (4:18). The dream in ch. 7 has the introductory formula, "I looked [. . . and behold]" (7:2) but not the concluding one. Prefacing a dream or vision with "behold" is common elsewhere in the Hebrew Bible (Gen. 37:7, 9; 41:2, 3, 17; Zech. 1:8; Amos 7:1, 4, 7; 8:1; Jer. 24:1) (Collins, *Daniel*, p. 162).

2:31–33 / For references to statues made with precious metals, see *ANEP*, p. 166. Concerning dreams of colossi, Gudea of Sumer and Egyptian pharaoh Merneptah are examples (A. L. Oppenheim, *The Interpretation of Dreams in the Ancient Near East* [Philadelphia: American Philosophical Society, 1956], p. 189). For further information on literary figures of huge humans representing the world, see references in Collins, *Daniel*, p. 162 n. 102.

The Persian text *Bahman Yasht*, referred to above, is also known as *Zand-î Vohûman Yasn* (Behramgore Tehmuras Anklesaria, ed. and trans., *Zand-î Vohûman Yasn and Two Pahlavi Fragments* [Bombay: Bhargava, 1957], pp. 101–2). For further discussion and references to other parallels to the statue, see Collins, *Daniel*, pp. 162–64; Montgomery, *Daniel*, p. 189.

2:36 / See the Additional Note on 2:31, 36a.

2:38 / The NIV moves the clause **wherever they live** to the latter part of the verse to go with "he has made you ruler over them all." In the Aramaic text it is earlier in the verse. It might go with "mankind." Then it would read, "Wherever mankind lives he has placed the beasts of the field and the birds of the air in your hands." Or it might go with all three: "Wherever they live, he has placed mankind, and the beasts of the field and the birds of the air in your hands."

2:40 / The Aramaic text has a repetition of the idea of iron breaking things. The NIV leaves both clauses in (**for iron breaks and smashes everything—and as iron breaks things to pieces**), but these two clauses make the verse a little awkward. The ancient translations in Greek, Syriac, and Latin have shorter readings, which might suggest that the MT is corrupt at this point. The NRSV opts for a shorter reading ("just as iron crushes and smashes everything"), leaving out the second clause. However, the more cumbersome reading is to be preferred here. It is more likely that the ancient versions shortened the verse to streamline it than that a scribe would add the additional clause. There is only a little help from Qumran. The fragmentary text of 4QDan^a is missing "for iron breaks and smashes everything—and as iron." But then it has part of the next word, "breaks." On the one hand, this evidence could be used to support the longer reading, because it has the second occurrence of "and as iron breaks." On the other hand, it is possible that the scroll only had the second reading and not both.

2:44 / Although the final form of the text clearly indicates a succession of four kingdoms, some have wondered whether the original story was instead about four kings. In support one might point to the fact that it begins by identifying one king, Nebuchadnezzar, as the head of gold, not a kingdom. Also, v. 44 says **in the time of those kings,** not "kingdoms." Some argue that the earlier story was about Nebuchadnezzar and three of his successors: Amel-Marduk, Neriglissar, and Nabonidus (see, e.g., P. R. Davies, "Daniel Chapter Two," *JTS* 27 [1976], pp. 392–401). One problem with this interpretation is that there was another king, Labashi-Marduk, between Neriglissar and Nabonidus, although he ruled for only a brief time. It is an intriguing interpretation, but it is hypothetical and not supported very well from the text of Daniel as it now stands (Collins, *Daniel*, pp. 169–70). If it is correct, then the story was later adapted in Maccabean times to a four-kingdom scheme.

2:45 / The NIV is a bit free with the Aramaic at this point. **This is the meaning** is not there, and the word translated **vision** is actually a verb, "you saw," rather than a noun. "Just as you saw" is a better rendering. Because v. 45 really is a continuation of v. 44, it should read something like this: "It will crush all those kingdoms . . . ; just as you saw the rock cut out of a mountain . . . —a rock that broke the iron, the bronze, the clay, the silver and the gold to pieces." In other words, the kingdom of God will destroy all human kingdoms, just as in the vision the rock destroyed all the materials in the statue.

The vision indicates that the **rock** is **cut out** (2:34) but not that it is out **of a mountain**. The rock becomes a mountain (2:35) but is not cut out from one. This leads some commentators to think that the phrase is not original. It is quite possible that "out of a mountain" was added later. On the other hand, one might ask whether all the details must be found in the dream description. The stone was cut out (2:34) of something. It is possible that the author of Daniel left this detail out of the dream narration but included it in the interpretation. There is no contradiction between the vision and the interpretation. What is remarkable is not that v. 45 has something not in the vision but that it says nothing about the rock becoming a mountain (2:35).

The reversal of the order of the nouns **the iron, the bronze, the clay, the silver and the gold** is not unusual, because the image is struck on its feet. However, the order within the set of the nouns is strange, because it has "clay" between bronze and silver, when it should go with "iron." Perhaps at one point it dropped out of the text and was added back in by a scribe in the wrong place.

§3 The Gold Image and the Blazing Furnace (Dan. 3:1–30)

There are a couple of loose links between chapter 2 and chapter 3. First, when the astrologers (Chaldeans) accuse the three friends, they refer to them as "some Jews whom you have set over the affairs of the province of Babylon" (3:12), alluding to their promotion in chapter 2 (2:49). Secondly, the term "image" generally connects chapter 2 to chapter 3. First, Nebuchadnezzar sees an image (2:31; NIV "statue"); then he erects one (3:1). It is unlikely, as some have suggested, that because Nebuchadnezzar was identified as the head of gold (2:38), he sought to make a statue of himself. The text does not indicate that the dream of chapter 2 inspired the image of chapter 3. Furthermore, the two are dissimilar, for in the dream statue, only the head is of gold, while in the real one, all of it is covered with gold. Also, there is no description of the object, so we cannot be sure that it was in the king's likeness. Finally, there are other points of disjuncture between chapter 3 and the earlier traditions. While chapter 2 is mainly about Daniel, with brief appearances by his friends, chapter 3 is exclusively about the three friends. Whereas earlier they are described as "young men" (1:4, 10, 13, 15, 17), here they are "men" (3:13, 21, 23, 24, 25). Before this, they are known by both their Babylonian and Hebrew names; here, only by their Babylonian names: Shadrach, Meshach, and Abednego. In chapter 2, Nebuchadnezzar witnesses the power of Israel's God and offers him praise (2:47), yet surprisingly, he seems not to remember that experience in chapter 3, for he exhibits such skepticism (3:15).

Not only is Daniel missing from Daniel 3, but there is no explanation in this chapter for his absence. As mentioned previously, this probably indicates that this story circulated separately. Mirroring chapter 3 is chapter 6, which concerns Daniel but omits the three friends. In fact, Shadrach, Meshach, and Abednego disappear after the furnace episode. Furthermore, chapter 3 is parallel to chapter 6. In both accounts, officials make accusations (3:8 and 6:24 use the same idiom) of breaking the law with respect to religion: in the former, the three disobey the king's decree to bow down before the statue; in the latter, Daniel breaks the king's decree prohibiting prayer. Shadrach, Meshach, and Abednego "pay no attention" to the king (3:12); Daniel is accused of the same thing (6:13). Both accounts contain the threat of death, as well as deliverance by an angel. In chapter 3, after the three Jews are denounced and thrown into the blazing furnace, God delivers them by his angel, who is present with them in the fire (3:25, 28). In chapter 6, Daniel is thrown into a den of lions, but God sends an angel to shut the mouths of the lions (6:22).

One interesting feature of chapter 3 is the repetition of lists, phrases, and words. The list of officials occurs three times (3:2, 3, 27). The musical instruments are itemized four times (3:5, 7, 10, 15). Twice we read "peoples, nations and men of every language" (3:4, 7; there is a third time in MT 3:31, but this verse really goes with what follows and is numbered as 4:1 in English). The phrase "fall down and worship" repeats frequently (3:5, 6, 7, 10, 11, 15 ["worship" twice]) as does "blazing furnace" (NIV; Aramaic: "burning furnace of fire"; 3:6, 11, 15, 17, 20, 21, 23, 26). "Image" is found often: with "of gold" (3:1, 5, 7, 10, 12, 14, 18); with "made" and "set it up" (3:1); with "I made" (3:15); with "that King Nebuchadnezzar had set up" (3:2 [NIV leaves out "Nebuchadnezzar"], 3 [twice but NIV leaves one out], 7); with "that King Nebuchadnezzar has set up" (3:5); that "you have set up" (3:12, 18); and with that "I have set up" (3:14). It also appears once with reference not to the statue but to the "image of his [the king's] face," rendered "attitude" in the NIV. Of course, the names Shadrach, Meshach, and Abednego recur (3:12, 13, 14, 16, 19, 20, 22, 23 [NIV omits], 26, 28, 29, 30). The Aramaic word *gubrin*, "men," turns up a number of times, although it does not always designate the three Jews, and it sometimes means "certain" (NIV "some"; 3:8, 12 [twice], 13, 20 [twice], 21, 22 [NIV "soldiers"], 23, 24, 25, 27 [NIV "them"]). The expression *sim teʿem* has two meanings: "to issue a decree" (3:10, 29) and "to pay attention" (3:12). The verb "change" shows up three times (3:19, 27 [NIV "scorched"], 28 [NIV "defied"]). Some commentators have seen a comic element in the repetitious style, reading it as satirical (e.g., Baldwin, *Daniel*, p. 102). To be sure, there are humorous aspects of the story, such as the ridiculous proportions of the statue, the furnace heated seven times over, and the raging king. No doubt the Jewish author is mocking the pagans for their idolatry. However, it is not clear that the storyteller intends to repeat the lists for comedic effect. Others argue that the purpose is to increase the sense of threat (Longman, *Daniel*, p. 98) or the feeling of Nebuchadnezzar's power (Gowan, *Daniel*, p. 64). It is difficult to ascertain whether these things are so. What can be said with confidence is that this repetitious style is characteristic of oral storytellers (Collins, *Daniel*, p. 192). The written form of Daniel 3, thus, preserves this echo of storytelling art.

The fiery-furnace story may have its roots in an event during the Babylonian exile. We know that ancient kings were inclined to raise large statues. Perhaps, at times, they even made it compulsory to worship them. There is also a report that Nebuchadnezzar roasted two men (Jer. 29:22). Nevertheless, the mention of Persian officials (see the commentary on 3:1–7) suggests a time after the Babylonian period, and the use of Greek terms for some of the instruments points to the Hellenistic era. Whether Nebuchadnezzar ever threatened Jews with martyrdom is not known, but it is well established that a certain Seleucid tyrant, Antiochus IV, did. In the book's final form, the target audience for Daniel 3 appears to be the persecuted Jewish community of the second century B.C. If this is so, the author or an editor included the story to encourage Jews not to participate in the Greek religion. During this period, there was a lot of pressure on Jews (and others) to assimilate to the Hellenistic culture, which was pervasive. It culminated in the proscription of Judaism by Antiochus Epiphanes. He installed an altar in Yahweh's temple in Jerusalem and offered unclean animals there in sacrifice to Zeus Olympios; this action is known as the "abomination that causes desolation" (Dan. 9:27; 11:31; see also Dan. 8:13; 1 Macc. 1:54). He forced Jews to abandon their religion and to eat pork sacrificed to Greek gods or be executed (1 Macc. 1:57, 60–63; 2 Macc. 6:9–11, 18, 31; 7:1–42). Some Jews denied their faith and participated in the pagan cult, but others were martyred, choosing death over apostasy. In this interpretation, the statue in Daniel 3 represents the detestable Greek cult, and the furnace is a cipher for the Seleucid soldiers who carried out the king's order to murder faithful Jews. The author of the book of Daniel hoped that God would intervene in history by delivering his people from death, just as he saved Shadrach, Meshach, and Abednego from the flames in the furnace. However, he was uncompromising in his attitude toward the king: even if God does not come to their rescue they should not worship the foreign gods or bow before images (3:18). In other words, it is better to lay down one's life than to renounce the faith.

3:1–7 / **Nebuchadnezzar** makes **an image of gold** (3:1), but the text does not supply a description, so it is unclear whether it is a statue of a god or of the king. The Christian writer Hippolytus (second–third century A.D.) thought it was an image of Nebuchadnezzar. He argued that the Babylonian king was so filled with pride after being described as the head of gold (2:38) that he made a whole gold statue of himself. Saint Jerome followed this interpretation (A.D. 342–420). Unlike in Egypt, where the pharaoh was worshiped as a god, it was unusual for Mesopotamian kings to claim divinity. However, they frequently made images of themselves as signs of their power. Support for a Jewish tradition that Nebuchadnezzar wanted to be worshiped can be found in the apocryphal book Judith. The commander Holofernes was directed to destroy all the shrines and idols, leaving only Nebuchadnezzar to be worshiped as a god (Jdt. 3:8). It is also tempting to see a parallel with Daniel 6, where the decree stipulates that for thirty days no one is to pray to any god or man except the king (Dan. 6:7, 12). Perhaps the narrator intends something similar here, that everyone is expected to worship the image of the king. Given the facts that some of the Hellenistic rulers were deified, and that Antiochus IV considered himself to be "Epiphanes," that is, the manifestation of a god, such a reading is more likely. The author appears to present Nebuchadnezzar as a cipher for the oppressive Seleucid monarch of the second century B.C. It is even possible that the writer is thinking of the abomination of desolation, with a statue of Zeus in the likeness of Antiochus IV (Rowley, "Unity of the Book of Daniel," p. 265), who also had coins with his visage in the fashion of Zeus. Against this, the text of Daniel does not say that this was an image of the king, and it makes no explicit connection between the dream image of chapter 2 and the real image of chapter 3. Also, according to most recent interpreters, Daniel 3:12, 14, and 18 equate the god with the statue. (See the commentary on 3:12.)

The statue was probably not solid gold but constructed of some other material and overlaid with gold. The height of **ninety feet** (in Aramaic, sixty cubits) is unusual but not unheard of: the Colossus at Rhodes was seventy cubits high. However, the dimensions are odd: ninety feet tall by only **nine feet wide** (six cubits). Such a statue would be disproportionately skinny. Perhaps the biblical writer described it this way in order to make the idol appear ridiculous. Alternatively, perhaps the writer was aware that the Babylonians favored a base-six number system and for that reason used the numbers sixty and six. One suggestion is that the object was shaped like a pillar, pole, or obelisk, with an idol or royal image at the top that had more human proportions. The location **on the plain of Dura** is uncertain. It could be a number of different places, for *dur*, "wall," or "fortress," is often found in geographical names in Akkadian.

The ones **summoned . . . to come to the dedication of the image** King Nebuchadnezzar **had set up** were all the important leaders (3:2). Since Daniel was appointed to a high position (2:48), one would expect him to have attended this gathering. It is inconceivable that he was present and bowed to the image along with everyone else while only his three friends refused. Various excuses have been invented to explain Daniel's absence, but they are not convincing. As discussed above, the stories found in Daniel likely have been edited together from different sources, one of which preserved the account of the three Jews; it was independent of traditions about Daniel.

The list of officials is interesting: **satraps, prefects, governors, advisers, treasurers, judges, magistrates** (3:2). After the list of specific administrators, there is the all-inclusive phrase, **and all the other provincial officials** (3:2). Only the terms for "prefects" and "governors" are Semitic, both being loan words from Akkadian. The third word, "governors," is the Aramaic equivalent of the Hebrew word used for Nehemiah's title (Neh. 5:14). The rest of the terms are Persian. This suggests that the story was composed in the Persian period or later, rather than in the Babylonian period, which it purportedly describes. The term "satrap" is especially curious since it was the Persian king Darius I (522–486 B.C.) who divided his realm into satrapies, not the Babylonian king Nebuchadnezzar. If the author of Daniel was an apocalyptic author of the second century B.C. rather than an earlier historian, he may not have been aware of this historical fact. In this case, modern scholars should not fault him, as the purpose of an apocalyptic author was not to write history as such but to write imaginative literature dealing with the coming of God's kingdom. The style of the book features repetition, so verse 3 repeats the list of officials from verse 2.

The **herald** addresses **peoples, nations and men of every language** (3:4; see also 3:7 ["all the peoples"] and 3:29; 4:1; 5:19; 6:25; 7:14). A question arises about how to reconcile that with the earlier verses, which indicate that only the leaders were summoned for the dedication ceremony (3:2–3). Perhaps the storyteller intends us to picture the leaders up front with a crowd of common folk gathered around them. If so, there should be other Jews present besides Shadrach, Meshach, and Abednego. Since many Jews were exiled to Babylon, we would expect more than three to disobey the king's command, yet no others are recorded. Another possibility is that we should think of a diverse group of officials from various countries. That would lead to the conclusion that only the administrators are present and only three of them are Jewish (four if we count Daniel, although he must have been absent). Upon further consideration, however, the best approach may simply be not to ask such detailed questions, because the answers may not have been very important to the storyteller.

The dedication of the statue includes music. When they hear the musical instruments (see Additional Note for 3:5), they are to **fall down and worship the image** (3:5). The author, who favors lists, now names the various instruments used: **horn, flute, zither, lyre, harp, pipes** (3:5). The list of instruments is similar to that of the officials (3:3) in that it gives several examples and then a general phrase to indicate others: **and all kinds of music** (3:5). Three of these words—"zither," "harp," and "pipes"—are of Greek origin, suggesting a late date for this story.

The penalty for disobedience is burning; they would **be thrown into a blazing furnace** (3:6). In the ancient Near East burning is mentioned in Hammurabi's Code (25, 110, 157). There is also an Old Babylonian text that refers to a victim being thrown into a furnace (Alexander, "New Light on the Fiery Furnace," pp. 375–76). In the Bible, burning is allowed as a punishment (Gen. 38:24; Lev. 21:9; Josh. 7:15, 25). The psalmist says, "At the time of your appearing you will make them like a fiery furnace. In his wrath the LORD will swallow them up, and his fire will consume them" (Ps. 21:9). Nebuchadnezzar burned the false prophets Ahab and Zedekiah (Jer. 29:22). In Jewish tradition, the high priest Joshua was cast into the flames along with them, but he was unharmed (*Tankhuma* 6; cited in Montgomery, *Daniel*, p. 196). Abraham also was supernaturally delivered from a fiery furnace for not worshiping a foreign god (Ginzberg, *Legends of the Jews*, vol. 1, pp. 198–203).

3:8–12 / Shadrach, Meshach, and Abednego remain firm in their faith. Despite the threat of the blazing furnace, they refuse to bow down and worship. As a result, **some astrologers** come **forward and** denounce **the Jews** (3:8). The word translated by the NIV as "astrologers" is actually the word for "Chaldeans," which is a better translation (see the NIV footnote). Though it is possible to take "Chaldeans" as an ethnic reference, it is more likely that one of the groups of professional advisers is indicated, as in Daniel 1:4 and throughout chapter 2 (e.g., 2:2). In chapter 6, it is after Daniel is about to be promoted over all the other administrators that some of them try to find a way to accuse him; jealousy seems to be the motivation. Here in chapter 3, it is not as obvious. It could be simply that as officers of the realm they felt obligated to report anyone who failed to obey the king. In other words, they were only doing their duty. However, the biblical writer may have intentionally mentioned Chaldeans instead of, say, satraps or prefects as a way of highlighting the contrast between the Jews, who are in contact with God, and the incompetent advisers who follow false religious practices and are charlatans with respect to divine power. Also, if we connect chapter 3 with chapters 1 and 2, where the Jews are promoted over others (1:20; 2:48), then professional rivalry might have played a role here, as in chapter 6. This is even more likely considering the words the Chaldeans use to report the three to the king. They mention that they are **some Jews whom you have set over the affairs of the province of Babylon** (3:12). Perhaps the Chaldeans are envious of the prominent positions the Jews enjoy. Furthermore, the term rendered **denounced** is a colorful term in Aramaic. Literally, it means they "ate their pieces" (also used in 6:24). It can be rendered "to slander" or "to accuse maliciously" (so RSV). In the light of this idiom, it makes sense to see these Chaldeans as going beyond duty and acting with hostile intent.

Does the Aramaic phrase "some Jews" (NIV) or "certain Jews" (NRSV) indicate an anti-Jewish attitude on the part of the Babylonians? There is a parallel in Esther 3:8–9:

> Then Haman said to King Xerxes, "There is a certain people dispersed and scattered among the peoples in all the provinces of your kingdom whose customs are different from those of all other people and who do not obey the king's laws; it is not in the king's best interest to tolerate them. If it pleases the king, let a decree be issued to destroy them, and I will put ten thousand talents of silver into the royal treasury for the men who carry out this business."

Of course, Daniel 3 is quite different from Esther 3, because Nebuchadnezzar does not issue a decree calling for the destruction of all Jews. Nevertheless, the story concerns more than just Shadrach, Meshach, and Abednego. It is being recounted because it applies to all the Jewish people. The three are being held up as examples to show the rest how to behave in the time of such a trial. The story has two horizons: one in the sixth century B.C. when the story is set (during the Neo-Babylonian Empire) and the other in the second century B.C. (during the Seleucid Empire) when the book of Daniel was possibly composed. In the context of the story, only the three are threatened, for even though the decree is addressed to all peoples, apparently only three Jews are present. In a later context, however, when there was more widespread oppression under Antiochus IV, the pressure was on all of God's people to conform or face death. The message of Daniel 3 is that Jews should not bow before the image of Zeus, eat pork, or participate in any pagan rites, even if threatened with death. In addition to how it applied in those two specific eras, the same message applies to Christians today or in any age who live under an anti-Christian government or who face social pressure to conform to non-Christian practices, at times at the risk of their lives or livelihoods.

In their denunciation, the enemies make three indictments: the Jews do not **pay attention to** the **king**, they do not **serve his gods**, and they do not **worship the image of gold** that he **set up** (3:12). The first accusation contains intriguing vocabulary. The Aramaic expression in verse 10 meaning "to make a decree" is very similar to the idiom meaning "to pay respect to" (NIV "pay attention to") (see the Additional Note on 3:12). So, there is a contrast in the speech of the Chaldeans: "You, O king, have made a decree" (v. 10), but these three Jews "have not paid respect to you" (v. 12). The second and third accusations relate to the discussion in verse 1 concerning whether the statue was of a god or of Nebuchadnezzar. The answer depends partly on the meaning of Daniel 3:12, 14, and 18. The NIV reads, "They neither serve your gods nor worship the image of gold you have set up" (3:12; similar translations appear in vv. 14, 18). The way it is worded suggests two different things: serving the gods and worshiping the image. This lends itself to the interpretation that the image might be of the king as opposed to one of the gods. While the wording of the Aramaic allows the phrases to be construed as two separate things, it is possible to take them together, since they are related to one another. One way to serve the god is to worship his gold image. This lends itself to identifying the god with the gold image. It is similar to the clause "fall down and worship" in verse 5. Just as falling down is worshiping, so here, serving the god may be equated with worshiping his image. In spite of the above discussion, though, it is impossible to say for sure whether the statue is of a god or of the king, because the text does not make this clear.

3:13–18 / At this point in the story, the king angrily summons the three to appear before him. Royal rage is a common element in court stories (see also Dan. 2:12; 3:19; Esth. 1:12; 7:7; 2 Macc. 7:3; 3 Macc. 3:1; 5:1, 30). Perhaps it is intended to be comical, ridiculing the king for his lack of self-control as he has an apoplectic fit. He gives them another chance to comply, threatening them with the fiery furnace.

There is an interesting structure to the king's speech in verse 15. It contains two "if" clauses. The NIV moves the first "if" clause later in the verse, after the musical instruments; it actually comes first in the Aramaic. The NIV also adds the phrase **very good**. Actually, most commentators and translators add something like this, treating the first part of the verse as an elliptical clause. To simplify the verse and to paraphrase, it would read something like this: "If you are ready to worship . . . ; but if you do not worship, you will be thrown into the furnace." They add "very good," or something like it, to fill in what is missing. "If you are ready to worship, [very good]; but if you do not worship, you will be thrown into the furnace." However, it might better be read thus: "If you are ready when you hear the music, you will bow down and worship; if you do not worship, you will be thrown into the furnace." There is a similar "if . . . if not" construction in verse 17.

The king not only threatens them but challenges their God. He asks, **"Then what god will be able to rescue you from my hand?"** (3:15). This statement appears to be further evidence that chapter 3 was originally independent of the previous chapters. If Nebuchadnezzar found that the Jews were ten times wiser than the rest of the advisers (1:20) and if he knew that their God was the greatest of the gods and the only God who could reveal dreams (2:47), one would expect him to be a little more restrained, especially after his exuberant praise for their God earlier (2:47).

The statement is reminiscent of chapter 2, where the royal advisers are stymied by the king's request to recount the dream: "No one can reveal it to the king except the gods, and they do not live among men" (2:11). These statements are designed to set the reader up for the miracles that follow, thus magnifying the greatness and power of God. In Daniel 2, the Babylonian wise men do not believe any sage can do what the king asks and do not believe that their gods will reveal the secret. Yet, Daniel succeeds by the help of his God. In Daniel 3, Nebuchadnezzar does not believe any god can deliver from his furnace, but the God of the Jews saves his loyal servants. Besides Daniel 2, another parallel to Daniel 3:15 is 2 Kings 18:33–35, where the Assyrian commander taunts Hezekiah and the people of Judah, boasting that no gods have been able to protect any nation from the Assyrian army. This time it is different, though, because God miraculously intervenes, sending his angel to slay the enemy soldiers (2 Kgs. 19:35). In the same way, a divine messenger delivers the three Jews from the furnace.

The motif of someone being in someone else's hand or power is scattered throughout the book of Daniel. The Lord gave Judah's king into Nebuchadnezzar's hand (1:2) as well as all humans and animals (2:38). To the king's challenge in Daniel 3:15, the Jews respond that their God is able to deliver them from his hand (3:17). God also delivers Daniel from the power (lit. "hand") of the lions (6:27). The holy ones will be given into the hand of Antiochus IV for a period of time (7:25). In Daniel's vision, the ram (Persia) has dominion at first such that no one is able save another from his hand (8:4). However, a male goat (Alexander the Great) comes along and displaces the ram; no one can deliver the ram from his hand (8:7; similar expressions occur in 11:11, 16, and 41). The theological significance of this is that ultimate power belongs to heaven. If earthly kings have authority for a time, it is only because God allows it, setting up whomever he wishes (5:21). Human kings and kingdoms will eventually all fall before the eternal, divine kingdom. In the meantime, the Lord may choose to intervene in history to rescue his faithful ones from fire (Dan. 3) or lions (Dan. 6).

According to the MT, the three address the king only by his name, not his title, in their response: **Shadrach, Meshach and Abednego replied to the king, "O Nebuchadnezzar . . ."** (3:16). One would not expect them to be so disrespectful. On the one hand, with a slight change to the text it is possible to read, "Shadrach, Meshach, and Abednego replied to King Nebuchadnezzar," which makes more sense (see the Additional Note on 3:16). On the other hand, characters do not always speak in stories as they do in real life, so it is best not to emend the text here. The words of their reply follow: **We do not need to defend ourselves before you in this matter** (3:16). This sounds a little defiant in English. It could be that they are not intending to be insolent; they are merely pleading "no contest." They are acknowledging that they are guilty of refusing to bow before the image. Alternatively, they are boldly rejecting Nebuchadnezzar's offer to spare their lives if they will worship the image; they refuse to compromise their faith.

Verses 17–18 are the most difficult in the chapter because of the two "if" clauses, which are not as easy to interpret as the similar construction in verse 15. They are also the most important verses theologically. In fact, they are profoundly consequential for the whole book. The NIV rendering of verse 17 is more of an interpretation than a translation: **If we are thrown into the blazing furnace, the God we serve is able to save us from it** (3:17). The Aramaic does not say, "If we are thrown into the blazing furnace." The NIV adds this clause to explain the Aramaic, which could be translated "If it is" or "If it be so." (See the Additional Note on 3:17.) A better translation of the sentence is "If our God whom we serve is able to deliver us . . ." The Jews are not saying, "If it be so that we are thrown into the furnace . . ." Neither are they saying, "If our God whom we serve exists . . ." Instead they are raising the issue of God's power.

The NRSV translates the second verb, "to save" or "to deliver," as a jussive: "If our God . . . is able to deliver us . . . let him deliver." This reduces the tension with the next verse, where doubt is introduced about whether God actually will rescue them. While traditionally, Shadrach, Meshach, and Abednego are portrayed as being certain of their rescue, it is incredible that they would be so naive as to think that just because God is able to deliver them, he necessarily would. They are sure of God's power, and hopeful regarding deliverance. They do not doubt that God can rescue, and they pray that he will. Such is the spirit of the book of Daniel, which was so helpful to the Jews of the Hellenistic era. They know that God will someday bring his kingdom, and they know that he is able to do so in their time, saving them from the persecution Antiochus IV

The prayer of their hearts is "Let him rescue us." This also becomes the prayer of all believers at all times.

The next problem concerns the end of verse 17. Does the phrase **from your hand, O king** go with what precedes or with what follows? If the former, then there is a compound object of the first occurrence of the verb "save": "If our God . . . is able to save us from the blazing furnace and from your hand, O king, let him save." If the latter, then it goes with the second occurrence of "save": "If our God . . . is able to save us from the blazing furnace, let him save from your hand, O king." Although either one is possible, the *waw*, "and," on the front of "from" seems to make the former more likely. The NIV follows the latter: **"and he will rescue us** from your hand, O king." (Most translations add "us," to make better sense, even though it is not in the text.) Either way, the Jews are confidently answering Nebuchadnezzar's challenge from verse 15. He threatens them with the blazing furnace and asks, "What god will be able to rescue you from my hand?" (3:15). They respond that their God is able to rescue them from the blazing furnace and from the king's hand. Their confession of faith triumphs over the king's skepticism concerning their God's ability to deliver them.

The second "if" clause comes in verse 18: "And if not." What verb does it refer back to? Initially, for the sake of parallelism, one would expect it to go back to the verb of the first "if" clause. Therefore, the larger structure would be: "If our God is able to save . . . let him save. And if not . . . we will not worship the image." In other words, if he is not able, they will still not bow before the statue. Alternatively, if we render the first clause "If our God exists," then the second one should be "And if not," that is, if he does not exist. But these are incomprehensible. If their God is not able to rescue them or if he does not exist, why should they be loyal to their religion and refuse to worship the image? The second "if" clause, therefore, must connect to the last verb in verse 17, "deliver": **"But even if he does not** [deliver], **we want you to know, O king, that we will not serve your gods or worship the image of gold you have set up"** (3:18). Support for this comes from the "if . . . if not" construction in verse 15. The "if not" clause does not go back to the verb of the first "if" clause. That would be "If you are ready . . . but if you are not ready . . ." Rather, the second "if" clause picks up on a later verb: "If you are ready . . . you will bow down and worship . . . but if you do not worship." So also in verse 17, the second "if" clause does not go back to the first but resumes from the more recent verb. (See Additional Note on 3:18.)

Putting all the above together, the flow of the passage is as follows. The king denies that there is any god who can deliver the three friends from the blazing furnace (3:15). They answer that if their God is able, he will deliver them, or perhaps they are praying, "Let him deliver" or "May he deliver" (3:17). They are speaking theoretically, of course, for they know that he is able. Yet, even if he does not deliver them, they would rather die being faithful to God than deny him by worshiping the image (3:18). They do not doubt the existence of God or his ability to save. They may even believe that God will deliver them. But even if he should choose not to, it would be better to lose one's life than to apostatize.

Whenever this story originated, whether in the Babylonian period or in the Persian period, its message spoke to the Jews living in the Hellenistic era who were being persecuted by Antiochus IV. They trusted that God would intervene miraculously in their day as he had in the time of Shadrach, Meshach, and Abednego. But if not, they remained as resolute as those three, preferring to die a martyr's death than to yield to the pressure of the king by worshiping idols. The author was not naive in thinking that God's people would always be rescued, for it is clear that he expected some to suffer and die for their faith (7:21, 25; 8:9–11, 24–25; 11:33). Similarly, every persecuted believer longs for the return of the Lord in his or her lifetime, even though he or she knows that it might be delayed further. The book urges readers to nourish such hopes, whatever their situations.

3:19–23 / The theme of royal rage repeats (see 3:13) as king **Nebuchadnezzar** becomes **furious** at the obstinacy of his three subjects. His anger manifests itself in his countenance. The NIV says **his attitude toward them changed** (3:19), but the Aramaic literally says, "the image of his face changed." The word for "image" is the same as the word for the statue. The following are better renderings: "the expression of his face was changed" (RSV); "his face was contorted" (NRSV). Acting out of his fury, the king orders **the furnace heated seven times hotter than usual** (3:19), which is ridiculous because the flames are already lethal. Raising the temperature will not make the men any more dead, but it will have the unintended consequence of destroying some of the king's own soldiers (3:22). This is part of the storyteller's art as he portrays the king as a buffoon.

The king then has the three Jews bound and thrown **into the burning furnace** (3:20). They are cast into the furnace **wearing their robes, trousers, turbans and other clothes** (3:21). Once again we encounter the author's delight in lists. There is some uncertainty about the first two articles of clothing, but there is a wide consensus that the third is some kind of head covering.

There is some poetic justice when **the flames of the fire** kill **the soldiers** (3:22) who brought the victims into the furnace. Just as Haman was hanged on his own gallows, which he had prepared for Mordecai (Esth. 7:10); just as those who accused Daniel were cast into the lions' den (Dan. 6:24); and just as the enemies of Susanna were put to death instead of her (Sus. 62), these men die in the fire they prepare for the three Jews. However, this story in chapter 3 is also different from the others in that the Chaldeans who denounce the three Jews are not burned, at least not in the MT. The Greek version, preserved in the Apocrypha in the Prayer of Azariah, elaborates on the fate of those outside: "And the flames poured out above the furnace forty-nine cubits, and spread out and burned those Chaldeans who were caught near the furnace" (Pr. Azar. 24–25 NRSV [= 3:47–48 LXX]). Of course, it does not specifically say that the Chaldeans who were incinerated were the same ones who had brought the accusation, but it may be implied. Because the text says they **fell into the blazing furnace** (3:23), a number of commentators have suggested that it was a type of kiln with an opening in the top and a door down below. They were dropped in through the top, but they exited through the door, through which Nebuchadnezzar was able to see the four men (3:25).

3:24–30 / Nebuchadnezzar's wrath turns to **amazement** as he not only sees that the three Jews are **unbound and unharmed** but also sees a **fourth** who **looks like a son of the gods** (3:24–25). The OT often mentions the "sons of God," which is a reference to the divine council of heavenly beings, or angels (see, e.g., Gen. 6:2, 4; Deut. 32:8 [LXX and NRSV marginal reading]; 1 Kgs. 22:19; Job 1:6; 2:1; 38:7; Pss. 29:1; 82:6). The KJV translation, "and the form of the fourth is like the Son of God," is misleading, suggesting a pre-incarnate appearance of Jesus. Such an interpretation reads the NT into the OT rather than discerning the original OT meaning. The author of Daniel clearly understands this fourth man to be an angel (3:28).

God visits his people in their trials. He speaks to Job out of the whirlwind (Job 38:1) and goes to be with his people in exile (Ezek. 1; 11:16). But the difference between Job and the Jews in exile on the one hand and the three Jews of Daniel 3 on the other is that the latter were unharmed while Job and the exiles really suffered; so did the Jews under Antiochus IV. The message of Daniel 3 compares to other promises in Scripture. Speaking of a different, future "fiery furnace," Yahweh dispels the fears of his exiled people about their safe return home: "When you walk through fire, you will not be burned; the flames will not set you ablaze.... Do not be afraid, for I am with you..." (Isa. 43:2, 5). Looking back on a "fiery furnace" that Israel survived in the past, the psalmist also testifies, "For you, O God, tested us; you refined us like silver.... We went through fire and water, but you brought us to a place of abundance" (Ps. 66:10, 12). Isaiah 43, Psalm 66, and Daniel 3 also speak words of reassurance to Christians today who feel themselves walking through fire. Whatever its intensity, they can remain faithful because they are not alone.

Nebuchadnezzar acknowledges the God of Shadrach, Meshach, and Abednego to be **the Most High God** and calls them to **come out** (3:26). When they exit, the various leaders notice that not only have they not been harmed, but not **a hair of their heads** has been **singed; their robes were not scorched, and there was no smell of fire on them** (3:27). This verse brings out the significance of the articles of clothing. The narrator details their apparel earlier (3:21) so that he can heighten the dramatic impact of the miracle here. The reader is amazed to learn that the fire has had no effect at all on their garments.

Nebuchadnezzar's praise of God in verse 28 is instructive for Jews (and Christians) facing persecution. **They trusted in him and defied the king's command and were willing to give up their lives rather than serve or worship any god except their own God** (3:28). God does not always rescue from death, as the martyrs of the second century B.C. learned (1 Macc. 1:57, 60–63; 2 Macc. 6:8–11, 18–31; 7:1–42). The book of Daniel encourages its Jewish audience to trust in the Lord, defy the Seleucid authorities, refrain from worshiping pagan gods, and be willing to sacrifice their lives. The same message is relevant for us today. We should put our trust in God and defy the world. We may not be tempted to bow down before graven images, but the things of the world attract us and draw us away from the Father. When we follow them we are engaging in a type of idolatry. First John tells us, "Do not love the world or anything in the world. If anyone loves the world, the love of the Father is not in him. For everything in the world—the cravings of sinful man, the lust of his eyes and the boasting of what he has and does—comes not from the Father but from the world" (1 John 2:15–16). Although Westerners are rarely threatened with martyrdom, they should be willing to lay down their lives for the Lord if put in that position, and they should remember that sometimes even today, people in other parts of the world are faced with the choice of being faithful to Jesus unto death or denying him in order to save their necks. Our Lord said, "Do not be afraid of those who kill the body but cannot kill the soul. Rather, be afraid of the One who can destroy both soul and body in hell" (Matt. 10:28). He also warned that "whoever acknowledges me before men, I will also acknowledge him before my Father in heaven. But whoever disowns me before men, I will disown him before my Father in heaven" (Matt. 10:32–33). Finally, in response to those who deny the relevance of apocalyptic to Western Christians because their sociological situation is different (they are secure rather than beleaguered), we note that persecution is not the only source of suffering. Christians everywhere are sometimes afflicted with painful illnesses or experience traumatic accidents. While God does not always save us from the fiery trials of life, as he did Shadrach, Meshach, and Abednego, he is present with us in our suffering, for he has promised never to leave or forsake us (Heb. 13:5).

The miracle prompts a new decree, that no one should **say anything against the God of Shadrach, Meshach and Abednego** (3:29) or they will face severe penalties. Daniel 6 ends similarly with Nebuchadnezzar praising God and issuing a decree. Houses being **turned into piles of rubble** (3:29) is among the standard penalties for disobeying a royal decree or for greatly displeasing the king (Ezra 6:6–12; Dan. 2:5). King Nebuchadnezzar earlier mockingly asked, "What god will be able to rescue you from my hand?" After this extraordinary demonstration of God's power, he is now able to answer his own question. He testifies that **no other god** but the God of the Jews **can save in this way** (3:29). This remarkable turnaround leads to the promotion of the three heroes once again (3:30; see also 2:48–49; cf. 6:28).

Additional Notes §3

3:2 / The term for **satraps**, *'akhashdarpenayya'* (Aram.), derives from *kshatrapawan* (Old Persian), meaning "protector of the realm" (Driver, *Daniel*, p. 36). The Greek text has *satrapas*, from which we get the English form. Aramaic *'akhashdarpenayya'*, "satrap," is attested in an Assyrian text from the eighth century B.C., but it is used of Median lords (Collins, *Daniel*, p. 183, citing E. Lipiński, review of A. Lacocque, *Le Livre de Daniel*, VT 28 [1978], p. 237). So, even though it predates Nebuchadnezzar, it is not a Semitic term, and it is unlikely that it was the title of a Babylonian office. Most scholars consider it anachronistic here.

3:3 / The phrase **that King Nebuchadnezzar had set up** occurs twice in this verse, but the second one is omitted by the Greek text of Theodotion. The NIV likewise omits it, but since repetition is typical of Dan. 3, it is better to follow the MT here and retain it. The NIV also omits the second occurrence of "the image." So, instead of "and they stood before it," the end of the verse should read, "and they stood before the image that King Nebuchadnezzar had set up."

3:4 / Although various suggestions have been made for the origin of the Aramaic term *karoza'*, **herald** (e.g., Aramaic, Persian, Hurrian), the evidence tips the scales in favor of the Greek word *kērux*, "herald" (Collins, *Daniel*, p. 183).

The phrase **peoples, nations and men of every language** recurs with regularity in Daniel and Revelation. These three groups are commanded to worship the image in v. 5; they do so in v. 7. Nebuchadnezzar issues them a decree preventing blasphemy against the God of Shadrach, Meshach, and Abednego (3:29). He addresses them again with a wish for their prosperity as he praises God, introducing the account of his madness and subsequent healing (4:1). Daniel acknowledges to Belshazzar that God gave Nebuchadnezzar power over "all the peoples and nations and men of every language" (5:19). King Darius writes an edict for the same three groups (6:25). Finally, the heavenly being who looks like a man receives eternal dominion over them (7:14). The influence of Daniel on the NT apocalypse is seen in the similar lists that appear in Rev. 5:9; 7:9; 10:11; 13:7; 14:6; 17:15.

3:5 / In the list of instruments, the first word, *qarna'*, is the normal word for **horn** and probably refers to a ram's horn. The second word, *mashroqita'*, from the root *shrq*, meaning "to hiss" or "whistle," is usually translated "pipe" or **flute**. The third term, *qitaros* (*kethib*)/*qatros* (*qere*), is from the Greek *kitharis*, or *kithara*. It is the word from which we get "guitar" and **zither**. It represents a stringed instrument and is usually translated "harp," "zither," or "lyre." The fourth term, *sabbeka'*, is not as clear. It is related to the Greek *sambukē* and is thought to be a triangular-shaped stringed instrument, hence "trigon" in RSV and NRSV; NIV renders it **lyre**. The fifth term, *pesanterin*, is the Greek *psaltērion*, or **harp**. The sixth and final term, *sumponyah* (of Greek derivation), is ambiguous. It probably represents a musical instrument, variously translated as "bagpipe" (RSV), "drum" (NRSV), or **pipes** (NIV). However, in certain contexts it might indicate "harmony," as the name implies, being the word from which we get "symphony."

3:12 / The expression *sim te'em* in v. 10 means "to give a command," or "to make a decree," but here in v. 12, *sim te'em* with *'al* means "to pay respect to" or "**to pay attention** to." Is there some sort of wordplay here? Both expressions occur within the speech of the Chaldeans. The king makes a decree or gives a judgment (*sim te'em*) that has an impact on Shadrach, Meshach, and Abednego. In response, they refuse to pay him a favorable judgment or respect (*sim te'em 'al*) by obeying his decree. The same situation is found in Dan. 6, where Daniel's envious colleagues accuse him of failing to pay respect or attention to the king (6:13) by obeying his decree restricting prayer. The contrast is not present in ch. 6, though, because the word for the decree in vv. 7, 8, 9, 10, 12, 13, 15 [8, 9, 10, 11, 13, 14, 16 MT] is not *te'em*. However, the expression *sim te'em*, meaning "to make a decree," does occur toward the end of the chapter, when the king commands his subjects to "fear and reverence the God of Daniel" (6:26 [6:27 MT]). It is used similarly in Dan. 3:29 and 4:6 [4:3 MT] and in Ezra 4:21; 5:13; 6:1, 3, 12. Interestingly, the word *te'em* also has the meaning "taste," as in Dan. 5:2.

In the statement "They neither serve your gods nor worship the image of gold you have set up," the Aramaic word for **gods** is actually vocalized (in the *qere*) as a singular, "god," which might point to the statue. Even if one argues for the plural form (the *kethib*), the meaning might still be singular (Montgomery, *Daniel*, p. 205). Furthermore, the conjunction separating "serve..." and "worship..." would normally be rendered "and." That leads to the following translation: "They do not serve your god, and they do not worship the gold image." The two verbs may therefore refer two different actions or they may be parallel descriptions of the same action.

3:16 / Rather than reading, **replied to the king, "O Nebuchadnezzar...,"** the LXX and other ancient versions read, "replied to King Nebuchadnezzar." The LXX reading is more believable, and it is possible to read the MT this way with only a minor change. The main problem is that after that minor change, the MT still has the order *malka' nebukadnetsar* (King Nebuchadnezzar) instead of the normal order *nebukadnetsar malka'* (3:1, 2, 3, 5, 7, 9, 24). We might invert the two (one possible solution suggested by *BHS*), but it is better to err on the side of caution, refraining from both emendations in this case. Furthermore, the MT has the more difficult reading, which is preferred. It would have been unacceptably rude to address the king as "Nebuchadnezzar." Therefore, it is more likely that a scribe would change the reading in the MT to the reading in the LXX than vice versa. A storyteller from the second century B.C., as the author may have been, perhaps would not be overly concerned about whether King Nebuchadnezzar of the sixth century was spoken to politely.

3:17 / The Aramaic does not say, **if we are thrown into the blazing furnace.** The text has *hen 'itay*, that is, "if" followed by the particle of existence. Some take this to mean "If it is" or "If it be so." Apparently, the NIV translators add "If we are thrown into the blazing furnace" at the beginning of the verse to explain "If it be so." Then they substitute "it" later in the verse, presumably to avoid the redundancy of having "blazing furnace" twice. (The Aramaic also has "our God"; it is not clear why the NIV omits "our.") If we opt for the reading "If it be so" in v. 17, we must look for the antecedent. If what be so? It is reasonable to look back to v. 15, where the king seeks to coerce the three friends' worship of the image by threatening them with death by burning. While there is a connection between the two verses because the three Jews in v. 17 are answering the king's statement in v. 15, it is unlikely that *hen 'itay* should be translated "If it be so."

Some argue that the particle of existence, *'itay*, goes with "God": "If our God whom we serve exists" (Goldingay, *Daniel*, p. 64; Hartman and Di Lella, *Daniel*, p. 158). If so, the Jews are making the point that the deity they espouse has power to deliver from flame. In other words, if there is such a God as the one the Jews profess (and they believe there is), then he certainly has control over the elements of nature, including fire. Grammatically, this is not the best interpretation, either, though. Both the "If it be so" and the "If God exists" understandings separate the particle *'itay* from the participle *yakil*, "being able." These should be connected by construing the particle of existence as a copula followed by a supplementary participle, yielding "If our God... is ['*itay*] able [*yakil*] to save us... he will save" (Montgomery, *Daniel*, p. 206; Collins, *Daniel*, p. 187). This is the superior translation. The Jews are saying, "If our God whom we serve is able to deliver us . . ."

3:18 / Taking the if clause in v. 18 to refer back to the verb of the first "if" clause seems to be incredible, as explained in the commentary. It is not a matter of making the text more orthodox (Collins, *Daniel*, pp. 187–88; P. W. Coxon, "Daniel III 17: A Linguistic and Theological Problem," *VT* 26 [1976], p. 408) but of making it believable.

3:23 / After verse 23 the LXX has a long interpolation in three sections: (1) the Prayer of Azariah (3:24–45 LXX = vv. 1–22 Apocrypha), (2) a prose narrative relating what happened to the three Jews while they were in the furnace (3:46–50 LXX = vv. 23–27 Apocrypha), and (3) the Song of the Three Young Men (3:51–90 LXX = vv. 28–68 Apocrypha). The consensus on 1 and 3 is that they are not original to Daniel. However, some think 2 might be original since it better explains what happened in the fire and the king's disturbed state in v. 24. Others think that these verses are not authentic since they relate that an angel came down to be with the men and to make things comfortable for them. This lessens the dramatic impact of vv. 24–25, where the king sees the heavenly being. One major difference between the two versions is that in the MT, the guards who put the men in are burned by the fire, whereas in the interpolation, the guards keep the fire going while some Chaldeans get burned (Hartman and Di Lella, *Daniel*, p. 163).

3:26 / The Hebrew equivalent (*'el 'elyon*) of the Aramaic term for **Most High God** is authentically Israelite, yet it is used by those outside the community of faith, such as Melchizedek, the Canaanite priest (Gen. 14:18, 19, 20, 22). Balaam, the Mesopotamian prophet (Num. 24:16) and the unnamed king of Babylon who seeks to exalt himself to the level of God (Isa. 14:14) similarly refer to God with the form *'elyon*, "Most High," by itself, without "God" (see also, e.g., Deut. 32:8; 2 Sam. 22:14; Isa. 14:14; Lam. 3:35; Hos. 11:7; cf. Mark 5:7; Luke 1:32; 6:35; 8:28; Acts 7:48; Heb. 7:1). The term *'elyon* is found often in the Psalms (Pss. 9:2; 18:13; 21:7; 50:14; 91:1); sometimes a divine name is in a parallel line, although the term also occurs with "God" (Pss. 57:2; 78:56) and with "Yahweh" (Pss. 7:17; 47:2). Elsewhere in Daniel, the Aramaic cognate is found with "God" (Dan. 4:2 [3:32 MT]; 5:18) and without "God" (Dan. 4:17, 24, 25, 32, 34 [4:14, 21, 22, 29, 31 MT]; 7:25). It accompanies *qaddishe*, "holy ones," in 7:18, 22, 25, and 27. "Most High" is not unique to Israel but is found in Phoenician and Aramaic, outside the Bible (see F. M. Cross Jr., *Canaanite Myth and Hebrew Epic* [Cambridge, Mass.: Harvard University Press, 1973], p. 51). The Greek counterpart, *hypsistos*, is frequenty found in Hellenistic writings (Collins, *Daniel*, p. 190; G. Bertram, "*hypsistos*," *TDNT* 8:614–20).

§4 The King Becomes a Beast-Man and Then Recovers (Dan. 4:1–37)

In terms of form, chapter 4 starts out as a letter from King Nebuchadnezzar addressed to all people everywhere. It begins in the first person with praise to God (4:1–3). Next, the king relates in his own voice the story of his dream (4:4–18). Then the account shifts to the third person for Daniel's interpretation (4:19–27) and for the narrative of how the dream was fulfilled (4:28–33). Finally, the text reverts back to the first person as Nebuchadnezzar reports his restoration (4:34–37). It ends as it began, with praise to God, thus forming an *inclusio*, or A-B-A pattern: verses 1–3 at the beginning parallel verses 34–35, 37 at the end. It is not clear why the text changes from first person to third and back to first. There is also an *inclusio* device framing the material in chapters 4–6. Daniel 4 begins with a royal document addressed to all the people in the realm, wishing them prosperity, mentioning signs and wonders, and confessing that God's kingdom is eternal (4:1–3); Daniel 6 ends the same way (6:25–27). This parallelistic structure delimits chapters 4–6 and indicates that this is a unit of material that probably circulated together at an earlier stage of the Danielic tradition.

Daniel 2, 4, and 5 go together because they all contain contest narratives that set Daniel against the other wise men of Babylon to see who can interpret. Of course, Daniel and his God always win. While in chapter 5 the contest consists of interpreting the writing on the wall, the other two center on dream interpretation. For this reason, chapter 4 is closer to chapter 2: Nebuchadnezzar has a dream; his wise men fail to interpret it; but God supplies the interpretation through his servant Daniel. However, here, unlike chapter 2, the king is willing to tell the content of the dream and does not threaten his counselors with death. Since Daniel was successful in interpreting the earlier dream (ch. 2) and was recognized by the king as being endowed with a divine spirit (4:8), one wonders why Nebuchadnezzar even asked his counselors. Why did he not go straight to Daniel? On this puzzle the text is silent, but it may be because chapters 2 and 4 were originally independent stories that have only loosely been tied together in the larger work. Parts of chapter

4 are in poetry, but there is debate about which verses. The NIV sets out only verses 3 and 34b–35 as poetry, while the NRSV includes also verses 10–12, 14–17, and 37b.

In chapter 4, King Nebuchadnezzar is on rather friendly terms with Daniel. Furthermore, in the MT the king is not vilified for destroying Jerusalem (though there is mention of it in the LXX). Therefore, this story possibly originated before the persecution of the Jews under Antiochus IV; otherwise we would expect the king to be portrayed more negatively. Nevertheless, the story took on new meaning in the second century. Epiphanes was sometimes called Epimanes, "the mad one," behind his back (for the meaning of "Epiphanes," see "Historical Background" in the Introduction). There is also a tradition that he repented when he was dying, acknowledging that humans should submit to God and not consider themselves to be his equals (2 Macc. 9:11–12). Readers of the second century and later would have seen in Nebuchadnezzar—a king who lost his human reason and acted beastly, but then came to his senses and praised God—a type of Antiochus IV.

The central themes of the chapter, that God can take away kingdoms and give them to whomever he will (4:17, 25, 32), even to the lowliest ones (4:17), and that God's kingdom is everlasting (4:3, 34), serve the overall apocalyptic thrust of the book. Thus, chapter 4 is reminiscent of chapter 2, which spells doom for the earthly kingdoms, and it anticipates chapter 7, where the beastly kingdoms are superseded by the kingdom of God, which is handed over to the lowliest ones, namely the Jews. Therefore, Daniel 4, like the work as a whole, provided a shot of hope for all the persecuted people of God suffering under the Seleucid tyrant. In turn, it comforts all who suffer under despots, whether they are Babylonian, Median, Persian Seleucid, Roman, or modern.

The story in this chapter was probably originally about the last Babylonian king, Nabonidus, rather than Nebuchadnezzar. There is no evidence that Nebuchadnezzar was driven from his throne for a period of time. However, one ancient text makes it clear that Nabonidus left Babylon for ten years, and another mentions a seven-year affliction. Also, in chapter 5, Belshazzar is called the son of the king who was humbled in chapter 4 (5:18–24). Nabonidus was Belshazzar's father, not Nebuchadnezzar. Nebuchadnezzar could have displaced Nabonidus in the story because he was better known, because he destroyed Jerusalem, and because of his prominence in the first three chapters of Daniel.

4:1–3 / Chapter 4 recounts the story of how King Nebuchadnezzar lost his kingdom for a time and later got it back. It portrays King

Nebuchadnezzar as being so grateful to God for restoring him to his throne that he wrote to everyone in his domain a public testimony of praise. It follows a letter form that was common from the Babylonian period down through the Persian and Hellenistic eras. It begins with the introduction of the sender: **King Nebuchadnezzar** (4:1). Next come the addressees: **To the peoples, nations and men of every language, who live in all the world** (4:1). "All the world" is only a slight exaggeration since Babylon controlled most of the territory known or settled at that time. This is followed by the salutation: **May you prosper greatly!** (4:1). More literally, he desires their peace to grow great, but *shelam*, "peace," is a rich word that can include "well-being" and "prosperity," so the NIV is on the mark. Almost the same form is used by King Darius (Dan. 6:25) and by Artaxerxes (in another Aramaic passage in the OT, Ezra 7:12). This kind of salutation continues in the NT epistles of Paul (1 Cor. 1:1–3) and Peter (1 Pet. 1:1–2; 2 Pet. 1:1–2). Wishing peace on others was encouraged by the Lord (Luke 10:5) as well.

The king praises **the Most High God** for his **signs** and **wonders** and for his **eternal kingdom** (4:2–3). There are a number of doxologies in the court stories of Daniel 1–6. In chapter 2, Daniel gives glory to God for revealing to him the dream and interpretation (2:20–23). After Daniel delivers the revelation, Nebuchadnezzar blesses the prophet's God for making known the mystery (2:47). Similarly, at the end of chapter 3, the king praises the Jewish deity and makes a decree proscribing blasphemy against him by "the people of any nation or language" (3:28–30). Likewise, Daniel 4 concludes with a hymn of praise uttered by King Nebuchadnezzar (4:34–35, 37). Not surprisingly, the end of chapter 6 also records royal worship, as King Darius exalts God for rescuing Daniel from the lions (6:26–27). This last passage closely parallels Daniel 4:1–3. Darius sends a decree "to all the peoples, nations and men of every language throughout the land" (6:25 // 4:1). It contains the salutation: "May you prosper greatly!" (6:25 // 4:1). It mentions God's kingdom, which "will not be destroyed" (6:26 // 4:3), and God's "signs and wonders" (6:27 // 4:2–3). Daniel 6 is also like Daniel 3 in making a demand on Gentiles, except that chapter 6 is stronger. Chapter 3 is negative—it only makes it illegal to speak against the God of the Jews (3:29); but chapter 6 is positive in promoting the Jews' religion—it requires others to "fear and reverence" Daniel's God (6:26).

Unlike chapters 2, 3, and 6, which only conclude with praise, chapter 4 both begins and ends with doxologies. This gave rise to confusion among some medieval biblical translators and interpreters. In the Latin Vulgate and in Bibles published in Hebrew, the verses labeled 4:1–3 in our

English versions are numbered with chapter 3 (3:31–33). However, the chapter breaks and verse numbers were inserted in the thirteenth century A.D. and not always in the right places. These verses clearly belong at the head of chapter 4 but were probably numbered with chapter 3 because of the pattern in chapters 2, 3, and 6: it was thought that the praise must come at the end of sections. In the LXX, these verses are moved to the end of chapter 4, probably for the same reason.

That the pagan Babylonian king would admit that the heavenly king, Israel's God, is worthy of glory would have been seen as a fulfillment of prophecy. In the later sections of the book of Isaiah, Yahweh calls Israel to be a light and a witness to the nations of the world. There are predictions that foreigners and even Gentile kings would one day bring their wealth to the Jews and acknowledge that they worship the true God (Isa. 42:6–7; 43:12; 45:14, 22; 49:7, 22–23; 60:3–12, 14, 16). The first readers of Daniel would have delighted in the portrayal of Daniel as a faithful witness and of Nebuchadnezzar, who destroyed Jerusalem and the temple, as a humbled worshiper of the Most High. Kings Nebuchadnezzar (Dan. 2:47; 3:28–29; 4:2–3, 34–35, 37) and Darius (Dan. 6:26–27) acknowledge God, and by promoting and prospering Daniel and his friends, these kings (and Belshazzar in chapter 5) also fulfill the predictions about wealth (Dan. 2:48–49; 3:30; 4:9; 5:29; 6:28).

The doxology continues: God's kingdom will never end; **his dominion endures from generation to generation** (4:3; cf. Ps. 145:13). This is an important theme in Daniel. It is repeated not only at the end of this chapter (4:34) but in Darius's doxology as well (6:26). Moreover, it recurs in the two apocalyptic visions found in the Aramaic section. God's kingdom is everlasting, in contrast to the earthly kingdoms, which will all be destroyed (2:44; 7:27). A contrast is implied in Daniel 4 also. By emphasizing the everlasting nature of God's rule, these opening verses highlight how different and inferior is the temporal, ephemeral kingdom of King Nebuchadnezzar. God remains on his throne, while Nebuchadnezzar's rule is interrupted (4:33) and renewed at God's pleasure (4:34). The power of human authority pales in comparison with that of the only true sovereign, for no one can reign on earth unless heaven allows it (4:17, 25, 32). Furthermore, this divine potentate is free to do as he wishes, without accountability to anyone (4:35).

God's "signs" are described as **great** and his "wonders" as **mighty** (4:3). The root of "great" is *rbb* (there is also a similar root, *rbh*, with a similar meaning), and the root of "mighty" is *tqp*. Words formed from these roots occur several times in Daniel 4. (The NIV does not always translate them with the English words "great" and "mighty," but they will be used here consistently to make clear the repetition.) Just as God's acts are "great" and "mighty" (4:3), the tree in the dream is "great" and "mighty" (4:11, 20; NIV "large" and "strong"). Nebuchadnezzar, identified as the tree, is likewise described as "great" and "mighty" (4:22; NIV "great" and "strong"). When he boasts of building "great" Babylon by his own "mighty" power (4:30), however, he is immediately driven from his throne. The author allows that Nebuchadnezzar is great and mighty, but he must not claim that he is the source of that greatness and might. Rather, Nebuchadnezzar must acknowledge "that the Most High is sovereign over the kingdoms of men" (4:17, 25, 32) and that all power comes from him. Nebuchadnezzar's arrogance regarding his own strength brings about the dissolution of his kingdom and the loss of his might. As Proverbs says, "Pride goes before destruction, a haughty spirit before a fall" (16:18). Nebuchadnezzar's humiliation and subsequent restoration are manifestations of God's signs and wonders, which are truly great and mighty.

4:4–9 / After the opening letter formula and hymn, Nebuchadnezzar proceeds to tell his story in the first person. Verses 4 and 5 exhibit a dramatic contrast between his initial state and his dream-affected state. At the outset, he is **at home . . . , contented and prosperous** (4:4), but then he has **a dream that** makes him **afraid** and **terrified** (4:5). How quickly things can change when God intervenes in human lives; encounters with God can be unsettling! Nebuchadnezzar was "troubled" after his earlier dream, too (2:1, 3). Belshazzar "was so frightened that his knees knocked together" and his face grew pale when he saw the handwriting on the wall (Dan. 5:6, 9). Daniel's response upon hearing the king's dream in chapter 4 runs along the same lines: he becomes "perplexed" and alarmed (4:19; see also Dan. 7:15; 8:17; 10:8–10; Rev. 1:17).

As in chapter 2, the king summons his **wise men** so that they can **interpret the dream** (4:6). Unlike chapter 2, the king tells them the dream (4:7) and refrains from threatening them if they fail. Of course, the reader is not surprised to find (also like chapter 2) that they cannot **interpret it** (4:7). **Finally, Daniel** comes **into** the king's **presence** (4:8). The narrator explains that Daniel **is called Belteshazzar, after the name of** Nebuchadnezzar's **god** (4:8). Apparently, the author of Daniel understood Daniel's Babylonian name to begin with "Bel," an alternate name for Marduk, the chief god of Babylon ("Bel" is found in Isa. 46:1; Jer. 50:2; 51:44). However, the name most likely derives from the Akkadian phrase *balatsu-utsur*, meaning "protect his life." In other words, there is no divine name expressed, although one might be understood. The explanation in this verse is, therefore, a popular etymology. Some see this as further evidence for the lateness of the book, since a sixth-century author living in Babylon probably would have known Akkadian.

We expect that Daniel will be able to provide the interpretation because we know what Nebuchadnezzar declares: **the spirit of the holy gods is in him** (4:8; cf. 4:9). Earlier in the book, the Babylonian advisers deny that the gods dwell with humans (2:11), but Daniel proves them wrong. The king remembers this and is confident that the Jewish sage will come through again. Daniel 4 is reminiscent of the Joseph story, where after interpreting Pharaoh's dream, Joseph is described as "one in whom is the spirit of God" (Gen. 41:38). (See the Additional Note on 4:8.)

The dream account is found in verses 10–17, but it is sandwiched between introductory and concluding elements. The writer is using the *inclusio* device (A-B-A pattern) again, to set the dream narrative in high relief. There are actually four elements that repeat at the beginning and end of this section. In both places, the text says that the Babylonian advisers fail: "When the magicians, enchanters, astrologers and diviners came, I told them the dream, but they could not interpret it for me" (4:7); "none of the wise men in my kingdom can interpret it for me" (4:18). That the spirit of the holy gods is in Daniel is found twice before and once after the dream (4:8, 9 and 4:18). Before recounting the dream, the king expresses faith in Daniel's ability to interpret: "no mystery is too difficult for you" (4:9); afterward he says that "none of the" others "can interpret" the dream, "but you can" (4:18). Finally, there is the request for the interpretation itself: "Here is my dream; interpret it for me" (4:9, before); "This is the dream that I, King Nebuchadnezzar, had. Now, Belteshazzar, tell me what it means" (4:18, after).

The king addresses Daniel as the **chief of the magicians** (4:9). Previously, Daniel and his friends distinguished themselves during their training, excelling over all others (1:18–20). By divine revelation, Daniel not only interpreted but gave the content of an earlier royal dream (ch. 2). As a result, Nebuchadnezzar promoted Daniel to the position of "chief prefect over all the wise men of Babylon" (2:48 NRSV). Finally, the Jewish prophet was recognized as being endowed with a divine spirit (4:8). Given this background, it is difficult to understand why the king even bothered with the other wise men (4:6–7); one would expect him to consult Daniel first. In the context of the narrative, however, there is greater dramatic effect and more pleasure for the reader to see the incompetent pagans fail once more. From the storyteller's perspective, it is more interesting and satisfying to bring Daniel in last to triumph over the Babylonian bunglers. Also, as mentioned above, chapters 2 and

4 were once independent traditions; when they were brought together in the book of Daniel, it was not thought important to smooth everything over. Finally, it is worth noting that verses 6–9, which tell of the attempt and failure of the Babylonian sages, are not in the Septuagint. It is possible that the Greek tradition preserves the original text and that verses 6–9 were added to the Aramaic version to fashion chapter 4 after chapter 2. On the other hand, it seems more likely that the LXX removed verses 6–9 because it did not make sense for the king to inquire of his charlatan magicians (Montgomery, *Daniel*, pp. 245, 247).

The king expresses confidence in Daniel: **no mystery is too difficult for you** (4:9). "Mystery" harks back to chapter 2, where this word occurs seven times (2:18, 19, 27, 28, 29, 30, 47). Then Nebuchadnezzar gives a directive: **Here is my dream; interpret it for me** (4:9). The Aramaic actually should be rendered "Tell the visions of my dream that I saw and its interpretation." However, that does not fit here. Such a statement would make sense in Daniel 2, where the king demanded that his sages supply both the content and meaning. But here the king narrates the dream, while Daniel only provides the interpretation. With a slight emendation (see Additional Note on 4:9) it is possible to read "here" instead of "visions." Then the verb "tell" would only go with "its interpretation," yielding "Here is my dream that I saw; tell its interpretation."

4:10–18 / Nebuchadnezzar recounts his dream: he saw **a tree in the middle of the land. Its height was enormous** (4:10); **its top touched the sky** (4:11). It produced abundant branches, leaves, and fruit. **Under it the beasts of the field found shelter, and the birds of the air lived in its branches; from it every creature was fed** (4:12). This seems to be a description of the cosmic tree, a fairly common motif in ancient Near Eastern art and iconography, though rare in texts (see the Additional Note on 4:10). It stands in "the middle of the earth" (not "in the middle of the land," as in the NIV, as if it were a local tree) and binds everything together: its branches reach up into heaven, while its roots touch the earth and spread down into the underworld. It is a sort of tree of life that provides food and shelter to all creatures and humans who dwell on earth. The king, who has an important role in maintaining the cosmic order, sometimes stands in for the tree in pictures, so it makes great sense that King Nebuchadnezzar should be identified with this tree.

Nebuchadnezzar saw not only a tree but **a messenger, a holy one, coming down from heaven** (4:13; also vv. 17, 23). The word translated "messenger" really means "watcher," as in someone standing watch or staying awake, not in the sense of looking (cf. NIV footnote). The term occurs frequently in Jewish works from the Greek and Roman periods, especially in *1 Enoch* (but also in *Jubilees*, the *Testaments of the Twelve Patriarchs*, and the Dead Sea Scrolls). It often refers to fallen angels but may also refer to faithful angels. Though the root is not used in the Bible outside Daniel for heavenly beings who are watchers, the concept might be there. For example, God stations watchmen (different root) on the walls of Jerusalem to pray; they are never silent, they never rest, and they are not to let God rest until he restores the holy city (Isa. 62:6). God himself is always watchful and vigilant, standing as a protective guard over his people: "he who watches over Israel will neither slumber nor sleep" (Ps. 121:4). Elsewhere in Daniel, heavenly beings are called angels (3:28), attendants (7:16 NRSV), men (9:21), or princes (10:13). These "watchers" are also called "holy ones" (4:13, 17, 23).

This illuminates our understanding of the term "holy ones [NIV "saints"] of the Most High" in Daniel 7:18. They are probably heavenly beings as well (7:18), rather than human "saints." The "watchers" are apparently part of God's heavenly council (see 1 Kgs. 22:19–23; Job 1–2; Ps. 82; 89:6–8; Isa. 6:1–8; Jer. 23:18–22). The Most High God, the heavenly king, has decided to have the tree cut down (4:23), and he has communicated this to his privy council composed of heavenly beings. Then **the decision is announced by** the watchers; **the holy ones declare the verdict** (4:17). One of them cries **in a loud voice: "Cut down the tree and trim off its branches; strip off its leaves and scatter its fruit"** (4:14). To whom is he calling? Presumably he is addressing other members of the heavenly council, because he uses plural imperatives, as is the case in Isaiah 40:1–2 (see Cross, "Council of Yahweh," pp. 274–77). Because Nebuchadnezzar's tree fails to bear the fruit of humility before God, it draws the wrath and judgment of God. Perhaps this is a point of contact with the NT, for John the Baptist rebukes the religious leaders of his day for not bearing the fruit of repentance: "The ax is already at the root of the trees, and every tree that does not produce good fruit will be cut down and thrown into the fire" (Matt. 3:10). The sad result of the tree's demise is that the **animals will flee from under it and the birds from its branches** (4:14).

Tree and vine imagery are common metaphors for kings and kingdoms in the Bible. Daniel 4 and Ezekiel 17 and 31 all have a tree with luxuriant branches where the birds make their nests and beneath whose boughs animals of all kinds find a home. They picture the ideal kingdom (and king) as a beneficent government whose prosperity aids everyone, even other nations. Jesus also uses the figure of the tree to represent the kingdom of God. It starts small, like a mustard seed, but grows into a great tree that provides a place for the birds to nest (Matt. 13:31–32; Mark 4:30–32; Luke 13:18–19).

The problem with human kingdoms, however, is that monarchs become preoccupied with their own greatness and, hence, lose their reason for being. In Daniel 4 and Ezekiel 31, the tree is cut down (in Ezekiel, it is cast down to Sheol [the grave; Ezek. 31:15]; in Daniel the punishment is temporary). In Ezekiel 17, only the top is broken off and later a vine is uprooted, but in the conclusion God talks of destroying trees (v. 24). In the Ezekiel texts, the tree is cut down because "it was proud of its height" (Ezek. 31:11; cf. 17:24). Pride is also the reason for the downfall of the tree in Daniel 4, whose "top touched the sky." This is reminiscent of the men who wanted to "make a name for" themselves by building the tower of Babel, which would reach "to the heavens" (Gen. 11:4). But God gives kingdoms to the "lowliest of men" (Dan. 4:17), so Nebuchadnezzar will be driven out until he learns to acknowledge God's sovereignty (Dan. 4:25, 32). As the final verse of the chapter says, "Those who walk in pride he is able to humble" (4:37). The indictment of pride continues in chapter 5. Belshazzar is rebuked for not humbling himself (5:22). Referring to the episode in Daniel 4, Daniel tells him to take a lesson from his father who "was deposed from his royal throne and stripped of his glory . . . until he acknowledged that the Most High God is sovereign" (5:20–21). In short, Daniel 4 tells Nebuchadnezzar's story using a common biblical metaphor for human kingdoms to underscore that the greatest of them is the lowliest one. Such a kingdom strives to acknowledge God's sovereign greatness rather than admiring its own.

Although the tree is to be felled, **the stump and its roots** are to **remain in the ground** (4:15). Actually, the word translated "stump" means "root," but it would be redundant and confusing to translate "root of its roots," so most modern versions render it "stump." Perhaps the MT represents a conflation of two readings with different words for "root" (Collins, *Daniel*, pp. 208, 210 n. 23). Leaving the root engenders hope for Nebuchadnezzar's future, just as stumps do in other passages (see Job 14:7). For example, Isaiah portrays Judah as a felled tree, but the stump is left, leaving a meager hope of new growth (Isa. 6:13). In another passage Isaiah is more hopeful, predicting the coming of a new David from the stump of Jesse (Isa. 11:1).

Exegetes have struggled with the Aramaic expression "leave its roots . . . in a band of iron and bronze [NIV **bound with iron and bronze**]" (4:15). It might be connected to the practice in Mesopotamia of putting metal bands on trees, perhaps for some religious purpose—except that here we no longer have a tree, only roots (Collins, *Daniel*, p. 226). Or, it is possible that the metal bands are attached to keep the tree from growing during the time of punishment and also to protect and preserve the roots from decay (Barr, "Daniel," p. 595). While there is no evidence from antiquity that ancient people did this (and therefore, most scholars now reject this once-popular view), there is much from the ancient world that we do not know, so we cannot rule it out. Perhaps the expression signifies some sort of psychological binding, since Nebuchadnezzar seems to lose his human reasoning (Driver, *Daniel*, p. 50). Alternatively, since this is a dream, the metal bands may be symbolic and need not correspond to what was normally done to roots in Mesopotamia.

A phrase from Jeremiah 27:2 may suggest their symbolic significance. The word for "band" in Daniel 4:15 (NIV "bound") is from the same root as the word for "bands" in Jeremiah 27:2. The prophet tells the people to show their loyalty to Babylon by wearing Nebuchadnezzar's "bands and yoke bars" (a literal translation; NIV "Make a yoke out of straps and crossbars and put it on your neck"). The metal band of Daniel 4:15, then, may symbolize submission: Nebuchadnezzar himself will be shackled when he becomes a beast-man, forced into submission to others, until he subjects himself to the heavenly sovereign. Finally, some have suggested the bound roots indicate that Nebuchadnezzar would be shackled while in his wild state. This view is supported by the LXX and is probably the best solution. At some point in verse 15 the imagery shifts from tree to human and beast. Verse 16 is clearly about Nebuchadnezzar and not about a tree, because it speaks of the transformation from man to beast. The part about being **drenched with the dew of heaven** (4:15) seems to be about the man, because the fulfillment of the dream mentions this detail regarding Nebuchadnezzar (4:33). If the metal band refers to chains used to restrain the wild man, then the shift already occurs at that point in verse 15. Instead of reading the phrase "in a band of iron and bronze" with what precedes, we should connect it to the following: "But leave its roots in the ground. In a band of iron and bronze, let him be fed with the grass of the field; let him be wet with the dew of heaven" (4:15; author's translation, leaving out one of the words for "root" and adding in "let him be fed" from 4:25, 32–33—see the Additional Note on 4:15).

Nebuchadnezzar is to become animal-like and live in the wild. He will "eat grass like cattle" (4:25, 32; see also v. 33). He will be covered with dew when he sleeps outside with the plants and animals. His **mind will be changed from that of a man,** and he will **be given the mind of an animal** (4:16). Some think this means that Nebuchadnezzar will become insane, but that is not what the text indicates; it says he will become bestial. Some even try to diagnose his illness as lycanthropy or zoanthropy, conditions where people lose touch with reality, believing they are animals. However, the biblical writer seems to be speaking of a metamorphosis. The narrative does not state that his human mind is deluded into fantasizing that he is an animal, but rather that it is transformed into an animal mind (4:16), which causes him to live like a beast and to resemble a beast (4:33). His mind is rearranged rather than deranged. To identify this with a known medical condition removes the wonder of the story, for this is a work of God, not necessarily a naturally occurring malady. (For two parallel stories from the ancient Near East, see the Additional Note on 4:16.) This motif in Daniel 4 of the animalistic earthly monarch anticipates the vision of Daniel 7, where four violent, evil empires are represented as beasts (7:1–8) and are destroyed by God's kingdom, represented by one who resembles a human being (7:13; NIV "one like a son of man"). The beastly kingdoms come from the sea, a symbol of chaos, while God's kingdom comes from heaven.

Nebuchadnezzar will remain in his bestial state until **seven times pass by for him** (4:16; repeated in vv. 23, 25, 32). This is usually understood to be seven years. It is interesting that another Babylonian king, Nabonidus, endured an affliction for seven years. We know about this from the Qumran text *The Prayer of Nabonidus*. Many scholars believe that the account in Daniel 4 developed from a tradition about Nabonidus rather than Nebuchadnezzar (for further discussion, see the Additional Note on 4:16).

This story calls to mind another figure from history: Antiochus IV Epiphanes. It may have been originally about Nabonidus; it may have developed into a story about Nebuchadnezzar; but when Jews in the second century B.C. read Daniel 4, they would have thought of the Seleucid king Antiochus IV. Like Nebuchadnezzar, he was certainly guilty of hubris. The book of Daniel records that Antiochus had "a mouth that spoke boastfully" (7:8). He set himself "up to be as great as the Prince of the host" (8:11). "He will consider himself superior" (8:25). "He will exalt and magnify himself above every god" (11:36) and "will exalt himself above them all" (11:37). He even called himself Epiphanes, "god manifest." The change in Nebuchadnezzar from human to beast with the consequent loss of human reason reminds us that behind his back some called Antiochus IV "Epimanes [the mad one]" instead of Epiphanes. Nebuchadnezzar's affliction and repentance are paralleled by Antiochus's final illness and deathbed conversion. His arrogance diminished and he "came to his senses" (2 Macc. 9:11 NRSV). This is similar to Daniel 4:34, when Nebuchadnezzar gets his human knowledge back. Antiochus declares, "It is right to be subject to God" (2 Macc. 9:12 NRSV). This is comparable to Daniel 4:34, where Nebuchadnezzar praises the Most High, and also to Daniel 4:17, which tells us the purpose of this chapter: that all may know that God is ruler over all. Antiochus repents, makes Jerusalem free, decides to become a Jew, and issues a letter to the Jews; then he dies (2 Macc. 9:13–29).

Whether the story in chapter 4 was originally about Nabonidus or Nebuchadnezzar, and whether it is primarily about one of those Babylonian kings or Antiochus IV, it is clear that the kingship of God is the chapter's central theological theme. It is written **that the living may know that the Most High is sovereign over the kingdoms of men** (4:17; see also vv. 25, 32). Nebuchadnezzar may think that he rules the world autonomously (4:1), but he learns otherwise when God humbles him by taking away his humanity. To be human is to acknowledge that there is a God above us and to submit to his authority. When Nebuchadnezzar realizes this, he will be restored to his throne. God established the proper governance structure in the garden of Eden, allowing humans to rule the earth under him. Humans have dominion over the fish of the sea, the birds of the air, and over all the animals (Gen. 1:28), but they are responsible to the one who created them and placed them in the garden.

God is the heavenly king, but he also allows some humans to rule over other humans as earthly kings over the earthly domain. **He gives** the kingdoms of men **to anyone he wishes and sets over them the lowliest of men** (4:17). "The Most High is sovereign over the kingdoms of men and gives them to anyone he wishes" repeats in verse 25, except it does not include the last part about the lowliest of humans. This statement applies to Nebuchadnezzar, because he will be brought low, made to be the lowliest of all, a beast-man. But this verse also prepares the reader for Daniel 7, where the kingdom is given to the "people of the holy ones of the Most High" (7:27 NRSV; NIV "the saints, the people of the Most High"), who will rule forever. They are perhaps in view as the lowliest people because they were persecuted by the evil king, Antiochus IV. The author of the book of Daniel expects the holy ones (7:18, 22, 25, 27, that is, heavenly beings; NIV "saints") and the Jews to receive "the sovereignty, power and greatness of the kingdoms under the whole heaven" (7:27). What is prophesied in Daniel 7 is applied to Jesus in the NT: "The kingdom of the world has become the kingdom of our Lord and of his Christ, and he will reign for ever and ever" (Rev. 11:15). Jesus left the glory of heaven to take the form of the lowliest of human beings. Paul explains this in Philippians: "And being found in appearance as a man, he humbled himself and became obedient to death—even death on a cross! Therefore, God exalted him to the highest place and gave him the name that is above every name" (Phil. 2:8–9). When Jesus returns, he will fulfill the vision of Daniel 7 by coming in the clouds as the Son of Man and conquering king (Matt. 24:30; Rev. 1:7).

4:19–27 / At this point the story shifts from a first-person account to a third-person narrative. It shifts back to first person in verses 34–37 as Nebuchadnezzar concludes the chapter in his own voice. This may be evidence of editing, or it may be literary artifice. For the latter it may be said that Nebuchadnezzar could not relate the part about his becoming beastly, because he had lost his senses (implied by 4:34). But there are two problems with that explanation. First, Nebuchadnezzar might have retained some memory of what happened to him or been informed by others. After all, the narrator had to be so informed. So, the king could have continued in the first person. Secondly, the author shifts too soon. The part about the fulfillment does not occur until verses 28–33. Therefore, verses 19–27 could have continued in the first person. One thing is clear: verses 19–33 are essential to the story. That means that if the change of voice in the narrative indicates editing, it only means that an editor changed the voice, not that these verses are a later addition. Whatever the case, the literary effect of the change is to introduce a narrator and a narrative frame into the story. The change divides the king's testimony into "before" and "after" segments, with narration in between them (vv. 19–33). This narrative section can be subdivided into Daniel's interpretation (vv. 19–27) and the subsequent recounting of the fulfillment (vv. 28–33). The result is a literary inclusion that both highlights the king's first-person accounts on either end, and also is centered around the third-person narrative that features Daniel's interpretation and the story of the dream's fulfillment in the middle.

Daniel is **greatly perplexed** and **terrified** (4:19) by the dream. Earlier we are told that King Nebuchadnezzar is "afraid" and "terrified" by it (4:5; see also 2:1, 3; 5:6, 9). When Daniel has his own dreams, he is likewise distressed: "troubled in spirit" and "disturbed" (7:15); "terrified" (8:17); "exhausted" and "ill" (8:27); without "strength," with a "face" that was "deathly pale," and "helpless" (10:8). The appearance of Jesus elicits a similar response from John on the island of Patmos: "I fell at his feet as though dead" (Rev. 1:17). Then Jesus laid his hand on him and told him not to be afraid (Rev. 1:17). The reports of physiological and emotional reactions to dreams and visions underscore how unusual and other-worldly those experiences are. In them conflicting realities collide, leaving their recipients physically overwhelmed and emotionally drained.

Since the dream portends evil for the king, Daniel softens the blow and politely supports his master by wishing it on his foes: **"My lord, if** only the dream applied to your enemies and its meaning to your adversaries!" (4:19). Verses 20–21 repeat the dream in slightly different words from those in verses 9–12. Daniel adds his interpretation, identifying the king with the tree: "you, O king, are that tree!" (4:22). Daniel elaborates by drawing out the metaphor. Just as the tree was tall and far reaching, so is Nebuchadnezzar's kingdom. Daniel says, **"You have become great and strong; your greatness has grown until it reaches the sky, and your dominion extends to distant parts of the earth"** (4:22). This is similar to the passage in chapter 2 where Daniel describes Nebuchadnezzar's extensive kingdom and identifies the king with the statue: "The God of heaven has given you dominion and power and might and glory; in your hands he has placed mankind and the beasts of the field and the birds of the air. Wherever they live, he has made you ruler over them all. You are that head of gold." (2:37–38). Before, Nebuchadnezzar was a head symbolizing sovereignty and gold representing wealth; now, he is a luxuriant tree signifying strength and the vast extent of his domain. The difference is that the earlier dream is more positive, because the destruction does not come until several kingdoms after Babylonia. In the vision of chapter 4, though, judgment will fall on Nebuchadnezzar in his lifetime. It is interesting that both dreams highlight dominion over the animals. The quote from Daniel 2 spells out the king's rule over "the beasts of the field and the birds of the air" (2:38). In Daniel 4, he is a wealthy and powerful king, represented by a tree that overshadows everything; his abundance and largess provide shelter for the beasts of the field and nests for the birds of the air (4:12, 21). Similarly, God says through Jeremiah: "Now I will hand all your countries over to my servant Nebuchadnezzar king of Babylon; I will make even the wild animals subject to him" (Jer. 27:6). Nebuchadnezzar is a kind of new Adam, having been given dominion over the earth and the animals (Gen. 1:26, 28; 2:19).

The **interpretation is a decree** of the Most High (4:24). The word translated "decree" is the same word rendered "decision" in verse 17. "Decree" should be used in both places. Although verse 17 says that it is a decree of the watchers (NIV "messengers"), as opposed to verse 24, which attributes the decree to God, the two are not really in tension with one another. As mentioned earlier (see the commentary on 4:17), this is simply another example of the heavenly council motif found in many passages in the OT. God, the heavenly king, makes his decisions in concert with his privy council. Then one of the members of the council announces it to the humans (Dan. 4:17), or a prophet witnesses the proceedings of the heavenly council and then relays the message to the people (e.g., 1 Kgs. 22:19–23; Isa. 6).

Daniel applies the dream to the Babylonian king. He will **be driven away from people and will live with the wild animals** (4:25). That the king will **eat grass like cattle** (4:25) is not in the MT version of the dream (4:15), but it shows up here in the interpretation (and also in 4:32, 33). However, the verb "to eat" or "to be fed" should be added before "grass of the field" in verse 15, based on the statement here and in verse 32 (see the Additional Note for 4:15). This will continue for **seven times** (which probably indicates seven years) until Nebuchadnezzar realizes **that the Most High is sovereign over the kingdoms of men and gives them to anyone he wishes** (4:25). The **roots** are left as a promise of restoration once Nebuchadnezzar admits **that Heaven rules** (4:26). "Heaven" is used here as a substitute for "God." This is the first and only example of this in the OT (Porteous, *Daniel*, p. 71). However, this practice is found frequently in the Jewish literature of the Hellenistic and Roman eras and then also in the NT (e.g., Matthew's "kingdom of heaven" compared to Luke's "kingdom of God"). Perhaps this is evidence for the lateness of the book.

Then Daniel counsels the king, **"Renounce your sins by doing what is right"** (4:27). The word "renounce" literally means "tear away" or "break off" in Aramaic (4:24 MT). By tearing away from an enemy or a wild animal, one is finding redemption, so at times the word may mean "to redeem." Likewise, the cognate Hebrew word can range from literal "breaking off," as of a yoke (Gen. 27:40), to "redeem," as from enemies (Ps. 136:24). The king is perhaps being told to break off his sin by doing right (that is, to stop sinning), or maybe to get free from sin by doing right. The expression "doing what is right" can be an idiom for almsgiving or giving money to the poor, especially in late OT times (Ps. 37:21; Tob. 12:7–10; Sir. 3:29–4:10). Although it is possible that the writer has this in mind, we should probably interpret it more broadly as good deeds. Since the time of the Reformation some Protestants have gotten worked up over this verse because it seems to teach works righteousness. However, even the NT teaches the importance of good works. Jesus proclaims that our righteousness must exceed that of the scribes and Pharisees if we are to enter the kingdom of heaven (Matt. 5:20). He encourages acts of righteousness (Matt. 6:1), which he defines as almsgiving, as long as they are done in secret (Matt. 6:2–4). In fact, the Lord tells the rich man that with respect to righteousness, he lacks only one thing: he must sell all his possessions and give the money to the poor (Mark 10:21). In Acts, Dorcas (Acts 9:36) and Cornelius (Acts 10:2) are praised for their good works. At one point, Jesus indicates that the difference between those who go to eternal punishment and those who go to eternal life is whether they feed the hungry, give drink to the thirsty, welcome the stranger, clothe the naked, care for the sick, and visit the prisoners (Matt. 25:31–46). Even Paul, who preaches salvation by faith (Eph. 2:8–9), insists that we have been "created in Christ Jesus to do good works" (Eph. 2:10). Therefore, it is incumbent upon us to announce the forgiveness of sins through the death of Christ but also to encourage the followers of Jesus to be rich in good works (1 Tim. 6:18).

Nebuchadnezzar would not have been surprised to be told to break off his **wickedness by being kind to the oppressed** (4:27), because this was not only an Israelite value. Kings were expected to care for the poor and downtrodden. In the prologue to his famous law code from the early second millennium B.C., Hammurabi claims that the gods have charged him to "promote the welfare of the people, . . . to cause justice to prevail in the land, to destroy the wicked and the evil, that the strong might not oppress the weak" (*ANET*, p. 164). A number of passages in the OT communicate this expectation of kings as well. In one case, the gods who are the members of the heavenly council (Ps. 82:1) are commanded: "Defend the cause of the weak and fatherless; maintain the rights of the poor and oppressed. Rescue the weak and needy; deliver them from the hand of the wicked" (Ps. 82:3–4). Because they fail to do this, they fall under the judgment of *'elohim* (God), the head of the council; they will lose their divinity and die like men (Ps. 82:6). By extension, what is expected of gods ruling over various lands would also be expected of the kings ruling under them (see also Ps. 72:1–2; Isa. 11:3–4; Jer. 22:15–16).

There is some hope for Nebuchadnezzar that by avoiding sin and doing more good deeds, he might prolong his current condition and postpone the judgment spelled out in the dream. There is no promise, though; Daniel merely says, **"It may be that then your prosperity will continue"** (4:27). Could he have put it off indefinitely? Since heaven made a decree, it would seem that the king's fate is inevitable, although it may be delayed. Scripture is ambivalent about decrees of heaven, however. At times it seems that nothing can be done to avert a prediction. When King Jehoash strikes the ground halfheartedly, he fixes the outcome of a slight victory over the Arameans (2 Kgs. 13:18–19). It is too late to strike the ground more and alter the course of the future once the prophecy is proclaimed. Poor Saul's rejection is not rescinded, even though he confesses his sin, asks for forgiveness, and worships God in Samuel's presence (1 Sam. 15:24–31). On the other side, we recall the familiar story of Jonah and Nineveh. Jonah predicts the Assyrian capital's destruction in forty days (Jon. 3:4). He then complains bitterly when God relents and changes his mind in response to Nineveh's repentance (Jon. 4:1–3). In another case, God decides to destroy the people because they have made a golden calf, but he changes his mind through the intercession of Moses (Exod. 32:14). It is pointless to speculate about what would have happened to Nebuchadnezzar had he continued walking in righteousness. As the story unfolds, he indeed sows the seeds of pride and reaps the harvest of God's punishment.

4:28–33 / God's judgments may be delayed, but his word will not fail. **All** that was in the dream happens **to King Nebuchadnezzar** (4:28). There is a delay of **twelve months** before the decree is fulfilled, when Nebuchadnezzar is **walking on the roof of the royal palace of Babylon** (4:29). The word "roof" is not in the Aramaic, but most modern translations supply it. In an extrabiblical account, Nebuchadnezzar is walking on his roof when a divine spirit comes upon him and he has an ecstatic experience in which he utters a sort of prophecy. He predicts the coming of Cyrus, "a Persian mule," and expresses his wish that the invader would "be driven through the desert, where wild animals have their dwellings, and birds roam" (Eusebius, *Preparation for the Gospel* 9.41.6; Eusebius cites as his source Abydenus, who cites Megasthenes). Of course, Nebuchadnezzar's curse is not effective in preventing Cyrus from taking over Babylon, but it is interesting that Nebuchadnezzar's punishment of being driven out to dwell with the wild animals (according to Dan. 4) is what he wishes for Cyrus.

What set things in motion was the king's boast: **Is not this the great Babylon I have built as the royal residence, by my mighty power and for the glory of my majesty?** (4:30). Babylon was truly a magnificent city, one of the wonders of the ancient world. As Nebuchadnezzar stands on his palace and surveys the gates, temples, streets, houses, and renowned hanging gardens, his heart swells with pride, and he makes this statement. He fails to acknowledge the God above who gave him the power to rule. Deuteronomy warns the wealthy not to "become proud" and "forget the Lord"; not to take credit for their possessions (Deut. 8:10–18); "but remember the Lord your God, for it is he who gives you the ability to produce wealth" (Deut. 8:18). Jesus tells of a man who acquires great wealth and boasts that he will now "take life easy; eat, drink and be merry" (Luke 12:19; cf. Dan. 4:4, where Nebuchadnezzar is "contented and prosperous"). But it is not to be; heaven intervenes. "God said to him, 'You fool! This very night your life will be demanded from you. Then who will get what you have prepared for yourself?' This is how it will be with anyone who stores up things for himself but is not rich toward God" (Luke 12:20–21).

So it is with Nebuchadnezzar. God interrupts his moment of self-congratulation. **A voice** comes **from heaven, "This is what is decreed for** you, King Nebuchadnezzar: Your royal authority has been taken from you" (4:31). The "voice from heaven" is a common feature of Jewish writings. The rabbis taught that prophecy ceased after the last OT prophets—Haggai, Zechariah, and Malachi—died. Yet God would occasionally speak from heaven. (See the Additional Note on 4:31 for references.) In this case it is a voice of judgment. Verse 32 is a repeat of verse 25, telling how the king will be **driven away . . . and will live with the wild animals,** and **will eat grass like cattle.** Just as Adam and Eve are expelled from the garden for wanting to lift themselves up to God's level (Gen. 3:5), Nebuchadnezzar is exiled from his throne for his pride.

That God **gives** kingdoms **to anyone he wishes** (4:32; see also vv. 17, 25) is affirmed throughout the OT. In the cyclical pattern of the book of Judges, God raises up enemy rulers to oppress Israel when the people fall into sin. During the monarchy, God uses Assyria as the rod of punishment against Judah (Isa. 10:5), but then he destroys Assyria for becoming lifted up with pride (Isa. 10:12–19). He gives Judah into the hands of Nebuchadnezzar, king of Babylon (Dan. 1:1–2). He raises up the Medes against Babylon (Isa. 13:17–22) and anoints Cyrus to conquer Babylon so that the Jews might return to their land and rebuild the temple of Yahweh (Isa. 44:28–45:4).

Verse 33 tells of the fulfillment of the dream but adds two new details: **his hair grew like the feathers of an eagle and his nails like the claws of a bird** (4:33). As noted earlier in the chapter, his mind was to be changed from a human one to that of a beast (4:16). This verse reports that his body has been transformed too. His hair has become thick like a bird's; his fingers and toes have become talons. There is a parallel to this language in the ancient story of Ahiqar. He experiences a reversal of fortune as well. As the Assyrian king's vizier, he is wealthy and powerful, but when falsely accused, he is condemned to death. A servant saves him and hides him in a pit, where his hair becomes long like a wild animal's and "his nails like the claws of an eagle" (Ahiqar, 5:11, cited from Charles, *Apocrypha and Pseudepigrapha*, vol. 2, p. 754). Later, he was vindicated and, like Nebuchadnezzar, restored.

4:34–37 / In this last segment of the chapter, the narrative reverts back to the first person. Nebuchadnezzar testifies concerning his recovery and restoration. It begins when, **at the end of that time,** he raises his **eyes toward heaven** (4:34). The decree indicates that his punishment will be for a limited period: "seven times" or "years" (4:16, 23, 25, 32), seven being the number of perfection or completion. However, the decree also says that he will remain in his beastly state until he acknowledges "that the Most High is sovereign over the kingdoms of men and gives them to anyone he wishes" (4:25, 32). Does his restoration occur because the time is up or because he acknowledges God's rule? Clearly both of these are significant to the writer. God determines the time, but human actions are important as well. Just as Nebuchadnezzar set in motion his downfall by his boast (4:30), so now he initiates his recovery by his turning toward God. By lifting his eyes to heaven, he is acknowledging the authority of God. This is one difference between humans and the animals: we are aware of God. This leads to the return of human reason, another distinctive feature that separates us from the beasts. Nebuchadnezzar states, "**my sanity was restored**" (4:34). The text more literally says, "my knowledge returned to me," or "my reason returned to me" (NRSV). These are better translations, because the story seems to be about a metamorphosis from human to beast and back again rather than temporary insanity. What commences with a symbolic gesture, lifting the eyes, leads to restoration of human reason, knowledge, or intelligence, which in turn leads to worship (4:34). Nebuchadnezzar finishes as he began (4:1–3), with praise. And the apocalyptist returns to dominant themes: God is sovereign (4:17, 25, 32, 34, 36) and his kingdom is eternal (2:44; 6:26; 7:27).

Of course, God's rule is not limited to human kings. **He does as he pleases with the powers of heaven** (4:35). This does not mean that God is capricious in his dealings with angels, for God's deeds are just and consistent with his nature. Rather, it affirms that the Most High exercises control over heavenly rulers as well as earthly ones like Nebuchadnezzar. According to the book of Daniel, there are spirits in the high places who govern kingdoms (Dan. 10:13, 20–21). Paul agrees, speaking of a hierarchy of evil rulers, authorities, and powers above (Eph. 6:12). In the last judgment God will "punish the powers in the heavens above and the kings on the earth below" (Isa. 24:21). **No one can hold back his hand or say to him: "What have you done?"** (Dan. 4:35). God may question us, but we must be careful how we address him. There is a fine line sometimes between the lament psalms and murmuring in the wilderness. Lamenting is not only allowed but encouraged, while murmuring is not. The believer who is suffering may complain bitterly to God (e.g., Ps. 22), but he or she must come meekly, as a supplicant. It is possible to complain in a faithless way (Exod. 16:7–8; Num. 14:27, 36; 16:11; 17:5); those who did so were condemned to die without entering the promised land. Humans must never think they can stand over God in judgment or put him on the witness stand to cross-examine him. When Job crossed over the line while contending with heaven, God turned the tables on him by firing at Job a withering stream of questions about creation, which he could not answer (Job 38:2–39:30; 40:7–41:34). This humbled Job and taught him not to question God in an arrogant or accusing way.

In Daniel 4, verses 36–37 repeat the thoughts of verses 34–35. Nebuchadnezzar gets his knowledge or reason back (vv. 34 and 36), and then he praises God (vv. 34–35 and 37). The NIV obscures this by translating, **At the same time that my sanity was restored, my honor and splendor were returned to me for the glory of my kingdom** (4:36). This rendering smooths things over to make verse 35 appear to resume the thought of verse 34 in order to develop it. The NRSV reading is superior: "At that time my reason returned to me." This means when the seven years were finished, or at the time when he turned his gaze heavenward. In other words, these verses form a doublet; two different versions of the conclusion of the story are preserved here.

Verse 34 (NRSV)	Verses 36–37 (NRSV)
my reason returned to me	my reason returned to me
I blessed the Most High, and praised	Now I, Nebuchadnezzar, praise and extol
and honored the one who lives forever	and honor the King of heaven

The two endings are not exactly alike, for the second one adds the information regarding the return to the throne, which is not contained in the first.

Once again we see that the God of the Jews is greater than the gods of Babylon. He is identified as the Most High (4:2, 17, 24, 25, 32, 34) and the king of heaven (4:37). He is the one who can interpret dreams, and he is the one who humbles Nebuchadnezzar. Overweening pride will be punished, for God does not allow hubris: **those who walk in pride he is able to humble** (4:37). God gives sovereignty "to anyone he wishes" (4:17, 25, 32), which means that he even allows pagans like Nebuchadnezzar to rule over the Jews, at least until the end (2:44–45; 7:26–27). In fact, after his ordeal, the Babylonian king becomes **even greater than before** (4:36). Apparently, foreigners do not necessarily need to convert to Judaism, but they should acknowledge the Most High God (4:17, 25, 32) and do righteous deeds (4:27).

Additional Notes §4

4:1–3 / These verses (or variants of them) are found at the end of chapter 4 in the LXX. The MT order is probably more original. It is more likely that a scribe would move them from the beginning to the end, than that he would move them from the end to the beginning, because he would be trying to make ch. 4 conform to chs. 3 and 6, both of which conclude with doxologies. Furthermore, moving it to the end breaks up the double *inclusio* framing ch. 4 and also framing chs. 4–6: both envelope constructions begin and end with praise. Finally, and most important, the king declares that he is about to tell what God has done (4:34 LXX). This clearly shows that it is an introduction rather than a conclusion. It should be at the head of the chapter, and the dream account should follow (Montgomery, *Daniel*, p. 248).

4:2 / See also 4:17, 24, 25, 32, 34. The Aramaic for **Most High God** is the equivalent of *'el 'elyon* in Hebrew. (See the Additional Note for 3:26.)

The terms **signs and wonders** occur a number of times in the Bible: e.g., Exod. 7:3; Deut. 4:34; 6:22; Neh. 9:10; Ps. 135:9; Jer. 32:20; Dan. 6:27; Mark 13:22; John 4:48; Acts 4:30; 5:12; Rom. 15:19; 2 Cor. 12:12; Heb. 2:4. In most cases in the OT they refer to the exodus.

4:4 / The Hebrew term for **prosperous** describes trees that are "luxuriant" or "flourishing" (Deut. 12:2; Hos. 14:8), or thriving humans who are compared to such trees (e.g., Pss. 37:35; 52:8 [52:10 MT]; 92:12–14 [92:13–15 MT]; Jer. 11:16). Perhaps this term was chosen deliberately because Nebuchadnezzar is likened to a huge, fruitful tree in his dream (Collins, *Daniel*, p. 222).

4:7 / The list of sages here—**magicians, enchanters, astrologers and diviners**—is similar to the one in 2:2, except that "sorcerers" appears there instead of "diviners." However, the word "diviners" is found in the list in 2:27. "Diviners" comes from the root *gzr*. This word in the singular is also used for the Jew who helped King Nabonidus find healing, in the Qumran text *Prayer of Nabonidus* (4QPrNab).

4:8 / The Aramaic for **the spirit of the holy gods** is *ruakh 'elahin qaddishin* (4:5 MT). Most modern versions translate "holy gods," in the plural. However, many commentators allow that it could be singular, "holy God." The most common term for "God" in Hebrew is the plural form *'elohim*, yet it is understood as singular in meaning when referring (as most of the time it does) to the God of Israel. In fact, the equivalent Hebrew expression, *'elohim qedoshim*, "holy God," occurs in Josh. 24:19.

The same ambiguity as in Daniel occurs when another pagan king, the Egyptian pharaoh, says Joseph is "one in whom is the spirit of God," or, as the NIV footnote says, "of the gods" (*'ish 'asher ruakh 'elohim bo*; Gen. 41:38). Here in Dan. 4, the NIV committee decided to use the plural with no marginal reading. In fact, however, what is true for the Hebrew of Genesis is true for the Aramaic of Daniel: either reading is possible. What is interesting is that in both passages it is a pagan who is speaking. Pharaoh may have intended "the spirit of the gods," because he was a polytheist, but the Israelites would have understood Joseph to be endowed with the "spirit of God." Likewise, Nebuchadnezzar's theology would have been expressed as "spirit of the holy gods," while the Jewish audience reading this book would have understood "the spirit of the holy God" to be influencing Daniel (the phrase also occurs in Dan. 5:11, 14).

4:9 / In the clause **here is my dream,** the MT (4:6) has *khezwe*, "visions" ("visions of my dream"), but it makes more sense here to read *khazi*, "see," "lo," "behold," "here" (Montgomery, *Daniel*, p. 226). Perhaps the *khezwe* migrated here from the next verse (4:10 [4:7 MT]), where it truly belongs. The word occurs with the meaning "take thought of" (Collins, *Daniel*, p. 223). The NRSV reads, "Hear the dream," following the Greek version of Theodotion, which adds *akouson*, "Hear."

4:10 / For further reading on the cosmic-**tree** motif see G. Widengren, *The King and the Tree of Life in Ancient Near Eastern Religion* (Uppsala: Lundequist, 1951); S. Parpola, "The Assyrian Tree of Life: Tracing the Origins of Jewish Monotheism and Greek Philosophy," *JNES* 52 (1993), pp. 161–208; B. N. Porter, *Trees, Kings, and Politics: Studies in Assyrian Iconography* (Fribourg: Academic Press, 2003).

4:15 / According to the MT (v. 12), the phrase **in the grass of the field** goes with what precedes: the roots of the former tree will "remain . . . in the grass of the field." However, it is possible that "the grass of the field" is missing a verb. When we compare this to 4:25, 32–33 and 5:21, we notice that grass is used differently. In those verses, it says the king eats "grass like cattle." For this reason, it may be that the verb "to eat" or "to be fed" was lost from 4:15. The LXX supports adding it back in here (Montgomery, *Daniel*, pp. 233, 235; Collins, *Daniel*, pp. 209–210, 227). On the other side, 4:15 is repeated in 4:23. Since 4:23 also does not have the verb "eat" or "to be fed," it supports leaving the MT (Goldingay, *Daniel*, p. 80 n. 12c). The response to that is that 4:23 may be a secondary exact repetition of 4:15 (Montgomery, *Daniel*, p. 235). If we add "to be fed" in 4:15, we should also add it to 4:23, as Collins does.

4:16 / Many scholars believe that the account in Daniel 4 developed from a tradition about Nabonidus rather than Nebuchadnezzar. There are a number of reasons for this. Both accounts concern a Babylonian king whose name begins with the god's name, "Nabu." Both are told in the first person. In both cases the affliction is caused by God and lasts seven years, although the afflictions are quite different: Nebuchadnezzar becomes beast-like while Nabonidus endures a severe skin ailment. Both use the term *ptgm*: in Daniel, it is the "decree" (NIV: "decision") of the Most High that the watchers proclaim (Dan. 4:17); in the Qumran text, it is the "decree" of God to afflict Nabonidus. Both texts place the king away from court: in the Bible Nebuchadnezzar is driven out into the wild; in the Qumran passage Nabonidus is in Teima, an oasis in the Arabian desert. Both use the term *gzr*, "diviner," although in Daniel it is used of those who could not interpret the dream (Dan. 4:7); in the *Prayer of Nabonidus* it is used of the Jewish healer. In both stories an exiled Jewish person is a miracle worker: Daniel who can interpret dreams; the unnamed diviner (*gzr*) in the Qumran text. Both have the motif of sin: Daniel tells Nebuchadnezzar to cease sinning and to act righteously (Dan. 4:27); in 4QPrNab, Nabonidus testifies that God forgave his sins (in the LXX, Dan. 4:30a has "I prayed concerning my sins in front of the Lord, the God of heaven"). Nebuchadnezzar inscribes a document to publish his testimony and to praise God (4:1–3, 34–37); Nabonidus was instructed by the Jewish diviner to record his story and to glorify God. Finally, both texts tell of a polytheistic king who learns something of the Jewish God.

Further support for the notion that chapter 4 was originally about Nabonidus comes from other texts and from other places in Daniel. We know nothing from Babylonian records of a seven year hiatus in Nebuchadnezzar's reign. However, records exist corroborating that Nabonidus was away from Babylon for ten years (*ANET*, pp. 305–6). During that time he left his son, Belshazzar, in command as vice-regent, who figures prominently in Daniel 5. Because he was away and because he neglected some of the gods and religious ceremonies of Babylon, he was hated by the priests and considered to be crazy (*ANET*, pp. 312–15). One of the historical difficulties in Daniel is its identifying Belshazzar as the son of Nebuchadnezzar (5:2, 11, 13, 18). However, if this story was originally about Nabonidus, then the historical problem vanishes. Daniel 5:18–21 records that Daniel reminds Belshazzar of what happened to his father, Nebuchadnezzar. But if we substitute Nabonidus for Nebuchadnezzar, all the details fit more closely, plus Nabonidus truly was the father of Belshazzar (Barr, 595). Also, the stories would represent the historical progression better: Nebuchadnezzar (chs. 1–3); Nabonidus (ch. 4); Belshazzar (ch. 5) (Cross, *Ancient Library of Qumran*, p. 167). How did the protagonist of the story get changed from Nabonidus to Nebuchadnezzar? There are a number of differences between the Qumran account and Daniel 4. If a common tradition stands behind Daniel 4 and the Qumran manuscript, it is hard to account for those differences. As stories are told and retold, variations develop, so it is possible that the changes were not conscious or intentional. However, it may be that Nebuchadnezzar was substituted for Nabonidus because he was better known. Nebuchadnezzar is mentioned elsewhere in the Bible (for example, in Neh. 7:6, plus numerous times in Kings, Chronicles, Ezra, Jeremiah, and Ezekiel), while Nabonidus is not.

Perhaps the best parallel, but in reverse, of Nebuchadnezzar being **given the mind of an animal** is the story of Enkidu in the Old Babylonian Epic of Gilgamesh. He is a wild man whose body is covered with hair. He eats grass with the gazelles, runs with wild animals, and drinks with them at their watering places. But a woman tames him, changing him into a human. This not only causes the animals to avoid him but causes physical changes in his body. He can no longer keep up with the animals, because his muscles become different. In Gilgamesh, a beast-man becomes human; in Dan. 4, a human king becomes a beast-man (though temporarily—he is later restored to his original state). See P. W. Coxon, "Another Look at Nebuchadnezzar's Madness," in *The Book of Daniel in the Light of New Findings* (ed. A. S. Van der Woude; Leuven: Leuven University Press, 1993), pp. 218–19.

4:17 / The theme of **the lowliest of men** being exalted and the proud being abased occurs frequently in the Bible: 1 Sam. 2:7–8; Job 5:11; Ps. 113:7–8;

Ezek. 17:24; Luke 1:51–53; 1 Cor. 1:26–31; 1 Pet. 5:6; also the theme of the proud being abased: Lev. 26:19; Deut. 8:2–3; Job 40:11; Ps. 18:27; Prov. 3:34; Isa. 2:11–17; Jer. 49:16; Ezek. 7:24; Dan. 4:37; Matt. 23:12; Luke 14:11; James 1:9–10.

4:23 / It may be that much of v. 23 is secondary (everything after **destroy it**). It repeats v. 15 almost verbatim, whereas in vv. 25–26 only portions of the earlier verses are repeated as part of the interpretation (Montgomery, *Daniel*, p. 241). But this would not be sufficient grounds for questioning this verse. The author may choose to quote a previous section and then interpret it. There is a parallel for that in the commentary on Habakkuk from Qumran (1QpHab 1–5; 7.3; 8.14–9.7; cited in Collins, *Daniel*, p. 229 n. 116). More important evidence for questioning this verse is that parts of it are missing from the LXX. On the other hand, there are many differences between the Greek and Aramaic texts, and it is not always possible to reconstruct the Aramaic text with confidence from the Greek. Since this is so, my inclination is to leave v. 23. Perhaps the author intended to begin with a longer quote and then continue with smaller, selective quotes or allusions.

4:25 / The element **you will eat grass like cattle** is not in the dream (4:15). Some would add in a verb for eating or being fed to v. 15 from vv. 25 and 32 (see the Additional Note on 4:15).

4:27 / The NIV supplies the word **renounce** for the Aramaic word *peraq* [4:24 MT], which means "to tear away" or "break off." As mentioned above in the commentary, if it denotes tearing away from something threatening or harmful, it might carry the extended meaning "to redeem" (cf. Zech. 11:16; Exod. 32:2); Lam. 5:8). The LXX translates *peraq* with *lytrōsai*, "redeem," in Dan. 4:27, but the notion of "redeeming sin" is obscure. People can be redeemed from sin, but how do they redeem sin? Some commentators (and the NRSV) move from "redeem" to "atone," but it is a questionable translation for the Aramaic word. It is preferable, therefore, to render the text more literally here: "Break off your sins with righteousness" (Driver, *Daniel*, p. 54).

4:31 / In Jewish writings there are many references to the *bat qol*, or **voice . . . from heaven** (lit. "daughter of a voice"). In the NT, Jesus hears a heavenly voice at his baptism, saying, "This is my Son, whom I love; with him I am well pleased" (Matt. 3:17; see also Luke 3:22). Another occasion is on the mount of transfiguration; God says, "This is my Son, whom I love; with him I am well pleased. Listen to him!" (Matt. 17:5). John records an instance after the triumphal entry when Jesus prays that the Father will glorify his name. God responds, "I have glorified it, and will glorify it again" (John 12:28). A voice also instructs Peter to eat things formerly considered unclean: "Do not call anything impure that God has made clean" (Acts 11:9). There are a number of examples in Revelation as well (e.g., Rev. 10:4, 8; 11:12; 14:13). For extrabiblical occurrences, see Collins, *Daniel*, pp. 230–31; O. Betz, "*phōnē*," *TDNT* 9:288–90, 298–99.

§5 The Writing on the Wall (Dan. 5:1–31)

We have seen evidence that the earlier chapters were independent traditions. For example, in chapter 1 the four Jews proved to be wiser than all the other sages, yet they are not asked to interpret the dream in chapter 2; Daniel is prominent in chapter 2 but missing from chapter 3. The author does not do a lot to provide smooth transitions between the different episodes, but there is some continuity in that the first four chapters feature King Nebuchadnezzar. The chasm between chapers 4 and 5 is greater than those between the other chapters because the text all of a sudden begins describing King Belshazzar's banquet without any background information or introduction. For example, the narrator does not record Nebuchadnezzar's death or supply any chronology for the period following his reign. So, even within the conceptual framework of the book, the movement is sudden. However, when we consider Babylonian history, it appears still more abrupt, for there were several kings and twenty-three years between the death of Nebuchadnezzar and the time of this account. Nevertheless, connections exist between this chapter and the previous ones.

Chapter 5 follows from chapter 4 because Belshazzar is portrayed as the son of Nebuchadnezzar, who is the king in that chapter (at least as it has come down to us—the story in chapter 4 probably originated with a tradition about Nabonidus, the actual father of Belshazzar; see the commentary on Dan. 4 and particularly the Additional Note on 4:16). The two chapters are also linked together because Daniel actually gives a summary of chapter 4 in Daniel 5:18–21. Chapter 5 is tied to chapters 2 and 4, because these all have revelations that need to be interpreted (dreams in chs. 2 and 4, and an inscription in ch. 5). Moreover, in all three cases, the wise men fail but Daniel succeeds. Daniel 5 is also joined to chapter 1: in chapter 5 the temple vessels figure prominently, while chapter 1 has set the stage for this story by mentioning that King Nebuchadnezzar brought the temple vessels to Babylon (1:2).

5:1–7 / The first verse of chapter 5 presents us with another historical problem in the book of Daniel by using the label **King Belshazzar**.

We have no evidence outside the Bible that he was crowned king (see also 7:1 and 8:1); on the contrary, the evidence goes against it. We know of Belshazzar independently from Akkadian texts. He was the son of King Nabonidus and called the "crown prince" (*ANET*, pp. 306, 310 n. 5). He was vice-regent and entrusted with some royal authority while his father was away in Teima (*ANET*, p. 313). However, he is never given the title "king" in Babylonian texts. Furthermore, it is apparent that he could not fulfill all the royal duties in the absence of Nabonidus. Only the king could perform certain rituals of the important Akitu Festival, or New Year celebration. While King Nabonidus was away, the Akitu Festival was not held (*ANET*, p. 306). Finally, King Nabonidus returned before Babylon's fall, so that whatever powers Belshazzar assumed earlier, while his father was gone, were no longer his at the time when Babylon was conquered, which is the setting for this chapter (Dan. 5:30). It seems, therefore, that this is a somewhat fictionalized account told for theological purposes.

Belshazzar gives **a great banquet for a thousand of his nobles and drinks wine with them** (5:1). The biblical text does not give the reason for the banquet, although the extrabiblical sources record a festival that took place the night Cyrus conquered Babylon (see the Additional Note on 5:1). At the banquet, Belshazzar gives a command **while he is drinking his wine** (5:2). More literally, the Aramaic says, "in the taste of the wine," meaning "when he had tasted the wine." This is often understood to mean "under the influence of the wine" (so NRSV). In other words, the alcohol has the effect of lowering the king's inhibitions, resulting in his act of indiscretion. He orders his servants **to bring in the gold and silver goblets that Nebuchadnezzar** took **from the temple in Jerusalem** (5:2). This sacrilege of calling for and drinking from the temple vessels, which is made an even greater desecration by including **concubines** (5:2) in the group, leads to the judgment against him later in the chapter. This verse links chapter 5 with chapter 1, which mentions that Nebuchadnezzar took "articles from the temple of God," which he "carried off to the temple of his god in Babylonia and put in the treasure house of his god" (1:2).

As already noted above, though Nabonidus was actually Belshazzar's father, here the text says that Nebuchadnezzar was **his father** (5:2), which presents a historical problem. To solve this, some interpreters have understood "father" to mean "ancestor." However, it is unlikely that Belshazzar was a descendant of Nebuchadnezzar either. Nabonidus was a usurper and therefore not in the line of Nebuchadnezzar. While it is possible that Belshazzar was related to Nebuchadnezzar through his mother or grandmother (Baldwin, *Daniel*, p. 23), or even through his wife (Driver, *Daniel*, p. 62), this is mere conjecture. Because this is tenuous, others suggest the meaning "predecessor" (the NIV footnote has both "ancestor" and "predecessor" as possibilities). But this is stretching the term "father" too much, because a predecessor is normally not just a previous king, but a previous king in the same dynasty or royal lineage.

However, when we look within Daniel 5 itself, there seems to be too much emphasis on the father-son relationship for it to be talking about a distant relative or previous unrelated king. The point later in the chapter is that this experience of being turned into a beast-man happened to Belshazzar's father, so he should have learned from that to humble himself. If, as has been suggested, the story in chapter 4 was really about Nabonidus rather than Nebuchadnezzar, then it makes more sense, for Belshazzar really was the son of Nabonidus. The name may have been changed to "Nebuchadnezzar" by accident, or perhaps it was changed intentionally, maybe because Nebuchadnezzar was well known, or because he destroyed the temple and brought to Babylon the temple vessels, which are featured so prominently in this chapter.

Belshazzar, **his nobles, his wives and his concubines** (5:3) dare to drink from the holy temple vessels. They are guilty not only of this sacrilege but of idolatry as well. They praise **the gods of gold and silver, of bronze, iron, wood and stone** (5:4). We are reminded of the *Prayer of Nabonidus*: "For seven years I continued praying [to] the gods made of silver and gold, [bronze, iron,] wood, stone, and clay, for I [used to th]ink that th[ey] really were gods" (4Q242; Wise et al., trans., *Dead Sea Scrolls: Revised Edition*, p. 342 [frags. 1–3, lines 11–13]).

It is intriguing that in Daniel, Nebuchadnezzar is not judged for destroying the temple and stealing the vessels, but Belshazzar is harshly condemned for drinking from them. Perhaps this is because the books of Kings and Jeremiah preach that the destruction of the temple was a judgment of God on the people of Judah for their sins. Also, Belshazzar may be intended as a cipher for Antiochus IV, if Daniel was written in the second century. The Seleucid king arrogantly entered the sanctuary and took the gold altar, lampstand, and various cups and vessels (1 Macc. 1:21–24). He also practiced idolatry and allowed sex acts with prostitutes in the temple (2 Macc. 6:1–5). The inclusion of the concubines in Daniel 5:2–3 may be an allusion to this.

The king's offenses precipitate a divine reaction: **Suddenly the fingers of a human hand appeared and wrote on the plaster of the wall** (5:5). Although the text does not say it is the hand of God, the fingers and hand are clearly supernatural, as it later plainly states what is obvious here: God "sent the hand that wrote the inscription" (5:24). This is reminiscent of the tablets of the covenant, which were "inscribed by the finger of God" (Exod. 31:18; Deut. 9:10). In the story of the exodus, the Egyptian magicians admit defeat, acknowledging that the gnat plague was "the finger of God" (Exod. 8:19). In that passage, God does not write, but he shows his power. Similarly, Jesus manifests divine power, casting out demons "by the finger of God" (Luke 11:20). Scripture also frequently uses the expressions "hand of the LORD" (e.g., Ezra 7:6; Isa. 41:20; Ezek. 40:1) and "hand of God" (2 Chron. 30:12; Eccl. 2:24; see also Eccl. 9:1).

So that the writing will be easier to read, it is placed on a plastered, or plain, unadorned section of the wall. So that it will be illuminated, it is placed **near the lampstand** (5:5). The king is overwhelmed with fear: **his face** turns **pale, his knees** knock **together,** and **his legs give way** (5:6). Panic is a common reaction to God's manifestations in Daniel. Nebuchadnezzar is frightened by his visions (2:1–2; 4:5). Similarly, Daniel is often alarmed or weakened in response to God's revelations (4:19; 7:28; 8:17, 27; 10:7–8). The king's terror sets the stage for yet another contest between Daniel and the wise men of Babylon (as in chapters 2 and 4).

The king calls **out for the enchanters, astrologers and diviners to be brought.** He then promises them great rewards. The one who can read the inscription and interpret it **will** first of all **be clothed in purple** (5:7). Purple was a sign of royalty or nobility in the ancient world; during the reigns of some Seleucid kings it indicated royal favor (1 Macc. 10:20, 62, 64; 15:43–44). Secondly, anyone who can read and interpret the message will **have a gold chain placed around his neck** (Dan. 5:7). This is reminiscent of Genesis, where Pharaoh clothes Joseph in fine linen robes and puts "a gold chain around his neck" (Gen. 41:42). Finally, **he will be made the third highest ruler in the kingdom** (Dan. 5:7). Joseph was rewarded by being promoted to a position second only to Pharaoh (Gen. 41:40–43). Similarly, this verse is usually understood to indicate that Daniel would be third in command, perhaps after Nabonidus and Belshazzar. However, it is possible that the term "third" is not to be taken literally but is merely a title for an officer (see the Additional Note on 5:7). Earlier, Daniel is made "ruler over the province of Babylon," with authority over "all its wise men" (Dan. 2:48; cf. 5:11). Later, Daniel is said to be one of three administrators over the 120 satraps (Dan. 6:2).

5:8–16 / Verse 8 seems to be an alternate tradition telling of the entrance of the **king's wise men,** because in verse 7 the king already addresses them and promises them rewards. Yet in verse 8 they apparently enter again. It is not clear why **they could not read the writing or tell the king what it meant** (5:8). The text does not say what language it was written in. Some have suggested that it was in some secret script that no one could read without special revelation from God, but then it is not clear how the king would be able to verify if an interpreter was telling the truth. Perhaps it was in Akkadian but written with unusual cuneiform signs (Goldingay, *Daniel*, p. 109). Alternatively, it could have been in Aramaic, written without vowels, which seems most likely. As such, it was cryptic, because the words could be vocalized or read several ways. Therefore, when it says the wise men could not read it, it does not mean that they could not recognize the letters; rather, they were unsure how to pronounce it. Without first reading it correctly, they had no hope of interpreting it.

The failure of his counselors increased the king's consternation. **King Belshazzar became even more terrified and his face grew more pale; also, his nobles were baffled** (5:9). Apparently the king and the nobles had forgotten about Daniel, because it does not occur to them to call for him. This is curious, for he had been successful previously in these types of situations and had been honored and promoted often enough because of his skill in interpreting dreams. It is especially surprising since the story gives the impression that the events of chapter 4 were fairly recent, having taken place in the time of Belshazzar's father. The text does not explain how God's servant passed out of mind at court, but it does tell us that **the queen** remembers. She **came into the banquet hall** (5:10) to inform the king. Since the king's "wives and concubines" were already present at the feast (vv. 2–3), "queen" here probably refers to the queen mother (see NIV footnote), Nebuchadnezzar's wife, because the writer understood Belshazzar to be Nebuchadnezzar's son. Nitocris, Nebuchadnezzar's second wife, was praised for her wisdom (Herodotus, *Hist*. 1.185; Collins, *Daniel*, p. 248 n. 66).

The queen at length tells of a man of remarkable qualities. He has the **spirit of the holy gods** and possesses their **insight and intelligence and wisdom** (5:11; see 2:48; 4:9). Most important is his ability **to interpret dreams, explain riddles and solve difficult problems** (5:12). She entreats the king to summon Daniel (5:12), and the king does so (5:13). He asks whether Daniel is **one of the exiles** (5:13; see 2:25), something the queen did not mention. Then the king repeats to Daniel the queen's praise of his amazing gifts (5:14; cf. v. 11). Next the king tells of the failed attempt of his advisers to **read** and **explain it** (5:15; cf. vv. 7–8) and reiterates the queen's high opinion of his interpretation skills (5:16). The king concludes by reviewing the proffered rewards: **purple** clothing, a **gold chain,** and promotion to **third highest ruler,** or perhaps appointment to high office (5:16; see the commentary and Additional Note on 5:7). He omits the queen's mention of Daniel's promotion to chief sage (5:11; 2:48; 4:9).

5:17–29 / Daniel is not interested in rewards. He says boldly, almost rudely, to the king, **"You may keep your gifts for yourself and give your rewards to someone else"** (5:17); Daniel had been more polite to King Nebuchadnezzar (4:19, 27). Verse 17 is in tension with verse 29, where Daniel accepts the gifts after all. However, the purpose of verse 17 is to show that Daniel is not venal like the prophets in Micah's day (Mic. 3:5). There was a tradition that prophets should not profit from the supernatural gifts they exhibit. Elisha refused payment for the healing of Naaman, but when his servant, Gehazi, sought and received silver and clothes, Gehazi was struck with leprosy (2 Kgs. 5:21–27). Even though he is not interested in wealth and power, Daniel is quite willing to **read the writing for the king and tell him what it means** (5:17).

Verses 17–23 recapitulate the story in chapter 4 of Nebuchadnezzar's transformation into a beast-man and his restoration. These verses are not in the LXX. This may be because they are not original; perhaps a redactor added in the comparison between Nebuchadnezzar and Belshazzar in order to show two different methods God employs on pagan kings (Collins, *Daniel*, p. 249). On the other hand, it is possible that the Greek translator left this part out because it repeats the story from chapter 4 (Montgomery, *Daniel*, p. 267). I think the latter is more likely.

The NIV leaves out the first word of verse 18: "you." The NIV has **O king, the Most High God . . .** The Aramaic actually reads, "You, O king . . ." This is significant because the Aramaic emphasizes the accusatory tone (the NIV sounds more conciliatory) and also because the thought is completed in verse 22 below. The address "You, O king" (5:18) is resumed with "But you his son, O Belshazzar" (5:22). In between is sandwiched the story of Nebuchadnezzar from the chapter before. The idea and development are as follows: As for *you*, O king, God gave your father sovereignty, but he became lifted up with pride. God had to humble him by turning him into a beast-man until he learned that "the Most High God is sovereign." But *you* did not learn from all this! (5:18–22).

Daniel recounts the story of Nebuchadnezzar from chapter 4 as a way of rebuking Belshazzar. He is holding up a portrait of the father to the son and saying, "Why can you not be more like your father?" Or, "Why did you not learn from your father?" One is reminded of Jeremiah, who reproved Jehoiakim for not being more like his father, Josiah, who did "justice and righteousness" (Jer. 22:13–19). One of the main tasks of the prophet was to rebuke kings for their sins. Samuel pronounced judgment on Saul for offering an illicit sacrifice (1 Sam. 13:8–14) and for failing to devote everything to destruction in his battle with the Amalekites (1 Sam. 15:1–23). Nathan criticized David for his sin with Bathsheba (1 Sam. 12).

Elijah condemned Ahab and Jezebel for the multitude of their abominations (1 Kgs. 21:20–26). Daniel is portrayed as an Israelite prophet here, except that he is facing a foreign king instead of one from his own people. Daniel 5 shows that God takes sin seriously, that he holds leaders accountable, and that he brings judgment on those who break his commands.

God gave Nebuchadnezzar **sovereignty** (5:18). An interesting parallel to this can be found in Jeremiah: God gave all nations and the animals into the hand of his servant Nebuchadnezzar (Jer. 27:5–7). Regarding human kingdoms, Daniel says that God **sets over them anyone he wishes** (Dan. 5:21). This also echoes something God said through Jeremiah about dominion: "I give it to anyone I please" (Jer. 27:5). Nebuchadnezzar was empowered **to put to death** and **to spare; to promote** and **to humble** (Dan. 5:19). Of course, it is God who ultimately has power to "put to death" and "bring to life" (Deut. 32:39; 1 Sam. 2:6–7), to bring one down and exalt another (Ps. 75:7), but he delegates that to earthly kings, who are divinely appointed to wield the sword in order to establish justice (Rom. 13:1–5). Yet, mortal kings must acknowledge that there is an authority over them as well, namely, the heavenly king. They need to know that **the Most High God is sovereign over the kingdoms of men** (Dan. 5:21). Nebuchadnezzar had to learn that the hard way, for when **his heart became arrogant and hardened with pride,** he lost his throne for a time (5:20). **He was driven away from people and given the mind of an animal,** being forced to live **with the wild donkeys** and eat **grass like cattle** out in the field **until he acknowledged** the rule of God (5:21).

But Belshazzar did not learn from his "father's" example. Daniel catalogs Belshazzar's sins:

1. he did not humble himself (5:22) but **set** himself **up against the Lord of heaven;**
2. he had **the goblets from** Yahweh's **temple brought to** him, and he and his **nobles,** his **wives,** and his **concubines drank wine from them;**
3. he **praised the gods of silver and gold, of bronze, iron, wood and stone;** and finally,
4. he **did not honor** the one true **God** (5:23).

By lifting himself "up against the Lord of heaven," Belshazzar reminds us of Isaiah's taunt song against the king of Babylon: "You said in your heart, 'I will ascend to heaven; I will raise my throne above the stars of God. . . . I will make myself like the Most High.' But you are brought down to the grave" (Isa. 14:13–15). He also anticipates the evil king Antiochus IV, "the little horn" who "grew as high as the host of heaven"

(Dan. 8:9–11) and who "shall exalt himself and consider himself greater than any god" (Dan. 11:36). Though the representation of Belshazzar is perhaps not quite so dark as the one in Isaiah 14 or the ones in Daniel 8 and 11, he is similar to the evil kings in those passages in incurring God's wrath for his overweening pride.

Belshazzar's offenses against heaven triggered heaven's response. God **sent the hand that wrote the inscription** (5:24). In previous times God appointed prophets to announce his word of condemnation on the kings of Israel and Judah. For example, God sent Micaiah to predict the death of King Ahab in battle (1 Kgs. 22:17–28) and Jeremiah to announce an ignominious death for King Jehoiakim (Jer. 22:18–19). Here he sends a hand to inscribe doom for Belshazzar.

According to the MT, the hand wrote the following inscription: **MENE, MENE, TEKEL, PARSIN** (5:25). The terms can be understood on several levels: first, as nouns referring to weights, which is the way the Aramaic words are pointed; secondly, as verbs, as in Daniel's interpretation; and thirdly, possibly as kings, a more esoteric (and dubious) meaning. As weights, the terms mean the following: "mene," a mina; "tekel," a shekel; and "parsin," halves (of a weight, usually half of a mina). A mina normally was equal to sixty shekels (sometimes fifty). "Parsin" could be understood as plural, "half-minas" (or possibly "half-shekels"); or dual, "two half-minas" (perhaps "two half-shekels"). "Mene," if spelled slightly differently, can be analyzed as coming from the root meaning "to count." If so, it might be possible to read the first occurrence of "mene" as a verb and the second as a weight: "counted: a mina, a shekel, and a half-shekel (or half-mina)" (Eissfeldt, "Die Menetekel-Inschrift," p. 109, cited in Collins, *Daniel*, p. 251). However, the root for the verb "to count" is different from that for "mina." For two reasons, it seems more likely that the repetition of "mene" was due to a scribal error. First, it is odd that there are two occurrences of "mene" when only one figures in the interpretation in verse 26. That makes it likely that a dittography has occurred and the original had only one "mene." Secondly, there is textual support for the shorter reading, as evidenced by the preface to chapter 5 of the Old Greek and by the Theodotionic version of the Septuagint.

Some have suggested that the second "mene" was added on purpose so that there would be four terms instead of three. It is thought that this would have been motivated by a desire to match the four terms to the four kingdoms of chapters 2 and 7 (Lacocque, *Daniel*, p. 100). However, there is no support for this in the interpretation itself. That is, there is no indication that the first "mene" stands for Babylonia, the second "mene" for Media, the "tekel" for Persia, and the "parsin" for Greece. In fact, there is a play on the word "parsin" meaning Persia, not Greece.

Just as there is reason to eliminate one "mene," so the form "parsin" is also questionable. The LXX points to an original reading of *prs*, which provides better parallelism and symmetry: three words with three letters each (see the Additional Note on 5:25). Verse 28 also supports the reading *peres* instead of *parsin*, because that is the form being interpreted there. The preferred reading is the one that explains the others: it seems slightly more probable that a scribe would change *peres* to *parsin* to make a more obvious connection to the Persians, who conquered Babylon, than that a copyist would shorten the word from *parsin* to *peres*. In conclusion, then, I think the writing on the wall was either *"mene' peres teqel"* or *"mene' teqel peres"* (both orders appear in the Greek), rather than *"mene' mene' teqel parsin"* as in the MT.

The Babylonian sages in the story were baffled with this inscription. If the letters were strung together without breaks between the words—like this: מנאתקלפרס (in Aramaic, reading from right to left; in Latin characters, from left to right: *mn'tqlprs*)—it would be confusing. Or, if in a block, reading each word from top to bottom with the vertical words going from right to left (from left to right in Latin characters), it would look like this:

m	*t*	*p*		פ	ת	מ
n	*q*	*r*		ר	ק	נ
'	*l*	*s*		ס	ל	א

This structure would be even more enigmatic, because the sages might try to read it from right to left in rows, which makes no sense. However, it is quite possible that the Mesopotamian diviners simply saw words for three weights—"mina," "shekel," "half,"—and did not know what sense to make of them beyond that (see the Additional Note on 5:25). Only Daniel, by the Spirit of God, could tell the significance of these cryptic terms.

Daniel *is* able to interpret the words, and when he does, it is intriguing that he does not construe them as nouns, the way they are vocalized in the MT, but as verbs. Daniel's explanation of the first term involves a pun. He tells the king, **God has numbered the days of your reign and brought it to an end** (5:26). As noted above, **Mene** (5:26) is a noun meaning "mina," a unit of weight, but the verb "numbered," while similar, is from a different root. So, the prophet makes a wordplay because the two words sound alike, interpreting "mina" as "numbered" in order to pronounce judgment and announce the termination of the Babylonian kingdom. There may be a further wordplay in the phrase "brought it to an end," because the verb in this clause can mean "to hand over." In business dealings one might count the money and then hand it over. In the same manner, God is counting the worth of Belshazzar's kingdom and handing that kingdom over (to its enemies). In other words, God is bringing the kingdom to an end. Wordplays are a common literary device in the OT; two prophetic examples immediately come to mind. Amos, upon seeing a basket of summer fruit (*qayits*), announces the end (*qets*) of Israel (Amos 8:2). When God shows Jeremiah a branch of an almond tree (*shaqed*), he gives the prophet the promise: "I am watching [*shoqed*] over my word to perform it" (Jer. 1:11–12 NRSV).

The second noun, **Tekel** (v. 27), or "shekel," comes from the root *tql*, which as a verb means "to weigh." Again there is a play on words, as the meaning of "tekel" is that the king has **been weighed on the scales and found wanting** (5:27). Belshazzar is not substantial enough to rule; lacking gravitas, he is too light. In fact, the writer may have had in mind the verb *qelal*, "to be light," as a further wordplay on *teqel* (Collins, *Daniel*, p. 252). This notion of being weighed by God is also found in 1 Samuel 2:3; Job 31:6; Psalm 62:9; and Proverbs 24:12.

The third term that Daniel interprets is **Peres** (5:28), not *parsin*. As already noted, this suggests that *parsin* is not original to verse 25 but was changed by a scribe secondarily. The root *prs* occurs three times in verse 28. The first is the noun *peres*, vocalized as the noun "half-mina" (or possibly "half-shekel"). The second is the passive verb form *perisat*, "is divided" or "is broken in two." The third is the term *paras*, "Persians." The prophetic meaning of *peres* is that Belshazzar's **kingdom is divided and given to the Medes and Persians** (5:28). There are thus two wordplays: *peres* ("half-mina") signifies the dividing (*perisat*) of the kingdom and also points to one of the two kingdoms following Babylonia, namely Persia (*paras*). This is a bit surprising, since in Daniel's scheme of things, Babylonia does not fall to the combined forces of Medes and Persians, nor is it divided between them. Rather, there are two successive kingdoms: Media and then Persia. This is clear from a statement just a few verses later: there is a Median kingdom between Babylonia and Persia headed up by Darius the Mede (5:31). To summarize, the text has "mina," "shekel," "half" (nouns); Daniel interprets them as "numbered," "weighted," "divided" (verbs).

We have discussed the terms as weights and verbs. There is another possible level of meaning. Certain scholars have read them in reference to various Babylonian kings. Proposals include Nebuchadnezzar,

Evil-Merodach, and Belshazzar; Nebuchadnezzar, Nabonidus, and Belshazzar; or Belshazzar, Nabonidus, and Nebuchadnezzar (see the Additional Note on 5:25). However, since the book of Daniel mentions Nebuchadnezzar, Belshazzar, and then Darius the Mede, perhaps those are the kings indicated. There may be something to this third level of interpretation, but it is rather speculative; there is no indication in the chapter that the weights refer to kings.

The king orders Daniel to be **clothed in purple,** decorated with a **gold chain,** and promoted to high office (or **third highest ruler;** see commentary and Additional Note on 5:7) (5:29). The text does not say why Daniel is willing to receive the promised rewards after initially refusing them (5:17). Once again, as in previous chapters, we see that God is the source of true wisdom. Time after time, Daniel is able to succeed where the Babylonian sages cannot. He recounts and interprets the king's dream (ch. 2); he later gives the meaning of another royal dream (ch. 4); and here he explains the cryptic inscription (ch. 5). God is still very active in imparting wisdom to his faithful servants, but it is often not as obvious as in the book of Daniel, because God's wisdom appears to be foolishness to the world (1 Cor. 1:18–2:16). Paul comments that not many Christians in his day "were wise by human standards" (1 Cor. 1:26).

5:30–31 / The judgment on Belshazzar is carried out swiftly. **That very night** he is **slain** (5:30). The lack of details concerning how this happened is striking. The report leaves it unclear whether, for example, a coup d'état or foreign invasion lies behind it. Many scholars connect the slaying of Belshazzar with the Persian conquest of Babylon led by Cyrus in 539 B.C. and draw on extrabiblical sources to fill in details. Xenophon's account of Cyrus's invasion of Babylon records that Gadatas and Gobryas entered the palace, found the king, and killed him (*Cyropaedia* 7.5.24–30). Unfortunately, it does not mention the king's name. Nabonidus was probably the actual king, although Daniel calls Belshazzar king as well. According to the Nabonidus Chronicle, Nabonidus fled after the battle of Sippar and was later captured when he returned to Babylon after Babylon fell (*ANET*, p. 306). If that is true, then either Xenophon's account refers to someone else or there is a contradiction. The Cyrus Cylinder is not very helpful; it merely says that Marduk handed Nabonidus over to Cyrus (*ANET*, p. 315). Some would see the Xenophon account as referring to the death of Belshazzar and corroborating Daniel 5:30. However, others doubt the trustworthiness of Xenophon's history (Collins, *Daniel*, p. 253).

Although God is transcendent, he sometimes intervenes in human history to save (as when he brought Israel out of Egypt in the exodus) and to destroy (as when he brought about the dissolution of the kingdom of Judah in 587 B.C.). In Daniel 5, God intervenes three times: first, by causing the inscription; second, by giving Daniel the interpretation so that the indictment and sentence can be announced to Belshazzar; and third, by bringing in the enemy army to Babylon to carry out the punishment. God acts in human history today, as well, by drawing sinners to himself, by watching out for his people, and by answering prayer. However, he does not always punish sin immediately; striking someone dead for transgression is rare in the church age (e.g., Acts 5:5). When Jesus returns, there will be a final judgment (Rev. 20:11–15). In the meantime, God has established human political structures to enforce law (Rom. 13:1–4).

With the death of the Babylonian king, **Darius the Mede takes over the kingdom** (5:31). In terms of history, this is surprising. We know of one Persian king named Darius who ruled from 522 to 486 B.C. (there were actually three Persian kings of that name). We also know that Cyrus, the Persian king, conquered Babylon (in 539) and ruled immediately after his conquest. There was no Median king—or any king, for that matter—between Nabonidus (or Belshazzar) and Cyrus. Outside the book of Daniel there is no record of a king named "Darius the Mede." Two things probably gave rise to this literary figure. The first was the four-kingdom program of chapters 2 and 7. This demanded that a kingdom such as Media be placed between Babylonia and Persia. The second was the record of prophecy. Isaiah and Jeremiah predicted that Babylon would fall to the Medes (Isa. 13:17–22; 21:1–10; Jer. 51:11) and that the Babylonians would be carousing just before the end (Isa. 21:5; Jer. 51:39, 57). Daniel 5 fulfills this imagery. The characterization of Darius the Mede in Daniel has been colored by the later Persian king Darius of history. Darius the Persian quelled two uprisings in Babylon (much later, in 522 B.C.); this may have caused the writer of Daniel to record Darius the Mede as the conqueror of Babylon in chapter 5. Also, Darius the Persian divided his empire into 20 satrapies; compare Darius the Mede with his 120 satrapies (Dan. 6:1). Attempts have been made to harmonize Darius the Mede with a historical figure of a different name, such as Gobryas or Cyrus, but these proposals are not convincing (see the Additional Note on 5:31).

Whatever the case, according to Daniel 5, Belshazzar, who put to profane use the temple vessels meant to serve only Yahweh, is gone, replaced by Darius the Mede. Once again, Daniel's interpretive insight has embarrassed his Babylonian counterparts and borne positive witness to the wisdom and sovereignty of Israel's God. As a result, like Joseph in Egypt, Daniel the Jew in Babylon has ascended to the upper ranks of imperial leadership.

Additional Notes §5

5:1 / The Aramaic for **Belshazzar** here is *belsha'tsar*. It is a close but not exact rendering of the Akkadian *Bel-shar-utsur*, "Bel, protect the king." ("Bel" [compare "Baal" in Hebrew and Ugaritic] refers to the Babylonian god Marduk.) In 5:30; 7:1; and 8:1 it is spelled *bel'shatsar*, which is even more divergent. Daniel's Akkadian name is similar: *Beltesha'tsar* (5:12), although the meaning is different, "protect his life" (see commentary and Additional Note on 1:7). Oddly, the Greek translators did not distinguish between the names but spelled them all *Baltasar*.

Although they do not mention Belshazzar or his **great banquet**, the ancient Greek writers Herodotus and Xenophon both record that there was a festival on the night that Cyrus conquered Babylon. Xenophon reports, "A certain festival had come round in Babylon, during which all Babylon was accustomed to drink and revel all night long" (Xenophon, *Cyropaedia* 7.15 [Miller, LCL]). Herodotus adds, "All this time they were dancing and making merry at a festival which chanced to be toward, till they learnt the truth but too well" (Herodotus, *Hist.* 1.191 [Godley, LCL]).

5:2 / The phrase **was drinking ... wine** is literally "in the taste of the wine." The root *t'm* means "taste" here, but it has a wide range of meaning. It occurs in 2:14; 3:12; and 6:14 with the sense of "discretion." Elsewhere in Daniel, *t'm* means "decree." In 6:2 (6:3 MT) it means "account" or "report." In 3:10, 29; 4:6 (4:3 MT); and 6:26 (6:27 MT) it means "decree" (BDB, p. 1094). In 6:13 (6:14 MT) it means (to pay) "attention."

5:3 / "Gold and silver goblets" are mentioned in v. 2. However, v. 3 in the MT has only **gold goblets**. Theodotion's Greek version adds "silver" in v. 3 as well. The RSV and NRSV follow Theodotion; NIV follows the MT.

In the phrase **the temple of God in Jerusalem,** the NIV omits "which is the house" between "temple" and "God." That is, it should read, "the temple, which is the house of God in Jerusalem." A more literal translation is "the temple, which is the house of God, which is in Jerusalem."

5:5 / Gibson suggests (M. D. Gibson, "Belshazzar's Feast," *ExpTim* 23 [1911–12], p. 181) that the terms written on the wall were common to the stewards occupied with weights and measures. They were working next to the banquet hall in a room that had these words on the wall for business purposes. One of the stewards was writing next to a lamp, which cast a shadow of a hand on the wall. Because the king was intoxicated, he thought he saw an actual hand making an inscription on the wall. Gibson still consider it a divine communication, though through natural, not supernatural agency. Although the article cited above is old and the interpretation has little to recommend it, it is mentioned because at least one more recent commentator follows it (Baldwin, *Daniel*, 124).

5:6 / The statement **his legs gave way** literally means something like "the joints of his hips were loosed." It is possible that we should understand the clause to mean that the king was so frightened that his bowels were loosed (A. Wolters, "Untying the King's Knots: Physiology and Wordplay in Daniel 5," *JBL* 110 [1991], pp. 117–22). The word for "joints" is from the root *qtr*, and the word for "loosed" is from the root *shr'*. In a kind of play on words, these words occur later in the chapter with a different meaning. "Loose joints" becomes "loosing knots" in the sense of untying knotty problems or solving riddles (5:12, 16). This sets up a contrast between the king, who is so weak he cannot stand (5:6), and Daniel, who is so strong spiritually and intellectually that he can "solve difficult problems" (5:12, 16).

5:7 / The Aramaic says that the individual will rule as a *talti*, or **third**. Hebrew may be helpful in understanding this verse. The cognate term *shalish* is translated "officer" (Exod. 14:7; 2 Kgs. 7:2, 17, 19; 9:25). It does mean third, but it referred originally to the third soldier in a chariot. Over time it came to mean an "officer" or "official."

5:11 / For a discussion of whether to translate **gods** or "God," see the Additional Note on 4:8.

The Aramaic has *umalka' nebukadnetsar 'abuk*, "King Nebuchadnezzar your father," within the verse. Then at the end of the verse it has the repetitious *'abuk malka'*, **your father the king.** The second phrase does not fit and is most likely not original. The NRSV rightly omits it. The NIV tries to make sense of it by moving it up to the first occurrence: "King Nebuchadnezzar your father—your father the king, I say—." But it is still awkward and redundant; also "I say" is not in the Aramaic.

5:11–12 / There is a question of syntax in vv. 11 and 12. The thought of v. 11 continues in v. 12, so there should probably not be a period after v. 11 as there is in the NIV. In Aramaic it reads, "King Nebuchadnezzar . . . appointed him chief of the . . . diviners because a keen mind and knowledge . . . were found in him, in this Daniel, whom the king named Belteshazzar." Also, the NIV, by starting a new sentence, moved the introduction of the name, "Daniel," to an earlier spot, smoothing over what is actually a bit rough in the Aramaic. The queen refers to **this man Daniel** as if he has been mentioned before in the context, which he has not. Therefore, this phrase appears to be an explanatory addition by a redactor (Collins, *Daniel*, p. 249).

5:12 / On the phrase **solve difficult problems**, see the Additional Note on 5:6.

5:25 / The first to understand the terms **MENE, MENE, TEKEL, PARSIN** as weights was C. S. Clermont-Ganneau, "Mané, thécel, pharès et le festin de Balthasar," *Journal Asiatique* 8 (1886), pp. 36–67; reprinted in *Recueil d'archéologie orientale* (Paris: Leroux, 1888), vol. 1, pp. 136–59. The problem with rendering the first "mene" as a verb is that the root for the verb "to count" is *mnh*, while the word in the text, "mene," vocalized *měnē'*, comes from the root *mn'*, "mina." While it is possible that *mnh* was corrupted to *mn'*, resulting

Additional Notes §5

in the repetition of the word *mene*, it seems better to eliminate one of them as a scribal error.

Two word orders are found in the Greek. The LXX reads, *manē phares thekel*. Theodotion has *manē thekel phares*. It is not clear which order to follow, but the LXX may be earlier, with Theodotion representing a revision toward the MT.

Those scholars who suggest the terms stand for kings offer differing opinions on which kings are indicated. H. L. Ginsberg (*Studies in Daniel* [Texts and Studies of the Jewish Theological Seminary of America 14; New York: Jewish Theological Seminary of America, 1948], p. 25) has suggested that they refer to Nebuchadnezzar, Evil-Merodach, and Belshazzar. D. N. Freedman ("The Prayer of Nabonidus," *BASOR* 145 [1957], pp. 31–32) prefers Nebuchadnezzar, Nabonidus, and Belshazzar. If we understand the weights to be mina, shekel, and half-mina, Freedman's order is a little puzzling: why would Belshazzar weigh more than Nabonidus? F. M. Cross agrees on those three kings, but rearranges the weights, arguing that they should be in descending order as in the LXX (mentioned above): mina, half-mina, shekel (cited in Collins, *Daniel*, p. 251 n. 102 as a "personal communication"). This also works better because Belshazzar was the lightest. Another alternative is to leave the order as it is and read half-shekel instead of half-mina; that way Belshazzar still comes out lightest. It is interesting, though, that the book of Daniel as we now have it does not mention Nabonidus. Rather, it mentions Nebuchadnezzar, Belshazzar, and then Darius the Mede. If these are the three kings indicated, then perhaps we should read mina, shekel, half-mina, because Belshazzar is the lightweight shekel who is singled out for judgment. Darius the Mede, on the other hand, is far heavier than Belshazzar, because he is able to conquer Babylon, though he is not as heavy as Nebuchadnezzar.

5:31 / Various attempts have been made to identify **Darius the Mede** as a historical figure known by another name. Some scholars identify Gobryas as Darius the Mede (J. C. Whitcomb, *Darius the Mede* [Grand Rapids: Eerdmans, 1959], p. 8), but this will not work. Gobryas was a governor of Babylon but never king; nor was he called Darius, as far as we know (Collins, *Daniel*, p. 31). Others suggest that Darius is an alternate name for Cyrus, but that cannot be supported from history either. They equate the two by rendering 6:28 as "the reign of Darius, even the reign of Cyrus the Persian" (Baldwin, *Daniel*, pp. 26, 132, following D. J. Wiseman; see the NIV footnote to 6:28). In fact the writer of Daniel understood there to be two separate reigns: "the reign of Darius and the reign of Cyrus the Persian" (6:28). This is clear from the sequence of kingdoms in chs. 2 and 7 and also from the sequence in the book of Daniel. Chs. 1–5 are set in the Babylonian period (chs. 1–4 in the time of Nebuchadnezzar; ch. 5 in the time of Belshazzar). Ch. 6 is set in the time of Darius the Mede, but it introduces Cyrus the Persian at the end of the chapter (6:28). The book then backs up and starts over: chs. 7–8 are set in the Babylonian period; ch. 9, Median; Daniel 10:1 gives a Persian context, but 10:20 indicates that Greece is next on the scene (Collins, *Daniel*, p. 31). It is curious that the text supplies the age of Darius the Mede: **sixty-two** (5:31). Some have seen in this a further interpretation of the weights in the inscription. If we leave the consonants *prsyn* in the text and vocalize the word as a dual, *parsayin*, then it represents two halves. Although it is normally understood to be half-minas, it might be construed as half-shekels. Using the rate of sixty shekels to the mina yields the number sixty-two: one mina equals sixty shekels, plus one shekel, plus two half-shekels, equals sixty-two shekels (Goldingay, *Daniel*, p. 112). However, as already noted, there is more support for reading *peres*, not *parsin*, and furthermore, the understanding of a half-mina would be more normal than a half-shekel. Finally, the text makes no attempt to tie the cryptic text to the age of the conqueror, so it may be reading too much into the verse to do so. The number **sixty-two** recurs later in Daniel's chronological schema (Dan. 9:25, 26). Much scholarly discussion has focused on the identity of Darius, because there is no such individual known from extrabiblical historical sources. On the contrary, there is good reason to question the existence of this figure.

§6 The Lions' Pit (Dan. 6:1–28)

In this familiar chapter, Daniel's enemies conspire to get him thrown into the lions' pit for making petitions to his God. Just as we wonder where Daniel is in chapter 3, so we wonder where Hananiah, Mishael, and Azariah (Shadrach, Meshach, and Abednego) are in chapter 6, for there is no mention of them. We can be sure that they, like Daniel, would have continued their daily prayers in spite of the threat of being devoured by wild animals, yet there is no explanation for their absence. This is likely because chapters 3 and 6 were originally independent stories. Moreover, there must have been other faithful Jews in the realm as well; but there is no accounting of them, whether any obeyed the king or defied him. These are representative accounts; they are not meant to be exhaustive, telling us what everyone did in that time. Furthermore, they are didactic, written in order to teach the Jewish people how to behave in a foreign, and sometimes hostile, environment. So they focus on exemplary individuals to make the stories more realistic and concrete. Chapter 3 focuses on Hananiah, Mishael, and Azariah, while chapter 6 focuses on Daniel.

In both chapter 3 and chapter 6, the heroes are faithful to God, willing even to die if necessary. In the first instance, the three refuse to worship an image, while in the second, Daniel refuses to stop praying. In both cases God delivers them by sending his angel. In chapter 3, however, the king makes the command on his own, and men just report the three Jews to the king; whereas in chapter 6, evil men devise a plot to trap Daniel by manipulating the king to issue a command. In chapter 3, the king is hostile to the three friends, ordering that they be thrown into the furnace; he becomes friendly when he sees they are saved. By way of contrast, in chapter 6 the king laments having to send Daniel to the lions and even tries unsuccessfully to save him. In chapter 3, the three express hope that God will save them; in chapter 6, the king hopes God will save Daniel, while Daniel himself is rather quiet. Also, the king in chapter 3 says, "Then what god will be able to rescue you from my hand?" (3:15); but the king in chapter 6 says, "May your God, whom you serve continually, rescue you!" (6:16). In chapter 3, those who reported the three youths to the king go unpunished, but the ones who throw them into the fire are burned to death (Dan. 3:22). In chapter 6, those who sought the death of Daniel are themselves thrown into the lions' pit and killed, as justice would demand (6:24). Both chapters end with the king issuing a decree: the former one is negative, prohibiting slander against the Jewish God (3:29); the latter one is positive, requiring everyone to worship this deity (6:26).

Historical questions arise here. It seems that the author of Daniel considers Darius the Mede to be the conqueror of Babylonia, since he "took over the kingdom" (5:31) from Belshazzar. In fact it was Cyrus the Persian who ruled Babylonia after the last king, Nabonidus. There was a later Persian king, Darius I, who ruled from 521 to 486 B.C., but he was not a Mede (following him were two more Persian kings named Darius). The Persians did have satrapies (provinces) but they numbered in the twenties, not 120 (6:1). From what we know of Darius and the Persian kings, it seems incredible both that the king would be duped by his advisers and that he would make an edict requiring such a narrow religious practice. The story may contain a historical kernel about a faithful Jew who was delivered from death, but the final account seems to be fashioned as a well-told story rather than as a historical record. Interestingly, the book of Esther also portrays a Persian king as gullible and easily manipulated by advisers to make an outrageous decree.

If the book of Daniel was written in the second century B.C., the story of the lions' pit was likely included because of its relevance to the Jews suffering persecution at the hands of Antiochus IV. Both King Darius and Antiochus proscribed practices central to the Jewish religion. However, the story of Daniel in the lions' pit was probably written before the second century B.C. Perhaps it originated in the late Persian period, when some of the details of the earlier Persian history had been forgotten. Then it was selected and adapted by the author of Daniel to address the Jews of his generation.

6:1–9 / Darius sets up 120 satraps to rule throughout the kingdom (6:1). The last verse in chapter 5 calls this king "Darius the Mede" (5:31). Here he is just called "Darius." It was actually Darius the Persian, otherwise known as Darius I Hystaspes (521–486 B.C.), who divided up his kingdom into satrapies, or provinces, governed by satraps (provincial governors). In Darius's inscriptions the number is much lower than 120, but it varies between 21, 23, and 29 (Montgomery, *Daniel*, p. 269). According to Herodotus there were 20 (Herodotus, *Hist.* 3.89). These larger satrapies were subdivided into smaller territories ruled by local governors. When Xenophon and other Greek historians use the term "satrap," they seem to include these lesser governors, who were not actually satraps. It is possible that the author of Daniel is doing the same thing, which would, of course, inflate the number. Alternatively, the writer may be exaggerating or arbitrarily choosing a number, since he is discussing an individual who cannot be located in history. The later king Xerxes (485–465 B.C.) is said to have had 127 satrapies (Esth. 1:1; 8:9).

Darius also appoints **three administrators over** the satraps, **one of whom is Daniel** (6:2). These offices cannot be corroborated from history. It may be that the author of Daniel 6 was influenced to introduce them here by the previous statement: "Daniel . . . was proclaimed the third highest ruler in the kingdom" (5:29; see also 5:7, 16). As noted above, what the NIV renders "third highest ruler" probably just means "high office" (see commentary and Additional Note on 5:7). The function of the three administrators is to make sure **that the king does not suffer loss** (6:2). Ostensibly, this was also the concern of the group that opposed the Jews who returned to Judah in the postexilic period. They requested that the Persian king stop the Jews from building lest he lose money and land (Ezra 4:13–16); he replied accordingly, expressing fear of circumstances "to the detriment of the royal interests" (Ezra 4:22). However, the group opposing the Jews was really motivated by self-interest and hostility toward the Jews. So it is with the conspirators in Daniel 6.

Daniel proves to be so superior to the other **administrators** and **satraps . . . that the king plans to set him over the whole kingdom** (6:3). On the one hand, it may be that the story in Daniel 6 has been influenced by the story of Joseph, who was second only to Pharaoh (Gen. 41:40). On the other hand, perhaps the writer was thinking of the *chiliarch*, who was the chief administrator under the Persian king. However, the narrative does not record the promotion of Daniel to this office at the end of the chapter, as one might expect from this verse and from the preceding narratives. At the end of chapter 2, Daniel was elevated over the province of Babylon and over the other wise men (2:48), and his Jewish comrades were also given key positions (2:49). At the close of chapter 3, Nebuchadnezzar promoted Shadrach, Meshach, and Abednego (3:30). Belshazzar gave Daniel third place in his kingdom at the conclusion of chapter 5 (5:29). What distinguishes Daniel are **his exceptional qualities** (6:3). A translation closer to the Aramaic would be "an excellent spirit was in him." This reminds us of earlier statements. Daniel "was found to have a keen mind [Aram. "excellent spirit"] and knowledge and understanding, and also the ability to interpret dreams, explain riddles and solve difficult problems" (5:12). In Daniel was "the spirit of the holy gods" (4:8, 9, 18; 5:11).

Apparently, Daniel's colleagues are jealous of his success. They try **to find grounds for charges against** him, but they fail **because he** is **trustworthy and neither corrupt nor negligent** (6:4). They then conclude that the only way to "find any basis for charges against him" will be if **it has something to do with the law of his God** (6:5). The translation "law" might be a bit misleading, as it can conjure up an image of the Torah scrolls. However, the conspirators are trying to trap Daniel, not by using a particular commandment, but rather through his practice of the Jewish faith, specifically his prayer habits. Therefore, it makes more sense in this context to construe the word as "religion." Perhaps, though, if the author was from the second century B.C., he wanted his audience to think of the Jewish law, since the Jews were being persecuted for observing the torah in his day. The story thus points to the later oppression under Antiochus IV, who destroyed copies of the law and punished those who followed it. While it is true that there is no widespread persecution of Jews in Daniel 6, it nevertheless hints at the later situation, because Daniel is a representative of the Jewish people. Just as his enemies seek to kill him for maintaining his practice of prayer, so the Seleucid king subjected Jews to torture and murder in the second century for practicing their religion. Therefore, Daniel 6 does suggest anti-Semitism (Lacocque, *Daniel*, p. 111). The term "law" also sets up a contrast between the law of God and the "law [or "laws"] of the Medes and the Persians" (Dan. 6:8, 12, 15). To Jews in the Maccabean period and to Jews and Christians in all periods, the unambiguous message is that we ought to obey God rather than people (Acts 5:29), even if it causes us to suffer: God's authority trumps human authority.

One difference between chapters 3 and 6 is that in the former, the three youths are enjoined to commit idolatry, a blatant sin of commission, while in the latter, Daniel is commanded only not to pray, which in later Jewish law would not have been a sin. Halakah requires a Jew to be willing to die if ordered to perform a sinful deed, such as worshiping an idol, but not when ordered to abstain from doing a religious practice, such as prayer, even though commanded by God to do so (Ginzberg, *Legends of the Jews*, vol. 4, p. 348; vol. 6, p. 435). However, the halakah was not written down until the Christian era, so it is hard to know what would have obtained in the time when the book of Daniel was written. The book certainly presents a Daniel doing what he feels is right, even if it means that he will die; he also may believe that to refrain from prayer would be a serious sin of omission. Once again, though, it is important to remember that the author of this book is more concerned to use Daniel's story to preach to the people of his day than he is to record history.

Consequently, in a sense, it does not matter how serious this temptation to cease praying was in that moment. The Jews under Antiochus IV, and Jews and Christians under later tyrants, would have grasped the message: do not stop practicing your religion, even though it means doing something illegal and threatens you with death.

Having resolved to trap Daniel for his religious devotion, the administrators go **as a group to the king** (6:6; also vv. 11 and 15). The Aramaic is a bit more colorful here, implying collusion, conspiracy, or even tumultuousness (see the Additional Note on 6:6). Indeed the writer may be ridiculing this plotting crowd, bustling about as a noisy throng. The sheer number of people involved in this plot does reach comic proportions. This is not merely a matter of rivalry between Daniel and the other two triumvirs. In addition to the 120 **satraps**, all the other officials are listed as well (6:6). They press the king to **issue an edict** forbidding anyone from praying **to any god or man, except the king**, for a **thirty**-day period (6:7). The king has the ultimate authority to enact laws, but his counselors can make suggestions. Similarly, in the book of Esther, Haman requests that the king issue a decree calling for the destruction of the Jews (Esth. 3:9). What is odd about Daniel 6:7, though, is that the Persians were known for their tolerance. As far as we know, they would never have proscribed prayer to other gods. It is even more incredible that they would disallow petitions to humans other than the king. The Persians did not divinize their kings, and even ancient Near Eastern cultures that did, such as the Egyptians, did not demand exclusive worship of any one god (with the exception of Pharaoh Akhenaten), much less of the king. Again, it makes more sense if we consider that Darius may be a symbol for Antiochus IV, whose policy amounted to exalting himself above the one true God. It seems, then, that from the very beginning this account was an intentional caricature of history. The author of Daniel is attempting to lambaste pagan religion in general and Antiochus IV in particular. In the same way today, a political cartoon may exaggerate the feature of a politician, or a comedian may, in doing impressions of public figures, overemphasize an accent, a gesture, or a facial expression for humorous effect.

The location of the lions is a bit surprising. Anyone violating **the decree** will be **thrown into the lions' den** or pit (6:7). Pits were dug to catch lions in antiquity, but the lions would normally have been removed afterward and placed in cages (Ezek. 19:4, 8–9). Mesopotamian kings would then set the lions free when they chose, in order to hunt them; we have reliefs of them engaged in this sport. The text conjures up an image of a pit with steep sides (because Daniel had to be lifted out [Dan. 6:23]), and a small hole at the top over which one could place a stone

(6:17). It does not seem that this would be a very practical way to keep lions for any length of time, but apparently they were actually held in "cages or pits" (Oppenheim, *Ancient Mesopotamia*, p. 46). Much later the Romans kept lions in a holding area under the Colosseum, known as a *hypogeum*, from which they could be raised and released for the games. Although Christians today are not normally threatened with real wild animals, lions can be metaphorical, as when the psalmist imagines his enemies as ravenous lions (Ps. 57:4; 22:13). Furthermore, the NT likens the devil to a "roaring lion looking for someone to devour" (1 Pet. 5:8). God can deliver his people from all ravenous beasts, whether physical, symbolic, or spiritual.

The officials ask the king to put the decree **in writing so that it cannot be altered—in accordance with the laws of the Medes and Persians, which cannot be repealed** (6:8). This raises a couple of questions. First, if the apocalyptist thought there was a separate Median kingdom ruled by one Darius that came between the Babylonian and Persian Empires, then why does he speak of "the laws of the Medes and Persians" as if the two peoples were a united kingdom already (which would have happened later after the Persians conquered Media). Secondly, if the passage is really about a Persian, not Median, king, why could he not change his mind and revoke the law? Scholars usually cite two passages to give credence to this notion. One is Hammurabi's law code, which lists stiff penalties for a judge who makes a decision in a case and later alters that judgment (HC 5; *ANET*, p. 167). But that involves a judge, not a king, and a legal decision, not the enacting or changing of a law. Presumably it is designed to prevent a judge from being pressured by the rich or powerful to reverse a judgment against them. The other passage records that King Darius once sentenced a man to death, but having later changed his mind, he could not reverse things (Diodorus Siculus, *Lib.* 17.30). However, this example may not be apt at all. Perhaps the reason Darius could not change his mind was because the man had already been executed (Goldingay, *Daniel*, p. 128).

If the king is sovereign and makes a law that turns out to be unjust, why can he not act to reverse that unjust law? According to Herodotus, there was a law that stated that "the King of Persia might do whatsoever he wished" (Herodotus, *Hist.* 3.31 [Godley, LCL]). Or, perhaps what was originally meant by the first part of Daniel 6:8 is that "it cannot be altered" by some subordinate. In other words, the royal authority is behind it; no one other than the king may change it or make exceptions. The second part of the verse probably was intended originally to say something about the enduring nature of the law. The point was not that it was inflexible and could not be changed but that it would last and not expire or lapse (Collins, *Daniel*, p. 268; cf. also Esth. 1:19; 8:8). However, in the context of this chapter, it is necessary that the law be immutable in order for the plot to proceed, because Darius does not want Daniel to die. If the king had simply rescinded the decree, there would have been no miracle. So, in the narrative his hands are tied; he is unable to rescue Daniel, even though he tries (Dan. 6:14–15).

The king is presented as somewhat ridiculous. Not only do the jealous administrators trap Daniel, but they trick the king into being their tool. Without thinking about the consequences, **King Darius** does what his administrators ask and puts **the decree in writing** (6:9). Darius is such a fool that he does not see through their plot and cannot do anything about it once he realizes his mistake; he is a prisoner of his own law. This is further evidence that this story is not meant to be a historical record. It has some points of contact with history: there was a king named Darius; there were satrapies. But the writer plays with the tradition, using it as the backdrop for his message. As already noted, his goal is not to teach history as such but to warn his audience to be faithful even unto death. Preachers today often use the Bible, history, or current events in similar ways to launch a moral, an object lesson, or a religious application.

The seemingly irrevocable nature of the king's decree reminds us of other passages in the Bible. Blessings once given cannot be rescinded. Isaac blesses Jacob, thinking it is Esau, but cannot change the blessing even though it was given under false pretenses and even after learning that he has been deceived (Gen. 27:30–40). A prophecy once uttered or acted out cannot normally be reversed (e.g., 2 Kgs. 13:14–19; see the commentary on 4:19–27). In the same way, vows must be paid. Jephthah does not feel he has the option of sacrificing anything other than his daughter, though he deeply regrets his vow (Judg. 11:29–40). In a similar story, also set in the Persian era, the decree to annihilate the Jews that Haman dupes King Ahasuerus into proclaiming can only be countermanded, not revoked (Esth. 1:19; 8:8).

6:10–17 / Daniel does not let the new law hinder his devotions. When Daniel discovers that the decree has been published, he goes home and prays **just as . . . before** (6:10). The NIV's "published" really just means that the king signed it. Daniel's practice of prayer includes getting down on his knees and praying toward Jerusalem (6:10). When Solomon dedicated the temple with prayer, he also knelt (1 Kgs. 8:54), and he mentioned that Israelites in the future would pray toward Jerusalem (1 Kgs. 8:35). In the LXX, Daniel deliberately opens his windows, which may be understood as an act of defiance. However, the MT simply notes that his windows have been opened (6:10). It is possible that this indicates the sort of windows that could not be closed: holes cut in the wall (Montgomery, *Daniel*, p. 274). In that case, he is neither trying to flaunt his spirituality nor trying to conceal it; he is merely following his usual custom. Of course this is also a necessary detail in the development of the story. If Daniel had prayed secretly, he would not have been apprehended, and there would be no story. Furthermore, the narrator must include the information about the open window so the reader knows how Daniel was caught. In connection with the notion of private prayer, one thinks of Jesus's teaching that his disciples should not be like the hypocrites, who pray to be seen by others, but should pray in secret (Matt. 6:5–6). Daniel prays three times a day (6:10). This is similar to the psalmist who cries out to God "evening, morning and noon" (Ps. 55:17).

It should be no surprise to the reader that the administrators spy on Daniel; nor are the administrators surprised to find Daniel violating the law. They fully expect this, because they devised the law to trap him. They go **as a group and** find **Daniel praying and asking God for help** (6:11). It is a bit ludicrous to imagine more than 120 men thronging to the king (see commentary on 6:6–7 and Additional Note on 6:6; see also 6:15) and then thronging outside Daniel's window (6:11). Then they move en masse back **to the king** to remind him of his **decree** (6:12). He confirms that **the decree** still **stands** (6:12). They then spring the trap by informing on Daniel and indicting him. By noting that he is **one of the exiles from Judah** (6:13), they are indicating their prejudice against foreigners and possibly even special antipathy toward Jews. They accuse Daniel of paying **no attention** to the king or to his **decree, for he still prays three times a day** (6:13).

Unlike Nebuchadnezzar in chapter 3, who angrily seeks to destroy the three faithful Jews, Darius is here portrayed as a friend of Daniel's. When it dawns on him that he has inadvertently imperiled the life of his top adviser, **he is greatly distressed** (6:14). As it turns out, he too is a victim of these plotting administrators. He determines **to rescue Daniel** and makes **every effort** to do so (6:14). We are not told what these efforts entail. Presumably he is looking for a legal way out so that he can avoid enforcing the law, but he does not find it. The sympathetic presentation of the king may reflect the Persian era, when the Jews got along fairly well with their overlords. However, it still speaks to the Jews who were commanded by Antiochus to stop practicing their religion or die. It has a timeless message as well for all believers in all times: be faithful to the Lord even if it means becoming a martyr, for there are worse things than death. As Jesus says, "Do not be afraid of those who kill the body but cannot kill the soul. Rather, be afraid of the One who can destroy both soul and body in hell" (Matt. 10:28).

The evil administrators remind the king of the immutability of the law: **no decree or edict that the king issues can be changed** (6:15; see the commentary on 6:8). The king acquiesces and gives **the order**, with the result that they throw Daniel **into the lions' den** (6:16). However, the king encourages Daniel to trust in his God: **May your God, whom you serve continually, rescue you!** (6:16). Grammatically, this may be translated more confidently, "Your God, whom you serve continually, will rescue you." The statement then parallels the profession of Shadrach, Meshach, and Abednego in chapter 3: "If we are thrown into the blazing furnace, the God we serve is able to save us from it, and he will rescue us from your hand, O king" (3:17). However, such a strong confession of faith does not seem to fit the context, for the king is nervous before (6:14) and after (6:18–20) he gives the order. If it is to be read in the more emphatic and positive manner, it probably reflects the belief of the author more than the king in the story.

After Daniel is cast into the pit with the lions, a **stone is placed over its mouth**. Then it is **sealed** with the **signet** rings of **the king and his nobles** (6:17). The rings are probably pressed onto a seal of clay. Such a seal would not prevent someone from removing the stone. Its purpose was rather to make sure that if someone did so, the seal would be broken and it would be known. In this way it would prevent both the conspirators from kidnapping him and the king from rescuing him (this is actually expressed in the LXX, though not in the MT).

6:18–24 / The king is so worried about Daniel that he cannot enjoy the normal daily pleasures. He spends the night without eating and without any entertainment (6:18). "Entertainment" might refer to music, dancers, or perhaps even concubines. Also he cannot sleep (6:18). So, as soon as the first light of dawn appears, the king gets up and hurries to the lions' den to see how Daniel fares (6:19). When he gets to the pit, he calls to Daniel (6:20). The king addresses Daniel as the servant of the living God (6:20). Unlike the lifeless pagan deities, who cannot speak, see, or hear (Ps. 135:15–18; Isa. 44:18), the God of Israel is alive (Deut. 5:26; Josh. 3:10; 1 Sam. 17:26; Ps. 42:2; Jer. 10:10; Dan. 6:26; Hos. 1:10). What is surprising is that King Darius exudes so much faith when he does not yet know whether Daniel's God is able to save. The use of the phrase "the living God" fits better in verse 26, where it is used again after Daniel leaves the pit; but here such a strong affirmation is puzzling, especially since the king speaks in an anguished voice (6:20). Because he is unsure, the king asks Daniel whether his God has been able to rescue him from the lions (6:20). This may be just a designation for the Jewish God that Darius has picked up from Daniel. If so, it is not a confession of faith on the part of the king but merely a way of referring to Daniel's God and distinguishing him from other gods.

Daniel responds politely with the formulaic **"O king, live forever!"** (6:21), which is used elsewhere by other royal servants or the queen (Dan. 2:4; 3:9; 5:10; 6:6), but this is the only place in Daniel where it is spoken by a Jew (cf. 1 Kgs. 1:31; Neh. 2:3). Daniel then assures his master that he is safe: **My God sent his angel, and he shut the mouths of the lions** (Dan. 6:22). Similarly, an angel rescues the three Jews from the fire earlier in the book (3:26). The writer of the letter to the Hebrews alludes to both events in one place by mentioning those "who through faith . . . shut the mouths of lions, quenched the fury of the flames" (Heb. 11:33–34). Angels are active in other passages in the OT as well. An angel delivers Jerusalem from Sennacherib in the time of King Hezekiah by slaying 185,000 Assyrian soldiers (2 Kgs. 19:35; Isa. 37:36). Two angels protect Lot and his family from a gang by striking them with blindness (Gen. 19:1–11). The angel of God guards the Israelites by coming between them and the Egyptians (Exod. 14:19–20). An angel saves Elijah by providing food and drink for him in the wilderness (1 Kgs. 19:1–8). In the NT an angel prevents the murder of Jesus by warning Joseph to flee to Egypt with Mary and their baby (Matt. 2:13–15).

Does Daniel 6 exemplify human dominion over the animals (see Gen. 1:28)? This is hardly in view, since Daniel is not presented as a lion tamer. Rather, God by means of an angel supernaturally intervenes. Does Daniel 6 anticipate the peaceable kingdom of Isaiah 11:6–9 and 65:25? It is true that when the kingdom of God comes, animals "will neither harm nor destroy" (Isa. 11:9). It is also true that the book of Daniel concerns the coming of the kingdom of God. But there is no indication in Daniel 6 that the writer is thinking about the return-to-paradise motif.

The text offers two reasons why Daniel is delivered. One is that he **was found innocent in** God's **sight** (Dan. 6:22; so also 1 Macc. 2:60). The other is that **he trusted in his God** (Dan. 6:23). A further point the author makes is that Daniel is not guilty of any charges brought by the other administrators. He has been completely loyal and has never **done the king any wrong** (Dan. 6:22). In fact, the time in the lions' pit may have been understood as a trial by ordeal (Num. 5:11–31). He is vindicated by enduring the trial without being harmed by the lions. Had he been culpable, he would not have survived.

God does not always save us from trials, but he saves us through our trials. God does not prevent the three youths from being cast into the furnace (Dan. 3); nor does he keep Daniel from being thrown into the lions' pit. However, he saves them from the effects. In those cases they seem not to have suffered. Just as no harm comes to the three youths from the fire (3:27), so **no wound is found on** Daniel from the lions (6:23). However, Job truly suffered, although God later rescued him from pain by healing him. Jeremiah complained bitterly about his sufferings (Jer. 20:7–8; see also Jer. 1:8). In the NT, God sometimes delivered his people from prison (Acts 4:18–20; 5:19–20; 12:1–10; 16:19–26), but other times they endured persecution (Acts 5:40–41; 2 Cor. 11:23–29). Just as Job's story cannot be taken as a promise that everyone will always be healed, so Daniel 6 cannot be understood as a promise that no one will ever be martyred. Yet it does bear witness that God sometimes acts in history to save his people from harm. In the parable of the unjust judge, Jesus encourages his followers to cry out for justice in this life and to believe that God will quickly respond (Luke 18:1–8). Furthermore, we know from other passages that if we do not get justice in this life, we will in the next, for there will be a final judgment (Acts 17:31; 2 Cor. 5:10; Rev. 6:10; 20:11–15).

The king gives **orders to lift Daniel out of the den** (6:23) and then summons **the men who** have **falsely accused Daniel** (6:24). They are given the same punishment they set for Daniel: they are **brought in and thrown into the lions' den, along with their wives and children** (6:24). From the biblical storyteller's vantage point, the destruction of the enemies is significant, to show that Daniel's survival is not an accident. In case someone should suggest that the lions were tame or were not hungry, the detail is supplied that before the victims reach **the floor of the den, the lions** overpower **them and** crush **all their bones** (6:24).

The Torah declares that it should be done to a malicious witness "as he intended to do to his brother" (Deut. 19:19). The wisdom tradition agrees that "a false witness will not go unpunished" (Prov. 19:5). Harm will come back in kind to the one who intends harm. "He who digs a hole and scoops it out falls into the pit he has made. The trouble he causes recoils on himself; his violence comes down on his own head" (Ps. 7:15–16; see also Pss. 9:15; 57:6; Prov. 26:27; 28:10). In Daniel 3, those who threw the three youths into the furnace are burned (Dan. 3:22). However, the parallel is not exact, because they are merely soldiers who are given a task and not the ones who turned the Jews in. A better example is the evil Haman, who was hanged on the gallows he had prepared for righteous Mordecai (Esth. 7:10).

The execution of the "wives and children" along with the conspirators is troubling to some modern readers. The Bible does not necessarily condone this, though. One could adopt a stance against Darius's judgment on the grounds that he was an unjust pagan. However, these deaths might not have been as offensive to ancient Israelites as they are to us. In the earliest form of the law, sins of the parents were visited on the descendants to the third and fourth generation (Exod. 34:7). There was a sense of corporate guilt in early Israel, which is illustrated by the stoning of Achan and his family after he took illicit spoil from Jericho (Josh. 7) and by the deaths of the rebels Korah, Dathan, and Abiram, along with all of their families (Num. 16:23–33). On the one hand, we might see the killing of the family members in Daniel 6 as being parallel to this tradition. On the other hand, later legislation restricted punishment to the guilty individual (Deut. 24:16; 2 Kgs. 14:1–6); this was affirmed by Jeremiah and Ezekiel as well (Jer. 31:29–30; Ezek. 18). According to those passages, the wives and children should not have been killed. Nevertheless, the biblical writer may have approved of this retribution. If so, it does not mean that readers today must agree; it is appropriate to be outraged at the slaughter of the innocents. Some Christians would go even further to argue that in the light of Jesus Christ, we should have a more sympathetic and compassionate attitude toward the enemies (Matt. 5:44–45; Luke 6:27–28, 35–36). While this is true, even the NT supports the notions of justice and retribution. We should not take justice into our own hands to seek vengeance on others, but we should allow for the vengeance and wrath of God (Rom. 12:17–21), and we should be glad for the civil authorities, who use their power to punish criminals (Rom. 13:1–5). Furthermore, while Daniel 6 records only the casting of the evildoers into a lions' pit, NT passages represent God consigning sinners to hell (Matt. 25:46; Rev. 20:11–15).

6:25–28 / Reminiscent of earlier chapters (2:46–47; 3:29; 4:34–37), the king extols the God of the Jews. Here he does this by writing to all the peoples, nations and men of every language throughout the land (6:25). He addresses them with a customary greeting: May you prosper greatly! (6:25). Then he issues a decree that all his subjects must fear and reverence the God of Daniel (6:26). This is an advance over the decree in chapter 3, which is intended merely to prevent a behavior; people are forbidden from saying "anything against the God of Shadrach, Meshach and Abednego" (3:29). Here, the decree promotes an activity, commanding the people to respect this God; they are to tremble in awe before him. The former proscribes verbal attacks on God; the latter prescribes everyone to honor him. During the exile God had called his people to be witnesses to the nations (Isa. 42:6; 43:12; 49:6), promising that one day kings and foreign peoples would acknowledge that the Jews worshiped the one, true God (Isa. 45:14–15; 49:7, 22–23; 56:6–7; Zech. 2:11; 8:20–23; 14:16–19). Here a king fulfills that prophecy.

Unlike idols, Daniel's God is **living** (6:26). As already noted, this confession of faith fits better here than previously (see the commentary on 6:20). The Jewish God also **endures forever** (6:26). Unlike human regimes, **his kingdom will not be destroyed, his dominion will never end** (6:26). This statement is also reminiscent of earlier parts of the book, such as Nebuchadnezzar's vision in chapter 2 (2:44) and his affirmations about the eternality of God's kingdom in chapter 4 (4:3, 34). It also anticipates the vision of the next chapter (Dan. 7), which records the arrival of God's everlasting reign. We are reminded that the book of Daniel is apocalyptic. Even though chapters 7–12 deal more with the end of time, the theme is not absent from the first half of the book. Finally, Daniel's God is a God of salvation: **He rescues and he saves. . . . He has rescued Daniel from the power of the lions** (6:27). This truth was intended to feed the hope of God's beleaguered people being devoured by the Seleucid "lions," that God may intervene in history to deliver them. Secondarily, it becomes a timeless message for every age.

The chapter concludes with a brief chronological note, locating Daniel's prospering in the interval of time from the reign of **Darius** to that of **Cyrus the Persian** (6:28). This calls to mind Daniel 1:21, which says that "Daniel remained there until the first year of King Cyrus." These two similar statements frame chapters 2 through 6, setting off this block from the preceding introductory chapter (ch. 1) and from the following, more apocalyptic chapters (chs. 7–12). Nevertheless, we must not forget that chapter 2 is also linked to chapter 7 by the theme of the four kingdoms and that chapters 2 through 7 form a chiastic structure, making them a unit. As further confirmation of their unity, it also bears mentioning that they are written in Aramaic. There is a further chronological reference to Cyrus in Daniel 10:1.

The book's author uses repetition for theological effect. Four times he uses the Aramaic word meaning "law" or "religion," but only once does it refer to God's "law" (v. 5); every other time it refers to the "law" of the Medes and Persians (vv. 8, 12, 15). In this way, he creates a tension between divine and human requirements, so that as the story plays out, Daniel remains faithful to Jewish law, or religion, by praying, even though he risks his life to do so.

Seven times we find words from the root meaning "to seek," "to ask," or "to pray." The conspirators "tried" or "sought" (v. 4) to find a way to trap Daniel. The edict was that no one should "ask" "a request" (v. 7; the two words from the root are rendered by the one word, "prays," in the NIV) from anyone except the king. Yet, Daniel continued "praying" (v. 11) to God. The evil administrators reminded the king of his decree against anyone who "prays" (v. 12) to a god and indicted Daniel because he "asks" "his request" (v. 13; NIV "prays") three times daily. This highlights the importance of praying to God rather than seeking after other gods or humans.

There are five occurrences of the verb meaning "to rescue." The king attempts "to rescue" (v. 14) Daniel, but fails. After casting Daniel into the pit of lions, Darius then expresses his hope that God will "rescue" (v. 16) Daniel. In the morning, he inquires whether God was able "to rescue" (v. 20) his servant. At the end, the king proclaims that God "rescues," because he "rescued" Daniel from the lions (v. 27). The purpose here is that readers may infer something about the nature of God from the story: God rescued Daniel from the wild animals because that is his nature—he is a God who rescues and saves. This is further intended to engender hope for those who, like Daniel, are persecuted for their faith; God is able to deliver them.

Finally, there is the root meaning "to harm," "to hurt," or "to destroy." The lions could not "hurt" Daniel, because he was blameless and had not done any "harm" (NIV "wrong") to the king (v. 22). After Daniel exits the pit, no "hurt" or "wound" (v. 23) is found on him. The closing edict affirms that God's kingdom will never be "destroyed" (v. 26). The theological intention is clear: just as ravenous beasts could not harm Daniel, so nothing can harm or destroy heaven's dominion. Daniel's experience is symbolic and prophetic.

There are parallels in Daniel 6 to the life of Jesus. Daniel's fellow administrators conspire against Daniel to ensnare him. Just so, the religious leaders conspired against Jesus (Matt. 26:3–5), and Judas betrayed him (Matt. 26:14–16). Daniel is arrested because he prays, contrary to the edict; Jesus was arrested after prayer in the Garden of Gethsemane because he defied religious authorities (Matt. 26:36–55). Darius struggles to save Daniel but is bound by law and pressured by his administrators, so he carries out the sentence (Dan. 6:14–15); Pilate was sympathetic to Jesus and washed his hands of the affair, but he felt pressure from the religious leaders, from the crowds, and from Rome (to keep the peace), so he allowed Jesus to be crucified (Matt. 27:18–24). The opening to the lions' pit is covered with a stone and sealed (Dan. 6:17); Jesus's tomb was treated similarly (Matt. 27:60, 66). Both come forth from their enclosures alive, although Jesus died, whereas Daniel did not. These parallel motifs to Daniel in Jesus's life do not "predict" events which Jesus later "fulfills." On the one hand, the parallels are close enough to say that maybe the Gospel writers thought of Daniel as a type of Christ. On the other hand, since they do not declare this unequivocally, perhaps the most we can say is that the parallels are remarkable but possibly coincidental.

Additional Notes §6

6:1 / On the term *'akhashdarpenayya'* (Aram.; 6:2 MT), **satraps**, see the Additional Note on 3:2.

6:2 / The Aramaic *sarak* (here in the plural; NIV **administrators**) comes from an Old Persian word meaning "head" or "chief" (Hartman and Di Lella, *Daniel*, p. 194; Driver, *Daniel*, pp. 71–72). In the OT it only occurs in this chapter, in vv. 2, 3, 4, 6, and 7 (vv. 3, 4, 5, 7, and 8 MT). However, it occurs in the Aramaic Targums, where it corresponds to the Hebrew *shoter*, "officer" (e.g., Exod. 5:6, 10; Deut. 1:15; 20:5) (Driver, *Daniel*, p. 72).

The Aramaic verb *nezaq*, **suffer loss**, is used three other times in the OT: "and the royal revenues *will suffer*" (Ezra 4:13); "*troublesome* to kings and provinces" (Ezra 4:15); "*to the detriment* of the royal interests" (Ezra 4:22). All four instances concern the possibility of loss to the king.

6:5 / The word *dat*, **law**, is a Persian loanword. It is used in 2:9, 13, and 15 in the sense of "penalty" or "decree." In 6:8, 12, and 15 (6:9, 13, and 16 MT), it refers to the "law" of the Medes and Persians (a different word is used for "decree" in these verses). But here in 6:5 (6:6 MT), it has a different nuance. In later Jewish writings, for example in the Talmud, it means "religion," which is the best meaning for the present context, because it has to do with Daniel's practice of prayer rather than a specific commandment. The term also occurs in Ezra 7:12, 14, 25, and 26, where it does signify "law."

6:6 / The root *rgsh*, translated here **went as a group**, is usually rendered "be in tumult" (BDB, p. 1112). The form here, *hargishu*, is in the *haphel* conjugation and means "to show tumultuousness," "come thronging" (BDB, p. 1112). It occurs in 6:6, 11, and 15 (6:7, 12, and 16 MT). The meaning is suggested from Syriac and fits the usage in the Targums. However, the root *rgsh* in Hebrew occurs parallel to the root *swd*, signifying secret counsel (e.g., Pss. 55:14; 64:2). Therefore, the term may connote "conspiring," "colluding," "plotting secretly" (Collins, *Daniel*, 265–66). That certainly makes sense here, for this group is secretly setting a trap for Daniel. On the other hand, the writer may be trying to paint a picture of a tumultuous throng. Porteous rules this meaning out for being too "ridiculous" (N. W. Porteous, *Daniel: A Commentary* [OTL; Philadelphia: Westminster, 1965], p. 90), but ridicule may have been the author's goal (Collins,

Daniel, p. 266). This type of literature is composed as a story rather than as a historical record, so the author may have been going for a caricature rather than a realistic portrait.

6:7 / The traditional rendering of *gob* (6:8 MT) is **den**, but it is really closer to Hebrew *bor*, "pit." We should picture something more like a cistern than a cave. People (and lions) could be lowered and lifted out from the top hole (vv. 17, 23 [vv. 18, 24 MT]). Similarly, Jeremiah was lowered by ropes into a cistern with a muddy floor (Jer. 38:6–13).

6:12 / The phrase *'al 'esar malka'*, **about his royal decree**, or "concerning the decree of the king" (6:13 MT), is a bit redundant considering that the administrators immediately say, "Did you not publish a decree?" The first two words, *'al 'esar*, "concerning the decree," have no parallel in the Greek, so they may be a later addition. It would be possible to delete them and read *malka'* as a vocative. We would then revise the NIV to read: "So they went to the king and spoke to him: O king, did you not . . . ?" However, the contested words do appear in 4QDan^b, albeit with a slight variation; therefore, it is best to read with the MT.

6:19 / The MT (6:20) has **dawn** twice, although they are two different words. The following, then, is a more literal translation than the NIV: "Then the king, at dawn, arose at dawn." The first term, *sheparpar*, is less common than the second term, so *negah*, the second one, looks suspiciously like a scribal gloss. Both terms, however, have strong textual support: both are in 4QDan^b and Theodotion. It seems that the second term is more specific, referring to the precise moment when the sun rises, whereas the first is broader, signifying the longer time period of dawn (Montgomery, *Daniel*, p. 279). Therefore, we should consider both original, with the second term giving greater specificity to the first. Consequently, the NIV is a good rendering; compare similarly the English expression "at the crack of dawn" (Hartman and Di Lella, *Daniel*, p. 196).

6:24 / Literally, the words **who had falsely accused Daniel** mean "who had eaten the pieces of Daniel." The idiom means "to slander," "to accuse maliciously," or "to denounce." It is used also in 3:8.

According to the MT, there were 120 satraps, all of whom apparently went as a group with the two administrators to the king (6:1–2, 4, 6 [6:2–3, 5, 7 MT]). However, the LXX at vv. 3, 4, and 24 indicates that only the two other administrators were accusers. In the MT version, after adding in the family members the number would be quite large, making the story seem fantastic. How could the pit be large enough? How could there be enough lions to harm so many people? It is possible that the LXX is original and that the MT exaggerated the number. On the other hand, it seems more likely that the MT is original; the Greek tradition perhaps reduced the number to make it more believable (W. S. Towner, *Daniel* [Interp; Atlanta: John Knox, 1984], p. 87). Three or four hundred people being cast into the lions' pit does seem absurd: "They might have died of suffocation rather than of the lions" (Collins, *Daniel*, p. 262, citing Wills, *Jew in the Court*, pp. 137–38). This suggests that Dan. 6 is not "a straightforward piece of history" but "a dramatized warning and promise of God's judgment on wickedness" (Goldingay, *Daniel*, p. 135).

6:26 / The terms rendered **fear and reverence** are better translated "tremble and fear," as in the NRSV. It is interesting that the same terms are used in 5:19, except that there they refer to the people cowering before the earthly king, Nebuchadnezzar, rather than revering God, as here. In the Greek tradition the text of 6:26 has been embellished to give even more glory to God than the MT. In the LXX, the king demands more than reverence: he requires that the people "worship and serve [*latreuontes*]" this God (6:26). Moreover, he boldly confesses that he will "worship and serve [*douleuōn*]" him all his life (6:27). Finally, he notes the futility of paganism: "for the idols made by hand are not able to save, as the God of Daniel redeemed Daniel" (6:27).

§7 The Four Beastly Kingdoms and God's Kingdom (Dan. 7:1–28)

Daniel 7 is centrally located in the book; it is also of central importance. It functions as a transitional unit, providing a hinge that connects the two halves of the work. Chapter 7 is tied to what precedes by its language: it is part of the Aramaic section, which runs from Daniel 2:4b through 7:28. It is also part of the chiastic structure of chapters 2–7 (see "Stage Three" under "Language Problem and Literary Development" in the Introduction), which have been carefully crafted into a unit. However, it is tied to what follows by its more apocalyptic flavor. By genre, chapters 7–12 are primarily eschatological visions, unlike chapters 1–6, which are court stories. This difference should not be overemphasized, though, because the first half of the book also contains visions, one of which is for the end times: chapter 2. Chapter 7 is similar to chapter 2 in predicting a series of four kingdoms followed by the coming of the final, eternal kingdom of God. Nevertheless, chapter 2 is different from chapter 7 in that it is couched within a court narrative. Also, chapter 2 does not point to the archenemy of the Jews in the second century B.C., Antiochus IV, whereas chapter 7 does, in the figure of the little horn.

A further connection between chapter 7 and what follows is that Daniel sees the visions and communicates them in the first person (except for 7:1 and 10:1), yet he cannot understand them; he needs an angelic mediator to provide him with the interpretations. This is surprisingly different from the opening half of the book, where others besides Daniel experience the visions (Nebuchadnezzar in chs. 2 and 4) and visitations (Belshazzar in ch. 5). These accounts are narrated in the third person (except for 4:4–18, 34–37), and Daniel acts as the skillful interpreter, receiving the secret meanings directly from God without the aid of a heavenly messenger.

Another way in which chapter 7 is like chapters 8–12 is that it vilifies the kings and kingdoms of the world, with special emphasis on the despicable deeds of Antiochus IV. In the first half of the book, Daniel and his friends are threatened at times, but the kings are not anti-Jewish. In fact, they can be quite amiable—for example, when Darius clearly sides with Daniel against the conspirators in chapter 6. In the second half of the book, the human potentates are much more malevolent. They are exceedingly evil and destructive (7:2–7), and one king (Antiochus Epiphanes) especially seeks to persecute Jews and abolish Judaism (7:21, 25; 8:10–14, 24–25; 9:26–27; 11:30–39). Chapters 1–6, taking their cue from the story of Joseph (Gen. 39:4, 21; 41:37–44), communicate that it is possible for Jews to prosper in the court of a pagan king. God gives his faithful servants, Daniel and his friends, favor with their Gentile rulers, so that they are promoted. This is not so in chapters 7–12, where the faithful are oppressed; there is little or no hope of favor or even peace with the tyrannical "little horn." Once again, this difference should not be stressed too much, for as it was shown in the earlier sections of the commentary, it seems the author even shaped the traditional material in chapters 1–6 to speak to the people of his day, living under Seleucid oppression in the second century B.C.

Finally, chapter 7 fits in the second half of the book, because of the chronology. The author intentionally signals a change here, with date formulas. In the first half of the book, the career of Daniel progresses through the reigns of Nebuchadnezzar (chs. 1–4), Belshazzar (ch. 5), and Darius the Mede (ch. 6), but chapter 7 jumps back to the first year of Belshazzar (7:1). Chapter 8 clearly follows this by being dated to Belshazzar's third year (8:1). When we get to chapter 9, we advance to the first year of Darius (9:1). The concluding section (chs. 10–12) of the book is located in the third year of Cyrus. So, chapters 1–6 start with Nebuchadnezzar's Babylon and finish with Darius the Mede; chapters 7–12 begin with Belshazzar's Babylon and end with Persia.

One theme unites the two halves of the book: God controls the earthly powers. This is evident in chapter 1 as God carries his people into exile and fills the four Jewish youths with wisdom so that they outshine the other sages (this is also apparent in chs. 2, 4, and 5: only Daniel can interpret; all the others fail). It is manifest in the vision of chapter 2, where God's kingdom displaces human empires. It is displayed in chapters 3 and 6 when God thwarts attempts to execute his servants. It dominates chapters 4 and 5, where heaven imposes judgments on two proud monarchs: one being humiliated, the other sentenced to death. Chapters 7–12 perpetuate the notion that God is sovereign over human authorities, revealing how he will subdue them by establishing his everlasting kingdom. Besides the unity, there is also movement forward in this theme as the book develops. Just as the kingdoms are more nefarious in Daniel 7–12, so God's power over them is more dramatic and pronounced. He delivers from execution (ch. 2), from fire (ch. 3), and from lions (ch. 6) in the first half, but the hope of the latter half is that God will intervene in human history to deliver his people from the terrible persecution they are undergoing, put Antiochus IV to death, and set up his glorious, eternal kingdom (Dan. 7–12). The final vision even includes a resurrection of the dead and judgment (12:1–2).

7:1–8 / The first verse is introductory in nature, informing the reader in the third person that Daniel had a dream. Once the dream begins (7:2), the chapter shifts to a first-person account. Daniel 10 utilizes the same pattern, with the first verse in the third person, followed by the vision (vv. 2 and following) related by Daniel in the first person. The text also gives the date for the dream: in the first year of Belshazzar king of Babylon (7:1). It is significant that Daniel wrote down his dream, because this book is apocalyptic. The classical prophets were predominantly preachers whose words were mostly collected and edited by their disciples. This is not to deny that they ever inscribed or dictated words, however. Isaiah, for example, narrated the account of his call vision in his own words (Isa. 6). God also instructed Isaiah to write certain things (Isa. 8:1; 30:8); so also Jeremiah (Jer. 30:2; 36:2) and Habakkuk (Hab. 2:2). Nevertheless, speaking is more characteristic of prophecy, while writing is more characteristic of apocalyptic literature (*1 En.* 81:6; 82:1; 2 Esd. 14:37–48; Rev. 1:11, 19; 14:13; 19:9; 21:5).

The last clause of verse 1 in the NIV is **He wrote down the substance of his dream** (v. 1). This clause introduces the dream vision itself, so it is better not to translate the Aramaic word here as "substance" but rather as "head" or "first." The meaning is not that Daniel recorded the gist of what he saw but rather that the dream account is coming next. That this is so is clear from verse 28, which signifies the close of the dream: "This is the end of the matter." The account of what Daniel saw, then, is framed by the introductory rubric in verse 1 and the concluding clause in verse 28. Therefore, the opening should be rendered something like this: "He wrote down the dream. The beginning of the words:" (7:1).

Verse 2 contains another introduction to Daniel's dream. The NIV has **Daniel said** (7:2), but the MT is actually longer: "Daniel answered and said . . ." The problem with this is that the dream was already introduced in the verse before. We expect Daniel to launch into his vision report after "The beginning of the words . . ." Not only is the second introduction redundant, but it is also missing from the Greek version. Consequently, we should probably omit "Daniel said" on the grounds that these words are not original.

At this point the dream narrative commences. Daniel recounts his **vision at night** (7:2). The first things he sees are **the four winds of heaven churning up the great sea** (7:2). In the Babylonian creation myth, the god Marduk is given a number of weapons to help him defeat Tiamat, the goddess of the sea. Among these weapons are the four winds: south, north, east, and west (*ANET*, p. 66). "Four winds" language is used later in Daniel (Dan. 8:8; 11:4) and is also fairly common elsewhere in the Bible (Jer. 49:36; Ezek. 37:9; Zech. 2:6; 6:5 [NIV footnote]; Matt. 24:31; Mark 13:27; Rev. 7:1). It is a way of saying "all directions." Some make a comparison to Genesis 1:2, where "the Spirit of God was hovering over the waters" (Hartman and Di Lella, *Daniel*, p. 211). But, in fact, there is a strong contrast between the two passages (Collins, *Daniel*, p. 294). In Genesis, God is creating the world, bringing order out of chaos. The Spirit or wind of God is not churning up the sea but calmly hovering, brooding, or moving gently over the surface of the waters. In Daniel the winds make the sea choppy, stormy, turbulent, and chaotic. Genesis is positive, for God has control over the waters and causes them to teem with good creatures (Gen. 1:20–22). Daniel is negative, for evil beasts will emanate from the chaos waters causing great destruction (Dan. 7:3–7).

"The great sea" (Dan. 7:2) is describing the deep, the chaos waters, or the primal watery abyss (Gen. 7:11; Pss. 77:16; 78:15; 106:9; 107:26; Isa. 51:10; 63:12–13; Amos 7:4). We can tell that the four kingdoms of Daniel 7 are wicked, because they are represented as **four great beasts that came up out of the sea** (7:3). They appear as creatures from the chaos waters below, in stark contrast to the transcendent one revealed later, who looks like a human being and is from above (7:13–14). In the ancient Near East, the sea was associated with dangerous beings and monsters. Tiamat, the goddess of the sea, went to war against the other gods in the Mesopotamian Creation Epic and was subdued by the warrior god Marduk (*ANET*, pp. 60–72). Closer to Israel, in Canaanite literature from Ugarit, Baal, the god of storm and fertility, defeated Yamm, the god of the sea (*ANET*, p. 131). Baal also did battle with Lotan, or Leviathan, the dragon or twisting serpent thought to live in the sea (*ANET*, pp. 137–38). The ancient Israelites knew these myths or ones like them and selectively appropriated some of their motifs, themes, and shared worldview for Israel's theology. However, in doing so, they also transformed the myths in order to undermine the foreign religions and to adapt the content to Yahwism. The sea may threaten, but Yahweh is stronger (Ps. 93:3–4); he stills the roaring sea (Ps. 65:7). He rebuked the sea so that it fled, and he restrained it with a boundary (Ps. 104:6–9). It was Yahweh, not Baal or Marduk, who defeated Rahab, the sea monster (Job 9:13; 26:12–13; Ps.

89:9–10; Isa. 51:9). He "crushed the heads of Leviathan," the sea monster or sea serpent (Ps. 74:13–14; Isa. 27:1). The NT apocalypse also draws on this motif as it describes a beast rising out of the sea (Rev. 13:1) or from the abyss (Rev. 17:8). It also describes the sea as "glass" (Rev. 15:2), for when Jesus returns, it will no longer be choppy and chaotic. In fact, when God finally makes the new heaven and earth, there will no longer be any sea (Rev. 21:1).

In verses 4–6, the first three beasts are said to be *like* other animals: a winged lion, a bear with tusks, and a winged leopard with four heads. The fourth beast is not compared to any known animal but is simply described as a powerful beast with iron teeth (7:7). Ezekiel has a vision of composite beasts, but the imagery is not very close. They have calf legs, human hands, wings, and four faces (human, lion, ox, eagle; Ezek. 1:4–10). Also, Ezekiel's creatures are heavenly beings, not beasts from the abyss. They are probably cherubim, since they are part of God's throne (Ezek. 1:22–28), after which the ark was fashioned; Yahweh is enthroned on, between, or above the cherubim (1 Sam. 4:4; 2 Sam. 6:2; 2 Kgs. 19:15; 1 Chron. 13:6; Pss. 80:1; 99:1; Isa. 37:16). A closer parallel can be found in Hosea, where God presents himself in imagery similar to that of Daniel. Like wild animals, he is about to pounce upon the Israelites for their sins: "I will come upon them like a lion, like a leopard I will lurk by the path. Like a bear robbed of her cubs, I will attack them and rip them open. Like a lion I will devour them; a wild animal will tear them apart" (Hos. 13:7–8). The sequence is close. Hosea has lion, leopard, bear, lion/wild animal; Daniel has lion, bear, leopard, wild animal. Daniel puts the bear before the leopard, while Hosea has the leopard before the bear; Hosea puts the fourth beast in parallel with "lion," while Daniel leaves it unspecified. There are other differences as well in the details of Daniel's beasts, such as wings. Daniel may also be drawing on the art and iconography of the ancient Near East, where images of hybrid creatures were quite common, especially in Mesopotamia (see *ANEP*, pp. 212–13).

The **first beast was like a lion** with **the wings of an eagle** (7:4). Just as the lion is the most exalted beast on four legs and the eagle is the most magnificent creature that flies, this first kingdom is the greatest. It signifies Babylonia, which, in the mind of the author, was the most powerful empire. Similarly, in the statue imagery of chapter 2, gold is the finest of the metals, so Daniel identifies the Babylonian king, Nebuchadnezzar, as the head of gold (Dan. 2:32, 36–38). Here, as Daniel continues to watch the winged lion, he sees **its wings ... torn off** (v. 4). On the one hand, this can be understood as a judgment, limiting the beast's speed and range. On the other hand, that it then stands **on two feet like a man** (see *ANEP*, p. 61, no. 192, for an example of a lion standing on his hind feet) and obtains **the heart of a man** (7:4) is clearly a reward, not a punishment; a blessing, not a curse. The writer is probably alluding to the healing of Nebuchadnezzar in Daniel 4. The Babylonian king was judged for his pride and driven out from his throne to live like an animal: "Let his mind be changed from that of a man and let him be given the mind of an animal" (4:16). The same Aramaic word is translated "mind" in Daniel 4:16 (4:17 MT) and "heart" in 7:4. Later, after being humbled, Nebuchadnezzar returned to his senses. Once he acknowledged "that the Most High is sovereign over the kingdoms of men and gives them to anyone he wishes," (4:25) then his "sanity was restored" (4:34). In other words, he was given the heart or mind of a man once more. This is further confirmation that the first kingdom is Babylonia.

The **second beast** has the appearance of **a bear** (7:5). Some see significance in the **three ribs in its mouth between its teeth** (7:5). It has been proposed that they represent three different kingdoms, three Babylonian kings, or three cities (for details on the various possibilities, see the Additional Note on 7:5). All of these suggestions are attempts to read too much into the text. The ribs only show that the bear has a voracious appetite; it is finishing off its last victim (Collins, *Daniel*, p. 298). The bear is **raised up on one of its sides** (7:5) perhaps because it is planning to spring on new prey after finishing the ribs. At that moment, a voice instructs the bear to **get up and eat** its **fill of flesh** (7:5). The bear represents Media, which is being "stirred up" to devour Babylonia (Jer. 51:11; see also 51:28).

The third beast looks **like a leopard** with **four wings** and **four heads** (7:6). Since the third empire is Persia, the four heads possibly represent the four Persian kings known to the Jews from biblical tradition (see also Dan. 11:2, which enumerates four Persian kings): Cyrus (Ezra 1:1–4, 7–8; 3:7; Isa. 44:28–45:4), Ahasuerus, or Xerxes (Ezra 4:6; Esth. 1:1–3), Artaxerxes (Ezra 4:7–8, 11, 23), and Darius the Persian (Neh. 12:22). Regarding the last king, there were actually three Persian monarchs named Darius. Perhaps Darius III is in view, because he was defeated by Alexander the Great. Another suggestion regarding the number four is that it represents the four points of the compass. It then highlights the universal reign of this kingdom. This fits in well with what is said of this beast: **it was given authority to rule** (7:6). Furthermore, this statement about the third kingdom here in chapter 7 corresponds nicely with the description of the third kingdom in chapter 2: it "will rule over the whole earth" (2:39). That no one can exercise dominion on earth without heaven's permission is a recurring theme in the book. "The Lord delivered Jehoiachin" into the hand of Nebuchadnezzar (1:2). Daniel instructs the Babylonian king that "the Most High is sovereign over the kingdoms of men and gives them to anyone he wishes" (4:17, 25, 32; cf. 5:21). The seer reminds Belshazzar: "The Most High God gave your father Nebuchadnezzar sovereignty and greatness and glory and splendor" (5:18).

The **fourth beast** is not compared to a specific known animal, and we are told that it is **different from all the former beasts** (7:7). It is ferocious: **terrifying and frightening and very powerful** (7:7). It is also described as having **large iron teeth** (7:7). The mention of iron connects this kingdom with the fourth kingdom of chapter 2, which is portrayed in two phases: (1) legs of iron and (2) feet of iron and clay (2:33, 40–43). A further correspondence between the two chapters can be seen in the destructive nature of the fourth kingdom: **it crushed and devoured its victims and trampled underfoot whatever was left** (7:7). Similarly, the fourth kingdom in chapter 2 will be "strong as iron—for iron breaks and smashes everything—and as iron breaks things to pieces, so it will crush and break all the others" (2:40). This is not merely a thematic correspondence, but a verbal one as well, for the words "crushed" (7:7), "breaks" (2:40), and "crush" (2:40) are all from the same Aramaic root (see the Additional Note on 7:7).

Chapters 2 and 7 both agree that there will be four empires and that the last one will be brutal. But Daniel's vision of the four beasts goes beyond Nebuchadnezzar's image of the four metals by providing greater specificity in its description of the fourth kingdom. This last beast has **ten horns** (7:7), which we are later told represent ten kings (7:24). This stands for the Greek Empire, with special emphasis on its development into the Seleucid kingdom. In addition, after the ten horns comes **another horn, a little one** (7:8), which represents an eleventh king (7:24). This king is arrogant, with **a mouth** that speaks **boastfully** (7:8). Later, a king is described who "will say unheard-of things against the God of gods" (11:36). These are clearly pointing to Antiochus IV, who "spoke with great arrogance" (1 Macc. 1:24 NRSV). Since both Daniel 2 and 7 are in Aramaic, contain the same four-kingdom schema, and describe the kingdom of God as a fifth kingdom that will destroy the previous ones and last forever, it follows that this common material is likely traditional. However, since there is nothing in chapter 2 about a succession of kings leading up to an especially evil tyrant, it seems that the author of the book added Daniel 7:7d–8, 11a, 20–22, and 24–25—the verses that envision the eleven horns. By doing this the author accomplishes three things. First, he breaks the monotony: chapter 7 does not just repeat chapter 2 with different imagery; it provides movement by carrying the thought further. Secondly, he makes it very clear who his target is. The previous chapters are more subtle, but now there is no mistaking the Seleucid ruler of the second century B.C. Thirdly, he prepares the way for the following chapters, where he will go into even greater detail about the little horn (ch. 8), the time of the end (ch. 9), and the Seleucid Empire, with its evil monarch who persecutes the Jews (ch. 11). In these ways the author shows how he was shaping the tradition to fit his larger apocalyptic purpose (for more detail, see the Additional Note).

The notion that there would be a succession of three or four empires could date from the Persian or early Greek period. The representation of Greece as the worst and most destructive kingdom could stem from Alexander's conquest. In the second century B.C., the extreme antipathy Antiochus IV showed the Jews could have provided impetus for the composition of this apocalypse. Antiochus pushed his program of Hellenization (1 Macc. 1:11–15), sold the high priesthood (2 Macc. 4:7–10), and plundered the Jerusalem temple (1 Macc. 1:20–23). Then he made Judaism illegal, desecrated the temple, and began to force Jews to worship the Greek gods or die (1 Macc. 1:54–61). The author of Daniel portrayed Antiochus IV as the little horn—the evil tyrant who made war against the holy ones—in order to express the hope that God would intervene in history to put an end to this brutal regime. The apocalyptist's prayer was that God's everlasting kingdom would replace this beastly one.

In his vision, Daniel not only sees the ten horns and the eleventh little horn, but he sees that **three of the first horns** are **uprooted before the little one** (7:8). While it is clear that the little horn is Antiochus IV, it is not so transparent which other kings are intended for the ten and the three. On the one hand, the ten might be kings contemporary with the eleventh. If so, the three could refer to the kings that Antiochus IV defeated: Ptolemy VI Philometor, Ptolemy VII Euergetes, and Artaxias of Armenia. On the other hand, it seems more natural to read the ten as a succession of kings, the last three of which were contenders who were pushed aside so that the eleventh could reign. In other words, the text is saying that the little horn will come after the ten kings (7:24) and will uproot three of them (7:8). Most scholars follow this view, but they debate which kings to include in the list of ten.

There is an extant king list from the Hellenistic era (*ANET*, pp. 566–67) that contains the following names (regnal years from Hartman and Di Lella, *Daniel*, p. 214):

1. Alexander the Great, 336–323
2. Philip Arrhidaeus (Alexander's brother), 323–316

3. Alexander IV Aegus (the son of Alexander the Great), 316–312
4. Seleucus I Nicator, 312–280
5. Antiochus I Soter, 280–261
6. Antiochus II Theos, 261–246
7. Seleucus II Gallinicus, 246–226
8. Seleucus III Soter, 226–223
9. Antiochus III the Great, 223–187
10. Seleucus IV Philopator, 187–175
11. Antiochus IV Epiphanes, 175–164

However, it is best to eliminate Philip and Alexander IV at the beginning, because they are not part of the Seleucid dynasty, which is clearly central to Daniel. Toward the end of the list, we should include the sons of Seleucus IV, Antiochus and Demetrius, who were rivals for the throne with Antiochus IV. It is true that, of these, Antiochus IV can be blamed for the death of only Antiochus son of Seleucus IV. Nevertheless, Seleucus IV was murdered (by Heliodorus), and Demetrius was held hostage in Rome. Thus all three were displaced, with the result that Antiochus IV captured the throne (Collins, *Daniel*, pp. 320–21). The eleven horns would, then, refer to the following:

1. Alexander the Great
2. Seleucus I Nicator
3. Antiochus I Soter
4. Antiochus II Theos
5. Seleucus II Gallinicus
6. Seleucus III Soter
7. Antiochus III the Great
8. Seleucus IV Philopator
9. Antiochus (son of Seleucus IV)
10. Demetrius (son of Seleucus IV)
11. Antiochus IV Epiphanes

Antiochus son of Seleucus IV can be considered a king because he was coregent with Antiochus IV before he was killed. Demetrius, however, was not crowned (at least, not before Antiochus IV—Demetrius did later reign as Demetrius I Soter). If the ten horns symbolize ten kings, then the biblical writer included Demetrius for reasons about which we can only guess. If so, strict historical precision apparently did not concern him. Perhaps he considered Demetrius to be the rightful king instead of Antiochus IV, so Demetrius might be king in his mind if not in history.

7:9–14 / The MT sets verses 9–10 out as poetry. Daniel has been seeing a vision of beasts emerging from the sea symbolizing four kingdoms. Now he sees a heavenly judgment scene with **thrones**. One throne is for God, **the Ancient of Days**, who sits upon it (7:9). The other thrones are intended for the rest of the heavenly court, the **thousands upon thousands** of other heavenly beings mentioned in the next verse: **the court was seated** (7:10). The background to this is the divine council motif, which is common in ancient Near Eastern texts. Among Israel's polytheistic neighbors there would be a chief god who was king and head of the pantheon. The lesser gods served as part of his court and privy council. In Israel, of course, there was only supposed to be one God. The other heavenly beings were not normally called deities, but they were part of his council (1 Kgs. 22:19–22; Job 1–2; Pss. 82; 89:6–8; Isa. 6:1–7; Jer. 23:18). Psalm 82 is unusual because it does seem to allow that the members of the heavenly assembly were gods (Ps. 82:1). But God judges them and condemns them to death (Ps. 82:6–7). It concludes with a prayer that God will "rise up" and "judge the earth" (Ps. 82:8). Psalm 96 also proclaims God as judge: "he comes to judge the earth. He will judge the world in righteousness and the peoples with his truth" (Ps. 96:13). In the NT, Jesus promises twelve thrones for his disciples so that they might judge Israel (Matt. 19:28). There are also thrones in heaven for the twenty-four elders (Rev. 4:4).

The phrase "Ancient of Days" is similar to the Canaanite expression "father of years" used of *'el* in the Ugaritic texts. There *'el* is also portrayed as old and wise with gray hair, just as here God's **hair** is **white like wool** (7:9). The expression "Eternal God" (Gen. 21:33) is also roughly parallel. Like his hair, God's **clothing** is also **as white as snow** (7:9). Similarly the clothes of Jesus at his transfiguration (Mark 9:3) and of the angel at Jesus's tomb (Matt. 28:3) were bright white. **Fire** is a common element of theophanies (Exod. 3:2; 19:18; Deut. 5:4; Ps. 97:3). Both fire (Ezek. 1:4, 13) and **wheels** (Ezek. 1:15–21) accompany Ezekiel's vision of God's glory. There are parallels for **river of fire** (7:10), "clothing whiter than snow," and **ten thousand times ten thousand** (7:10) in *1 Enoch* 14 (Collins, *Daniel*, p. 300). In short, Daniel 7:9 draws on well-known imagery of the biblical world.

Once the court is seated, the judgment can commence. For this purpose **the books** are **opened** (7:10). Daniel also mentions "the Book of Truth" (10:21) and a book that lists those who "will be delivered" (12:1). Malachi mentions a "scroll of remembrance," which is a record of "those who revered the LORD and honored his name" (Mal. 3:16). The books spell doom for the fourth beast: **Then I continued to watch . . . until the** beast was slain and its body destroyed and thrown into the blazing fire (7:11). The connection between the court and the destruction of the beast is even closer in verse 26 in the interpretation section of the chapter. The mention of **the boastful words the horn was speaking** (7:11) specifically ties the judgment of Greece to the arrogance of Antiochus IV.

The fourth beast is destroyed, but the other three are not. **Stripped of their authority,** they are **allowed to live for a period of time** (7:12). This is puzzling because the beasts seem to represent a succession of empires. Presumably, each new kingdom destroys the previous one, yet somehow they survive. There is a parallel tension in Daniel 2. There we saw that on the one hand, the fourth kingdom destroys the earlier kingdoms (2:40), yet on the other hand, they must survive because it is God's ultimate kingdom that destroys the others (2:44). In the dream imagery, the stone strikes the feet—the last kingdom—but that brings down the whole statue, which symbolically contains all the kingdoms (2:45). Apparently, the author of Daniel has in mind the vestiges of the former kingdoms and peoples. By the time of Antiochus IV the vast empires of Babylonia, Media, and Persia had disappeared; they had been "stripped of their authority." Yet, there were small territories ruled by the remnants of those peoples, so it still might be said that the other beasts/kingdoms survived. The "period of time" probably refers to the time between the destruction of the fourth beast/kingdom and the coming of the kingdom of God. When that happens, all the "peoples, nations and men" will be expected to submit to God and to serve his kingdom (7:14; cf. v. 27).

The next thing Daniel sees in his **vision at night** is **one like a son of man** (7:13). The term "son of man" (*bar 'enash*) actually means "man," "a human being," or "mortal." The Hebrew equivalent (*ben-'adam*) is used frequently this way in Ezekiel when the prophet is addressed by God or an angel. For example, the word of the Lord comes to Ezekiel, saying, "Son of man, I have made you a watchman for the house of Israel" (Ezek. 3:17). The same usage is found in Daniel. The angel Gabriel addresses Daniel, "Son of man, . . . understand that the vision concerns the time of the end" (Dan. 8:17). The contrast is between heavenly beings (including God) and humans. That it clearly means "man" or "human" can be seen where it is parallel with "man," as in Numbers 23:19 ("God is not a man that he should lie, nor a son of man, that he should change his mind") and Psalm 8:4 ("What is man that you are mindful of him, the son of man that you care for him?"). So, if "son of man" means "human being," then "one *like* a son of man" means one who looks like a human being, in this case a heavenly being who looks human. The construction is parallel to those used in describing the first three beasts. The first was "like a lion" (7:4); the second "looked like a bear" (7:5); and the third "looked like a leopard" (7:6). Yet this is a heavenly figure. Angels often look like humans, throughout the Bible and also in Daniel. In Daniel 8:15 the heavenly one looks "like a man." The archangel Gabriel is called a "man" in Daniel 9:21 (similarly 10:5, 16). God looks like a man in Ezekiel 1:26. It should not surprise us if God and his heavenly attendants look like us, or rather, we look like them, for we are made in their image (Gen. 1:26–27). God is not anthropomorphic, but we are theomorphic, for we were made in his image, not he in ours. While some people today think the image of God is something spiritual, at least some ancient Israelites would have thought it physical, as for example when God appeared to Abraham as a man (Gen. 18:1–19:1) and when God, resembling a man, wrestled with Jacob (Gen. 32:22–32).

Although the one Daniel sees appears to be human, it is in fact a heavenly being, for it was **coming with the clouds of heaven** (7:13). Unlike the beasts, which come from the unruly chaos waters of the abyss, this humanlike figure comes from above. The cultural background to this is clearly the Canaanite myth of Baal, the warrior god and storm god, who rode through heaven on his cloudy chariot. The Israelites appropriated this imagery for their warrior deity, Yahweh. For example, Psalm 104 says, "He makes the clouds his chariot and rides on the wings of the wind" (Ps. 104:3). Similarly, Psalm 68 reads, "extol him who rides on the clouds—his name is the LORD [*Yah*]" (Ps. 68:4).

This presents a problem, though, because in Israel the cloud rider is normally Yahweh. Yet, we already saw that Yahweh is the "Ancient of Days." Then this transcendent one, with human appearance, approaches **the Ancient of Days and is led into his presence** (7:13). There seem to be two divine figures here, which is confusing. This was not a problem for the Canaanites, who were polytheists, but it is curious to find this imagery in Jewish literature. Canaanite El was the head of the pantheon, the king, the "father of years," the wise old judge with hoary head who sat on his throne. Baal was the young warrior / storm god. After defeating Yamm, the god of the sea and rivers, Baal approached El. It was requested that a palace be built for Baal that he might be worshiped as king (*ANET*, pp. 129–35). Here, the Ancient of Days is parallel to El; the one like a human being is similar to Baal. Just as Baal is proclaimed king in Canaanite texts, the one like a human in Daniel gets a kingdom. He is **given authority, glory and sovereign power. . . . His dominion is an everlasting dominion that will not pass away, and his kingdom is one that will never be destroyed** (7:14). The best solution is to see this one like a human as a being (or collective—"beings"—see below on the "saints of the Most High") subordinate to God. The Israelites appropriated the divine council motif but subordinated the other heavenly beings to God. They took away the divinity of these beings and made them servants, messengers, and attendants of the one true God. So, with this Baal motif, they must have thought of this one like a human being as subordinate to God. Although it is usually Yahweh who as sovereign deity rides forth on his cloudy chariot, this must be an exception, since the Ancient of Days is clearly the king of heaven.

To sum up this section, Daniel sees a vision of four beasts/kingdoms emerging from the sea, the fourth of which is exceedingly wicked. This is followed by the setting up of the heavenly court, which pronounces judgment on the fourth kingdom and destroys it. Verses 13 and 14 portray the coming of God's kingdom. It is in strong contrast to the previous kingdoms. They are like wild, violent animals; this one is like a human being. They are from below, from the sea, from chaos; this one is from heaven. Their kingdoms and power are temporal, ephemeral; this one has eternal dominion.

7:15–18 / In this next section, a heavenly being gives Daniel the interpretation of his dream/vision. Daniel's response to the vision is consternation. He is troubled in spirit and disturbed by the visions that passed through his mind (7:15). It is curious that a similar statement is made at the end of this same chapter (7:28). This is a recurrent motif in Daniel: Nebuchadnezzar (2:1; 4:5) and Daniel, later in the book (8:27; 10:16–17). Similarly, Pharaoh was troubled about his dream (Gen. 41:8). In the Bible, dreams typically leave their recipients troubled, for the dreams often portend imminent, disturbing events.

In his anxiety, Daniel approaches **one of those standing there and asks him the true meaning of all this** (7:16). It is possible that Gabriel is the one Daniel approaches (8:16; 9:21). In Daniel 1–6, Daniel does not need angels to interpret dreams and visions. Rather, he is the interpreter, getting insight directly from God. In chapters 7–12, however, there are intermediaries. This shows the more apocalyptic character of the second half of the book. The tendency in classical prophecy is for God to speak directly to the prophet. The development of apocalyptic literature begins in the exile, where angels are prominent, such as in Ezekiel 40–48. Zechariah, in the postexilic period, carries this further. The interpreting angel is central in Zechariah 1–7.

The angel is happy to help Daniel: **he told me and gave me the interpretation of these things** (7:16). He first explains that **the four great beasts are four kingdoms** (7:17). These empires **rise from the earth** (7:17).

This does not contradict verse 3, which tells us they come from the sea, a place symbolic of chaos and evil. These kingdoms are from below, from the earth, not from heaven, as is the kingdom of God.

Now we come to a big surprise indeed. Who is the one like a human being, introduced in verse 13? There it seems to be an individual. Yet, the angel apparently reveals now that it is a group. In verse 14, in the vision, the dominion is given to the human-like heavenly being. But in verse 18, in the interpretation, the kingdom is given to a plurality: **the saints of the Most High will receive the kingdom and will possess it forever** (7:18). The "saints of the Most High" in the interpretation clearly correspond to the "one like a son of man" in the vision (Hartman and Di Lella, *Daniel*, p. 219). These "saints" or "holy ones" are not the earthly believers. Rather, they are heavenly beings. While the term may at times refer to humans (e.g., Ps. 34:9), such usage is rare in the Old Testament. Outside of the Bible, in ancient Near Eastern texts, the term is used for heavenly beings (for the references in Ugaritic, Phoenician, and Aramaic and also in the DSS, see Collins, *Daniel*, p. 314). In other passages in the OT, this is also the norm. For example, Deuteronomy says, "The LORD came from Sinai. . . . He came with myriads of holy ones" (Deut. 33:2). Psalm 89 reads, "The heavens praise your wonders, O LORD, your faithfulness too, in the assembly of the holy ones" (Ps. 89:5; see also Job 15:15). Finally, it is clear from the book of Daniel that this is the understanding. Earlier in the book, Nebuchadnezzar saw "a messenger, a holy one, coming down from heaven" (Dan. 4:13). What he decrees is the judgment of heaven: "The decision is announced by messengers; the holy ones declare the verdict" (Dan. 4:17). In these passages, the term "holy ones," or "saints," undeniably refers to heavenly beings. So it is with Daniel 7:18.

One objection concerning this view is that the evil king, represented by the horn, defeats some of the saints (7:21), which seems impossible. Yet that is what the book teaches. The little horn, which stands for Antiochus IV, brings down some of the host of heaven and tramples them (8:10–12). What the author of Daniel envisioned was spiritual warfare (10:12–13, 20): when there is conflict below, it is related to conflict in the heavenly arena. From a human standpoint, Antiochus IV persecuted Jews on earth, but from the apocalyptist's point of view, this could not have happened unless evil spirits triumphed over some of the angels. This is therefore a kind of theodicy, explaining evil on earth by citing warfare in heaven. Of course, God's army ultimately triumphs, which would have been of great encouragement to the persecuted Jews.

7:19–27 / Although the angel gives the interpretation in verses 15–18, it is brief, and Daniel is not content with it. He desires further elaboration of the meaning. Specifically, he wants **to know the true meaning of the fourth beast, which was different from all the others and most terrifying** (7:19). He also is curious **to know about the ten horns** (7:20). In this passage, Daniel also wishes for more information concerning **the horn that looked more imposing than the others and that had eyes and a mouth that spoke boastfully** (7:20). Although the vision seems to have ended in verse 14, Daniel now sees **this horn . . . waging war against the saints and defeating them, until the Ancient of Days** comes and pronounces **judgment in favor of the saints of the Most High, and the time comes when they possess the kingdom** (7:21–22). This marks a sudden jump back into vision material and the repetition of verse 18. The author of the book of Daniel added this into the traditional story to reflect his historical situation: one of intense persecution that had implications in the cosmic realm. The literary effect is to give hope to the Jews because the suffering will be temporary. Later divine judgment on the horn will, in the end, leave the holy ones in heaven and the faithful Jews on earth in possession of the kingdom.

The angel now reveals that the **fourth beast** is a **fourth kingdom** that will conquer **the whole earth** (7:23). The **ten horns** stand for **ten kings who will come from this kingdom** (7:24), after whom an eleventh **king will arise** who **will subdue three kings** (7:24). **He will** also **speak against the Most High and oppress his saints** (7:25). The word "oppress" means "to wear out," as with clothing. In addition, this evil king will **try to change the set times and the laws** (7:25). This is God's prerogative; "he changes times and seasons" (2:21). While some think that changing the times has to do with changing the Jewish calendar, it probably has more to do with forbidding Jewish practices on Sabbaths and festivals rather than specifically tampering with the actual numbering of the days and months (1 Macc. 1:41–50; see Collins, *Daniel*, p. 322). The persecution of the saints will last **for a time, times and half a time** (7:25). This is a cryptic way of saying three and a half years—that is, a year, two years, and half a year (for similar references, see Dan. 8:14; 9:27; 12:7, 11–12; Rev. 12:6, 14; 13:5).

With verse 26, we return once again, for the last time, to hear the denouement of the story. **The court will sit** and bring an end to the fourth beast (7:26). Then **sovereignty** will be given **to the saints, the people of the Most High** (7:27). The MT has "to the people of the holy ones of the Most High." The NIV switches "saints" and "people" and interprets the two terms to be in apposition with each other. While that is possible, we have seen that "the holy ones" indicates heavenly ones. Therefore, "the people of the holy ones of the Most High" points to the Jews who are the people of the heavenly host of the Most High, or God. Just as the persecution of the Jews results from the trampling of angels by evil spirits, so the liberation and reign of the Jews will result from the defeat of the evil kingdom and the triumph of the angels. The angels receive the power from God, but that translates into dominion for the people on earth as well.

7:28 / The chapter is delimited by "the beginning of the words" in verse 1 and "this is the end of the matter" in verse 28. Once again Daniel testifies to his consternation. He then concludes by noting, I kept the matter to myself (v. 28). Why Daniel keeps silent is not stated. Perhaps it is because he is awestruck and overwhelmed by what he has seen. Or, maybe we should connect this with the end of the book, where Daniel is instructed to "close up and seal the words of the scroll until the time of the end" (12:4). In other words, he understands himself to be forbidden to reveal to the people of his day what he has seen. In this way, the second-century author emphasizes his hope that what is written in the vision is about to happen.

Daniel 7 is of the utmost importance for understanding both the identity of Jesus and the plan of God for the end times. When the book was written, "son of man" was not a title, but rather the vision referred to a transcendent one who looked like a man. Originally it was probably understood to be an angel or archangel—Michael is the best candidate, since he figures prominently in the deliverance of the Jews (12:1). However, in the NT, Jesus uses "Son of Man" as a title for himself (for example, Matt. 8:20; 9:6; 11:19). Although he sometimes uses it to mean "man," he identifies himself with the figure in Daniel's vision at other times, predicting that he will return in power and glory riding on clouds (Matt. 19:28; 24:27, 30; 26:64). John also utilizes the imagery for Jesus in his apocalypse (Rev. 1:7, 13; 14:14). Daniel's vision in chapter 7 gives us hope for the future. Jesus will return to raise from the dead those believers who have died (1 Cor. 15:22–26; 1 Thess. 4:14–17), to gather together his living followers, and to set up God's kingdom in its fullness. The oppressive regimes of this world will disintegrate as they are replaced by the eternal, righteous, reign of God. This leads us to cry "Maranatha" (1 Cor. 16:22) and to pray "Your kingdom come . . . on earth as it is in heaven" (Matt 6:10). For those who are suffering persecution for the name of Jesus, Daniel 7 holds out the certain hope of the eventual triumph of God's kingdom and with it the vindication of God's people for their faithfulness. It calls them to endure and persevere through their present trials with an eye fixed on the horizon awaiting their great future.

Additional Notes §7

7:1 / The Aramaic has *daniye'l khelem khazah wekhezwe re'sheh 'al mishkebeh*: "Daniel saw a **dream** and **visions** of his head upon his bed." The LXX has only one term, *horama*—"dream" or "vision"—instead of two, "dream and visions," as in the MT. Since the pair occurs several other times (2:28; 4:2 [4:5 Eng.]), it is more likely that one term dropped out of the Greek than that a second term was added to the Aramaic. Therefore, the MT is preferable.

A more literal translation of **he wrote down the substance of his dream** (Aram. *be'dayin khelma' ketab re'sh millin 'amar*) is "then he wrote the dream; the head of words he said." In better-sounding English: "Then he wrote down his dream, thus beginning his account" (Hartman and Di Lella, *Daniel*, p. 202). Goldingay omits *'amar* because its equivalent is missing from the LXX and because it is possibly a scribal gloss: "He wrote the dream down. The beginning of the account:" (Goldingay, *Daniel*, 142); Collins translates the second clause "he began to speak" but omits it because it is missing from Theodotion's Greek version and because it seems unlikely to fit in the gap of 4QDan^b. I retain it because it is part of the structure of the chapter. Alternatively, we might read *re'sh millin*, "the beginning of words" (as though followed by a colon), leaving out *'amar*, "he said." Of course, it is possible that the structure was added later, but that is not clear. The dream does seem to have several introductions, but the one at the beginning of v. 2 is more suspect.

7:2 / Goldingay argues that **the great sea** refers to the Mediterranean Sea (Goldingay, *Daniel*, p. 160). In other places that is so (e.g., Josh. 1:4; 9:1; 15:47; 23:4; Ezek. 47:10, 15, 19, 20), but not here (Collins, *Daniel*, p. 295; Hartman and Di Lella, *Daniel*, p. 211). Most of the nations indicated here (Babylonia, Media, Persia) do not border the Mediterranean Sea. In 7:2 the Aramaic *yamma' rabba'*, "the great sea," is referring to what is in Hebrew the *tehom rabbah*, "the great abyss" (Montgomery, *Daniel*, p. 285).

7:4 / The first and third animals are composed of animal bodies with birdlike **wings**. This has caused some to comment that they violate the Torah with respect to mixing of breeds (Gen. 1:11–12, 21, 24, 25; Deut. 22:9–11; see Goldingay, *Daniel*, p. 161; T. Longman III, *Daniel* [NIVAC; Grand Rapids: Zondervan, 1999], p. 183). Of course these are not creatures of our world, but in the understanding of those who wrote and read this literature, there is no indication that these animals resulted from crossbreeding. Perhaps in the minds of the authors and their readers these are separate species, created after their kind. It is true that demons are represented in ancient Near Eastern art as hybrid animals, but in the Bible so are heavenly beings. The cherubim are winged beings with animal bodies and some human features (Ezek. 1), and the six-winged seraphim probably have serpentine bodies (Isa. 6).

7:5 / Instead of **ribs,** some read "fangs" or "tusks," based on Arabic usage of the cognate word (R. Frank, "The Description of the 'Bear' in Dn 7,5," *CBQ* 21 [1959], pp. 505–7). But the normal meaning in Aramaic is "rib." Hartman and Di Lella follow Ginsberg (*Studies in Daniel*, pp. 12–15) in rearranging the text so that the tusks go with the lion rather than the bear. They then interpret the three tusks as symbolizing three Babylonian kings (Hartman and Di Lella, *Daniel*, pp. 209, 212). There is no manuscript evidence for Ginsberg's rearrangement.

Over the centuries, scholars have sought to identify the three ribs with kingdoms: Assyria, Babylonia, and Media (Hippolytus, third cent. A.D.); Babylon, Assyria, and Syria (G. H. Ewald, nineteenth cent. ; Babylonia, Media, and Persia (Jerome, fourth cent. A.D.); Babylonia, Media, and Lydia (L. Berthold, nineteenth cent. A.D.); Ararat, Minni, and Ashkenaz (R. J. M. Gurney, "The Four Kingdoms of Daniel 2 and 7," *Them* 2 [1977], p. 43); or perhaps Urartu, Mannaea, and Scythia (J. H. Walton, "The Four Kingdoms of Daniel," *JETS* 29 [1986], p. 30). Another suggestion is that they are three Babylonian kings: Nebuchadnezzar, Evil-Merodach, and Belshazzar (Lacocque, *Daniel*, p. 140). According to the medieval rabbi Ibn Ezra, the three ribs are three cities conquered by the Medes (cited in Lacocque, *Daniel*, p. 140, n. 78).

In the phrase **on one of its sides,** Hartman and Di Lella consider the number "one" to be significant, pointing to Darius the Mede, the one Median king with whom the author was familiar (Hartman and Di Lella, *Daniel*, pp. 212–13). As with the symbolism of the three ribs, this is not at all clear.

7:6 / Those who say this animal is Greece interpret the **four heads** as the four Diadochi, or successors of Alexander (S. R. Miller, *Daniel* [NAC 18; Nashville: Broadman & Holman, 1994]). However, it is clear that the author had Persia in mind, because his four-kingdom scheme is Babylonia (7:1; 8:1), Media (9:1), Persia (10:1), and Greece (10:20). For further discussion of the four kingdoms, see the Introduction and the commentary on Dan. 2.

7:7 / The NIV reverses the terms **crushed and devoured.** The MT has *'akelah umaddeqah*, "devoured and crushed." The term "crushed" comes from the root *dqq*. It is also used in vv. 19 and 23 in the same way, describing the crushing action of the fourth kingdom. It occurs in ch. 2 with reference to the fourth kingdom, which "breaks" and "will crush" all other kingdoms (2:40). But it also describes what the kingdom of God will do. It is represented as a rock that "smashed" the fourth kingdom of iron and clay (2:34). Later in the interpretation section, the kingdom of God "will crush" all the others like the rock that "broke" the other metals (2:44–45). Finally, it is used of the lions, which broke in pieces all of the bones of those cast into the den (6:24).

7:8 / Ch. 7 may have undergone some development over time. If the earlier version put forth a ten-king scheme understanding Antiochus IV as the tenth and final king, that means that all of the references to the eleventh horn in the vision and the interpretation are secondary. The verses thought to be secondary are as follows: 7:7d–8, 11a, 20–22, and 24–25 (Hartman and Di Lella, *Daniel*, pp. 208–10, following Ginsberg, *Studies in Daniel*, pp. 5–23, 63–75). We cannot be sure that the developmental view is correct. It is possible that the original author used different language when talking about the eleventh king simply because Antiochus IV was different from all previous kings (Collins, *Daniel*, p. 279). Still, I think there is enough evidence to tip the scales slightly in favor of the two-editions view.

If one is not convinced that we can know which names the author had in mind, there is another solution. It is possible that the number ten was chosen as a round figure to indicate an indefinite number of rulers in the Greek kingdom that preceded Antiochus IV (Goldingay, *Daniel*, p. 179). However, in this interpretation, the number **three** is still a problem.

7:13 / The NIV uses traditional language in rendering *kebar 'enash* literally as **one like a son of man.** The NRSV rendering is superior: "one like a human being." Its Hebrew equivalent (*ben-'adam*) also occurs in other books (e.g., Num. 23:19; Pss. 8:4 [8:5 MT]; 80:17 [80:18 MT]; 144:3; Job 25:6; cf. Isa. 51:12; Jer. 49:18; 50:40).

7:17 / The Aramaic actually says "kings," not **kingdoms.** However, the Greek has "kingdoms," which may be original. In Aramaic, *malkewan*, "kingdoms," is very similar to *malkin*, "kings"; the change could have resulted from scribal error. But it is possible to keep the MT reading, "kings," and understand it as symbolic. Kings are symbols for kingdoms. In any case, it is clear from the chapter that the beasts represent empires and not individual kings.

§8 The Vision of the Ram and the Male Goat (Dan. 8:1–27)

Here in chapter 8 the language reverts back to Hebrew. When the Aramaic section began, the narrator introduced it by saying, "The astrologers answered the king in Aramaic" (2:4). There is no explanation given in chapter 8 for the change back. The author inherited the Aramaic material (2:4b–7:28) but shaped it for his purposes. He then added chapters 1 (actually, 1:1–2:4a) and 8–12 in Hebrew.

Chapter 8 is linked to chapter 7 explicitly by informing the reader that this vision came after the earlier one (8:1). The two chapters share some similarities but also are distinguished by certain differences. Both begin with a chronological heading locating the vision in the reign of King Belshazzar: chapter 7 is dated to his first year, chapter 8 to his third. Both use animals to symbolize kingdoms, but in chapter 7 they are fantastic creatures (e.g., lionlike with wings [v. 4]), whereas those of chapter 8 are normal (a ram [v. 3] and a goat [v. 5]). In both cases the seer needs a heavenly being to supply the interpretation of the vision (7:15–16; 8:15–16). However, in the former the angel is not named, while in the latter he is called Gabriel (8:16). Both visions feature a little horn (7:8; 8:9), which represents an arrogant king (7:20; 8:11, 25) who attacks heaven (7:21, 25; 8:10–11, 25) and Judaism (by trying to change the set times and law [7:25]; by removing the sacrifice, bringing low the sanctuary, destroying copies of the Torah, and killing Jews [8:11–12, 25]). Both vision accounts close by recounting Daniel's dramatic response to the supernatural experience ("deeply troubled," "pale" [7:28]; "exhausted," "ill," and "appalled" [8:27]).

Chapter 8 also covers some of the same ground as chapter 7, but it focuses on the last two kingdoms. Leaving out Babylonia and only touching on Media, chapter 8 depicts Alexander's conquest of Persia. It then recounts the period of the Diadochi (Alexander's successors), the rise of "the little horn" (Antiochus IV), and his subsequent desecration of the temple. Both chapters 7 and 8 record the ascent of the evil tyrant, but chapter 8 supplies much more detail. Both speak of his downfall, too. However, unlike chapter 7, chapter 8 does not go beyond that to describe the coming of the kingdom of God, although it does talk about an "end" (8:17, 19). Finally, chapter 7 is a bit more mysterious than chapter 8. It outlines four kingdoms (like Dan. 2) but does not identify them. In contrast to that, Daniel 8 names the kingdoms of Media, Persia, and Greece. Also, while it seems clear in both chapters that the little horn stands for Antiochus IV, it is more obvious in chapter 8 because of the additional details. Both chapters announce a limit to the wicked monarch's reign, but "a time, times and half a time" (7:25) is more cryptic; "2,300 evenings and mornings" (8:14) is more concrete.

8:1–2 / Daniel's first vision, recorded in chapter 7, is dated to the first year of Belshazzar. Chapter 8 tells us that Daniel again had a vision (8:1). This second vision is dated to the third year of King Belshazzar's reign (8:1). The wording is almost exactly the same as in Daniel 1:1, "In the third year of the reign of Jehoiakim." This is not surprising as both were written by the same person. The author alludes to chapter 7 by noting that this vision was after the one that had already appeared to Daniel (8:1).

In the Hebrew, verse 2 feels choppy and awkward because it seems to contain too many introductory clauses: "and I saw in the vision"; "and it was when I saw"; "I was in Susa"; "and I saw in the vision"; "and I was by the Ulai canal." The second clause, "and it was when I saw," is absent from the LXX and is likely the result of scribal embellishment. The verse may be a conflation of two readings: one placing Daniel in Susa and the other placing him by the Ulai Canal. The NIV makes the English translation smoother than it actually is in the original language: **In my vision I saw myself in . . . Susa . . . ; in the vision I was beside the Ulai Canal** (8:2).

It is not clear whether Daniel only *saw* himself in Susa in the vision or whether he was actually there. Ezekiel was transported to places in his visions (Ezek. 8:3; 11:24; 40:2); maybe it was the same with Daniel. Alternatively, Daniel could have been in Susa bodily when he saw the vision. The Syriac version supports the former interpretation; Josephus supports the latter (*Ant.* 10.269). The NIV seems to be following the Syriac, interpreting the text to mean that the trip to Susa was only going on in Daniel's head. It removes the ambiguity by adding "my" and "myself," which are not in the Hebrew, and leaving out "I was in Susa," which is in the text: "In my vision I saw myself . . . in Susa" (NIV 8:2). Perhaps the location of Susa is significant because of the content of the vision; the next verse (8:3) describes a two-horned ram that represents Persia (although the smaller horn stands for Media, which Persia absorbed [8:20]). Susa, located east of Babylon, between Persepolis in the south and Ecbatana in the north, was an important administrative capital for the Persian kings. "**The citadel** of Susa" (8:2) means the fortified place that was Susa; it does not refer to a separate stronghold inside the city (Goldingay, *Daniel*, p. 196). A better translation might be "the citadel, Susa" (cf. Neh. 1:1; Esth. 1:2, 5; 2:3, 5, 8; 3:15; 8:14; 9:6, 11, 12). That Daniel receives his vision by the Ulai Canal just to the northwest of Susa is reminiscent of Ezekiel's experience by the river Chebar in Babylon (Ezek. 1).

8:3–12 / This section contains the narrative of the vision itself. Daniel looks up and sees a ram with two horns (8:3). Later in the chapter, the interpretation identifies the ram as "the kings of Media and Persia" (8:20). Those who interpret the four kingdoms of chapters 2 and 7 as Babylonia, Medo-Persia, Greece, and Rome sometimes use this verse to buttress their position, arguing against separate Median and Persian kingdoms. In their view, the book indicates a combined Medo-Persian Empire, because the two horns are in one animal (Baldwin, *Daniel*, p. 65). On the contrary, the author of Daniel still acknowledges that they are distinct powers, because they are represented by separate horns and because one horn was longer than the other but grew up later (8:3). That indicates an awareness that the Persian kingdom came after the Median and absorbed it, because it was more powerful, which is in harmony with the rest of the book. Therefore, the ram must actually represent Persia. This is supported by subsequent verses that record the defeat of the ram (Persia) by the goat (Greece). Media and Persia are paired elsewhere in Daniel and in the OT (Dan. 5:28; 6:8, 12, 15; 8:20; Esth. 1:14, 19; 10:2).

Daniel observes **the ram charging toward the west and the north and the south** (8:4). History bears witness to Persian expansion. Cambyses (529–522) stretched the southern border toward Egypt. Darius (522–486) increased territory northward toward Scythia and westward toward Greece. It is odd that the ram does not charge toward the east, because Persia did conquer in the direction of India (Esth. 1:1). It is possible, however, that "east" was in the original text and dropped out by haplography (see the Additional Note on 8:4). In any case, "the ram" was a formidable force in its day: **no animal could stand against him, and none could rescue from his power** (8:4). The picture of this ram butting other animals out of its way is compelling and apt. Although initially no army was able to "stand against" Persia, they eventually succumbed to Greece. A few verses later the text records that Persia (the "ram") "was powerless to stand against" Greece (the "goat"; 8:7). What the book later says of Antiochus III ("the king of the North") is also parallel: "no one will be able to stand against him" (11:16).

In Daniel's vision, the ram **did as he pleased** (8:4). It is entirely appropriate that God can do "as he pleases" (4:35), because he is king of the universe. He is also all-good as well as all-powerful, so his sovereign might is directed toward salutary ends. However, when human kings accrue great power so that they can do whatever they wish, it is of questionable value. While it is not obviously negative here regarding Persia, it may be implied. This idiom is used three other times in Daniel. A "mighty king" of Greece "who will rule with great power"—a reference to Alexander the Great—will "do as he pleases" (11:3). The "king of the North"—Antiochus III—also "will do as he pleases" (11:15–16). Finally, another "king of the North"—this time Antiochus Epiphanes—"will do as he pleases" (11:36). In that context it is extremely negative, for he uses his power to do evil deeds, such as desecrating the temple (11:31).

Another similarity between the ram (Persia) of chapter 8 and Antiochus IV is that the ram **became great** (from the root *gdl* [8:4]). Once again, it may have negative connotations, in this case implying arrogance. Antiochus IV (the "king of the North") "will exalt and magnify [*yitgaddel*] himself" (11:36); he (the "little horn") speaks "boastfully" (7:8, 20). Alexander (the "goat") "became very great" (*higdil* [8:8]), which might also mean he "magnified himself." In other contexts with humans, it may suggest more than pride; it may even indicate rebellion (Pss. 35:26; 55:12 [55:13 MT]; Jer. 48:26, 42; Zeph. 2:10). When this verb is used with God as the subject, it tells of his great deeds (1 Sam. 12:24; Ps. 126:2–3). In contrast, the author of Daniel looks askance at human hubris.

Next, the scene changes. A new animal enters the stage: **a goat with a prominent horn between his eyes** comes **from the west** (8:5). The goat represents the Greek kingdom, and the horn represents Alexander (8:21), who initiated his conquest of the then-known world by advancing eastward from Macedonia. The word translated "prominent" literally means "sight" or "vision." A "horn of sight" is a visible, noticeable, eye-catching, or conspicuous horn. He crosses **the whole earth** (8:5): "He advanced to the ends of the earth, and plundered many nations. When the earth became quiet before him, he was exalted, and his heart was lifted up" (1 Macc. 1:3 NRSV). That he accomplishes all this **without touching the ground** (8:5) indicates the incredible speed (eleven years) with which Alexander took over the world. It seems to suggest flight, but it does not mention wings. However, the third beast in chapter 7, which represents Greece, has four wings (Dan. 7:6). Other conquerors also flew over the earth: the Babylonians "fly like a vulture swooping to devour" (Hab. 1:8); Cyrus runs through the nations "scarcely touching the path with his feet" (Isa. 41:3 NRSV).

The he-goat (Greece) now displaces the ram (Persia). The goat charges at the ram **in great rage** (8:6). He attacks **the ram furiously, striking the ram and shattering his two horns** (8:7). The graphic image of a goat butting heads with a ram, dehorning him, knocking him to the ground, and trampling on him (8:7) corresponds well to history. Alexander crushed the Persian army in a series of decisive victories climaxing in two final battles: he dealt a crippling blow to it at Issus in 333 B.C.; he finished it off near Arbela in 331.

Some of the expressions used here occur elsewhere in Daniel. First, **the ram was powerless to stand against him** (8:7). As already noted, this is in contrast to what was said earlier of the ram, that "no animal could stand against him" (8:4): after reaching its peak, Persia declined and fell. This clause also anticipates the description of the "king of the North" (Antiochus III): "no one will be able to stand against him" (11:16). Secondly, the goat "knocked" the ram "to the ground and trampled him" (8:7). Just so, the exceedingly violent fourth beast of chapter 7 "trampled" its victims "underfoot" (7:7). Also, the little horn (Antiochus Epiphanes) "threw some of the starry host down to the earth and trampled on them" (8:10; cf. v. 13). Thirdly, "the goat was enraged against the ram" (8:7 translated more literally; the NIV renders the verb as an adverb, "furiously"). Similarly, "the king of the South will be enraged" (11:11 literal translation; NIV "will march out in a rage").

At this point the NIV records that **the goat became very great** (8:8). This is a possible translation that is also followed by the NRSV. However, another plausible rendering is "the he-goat magnified himself exceedingly" (RSV). There is a progression in hubris from one kingdom to the next, climaxing in the little horn, who tries to elevate himself to the level of heaven (8:10–11). **At the height of his power** the **large horn is broken off** (8:8). Surprisingly, in 323 B.C. Alexander the Great died in the prime of life at age thirty-two in Babylon. **In its place four prominent horns grew up** (8:8). It is better to read "four others" instead of "four prominent horns" (see the Additional Note on 8:8). These horns signify four rulers. For more than twenty years there was turmoil following the death of Alexander as various generals jockeyed for power and territory. During that time, the empire was divided into four main kingdoms headed by four generals, known in the histories as the Diadochi, or successors. But there were different generals at different times. Some scholars, following Jerome, identify the four horns as Philip Arrhidaeus (Alexander's brother), who gained Macedonia; Antigonus Monophthalmus ("the one-eyed"), who took over Asia Minor (modern Turkey); Ptolemy Lagus, who controlled Egypt; and Seleucus Nicator, who claimed Syria and Babylon

(Collins, *Daniel*, p. 331). However, Philip was incompetent, propped up by other generals, and eventually murdered. Antigonus died attempting to take over Greece. The final division was settled after the battle of Ipsus in 301. Therefore, it is better to follow other scholars who point to this slightly later period and identify the four as Cassander (Macedonia and Greece), Lysimachus (Asia Minor), Ptolemy (Egypt), and Seleucus (Babylon and Syria) (e.g., Montgomery, *Daniel*, p. 332; Driver, *Daniel*, p. 115; for a more detailed history of the period, see Koester, *Introduction to the New Testament*, vol. 1, pp. 13–15, and Will, "Succession to Alexander," pp. 23–61).

The four winds of heaven (8:8) are the four points of the compass: south (Egypt), west (Macedonia and Greece), north (Asia Minor), and east (Babylon and Syria). Because the Seleucids controlled the land between Babylon and India, they are thought of here as representing the east. However, the Seleucids also held Syria, to the north, and fought with Egypt, to the south, eventually wresting the land of Israel from the Ptolemies. For this reason, the Seleucid is called "the king of the North" numerous times in chapter 11 (e.g., 11:6, 11, 13).

With the development that **out of one of them** comes **another horn** (8:9), the vision leaps ahead from the fourth century to the second, to the time of Antiochus IV (175–164 B.C.). He indeed came from one of the four horns: the line of Seleucus. Truly he **started small** (8:9). He had been held hostage in Rome for fourteen years, waiting in the wings while his brother Seleucus IV reigned. When that brother was assassinated, he was able to ascend to the throne. He then **grew in power to the south and to the east and toward the Beautiful Land** (8:9). He launched two campaigns against Egypt in the south. He fought against the Parthians in the east. However, it is clear from the following verses that the writer is most concerned about Epiphanes's attack on Jerusalem. The MT only has "the beauty." Although the word "land" is not found in this verse, it makes sense to supply it from occurrences of "the Beautiful Land" (Dan. 11:16, 41; for similar expressions see Pss. 48:2; 50:2; 106:24; Jer. 3:19; Ezek. 20:6, 15; Zech. 7:14; Mal. 3:12). It would also be possible to render it "the beautiful holy mountain" (Dan. 11:45), which points to Mount Zion. Perhaps this would be the better translation since the following verses (8:10–13) emphasize the damage to the sanctuary and the removal of the sacrifice in Jerusalem.

The horn advanced not only geopolitically but cosmically as well. The horn grows **until it reaches the host of the heavens** (8:10). The motif of lifting oneself up to heaven occurs in ancient Near Eastern myths and also in Isaiah 14, to which this passage is probably alluding. Using the

Canaanite figure "morning star" (Isa. 14:12), Israel's remnant taunts the king of Babylon for trying futilely to elevate his throne above the "stars of God" so that he could rule over the heavenly assembly (Isa. 14:13). He vainly boasts, "I will ascend above the tops of the clouds; I will make myself like the Most High" (Isa. 14:14). But he will not ultimately succeed; on the contrary, he will be "brought down to the grave, to the depths of the pit" (Isa. 14:15). So it would be with the tyrant Epiphanes, who would succeed only for a time (Dan. 8:12, 24–25a); then he would be destroyed (Dan. 8:25b). Indeed, he died a painful and ignominious death (1 Macc. 6:8–16; 2 Macc. 9:5–28).

The Hebrew term for "host" (8:10) frequently refers to the heavenly beings who are part of God's army (1 Kgs. 22:19). In fact, God is called "Yahweh of hosts" over two hundred times (e.g., 1 Sam. 1:3, 11; 4:4; Ps. 46:7, 11; Isa. 1:9, 24; consult the NRSV, which has "LORD of hosts"; NIV's "LORD Almighty" is not the best rendering). When earthly armies clashed below, it was understood that the heavenly armies also engaged above. That is why the "commander of the army ["host"] of the LORD" (Josh. 5:14) makes an appearance to Joshua, the earthly commander, at the beginning of the conquest. At other times "host" simply means the heavenly bodies—the sun, moon, and stars, or just the stars (Gen. 2:1 [NIV "array"]; Ps. 33:6). Yet there is a connection between these two notions. The stars are part of God's host, fighting for Israel from heaven in the story of Deborah (Judg. 5:20). It is well known that people in the ancient world worshiped the stars as heavenly beings, something that the Israelites were warned not to do (Deut. 4:19). In short, Antiochus IV, in attacking the temple, was actually warring against the host of heaven, who were understood as both heavenly beings and stars. At his death he is described as a man who "had thought that he could touch the stars of heaven" (2 Macc. 9:10 NRSV).

What is truly amazing about Daniel 8 is that Antiochus IV is somewhat victorious in his attack on heaven. He actually throws **some of the starry host down to the earth and** tramples **on them** (8:10). Whether the biblical writer is merely acknowledging that the evil king was able to stop the Jerusalem sacrifice and persecute Jews for a time, or whether he is really affirming that in the heavenly battle some of the good angels were defeated and thrown down, is difficult to say. It is bold imagery to say the least. While it may seem incredible to the modern Christian reader, the latter meaning is quite believable for this Jewish writer of the second century B.C. This was his way of wrestling with the problem of evil. How was it possible for this wicked monarch to prevail over the Jews? How was it conceivable for him to desecrate the holy temple? The author's conclusion was that some of God's angels must have been defeated. This theme is borrowed by the NT, for in John's vision also, the dragon "swept a third of the stars [understood to be angels] out of the sky and flung them to the earth" (Rev. 12:4). However, the enemy does not triumph for long. Then "there was war in heaven" between "Michael and his angels" and "the dragon and his angels," resulting in the dragon's defeat, so that "they lost their place in heaven" (Rev. 12:7–8). Isaiah 14, a taunt song against the king of Babylon, mentioned above, and Ezekiel 28, a taunt song against the king of Tyre, are later used in Christian theology to explain the fall of Satan and his angels. Similarly, in the "Isaianic Apocalypse" (Isa. 24–27), rebellious members of the heavenly host are destined for punishment (Isa. 24:21). This theme is advanced in the NT also: Jesus sees "Satan fall like lightning from heaven" (Luke 10:18).

The horn is exceedingly arrogant. **It sets itself up to be as great as the Prince of the host** (8:11). Who is this figure, "the Prince of the host"? Because Michael the archangel is called "prince" (10:21) in the book of Daniel, some would say that he is in view here. However, he is only "one of the chief princes" (10:13), not "the Prince of the host," which suggests a more exalted person. Because priests are sometimes called "prince" (1 Chron. 24:5 [NIV "officials"]; Ezra 8:24 [NIV "leading"]), the high priest Onias III (murdered in 171 B.C.; 2 Macc. 4:33–35; Dan. 9:26) has been suggested. But the term "prince" is used only of angels in Daniel. Furthermore, the superlative term "Prince of princes" is used later in the chapter (Dan. 8:25) to indicate the greatest of all princes or rulers—in other words, God. Finally, Daniel 8:11 is parallel to Daniel 11:36. In the former, Antiochus IV exalts himself up to the Prince of the host; in the latter, he exalts himself above the gods and slanders the "God of gods." Therefore, "the Prince of the host" must be God, not an angel or priest. Once again we are reminded of the self-vaunting king of Babylon in Isaiah 14: "I will make myself like the Most High" (Isa. 14:14). With that in mind it is interesting to note that Antiochus IV called himself "Epiphanes": "God manifest." How far he carried this is not clear. Perhaps he did not go so far as to establish a cult for himself with temple and sacrifice. Nevertheless, by calling himself "Epiphanes" and by profaning the temple, he must have appeared to the Jews to be elevating himself to the level of God. Isaiah 14 and Daniel 8 are paralleled in the account of Antiochus's death: he who "thought in his superhuman arrogance" that he could control the ocean's waves and weigh the mountains (2 Macc. 9:8 NRSV) was reduced by pain and disease so that he confessed, "It is right to be subject to God; mortals should not think that they are equal to God" (2 Macc. 9:12 NRSV).

Then the horn takes **away the daily sacrifice from** the Prince of the host (8:11). The Torah stipulates that every morning and evening, the Israelites were to offer a lamb as a whole burnt offering, along with a grain offering and a drink offering of wine (Exod. 29:38–42; Num. 28:2–8; cf. Ezek. 46:13–15, which has only a morning offering with different measurements and no wine). Antiochus IV issued a command "to forbid burnt offerings and sacrifices and drink offerings in the sanctuary" (1 Macc. 1:45 NRSV; see also Dan. 11:31). In place of the holy and legitimate sacrifices, the Seleucids offered illicit offerings (perhaps even swine [1 Macc. 1:47]) to Olympian Zeus in the Jerusalem temple (1 Macc. 1:59; 2 Macc. 6:2, 4–5). This is called the "abomination that causes desolation" (Dan. 11:31; 12:11; see also 8:12, 13; 9:27; 11:31).

As a result, **the place of his sanctuary is brought low** (8:11). Antiochus IV did not completely destroy the temple, as the Babylonians had done in 587 B.C. and as the Romans later did in A.D. 70. However, he badly damaged and profaned it. He plundered the temple, stripping it of its sacred furnishings (altar, lampstand, table for the bread of Presence), stealing the silver and gold vessels and utensils (1 Macc. 1:20–24), so that it became "desolate like a desert" (1 Macc. 1:39 NRSV). "The sanctuary was trampled down" (1 Macc. 3:45 NRSV). The gates had been burned, the priests' quarters were in ruins, and wild bushes were growing in the courts (1 Macc. 4:38). We do not know how extensive the damage was, but we are told that after driving out the pagans, the Jews had to reconstruct the sanctuary (1 Macc. 4:47–48).

Verse 12a is full of difficulties. The NIV has **Because of rebellion, the host [of the saints] and the daily sacrifice were given over to it** (8:12). I have placed the phrase "of the saints" in brackets because it is not in the MT. Nor should it be added in, for the context is the heavenly host or angels, not the Jewish saints. The phrase "to it" is also not original but supplied by the translator. This addition is acceptable, to explain that they are handed over to the horn or evil ruler. Rendering "because of rebellion" is problematic as it implies that what happens is a punishment for the sin of the host. If the heavenly host is in view (which is my position), then rebellion or transgression is out of the question. (There is no clear teaching in the OT about a large group of angels rebelling and being expelled from heaven. However, even if we embrace this tradition, it is usually understood to be a unique event. The members of the heavenly host here [8:12] are faithful, not rebellious.) If the writer intends the Jewish saints, then it is still unlikely, for the book of Daniel blames the wicked king, not the persecuted saints, for the desecration of the temple. In other words, this verse is speaking about the transgression of

Antiochus IV, not that of the Jewish people (Collins, *Daniel*, p. 335; see also 8:13; 9:24).

Literally, the Hebrew of verse 12a says, "and a host will be given on the continual burnt offering in transgression." The problem is how to make sense of this. I propose leaving out "host," because it is not in the Greek and because its gender (masc.) does not agree with the verb (fem.) "will be placed" or "given" (see the Additional Note on 8:12). The preposition "in," though, needs to be retained. I would translate it as: "It will be given against the whole burnt offering in transgression." The meaning is that God will allow it—the horn—to go against the whole burnt offering in its (the horn's) transgression. In other words, Antiochus IV will sin by removing the daily sacrifice. "It will be set over the daily offering in an act of rebellion" (Goldingay, *Daniel*, p. 195).

The NIV reading in verse 12b—**It prospered in everything it did, and truth was thrown to the ground** (8:12)—may be improved on. The Hebrew text has "it will throw truth to the ground; it will act and prosper." The NIV reverses the clauses, turns an active verb into a passive ("was thrown"), and translates in the past tense. The first verb in the sentence ("will be given") is clearly future, and the others should be read that way as well (see the Additional Note on 8:12). "Horn" is the antecedent of "it." "Truth" is best taken as a reference to the Torah, because Antiochus had the books of the law torn and burned (1 Macc. 1:56). The NIV's "It prospered in everything it did" is an acceptable rendering of the Hebrew, except that it is in the past tense. Similarly, the RSV translates in the past tense, but it also adds in "the horn": "and the horn acted and prospered." Although a bit wooden and overly literal, the following probably communicates the meaning of the verse best: "And it [the horn] will be given against the continual burnt offering in [the course of] transgression; and truth will be cast to the ground; and he will act and prosper."

8:13–14 / The account transitions from vision to audition, as Daniel hears the angels' voices. A holy one is speaking (8:13), although we are not told what he says. Perhaps he gave the concluding statement in verse 12 about the evil king prospering, since that would be hard to view. It is possible for the seer to observe the little horn casting down stars and trampling them (8:10), taking away the sacrifice (8:11–12), damaging the temple (8:11), and throwing down the Torah scrolls (8:12). However, it is more difficult to envision someone "acting" and "prospering" (8:12), which the angel might have communicated orally, but the text does not specify.

Then, **another holy one** speaks to the first one: **How long will it take for the vision to be fulfilled . . . ?** (8:13). The question "How long?"

is common in the lament tradition of the Psalms (Pss. 6:3; 13:1–2; 35:17; 74:10; 79:5; 80:4; 89:46; 90:13; 94:3). The prophets utilize the query as well (Isa. 6:11; Jer. 4:21; 12:4; 47:6; Hab. 1:2; Zech. 1:12); it is also used one more time in Daniel (Dan. 12:6). Zechariah 1:12 is similar to Daniel 8:13 in that it involves a vision and dialogue with heaven (an angel speaks to the prophet and God speaks through an angel [see Zech. 1:7–17]). Isaiah 6:11 is like Daniel 8:13, because God actually answers the question, although not with the same specificity as in Daniel. Instead of measuring out a period of time in days, months, or years, the Lord replies that the punishment will continue "until the cities lie ruined and without inhabitant, until the houses are left deserted and the fields ruined and ravaged, until the LORD has sent everyone far away and the land is utterly forsaken" (Isa. 6:11–12). In the other passages, God's people have experienced harm, leading them to cry out to God for deliverance and ask how long their suffering must continue. The emphasis is on the present distress and the prayer for deliverance. They are not looking for an answer in terms of a specific amount of time; rather, they are saying that they have suffered enough and God should act on their behalf. But in Daniel, the emphasis is different. The angel is actually asking the temporal question: How long will it take for these things in the vision to transpire? Furthermore, he receives a precise answer with an exact number of days.

Verse 13 is awkward. Literally, it says, "For how long is the vision—the continual burnt offering, the transgression that desolates, giving and sanctuary and host trampling?" The NIV paraphrases the opening of the statement by adding "to be fulfilled." This smoothes out the translation, yielding "How long will it take for the vision to be fulfilled?" The NIV also adds **the vision concerning** (8:13). Though not in the Hebrew text, this phrase probably does show the proper relationship between the two parts of the verse, as the following words are in apposition to "vision" and sum up its content. After this, the NIV is again a bit paraphrastic: **the daily sacrifice, the rebellion that causes desolation, and the surrender of the sanctuary and of the host that will be trampled underfoot** (8:13). Instead of deleting the "and" before "sanctuary" (in the literal translation "giving and sanctuary and host trampling"), it is better to read it with the word before, construing it to be the third-person singular pronominal suffix "his": "his giving over [NIV "surrender"] of the sanctuary and of the host." The "his" refers to God, who allows the temple to fall into the hands of the unclean Greeks and be desecrated. The NIV's "that will be trampled underfoot" can be put more simply: "for trampling." A more accurate translation, then, would be "For how long is the vision—the continual burnt offering, the transgression that desolates, his giving over of the sanctuary and the host for trampling?"

The answer to the angel's question "How long?" is **2,300 evenings and mornings** (8:14). Although the beginning of the time period is not specified, the end of it is: when **the sanctuary will be reconsecrated** (8:14), which was Kislev 25, 164 B.C. (1 Macc. 4:52). Some think the number indicates 2,300 days, because evening and morning make one day, as in Genesis 1 (e.g., Gen. 1:5). This would be more than six years. Counting back from 164, this would bring us to 170, which is close to 171, when the high priest Onias III was murdered (Dan. 9:26; 2 Macc. 4:23–38; see Miller, *Daniel*, pp. 229–30). However, there is no hint of this event in the vision of chapter 8. The focus—especially in verses 11–13, where the time question is asked—is on the continual burnt offering. This sacrifice was offered twice daily, every morning and evening. Most commentators, therefore, understand the number to signify 2,300 morning and evening sacrifices. In other words, the time indicated is half that, or 1,150 days. This would be the number of days between the time when the sacrifice was taken away and the time when it was restored. The trouble is, the period from the institution of the pagan sacrifice in Jerusalem to the reconsecration of the temple was three years and ten days (1 Macc. 1:54; 4:52–53). That would be 1,105 days using a solar calendar, and 1,090 days using a lunar calendar of thirty days per month. So, the Daniel figure of 1,150 days does not exactly agree with the number from Maccabees. One could try to harmonize by saying that the sacrifice was stopped some fifty or so days before the pagan sacrifice began (Archer, "Daniel," p. 103), but this is pure conjecture; there is no support for this from history. It is better to let the tension stand, allowing that the number is a close approximation. While we may not be able to make the numbers jibe exactly with history, the main point of the passage is certain and true: God will bring an end to Epiphanes's evil regime, restore the holy sacrifice, and save his people from persecution.

8:15–26 / This next section contains the interpretation of the vision. Verses 15–19 serve as an introduction, while the interpretation itself begins in verse 20. After seeing the vision, Daniel tries to understand it (8:15). Then he notices in front of him **one who looks like a man** (8:15). As elsewhere in Daniel, this refers to a celestial being (3:25, 28; 7:13; 10:16, 18). There follows a man's voice, instructing Gabriel to tell Daniel the meaning of the vision (8:16). Since God is represented in various places in the Bible as being like a man (e.g., Ezek. 1:26), it is possible that the voice is that of God. A "man's voice" simply means a human voice, which

God would use in communicating with humans. It is also possible that it is another angel who speaks, maybe Michael (Collins, *Daniel*, p. 336). This is the first time in the Bible where an angel is named, and the only two named angels in the Bible are Gabriel, whose role is to reveal or announce (Dan. 8:16; 9:21; Luke 1:19, 26), and Michael (Dan. 10:13, 21; 12:1; Jude 9; Rev. 12:7), whose role is more to fight. Others are mentioned in Jewish literature, such as Uriel and Raphael.

Daniel is **terrified and** falls **prostrate** (8:17). It is common for people to fall on their faces when they are in the presence of God or an angel (Gen. 17:3; Josh. 5:14; Judg. 13:20; Ezek. 1:28; 3:23; 9:8; 43:3; 44:4; Dan. 10:9; Matt. 17:6; 28:4; Rev. 1:17). Gabriel addresses Daniel as **son of man** (8:17), or "human being." This is the only place in the book where he is called this, although Ezekiel is called "son of man" frequently. We are reminded of Daniel 7:13, where one appears in heaven who looks like a "son of man," or "human being."

Gabriel tells the seer that **the vision concerns the time of the end** (8:17). We must be careful not to interject our own views of eschatology at this point but to consider the meaning in light of the original historical context. If the context of the book of Daniel is the second century B.C., the vision focuses on Antiochus IV and his desecration of the temple. (Readers who prefer an earlier historical context may still interpret the latter events as the fulfillment of what they deem to be an earlier prophecy.) When the angel asks, "How long?" (8:13), an answer is given in terms of days culminating in the purification of the sanctuary (8:14). The "time of the end," therefore, has to do especially with the end of the sacrilege and the restoration of sacrifice. It involves the end of Antiochus IV and his oppressive rule but does not necessarily entail the end of history, time, and the world. Regardless, based on chapters 2 and 7, the author of Daniel was expecting the dramatic in-breaking of God's kingdom once Antiochus IV was destroyed. Yet he also believed that history and the world would continue eternally under the rule of God.

Eschatology (one's view of the end time) developed over the centuries. The prophets looked for a limited end within time, after which God would act again to bring salvation. For example, Amos saw the end of Israel at the hands of the Assyrians (see Amos 8:1–2 NRSV), but after that a period of restoration (Amos 9:11–15). Similarly, Hosea envisioned Israel's demise (Hos. 13:9), followed by healing and renewal (Hos. 14:4–7). This prophetic eschatology evolved into apocalyptic eschatology, which looked for a more radical end, leading to a more glorious act of God afterward. Some even spelled out a complete end of this world followed by the creation of a new heaven and earth (Isa. 65:17; 66:22; Rev. 21:1). Yet even in this scenario, life still goes on in the world to come. The book of Daniel does not predict a new heaven and earth, but it is closer to apocalyptic eschatology than to prophetic, because it foresees a resurrection of the dead and some sort of judgment resulting in "everlasting life" for some and "shame and everlasting contempt" for others (Dan. 12:2); Daniel is guaranteed a reward when he rises (12:13). Besides in Daniel 8:17, the Hebrew word *qets*, "end," occurs several more times in Daniel (8:19; 9:26 [twice]; 11:6, 13, 27, 35, 40, 45; 12:4, 6, 9, 13 [twice]). Without question there are supernatural eschatological elements, but the main emphasis seems to be on the end of Antiochus IV and his suppression of Judaism (11:45). In fact, his very destruction was seen as a divine act (8:25).

While Gabriel is **speaking to** him, Daniel is **in a deep sleep, with** his **face to the ground** (8:18). Verse 17 already mentions that Daniel "fell prostrate" (see above for references to similar passages). This verse adds that he "was in a deep sleep." The verb meaning "to be in a deep sleep" appears again in Daniel 10:9 (see also Judg. 4:21; Jon. 1:5–6). The noun from the same root, "deep sleep," is even more remarkable, often indicating a sleep caused by God (e.g., Gen. 2:21; 15:12; 1 Sam. 26:12; Job 4:13; 33:15). Perhaps the text is saying that Daniel went into an ecstatic state. In that case "sleep" might be misleading, as it has the connotation of being tired, disinterested, bored, or unconscious. In fact, a prophet is in a heightened state of consciousness when receiving revelation. Therefore, it might be better to translate, with the NRSV, "I fell into a trance." Then the angel touches him and raises him to his feet (8:18). Ezekiel had the same experience (Ezek. 2:2). It happens to Daniel again later (Dan. 9:21; 10:10, 16, 18). The phenomenon is also found elsewhere (*1 En.* 60:4; *4 Ezra* 5:15; Rev. 1:17).

The angel announces that what he is **going to tell** Daniel **will happen later in the time of wrath** (8:19). Does "wrath" refer to the wrath of Antiochus or the wrath of God? (See the Additional Note on 8:19.) The correct answer is that it applies to both. The "time of wrath" (8:19; 11:36) speaks of a period of Gentile domination that will be "completed" (11:36) when the Seleucid king dies. So, the persecution of the Jews in the second century B.C. was an expression of Antiochus IV's wrath. But God allowed it because of the sin of certain Jews who were unfaithful. These apostates tried to undo their circumcision and "abandoned the holy covenant" (1 Macc. 1:11–15 NRSV). They "sacrificed to idols and profaned the sabbath" (1 Macc. 1:43 NRSV). They "forsook the law" and "did evil" (1 Macc. 1:52–53 NRSV). Although many remained faithful, "very great wrath came upon Israel" (1 Macc. 1:64 NRSV). This last verse does not say it was the wrath of God, but that is implied by the context (compare the similar statement in 2 Kgs. 3:27). Therefore, the wrath of the Seleucid king was to a certain extent a consequence of the wrath of God. However, studying the examples of the Assyrians and Babylonians, whom God used to punish his people, helps to soften that last statement. The Assyrians were indeed the club in God's hand (Isa. 10:5), but when they became lifted up with pride (Isa. 10:12–15), God decided to destroy them (Isa. 10:16–19, 24–26). Likewise, the Babylonians were used by Yahweh to chasten Judah (Hab. 1:6). But they also became guilty of hubris (Hab. 2:4), so that Habakkuk pronounced woes on them (Hab. 2:6–19). The result was that those who plundered others would in turn be plundered (Hab. 2:8). The exile was an expression of God's wrath (Zech. 1:12), but after a time, God became "very angry" with the nations and decided to deliver his people from captivity (Zech. 1:14–17). So, here in Daniel, God allowed Antiochus IV to oppress his people because of sin. However, the ruthless tyrant greatly exalted himself (Dan. 8:11; 11:36), which set in motion his demise. The message of Daniel is that God will act to deliver his people and to punish this abundantly wicked king.

Some modern scholars are reluctant to allow any place for sin, judgment, or the wrath of God in the persecution of the Jews in the second century B.C. This is understandable since we are aware of the centuries of persecution that Jews have endured. We are especially uncomfortable knowing how much Jews have suffered at the hands of people who professed to follow Jesus Christ: the pope authorized the torture of Jews during the Inquisition; Jews were attacked during pogroms as the "Christ killers"; some so-called Christians in Europe sympathized with the Nazis. We would be horrified at the suggestion that such events as the Holocaust came about because of God's wrath on the Jews for their sins. We would excoriate those who committed hate crimes against the Jews and denounce all such actions as antithetical to true Christianity. Indeed, we must continue to speak out against anti-Semitism today. But we must also be careful to interpret texts such as Daniel and 1 Maccabees in light of their original historical context, even when their views go against our modern sensibilities. While the stress there is on the sin of Antiochus IV, the theme of God's wrath is also present, including the concomitant notions of Israel's sin and punishment.

The phrase "later in the time of wrath" is further elucidated by the statement that **the vision concerns the appointed time of the end** (8:19). Similar expressions occur in Daniel 11:27 ("an end will still come at the appointed time"); 11:35 ("until the time of the end, for it will still come at the appointed time"; for just "appointed time," see 11:29); 10:14 ("what will happen to your people in the future, for the vision concerns a time yet to come"); and 12:4 ("until the time of the end"). This may be an allusion to Habakkuk 2:3 ("For the revelation awaits an appointed time; it speaks of the end"), where "appointed time" is parallel to "end."

Following the introductory material in verses 15–19, verse 20 begins the actual deciphering of the vision. As mentioned above (see the commentary on 8:3), **the two-horned ram . . . represents the kings of Media and Persia** (8:20), and the **shaggy goat is the king of Greece** (8:21; see the commentary on 8:5). The word translated "shaggy" in the NIV actually means "he-goat." It is probably not original (see the Additional Note on 8:21). **The large horn . . . is the first king** (8:21), or Alexander the Great (see the commentary on 8:5). **The four horns that replaced the one that was broken off represent four kingdoms** (8:22). The text says "kingdoms," but the horns represent both kings and kingdoms. Initially, the horns stand for four kings, which we earlier identified as the Diadochi: Cassander, Lysimachus, Ptolemy, and Seleucus. But there were many kings after Alexander, so the author emphasizes the kingdoms, which were the territories headed up by the successors to Alexander. These heirs to Alexander's throne did **not have the same power** (8:22) as he. The diminishing of strength is communicated earlier, in Nebuchadnezzar's vision, by representing Alexander's empire as iron but the dominions of the Diadochi as iron mixed with clay (2:33, 40–43).

In Daniel's vision, "out of one of them came another horn" (8:9). The "one" spoken of is Seleucus, the most important of the Diadochi, because he founded a dynasty that led up to Antiochus IV—**a stern-faced king** (8:23). In the time of Moses, God threatened his people with covenant curses if they should disobey his law. One curse is that he will bring against them "a fierce-looking nation" (Deut. 28:49–50). The Hebrew expression rendered "stern-faced" in Daniel 8:23 is the same as the one rendered "fierce-looking" in Deuteronomy. This lends support to what was said earlier about "the time of wrath" (Dan. 8:19), that at least partly it has to do with the wrath of God. Antiochus is also **a master of intrigue** (8:23); that is, he is "adept in duplicity" (Collins, *Daniel*, p. 339), "a master of dissimulation, able to conceal his meaning under ambiguous words, and so disguising his real purposes" (Driver, *Daniel*, p. 123). He will "seize" the kingdom "through intrigue" (Dan. 11:21). He practices deceit (8:25; 11:23, 27). He will come to power **when rebels have become completely wicked** (8:23). "When the transgressors have reached their full measure" (RSV) is a better translation, because it communicates the idea that sins mount up to a point of climax, a notion found in several other places as well. God tells Abraham that his promise of land will be delayed for four generations, because "the sin of the Amorites has not yet reached its full measure" (Gen. 15:16). God punishes his own people quickly when they sin, because of his kindness for them, not wanting them to stray too far. But "in the case of the other nations the Lord waits patiently to punish them until they have reached the full measure of their sins" (2 Macc. 6:14; see also Wis. 19:1–4). Similarly, those who hinder the preaching of the gospel "heap up their sins to the limit. The wrath of God has come upon them at last [or "fully"]" (1 Thess. 2:16).

The stern-faced king **will become very strong, but not by his own power** (8:24). Literally, the Hebrew text says, "his power [will be] great, but not by his power," which seems self-contradictory. The phrase "not by his own power" is, therefore, suspect and may have been duplicated here erroneously from the Hebrew text of verse 22. The Greek text does not support it, but if it is original, it might mean that his strength is not his own; that is, it comes from God. This would not imply that God condones Antiochus's actions, only that God allows them, for no one can do anything unless God permits it (Montgomery, *Daniel*, p. 350), a recurring theme throughout the book of Daniel (1:1–2; 2:21; 4:17, 25, 32, 35; 5:21; 7:6). Alternatively, it might mean that he becomes a powerful king, not through his power but through his intrigues (Driver, *Daniel*, p. 123). The RSV and NRSV leave out the phrase, which is preferable to the NIV.

The king's strength will be followed by **astounding devastation, success in whatever he does**, and destruction of **mighty men and the holy people** (8:24). Furthermore, he will excel in **deceit** and will magnify himself. **When the people feel secure, he will destroy many** (8:25). This probably refers to the time that Antiochus IV sent his "chief collector of tribute" to Jerusalem (1 Macc. 1:29 NRSV): "Deceitfully he spoke peaceable words to them, and they believed him; but he suddenly fell upon the city, dealt it a severe blow, and destroyed many people of Israel" (1 Macc. 1:30 NRSV). Antiochus IV takes **his stand against the Prince of princes** (Dan. 8:25). This happens when the evil monarch dares to remove the holy sacrifices and replace them with pagan ones. As stated above concerning the Prince of the host (see the commentary on 8:11), "the Prince of princes" (8:25) is a reference to God, though some scholars consider it to refer to Michael (e.g., Lacocque, *Daniel*, p. 173). Yet, in spite of all Antiochus's success, God will not allow his evil deeds to go on indefinitely, nor will he escape punishment. **He will be destroyed, but not by human power** (8:25). Another reference to his demise can be found in Daniel 11:45, which simply says that while campaigning "he will come to his end." More detailed accounts of his death are recorded in 1 Maccabees 6:1–16 and in 2 Maccabees 9:5–29. While they do not agree in all the details, they both report that while in a foreign land he was struck with a sudden illness that led to his death. In the first passage, Antiochus IV acknowledges that his sins against God and against the Jews brought on his misfortunes (1 Macc. 6:12–13). In the second passage, the narrator says that God "struck him with an incurable and invisible blow" (2 Macc. 9:5 NRSV). On the one hand, it is possible to see this as a fulfillment of Daniel 8:25, for the king was not killed by a human; God destroyed Antiochus IV by sending him a terminal illness. One might then see the subsequent Maccabean revolt and Hasmonean dynasty as at least partial manifestations of the kingdom of God, as predicted in Daniel 7. On the other hand, the author of Daniel says that during the intense persecution, the Jews "will receive a little help" (Dan. 11:34)—probably a nod to the Maccabean uprising. The author does not put his trust in men or in armies; only a meager help is available from that quarter. He does not expect salvation to come from a revolt; rather, it will come from above, from God. Antiochus will die, "but not by human power" (8:25). This last phrase calls to mind the stone cut out of the mountain, "but not by human hands" (2:34, 45). When reading these verses along with Daniel 7 and 12, we get the impression that the author had something much more dramatic and glorious in mind. He expected Michael to appear in the clouds and to slay Epiphanes directly in battle. Moreover, he also anticipated a resurrection of the dead accompanied by rewards and punishments. Finally, he envisioned something more enduring—an eternal kingdom, which the Hasmonean rule was not.

Gabriel ensures the veracity of the vision (cf. Dan. 10:1; 11:2; 12:7; Rev. 19:9; 21:5; 22:6) and instructs the seer to **seal up the vision, for it concerns the distant future** (Dan. 8:26; see also 12:9). If God's purpose was that the book be sealed up until the time of the end (Dan. 12:9), one must explain why the content of the book has been made known before the end has come. Understanding the text as being intended for Jews in the second century resolves this potential difficulty. If we assume the writer has taken on the guise of Daniel of the sixth century B.C. as a literary device, verse 26 explains why the book was made known in the second century B.C. After writing down his vision, Daniel sealed it up, because it did not concern the exiles but was intended for the Jews of the Hellenistic era, who would discover it, open it, read it, understand it, and be encouraged by its message. This is seen as a strong argument for dating the book to the second century B.C.

8:27 / The chapter concludes with an account of Daniel being overwhelmed by the vision. He is exhausted and lies ill for several days (8:27; cf. 4:19; 7:28). That he subsequently gets up and goes about the king's business does not necessarily contradict Daniel 5:10–16, which shows that Belshazzar did not know Daniel. It may be that Daniel was getting his orders from one of the king's subordinates. Daniel is appalled by the vision (cf. 4:19); it is beyond understanding (8:27; cf. 12:8). This cannot mean he has no understanding of the vision since he has just received the interpretation. It means rather that he cannot fully comprehend it, because he is not familiar with the people and events of which it speaks. The meaning will not become transparent until the time of Antiochus IV.

Additional Notes §8

8:2 / The NIV adds **my** before **vision** and **myself** after **I saw**; these are not in the MT. A more literal translation follows:

Hebrew Text	and I saw in the vision, and it was when I saw, I was in Susa
LXX	and I saw in the vision, and I was by the Ulai Canal

It is clear that the two halves of the verse are very similar. Both begin with *wa'er'eh bekhazon*, "and I saw in the vision." The second *wa'er'eh bekhazon* may have been introduced by a scribe who accidentally repeated the first one, or v. 2 might conflate two variant readings, one that placed Daniel in Susa, and another that placed him by the Ulai Canal. Concerning the beginning of the verse, 4QDan[a] supports the longer MT reading, while the LXX leaves out "it was when I saw . . ." We should follow the LXX; "and it was when I saw" is redundant and probably not original. If the two parts of the verse go back to variant readings, the second is probably earlier because of later references to the canal (8:3, 6, 16). The first part of v. 2 might then have been added to explain where the canal was.

The word translated **Canal** is spelled *'wbl*. Some ancient witnesses, such as the LXX, the Syriac, and the Vulgate, read "gate." Since the city of Susa is not right on a river, some think it better to translate it this way, placing Daniel in the city by the gate that faced the Ulai river, located outside the city (Goldingay, *Daniel*, pp. 194, 196, 208). However, *'wbl* may be related to *yubal* (Jer. 17:8) and to *yabal* (Isa. 30:25; 44:4), "stream" (thus BDB, p. 385). There are no rivers right next to the city, but a nine-hundred-foot-wide canal bed, connecting two nearby rivers, has been found running near the ruins of Susa. This may well be the Ulai (Driver, *Daniel*, p. 112). Therefore, the reading in the MT is preferred.

8:3, 5 / Some scholars have attempted to find parallels outside the Bible to the **ram** and the **goat**. For example, there is an ancient reference to the Persian king bearing a ram-shaped emblem (Ammianus Marcellinus, *History* 10.1; Goldingay, *Daniel*, p. 208). Others have tried to find connections with signs of the zodiac. However, such efforts have not proven to be very fruitful in illuminating the text. Nor is it at all clear that the author was aware of such parallels or that he was consciously alluding to them (Hartman and Di Lella, *Daniel*, p. 234).

8:4 / One suggestion for why east is not included in the list of directions is that the author intentionally left it out, for one of two reasons: because to an Israelite, Persia was the east, or because the author lacked interest in lands east of Persia, where there were few or no Jews (Hartman and Di Lella, *Daniel*, p. 234). More likely, however, "east" was in the original text. The LXX, Papyrus 967, and 4QDan[a] include all four directions, although they each present the list in a different order. While we cannot be sure of the order, it is probable that "east" is original. If "east" stood first in the list, it might help to understand why it dropped out. The word immediately preceding the directions is *mingeakh*, "charged," which is somewhat similar to *mizrakh*, "east." This similarity might have caused haplography (Collins, *Daniel*, p. 325, n. 11).

8:5 / The NIV's **goat** oversimplifies the word's sense. The MT's *tsepir ha'izzim* is literally "the he-goat of the she-goats," meaning something like "the buck of the herd" (Goldingay, *Daniel*, p. 196); cf. "he-goat" (RSV) or "male goat" (NRSV); 8:8, 21. *Tsapir*, "he-goat," is an Aramaic loanword; see the parallel Aramaic expression *tsepire 'izzin* in Ezra 6:17 (Hartman and Di Lella, *Daniel*, p. 224). (See also the Additional Notes on 8:3 and 8:21)

The word *khazut*, **prominent**, is from the root *khazah*, "to see," and has the more literal meaning, "vision" or "sight" (Isa. 21:2; 29:11). (See the Additional Note on 8:8).

8:8 / The Hebrew does not have **horns**. It is supplied in the various translations. The text reads *khazut 'arba'*, "sight of four," which is an odd construction. "Sight" is usually rendered "conspicuous" here, as in v. 5; hence "prominent horns" in both. The LXX has "other" instead of "sight." This makes better sense for two reasons. First, because "four others" fits the passage better than "sight of four." Second, from a historical standpoint the other horns (the Diadochi) were not very prominent compared to the first (Alexander), which was broken off (Driver, *Daniel*, p. 114). But the most important reason for reading "other" instead of "sight" is that they are somewhat similar in Hebrew, and this could explain the scribal error. The occurrence of the word *khazut* in v. 5 affected the change of *'akharot*, "other," to *khazut*, "sight" or "prominent," in v. 8 (Collins, *Daniel*, p. 325).

8:9 / Where the NIV translates **another horn, which started small**, the MT has "one horn from a small," which is awkward. Dan. 7:8 has *qeren 'okhori ze'erah*, which is Aramaic for "another horn, a small one." The same expression in Hebrew would be *qeren 'akheret tse'irah*. That is more likely the original reading in 8:9, which then became corrupted into MT's *qeren 'akhat mitse'irah* (Montgomery, *Daniel*, p. 333). Therefore, the NIV is right to correct the text from "one horn" to "another horn." However, "which started small" is too paraphrastic. "Another horn, a small one" is the superior translation. This is not a minor point but crucial for the interpretation of the book. The NIV translation obscures the connection between the little horn of ch. 7 and the little horn of ch. 8.

For a proper interpretation of Daniel, it is important to see how ch. 8 follows from ch. 7 and that the little horns are identical, both representing Antiochus IV. While this identification cannot be avoided in ch. 8, some interpreters do not see this connection in ch. 7 because they understand the little horn there to be the Antichrist at the end of time when Jesus, the Son of Man, returns. A better way to read Daniel is to acknowledge that for its author, the little horn signified Antiochus IV in both chs. 7 and 8. However, in the light of history and God's new revelation in Jesus Christ, we can now see that it also has a later fulfillment in the Antichrist spoken of in the NT.

8:10 / The NIV combines two Hebrew phrases into one: **some of the starry host**. More literally, the Hebrew reads, "some of the host and some of the stars." This shows the ambivalence in the term "host," which may be either heavenly beings or stars. The literal reading suggests two groups are being cast down, when in actuality "some of the stars" explains "some of the host." Therefore, the important point to understand is that "starry host" also refers to heavenly beings and not simply to what modern people understand scientifically by "stars."

8:11 / The verb *higdil* means "it magnified." Though the verb is not reflexive by form, it is necessary to add "itself" to make good sense in English. Thus NIV: **It set itself up**; similarly RSV: "It magnified itself." NRSV has "it acted arrogantly." Another possibility is "it grew great" (Collins, *Daniel*, p. 325). Note that the text has shifted from feminine verbs (8:10), in agreement with the feminine noun "horn," to a masculine verb. Perhaps this is a grammatical mistake (Montgomery, *Daniel*, p. 335) or perhaps the author was thinking of the king himself instead of the horn.

The root *shlk* usually means "to throw" or "cast." The NIV reads **was brought low**. The RSV is more literal: "the place of his sanctuary was overthrown." Unfortunately, that might give some the misleading impression that the temple was leveled in the second century B.C., when it was not. Perhaps the meaning is more figurative, referring to the temple's defilement (Collins, *Daniel*, p. 334) or its being put out of commission (Goldingay, *Daniel*, p. 211). The verb *hishlik* has the sense of "despise" in reference to God's torah (Neh. 9:26; NIV "they put your law behind their backs"; Montgomery, *Daniel*, p. 336). Similarly, the laying of the foundation of the second temple in the time of Zerubbabel was a ritual act, a religious ceremony, and not merely an engineering feat (see C. L. Meyers and E. M. Meyers, *Haggai, Zechariah 1–8* [AB 25B; Garden City: Doubleday, 1987], pp. 246–53).

8:12 / The word **host** does not fit here very well. It is missing in the LXX, which seems to represent an earlier form of the text than MT. Although *wetsaba'*, "host," is normally masculine, it is paired here with an imperfect third-person singular feminine verb: *tinnaten*, "will be given" (NIV **were given**). There is possibly one other place where the noun *tsaba'* takes a feminine verb (Isa. 40:2), but the reading is contested. The fact that the other three verbs in Dan. 8:12 are also feminine suggests that the author had in mind the feminine noun *qeren*, "horn," as the subject, not the masculine noun *tsaba'*, "host." In other words, "it [the horn] will be given against the daily sacrifice in transgression; and it will cast [if read as imperfect] truth to the ground, and it will act and prosper." Therefore, "host" should be deleted from v. 12. It is remarkable that the tense shifts to the imperfect in this verse. Most commentators translate as past tense in spite of this (NIV, RSV, and NRSV) or consider the future tense to be "out of place" (Montgomery, *Daniel*, p. 336). Even though Daniel has been recounting what he has seen in his vision in the past tense, however, the author may have changed tense to indicate what will happen in the future (Goldingay, *Daniel*, p. 211). Just as he shifted from feminine verbs to masculine in v. 11 (see the Additional Note to 8:11), he shifted from past to future tense in v. 12. Ancient Semitic writers may not always be as consistent as ancient Greek or modern English writers.

Various other solutions have been proposed for the interpretive difficulties of v. 12. The commentary follows the LXX in omitting "host," but an alternative solution is to interpret "host" or "army" as "warfare." This yields the reading "warfare will be given or made against the continual burnt offering" (the Hebrew preposition translated "on" can mean "against" in this context). But this reading is doubtful since the same Hebrew word occurs in verses 10 and 11, where it clearly means "host." A better solution is to read "a host will be given over together with the daily offering, in [the course of] transgression" (Collins, *Daniel*, pp. 326, 333–35). The word "on" can mean "in addition to" or, in this case, "together with." The idea is that some of the heavenly host along with the burnt offering will be given over to Antiochus IV. Although it is hard for us to comprehend, this interpretation is supported by Daniel 7:25, where the "saints," or "holy ones"—that is, the heavenly beings, or angels—are given to the arrogant horn for a time. It is also supported by Daniel 8:10, which reveals that he will cast down some of the heavenly host. Thus, if one prefers to read "host" with the MT in verse 12, then this is the best path to follow.

8:13 / In Hebrew **the rebellion that causes desolation** is *happesha' shomem*. The second word looks very much like *shamayim*, "heaven." The chief god of the Greeks was called Zeus Olympios, which in Hebrew might be *ba'al shamayim*, "lord of heaven." It has been suggested that the term *happesha'*, "the rebellion," is used as a substitute for *ba'al*, "lord," here as a polemic against the Seleucid religion (see references in Goldingay, *Daniel*, p. 212). In other words, the Jews were ridiculing pagan religion by saying that the Greeks' "lord of heaven" was really "the rebellion that causes desolation." While this is quite possible, we cannot be certain. It is also conceivable that *shomem*, "desolation," was used here to ridicule Antiochus IV specifically. We know that he called himself "Epiphanes," "God manifest"; we also know that behind his back some changed it to "Epimanes," "the mad one." In later Hebrew the root *shmm* can have the meaning "be demented" (Lacocque, *Daniel*, p. 164), which could be pointing to the king, but it is not clear that this usage is as old as the second century B.C.

The Gentiles **trampled** the sanctuary in the time of Antiochus IV (1 Macc. 3:45, 51). The Jews then fortified Jerusalem so that the Gentiles could not trample down the walls (1 Macc. 4:60). Jesus predicted that "Jerusalem will be trampled on by the Gentiles until the times of the Gentiles are fulfilled" (Luke 21:24).

8:14 / It makes no sense for the angel to speak to Daniel (**he said to me**), as in the MT. One angel asks another angel a question (8:13). The angel addressed by the question then answers the questioning angel (8:14). We should therefore follow the LXX, which reads "to him" instead of "to me."

8:16 / The root *gbr* means "to be strong" or "mighty." The noun *geber* means "man," at times with the connotation of "mighty man" or "warrior." The name **Gabriel** is often interpreted as "the man of God" or "the hero of God," but "my mighty one is God" or "my hero is God" is preferable (Collins, *Daniel*, p. 336). A wordplay is evident here because the word for "man" in v. 15 is *geber*: Daniel sees one who looks like a *geber* (man), whose name turns out to be Gabriel.

8:17 / The term *qets*, **end**, prominent in Daniel (see 8:19; 9:26 [twice]; 11:6, 13, 27, 35, 40, 45; 12:4, 6, 9, 13 [twice]), echoes language of other prophets (Jer. 51:13; Lam. 4:18; Ezek. 7:2, 3, 6; Amos 8:1–2; Hab. 2:3). For the closely related term *'akharit hayyamim*, "the last days," see, e.g., Isa. 2:2; Jer. 23:20; 30:24; Ezek. 38:16; Dan. 10:14; Hos. 3:5; Mic. 4:1.

8:19 / Scholars are divided into two camps with respect to *za'am*, **wrath** or "indignation," and whether it refers to the wrath of Antiochus or the wrath of God. In support of the former, the verb *za'am*, "to be angry" or "indignant," is used of Antiochus later: "he will . . . vent his fury [*weza'am*] against the holy covenant" (11:30). Also, the tenor of the book of Daniel is that the Jewish people are victims of the evil king Antiochus IV, not objects of God's judgment. Except for ch. 9 (see, e.g., 9:7–8), they are not presented as sinners on the receiving end of God's anger in punishment for their guilt (Collins, *Daniel*, p. 339). On the other hand, in support of the latter notion, "wrath" almost always refers to God's indignation (verb: Zech. 1:12; Mal. 1:4; Ps. 7:11 [7:12 MT]; noun: Jer. 10:10; Ezek. 22:31; Nah. 1:6; Hab. 3:12). In one instance, the Assyrians are the rod of wrath in God's hand to punish Israel for their iniquities (Isa. 10:5). In another, the Babylonians are the means of reproof (Hab. 1:6–11). Perhaps Antiochus was viewed as an instrument of punishment at a later time (Hartman and Di Lella, *Daniel*, p. 237).

8:21 / For **shaggy goat**, the MT has *hatsapir hassa'ir*, "the he-goat the he-goat." The NIV translates the second word for "he-goat" as "shaggy." To be sure, it comes from the root *s'r*, meaning "hair," so the NIV is doing the best one can with this text. The first occurrence of "goat," in v. 5, has *tsepir-ha'izzim*, "the he-goat of the she-goats," meaning "he-goat" (see the Additional Note on 8:5). The LXX has almost the same expression in both verses 5 and 21. We should therefore delete *hassa'ir* so the Hebrew text reads *tsapir* or *tsepir ha'izzim*, "the he-goat."

The word for Greece is *yawan* in Hebrew, which is related to "Ionian." This is probably because the Ionian Greeks of Asia Minor were closer to Israel than those of the Greek islands. They also traveled and traded in the east and first introduced Greek civilization there (Driver, *Daniel*, p. 122).

§9 Daniel's Prayer and the Seventy Weeks (Dan. 9:1–27)

Chapter 9 is unique for three reasons. First, it starts with Daniel reading a prophetic text rather than receiving a vision as in the surrounding chapters (chs. 7, 8, and 10). Second, the particular name of Israel's God, Yahweh, is only found in this chapter (vv. 2, 4, 8, 10, 13, 14, 20). Third, most of the chapter is taken up with a prayer. Elsewhere, the author makes clear that Daniel believed in talking to God (2:18; 6:10), but only here does he record the lengthy text of one of the prophet's supplications (9:4b–19). Although Daniel 9 is mainly occupied by the prayer, the chapter transitions to apocalyptic revelation toward the end. God communicates his message to the seer via Gabriel (9:21). In this way the author links chapter 9 to chapter 8, by the appearance of the same heavenly messenger: "Gabriel, the man I had seen in the earlier vision, came to me" (9:21). Another possible link between these two chapters is the theme of understanding, except that here it is a point of contrast. While chapter 8 ends with the note that the vision was "beyond understanding" (8:27), chapter 9 begins with the statement that Daniel "understood" Jeremiah's prophetic message (9:2), although ironically it will be the angel that will bring additional "insight and understanding" (9:22) into the prophecy, new thoughts that Daniel on his own had not anticipated.

This chapter may be considered a midrash on Jeremiah 25:11–12; 29:10–14, because it represents an attempt to reinterpret earlier authoritative texts, in this case Jeremiah's predictions about the seventy years of desolation, in order to apply them to a later situation. The exile had ended in the latter part of the sixth century B.C., when the Persians defeated the Babylonians and allowed the Jews to return to Jerusalem to rebuild the temple. However, the Jews of the second century B.C. were still being persecuted in and around Jerusalem under Antiochus IV, so they continued to witness the desolation of the land. This caused them to look for another fulfillment of Jeremiah's prophecies. The angel provided a new understanding of the seventy years that made the promise relevant to the faithful ones of the Seleucid period.

Some scholars question whether the prayer (9:4b–19) is original because of the ways it differs from the rest of the book. To begin with, the Hebrew of the prayer is superior to the surrounding material: the remainder of the chapter fits with chapters 8 and 10–12 by being rougher and containing Aramaisms (Hartman and Di Lella, *Daniel*, p. 246). In response, one could argue that the author of the book chose a stock prayer in more classical Hebrew and inserted it here. If such is the case, then while he did not compose the prayer, it is still "original" in the sense that it was not added by a later redactor but was part of the first edition (Collins, *Daniel*, p. 347).

Next, one might expect a petition for illumination, since the angel brings a new explanation of the seventy years. Yet surprisingly, we find a penitential prayer that makes no reference at all to Jeremiah or to the seventy years. On the other side, one might counter that this charge is unwarranted, because Daniel did not imagine that he needed a new interpretation. He already thought he understood the meaning of the seventy years (9:2). Instead of looking for a new revelation, he was acting on his belief that repentance and confession would bring about the deliverance of his people. This was the common understanding of the exiles in Babylon; if the author of Daniel was from the second century, in taking on the guise of a sixth-century Daniel he was being careful to represent the seer in a way that was appropriate to the exilic period.

Then, there is the observation that one could remove the prayer without losing anything significant, because it is possible to jump from verse 3 to verse 21 without sacrificing coherence. Furthermore, duplications where the prayer begins and ends suggest redactional activity: verses 3 and 4 are competing introductions, and verses 20 and 21 are independent transitions from the prayer to the appearance of Gabriel. These are strong objections, but if the prayer is removed, the chapter is unusually short compared to the rest of the book. Of course, the rejoinder is that the shortness of the chapter might be what prompted an editor to supply a prayer. Also, the next section of the book, Daniel 10:1–12:4, is really one unit, even though it is now divided into three chapters and is unusually long. So, there does not have to be uniformity of length between the various chapters in the book.

Finally, there is a theological contrast between the prayer and the rest of Daniel. The rest of the book fixes blame for the suffering of the Jews on evil oppressors, such as Antiochus IV; in his prayer, Daniel makes the people responsible for their torments because they broke God's laws, thus bringing the covenant curses down on themselves (9:7–14). This is a persuasive point, but not unassailable. The theology of retribution found in Kings, Lamentations, and Jeremiah is also implied in the first chapter of Daniel: "And the Lord delivered Jehoiakim the king of Judah into his [Nebuchadnezzar's] hand, along with some of the articles from the temple of God" (Dan. 1:2). Furthermore, the author may have agreed that Jerusalem's destruction in the sixth century resulted from disobedience while questioning that theology for his own day, believing instead that the persecuted Jews were innocent, while Antiochus IV was blameworthy. In addition, the author was aware that Israelite society was always mixed. In the sixth century, it seems that the leaders and most of the people worshiped idols, so that destruction was inevitable. But there were faithful ones like Jeremiah who remained true to Yahweh's covenant, and the righteous suffered along with the wicked. So it was in the second century. Many Jews assimilated to the pagan Greek culture, while there were pious ones who resisted compromising their faith, such as the apocalyptist and other wise ones, some of whom were martyred (11:33–35). So, the author may be viewed as consistent, attributing the continuing desolation to the sins of the evil Jews as well as to the sins of the Seleucids. Thus, when he portrays Daniel confessing sin, he is thinking of the renegade, hellenized Jews who broke God's laws, not the righteous ones. That being said, the careful reader still notices the divergence between this chapter and the others in Daniel.

In conclusion, there are good reasons for questioning whether the prayer belongs to the earliest stratum of the book, but the evidence is inconclusive. Good arguments have been made on both sides of the debate. I incline to the view that the prayer is a later interpolation, while I acknowledge that it is not clear and that the prayer does fit very well in the chapter and in the purported sixth-century setting.

Daniel 9 exhibits the envelope construction, or A-B-A pattern. It begins with Daniel reading Jeremiah's prediction of seventy years of exile (9:1–2). This leads Daniel into prayer (9:3–19). The chapter concludes with a visitation from the archangel Gabriel, who helps Daniel to understand more fully the meaning of the seventy years and the time leading up to the end. However, the interpretation of the "seventy 'sevens'" (9:20–27, esp. vv. 24–27) remains very controversial. As Driver says, "Probably no passage of the Old Testament has been the subject of so much discussion, or has given rise to so many and such varied interpretations, as this. . . . The prophecy *admits of no explanation, consistent with history, whatever*" (Driver, *Daniel*, p. 143). Montogomery summarizes the problem: "The history of the exegesis of the 70 Weeks is the Dismal Swamp of O.T. criticism" (Montgomery, *Daniel*, p. 400).

9:1–2 / While chapter 8 is dated to the third year of King Belshazzar, chapter 9 is dated to the first year of Darius the Mede (9:1), who was mentioned earlier, in Daniel 5:31 and 6:1 (see the commentary on those verses). Here, the additional detail is given that he was the son of Xerxes (9:1). There are two main problems with verse 1. First of all, we know of no Darius the Mede from history, although there were several Persian kings named Darius. Secondly, the order should probably be reversed, because if we are to equate Darius the Mede with Darius I (the Persian), we know from history that the latter was not the son but the father of Xerxes. According to the present verse, Darius "was made king over the kingdom of the Chaldeans" (9:1, author's translation; NIV **was made ruler over the Babylonian kingdom**).

In the first year of his reign (9:2) is redundant at first glance (see 9:1). However, the author might have intentionally repeated the date for emphasis. According to Daniel, Belshazzar was the last Babylonian king (although historically it was Nabonidus); he was succeeded by Darius the Mede (5:30–6:1; although historically it was Cyrus the Persian). The repetition of "first year" might aim to highlight the dawn of a new era fraught with possibilities, both good and bad. With the end of the Babylonian kingdom, some Jews might have begun to wonder about God's timetable. Was God planning to deliver his people from captivity? The date was emphasized to explain why Daniel's thoughts turned to God's promise of deliverance through Jeremiah (Porteous, *Daniel*, p. 135; Driver, *Daniel*, p. 127).

Daniel has been reading **the Scriptures** (9:2), literally, "books" (so RSV and NRSV). Some would shy away from translating the word as "Scriptures," considering it anachronistic or possibly misleading if it is understood in the modern sense of a fixed set of religious writings. Even as late as the second century B.C., the biblical canon was still fluid and not completely fixed. That would even be truer for the sixth century B.C. (for those who prefer an early date for the book). Perhaps the term "Scriptures" may be used so long as it is understood that the canon was still open at that time. Nevertheless, to avoid confusion, "books" is preferable. Either way, the author of Daniel clearly considered Jeremiah to be authoritative, and Daniel acknowledges that the prophet's words are **the word of the LORD** (9:2). Like all believers, he sought insight into his day from God's revealed word.

This is an early example of the practice of citing, interpreting, and appropriating previous inspired texts, which became common at Qumran, in other Jewish literature, and in the NT (Gowan, *Daniel*, p. 127; Anderson, *Signs and Wonders*, p. 106). In fact, Jews and Christians still do this today.

Just as the author of Daniel was attempting to make Jeremiah relevant for his generation, so preachers in our time seek to apply the Bible to our modern situations. Likewise, when we read it devotionally, we listen for a message from the Lord specifically for us, because we believe God still speaks to his people through his word. Scripture is meant to teach us and to give us encouragement and hope (Rom. 15:4). God inspired the holy writings in order to instruct us in the way of salvation, to train us in righteousness, and to equip us for every good work (2 Tim. 3:14–17).

Some have seen a tension between the seer's confession that he **understood** (9:2) and the fact that he needed revelation from the angel later (Hartman and Di Lella, *Daniel*, p. 241). However, Daniel does understand **Jeremiah** on one level (9:2). **The prophet predicted that the desolation of Jerusalem would last seventy years** (Dan. 9:2; see Jer. 25:11–12; 29:4–14). According to the internal chronology of the book of Daniel, that period was almost finished. The author dates the first deportation to 605 B.C. (Dan. 1:1–2). Babylon falls in 539, some sixty-six years later. So Daniel determines to fast and pray in order to sanctify himself and prepare for the time of restoration, which is just around the corner. He believes he understands Jeremiah quite well and has no reason to think he needs further illumination. However, heaven will reinterpret the seventy years in a way that no one could guess from reading Jeremiah. Concerning the seventy years, historians date the first deportation to 597 B.C. rather than to 605. Even so, it might be possible to use 605 as the start date for Jeremiah 25:11–12, since it mentions the time the nations "will serve the king of Babylon" (Jer. 25:11), and that is the year that Babylon obtained hegemony over Judah. Jeremiah 29 is more difficult, because it seems to describe the seventy years as the time of captivity (Jer. 29:4–14), which was actually only fifty-nine years (597–538). Some other verses are relevant to this discussion. Zechariah appears to reckon the seventy years as spanning the time from the destruction of the temple (587) to its rebuilding (515); this is close at seventy-two years (Zech. 1:12–17). The Chronicler focuses on Jeremiah's description of desolation, counting seventy years from the fall of the temple (587) to the time of Cyrus's decree to return (538); but that was actually only forty-nine years (2 Chron. 36:19–22). A number of scholars think we should not take the number literally (Lacocque, *Daniel*, p. 177; Collins, *Daniel*, p. 349; Goldingay, *Daniel*, p. 239; Hartman and Di Lella, *Daniel*, p. 247). Perhaps it is just a round number for a long period, to contrast with the false prophets who predicted a short exile (Jer. 29:8–10). Another possibility is that Jeremiah came up with the number by adding up the years of ten sabbaticals (Lev. 25:2–7; Deut. 15:1–11; 2 Chron. 36:21); or he might have chosen seventy to symbolize a lifetime because this is roughly the number of years humans are allotted (Ps. 90:10). The former option would, in fact, combine two symbolic numbers, ten and seven, each of which connotes completeness.

9:3–14 / Daniel's prayer follows his meditation on the seventy years. So he turns to the Lord God (9:3), which probably means toward the holy city. When Solomon dedicated the temple, he prayed that his people, if taken captive, would pray toward the land of Israel, Jerusalem, and the temple (1 Kgs. 8:48). Daniel earlier petitioned God with his window open toward Jerusalem (Dan. 6:10). It should be noted that in chapter 9 he is not seeking revelation but is preparing for the return to Jerusalem by confessing his sin and the sin of his people (9:20). The prophets (e.g., Jeremiah and Ezekiel), the books of Kings, and Lamentations blame Judah for the exile, for it was their sin that brought the judgment of the Babylonian captivity. And the Jewish people knew that if they went into exile, they were to repent and confess their sin, so that God would remember his covenant, forgive them, and deliver them (Lev. 26:40–45; 1 Kgs. 8:46–51). Accordingly, Daniel pleads with God in prayer and petition, in fasting, and in sackcloth and ashes (9:3). These elements are repeated in other stressful situations. When threatened with death in the time of Esther, the Jews fast, wearing sackcloth and ashes (Esth. 4:1–3). After Jonah prophesies in Nineveh, the people pray and fast in sackcloth and ashes, hoping that God will relent from his decision to destroy their city (Jon. 3:6–9). In addition to these gestures (praying, fasting, and wearing sackcloth and ashes), God also expects us to care for the needy and to refrain from strife and quarreling (Isa. 58:4–10). While it is true that fasting is sometimes a means of preparing to receive revelation (Exod. 34:28; Deut. 9:9), there is no indication that Daniel is fasting for that reason. In the next chapter it is different because there Daniel is fasting to "gain understanding" (Dan. 10:2–3, 12).

The beginning of this prayer most closely resembles Ezra's devotions, when he "was praying and confessing, weeping and throwing himself down before the house of God" (Ezra 10:1). Likewise, in Nehemiah's day they "gathered together, fasting and wearing sackcloth and having dust on their heads.... They stood in their places and confessed their sins and the wickedness of their fathers" (Neh. 9:1–2). For other similar prayers in the OT, see, for example, 1 Kings 8; Ezra 9:6–15; Nehemiah 1:5–11; 9:5–37; Jeremiah 32:16–25. In sum, these traditional, symbolic gestures set the scene for the next step, the moment when Daniel follows up those actions by next putting into words his confession, repentance, and petition.

At first glance, verse 4 begins with what sounds like a second introduction to the prayer: **I prayed to the Lord my God and confessed** (9:4). In fact, its specific function seems to be to introduce the words of the actual prayer itself. Daniel begins his prayer with praise, acknowledging that **God is great and awesome** (9:4). This is instructive for the contemporary practice of prayer. We often come to the Lord with our long lists of needs, which of course he delights to hear; but we sometimes forget to worship and adore him for who he is and to thank him for the innumerable things he has already done for us. In addition to being worthy of praise, God is faithful, for he **keeps his covenant of love with all who love him and obey his commands** (9:4). This verse is almost identical to Nehemiah 1:5, and the second part calls to mind Deuteronomy 7:9. A covenant is a sort of contract, treaty, or agreement, such as the ones God made with Noah (Gen. 9:1–17), Abraham (Gen. 15; 17), Moses (Exod. 20–35), and David (2 Sam. 7; Pss. 89:1–37; 132). God is still a covenant-keeping God, for he made a new covenant in the blood of Jesus (Luke 22:19–20; see also Matt. 26:26–29). In the covenant with Moses and the Israelites, God first saved his people from slavery in Egypt and subsequently brought them to Sinai to give them his law. So it is in the new covenant: first he demonstrates his love for us by saving us through the death of Christ (Rom. 5:8–9); then he calls us to respond in love and obedience: "If you love me, you will obey what I command" (John 14:15; see also 13:34–35; 14:21, 23; 15:10, 12–14, 17).

Unfortunately, God's covenant people did not obey his commands, so Daniel's prayer then moves into a confession of sin whose pattern is comparable to one followed by Nehemiah (Neh. 1:6–7). The stacking up of five verbs for sin accentuates the transgression of the people: **we have sinned and done wrong. We have been wicked and have rebelled; we have turned away from your commands and laws** (Dan. 9:5). It is no coincidence that the first three verbs in this verse parallel those in Solomon's prayer when he dedicated the temple to Yahweh, because the wise king stipulated that should his people go into exile, and there repent, they should say, "We have sinned, we have done wrong, we have acted wickedly" (1 Kgs. 8:47). This is precisely the setting for Daniel and his people, and, therefore, to invoke words from the king's prayer seems the appropriate response in Daniel's prayer. Daniel singles out the **kings, princes,** and **fathers** (Dan. 9:6, 8; cf. Jer. 44:21), along with the rest of the people. Nehemiah implicates the priests with guilt as well (Neh. 9:34) and includes priests and prophets in his list of recipients of hardship (Neh. 9:32). The NT demands repentance (Acts 2:38; 3:19; 5:31; 17:30; 20:21; 2 Cor. 7:9–10; 2 Pet. 3:9) and confession of sin (1 John 1:9) as well as the OT.

There is a stark contrast between God, who is **righteous** (Dan. 9:7, 14), and the Israelites, who **are covered with shame** (9:7, 8). Because the Israelites did not listen to God's **servants the prophets** (9:6), they were **scattered** to other **countries** for their **unfaithfulness** (9:7). Similarly, Nehemiah notes: "By your Spirit you admonished them through your prophets. Yet they paid no attention, so you handed them over to the neighboring peoples" (Neh. 9:30). In spite of all this, God **is merciful and forgiving** (Dan. 9:9). Nevertheless, because the people **have not obeyed the Lord** (9:10), he has caused **the curses and sworn judgments written in the Law of Moses** to be **poured out** on them (9:11). The curses are recorded in Leviticus 26:27–45; Deuteronomy 27:15–26; 28:15–68; and 29:20. God elsewhere is said to "pour out" his wrath (Jer. 7:20; 42:18; 44:6; 2 Chron. 12:7; 34:25; Ps. 79:6). Some people erroneously imagine that wrath is an attribute of God only in the OT, but according to the NT apocalypse, in the end of time God will pour out seven bowls of wrath (Rev. 16:1); so, there is continuity between the OT and the NT. The Lord has **fulfilled the words spoken against** Israel by **bringing upon** them **disaster** (Dan. 9:12). In this way God shows that he keeps his word, whether for blessing or for punishment. As noted in the introduction to this chapter, most of Daniel emphasizes God's judgment on the wicked kingdoms of this world for persecuting his people. This chapter also lays blame on Israel: the exile was a consequence of disobedience.

In spite of the chastisement, the Israelites still failed to repent: **we have not sought the favor of the Lord our God by turning from our sins and giving attention to your truth** (9:13). The idiom "to seek the favor of" connotes "to mollify, pacify, appease" (BDB, p. 318). Ostensibly, this prayer comes from the exilic period, when the Jews could not do this through sacrifice, because the temple was in ruins. They were to appease God in this time (as today) by showing contrition and by humbly confessing their iniquities. The word translated "giving attention" comes from the root *skl*, which occurs a number of times in Daniel, where it often has more the sense "to be wise" or "to understand." The connection between these two concepts is transparent: to give attention is to turn the mind toward, to consider, to ponder, and therefore to understand. The book both begins and concludes with an emphasis on this motif: Daniel and his friends are wise (1:4, 17); at the end of history, the wise will instruct others, although some of them will fall (11:33, 35); and the wise will shine like the stars (12:3), be purified, and stand in contrast to the wicked (12:10). Here, more toward the middle of the book, the word occurs in the prayer to chide the Jews for not paying attention to God's truth. However, it is interesting that the root is also found in the apocalyptic section of this chapter. The angel comes to give Daniel insight (9:22) and directs him to understand the message from heaven (9:25).

Daniel's prayer continues: **The Lord did not hesitate to bring the disaster upon us** (9:14). The verb "did not hesitate" literally means "to keep watch," so this is better rendered, "Yahweh kept watch over the calamity and brought it upon us" (author's translation; cf. the NRSV: "So the Lord kept watch over this calamity until he brought it upon us"). The same expression is used in Jeremiah when God announces, "I am watching over my word to perform it" (Jer. 1:12 NRSV). The Lord ensures that his promises are fulfilled, even if they are assurances of punishment, as in this case, where he has made sure that the deserved judgment has come upon Judah. Similarly, God says, "I am watching over them for harm, not for good" (Jer. 44:27; cf. also 31:28).

9:15–19 / Daniel prays, **"Now, O Lord our God, . . . we have done wrong"** (9:15). "Now" signals the change from penitence to petition for deliverance, as in other biblical passages (Exod. 32:32; 1 Sam. 12:10; 15:25; 1 Chron. 21:8; Ezra 9:8, 10; Neh. 9:32; see also, in the Apocrypha, Bar. 2:11; Pr. Azar.; Sg. Three vv. 10, 18). The supplicant appeals to history with hope for the future: You **brought your people out of Egypt with a mighty hand** (Dan. 9:15). Just as God delivered the Israelites from bondage in Egypt and brought them to the promised land in the time of Moses, so the Jews hoped that God would deliver them from Babylonian captivity and restore them to the land of Israel. Indeed, the return from exile was understood to be a new exodus (Isa. 40:3–5; 43:16–19; 48:20–21; 51:9–11). The actual request for salvation comes in the next verse: Daniel prays that God will **turn away** his **anger** and his **wrath** (Dan. 9:16). In doing so, he appeals to God's mighty deeds, his reputation, and his mercy.

Daniel then prays, **"Now, our God, hear the prayers and petitions of your servant"** (9:17). Daniel builds his case before the heavenly bar. First, he grounds his petition in **all** of God's **righteous acts** (9:16). These are the powerful acts of deliverance that Yahweh performed in times past (Judg. 5:11; 1 Sam. 12:7; Mic. 6:5; Ps. 103:6). Daniel has already alluded to the exodus; now he invokes the other occasions when God acted in history to vindicate his people, implying that it is in God's nature to save or at least that it is characteristic of his previous work. Second, Daniel points to God's reputation: **For your sake, O my God, do not delay, because your city and your people bear your Name** (9:19; see also vv. 15, 18). This is boldly anthropomorphic, because it is the way we try to influence human judges to do what is right. They may be spurred into action by appeals to their vanity, whereas God is sovereign and free. Nevertheless, this way of praying is part of an honorable tradition in the OT. Similarly, the psalmist cries out for divine intervention so that the enemies will no longer revile God's name (Pss. 74:10, 18; 79:9–10). Third, Daniel does not depend on works to earn God's favor but looks for grace: **We do not make requests of you because we are righteous, but because of your great mercy** (Dan. 9:18). When we call on God, we can claim no righteousness of our own (Ps. 143:2; Isa. 64:6; Rom. 3:23). All we can do is cite God's righteousness and trust in his kindness (Rom. 3:21–26). This is something of a paradox, though, because on the one hand righteousness is credited to our account by faith (Rom. 4:1–25), while on the other hand Jesus demands that we keep his commands (Matt. 5:17–19), that we do good works (Matt. 5:16; 25:31–46), and that our righteousness exceed that of the scribes and the Pharisees (Matt. 5:20). When Daniel confesses his **sin and the sin of** his **people Israel** (Dan. 9:20; cf. vv. 15, 16), he expects that although they deserve judgment, God will **forgive** (9:19) because he is compassionate.

The prayer manifests a special interest in **Jerusalem** (9:7, 12, 16 [twice]), God's **city** (9:16, 18, 19) and **holy hill** (9:16), and also for the **people** (9:16, 19), who have become **an object of scorn to** their neighbors (9:16). Both the city and the people are said to be called by God's **Name** (9:18–19). This is not simply a matter of God's reputation, as mentioned above; it also indicates the influence of deuteronomistic theology, namely, that God would choose a place for his name to dwell (Deut. 12:5; 14:23; 16:2; 1 Kgs. 8:29; Jer. 7:10–11). The prayer also shows concern for the temple: **O Lord, look with favor on your desolate sanctuary** (Dan. 9:17). When the Hebrew expression is translated as "look with favor" (NIV), the reader misses the allusion to the Aaronic benediction (Num. 6:25). Instead, the phrase should be rendered more literally, "cause your face to shine." The root from which the word "desolate" comes is found several times in Daniel: "the rebellion that causes desolation" (Dan. 8:13); "desolations have been decreed" (Dan. 9:26); "abomination that causes desolation" (Dan. 9:27; 11:31; 12:11). If the author of the book of Daniel was from the second century, while he referred to the destroyed temple of Solomon, he was probably actually thinking of a contemporary temple "desolation," the desolating sacrilege that King Antiochus IV committed in the Jerusalem temple.

The prayer closes with a powerful cry to God: **O Lord, listen! O Lord, forgive! O Lord, hear and act!** (9:19). The threefold repetition of "Lord" is arresting and intended to get God's attention. The four imperative verbs communicate "a sense of urgent insistence" (Collins, *Daniel*, p. 351). "Listen" and "forgive" are reminiscent of Solomon's prayer: "Hear the supplication of your servant and of your people Israel when they pray toward this place. Hear from heaven, your dwelling place, and when you hear, forgive" (1 Kgs. 8:30). Finally, another vocative, **O my God,** and one last desperate request, **do not delay,** give the prayer a poignant, climactic closing (9:19).

9:20–27 / The prayer is mostly traditional material, but this last section of the chapter moves into the apocalyptic genre again. Just as the prayer was introduced twice (vv. 3 and 4), so there are two verses that mark the transition from the prayer to the revelation of Gabriel. Verses 20 and 21a are doublets. Verse 21a seems to be more likely original; verse 20 was added later, perhaps when the prayer was added (if it was a later addition). Verse 20 is not a complete sentence, as it is meant to lead into the introduction of Gabriel, just as verse 21a does now. It is closely tied to the prayer and supplies a précis of it: **While I was . . . confessing my sin and the sin of my people Israel and making my request to the Lord my God for his holy hill** (9:20). In contrast, v. 21a is more terse: **while I was still in prayer** (9:21a). If the prayer is an interpolation, then verse 21a was probably intended to follow from verse 3 like this: "So I turned to the Lord God and pleaded with him in prayer and petition, in fasting, and in sackcloth and ashes [9:3]. While I was still in prayer, **Gabriel, the man I had seen in the earlier vision, came to me** [9:21]."

Along with other key OT figures, Daniel demonstrates the importance of intercessory prayer. Abraham argued with God over Sodom and Gomorrah, although they were still destroyed because there were not even ten righteous people to be found (Gen. 18:23–33). Moses prayed for his sister, Miriam, so that she was healed of leprosy (Num. 12:13). He also interceded on behalf of Israel after they made a golden calf; God had decided to destroy them, but Moses convinced him to change his mind (Exod. 32:1–14). The NT instructs us to intercede for all people, especially for those in authority (1 Tim. 2:1–4) and for our fellow believers (Eph. 6:18). Regarding Daniel's prayer, it is noteworthy that even though he is a righteous prophet, he does not stand arrogantly aloof over his people; rather, he humbly confesses his sins along with theirs (Dan. 9:20). We must remember Jesus's warning not to be self-righteous when we pray: we cannot impress God with our good deeds, as the Pharisee attempted to do, but must cry out with the tax collector, "God, have mercy on me, a sinner" (Luke 18:9–14).

The phrase "in the earlier vision" (9:21) could be rendered, "in the vision at the beginning," which raises the question of how far back it is pointing. Some think that "at the beginning" refers to Daniel's first vision (Dan. 7:15–16; Collins, *Daniel*, p. 351). There Daniel, troubled by what he has seen, approaches one of the heavenly beings, who then provides the interpretation; but that angel is anonymous. While it is possible that the present verse is identifying that unnamed angel as Gabriel, it is more natural to understand "at the beginning" as meaning "at first," that is, at the first place where the text mentions this heavenly being. In other words, it refers back to Daniel 8:16, where Gabriel is introduced by name. In that verse a heavenly voice directs Gabriel to instruct Daniel. Therefore, just as chapter 8 is linked to chapter 7 ("In the third year of King Belshazzar's reign, I, Daniel, had a vision, after the one that had already appeared to me" [8:1]), Daniel 9 is connected to chapter 8 by the common figure of Gabriel, the angelic interpreter.

The word translated "came" (9:21) normally means "touched," as in the surrounding chapters. In both cases Daniel seems to go into a trancelike state ("deep sleep" [8:18; 10:9]), with his face to the ground, until a heavenly being touches him (8:18; 10:9–10, 15–16, 18). However, in chapter 9 the situation is not the same, because (1) Daniel remains conscious and (2) the prepositions following the verbs are different (see the Additional Note on 9:21). Here the verb apparently has the connotation of reaching, with the sense of arriving or coming to Daniel, although we cannot rule out the meaning "to touch."

The phrase **in swift flight** (v. 21) is questionable in Hebrew (see the Additional Note on 9:21). It seems more plausible to read "being weary in weariness." If so, was it the angel who was tired from his journey? Then the gist is "Gabriel arrived in extreme weariness." To some it seems "absurd" (Montgomery, *Daniel*, p. 371) that angels could become weary, but we must remember that in the imaginative world of this author, angels can be cast down by human kings (7:21; 8:10) and can be delayed by spiritual adversaries (10:12–13). If so, they could certainly experience fatigue. Nevertheless, it is possible that the construction describes Daniel, who is tired after fasting and praying. The sentence, then, should read something like this: "While I was still in prayer, being extremely weary, the man Gabriel, whom I had seen in the vision at the beginning, touched me." Note that here we have opted for the meaning "touched" instead of "came" (see above discussion), which creates a closer parallel with chapters 8 and 10, where the weakened Daniel is touched by the angel and strengthened (8:18; 10:9–10, 15–16, 18). Admittedly, this translation is a bit forced, given the current word order ("being extremely weary" comes after "the man Gabriel . . . at the beginning"); but perhaps we need to conclude that the verse was jumbled at some point, because it is awkward as it is. Maybe it originally conveyed the idea that the angel fortified the exhausted seer by touching him so that he could receive the heavenly messenger's interpretation.

Gabriel announces, "**Daniel, I have now come to give you insight and understanding**" (9:22). The pattern in chapters 7–12 is for a heavenly mediator to explain Daniel's visions to him (7:15–16, 23; 8:15–19; 10:4–20).

In the NT, Gabriel appears to Zechariah to announce the birth of John the Baptist (Luke 1:11–20) and to Mary to announce the birth of Jesus (Luke 1:26–38). Although God mainly speaks to the church through Scripture (see the commentary on 9:2), he occasionally communicates through subjective means such as angels, revelations, visions, dreams, tongues and interpretation, and prophecy (1 Cor. 14:26–31). However, we must be careful always to judge such messages by the Bible and by historical Christian doctrine (1 Cor. 14:29; 1 Thess. 5:21; 1 John 4:1). Whenever anyone teaches or preaches, we should be like the Bereans by examining the Scriptures to see whether the content is sound (Acts 17:11). Even if an angel appears to us, we are not obligated to pay attention if the supposed revelation is contrary to God's Word; in fact, such an angel would be cursed (Gal. 1:8–9).

Gabriel tells Daniel that as soon as Daniel **began to pray, an answer was given** (9:23). In Daniel 10, also, a heavenly messenger is dispatched in response to what the seer does—in that case, fasting—but he is delayed for three weeks (Dan. 10:12–13); here, heaven responds to both Daniel's prayer and his fasting. It is better to translate more literally here, "a word went out." The NIV's "an answer was given" seems to imply that Gabriel is bringing a specific reply to Daniel's prayer. However, Daniel was not asking for revelation in his prayer, which is what the angel has brought; he was confessing sin. At the same time, there is clearly a relationship between the prayer and the sending of the angel. If it were a coincidence, the angel would not have said, "as soon as you began to pray," alluding to the "prayer and petition" with "fasting" and "sackcloth and ashes" (9:3) at the start of the chapter. The best way to understand the connection is that God sends a messenger because Daniel prays, but not necessarily because of what Daniel prays (Collins, *Daniel*, p. 352). Besides the misleading connection between the prayer and the revelation, there is another reason why it is important to translate "a word went out" instead of "an answer was given": so that the reader can catch the similarity with "from the going out of a word" in verse 25, which the NIV renders "from the issuing of the decree" (or "word" [see NIV footnote]; see the commentary on 9:25). Daniel is described as being **highly esteemed** (9:23); he is similarly praised in the next chapter (10:11, 19).

Gabriel proceeds to explain the vision and its message: **Seventy "sevens" are decreed** (9:24). What does "seventy 'sevens'" mean? It is usually construed by commentators as seventy weeks of years (so the

RSV translation; cf. NRSV "seventy weeks"), meaning that each "seven" (or "week") is a grouping of seven years. Thus, the total number of years is seventy times seven, or 490 years. That interpretation is supported by the Torah, which speaks of a jubilee year after "seven sabbaths of years" (Lev. 25:8–12). Sabbath is the seventh day, so a sabbath of years is seven years. Seven sabbaths of years is therefore forty-nine years, followed by the fiftieth year, which is the jubilee. At that time, indentured servants were supposed to be set free and be allowed to return to their families and their property. The revelation in Daniel 9 multiplies the sabbath of years by a factor of ten: instead of seven sabbaths of years, there are seventy. Then the 490 years are subdivided into other periods of time representing historical events leading up to the end of the age (9:26–27). This interpretation makes the most sense, although, as it will be seen in the following section, it is difficult to see how the periods of time jibe exactly with history.

Periodization of history is a common feature of apocalyptic literature. The author of the *Sibylline Oracles* divides history into ten kingdoms or periods. The Book of the Watchers (*1 En.* 10:11–12) uses a plan of seventy generations. The Apocalypse of Weeks (*1 En.* 93; 91:11–19) carves out ten weeks, with the exile occurring late in the sixth week, the period of restoration after the exile being the seventh week, followed by three weeks of judgment, leading into eternity (Collins, *Daniel*, p. 353). Daniel 2 and 4 divide history into four historical kingdoms, culminating in the fifth kingdom—the kingdom of God; in chapter 9, the scheme is 7 weeks (49 years), 62 weeks (434 years), and 1 week (7 years).

Six infinitives carve out the things determined by heaven to take place by the end of the 490 years. God has decided

1. **to finish transgression;**
2. **to put an end to sin;**
3. **to atone for wickedness;**
4. **to bring in everlasting righteousness;**
5. **to seal up vision and prophecy;**
6. **to anoint the most holy (9:24).**

What is the relationship between these clauses? Is there a pattern or a progression? Some have discerned two groups of three: 1–3 are more negative, addressing the elimination of sin, whereas 4–6 are more positive, anticipating the coming kingdom of God and the cleansing of the temple. This view has merits but is not attentive enough to details. For example, number 3 deals with sin, as do the first two, but is positive in focusing on atonement, as opposed to numbers 1 and 2, which are negative and parallel to each other in the notion of eliminating evil. Others incline to an A B C / A′ B′ C′ pattern—that is, 1 corresponds to 4, 2 to 5, and 3 to 6—but this is not wholly convincing. Finishing transgression (1) naturally leads to the arrival of everlasting righteousness (4). Atonement rituals (3) can be related to the reconsecration of the Jerusalem sanctuary by anointing the most holy place (6). But the middle pair is problematic in that it is difficult to see how putting an end to sin (2) corresponds to sealing up the vision and the prophecy (5) (see Porteous, *Daniel*, p. 140). The best solution seems to be three consecutive pairs: 1 and 2; 3 and 4; 5 and 6. On the negative side, God will do away with transgression (1) and sin (2). On the positive side, God will atone for iniquity (3), thus restoring righteousness (4). This will ultimately lead to the fulfillment, in the sense of an authenticating seal, of prophetic visions (5) and the restoration of sacrifice in the newly purified, anointed temple (6) (Gowan, *Daniel*, pp. 132–33).

The noun "transgression" (9:24) is the same one used in Daniel 8:12 and 13 (NIV "rebellion") for the sin of Antiochus IV in defiling the temple (the participle "transgressors" is found in 8:23 [NIV "rebels"]). For that reason, this passage is probably predicting an end to his evil activities. However, since the context of Daniel 9 is the seer's prayer for forgiveness, the author may be thinking of the transgressions of the apostate Israelites as well. "To put an end" may mean "to complete." Perhaps the idea is similar to the expression used in chapter 8: "When the transgressors have reached their full measure" (8:23 RSV; NIV "when rebels have become completely wicked"). In other words, the notion here in Daniel 9:24 of finishing transgression and putting an end to sins may be that sin will have reached its limit, precipitating God's action.

The most controversial of the six infinitival constructions is the last: "to anoint the most holy" (9:24; see NIV footnote: "Or *Most Holy Place*; or *most holy One*"). What makes it controversial is that some Christians have interpreted the phrase to mean "to anoint the most holy *one*," meaning the Messiah, or Jesus (Young, *Daniel*, p. 201; see also Baldwin, *Daniel*, p. 169, who sees both temple and Messiah here). This reference to the Messiah does not appear to be either the original meaning of the verse or the author's intention. Rather, Christians have read Jesus into the OT and reinterpreted this passage as a prediction of the coming Messiah, or "anointed one." In the context of the book of Daniel, however, there is no doubt what this is speaking about, because the concern of the author is for the temple. He is distressed about its desecration and longs for its reconsecration, at which time he envisions an anointing, just as Moses anointed the tent of meeting (Exod. 30:26) and the tabernacle (Exod. 40:9). Therefore, the best translation is "a most holy place." First, "place" needs to be supplied to make it clear that it designates the holiest place in the temple, that is, the holy of holies. Secondly, even though there is only one most holy place, the object is indefinite in Hebrew, so it should be rendered "a most holy place," not "the most holy place."

The seventy weeks of years, or 490 years, is further subdivided into three unequal blocks of time. The first is seven weeks, or forty-nine years: **From the issuing of the decree to restore and rebuild Jerusalem until the Anointed One, the ruler, comes, there will be seven "sevens"** (9:25). The NIV's "from the issuing of the decree" calls to mind a human king's edict. The Hebrew expression may denote a royal decree, but it is not necessarily the case here. It might instead be a prophetic word or a word that God speaks from heaven. Therefore, it is preferable to translate the phrase as "from the going forth of the word," because it is more literal and more open ended. In addition, there is also a connection with verse 23, "a word went forth," which the NIV obscures by its translation "an answer was given."

The first option for identifying the going forth of the word is to look to Jeremiah. Some scholars have argued that we should use his prophecies about the seventy years. The first oracle concerning this is dated to 605 and speaks of the demise of Babylon (Jer. 25:1, 11–12). The second one (Jer. 29:10) is dated to the time of the first deportation in 597 and predicts the return to the land. However, neither one addresses the rebuilding of Jerusalem, which is important for Daniel 9:25. Other passages in Jeremiah announce a future reconstruction of the city (Jer. 30:18–22; 31:38–40), but they are more difficult to date, so it is not clear when to start the counting of the "seven 'sevens.'" (Some would even date Jer. 31:38–40 to the postexilic period.) A second choice is to associate the word that goes forth with the decree of Cyrus in 538 B.C. Some object that his decree allowed rebuilding only the temple, not Jerusalem, but in response it can be pointed out that even though the Jews could not build fortifications around the city in the time of Cyrus, they certainly did build houses for themselves. Therefore, it can truly be said that Cyrus's decree allowed the rebuilding of Jerusalem. A third option is to focus on Ezra's return in 458, but there was no decree to restore and rebuild Jerusalem and no building activity. A fourth alternative is to date the decree to 445, when Artaxerxes I gave Nehemiah permission to rebuild the walls of Jerusalem. There is no record of a public decree in the time of Artaxerxes, though one may be implied in Ezra 4:19–21, which says the Jews should stop building until a decree is issued; but no decree is recorded. Nevertheless, when the king grants Nehemiah's request to fortify the Jewish capital, that can constitute a "going forth of the word."

The trouble with all of the above dates is that none of them yields anything significant. "Seven 'sevens'" (9:25) is forty-nine years. When we subtract forty-nine from the above dates, we do not in any case arrive at a historical juncture in which a known anointed one emerges, as specified in verse 25 (see the Additional Note on 9:25). Interestingly, one starting date that does produce a noteworthy year is 587, the year of the destruction of the temple: 587 − 49 = 538, the date of Cyrus's decree. Unfortunately, though, there is no historical record of a word going forth to rebuild Jerusalem at the beginning of this period in 587. Rather, it is in 538, at the end of the block of time, that Cyrus issues his edict allowing the restoration of Zion. Neither is there the appearance of an anointed one, unless one chooses Cyrus. To be sure, he is called Yahweh's anointed in Isaiah 45:1, but we expect the first anointed one (Dan. 9:25) to be a priest, because such is the case with the second one (9:26; see below). An additional objection to picking 587 is that even though Jerusalem fell that year, we do not know whether the author of Daniel knew that. In other words, we have no idea when he would have dated the destruction of Jerusalem. The fact that he dates the first deportation to 605, which is not supported from history, and sets chapter 9 in the reign of Darius the Mede, who seems to be fictional, calls into question the attempt to find an exact date (Collins, *Daniel*, pp. 354–55).

The best solution to the problem of the "going forth of the word" is to think of it as a word from heaven. There is probably a connection between "a word went forth" (9:23; NIV "an answer was given"), which explains the dispatching of Gabriel to Daniel with a message from God, and "the going forth of the word" (9:25; NIV "the issuing of the decree") concerning the rebuilding of Jerusalem. If so, then this is not about a royal decree from a human king or even a prophetic oracle that we have access to, as in the case of Jeremiah, but a word that God speaks in heaven (Collins, *Daniel*, p. 355, although Collins identifies the word with Daniel's prophecy). Since Jeshua, the high priest who supports Zerubbabel in the rebuilding of the temple, is probably the anointed one in view in Daniel 9:25 (see below), we should look to that era. We do not know the exact date of his return to Judah from Babylon, but he was on the scene by 520, because the temple took five years to build and was completed in 515. If we allow that he returned a couple of years before the construction activity, we could start with 522. Adding on to 520 the forty-nine years (seven weeks of years) yields 571. So, maybe in 571 or so, God decrees in heaven that Jerusalem should be rebuilt in the future.

The fulfillment begins to take place in 538 when Cyrus allows Jews to return and restore the holy city. Jeshua, the anointed one spoken of here in Daniel 9:25, returns to the land in about 522 and begins his high-priestly ministry. Alternatively, we could still opt for 587, if we did not feel the need to be too precise. We might say that God spoke from heaven at the time of Jerusalem's destruction, predicting its future restoration. Around the time of the return, in 538 (but actually several years later, so more than the specified forty-nine years), Jeshua, the anointed one, appears (Seow, *Daniel*, p. 148).

In the next part of verse 25, the NIV misreads the Hebrew text by making it definite. The MT has "an anointed one, a ruler" or "an anointed one, a prince" (see NIV footnote), not "the Anointed One, the ruler" (NIV). There are actually two anointed ones in Daniel 9:25–26, and it is most natural to take them to be the high priests Jeshua and Onias III. In the restoration blueprint of Ezekiel (Ezek. 34:23–25; 37:24–28; 44:9–16) and Jeremiah (Jer. 33:17–18), there would be a dyarchy: two rulers. One would be a descendant of David, and the other would be a Zadokite priest. Zechariah, a prophet of the restoration era, agrees with this scheme, envisioning two anointed ones leading the people (Zech. 4:3, 11–14): Zerubbabel the descendant of David and Jeshua (or Joshua) the high priest. Some scholars point to Zerubbabel as the fulfillment of Daniel 9:25, but because of Daniel's concern for the temple and because the anointed one in Daniel 9:26 is probably the priest Onias, the anointed one here is probably Jeshua the high priest, rather than the Davidic descendant.

After the seven weeks comes a second period of time, which will last for **sixty-two "sevens"** (9:25), or 434 years (62 × 7). In Hebrew, there is clearly a break between the "seven 'sevens'" and the "sixty-two 'sevens'" (9:25), marking the numbers off as separate segments (contra the NIV, which seems to ignore the break, implying one block of sixty-nine weeks of years, or 483 years). The only reason to record two numbers is to designate two time periods. The best translation would be "from the going out of a word to restore and build Jerusalem until an anointed one, a prince, there will be seven weeks. Then for sixty-two weeks it will be built again" (author's translation; cf. NRSV). NIV may reflect a traditional messianic interpretation that, by adding the numbers together, indicates a single anointed one, whom it identifies as Jesus. However, this move seems untenable if the text describes two periods of time and two anointed ones. The first anointed one appears after the seven weeks of years while the second is cut off after the sixty-two weeks of years (9:26). Furthermore, the numbers do not work out exactly (see the Additional Note on 9:25). Most important, the text indicates the cutting off of an anointed one

(Dan. 9:26), not his anointing. In conclusion, there must be two anointed ones in Daniel 9, and it is best to take them to be Jeshua and Onias III.

According to the apocalyptist, during this second period of time Jerusalem **will be rebuilt with streets and a trench** (9:25). The returning Jews began to reconstruct the city with "streets" or "plazas" in 538, but the mention of a "trench" or "moat" suggests a later time. In 445, Nehemiah arrived with permission from the Persian king to erect a defensive wall around the holy city. A dry moat would have been dug around the outside of the wall to provide greater protection by increasing the distance between the ground and the top of the wall and by making it more difficult for an enemy to reach the wall. The book of Nehemiah (Neh. 4) makes it very clear that the local peoples provided intense opposition, so that the wall was definitely completed **in times of trouble** (9:25).

Gabriel's interpretation of the vision continues: **After the sixty-two "sevens," the Anointed One will be cut off and will have nothing** (9:26). Once again, by capitalizing "the Anointed One" the NIV is intentionally reading the NT into the OT (cf. NIV footnote to 9:25). This probably does not refer to the crucifixion of Jesus (see above). Rather, it points to Onias III, the high priest who was murdered in 171 B.C. (Dan. 11:22; 2 Macc. 4:23–34). He was the legitimate high priest, but when his brother, Jason, a supporter of the royal hellenization program, offered the king money, Antiochus IV deposed Onias and replaced him with Jason (2 Macc. 4:7–10). Later, Menelaus stole the office from Jason by offering even more money (2 Macc. 4:24), which he obtained by selling some of the gold temple vessels (2 Macc. 4:32). When Onias denounced him, Menelaus had Onias killed (2 Macc. 4:34).

The people of the ruler who will come (9:26) are the Seleucid soldiers of Antiochus IV. The NIV records that they **will destroy the city and the sanctuary** (9:26). This is a correct translation, but the verb "to destroy" can also mean "to damage," "ruin," "spoil," "corrupt," or "pervert" (BDB, p. 1008). The Syrians did not completely destroy Jerusalem and the temple as the Babylonians did earlier and as the Romans did later, but they caused much damage (1 Macc. 1:20–35; 2 Macc. 5:11–21) and in effect destroyed the sanctuary by replacing the worship of Yahweh with the cult of Zeus. Therefore, the temple structure remained, but it was completely corrupted and polluted by pagan rites. Just as the book of Daniel decrees that **war will continue until the end, and desolations have been decreed** (9:26), so Jesus, in listing signs of his return, announces: "When you hear of wars and rumors of wars, do not be alarmed. Such things must happen, but the end is still to come" (Mark 13:7). In other words, according to Jesus, the signs for which to watch that signal the "end" he has in mind compare to the ones Daniel mentioned, "war" and "desolations."

The last period of time is one week of years, or seven years, but it is further subdivided into two halves: **He will confirm a covenant with many for one "seven." In the middle of the "seven" he will put an end to sacrifice and offering. He will also set up an abomination that causes desolation** (9:27). The seven-year span spoken of is from the death of Onias III, in 171, to 164, when the Jews were fighting the Seleucids to regain control of the temple. The covenant mentioned is recorded in 1 Maccabees: "In those days certain renegades came out from Israel and misled many, saying, 'Let us go and make a covenant with the Gentiles around us, for since we separated from them many disasters have come upon us.' This proposal pleased them, and some of the people eagerly went to the king, who authorized them to observe the ordinances of the Gentiles" (1 Macc. 1:11–13 NRSV). "In the middle of the 'seven' [i.e., "week"]" indicates three and a half years, which relates to "time, times and half a time" (Dan. 7:25; 12:7; cf. 8:14; 12:11, 12). One thing seems clear from the context of the book of Daniel: the author is pointing to the evil deeds of Antiochus IV, who made Judaism illegal, stopped the holy sacrifices in the Jerusalem temple, and committed the desolating abomination in 167 B.C. by offering sacrifices to Zeus Olympios in Yahweh's sanctuary (Dan. 8:13; 9:27; 11:31; 12:11; 1 Macc. 1:54; 2 Macc. 6:5). Even though the time between the pollution and the cleansing was only three years (the Hebrew month Chislev 167 to Chislev 164), the reference to the Maccabean period seems obvious. However, Jesus predicted that there would be another fulfillment of this prophecy: "So when you see standing in the holy place 'the abomination that causes desolation,' spoken of through the prophet Daniel—let the reader understand—then let those who are in Judea flee to the mountains" (Matt. 24:15–16; cf. Mark 13:14). Perhaps this was fulfilled in A.D. 70, when the second temple was destroyed; other commentators argue for a future fulfillment when an Antichrist arises at the end of time (2 Thess. 2:4). Christians have to reckon with the fact that Satan is the god of this world (Matt. 4:8–9; 2 Cor. 4:4), so that sometimes evil rulers persecute the believers; such is the context of the book of Revelation, when many followers of Jesus were martyred at the hands of the Romans.

The Hebrew for "abomination that causes desolation" (9:27) appears to be a wordplay on the Semitic designation for Zeus Olympios (see the Additional Note on 9:27). In this way the biblical writer denigrates the pagan deity, for to him Zeus is not the Lord of Heaven but a desolating abomination. The sacrilege caused by Antiochus Epiphanes will continue **until the end that is decreed is poured out on him** (9:27). His death was already alluded to in the previous verse (9:26); it is also predicted in chapter 11: "Yet he will come to his end, and no one will help him" (11:45). The life of Antiochus IV did indeed finally come to an end (1 Macc. 6:8–16; 2 Macc. 9:5–28). Although the end of all things did not take place in the second century B.C., as the apocalyptist hoped, still the message of the book is absolutely infallible: God will one day destroy evil and bring his everlasting kingdom of righteousness.

In sum, if this reading is correct, the first anointed one would be Jeshua and the second Onias III. The events of the last week are in the time of Antiochus IV. The trouble is with the middle period, because 434 years is too long. If we take 522 to be the end of the first period and 171 to be the beginning of the third period, then the second period should only be 351 years long. Perhaps 434 is "a round number rather than a miscalculation" as some scholars aver (Collins, *Daniel*, p. 356). Or, it could be that the 434 years (62 weeks) are simply what was left over. In other words, the author, having started with the symbolic number 70 (from Jeremiah), multiplied it by the number 7, which is also symbolic, to get 490 years. Then he carved out the first period of 49 years (7 weeks × 7 years) to highlight Jeshua, and the last period of 1 week (7 years) to expose the tyranny of Epiphanes. What remains is the middle block of 62 weeks, which possibly is not meant to be taken literally. It is all about the sevens! If the author of Daniel reduced the number of years for the middle period, it would not fit the pattern. In short, even if the numbers do not work out exactly, overall there are enough other clues in the book to point us to the second century B.C.

Some readers of Daniel might argue that since the numbers do not work out perfectly in any scheme, we might just as well espouse the messianic interpretation. However, if God in the sixth century B.C. wanted to predict the death of Jesus in the first century A.D., one would expect him to be more accurate. On the other hand, if an apocalyptic writer of the second century B.C. was using history to denounce the evil Seleucid king Antiochus IV, he might very well have guessed too high for the number of years between Jeshua and the death of Onias III. In fact, there are examples of ancient writers doing just that—overestimating when figuring chronology (see Driver, *Daniel*, p. 146). Alternatively, as mentioned above, the author may have known that the number was not exact but may have been constrained by the pattern of heptads. Therefore, the interpretation that ties Daniel to the time of Epiphanes seems to be more persuasive (Driver, *Daniel*, p. 150).

Some readers may use Daniel 9 to try to develop a timetable for future end-time events, but such efforts are always inconclusive. Because the focus of Daniel is on the Maccabean age, we can only speak with clarity and confidence about interpretations for that generation. To be sure, parts of the book may be fulfilled again before Jesus returns, but we cannot predict exactly what or when. However, one thing is certain: God will one day destroy all evil human kingdoms and set up his righteous, eternal reign in an obvious way. In the meantime, his more hidden kingdom has already been inaugurated by our Lord in his first advent (Matt. 4:17; 10:7; 11:11–12; 12:28; Luke 10:9; 11:20; 16:16; 17:20–21), so that he rules in the hearts of his disciples. We can advance his kingdom in a number of ways. First of all, we can allow him to be Lord of our lives. Second, we can tell others the good news about the Messiah so that they allow his rule in their lives too. Third, we can pray for God's kingdom to come in its fullness, as we do when we say the Lord's Prayer: "Your kingdom come, your will be done on earth as it is in heaven" (Matt. 6:10); Paul also teaches us to pray for the second advent: "Maranatha," that is, "Come, O Lord!" (1 Cor. 16:22). In these ways we can contribute to the growth of heaven's dominion until the end: "Then the end will come, when he hands over the kingdom to God the Father after he has destroyed all dominion, authority and power. For he must reign until he has put all his enemies under his feet. The last enemy to be destroyed is death" (1 Cor. 15:24–26).

Additional Notes §9

9:1 / For **Xerxes**, the Hebrew has *'akhashwerosh*, which comes into Latin, and later English, as "Ahasuerus" (this name occurs in Ezra and numerous times in Esther; see the NRSV). The NIV supplies this in a footnote, but inserts in the text "Xerxes," the Greek name for this king.

The Hebrew has the passive *hophal* form *homlak*, "to be made king" or "to be caused to reign" (NIV **who was made ruler**). The verbal root *mlk* occurs often in the *hiphil*, the corresponding active conjugation, but only here in the *hophal*. To Calvin the *hophal* indicated that the figure in question was a viceroy, a point often repeated by scholars "who want to identify Darius with Gubaru, but the term clearly refers to kingship" (Collins, *Daniel*, p. 348). Apparently, it was not for apologetic reasons that the NIV translator used "who was made ruler" instead of "became king," because v. 2 in the NIV has "in the first year of his reign" (not "rule"). One might argue that the *hophal* form intends to suggest an unusual (perhaps violent) transfer of royal power, but it is better to translate it as "became king" in v. 1.

9:2 / The convention in English Bibles is to represent the proper name for Israel's God, "Yahweh," as **the Lord** (using small capital letters). "Yahweh" only occurs in ch. 9 in Daniel: vv. 2, 4, and 20 outside the prayer; vv. 8, 10, 13, and 14 (twice) within the prayer. Besides the name Yahweh, there are other words or roots that occur in both the prayer and the framework of this chapter listed in the following table:

Word or Root	Framework	Prayer
yrwshlm, "Jerusalem"	vv. 2, 25	vv. 7, 12, 16
skl, "to be wise" or "to pay attention"	vv. 22, 25	v. 13
shwb, "to return" or "restore"	v. 25	v. 13
shmm, "to be desolated"	v. 27	vv. 17, 18
ntk, "to pour out"	v. 27	v. 11
tkhnh/tkhnwn, "supplication"	vv. 3, 20, 23	vv. 17, 18

This shows that the prayer is now an integral part of the chapter. It is not clear whether that is because the prayer is original or because the redactor who added it was careful to choose words for the prayer that linked it to the surrounding material.

9:9–10 / Although vv. 4b–19 constitute a prayer, directed to God, the author shifts to the third person (note the **him** and **he**) in vv. 9–10 for didactic purposes. In vv. 4b–8 the prayer addresses God, but in vv. 9–10 the author teaches his audience about God's grace and their guilt. He reverts back to the second person in the first part of v. 11: "your law" and "you."

9:11 / In the second half of this verse, the author switches to the passive voice and the third person. Instead of addressing God by saying, "You have poured out your curses," he says they **have been poured out.** Also, since he is no longer speaking in the second person, he says **servant of God** instead of "your servant," and according to the MT he actually says, "because we have sinned against *him*," not **you,** as in the NIV (although a few ancient manuscripts have "you"). The text continues in the third person until the end of verse 13.

9:12 / The NIV incorrectly switches back to the second person with **you,** omitting the pronoun "his," which modifies "words"; the Hebrew remains in the third person: "He has fulfilled his words."

9:13–15 / In v. 13, the prayer briefly addresses God again in the second person. The third person returns in v. 14. In v. 15, the prayer changes back to the second person and continues this way until it ends in v. 19.

9:13 / Expressions similar to **just as it is written in the Law of Moses** occur in Josh. 8:31 and 1 Kgs. 2:3. The phrase "as it is written" was the standard way to quote the Hebrew Bible in the Dead Sea Scrolls, the Talmud, and in the NT (e.g., Mark 7:6; 9:13; 14:21; etc.).

9:21 / In chs. 8 and 10 the verb *naga'*, "touch" (translated in 9:21 as **came**), takes the preposition *be* with the object (8:18; 10:10, 18) or *'al*, "on" or "upon" (10:16). In contrast, Dan. 9 uses *'el*, "to" or "unto," suggesting movement toward. The verb *naga'* has a range of meaning: "to touch," "to reach," or "to strike." While here the verb has the sense of arriving or coming to Daniel, we cannot rule out the meaning "to touch," because this verb is used in that sense with the preposition *'el* in some instances (e.g., Hag. 2:12; Num. 4:15). In that case, maybe we should think of the angel as touching Daniel after all, along the analogy of chs. 8 and 10.

The phrase **in swift flight** is questionable in Hebrew. There are actually two words here (*mu'ap bi'ap*) that appear to be from the same root, but there is a debate about whether the root is *'up*, "to fly," or *ya'ap*, "to be weary," since they have two of the same radicals. The NIV derives the construction from the former, and since there is a double occurrence, construes it intensively, "in swift flight" (or perhaps NIV is following some of the ancient Greek manuscripts that actually have the word "swiftly" in the text). However, it is not likely that the second word can be explained from the root "to fly." Because of that we should perhaps translate "flying in weariness," taking the first word from "to fly" and the second from "to be weary." Another option is to eliminate the second word as a dittography (a scribal error that occurs when something is accidentally duplicated). Against the whole notion of using "to fly" is the fact that angels are not described as winged beings in the Bible. Seraphs (or seraphim; see Isa. 6:2 RSV) and cherubs (cherubim; see, e.g., Exod. 25:18–20; 2 Sam. 22:11; 1 Kgs. 6:23–28; Ezek. 10:5) have wings, but angels look like human beings (Dan. 8:15; 9:21; 10:16). Perhaps angels can fly without wings, but the text is not clear here. Therefore, it seems more plausible to read "being weary in weariness," from the alternate root *ya'ap* (so, BDB, p. 419).

9:22 / The Hebrew text has *wayyaben*, "and he made known" (NIV **he instructed**), but it lacks the expected object (**me**). Some Greek and Latin manuscripts supply "to me," which is suspect—a scribe probably added the object to improve the text; the NIV is apparently following this tradition. The Syriac and Old Greek preserve what is more likely the original reading: "and he came." In the Hebrew consonantal text this would be *wyb'*, which has only one letter different from the MT: *wybn*. Perhaps *wyb'*, "and he came," was corrupted to *wybn*, "and he made known," by influence of *bynh* (*binah*), "understanding," at the end of the verse.

The angel is to give Daniel **understanding** (*binah*). Words from root *byn*, "to understand," recur in Daniel (8:16, 17; 9:23; 10:11, 12, 14; 11:33), as do *hiphil* forms of the root *sakal*, "to give **insight**" (9:22, 25; 11:33, 35; 12:3, 10). Both roots also occur at the beginning of the book, in the description of the ideal qualities of Daniel and his friends (1:4, 17). The repetition of the roots underscores that the significance of the visions is not obvious to the average person; rather, their content is so mysterious and hidden that only highly skilled and divinely aided interpreters can understand them.

9:24 / The word for **sevens**, *shabu'im*, denotes a "heptad" or "period of seven" (BDB, p. 988). The NIV translation is therefore correct, although it leaves the meaning open. The NRSV renders the text "seventy weeks," interpreting *shabuʿim* to mean "weeks," which is normally *shabuʿot*; but here in Dan. 9, the word has the *-im* plural ending instead.

9:25 / Subtracting the **seven "sevens"** (forty-nine years) from the options listed in the commentary above for when the word went forth does not yield a year in which an anointed one emerged. The dates work out as follows:

"Going forth of the word"	Date	Date 49 years later
Jeremiah's first oracle (Jer. 25)	605 B.C.	556 B.C.
Jeremiah's second oracle (Jer. 29:10)	597 B.C.	548 B.C.
Decree of Cyrus	538 B.C.	489 B.C.
Ezra's return	458 B.C.	409 B.C.
Artaxerxes I's permission to rebuild Jerusalem's walls	445 B.C.	396 B.C.

Some say that 556 B.C. (option one) is a significant year because it is close to the accession year of Cyrus in 558. However, Cyrus did not conquer Babylon until 539 and did not liberate the Jews with his decree to restore Jerusalem until 538. According to Dan. 9:25, in order for 556 to work, the rebuilding of Zion during the sixty-two weeks would have had to begin around that time.

Combining the **seven** weeks and the **sixty-two** weeks does not yield a number that points to Jesus. Those who hold such a view usually start with the "decree" of Artaxerxes I in 445. Combining the two periods produces 483 years (49 + 434). Subtracting 483 years from 445 B.C. brings us to A.D. 38. However, since Jesus was probably born in 4 B.C. and crucified in A.D. 29, the dates are off by nine years. Others start with Ezra's return in 458, which lands us at A.D. 25 (= 458 – 483). They then say that this is the year of Jesus's baptism and anointing, because the Holy Spirit came upon him at that time. Yet it still seems to be off by a year. If Jesus was born in 4 B.C., then he began his public ministry thirty years later, in A.D. 26. Besides, there was no decree in 458 B.C. to rebuild Jerusalem (9:25).

The ancient versions were confused by the word *kharuts*, **trench**, because it occurs only here in the whole OT with this meaning. The Old Greek has "length," while Theodotion's Greek version and the Vulgate render it "walls." The translation "trench" or "moat" is now secure, since the root is attested with this meaning in Akkadian and Aramaic (Zakir Inscription) as well as in the Qumran *Copper Scroll*.

9:26 / The commentary argues that the 7 weeks and 62 weeks represent two successive, separate eras. It is interesting, however, that if we add 434 (sixty-nine weeks of years) to 171 (the year of Onias's death), we get 605, which is a significant year—the year Nebuchadnezzar became king. It is also the year Daniel uses to date the beginning of the exile. The trouble, though, is that there is no way to reconcile that with the first seven weeks of years, for 605 + 49 = 654, which is not a significant year. Also, it would be odd for there to be a word going forth to declare the rebuilding of Jerusalem in 654, when Jerusalem was still standing.

An attractive solution is to use 587, the year Jerusalem was destroyed, for the one number (587 − 49 = 538) and 605 for the other (605 − 434 = 171) (Lacocque, *Daniel*, p. 178). Although it produces two significant dates, the numbers in the text of Daniel seem to be consecutive. We might try starting from the same point in time for both periods, as though the years are concurrent. For example, we could start with 587. We already know that 587 − 49 = 538, the year of Cyrus's decree, but 587 − 434 = 153, which is not an important year. Starting with 605 also fails to produce any helpful results. Although 605 − 434 = 171, the year of Onias's assassination, 605 − 49 = 556, which is an insignificant year. In sum, from a modern perspective, the chronological calculations proposed for Dan. 9:26 are best accepted tentatively. Some scholars even think the numbers given there simply symbolize long and short periods of time rather than precise chronology.

The curious Hebrew construction for the phrase **and will have nothing** has been interpreted variously. The Old Greek reads, "and will not be." Theodotion expands the text to "and there is no judgment in him" or "in it." Some connect this clause with the following noun: "and will not have the city"; or they connect it with the following two nouns: "and will have neither the city nor the sanctuary" (Goldingay, *Daniel*, pp. 226, 230). Perhaps it is best to interpret the clause in the light of the similar expression "and no one will help him" (11:45; Collins, *Daniel*, pp. 356–57). Just as the wicked tyrant, Antiochus Epiphanes, will die with no one to help him (11:45), so the high priest, Onias, will be murdered without anyone to assist, defend, or deliver him (9:26).

9:27 / The term **abomination that causes desolation** is *shiqquts meshomem* (cf. 11:31; 12:11), which is a wordplay on *Baʿal Shamem*, "Lord of Heaven," a Semitic designation of Zeus Olympios. (See the Additional Note on 8:13.) The phrase thus cleverly refers to a pagan deity in relation to the Jerusalem temple, an outrage that only Semites were likely to catch from the wordplay.

The NIV uses brackets in the phrase **on a wing [of the temple]** to show that it is emending the text. A more literal translation of the Hebrew is "on the wing of abominations." The word "temple" comes from the Greek versions, but they do not have the word "wing." A simpler emendation is to change *ʿal kanap*, "on a wing," to *ʿal kannam*, "on their place" (Hartman and Di Lella, *Daniel*, p. 240). In other words, abominations will displace the sacrifices and offerings. To put this together with the entire clause, we should read "and in their place will be the abomination that causes desolation."

§10 The Final Revelation: Prologue (Dan. 10:1–11:2a)

Chapters 10 through 12 form one long unit containing the last apocalypse of the book. This unit can be subdivided into three smaller sections: the prologue (10:1–11:1), the body (11:2–12:4), and the epilogue (12:5–13). The proper divisions do not line up with the chapter breaks in our modern Bibles because those chapter breaks are not original; they were inserted long after the Bible was completed and not always in the most helpful places. The prologue sets the stage for the Final Revelation by introducing it: telling when the vision came, where Daniel was, how he fasted, his disposition when he saw the vision, the appearance of the heavenly being(s), and the spiritual warfare preceding the giving of the vision. The body of the unit, after briefly mentioning Persia and Alexander the Great, goes into much more detail about the Hellenistic era, focusing on the wars between the Seleucids and the Ptolemies and events leading up to the desecration of the temple (known as the abomination that makes desolate), and concludes with the death of Antiochus IV and the resurrection of the dead. This is followed by an epilogue, which comes back to the question "How long?" (12:6), introduced earlier (8:13). The earlier answer (8:14) is revised with three further answers (12:11–13), and with this the book ends.

10:1 / Just as chapter 10 introduces the concluding vision of the book of Daniel (which is contained in chapter 11), so the first verse introduces the rest of the chapter. It does so by establishing the date of the revelation. Similarly, the apocalypses of chapters 7, 8, and 9 also begin with date formulas. Chapter 10 begins in the third person but shifts to the first person in verse 2. This is like chapter 7 but unlike chapters 8 and 9, which begin and remain in the first person.

There is a difference between the date here—**in the third year of Cyrus** (10:1)—and Daniel 1:21, which says, "Daniel remained there until the first year of King Cyrus." Chapter 1 seems to be giving the beginning (1:1) and ending (1:21) of Daniel's career as sage and visionary. Of course, it is not an outright contradiction, because Daniel 1:21 does not explicitly say that Daniel died or stopped seeing visions then. Perhaps Daniel 10:1, aware of the claim of 1:21, intends to signal simply that Daniel's career extended two more years. In Daniel 10:1, Theodotion agrees with the MT ("third year"), unlike the LXX, which dates the final vision to the "first" year of Cyrus, in agreement with Daniel 1:21. That very agreement makes it suspect, however, so the Hebrew version is probably original, because it is the more difficult reading. (For the title **king of Persia**, see the Additional Note on 4:1).

As for the date itself, it is usually reckoned to be 536 or so, the third year after Cyrus began to reign over Babylon (539). To be sure, Cyrus became king over Anshan in about 558 (although he was a vassal of Media) and overthrew Media by about 550, so one could construe his third year to be much earlier. However, the focus of the book of Daniel is on Babylon, where the Jews were exiled. The previous date given was "the first year of Darius" (9:1), who in the mind of the author came between Belshazzar and Cyrus. It is not likely that the apocalyptist would back up before that. Therefore, "the third year of Cyrus" must point to a time after he conquered Babylon. If the Hebrew date is correct (as opposed to the Greek—see above), then Daniel would have been alive and present in 538 B.C., when Cyrus issued his decree allowing the Jews to return to the land of Judah. The text does not mention the decree or give a reason why Daniel remained in exile. This seems strange when one considers how important the return from exile was to the Jewish people in the late sixth century. It can be seen as evidence for the late date of the book, because an author living in the second century would be so much more concerned about deliverance from the Seleucids, as the author of Daniel appears to be when he passes over the restoration period without comment. It is intriguing that the third year of Cyrus (536 B.C.) falls exactly seventy years after 606 B.C., the year with which Daniel begins (1:1). However, neither here nor in chapter 9, which makes so much of the motif of seventy years, does the author call attention to this or draw out any inferences or conclusions. Consequently, it may not be significant.

It is curious that the author would mention Daniel's alternate name, **Belteshazzar** (10:1), here. Except for this occurrence, it is used only in the court stories of chapters 1–6; it has not been used since Daniel 5:12. Also, it is a Babylonian name, while this revelation comes in the Persian era, after the fall of the Babylonian kingdom. Perhaps the author is attempting to draw a connection between the court narratives and the apocalyptic material.

Part of the purpose of verse 1 was to assure the reader that the **revelation . . . given to Daniel** (literally, "a word was revealed to Daniel") was trustworthy: **its message was true** (10:1; cf. 8:26). This assurance is reiterated at the end of the prologue subunit and thus delimits the introduction to the body of the Final Revelation (10:21; 11:2). What comes next in verse 1 is difficult. In the text the NIV has **and it concerned a great war** (10:1). While the word *tsaba'* is usually translated "army" or "host," it is here rendered "war." In Hebrew it is modified by the adjective "great," resulting in "a great war." If this is the correct meaning, it refers to the terrestrial battles outlined in the revelation in chapter 11 and also, possibly, to the celestial battle, which gets briefer treatment (10:13, 20–21; 12:1). There is an alternate reading, though, in the NIV margin: "true and burdensome." Taking that as following from the previous clause would yield: "its message was true and burdensome." However, the word *tsaba'* can mean "service." In Isaiah 40:1–2, God comforts his people, informing them that they are about to be released from exile in Babylon: their "hard service [*tsaba'*] has been completed." Similarly, Job 7:1 says, "Does not man have hard service on earth?" (see also Job 14:14). If "service" is the appropriate definition here, then "great service" might indicate the important task Daniel accepted in communicating the revelation. The term "great" might even mean "burdensome," as in the NIV alternate reading. But the NIV translates two words, "great service," as one, "burdensome"; it would be better to include "service" in the translation to read "a burdensome service," not just "burdensome." That, however, seems to be reading too much into the text; it is best to render it simply: "its message was true and a great service."

The last part of the verse summarizes the revelation: **The understanding of the message came to him in a vision** (10:1). The NIV is paraphrastic, leaving out one of the words from the root *byn*, "to perceive," "consider," "understand." The Hebrew has "he perceived the word and had understanding in the vision." This wording is similar to Daniel 9:23: "perceive the word and understand the vision" (author's translation). The "word" refers to the message that God is about to give to Daniel. To what does the term "vision" refer? The word used here for "vision" in Daniel 10:1 is also used in verses 7 and 8. In the context of verses 5–8, what Daniel sees is a heavenly figure, so perhaps that is the answer. Yet, that is not the whole answer, because the main purpose of chapter 10 is to prepare the reader for the revelation found in chapter 11. Thus, the heavenly being is not the message but the messenger. Daniel is to perceive and understand not the supernatural figure but the information he brings. This is corroborated by verse 14, which explains that the vision has to do with what will happen to the Jews in the latter days. Even though the word for vision in verse 14 is different from the word used in Daniel 10:1, 7, and 8, it is clearly in continuity with verse 1, because the angel explains that he has come to make Daniel "understand" (from the root *byn*). The problem with this is that chapter 11 does not seem to be a vision but rather an audition; that is, Daniel does not see images but hears words as the heavenly messenger recounts to the seer what is to come (11:2 and following). "Vision" need not be construed narrowly as something one sees, as in the visions of chapters 2, 4, and 7, but can be used more broadly for "revelation," whether seen or heard (see the commentary on 10:14).

10:2–9 / Here the narrative becomes a first-person account. Daniel relates that he has mourned for three weeks (10:2). Literally, the text says, "three weeks [of] days." This is most likely in order to distinguish the term from the "weeks of years" implied in the previous chapter, although similar expressions do occur elsewhere (Gen. 41:1: "two years [of] days"; Deut. 21:13: "a month [of] days"; 2 Sam. 13:23: "two years [of] days"). Daniel's mourning includes fasting, though it is not a total fast. He abstains from choice food (Dan. 10:3): "delicacies" (RSV) or "rich food" (NRSV). The same word rendered "choice" here is used three other times in reference to Daniel, who is "highly esteemed" (Dan. 9:23; 10:11, 19). He also refuses meat and wine (10:3). He might have eaten bread and vegetables, and of course he would have drunk water. This reminds us of the diet of chapter 1, when Daniel was beginning his time of training for the king's service, on which occasion he refused the king's wine and rich food (1:8, 12, 15–16). This also reminds us of chapter 9, where Daniel fasted in sackcloth and ashes and subsequently received a revelation. There is a significant difference between these two chapters, however. In chapter 9, Daniel fasts in connection with his penitential prayers; there is no indication that he is seeking revelation. Rather, he is confessing his sins and the sins of his people (9:20). In contrast, in chapter 10, Daniel seems to be seeking information from God. It does not indicate this at the beginning, but neither does it mention anything about confession of sin. Later, though, the angel explains why Daniel was fasting: "You set your mind to gain understanding and to humble yourself before your God" (10:12). While visions and revelations are dependent on God and cannot be coerced from the human side, it was understood that individuals could do things to prepare themselves to receive a message from God. This was true in the prophetic tradition (1 Sam. 3:2–21; 10:9–13; 2 Kgs. 3:15), but much more so in the apocalyptic tradition. After receiving some "signs," Ezra is told that if he will "pray," "weep," and "fast for seven days," he will "hear yet greater things than these" (2 Esd. 5:13 NRSV). He obeys

(2 Esd. 5:20) and begins "to speak words in the presence of the Most High" (2 Esd. 5:22–31 NRSV), after which he receives more revelation (see also 2 Esd. 6:35–59; 7:1–44; 2 Apocalypse Baruch 5:7; 9:1–2; 12:5; 20:5–6; 21:1; 47:2; *Ascension of Isaiah* 2:10–11; *Testament of Reuben* 1:9–10). Finally, Daniel refrains from using lotions (Dan. 10:3). Oils and lotions helped to keep the skin moist in the Near East, where the weather is often dry. Because it was also frequently hot, they would add perfume to these ointments as a kind of deodorant. When mourning, people customarily did not to anoint themselves with such lotions (2 Sam. 12:20; 14:2; Isa. 61:3), for they were signs of joy. It is appropriate for us to seek God by mourning, praying, and fasting today (Matt. 9:14–15; Acts 13:2; 14:23), but by way of contrast, Jesus taught his followers to use oil and to wash their faces so that they could fast in secret and thus avoid parading their spirituality (Matt. 6:16–18).

The date is given as **the twenty-fourth day of the first month** (10:4). The OT contains different traditions regarding the New Year. According to one tradition, it was in the fall (Exod. 23:16; 34:22); according to another, in the spring (Exod. 12:2; Lev. 23:5, 23–25). Some scholars consider the former to be preexilic and the latter to be postexilic, because the Babylonians had their New Year in the spring; presumably the time in exile influenced the change among the Jews. If we follow that reasoning, the first month would be Nisan (Neh. 2:1; also called Abib or Aviv: Exod. 23:15), which corresponds to March or April. This means that Daniel would have fasted through the feast of Passover, which was celebrated from the fifteenth to the twenty-first of the first month. Some commentators see significance in this because the feasts were made illegal during the oppression of Antiochus IV: "her feasts were turned into mourning" (1 Macc. 1:39 NRSV); "And the king . . . directed them . . . to forbid burnt offerings and sacrifices and drink offerings in the sanctuary, to profane sabbaths and festivals, to defile the sanctuary and priests" (1 Macc. 1:44–46 NRSV). However, the text of Daniel does not hint at any such significance to the date.

Daniel was standing **on the bank of the great river, the Tigris** (10:4). In the three other OT occurrences, "the great river" is clearly identified as "the Euphrates" (Gen. 15:18; Deut. 1:7; Josh. 1:4; see also Rev. 9:14; 16:12). Even more often the Euphrates is simply designated "the River" (Gen. 31:21; Exod. 23:31; Num. 22:5; Josh. 24:2–3, 14–15; 2 Sam. 10:16; 1 Kgs. 4:21, 24; 14:15; 1 Chron. 19:16; 2 Chron. 9:26; Pss. 72:8; 80:11; Isa. 7:20; 8:7; Jer. 2:18; Zech. 9:10). Twice, in Jeremiah, the phrase "the River Euphrates" appears (Jer. 46:6, 10). The Tigris is actually mentioned by name in only one other place in the Bible, in connection with the garden of Eden (Gen. 2:14). Also, Daniel lived in Babylon, near the Euphrates. Therefore, "the Tigris" is probably a textual error (see the Additional Note on 10:4). The same river (i.e., the Euphrates) is intended later when Daniel mentions the angels by the river (Dan. 12:5–7). Daniel had earlier been by a canal, either in a vision or when he received a vision (Dan. 8:2). Similarly, Ezekiel was "by the Kebar River" when he saw a revelation (Ezek. 1:1).

Daniel begins the description of what he saw with the introductory statement **I looked up and there before me was . . .** (10:5). The Hebrew reads: "I lifted up my eyes and saw and behold . . ." The same formula is used to introduce the vision of the ram earlier in the book (8:3). What Daniel sees here is **a man** (10:5). Of course, it is not actually a man, that is, a mortal, a human being, but a heavenly being who looks like a man (see 7:13; 8:15–16). The angelic visitor is **dressed in linen** (10:5). Linen was associated with priestly attire (Exod. 28:5, 6; Lev. 6:10; 16:4, 32; 1 Sam. 2:18; 22:18). More important, Ezekiel's heavenly visitor was also clothed in linen (Ezek. 9:2, 3, 11; 10:2, 6, 7). This tradition is carried on in the NT as well: the seven angels (Rev. 15:6), the Lamb's bride (Rev. 19:8), and the armies of heaven (Rev. 19:14) all wear linen. Linen thus represents holiness. The OT priests wore a "sacred linen tunic" (Lev. 16:4), and the author of Revelation tells us that "fine linen stands for the righteous acts of the saints" (Rev. 19:8). The word "linen" in Ezekiel 9:2, 3, and 11 is translated in the LXX by the word *podērēs*, which is "a robe extending to the feet." The same word is used for the garment that Jesus wore when he appeared to John (Rev. 1:13). The angel in Daniel's vision also wears **a belt of the finest gold around his waist** (10:5; see the Additional Note on 10:5). Similarly, in Revelation, Jesus has "a golden sash around his chest" (Rev. 1:13).

There are several parallels between Daniel 10:6 and Ezekiel 1.

Daniel 10:6	Ezekiel 1
"His body was like chrysolite"	"they sparkled like chrysolite" (Ezek. 1:16)
"his face like lightning"	"lightning flashed out of it" (Ezek. 1:13); "the creatures sped back and forth like flashes of lightning" (Ezek. 1:14)
"his eyes like flaming torches"	"the appearance of the living creatures was like burning coals of fire or like torches" (Ezek. 1:13)
"his arms and legs like the gleam of burnished bronze"	"their feet . . . gleamed like burnished bronze" (Ezek. 1:7)
"and his voice like the sound of a multitude"	"I heard the sound of their wings, like the roar of rushing waters, like the voice of the Almighty, like the tumult of an army" (Ezek. 1:24)

Although the word translated "body" (Dan. 10:6) can mean corpse, it is used for the bodies of the heavenly beings in Ezekiel's vision (Ezek. 1:11, 23) just as it is in Daniel. Chrysolite (Heb. *tarshish*) is some kind of stone or mineral, named after the place where it was mined. The same stone was one of the stones on the breastplate of the high priest (Exod. 28:20; 39:13). It is variously translated "beryl" (thus RSV, NRSV), "topaz," or "chrysolite" (NIV). We are not certain of the location of Tarshish, except that it is out in the Mediterranean Sea (Jon. 1:3). Tharsis, also known as Tartessus, in the southwest part of Spain, is an excellent candidate, since it was known for its metals and stones. Lightning is common in theophanies (Pss. 18:12, 14; 29:7; 97:4); it attended the appearance of Yahweh on Mount Sinai (Exod. 19:16; 20:18).

Who is this figure in Daniel 10:5–6? Some Christians have seen it as a preincarnate appearance of Jesus (Young, *Daniel*, p. 225). As mentioned above, there are certainly clear parallels with John's vision of Jesus on the island of Patmos. Jesus is "like a son of man"; he has "a robe reaching down to his feet" and "a golden sash around his chest"; "his feet were like bronze glowing in a furnace," and "his voice was like the sound of rushing waters" (Rev. 1:13–15). From earliest times Christians identified Jesus with the figure of Daniel 10 (as well as with the one like a son of man in Daniel 7:13). However, the similarities do not prove the identification, because angels might have some or all of the same characteristics. Furthermore, even if we were to make such an identification in the light of the NT, we would still want to ask what the earliest interpretation was. What did the author of Daniel think? What would the earliest audience of the book have thought? Since Jesus had not been born yet, they certainly would not have thought of him in particular, but even a messianic figure is not probable, as this being needed to be rescued by Michael (Dan. 10:13; see also the Additional Note to 10:10). Some scholars (e.g., Montgomery, *Daniel*, pp. 419–20; Porteous, *Daniel*, p. 151) think it is another appearance of Gabriel (see Dan. 8:15–18 and 9:20–23 for the earlier appearances). Although this is possible, the figure of chapter 10 is not named, so we cannot be sure; since the text does not identify the angel, neither should we. Unfortunately, we cannot say more than that.

Besides the question of the celestial being's identity, there is the question of how many of the beings appear in this chapter. Some interpreters see a new personage in verse 10 ("A hand touched me . . ."), while others argue for an additional actor entering the stage in verse 16 ("Then one who looked like a man touched my lips . . ."). Chapter 12 is occasionally cited to support this more complex interaction of spirits. However, Daniel 10 is quite different from Daniel 12:5–6. Although the former is not crystal clear, it only explicitly mentions one heavenly creature; the latter is unambiguous: there are three heavenly beings described. The most elegant interpretation is the simplest, namely, that there is only one angel present in chapter 10.

Daniel is not alone, but he is **the only one who** sees **the vision. The men** who are with him must be aware of something, though, because **such terror** overwhelms them that they flee and hide themselves (10:7). Perhaps they are like those who accompanied Paul when he journeyed to Damascus. Paul saw and heard the risen Christ, while his companions only saw a light, but not a figure; they heard a sound but could not comprehend words (Acts 9:7; 22:9). Similarly, in the theophany at Sinai, the people "heard the sound of words but saw no form; there was only a voice" (Deut. 4:12). Likewise, once when God spoke from heaven in the time of Jesus, the crowd thought it was thunder (John 12:28–29). On the other hand, it is possible that when Daniel falls to the ground and goes into a trance (10:9), this behavior is enough to frighten his associates away.

Daniel does not run away in fright, but he is profoundly affected by **this great vision** (10:8). This refers not to some other vision that is going on in his head but to the sight of the heavenly being. However, as stated earlier, the main "vision" of this last unit (chs. 10–12) is the content of Daniel 11:2–12:4, as referenced in Daniel 10:1 and 14. The line-by-line description of his very evident physical reactions to the sight shows how overwhelming such encounters are for humans. The sudden, close proximity to deity is, quite simply, a shock to Daniel's system. He has **no strength left** (10:8). Saul likewise was enervated after seeing Samuel brought up from the grave by the medium from Endor (1 Sam. 28:20). Daniel's **face** turns **deathly pale** (10:8), a frightening, ghostly appearance. (For the Hebrew of this expression, see the Additional Note on 10:8) And Daniel is also **helpless** (10:8; literally, "retained no strength"). The same phrase is repeated in verse 16 and again in the next chapter of the king of the South's daughter. In the latter case the NIV translates more literally, "she will not retain her power" (Dan. 11:6; see also 2 Chron. 13:20; 22:9). In modern terms, Daniel felt like he just "had the stuffing knocked out of him."

Daniel falls **into a deep sleep** with his **face to the ground** (10:9), almost a moment of relief. The Hebrew has a double reading: "on my face, face to the ground." The NIV is correct to translate "face" only once. This verse is very similar to Daniel 8:18: "I was in a deep sleep, with my face to the ground." There, as here, it might be better to render the idiom as "fell into a trance" instead of "fell into a deep sleep," because Daniel was in the process of receiving revelation (see the commentary on

8:18). The root for the expression "deep sleep" is *rdm*, which may suggest a divinely induced sleep (Gen. 2:21; 15:12; 1 Sam. 26:12; Job 33:15). Joshua also fell prostrate when he met a heavenly visitor, the commander of Yahweh's army (Josh. 5:14). Similarly, Ezekiel (Ezek. 1:28) and John (Rev. 1:17) fell face down when they beheld visions, as did the disciples on the Mount of Transfiguration (Matt. 17:6–7).

Terrifying and unsettling emotional reactions to dreams and visions are a recurring theme in the book of Daniel (2:1, 3; 4:5, 19; 5:6, 8–9; 7:28; 8:27). Terror, bewilderment, ghostlike looks, and physical exhaustion are the human symptoms that attest the presence of direct, divine intervention through visions and auditions. They confirm the truthfulness of the message being delivered—it must be believed—and dramatically demand that its recipients respond to it as a momentous matter of life and death.

10:10–12 / While Daniel is prostrate in a trance, a hand touches him and sets him trembling on his hands and knees (10:10; the Hebrew actually has "knees and hands"). Presumably this is the same angel who has appeared in verses 5 and 6. Once again, this is similar to chapter 8: "Then he touched me and raised me to my feet" (8:18). The difference here is that Daniel does not get to his feet at once but has to be helped up gradually, in stages. First he gets to his knees and hands, which results from the angel's strengthening touch. The translations vary on how gentle the touch was. "He moved me" or "raised me" (Hartman and Di Lella, *Daniel*, p. 264) is probably a little weak. The verb means "to shake" or "cause to totter" (BDB, p. 631). "Roused me" (NRSV) and "set me trembling" (NIV) are a little more forceful. "Shook me" (Collins, *Daniel*, p. 361; Goldingay, *Daniel*, p. 272) is strongest, and perhaps the most accurate. Just as God strengthened Daniel through the angel's touch, Jesus communicated power and commissioned his church to minister healing through the laying on of hands (Matt. 9:27–30; Mark 8:23; Luke 4:40; Acts 28:8).

Whoever touched Daniel in verse 10 now says to him, **"Daniel, you who are highly esteemed"** (10:11; as mentioned earlier, the same word translated "esteemed" here is used for the food Daniel denies himself in v. 3). Because it was Gabriel who said these same words to Daniel previously (9:23), some identify the angelic messenger as Gabriel; this is unwarranted. Daniel is addressed this way a third time in Daniel 10:19 (although this may be part of a doublet).

Not only is Daniel praised, he is given instructions. He must **consider carefully the words** that the heavenly being is **about to speak** (10:11). The Hebrew root *byn*, "to consider," "perceive," "know," "understand," occurs often in Daniel. Here it means "to give heed to" or "pay attention to" the divine message. It is used similarly in Daniel 8:5, where Daniel is "thinking about" the first part of the vision he is seeing. It is used again in Daniel 9:23, which is a close parallel to this verse. There as here, a heavenly being tells Daniel that he is "highly esteemed," after which he tells Daniel to "consider the message."

Daniel is then told to **stand up**, which he does, but he is **trembling** (10:11). Words from the Hebrew root *rʿd*, "to tremble," are only used a few times in the OT. One of those places is in Ezra 10. Like Daniel (Dan. 9:3, 20; 10:2), Ezra was praying, confessing, and weeping because of the sins of the people (Ezra 10:1). Like Daniel (Dan. 9:3; 10:3), Ezra fasted (Ezra 10:6). In both places there is also trembling, although the circumstances are different. In the time of Ezra, the people were trembling because of their sinful state and because of the rain (Ezra 10:9; NIV "greatly distressed"); Daniel trembles because of an awesome vision he has seen (Dan. 10:4–11). There seems to have been an emphasis on trembling before the Lord in the postexilic period. Although it is a different word for trembling (from the root *khrd*—the root from which we get "Haredi" and "Haredim," designations of the ultraorthodox Jews in Israel today), the book of Ezra also talks about those who tremble at the words of God (Ezra 9:4) and those who tremble at the commandment of God (Ezra 10:3). God's delight is not in temples and animal sacrifice but in the one "who is humble and contrite in spirit, and trembles at my word" (Isa. 66:2; cf. 66:5). Daniel is portrayed as just such a person. He humbles himself (Dan. 10:12) and trembles because of the vision but also in the context of receiving words from God (Dan. 10:11).

The angel assures Daniel by telling him **not to be afraid** (10:12); the scene is repeated in verse 19. When Gideon saw the angel of Yahweh, he was very frightened also, so that Yahweh encouraged him: "Peace! Do not be afraid. You are not going to die" (Judg. 6:22–23; see also Gen. 15:1; 26:24). This experience is even more common in the NT (Matt. 28:5; Luke 1:13, 30; 2:10; Acts 27:24). One close parallel is found in the NT apocalypse: after John sees Jesus, he falls prostrate at his feet; then the Lord touches him and says, "Do not be afraid" (Rev. 1:17). Another is on the Mount of Transfiguration: after seeing Moses and Elijah with the glorified Jesus, the disciples "fell facedown to the ground, terrified. But Jesus came and touched them. 'Get up,' he said. 'Don't be afraid'" (Matt. 17:6–7). The reason for Daniel's fasting and praying is **to gain understanding and to humble** himself **before his God** (10:12). This indicates that he is preparing himself to receive divine revelation. This contrasts with chapter 9, where his prayer is focused on "confessing [his] sin and the sin of [his] people Israel" and seeking the deliverance of Jerusalem

(9:20). In that passage he also receives a revelation, but the text does not say he is seeking it.

The heavenly being goes on to explain the three-week delay. He was sent out on the **first day** of Daniel's fasting and praying because Daniel's **words were heard** and the messenger was sent **in response to them** (10:12). Similarly, in chapter 9, a messenger was sent "as soon as [Daniel] began to pray" (9:23). In the earlier instance, however, the angel arrived "while [Daniel] was still in prayer" (9:21). In chapter 10, the angel was detained for **twenty-one days** because **the prince of the Persian kingdom resisted** him for that period of time. In fact, it seems that he was only able to break free because **Michael, one of the chief princes, came to help** him (10:13). The name Michael means "Who is like El?" or "Who is like God?" The implied answer is "No one." In other words, no other god is as great as Israel's God, for he is incomparable. This implies a henotheistic theology (worshiping one God without denying the existence of others) rather than absolute monotheism (belief that there is only one God). Answers to our prayers are sometimes delayed too, which prompts Christians occasionally to invoke the vision of Daniel 10 as the reason. Jesus does not present the same rationale, but in the story of the unjust judge, he teaches us to persevere in prayer (Luke 18:1–8). Like Daniel, we should continue to pray, even if we do not see immediate results.

When the author speaks of "the prince of the Persian kingdom," he is speaking about not an earthly potentate but a heavenly being. This is clear from the mention of Michael, who is certainly not an earthly ruler but "one of the chief princes," that is, an archangel. Earlier, the apocalyptist described the evil tyrant as exalting himself as high as "the host of the heavens" (8:10), as high as the "Prince of the host" (8:11); he will even enter into conflict with "the Prince of princes" (8:25). In the time of Joshua, the commander of Yahweh's metaphysical army is also called "the Prince of the host of Yahweh" (Josh. 5:14, 15; NIV has "commander of the army of the LORD," but the word for "commander" is the same Hebrew word that is here translated "prince," and NIV's "commander of the army" is the same expression rendered "Prince of the host" in Dan. 8:11). Jewish texts identify several archangels: Uriel (2 Esd. 4:1; 5:20; 10:28); Jeremiel (2 Esd. 4:36); Suru'el, Raphael, Raguel, Michael, Saraqa'el, Gabriel (*1 En.* 20:1–7); Surafel (*1 En.* 9:1); and Michael, Raphael, Gabriel, Phanuel (*1 En.* 40:8–10; 54:6; 71:3). Other texts sometimes supply the names of demons as well. The OT mentions only two archangels, and these are both in the book of Daniel: Gabriel (8:16; 9:21) and Michael (10:13, 21; 12:1). Daniel also portrays this remarkable scene of conflict in the heavens between the archangels and what are presumably evil spirits or demons (10:13, 20–21). The above Jewish texts and the Daniel references demonstrate that angelology and demonology experienced greater development in the late OT period. The NT inherits this understanding and carries it forward, by including Gabriel (Luke 1:19, 26) and Michael (Jude 9; Rev. 12:7) in its message.

10:13 / In order for the celestial one addressing Daniel to reach the prophet, he had to leave Michael behind to engage the evil spirit. For the last part of verse 13, the NIV has **I was detained there with the king of Persia** (10:13), but the Hebrew actually reads, "I was left there with the kings of Persia," which is puzzling. What it should say is "I left him there with the prince of the kingdom of Persia" (see the Additional Note on 10:13). What is being described here is a battle between angels. The heavenly being over Persia resists the angel who is sent to give Daniel revelation. Apparently they wrestle, or perhaps their forces do battle, for twenty-one days, until Michael comes to win the victory. First of all, the background to this can be found in ancient Near Eastern polytheism. The understanding was that there were various gods over the separate nations. When the earthly armies clashed below, the heavenly armies of the respective deities were thought to fight above. Ancients also believed that there was a chief god who was head of the divine council, the assembly of the gods. Second, the background to Daniel can be found in the Bible, as we see how Israel elsewhere appropriated and adapted this imagery: "When the Most High gave to the nations their inheritance, when he separated the sons of men, he fixed the bounds of the peoples according to the number of the sons of God [supported by LXX, 4QDeut^j, and 4QDeut^q; MT has "Israel" in place of "God"]. For the LORD's portion is his people, Jacob his allotted heritage" (Deut. 32:8–9 RSV). In Israel there was only one God, so the divine council among Yahwists was composed of angels, known as the "sons of God" (see also Job 1:6 and 2:1, where the Hebrew expression "sons of God" is rendered in the NIV as "angels"). Yahweh put these heavenly beings in charge over the many nations, but he retained Israel for himself (see also Sir. 17:17). Obviously, Israel's God presided over the others and held them accountable, as can be seen in Psalm 82, where surprisingly, these ruling spirits are called "gods." There God is presented as the head of the council of gods (Ps. 82:1; for other examples of the divine council motif, see Gen. 1:26; 11:7; 1 Kgs. 22:19–23; Pss. 89:6–10; 97:7–9; Isa. 6:1–8; Jer. 23:18–22). In that capacity, he acts as divine judge, condemning the perverse patron spirits for not bringing justice to their peoples (Ps. 82:2–7). Similarly, in the "Isaianic Apocalypse" (Isa. 24–27), Yahweh "will punish the powers in the heavens above and the kings on the earth below" (Isa. 24:21). The idea of gods being appointed to the nations is also implied in Deuteronomy 4:19 and 29:26, which speak of alternate powers being allotted to the nations outside Israel.

Just as Michael is a conquering warrior in Daniel, so he is also in the NT apocalypse: "And there was war in heaven. Michael and his angels fought against the dragon, and the dragon and his angels fought back" (Rev. 12:7). Michael prevails there, as well, with the result that Satan and his angels are ejected from heaven and cast down to earth (Rev. 12:8–9). Michael's battle with the dragon closely parallels other battles between the gods, which are quite common in ancient Near Eastern mythology. For example, Marduk engages in combat with Tiamat, goddess of the sea, in the Babylonian Creation Epic (*ANET*, pp. 60–72, 501–3). Closer to Israel, Baal, a Canaanite deity, fights with Yamm and Lothan (= Leviathan), who represent sea and dragon (or sea monster) respectively (*ANET*, pp. 129–31, 137–38). In an OT echo of this, Yahweh has crushed Rahab, the dragon or sea monster (Job 26:12; Ps. 89:10; Isa. 51:9), and will one day punish "Leviathan the gliding serpent, Leviathan the coiling serpent; he will slay the monster of the sea" (Isa. 27:1). Usually, the Bible emphasizes the battle between Yahweh and the earthly foes (Josh. 10:11; Judg. 5:19–20). But the emphasis on battle between Yahweh and the dragon or between angels in heaven shows a recrudescence of myth in late OT times, especially in apocalyptic literature (Cross, *Canaanite Myth*, p. 343). In other words, mythological themes, which had been suppressed in the preexilic period, broke out again and came to the fore in exilic and postexilic literature. This became even more pronounced with the emergence of apocalyptic literature.

An interesting passage in 2 Maccabees describes an apparition of heavenly warfare: "there appeared over all the city golden-clad cavalry charging through the air" with "attacks and counterattacks made on this side and on that" (2 Macc. 5:2–4). The Dead Sea Scrolls recount a cosmic battle between the sons of light and the sons of darkness (*The War Scroll* [1 QM]). In the NT, Christians are participants in this activity of spiritual warfare through prayer. Paul teaches that "our struggle is not against flesh and blood, but against the rulers, against the authorities, against the powers of this dark world and against the spiritual forces of evil in the heavenly realms" (Eph. 6:12). He counsels us to put on our spiritual armor, to stand against the devil, and to pray (Eph. 6:10–18). We do not need to fear the evil spirits, because the Holy Spirit in us is greater than Satan, who is in the world (1 John 4:4). When we resist the devil, he will flee from us (James 4:7; 1 Pet. 5:8–9). In addition, we can take comfort in knowing that nothing can separate us from the love of Christ—not even angels or demons (Rom. 8:35–39). Our confidence in Almighty God empowers us to sing with Martin Luther ("A Mighty Fortress Is Our God"),

> The prince of darkness grim,
> We tremble not for him;
> His rage we can endure,
> For lo! his doom is sure;
> One little word shall fell him.

10:14–15 / Daniel 10:14 really resumes the thought of verse 12. Daniel determined "to gain understanding," and the angel declared, "I have come" (10:12). Here, the angel announces, "Now I have come to explain," or "I have come to cause you to understand" (10:14). This makes verse 13 a parenthetical report on the twenty-one-day delay. The content of the revelation is what will happen to Daniel's people in the future (10:14). The equivalent expression in Aramaic occurs in Daniel 2:28, where the NIV translates, "in days to come." Indeed, it can at times be general in reference to the future (e.g., Gen. 49:1; Num 24:14; Deut. 4:30; 31:29), but here and in Daniel 2:28 it is eschatological, meaning "in the end of days" or "in the latter days" (see the Additional Note on 10:14 and the commentary on 2:28). As will be made clear in chapter 11, the focus appears to be on the events of the second century B.C., specifically connected to evil deeds of Antiochus IV. This might puzzle some readers, because, of course, the end did not come in the second century B.C. However, we need not conclude that this is a false predictive prophecy. Rather, the author of Daniel apparently was pronouncing judgment on Epiphanes for desecrating the temple and for persecuting the Jews, speaking in hope that God would destroy the kingdom of the Seleucids and establish his everlasting kingdom in that time. Therefore, we must reinterpret the message, projecting it to the future end of time, when the resurrection of the dead and the final judgment will occur (12:1–4, 13), even though the author believed that all things would be fulfilled in his lifetime. He is, in truth, speaking about the latter days, which from our perspective this side of the New Testament are still to come.

The next clause, **for the vision concerns a time yet to come** (10:14), is not so transparent in Hebrew. Literally, it means "there is yet a vision for the days," which is fairly opaque. The expression "the days" probably refers to "the latter days" earlier in the verse. It is usually taken to mean that another vision will be given for the latter days; hence the NRSV translation: "For there is a further vision for those days." Perhaps this points to the revelation of chapters 11 and 12. The former vision was of the heavenly being (10:5–6), while the additional vision concerning the end of days is given in the following chapters. The term *khazon*, "vision," may denote "divine communication in a vision, oracle, prophecy" (BDB, p. 303). "Vision," then, is used broadly here for revelation in an oracle rather than in a vision, since chapters 11 and 12 seem to be more a record of what the angel says than of what Daniel sees. While it is possible that Daniel sees visions of the things described, the text does not say so. Perhaps Daniel 10:14 is related to Habakkuk 2:3: "For there is yet a vision for the appointed time; it pants for the end" (author's translation; NIV "For the revelation awaits an appointed time; it speaks of the end"). In addition, it bears some resemblance to Daniel 8:17, "the vision concerns the time of the end" (see commentary and Additional Note on 8:17), and 8:19, "because the vision concerns the appointed time of the end." (Note also Dan. 8:26, "but seal up the vision, for it concerns the distant future," which is similar to Dan. 12:4, "close up and seal the words of the scroll.")

While the angel is **saying this to** Daniel, Daniel bows **face toward the ground** (10:15). This seems like a doublet of verse 9, where Daniel is in a deep sleep with his face to the ground. If Daniel has been touched (v. 10) and set upon his feet (v. 11), what is he doing with his face to the ground again, especially since the intent of the angel was to allay his fears (v. 12)? This is similar to the doublets in earlier chapters (see the commentary on 4:34–37 and 9:3–4, 20–21). Daniel becomes **speechless** (10:15), because his experience has been so overwhelming. In contrast, when Zechariah met Gabriel, he was struck dumb as a judgment because he refused to believe the angel's words (Luke 1:20). Daniel's speech is restored when **one who** looks **like a man** touches his **lips** (Dan. 10:16; Hebrew actually has the plural: "one who looked like human beings"; see the Additional Note on 10:16). This is reminiscent of the one like a human being (NIV "like a son of man") in Daniel 7:13. An angel, "who looked like a man," appeared in Daniel 8:15; then Gabriel is designated a "man" (9:21). Earlier in chapter 10 there is the vision of "a man dressed in linen" (10:5), and later the expression "one who looked like a man" occurs again (10:18)—neither of these is a mortal. Not only do heavenly beings resemble humans, but God himself is described as "a figure like that of a man" by the prophet Ezekiel (Ezek. 1:26). This should not be surprising, since humans are made in the image of God and the angels, as is evident in creation when God says to his celestial council, "Let us make man in our image, in our likeness" (Gen. 1:26). This image would have been understood by some in the OT as a physical resemblance.

Touching of lips is prominent in the call visions of two important prophets: a seraph applies a hot coal to Isaiah's lips to purge him of sin and prepare him to prophesy (Isa. 6:6–7); God touches the mouth of Jeremiah with his hand to put his words in his mouth (Jer. 1:9). Since prophets speak for God, it is significant that he commissions these prophets with actions involving the lips. With Daniel it is otherwise, for he has been in God's service for years; the touch serves to revive his ability to talk. He is touched and strengthened again in verse 18.

10:16–19 / Able to speak once more, Daniel explains his state of dumbfoundedness. He is **overcome with anguish because of the vision** (10:16). The idiom "I am overcome with anguish" is literally "my pains were turned upon me." The Hebrew word for "pains" conjures up the image of a pregnant woman in labor (1 Sam. 4:19). The same word is used by Isaiah, who similarly felt extreme anguish like the "pangs" of a woman giving birth because of a vision of destruction he witnessed (Isa. 21:1–4). Daniel confesses, "I retain no strength" or "I have no strength" (Dan. 10:16; NIV I am helpless). The same expression is found in verse 8 (see also Dan. 11:6; 2 Chron. 13:20; 22:9).

Daniel is amazed that he can converse with such an awesome being: **How can I, your servant, talk with you, my lord?** (or perhaps the first and second parts of the verse are linked; to paraphrase: "How can I carry on a conversation with you when I am so weak?"; see the Additional Note on 10:17). He is still weak from the encounter: **My strength is gone and I can hardly breathe** (10:17). This leads to a third touch in the text as we have it now (see 10:10, 16), from **the one who looked like a man** (10:18; see the Additional Note and commentary on 10:16). Just as in chapter 8 (Dan. 8:18; see also Rev. 1:17), this revives Daniel and gives him **strength** (10:18). The angel addresses Daniel as he did earlier: **O man highly esteemed** (10:19; see 9:23; 10:11); and he repeats what was said before: **Do not be afraid** (10:19; see v. 12). Moreover, he speaks encouraging words: **Peace! Be strong now; be strong** (10:19). In Hebrew the expression is literally "Peace be to you." This is normally a greeting, wishing peace on the one greeted (e.g., Gen. 43:23 MT; Judg. 6:23; 19:20 MT). However, the angel has been with Daniel for a while, so here it may be a declaration regarding Daniel's state, since he has been afraid: "You are well," or "You are safe" (thus NRSV, Hartman and Di Lella, *Daniel*, p. 265). The repetition of "Be strong" twice here is unusual. We expect "Be strong and courageous," as elsewhere (see the Additional Note on 10:19). This last is often used in farewells in Hebrew and classical tradition (Deut. 31:6, 7, 23; see Montgomery, *Daniel*, p. 415). It is interesting, then, that we find both the Hebrew "Hello" and "Good-bye" in this one verse. Next, Daniel encourages the heavenly visitor to **speak, now that he has given** him **strength** (10:19).

10:20–11:2a / The angel commences with a question: **Do you know why I have come to you?** (10:20). Of course Daniel should know, because it was revealed to him in verses 12 and 14. The angel has been sent in response to Daniel's prayer and desire for knowledge and will disclose the future of the Jews. This repetition is probably a doublet: two versions of the story have been brought together here. If so, then verse 14 is from a source in which the angel tells his purpose early; verse 20 is from an alternate source that has not yet revealed the purpose of the visit. Whatever the case, in the present text the literary effect of the angel's question must be rhetorical. Its purpose is to remind Daniel (and the reader) of the purpose that has already been stated and to highlight it (Driver, *Daniel*, p. 161). The answer to the question found in verse 20 is given in verse 21a: **I will tell you what is written in the Book of Truth.** It is possible that originally the answer immediately followed the question, because the material about the war with the princes of Persia and Greece seems intrusive. Perhaps the redactor, to smooth this over, added the adversative conjunction but to the beginning of verse 21. The logic is this: the angel needs to return soon to Michael to support him in the battle against Persia, *but* before he goes, he will give Daniel a revelation.

The parallel to verse 21a in the alternate account is found in Daniel 11:2a: **I tell you the truth.** It is clear that Daniel 10:21a and 11:2a are a doublet, because they are so close, actually closer than the NIV shows. Both have the verb "I will tell," the object "you," and the word "truth." There are three differences: (1) they begin with different words, (2) they have slightly different word order, and (3) verse 21a adds "what is written in the book." Here is a comparison (author's translation):

| Daniel 10:21a | "But I will tell you what is written in a book of truth." |
| Daniel 11:2a | "And now, truth I will tell you." |

The "Book of Truth" is apparently a record of what God has determined for the future. The word "truth" emphasizes the trustworthy nature of what is inscribed in this writing: what is recorded will surely come to pass. The author of the book of Daniel recounts in chapter 11 a series of historical events. If he is indeed writing in the second century B.C., these events have already happened. But as a literary device, he places them in the time of Daniel in the exile as a way of communicating his belief that God has predetermined the future and recorded what will transpire before it takes place. The psalmist has a similar theology, expressed on a more individual level: "All the days ordained for me were written in your book before one of them came to be" (Ps. 139:16). The theme of God's sovereignty is woven into the book of Daniel (see, e.g., Dan. 4:17, 24, where Nebuchadnezzar's fate is decided by heaven). *First Enoch* also emphasizes books or tablets that tell the future destinies (see esp. *1 En.* 106:19–107:1; see also 81:1–2; 93:2–3; 103:2–3). Predestination is a motif evident in the writings from the Jewish community gathered at Qumran (4Q180), which was active not long after the time when Daniel may have been written. Some Jews consider that their fate for the coming year is determined and inscribed in a book between Rosh Hashanah and Yom Kippur. The fixing of fates may have come into Judaism by Babylonian influence (see *ANET*, p. 67) from the time of the exile (Collins, *Daniel*, p. 376). Besides the book of truth, two other books are described in Daniel: the book of life (Dan. 12:1; see also Exod. 32:32–33; Ps. 69:28; Luke 10:20; Phil. 4:3; Rev. 3:5; 13:8; 17:8; 20:12, 15; 21:27), containing the names of those who belong to God, and the books of judgment (Dan. 7:10; see also Rev. 20:12), containing records of people's deeds.

Some commentators are troubled by the notion of determinism found in Daniel (Towner, *Daniel*, p. 154), but this teaching offers comfort to believers today, just as it did to the faithful Jews of the late OT era. It is encouraging to know that God has determined that one day he will punish the evil tyrants, destroy their oppressive regimes, and establish his everlasting kingdom of righteousness (Dan. 2; 7; 11; 12; according to Matt. 24:36, God has predetermined a particular day and hour). It engenders hope to read that in the future God has a plan to raise the dead (Dan. 12:2). We need to be reminded that God is still on his throne, even though sometimes he allows us to suffer in this world. Furthermore, it is important to point out that in Scripture predestination is balanced out with affirmations of human free will. Although God hardened Pharaoh's heart (Exod. 7:3), which emphasizes determinism, it is also true that Pharaoh hardened his own heart (Exod. 8:15, 32, 9:34), which shows free will. In reflecting on Pharaoh in the exodus story, Paul strongly argues for predestination (Rom. 9:15–24), yet in the next chapter he quotes Joel 2:32 favorably, proclaiming that anyone may decide to call on the Lord and be saved (Rom. 10:13). Likewise, Jesus teaches that we cannot come to him unless the Father draws us to him (John 6:44, 64); on the other hand, he also extends an open invitation to all who choose to believe (John 3:16, 18).

The importance of God's election is to show us that all glory for our salvation goes to God, while the significance of human free will is to show that we are responsible before God for our choices. Daniel does not lack that balance, for it carries the theme of human freedom as well as that of God's sovereignty. In fact, the book is permeated with admonitions to choose to obey God, by way of example. Jews should be like Daniel and his friends in keeping the dietary rules (ch. 1). They should not worship images (ch. 3) or cease practicing their religion (ch. 6), even when threatened with death. They should model themselves after the wise, who resist pressure to "forsake the holy covenant" (11:30), choosing to suffer rather than to apostatize (11:32–35). The apocalyptist is setting before his people two options: either be faithful to God and to Judaism, which will result in God's favor, or assimilate to paganism and face God's wrath. None of these stories makes sense without human volition as an assumption. Even the final judgment (12:1–3) is meaningless without individual choice, for how can humans either be judged righteous and worthy of "everlasting life" or be judged guilty and worthy of "shame and everlasting contempt" (12:2) unless they distinguish themselves by deciding to follow one path or the other? In spite of the fact that a tension exists between divine election and human free will, which perhaps cannot be fully resolved in this life, we must allow both voices in Scripture to be heard, and we should strive to be balanced in our preaching and teaching on this topic.

After conveying his message for the future, the angel **will return to fight against the prince of Persia** (10:20), after which **the prince of Greece will come** (10:20). The phrase **and when I go** (10:20) does not mean when the angel goes to fight the prince of Persia, because the Greek Empire would not displace the Persian until about two hundred years later. It must mean when he goes away from the battle after fighting with the prince of Persia. In other words, after defeating Persia, he will leave that battle, allowing Greece to take over, which will initiate a new struggle with the prince of Greece (Driver, *Daniel*, p. 161). The only one to help him is **Michael,** who is Israel's prince (10:21).

In the first year of Darius the Mede, the angel of chapter 10 takes his **stand to support and protect** Michael (11:1). Many commentators consider the date in the time of Darius the Mede (11:1a) to be a later addition (e.g., Montgomery, *Daniel*, p. 416). This reference to Darius may be an explanatory comment by a scribe who wanted to identify the angel with Gabriel, because Gabriel is the messenger angel of chapter 9, which is dated to the time of Darius the Mede (9:1, 21). Also, it might have been added by someone who thought this was a new section and felt it needed a date formula like the beginnings of chapters 7, 8, 9, and 10; apparently he did not recognize that chapters 10 through 12 are one unit

(Porteous, *Daniel*, p. 155). If so, this individual also made the mistake of going back in time, for in the mind of the author of Daniel, Darius the Mede ruled before Cyrus. So, the progression is from the first year of Belshazzar (7:1) to the third year of Belshazzar (8:1) to the first year of Darius the Mede (9:1) to the third year of Cyrus (10:1). Now all of a sudden, the text reverts to the first year of Darius the Mede (Dan. 11:1). If it is a gloss, though, it is an early one, since the MT is supported by 4QDan^c.

Additional Notes §10

10:1 / Cyrus used various titles, such as "the king," "the great king," or "the king of kings," before he vanquished Babylon in 539 B.C. After 539 he added the title "king of Babylon" or "king of the lands" (Montgomery, *Daniel*, p. 405; Collins, *Daniel*, p. 372). However, it seems he did not use the title **king of Persia** as here (Williamson, *Ezra, Nehemiah*, pp. 9, 11). The Nabonidus Chronicle calls Cyrus "king of Persia" (*ANET*, p. 306) before the fall of Babylon. In the Bible, this title is frequently used in late texts (e.g., 2 Chron. 36:22, 23; Ezra 1:1, 2; 3:7; 4:3, 5).

10:4 / Instead of **the Tigris** (Heb. *khiddaqel*), which may be a scribal error, the Syriac version has "the Euphrates," which makes much more sense. On the other hand, because it makes more sense, it is suspect: a scribe might have changed "Tigris" to "Euphrates" for that very reason. Perhaps the text originally had "the great river," which denoted the Euphrates, and a scribe, in an erroneous effort to identify it, inserted "the Tigris."

10:5 / The phrase **of the finest gold** is *beketem 'upaz*, literally, "with gold of Uphaz" (so RSV; NRSV "with . . . gold from Uphaz"). The more common word for gold is *zahab*. The word used here, *ketem*, tends to be used in poetic passages (e.g., Job 28:19; 31:24). The expression "gold of Ophir" is used three times with the word *ketem* (Job 28:16; Ps. 45:9; Isa. 13:12). Ophir was a place in Arabia or Africa with which the Israelites traded and from which they brought back gold (1 Kgs. 9:28; 10:11; 22:48). We might wish to understand the phrase "gold of Uphaz" along the same lines, that is, that Uphaz is a place, except that there is only one other such reference in the Bible, in Jer. 10:9. Otherwise, we know of no place by this name. In contrast, "Ophir" occurs at least twelve times in the Bible and once in an ancient Near Eastern text. It is quite possible that "Uphaz" is a corruption of "Ophir." In fact, the Syriac version supports the reading "Ophir" in Jer. 10:9. Another possibility is that "Uphaz" is a corruption of Hebrew *paz* from the root *pzz*, meaning "fine" or "refined." The phrase *ketem paz*, "pure gold," occurs in Song 5:11. Apparently the NIV is following this line by translating "finest gold."

10:8 / Some commentators think that Daniel's reaction to this figure is more dramatic (10:7–11:1) than his reaction to Gabriel in chapter 8 (8:27; there is no similar reaction in ch. 9), with the result that the author intends us to think of someone even higher in the chain of command than Gabriel or Michael (R. H. Charles, *A Critical and Exegetical Commentary on the Book of Daniel* [Oxford: Clarendon Press, 1929], pp. 256–68; A. Jeffery, "The Book of Daniel: Introduction and Exegesis," *Interpreter's Bible*, vol. 6 [New York: Abingdon-Cokesbury Press, 1956], p. 502). This is not convincing, because the reactions are comparable. Even if the description in ch. 10 is more dramatic, it may simply be because it falls later in the book and is part of the climactic revelation. Furthermore, it is likely that Daniel appears to need touching and strengthening more than once in ch. 10 only because the author or an editor has included doublets, not because Daniel is more overwhelmed.

The statement **my face turned deathly pale** is literally "my splendor [*hod*] was changed upon me for disfigurement"; cf. a similar Aramaic clause in 7:28 ("my countenance [*ziw*] changed upon me"; NIV "my face turned pale"). Why MT has "splendor" (*hod*) while its Aramaic parallel has "countenance" (*ziw*) is uncertain. Unlike the latter, Dan. 10:8 also adds *lemashkhit*, "for ruin" or "for disfigurement." Perhaps the author of Daniel was thinking of Yahweh's suffering servant, who was portrayed as having a disfigured (*mishkhat*) appearance (Isa. 52:14).

10:10 / Because Miller (*Daniel*, pp. 281–83) identifies the figure of vv. 5–6 as God in the form of Christ, he is forced to argue that this verse introduces a new heavenly being. In other words, the **hand** of a different creature touches Daniel. Miller is pressed into this position for two reasons: this individual is merely a messenger, and he is not all-powerful. In his view, God sends but is not sent, as the one in this section is (10:11). This understanding may be questioned, though, because in John's gospel, Jesus is sent by the Father (e.g., John 3:34; 4:34; 5:23, 24, 30, 36–38). More important, this celestial one could not overcome the powerful spirit being who exercised control over Persia without the help of the archangel, Michael, which would not be true of God or Jesus. However, to consider vv. 5–6 as a christophany is reading the NT into the OT. Furthermore, there is no indication in the text that a new actor enters the stage in v. 10. Therefore, it is more natural to understand this heavenly being to be the one who appears in vv. 5–6 (Driver, *Daniel*, p. 156; Hartman and Di Lella, *Daniel*, p. 281).

10:12 / The Hebrew idiom *natatta 'et-libbeka*, **you set your mind**, is literally, "you gave your heart." The expression is found only in late texts (1 Chron. 22:19; 2 Chron. 11:16; Eccl. 1:13, 17; 7:21; 8:9, 16).

God tells the Israelites "to afflict your souls" (Lev. 16:29; NIV "deny yourselves"; or "you must fast," NIV footnote) on the Day of Atonement (see also Lev. 16:31; 23:27, 32; Num. 29:7). The verb rendered here **humble** is from the same root, so it implies fasting. Just as Daniel humbled himself (Dan. 10:12) by fasting (Dan. 10:3), so Ezra says: "There, by the Ahava Canal, I proclaimed a fast, so that we might humble ourselves before our God" (Ezra 8:21).

10:13 / The MT's *notarti sham* (NIV **I was detained there**) is difficult to translate. It really means "I remained there," or "I was left there," but that hardly makes sense, because the angel who is speaking did not stay behind. On the contrary, he escaped and went to Daniel. It was Michael who remained behind to fight or detain the spirit being or prince of Persia. BHS proposes *we'oto hotarti sham*, "I left him there" (thus RSV and NRSV), a reading supported by the Greek. The NIV translation is an attempt to clarify in English what is muddy in Hebrew. BDB (p. 451) suggests, "I was left over there beside the kings [i.e., I had nothing more to do . . .]." In other words, once Michael took over the battle, this angel was free to leave. This seems a stretch also, so it is probably best to emend the Hebrew text along the lines of the Greek. Repointing *notarti* (niph. "I was left") to *hotarti* (hiph. "I caused to be left") and adding the direct object *'oto* ("him") yields the more sensible rendering "I left him." Rather than **the king of Persia**, the Hebrew actually has *malkey paras*, "the kings of Persia," but this is problematic. It seems unlikely that the apocalyptist would also use "kings" to refer to the demons when he previously used "prince." The LXX and Theodotion suggest that we should add *sar*, "prince," here and read *malkut paras*, "the kingdom of Persia," with 6QDan rather than read *malkey paras*, "the kings of Persia," with the MT. Therefore, the text should say, "the prince of the kingdom of Persia," as earlier in the verse (thus NRSV).

10:14 / The expression *be'akharit hayyamim* (NIV **in the future;** cf. 2:28 [Aram.]) occurs fourteen times in the OT, sometimes referring generally to the future (Gen. 49:1; Num. 24:14; Deut. 4:30; and 31:29). However, it is often eschatological in the prophets (Isa. 2:2 [cf. Mic. 4:1]; Hos. 3:5; Ezek. 38:16) and in Dan. 2:28.

In Hebrew, **for the vision concerns a time yet to come** is literally "for there is yet a vision for the days." Since "days" (*hayyamim*) is definite ("the days"), it refers to particular days, presumably "the latter days" mentioned earlier in the verse; cf. 8:17 ("the time of the end"; cf. Dan. 11:27, 35; 12:4) and 8:19 ("the appointed time of the end"; cf. Dan. 11:29 [NIV "set time"]. The above are all influenced by Hab. 2:3 ("for there is yet a vision for the appointed time; it pants for the end").

10:16 / The phrase **one who looked like a man** literally reads "like a likeness of sons of man," or in better English as "one who looked like human beings do." The LXX reads "hand of a man" instead of "sons of man," perhaps influenced by the use of *naga'*, "to touch," here and in v. 10. Some think a new angel is introduced here, but there is no evidence to support that; cf. the commentary at verse 10.

10:17 / The Hebrew for **my strength is gone** means literally "strength will not stand in me." Before this, Hebrew has the adverbial *me'attah*, "from now," left untranslated in the NIV. This word is problematic because it usually means "henceforth," which does not make sense here since Daniel will not be without strength from this point forward. Maybe we should take it to mean "just now," i.e., he was weak just now because of the vision, but only temporarily (thus RSV:

"For now no strength remains in me"). Perhaps the adverb introduces a circumstantial clause linked to the first clause: "How can I talk with you while in these circumstances I will be powerless?" While all of these are possible, it seems best to go back to the first, more literal, reading, because Daniel does not know that the angel will revive him. Tentatively, we take it as an expression of Daniel's fear that from now on he will have no strength.

10:18 / The expression **the one who looked like a man** here is different from 10:16. There it is *kidmot bene 'adam*, "like a likeness of sons of man" (NIV "one who looked like a man"). Here it is *kemar'eh 'adam*, literally, "like the appearance of a human being." The same expression but with the addition of *demut*, "likeness," is found in Ezek. 1:26: "a figure like that of a man" (*demut kemar'eh 'adam*, lit. "a likeness like an appearance of a man"). Dan. 10:18 is close to 8:15, except that the earlier passage uses a different word for man: *kemar'eh-gaber*, "like the appearance of a man." For other similar expressions in Daniel, see references in the commentary on 10:16. The word *mar'eh*, "appearance," occurs often in Ezekiel (e.g., Ezek. 1:5; 8:2; 10:1; 40:3; 42:11).

10:19 / For **be strong now; be strong,** the MT has *khazaq wakhazaq*, "be strong and be strong." The more common expression is *khazaq we'emats*, "be strong and courageous" (Deut. 31:7, 23; Josh. 1:6, 7, 9, 18; plural forms Deut. 31:6). That reading is supported here by several Hebrew manuscripts and by the LXX, so we should correct the text to "Be strong and courageous!" (Hartman and Di Lella, *Daniel*, p. 256).

10:21 / The nouns **Book** and **Truth** are indefinite in Hebrew. Like the NIV, most commentators ignore this and translate the phrase as if definite, which is possible in Hebrew. However, Goldingay renders it correctly, without the article, "a reliable book" (Goldingay, *Daniel*, p. 272), taking "truth" to mean that the book is trustworthy rather than indicating some notion of "objective truth" (Goldingay, *Daniel*, p. 276).

In the phrase **your prince,** "your" is plural in Hebrew. Therefore, Michael is not merely Daniel's prince, but Israel's. "Your" refers to all the Jews.

11:1 / Hebrew *'omdi*, "my standing" (NIV **my stand**), is awkward, literally, "I—in the first year of Darius the Mede—my standing was to support and strengthen him." Some scholars change it to the participle *'omed*, "standing." The Greek reads "me" instead of the MT's **him.** By making those two changes, and eliminating the reference to Darius the Mede, which may be a scribal insertion, it is possible to read this as a continuation of 10:21b: "no one supports me against them except Michael, your prince, standing to support and protect me" (paraphrased in NIV language from Montgomery, *Daniel*, p. 416). This is very attractive because it makes sense of a difficult passage. However, 4QDan^c clearly reads *'amadti*, "I stood," showing that the MT's *'omdi*, "my standing," may need correction; neither should we emend to *'omed*, "standing," for 11:1 does not continue from 10:21b. The Dead Sea Scroll also reads "him," not "me," and supports retaining "in the first year of Darius the Mede." Therefore, the NIV is fine as it is.

§11 The Final Revelation: The Body (Dan. 11:2b–12:4)

We enter now into the body of the last main revelation of the book of Daniel. There has been some progression in the visions of the book from a more general scope, encompassing larger blocks of history, to a more narrow focus on shorter periods of time. So, for example, Daniel 2 spans four and a half centuries by outlining the four human empires of Babylonia, Media, Persia, and Greece, which are swept away by the fifth—the eternal kingdom of God. Aside from the fact that the fourth empire will have two phases (a stronger, "iron" phase [2:33, 40], corresponding to the rule of Alexander, and a relatively weaker, "iron and clay" phase [2:33, 41–43], corresponding to the divided kingdoms of the Diadochi), there is little detail. Daniel 7 sets out the same four empires as in Daniel 2 but includes more detail about the Greek dominion, especially the Hellenistic era, including the "little horn," which represents Antiochus IV (7:8, 11, 20–26). Then Daniel 8 ignores Babylonia and Media, expands on Persia and Greece, and builds up to a climax with an account that highlights the oppressions of Epiphanes. While the apocalyptic section of chapter 9 is brief (vv. 20–27) and does apparently include an allusion to the Babylonian captivity and return (v. 25), its emphasis is on the desolating sacrilege of the second century B.C. In chapter 11, as in chapter 8, the author also omits Babylonia and Media, so that he can primarily survey the history from the time of Persia down to the persecution of the Jews under the Seleucids.

This Final Revelation briefly summarizes the Persian stage and touches on Alexander the Great (two verses—11:2–3); then it goes into much more detail about the Hellenistic era, focusing on the wars between the Seleucids and the Ptolemies (seventeen verses—11:4–20); the climax comes as the chapter devotes the lion's share of space to Antiochus IV by chronicling events leading up to the desecration of the temple—known as the abomination that makes desolate, or the desolating sacrilege—which in turn is followed by the evil king's death (twenty-five verses—11:21–45); the Final Revelation concludes with the appearance of

Michael, a resurrection of the dead, and a judgment (four verses—12:1–4). (Concerning the type of literature here, see the Introduction on "Genre.")

11:2b / The context here is the time of the Persian king Cyrus (10:1). After this, **three more kings will appear in Persia, and then a fourth** (11:2b). There were actually thirteen Persian kings after Cyrus, but the apocalyptist either intentionally abbreviated the Persian period or was not aware of the particulars of Persian history. If the latter, this is further evidence for the late date of Daniel: the author is very careful to give the minute details of the Hellenistic period in which he lives, but very sketchy on the Babylonian and Persian history of the more distant past. When the NIV translates "and then a fourth," it is interpreting the Hebrew text, which is actually ambiguous. It should read something like this: "three more kings will appear in Persia, and the fourth will be far richer." One way to take this is as indicating a fourth king after Cyrus, as the NIV takes it. In other words, three kings will arise after Cyrus, and then a fourth king will arise after that, so that including Cyrus, five kings are in view. However, another way to read it is that the fourth king is the same as the third one after Cyrus. According to this interpretation, four kings are articulated: Cyrus plus the three who follow him. It seems more natural to take the text this latter way. Further support can be found from the leopard of chapter 7, which represents Persia (7:6). It has four wings and four heads, perhaps to symbolize four kings of Persia.

Scholars are divided over which kings are intended. One possibility is to identify them using the kings mentioned in the Bible, since these likely would have been known to the author of Daniel: Darius I Hystaspes (522–486 B.C.; see Ezra 4:5, 24; 5:5–7; 6:1, 12–15); Xerxes I (486–465 B.C., called Ahasuerus in the Bible; see, e.g., Ezra 4:6; Esth. 1:1–2, 9, 15–17, 19 NRSV); Artaxerxes I Longimanus (465–424 B.C.; see, e.g., Ezra 4:7–8; 6:14; 7:1, 7; 8:1; Neh. 2:1; 5:14; 13:6); and perhaps Darius III Codomannus (336–331 B.C.; see Neh. 12:22), who has the advantage of being the last Persian king. Based on the five-king hypothesis, these kings would be the four who came after Cyrus. If we use the four-king point of view, we might ignore Darius I and include the other three. This view has gaps in time, and many kings are skipped, but its strength is that it takes us down to the time of Alexander, who is mentioned in the next verse (Dan. 11:3). One weakness is that the text says this last king **will be far richer than all the others** (11:2b) and that that wealth will engender conflict with Greece (see below and the Additional Note on 11:8). The statement about wealth does not fit Darius III too well, but it may be that the author thought of Persia's wealth as reaching its pinnacle with the last king (Hartman and Di Lella, *Daniel*, p. 288).

Another possibility is to use the four kings immediately following Cyrus, thus following the five-king view. They were Cambyses (530–522 B.C.), Gaumâta (seven months of 522 B.C., who claimed to be Bardiya or Smerdis, Cambyses's brother), Darius I Hystaspes (522–486 B.C.), and Xerxes I (= Ahasuerus; 486–465 B.C.). It is convenient to have Xerxes as the last king in the series, because he was known for his great wealth, which he used to amass arms and men for battle against Greece (Driver, *Daniel*, p. 163), although unfortunately for him, he was defeated at Salamis in 480 B.C. If the four-king view is correct, it is still possible to end with Xerxes by eliminating Gaumâta, since he ruled for such a short time and was of dubious legitimacy. Therefore, the biblical writer may not have known of him or may have chosen to exclude him. The four kings then are Cyrus, Cambyses, Darius I, and Xerxes I. The strengths of this view are, first, that these are the kings who arose after Cyrus and, second, that Xerxes was known for wealth and war against Greece. The weakness of this view is that there is a large gap between Xerxes (486–465 B.C.), in verse 2, and Alexander (336–323 B.C.), who is introduced in verse 3. However, no matter what view we take, there will be gaps, because the text is not exhaustive, as it leaves out many of the kings. The author's concern is not to supply a comprehensive history of Persia, as he is pressing on to the Hellenistic era so that he can focus on the Seleucids and especially on Antiochus IV.

The last part of verse 2 is very difficult to translate. The NIV has **he will stir up everyone against the kingdom of Greece,** but the Hebrew does not have the word "against." Literally, it might be translated "he will stir up everything [or everyone], the kingdom of Greece." Alternatively, it might be rendered "the whole [meaning the wealth of the king mentioned previously] will stir up the kingdom of Greece" (similarly Barr, "Daniel," p. 601). In other words, this king's wealth will incite conflict, because Greece will envy the wealth of Persia (see the Additional Note on 11:2b). It is also possible that "the kingdom of Greece" is a gloss. These differences in the translation may tip the scales slightly in favor of making Darius III the last king in the list. First of all, if the phrase is talking of the stirring of the kingdom of Greece rather than "stirring up everyone against the kingdom of Greece," it seems to describe Alexander's defeat of Darius III and Persia. Secondly, Greece could not properly be called a "kingdom" in the time of Xerxes but could in the time of Alexander.

11:3–4 / Then a mighty king will appear (11:3), or perhaps more to the point, "a warrior king" (Driver, *Daniel*, p. 164). Alexander moved east and conquered everything from Greece to what is today Pakistan.

He truly was able to rule with great power and do as he pleased (11:3). Similarly, the ram (Persia) "did as he pleased" (8:4). The expression is used earlier of God, who "does as he pleases" (4:35). God is loving and good as well as sovereign, so we can be confident that what pleases him is just. It is more problematic here when used of Alexander, and actually negative when used later in the same chapter of Antiochus III (who "will do as he pleases," such that he "will have the power to destroy" [11:16]) and of Antiochus IV ("who will do as he pleases," with the result that "he will exalt and magnify himself above every god and will say unheard-of things against the God of gods" [11:36]). The description in Daniel continues: after he has appeared, his empire will be broken up (11:4). It is amazing how quickly Alexander rose and fell. After acceding to the throne in 336, he completed his vast empire by 327. Unfortunately for him, he did not have much time to enjoy the fruits of his impressive military victories, for he was cut down by a fever in Babylon in 323 at the age of only thirty-two. Earlier in Daniel, he is represented as a goat with a large horn: "At the height of his power his large horn was broken off" (8:8).

When Alexander died, his kingdom was **parceled out toward the four winds of heaven** (11:4). This clearly alludes to the division of his kingdom by the Diadochi, or successors. In chapter 8, when the horn is broken off, it is replaced by four other horns, who "grew up toward the four winds of heaven" (8:8). These are most likely the kingdoms of Cassander (Greece and Macedonia), Lysimachus (Thrace and Asia Minor), Seleucus (Syria and Mesopotamia), and Ptolemy (Egypt and Israel). When Alexander died, he left no male heir behind to succeed him, although his wife, Roxane, was pregnant at the time. She gave birth to a son following Alexander's death, but sadly the child did not stand much chance of survival. He was used as a pawn by generals pretending to protect him, until it was no longer necessary or advantageous. Then he was murdered, as were Roxane; Alexander's mentally handicapped half-brother, Philip Arrhidaeus; and Herakles, who claimed to be Alexander's illegitimate son. In the intrigues for power after the great warrior's demise, all possible claimants were eliminated, with the result that Alexander's kingdom did **not go to his descendants** (11:4). It is also true that his divided empire did not **have the power he exercised** (11:4), which was also the meaning of the image in chapter 2. Alexander's empire is there represented by iron, but the second phase of the Greek kingdom, under the Diadochi, is represented by a mixture of iron and clay (2:33, 40–43). Likewise, in chapter 8, the "four kingdoms that will emerge from his nation . . . will not have the same power" (8:22).

11:5–9 / Alexander is gone and his domain divided. The author now proceeds to go into much more detail about the wars between the Seleucids and the Ptolemies. In each case, the Seleucid king in question is called "the king of the North" and the Ptolemaic king is called "the king of the South." These directional designations are from the perspective of the Jews in Jerusalem, who are really the main concern of the biblical writer. The first king of the South, who became strong (11:5), was Ptolemy I Soter (323–285), sometimes called Lagi or Lagide because he was the son of Lagus. The word *negeb*, "South," in the Bible usually denotes the area immediately south of Judah, but in Daniel 11 it refers to Egypt. Ptolemy I had been one of Alexander's generals. He took control of Egypt and the land of Israel when Alexander died, and he ruled as satrap until 305, when he began to use the title "king." Seleucus I Nicator (312–280), who had been a cavalry officer under Alexander, was given the satrapy of Babylon. However, Antigonus Monophthalmus ("the One-Eyed"), who initially obtained parts of Asia Minor (Phrygia, Pamphylia, and Lycia—central and southern sections of modern-day Turkey), wanted to expand his rule. He eventually acquired all of Asia Minor and began to push eastward. Pressured by Antigonus, Seleucus fled for protection to Egypt and served briefly under Ptolemy. Therefore the text is correct in saying that Seleucus was one of his commanders (11:5). Ptolemy subsequently helped Seleucus defeat the army of Antigonus (led by Antigonus's son, Demetrius) in 312. Seleucus not only reclaimed his territory in Babylon, but over time he recovered much of Alexander's empire. His territory reached from the Punjab region (in modern-day Pakistan) in the east to the western shore of Asia Minor in the west, as well as southward into Syria. Ptolemy retained hegemony over Judea in addition to Egypt, but Seleucus's kingdom was much more extensive. Seleucus truly became even stronger than he (Ptolemy) and ruled "a dominion greater than his," that is, Ptolemy's (11:5; this translation is preferable to NIV's **will rule his own kingdom with great power**; see the Additional Note on 11:5).

There was conflict between the Seleucids and the Ptolemies over parts of Syria, Phoenicia, and Israel. However, **after some years** they became **allies** (11:6). Ptolemy II Philadelphus (285–246) decided to arrange a treaty marriage (about 250 B.C.). He offered up his daughter Berenice to be wed to Antiochus II Theos (261–246). In exchange, Antiochus was required to divorce his wife, Laodice, and ensure that her sons would not inherit the Seleucid throne but rather the offspring of Berenice would. Berenice, then, is **the daughter of the king of the South** who went **to the king of the North to make an alliance** (11:6). After Antiochus put Laodice aside and married Berenice, the new couple produced a son.

Unfortunately, Berenice did **not retain her power** (11:6). When her father died, Antiochus broke faith with her and ignored his treaty by reuniting with Laodice. Whether in bitterness for being divorced earlier or in fear of being divorced again should Antiochus change his mind once more, Laodice murdered Antiochus with poison. She also arranged the deaths of Berenice, her baby boy, and their Egyptian attendants. Berenice was **handed over, together with her royal escort and her** child (11:6, NIV alternate reading in footnote; the main text of the NIV reads "father" instead of "child"). Antiochus's offspring did **not last** (11:6; NIV has "power" in the text but "offspring" as an alternate reading in the footnote). As her husband, Antiochus is probably also in view as **the one who supported her** (11:6) or "who got possession of her" (RSV).

After the above events, Laodice's son Seleucus II Callinicus (246–226) ascended the throne. **In those days** (11:6), meanwhile, **one from** Berenice's **family line** arose **to take her place** (11:7)—that is, her brother, Ptolemy III Euergetes (246–221), who inherited the Egyptian throne. He attacked **the forces of the king of the North** and entered **his fortress** (11:7). Ptolemy III sought to avenge his sister by overrunning the Syrian kingdom. He plundered the Seleucid fortresses of Seleucia and Antioch. He put Laodice to death and was **victorious in his fight against** the armies of the northern provinces (11:7), capturing territory as far north as Asia Minor. His spoils included **valuable articles of silver and gold** (11:8). He not only carried this vast wealth **off to Egypt** but seized many of **their gods** and **metal images** as well (11:8). The idols of other nations were commonly carried into exile and displayed as trophies of war as a way of showing that the conqueror's gods were more powerful (Isa. 46:1–2; Jer. 48:7; 49:3). Although the Israelites did not have an image of God, they had an ark, which when captured was placed in the shrine of Dagon (1 Sam. 5:2).

Apparently, Ptolemy also returned some gods to Egypt that had been stolen earlier by the Persians. Because of the wealth he brought back and because of the restoration of the gods, Ptolemy was given the title Euergetes, or "Benefactor," by his people. Yet, Ptolemy III did not completely subjugate the Seleucid Empire. Perhaps he was only interested in plunder and in punishing Seleucus II for his sister's death; possibly his army was weakened by the conflict, in spite of his victories; or it may be that he was compelled to return to Egypt to quell a revolt there. In any case, the conflict ended and **for some years he** left **the king of the North alone** (11:8). Seleucus II successfully recovered his lost ground in Asia Minor and northern Syria but was pushed back when he attacked Ptolemy's territory farther south (ca. 242–240). **The king of the North** invaded **the realm of the king of the South,** but he was forced to **retreat to his own country** (11:9).

11:10–19 / The **sons** of Seleucus II then prepared **for war** (11:10). Seleucus II had two sons. Seleucus III Ceraunos (226–223) was murdered after a brief period on the throne, but Antiochus III the Great (223–187) succeeded his brother and enjoyed a long and powerful reign. He assembled **a great army, which** swept **on like an irresistible flood** (11:10). More literally, the text uses two verbs, meaning "to flood" and "to pass through." These same two verbs are used by Isaiah to describe the overwhelming tide of the Assyrian invasion (Isa. 8:8; the root for "to flood" is found also in Dan. 9:26; 11:22 [twice], 26, and 40).

Antiochus III was able to recapture southern Syria, Phoenicia, and parts of Israel (219–218 B.C.). He would **carry the battle as far as his fortress** (11:10). It is not clear whether "his" refers to Antiochus's or Ptolemy's fortress, or which fortress is intended. It might be Seleucia, the port of Antioch, in Syria, or one of the fortresses in the southern part of Israel, such as Raphia or Gaza. The latter is attractive because the Hebrew for "his fortress" is *maʿuzzoh*, which could be a play on the word Gaza (*ʿazah*; Driver, *Daniel*, p. 170). Ptolemy IV Philopator (221–203), **the king of the South,** marched **out in a rage** and fought against Antiochus III, **the king of the North** (11:11), at Raphia in 217 B.C. "The king of the North" raised **a large army** of some 70,000 men, but it was **defeated** by Ptolemy's similarly numerous host. As a result, **the king of the South** was **filled with pride** (11:12).

Unfortunately for Egypt, the victory was short-lived. Ptolemy did **not remain triumphant** (11:12), because he failed to press his advantage. He should have followed up his victory by pursuing Antiochus III northward. Instead, he contented himself with routing Antiochus's force and retaining control of Israel and southern Syria. For some fourteen years, Antiochus carried out further successful campaigns, especially in the east, mostly reconquering lost territory. When Ptolemy IV died in 203, he left a young son (less than ten years old) as his heir: Ptolemy V Epiphanes (203–181). Then Antiochus III, **the king of the North,** decided to seize the opportunity. He mustered **another army, larger than the first** (11:13), and went on the offensive. As for the **many who will rise against the king of the South** (11:14), this may refer to external forces, such as Philip V of Macedonia, who made an alliance with Antiochus, as well as to internal revolts that erupted at this time in Egypt. The uprisings came partly as a response to Agathocles, the highly unpopular minister who wielded great power earlier during the reign of Ptolemy IV. At the death of Ptolemy IV, Agathocles was poised to become even more oppressive, since Ptolemy V was too young to rule on his own. However, Agathocles was assassinated in one of the riots.

The next section of chapter 11 is somewhat impenetrable. **The violent men among your own people will rebel** (11:14) may be describing a party of Jews who opposed Egyptian rule and favored the Syrians. During Antiochus III's attack, when he seized Judah at first, perhaps some of the Jews helped the invaders. However, Scopus, Ptolemy V's general, was able to repel the Syrians, taking Judah back. Another possibility is that these pro-Seleucid Jews carried out against Scopus an insurrection that he quelled. Either way, for the moment they stumbled (the Hebrew term *wenikshalu* [from the root *kshl*] is feebly represented in the NIV, which simply says they rebelled **without success** [11:14]) because Scopus was in control. It is unclear what **vision** they were seeking **fulfillment** of by their sedition (11:14). Since they failed, we might argue that the author of Daniel is representing them negatively as having followed a false vision. The author opposes their action on behalf of Antiochus III, because the latter was the father of the wicked Antiochus IV. Perhaps the author means they were seeking fulfillment of the vision of the end and the coming of the kingdom of God. If so, they were mistaken about the timing and their ability to bring it about. Later, Daniel uses a word from the same root (*kshl*) to describe those who will stumble (NIV "fall") in the time of Antiochus IV (11:33–34). At that time they "will receive a little help" (11:34). This probably refers to the Maccabean revolt, which could help a little but could not usher in the end. The author does not have confidence in human attempts to establish God's kingdom.

Although Scopus drove out the Seleucid army and enjoyed a brief period of renewed control over Israel, he could not hold on to it. **The king of the North** built **up siege ramps** and captured **a fortified city** (11:15), which probably refers to Sidon. When Antiochus III returned, he won a great victory over Scopus at Paneas, one of the sources of the Jordan River (later called Caesarea Philippi in Roman times: Matt. 16:13; Mark 8:27). Scopus moved the remnant of his army to Sidon, where he was besieged and forced to surrender in 198 B.C. The Egyptian army was **powerless to resist** (11:15). **The invader,** Antiochus III, could **do as he** pleased; **no one** could **stand against him** (11:16). (Similar things are said of Persia [8:4], Alexander the Great [11:3], and Antiochus IV [11:36]). The land of Israel, **the Beautiful Land** (11:16; see also Dan. 8:9; 11:41; and Jer. 3:19), had passed from Egyptian hands to Syrian. As time went on, this produced disastrous consequences for the Jewish people, but initially they welcomed the change. When Antiochus entered Jerusalem, they cheered the Syrian army, offered them food, and helped drive out the Egyptian guard that had been stationed there. To reward them, the king in turn gave them some tax relief (Josephus, *Ant.* 12.3.3).

Antiochus now determined **to come with the might of his entire kingdom** (11:17) against Egyptian territory. The text actually does not say which king came against another, but it seems best to read this statement in connection with Antiochus's campaign against Ptolemaic possessions on the southern coast of Asia Minor. Next, the MT has "and upright ones with him and he will make" (11:17), which is confusing. It is better to read **and** "he" **will make an alliance** "with him" (11:17), following the Greek. The NIV adds **with the king of the South** (11:17), which is not in the Hebrew, although the "him" does refer to Ptolemy. Antiochus had ambitions of taking over more of Asia Minor and parts of Europe, farther west. Politically, he felt the need to make peace with Egypt, so he gave Ptolemy V Epiphanes **a daughter in marriage** (11:17), namely, Cleopatra I. Apparently, he also had an ulterior motive: he was hoping that out of loyalty to her father she would help him overthrow Ptolemy. Therefore, he arranged the marriage not only to buy peace but also "to destroy him," that is, the Egyptian king (NIV **in order to overthrow the kingdom** [11:17]; see the Additional Note on 11:17). Much to his chagrin, she turned out to be more loyal to her husband than to her father. Furthermore, Rome threatened the expansion of Antiochus, with the result that **his plans did not succeed** (11:17).

Antiochus III next turned **his attention to the coastlands** and took **many of them** (11:18). In 196 he campaigned in Asia Minor, subduing areas along the coast. He continued westward across the Hellespont into Thrace and Macedonia. By 192 he was advancing southward through Greece—action that Rome could not tolerate. The Romans did not want Antiochus III to get too much land and power, so at this point they intervened. The Roman **commander** Lucius Cornelius Scipio (later awarded the title Asiaticus for his victories over Antiochus) **put an end to his insolence** (11:18) by vanquishing the Seleucid king at Thermopylae in 191. "Insolence" may refer to his haughty attitude toward the Romans, who had warned him not to invade Greece; he defied them by doing so. Antiochus retreated into Asia Minor, where he was pursued by the Roman army. At Magnesia (not far from Ephesus), Scipio dealt the Syrians a second crushing defeat. At Apamea (ca. 189), he subsequently imposed upon Antiochus a humiliating peace agreement, forcing him to relinquish his territory in Greece, Macedonia, Thrace, and almost all of Asia Minor (he retained only Cilicia). In addition Antiochus was required to pay huge reparations and to leave his son, Antiochus IV, as a hostage in Rome. He had no recourse but to **turn back toward the fortresses of**

his own country (11:19) in order to raise money to pay Rome. Out of desperation he decided to rob the temple of Bel in Elymais (in Persia) in 187. In the process he was killed by an angry mob of locals: he stumbled and fell, **to be seen no more** (11:19).

11:20 / Verse 20 is transitional: its purpose is to move the reader from the great king Antiochus III, whose large ambition and fateful conquests brought the Jews into his domain, to Antiochus IV, whose overweening pride and oppressive actions brought him into conflict with the Jews. The immediate successor of Antiochus III was his son Seleucus IV Philopator. Saddled with indemnity and tribute payments to Rome, he sent out a tax collector to maintain the royal splendor (11:20). A dispute had arisen between Onias III, the high priest, and Simon, the "captain of the temple" (2 Macc. 3:4 NRSV). When Simon's will was stymied, he sought revenge by arranging an assault on the temple treasury; he went to Apollonius, the governor, to report that the temple contained fabulous wealth. Apollonius reported the matter to the king, who sent Heliodorus, his head official (the "tax collector"), to Jerusalem to claim the temple's funds. According to Jewish tradition, Heliodorus's mission was not successful, because a visitation from heaven thwarted him. A rider on a horse and two men appeared, who beat Heliodorus until he collapsed and was carried away (2 Macc. 3).

The NIV has **In a few years, however, he will be destroyed** (v. 20). Literally, the Hebrew says, "in a few days." Perhaps the writer used this expression to signify the shortness of Seleucus's reign—only twelve years (187–175). Alternatively, it is also possible that the author refers to the plot to murder the king, which only took a few days to plan and carry out. After Antiochus IV (the son of Antiochus III and brother of Seleucus IV) had been a hostage for about fourteen years, Demetrius, the son of Seleucus IV, was sent to Rome to take his place. While Antiochus IV was on his journey home, Heliodorus, mentioned above, had the king killed. Thus Seleucus IV was **destroyed, yet not . . . in battle** (11:20). The text also says he did not die **in anger** (11:20). If this means the anger of battle, then it could make sense (NAB "not in conflict"). However, it is also possible that the word translated "anger" should actually be rendered "publicly" (NEB "openly"; JB "publicly"), because Seleucus did not die in plain view or in a war but secretly by murder.

11:21–24 / This section introduces and then focuses on the wicked Seleucid king Antiochus IV (175–163). Daniel announces that he (Seleucus IV) will be succeeded by a contemptible person (11:21).

Although Heliodorus was able to murder his master, he did not obtain the kingdom, because Eumenes, the king of Pergamum, assisted Antiochus IV so that he could invade and seize it (11:21). The author unleashes his ire on Antiochus IV, calling him "contemptible" because he desecrated the temple and persecuted the Jews. Earlier he was decried as one who "spoke boastfully" (7:8, 20; cf. 7:11) and who "will speak against the Most High and oppress his saints" (7:25). He exalts himself to the sky, casts down members of the heavenly host, makes himself equal to the Prince of the host, stops the daily sacrifice, damages the temple, and throws truth to the ground (8:10–12). He is "a stern-faced king, a master of intrigue," who "will cause astounding devastation" and "will destroy mighty men and the holy people" (8:23–24). He will "cause deceit to prosper" and "consider himself superior"; "he will destroy many and take his stand against the Prince of princes" (Dan. 8:25). Other Jewish writers depict Antiochus IV as "a sinful root" (1 Macc. 1:10 NRSV) and "an arrogant and terrible man" (4 Macc. 4:15 NRSV). He is characterized as one who has not been given the honor of royalty (11:21). The legitimacy of his reign is questioned because his nephew, Demetrius (held hostage in Rome), the son of Seleucus IV, was next in line (and in fact did become king later: 162–150). Antiochus Epiphanes grasped the crown through intrigue (11:21). This may refer to the arrangement whereby Antiochus initially ruled as coregent with another nephew (also called Antiochus), one of Seleucus IV's sons—an arrangement that Antiochus IV violated when he had the youth murdered in order to become the sole king.

The NIV has **Then an overwhelming army will be swept away before him** (11:22). This gives the impression that there was a specific army that Antiochus destroyed at the beginning of his rule. It may be that the writer conceives of battles at the time of Antiochus's accession, but since the second half of the verse refers to a later event (the death of Onias III), it is more likely that this verse gives a summary of Antiochus IV's career. In other words, events are not in strict chronological order here. Because of this, we should leave out the word "then," which is an optional rendering of the conjunction and gives a false impression that the events of verse 22 follow in time those of verse 21. This statement is, rather, a general comment on the warring nature of this monarch and armies he defeated over time, not a reference to a particular battle. In addition, the last phrase of the verse lacks a verb: "and also a prince of a covenant" or "and also a covenant prince." The NIV takes the verb *weyishaberu*, "and they will be broken," with what follows it: **both it and a prince of the covenant will be destroyed** (translating "destroyed" instead of "broken"; 11:22); but it should be read with what goes before it: forces will be utterly swept away before him and broken—and also a covenant prince. The verse's ending is dangling, yet the meaning is clear: a covenant prince will fall. This is a reference to the murder of Onias III in 170 B.C. (see also 9:26). He had been high priest but was deposed for resisting the hellenizing program of Antiochus IV. Although it was not the king who ordered the killing of Onias but a rival high priest, Menelaus, the slaying was the result of the king's policy of selling the high priesthood to the highest bidder and to someone sympathetic to assimilation. Therefore, the biblical writer is being fair and accurate in laying the blame at the door of the Syrian monarch.

Antiochus was not a man of integrity. **After coming to an agreement,** he would **act deceitfully** (11:23). Some scholars look for a historical point of reference here. Perhaps the "agreement" alludes to the help Pergamum gave to Antiochus (Collins, *Daniel*, p. 382). If they supported him with the understanding that he would protect the interests of Seleucus IV's sons (Goldingay, *Daniel*, p. 299), they were mistaken, for he "acted deceitfully" by murdering the son who shared the throne with him. Another possibility might be the duplicitous expressions of goodwill the Syrian king offered to the Egyptian king, Ptolemy VI Philometor (181–146), Cleopatra's son and Antiochus's nephew (Driver, *Daniel*, p. 182). Or, the author might be thinking of the king's dealings with the Jews when he deposed and appointed high priests according to the money and loyalty they offered him (Montgomery, *Daniel*, p. 451) or when he made Judaism illegal (9:27). Finally, because it is not clear what event is in view, it may be best to consider this simply another general statement about Epiphanes's character. He did not need a huge force initially. Because he had the support of Pergamum, was related to Seleucus IV, and was willing at first to accept coregency, he had a much better claim than Heliodorus, who fled. There may have been some resistance, but he did not need a huge army to establish himself on the throne. Rather, **with only a few people** he was able to **rise to power** (11:23).

A lot of wealth went through the hands of Antiochus IV. **When the richest provinces** felt **secure,** he would **invade them** and take their possessions. He would then **distribute plunder, loot and wealth among his followers** (11:24). In this regard he was able to **achieve** much more than **his fathers** or **his forefathers** (11:24). At a point when his treasury was empty he determined to go to Persia to collect more taxes: "He feared that he might not have such funds as he had before for his expenses and for the gifts that he used to give more lavishly than preceding kings" (1 Macc. 3:30 NRSV). He sometimes doled out resources to build up cities in his realm, and he also gave generously to temples (Polybius, *Hist.* 26.10).

The text does not tell us which **fortresses** he plotted to **overthrow** (Dan. 11:24). However, the author of Daniel may be alluding to Antiochus's first war with Egypt. His forces "captured the fortified cities in the land of Egypt, and he plundered the land of Egypt" (1 Macc. 1:19 NRSV). The Seleucid king would not always be successful, however. He would plan attacks—**but only for a time** (Dan. 11:24). This means that God, who is in control, had determined an end to his activities (see also 11:27, 35).

11:25–28 / The author now details Antiochus's first invasion of Egypt (ca. 170 B.C.): with a large army he stirred up his strength and courage against the king of the South (11:25). The same event is chronicled in 1 Maccabees: "When Antiochus saw that his kingdom was established, he determined to become king of the land of Egypt, in order that he might reign over both kingdoms. So he invaded Egypt with a strong force, with chariots and elephants and cavalry and with a large fleet" (1 Macc. 1:16–17 NRSV). Ptolemy VI Philometor, Antiochus's nephew, attempted to wage war with a large and very powerful army, but he was unable to stand (11:25). Ptolemy's failure resulted from plots devised against him (11:25) and from **those who eat from the king's provisions** (11:26). This may be pointing to Ptolemy's two counselors, Eulaeus and Lenaeus, who encouraged the king to try to recover from Antiochus land that had previously belonged to Egypt. This foolish plan may have precipitated the Syrian invasion. Ptolemy's army was swept away, and many fell in battle (11:26; similarly "many were wounded and fell" [1 Macc. 1:18 NRSV]). After his army was defeated by Antiochus, "Ptolemy turned and fled before him" (1 Macc. 1:18 NRSV), but he was captured. Antiochus was able to take the important fortress of Pelusium (Dan. 11:24; 1 Macc. 1:19).

When Ptolemy VI had become king of Egypt, he was a teenager. Because of his youth, he had perhaps been controlled too much by his advisers. Antiochus now proceeded to subdue Egypt, professing that he was securing it for his nephew, Ptolemy. This is probably what the book of Daniel means when it says that **the two kings, with their hearts bent on evil, will sit at the same table and lie to each other** (11:27). Antiochus pretended to have an avuncular concern, while Ptolemy had to express false gratitude (Driver, *Daniel*, p. 184). However, the meetings and lies were **to no avail** (11:27); the strife between them would continue. Its end would not come until some future **appointed time** (11:27).

After his conquest, Antiochus began his return **to his own country with great wealth** (Dan. 11:28; see also 1 Macc. 1:19), leaving Egypt in the control of his vassal nephew, Ptolemy VI Philometor. **But his heart was set against the holy covenant** (Dan. 11:28). On his way back to Syria,

Antiochus stopped to **take action against it** (11:28) in Jerusalem. He plundered the holy temple, stealing most of its wealth: "He arrogantly entered the sanctuary and took the golden altar, the lampstand for the light, and all its utensils. He took also the table for the bread of the Presence, the cups for drink offerings, the bowls, the golden censers, the curtain, the crowns, and the gold decoration on the front of the temple; he stripped it all off. He took the silver and the gold, and the costly vessels; he took also the hidden treasures that he found" (1 Macc. 1:21–23 NRSV; cf. Dan. 1:2; 5:1–4, 5, 22–30). In addition to sacking the Jerusalem sanctuary, Antiochus killed many Jews (1 Macc. 1:24), after which he returned home.

11:29–35 / At the appointed time (11:29), Antiochus conducted a second campaign in Egypt (ca. 168 B.C.). What led up to this was a surprising turn of events. Ptolemy Philometor had a brother, Ptolemy Physcon (later called Euergetes), who earlier had been a rival for the throne. However, the two brothers now united to form a league in opposition to Antiochus Epiphanes, which so angered the Seleucid king that he decided to invade the South again (11:29). However, this time the outcome was different from what it was before (11:29). The reason for Epiphanes's failure was the intervention of Rome. The text mentions "ships of Kittim" (NIV **ships of the western coastlands**; see the Additional Note on 11:30) that will oppose him, and he will lose heart (11:30). This refers to the Roman legate Gaius Popilius Laenas, who came by sea with a contingent from Rome and forced a reluctant Epiphanes to withdraw his army. (For more details, see "Historical Background" in the Introduction.) This experience was not merely a defeat but a major humiliation in front of the Egyptians, the Romans, and his own army. As a result, he was already enraged when he entered the land of Israel.

Unfortunately for the Jews, events there only increased his wrath. Apparently a rumor reached Jerusalem that Antiochus had been not only defeated but killed. Jason, who had been deposed as high priest earlier by Antiochus, sought to take advantage of this situation by assembling an armed force to reinstate him in the office. Menelaus, the high priest whom Antiochus had appointed to replace Jason, hid in the citadel. Antiochus, thinking there was an open revolt against him, responded violently (2 Macc. 5:5–11): he vented **his fury against the holy covenant** by persecuting the devout Jews, and he showed **favor to those** Jews who forsook **the holy covenant** (11:30) and who embraced Hellenistic culture and religion.

Antiochus's **armed forces** arose **to desecrate the temple fortress** (11:31). They forced Jason to flee and reestablished Menelaus as high priest. They abolished **the daily sacrifice** (11:31; see also 8:11). The king sent out letters "to forbid burnt offerings and sacrifices and drink offerings in the sanctuary, to profane sabbaths and festivals, to defile the sanctuary and the priests, to build altars and sacred precincts and shrines for idols, to sacrifice swine and other unclean animals, and to leave their sons uncircumcised. They were to make themselves abominable by everything unclean and profane" (1 Macc. 1:45–48 NRSV). Moreover, the royal officers dedicated the Jerusalem temple to Olympian Zeus (2 Macc. 6:2) and **set up the abomination that causes desolation** (11:31; see also Dan. 8:13; 9:27; 12:11; Matt. 24:15; Mark 13:14). This seems to have been a pagan altar installed on top of Yahweh's altar of burnt offering (1 Macc. 1:54, 59). On it were sacrificed "abominable offerings" (2 Macc. 6:5 NRSV), thought to be swine, which were ritually unclean animals according to Jewish law.

With flattery Antiochus corrupted **those who** had **violated the covenant** (11:32). An example of the influence the Syrians tried to exert can be seen when the king's officers came to the village of Modein. There they attempted to entice Mattathias and his sons to participate in a pagan sacrifice. They said to Mattathias: "You are a leader, honored and great in this town, and supported by sons and brothers. Now be the first to come and do what the king commands, as all the Gentiles and the people of Judah and those that are left in Jerusalem have done. Then you and your sons will be numbered among the Friends of the king, and you and your sons will be honored with silver and gold and many gifts" (1 Macc. 2:17b–18 NRSV). In this case it was unsuccessful, though, because Mattathias confessed that he and his family would "continue to live by the covenant of our ancestors" (1 Macc. 2:20 NRSV). When a Jew stepped forward to participate in the sacrifice, Mattathias killed him as well as the officer and tore down the altar (1 Macc. 2:23–26). Thus began the Maccabean revolt. Elsewhere there were apostate Jews who were all too happy to abandon their religion in order to please the king: "Many of the people, everyone who forsook the law, joined them, and they did evil in the land" (1 Macc. 1:52 NRSV). However, others remained faithful: **the people who** knew **their God** were resolute in their actions (Dan. 11:32), refusing to eat pork or meat sacrificed to pagan gods: "But many in Israel stood firm and were resolved in their hearts not to eat unclean food. They chose to die rather than to be defiled by food or to profane the holy covenant; and they did die" (1 Macc. 1:62–63 NRSV).

"The wise ones" (Heb. *maskilim*; here in 11:33, 35 and also in 12:3, 10) among the Jews are highlighted for special treatment: **those who are wise will instruct many** [*rabbim*] (11:33). While some commentators (e.g., Hartman and Di Lella, *Daniel*, p. 299) identify "the wise ones" with the

Hasideans or Hasidim (Heb. *khasidim* "pious ones"), who are mentioned in the books of Maccabees (1 Macc. 2:42–44; 7:13; 2 Macc. 14:6), it is an unlikely connection. Whereas the Hasideans were soldiers in Judas Maccabeus's army, the apocalyptist who wrote Daniel apparently was not. He is not looking for deliverance to come from below, by human means. On the contrary, he is looking for the kingdom of God to come from above, brought from heaven to earth by a supernatural act of God, as portrayed in Daniel 7 (Collins, *Daniel*, p. 385). The author of Daniel identifies with this group known as "the wise ones" and considers himself a member. They are the ones who understand the revelations concerning the end times and the coming kingdom of God. These will bear the responsibility for teaching "the many," that is, the masses of untutored ones. It is possible that this is an allusion to the Suffering Servant in Isaiah 40–55, because of the use of "wise" and "many." Yahweh's servant "will act wisely" (*yaskil*; Isa. 52:13) and "will justify many" (*rabbim*; Isa. 53:11; cf. Dan. 12:3; see Ginsberg, "Oldest Interpretation of the Suffering Servant," pp. 400–404). He will do this through vicarious suffering. Likewise, here in Daniel the wise ones will suffer intense persecution: **they will fall by the sword or be burned or captured or plundered** (11:33).

When the wise ones **fall, they will receive a little help** (11:34). The help is usually associated with the Maccabean revolt. The apocalyptist does not expect ultimate deliverance to come from that quarter, but he acknowledges the Maccabees' attempts to drive out the Syrian Greeks during the time of persecution. If this interpretation is correct, then this verse (and perhaps the whole book, except for the epilogue, Dan. 12:5–13) can be dated to the interval between 167 and 164 B.C. It must be after the beginning of the persecution and the revolt, because these are alluded to, but before the final victory in 164, when it would be apparent that the armed struggle was more than "a little help."

Not all who follow the teachings of the wise ones, the ones who truly understand the revelations about the future, are trustworthy. Daniel warns that **many who are not sincere will join them** (11:34). This might refer to the Hasideans (Collins, *Daniel*, p. 386). They agreed with the wise ones about being faithful to Jewish practice but disagreed about how Antiochus Epiphanes would be overthrown. The wise ones believed God would do it directly, while the Hasideans believed they should go on the offensive. Some of the Hasideans may have formed alliances with the wise ones without being forthright about their differences. Another possibility is that the insincere ones were the apostate Jews. Before the Maccabean revolt, they were protected by the king's army. After the revolt began, they were attacked by the pious Jews (1 Macc. 1:44; 3:5–8), which might have forced some to join the resistance, although they did not not join earnestly, but only because they were coerced (Goldingay, *Daniel*, p. 303).

Some of the wise will stumble, that is, be martyred, **so that they may be refined, purified and made spotless until the time of the end** (11:35). This may hint at a concern for "individual salvation" (Collins, *Daniel*, p. 386), or it may express hope for the resurrection (12:1–3; see Lacocque, *Daniel*, pp. 230–31). It can also be read in such a way that "they" refers to the survivors, not the martyrs. In that case it means that although some will be killed, their deaths will have the effect of purifying the rest of the faithful community. "To refine" and "to purify" are drawn from the metal-production industry. Metals would be heated in the fire to burn off impurities. The term translated "made spotless" in the NIV comes from clothing production and actually means "made white." The same three verbs are repeated in the next chapter: "Many will be purified, made spotless and refined" (Dan. 12:10; see also Rev. 3:18). It is important to recognize the theme of threats to the Jews as a unifying link between the court stories in the first half of the book and the visions in the second half. Daniel and his friends could have been forced to transgress the Jewish dietary laws or to face punishment if they had failed their health test (Dan. 1:8–15). Shadrach, Meshach, and Abednego were cast into the fiery furnace for refusing to bow down before the image (Dan. 3), and Daniel was thrown to the lions for praying to his God when it was forbidden (Dan. 6). So it is that persecution of the Jews is expressed or implied also in chapters 7–12 (Dan. 7:21, 25; 8:10–13; 9:26–27) and especially here in chapter 11, where martyrdom is explicit.

The end will come when God determines it, at his **appointed time** (11:35; see also Dan. 8:17, 19; 10:14; 11:27, 40, 45; Hab. 2:3). This was a word of comfort, because the persecution could not continue any longer than God permitted (Hartman and Di Lella, *Daniel*, p. 301). Included in the end would be the death of Antiochus Epiphanes (11:40–45). This notion of an appointed end is mirrored in the NT in the teaching of Jesus that the Father has determined a time for the return of Christ, which no one knows—not the angels and not even the Son (Matt. 24:36). For those who are troubled about the doctrine of predestination, the Bible does not teach that humans are automata or puppets on strings. God has not predetermined every move we make, so we really do have freedom when it comes to individual decisions, whether trivial (e.g., deciding which shirt to wear in the morning) or significant (e.g., choosing whether to follow God or the world). Nevertheless, he is the sovereign Lord of history who directs its course and will bring all things to fulfillment in his time.

11:36–39 / The king, Antiochus IV, will do as he pleases (11:36). The same is said of Persia (the ram; 8:4), Alexander the Great (11:3), and Antiochus III (11:16). However, the legitimacy of their power is questionable, and their dominions are temporal. God also does as he pleases (4:35), but his reign is just and his kingdom is eternal (4:34).

The statement **He will exalt and magnify himself above every god** (11:36) repeats an earlier theme: the hubris of Antiochus IV. He set himself up "to be as great as the Prince of the host," that is, God (some say it is Michael, but see the commentary on 8:11). This may be an allusion to the figure who seeks to lift himself to the level of God in Isaiah 14 and Ezekiel 28 (Collins, *Daniel*, p. 386). The measure of his self-aggrandizement can be seen in the coins Antiochus IV minted where in his likeness he fashioned himself as Zeus. The epitome of arrogance is apparent also in the inscription he put on some of these coins in the latter part of his reign: "Of King Antiochus, God Manifest, Victory-Bearer." The title "Victory-Bearer" was an epithet of Zeus Olympios (Driver, *Daniel*, pp. 191–93) and Apollo (Collins, *Daniel*, p. 387). Because Antiochus was such a megalomaniac, behind his back some mockingly called him Epimanes, "the mad one," instead of Epiphanes, "God manifest." In an echo of Daniel 11:36, the apostle Paul predicts that the coming Antichrist "will oppose and will exalt himself over everything that is called God or is worshiped, so that he sets himself up in God's temple, proclaiming himself to be God" (2 Thess. 2:4).

Verse 36 continues: the king **will also say unheard-of things against the God of gods** (11:36). This is reminiscent of the horn with "a mouth that spoke boastfully" (7:8) and that "will speak against the Most High" (7:25). Although we do not have specific examples of Antiochus's blasphemies from history, this claim is believable, knowing this king's character. In Hebrew, "x of x" indicates the superlative, as in "Song of Songs" (Song 1:1), which is "the greatest song"; "holy of holies" or "the Most Holy Place" (Exod. 26:33, 34); and "vanity of vanities," which means "most vain" (Eccl. 1:2; NIV "meaningless"). The term "God of gods," then, means "the greatest God," which for Israelite monotheists signified the one true God, who was and is greater than all other "gods" (falsely so called).

The king **will be successful until the time of wrath is completed, for what has been determined must take place** (11:36). Daniel uses language similar to Isaiah's (Isa. 10:23, 25; see the Additional Note on 11:36). The "time of wrath," or "indignation," most likely refers to the fury of Antiochus vented against the Jews (Collins, *Daniel*, p. 386; some take it to speak of the wrath of God: e.g., Lucas, *Decoding Daniel*, p. 289, and Hartman and Di Lella, *Daniel*, p. 237). Heaven will not allow this period to go on indefinitely, for God has decreed a set time for it to end.

It is not clear how Antiochus showed **no regard for the** various **gods** (11:37). In fact, Polybius gives him credit for worshiping many gods (Polybius, *Hist.* 30.25–26). Perhaps this verse refers to the fact that he plundered temples to fill his treasury. By putting himself ahead of the cults he robbed, he showed that he exalted **himself above them all** (11:37). The god **desired by women** (11:37) is usually identified as Tammuz, a Babylonian god who was loved by Ishtar and who died young; his female devotees would mourn his death (Ezek. 8:14).

The identity of the **god unknown to his fathers** whom the king honors **with gold and silver, with precious stones and costly gifts** (11:38) is something of a puzzle. We know that Antiochus set up a shrine to Zeus Olympios (2 Macc. 6:2). Because of the reference to the fertility cult, it seems likely that Zeus was identified with the Syrian god *Ba'al Shamem* (2 Macc. 6:4; cf. Additional Notes on Dan. 2:18; 8:13; and 9:27). This is further supported by the phrase *shiqquts shomem*, "desolating abomination" (Dan. 9:27; 11:31; 12:11), which is probably a deliberate corruption of *Ba'al Shamem*, intended to ridicule the pagan deity. The problem is the expression "unknown to his fathers." Zeus was certainly known and worshiped by previous Seleucid kings. *Ba'al Shamem* must have been known as well. The main god of the Seleucids, though, had been Apollo. Since Antiochus advanced the cult of Zeus / *Ba'al Shamem* at the expense of Apollo's cult, the text may simply mean that Zeus / *Ba'al Shamem* was not known in the sense of "recognized" or "acknowledged." In addition, the writer may be exaggerating in order to deride Antiochus (Collins, *Daniel*, p. 388).

Antiochus apparently trusted in Zeus for protection, as a **god of fortresses** (11:38). Verse 39 also mentions fortresses. The NIV goes too far with the translation: **he will attack the mightiest fortresses with the help of a foreign god** (11:39). More literally the MT says: "he will deal with the mightiest fortresses with [the help of] a foreign god." With a slight repointing of the text, it can be read: "he will deal with those who enclose fortresses—people of a foreign god." This makes more sense and connects better with the next two parts of the verse, because all three clauses are about people: **He will greatly honor those who acknowledge him. He will make them rulers over many people** (11:39). The fortress in view is the hated Akra, a citadel in Jerusalem built and guarded by "sinful people" (1 Macc. 1:34 NRSV), who may have included apostate Jews. However, Antiochus apparently placed a garrison of pagan Gentile soldiers there as well (1 Macc. 6:18–21) to control the city, attack the religious Jews, and "defile the environs of the sanctuary, doing great damage to its purity" (1 Macc. 14:36–37 NRSV; Montgomery, *Daniel*, pp. 460, 463). Not only did he "honor them" and "make them rulers," but he increased their real-estate holdings by stealing from the faithful Jews in order to **distribute** their **land** to the renegades and pagans **at a price** (11:39).

11:40–45 / Verses 40–45 pose some difficulties, not because the content is unclear but because the events recounted up to this point have dovetailed so well with external historical records while in contrast, the events of the last section of chapter 11 bear no relation to the end of Antiochus Epiphanes's life as we know it. For this reason some understand that a major shift takes place here so that the biblical writer is no longer describing the life of the oppressor of the second century B.C. but is depicting the Antichrist at the end of time. However, the notion of the Antichrist is anachronistic, since its source is the NT in the Roman era (1 John 2:18, 22; 4:3; 2 John 7). While the author of Daniel would not have thought in those terms, Christian commentators sometimes do. This interpretation goes back at least as far as the third century A.D. to Hippolytus, who saw the Antichrist in Daniel 11, beginning with verse 36. Jerome, who spanned the fourth and fifth centuries, marked the shift at verse 21, while John Chrysostom, who was roughly contemporary with Jerome, took the entire chapter to be about the Antichrist (Montgomery, *Daniel*, pp. 468–70). Some readers aver that it is the nature of biblical prediction to mix events of the distant future with events closer to the time of the prophet (Baldwin, *Daniel*, p. 202), but this is debatable.

While these verses may turn out to have some correspondence to events at the end of history, we cannot be certain of that. What does seem clear from reading Daniel 11 is that the biblical writer thinks he is continuing in verses 40–45 with the same story he began in verses 2–39, for there is no indication in the text that he has jumped ahead in time over many centuries. However, most modern scholars agree that he was recounting known historical events of his day up to verse 39, but that at verse 40 he has shifted to the future. In other words, he reports on what has happened to Antiochus IV until he gets to verse 39, after which he anticipates the fate of this blasphemer. The reason for thinking this is, as mentioned above, that the events "predicted" in verses 40–45 cannot be corroborated from historical sources. If these verses are intended to be understood as prophecy, then they seem to be in error. Therefore, we are forced to one of several possible conclusions.

1. These verses are intended as prophecy and are then false prophecy, because the events predicted did not come to pass. This would have

serious implications for our understanding of Scripture, especially for these particular verses.

2. The verses are intended as prophecy and either came to pass in history, perhaps some time after Antiochus IV, or will come to pass at the end of time with relation to some future Antichrist or tyrant who will persecute the faithful followers of God or Jesus Christ. The problems with this view are that it does not fit any known history and that there is no indication the author is talking about someone other than Antiochus IV Epiphanes. Furthermore, there is no clue that he jumps to the distant future. Some claim that the beginning of verse 40 ("At the time of the end") is such a sign, but this is not credible, because he has been talking of the end all along (11:27, 35, 36). Clearly, the writer thought the end was imminent and connected to the downfall of Antiochus IV. Finally, with regard to applying verses 40–45 to the Antichrist, there is no way to verify or falsify this hypothesis since the events are still to come.

3. The verses are not intended as prophecy but as a hope for what would happen to this wicked king who persecuted God's people. They are words of judgment on an evil oppressor, a denunciation of Antiochus and a call for heaven to answer by bringing justice. They are an expression of faith in a God who cannot allow such evil to continue unabated. They are the voice of an apocalyptic visionary who expected Antiochus to die in the holy land, who expected deliverance to come from above, and who expected the kingdom of God to arrive in his lifetime. In fact, Antiochus died in Persia; the deliverance of Jerusalem came from the Maccabean revolt; and the kingdom of God has still not appeared in its fullness. Yet, the author of Daniel is not a false prophet, because the literary genre is not prophecy. It is more akin to the imprecatory psalms, where the psalmist is pronouncing curses on a wicked fiend, so he is not really claiming to predict the future under the influence of the Holy Spirit. As Lucas explains, "This would then be not so much a prediction as a promise to the reader that Antiochus will meet an end befitting his blasphemous arrogance and his acts against God and against those who are faithful to God" (Lucas, *Decoding Daniel*, p. 293). Or, perhaps they are predictions, albeit human conjecture based on what the author thinks will happen according to certain Scriptures he is considering (for suggestions about these Scriptures and a discussion of them, see the commentary on 11:45).

A careful reading of Daniel and history leads to the conclusion that the third option is most compelling. Verses 40–45 are an expression of the apocalyptist's creative imagination; they are part of his vision for how things should turn out, given Epiphanes's intolerable hubris (Lucas,

Decoding Daniel, p. 293; Goldingay, *Daniel*, p. 305; Hartman and Di Lella, *Daniel*, p. 192). Although things did not transpire exactly as he hoped, that does not discredit his vision. This is similar to the NT, where the Christians in the early church believed that Jesus would come back in their lifetime. The fact that our Lord has delayed his return does not invalidate the apocalyptic message of the NT. Also, the seer, the humanlike figure talking with Daniel, was partly correct, in that the Seleucid tyrant did come to an ignominious end. He was also correct that one day in the future, God will bring his everlasting kingdom of justice and peace to earth, at which time he will raise everyone from the dead and judge them.

As he describes in chapter 11, the author of Daniel expects a series of events to lead to the death of Antiochus and the resurrection of the dead. Another war between Egypt and Syria will signal **the time of the end** (11:40). **The king of the South will engage** the king of the North in **battle** (11:40). The writer anticipates a final confrontation between Egypt and Syria, initiated by Egypt. Although, according to Jerome, Porphyry reported another war between Ptolemy VI Philometor and Antiochus IV, his account has Antiochus invading Egypt again rather than defensively staving off an attack. Since there is no evidence for this third war from contemporary records, it seems likely that Porphyry was simply following this verse in Daniel rather than historical sources. Furthermore, considering the humiliation Antiochus experienced at the hands of Rome in the previous conflict, it is improbable that he would ask for more of the same by attacking Ptolemy, for Rome was still guarding Egypt (Driver, *Daniel*, p. 197).

The apocalyptist expresses confidence in the superiority of Antiochus's forces: Antiochus will **storm out against** Egypt with an army (**chariots and cavalry**) and a navy (**a great fleet of ships**) (11:40). Although **Edom, Moab and the leaders of Ammon will be delivered from his hand** (11:41), **Egypt will not escape** (11:42). Antiochus will take possession of **all the riches of Egypt** and will conquer the **Libyans and Nubians** as well (11:43). He **will** also **invade many** other **countries** (11:40), including Israel—**the Beautiful Land** (11:41)—where "tens of thousands" of Jews **will fall** (11:41). Instead of campaigning in the south, Antiochus actually spent his last year and a half fighting in the northeastern region of his realm. Rather than being overwhelmed with **the treasures of gold and of silver** (11:43), he was strapped for funds. This lack of funds was, in fact, the impetus behind his last venture; he wanted to collect tribute money from his eastern provinces.

The visionary writer imagines **reports from the east and the north** that **will alarm** Antiochus (11:44). This calls to mind Sennacherib's invasion of Judah in 701 B.C. When he threatened Jerusalem, God gave Isaiah a word for King Hezekiah: "Listen! I am going to put such a spirit in him that when he hears a certain report, he will return to his own country, and there I will have him cut down with the sword" (2 Kgs. 19:7; cf. Isa. 37:7). In Daniel 11:44 the word for "reports" is *shemu'ot*; the same word in the singular (*shemu'ah*) is used in 2 Kings 19:7 and Isaiah 37:7. These tidings will cause the king of the North to **set out in a great rage to destroy and annihilate many** (11:44). This is similar to verse 30: "Then he will turn back and vent his fury against the holy covenant." But he will not succeed this time; rather, he will come to his end.

The king **will pitch his royal tents between the seas at the beautiful holy mountain** (11:45). Because Antiochus died in Persia, some have tried to locate "the seas" and "the beautiful holy mountain" in the east somewhere. This is not tenable, though, for the reference is clearly to Judah. "The seas" must be the Mediterranean (a poetic plural as in Deut. 33:19; Judg. 5:17), and "the beautiful holy mountain" can hardly be anything other than Mount Zion in Jerusalem. Israel is called "the Beautiful Land" in verses 16 and 41; "beautiful" occurs alone in Daniel 8:9 (NIV "Beautiful Land"). The author seems to be projecting earlier Scriptures upon the evil king, Antiochus. For instance, because the Assyrians threaten Judah, Isaiah pronounces judgment on them, predicting that they will fall in the vicinity of "the mount of the Daughter of Zion, at the hill of Jerusalem" (Isa. 10:32 gives the threat and location; see 10:33–34 for the word of judgment). In another example, the prophet declares, "I will break the Assyrian in my land; and on my mountains I will trample him down" (Isa. 14:25). The motif of Jerusalem being besieged and then delivered also figures poetically and generally in Isaiah 29:1–8 and Psalms 2, 46, 48, and 76. Similarly, Ezekiel condemns Gog: "I will . . . send you against the mountains of Israel. . . . On the mountains of Israel you will fall" (Ezek. 39:2, 4). Joel announces that God will gather the nations to the "Valley of Jehoshaphat" (which might be symbolic for Jerusalem) for judgment (Joel 3). The apocalyptic vision of Zechariah 14 reports that God "will gather all the nations against Jerusalem to fight against it" (Zech. 14:2), only to appear himself in order to fight against those nations and deliver the holy city (Zech. 14:3–9). This motif figures in Jewish works outside the Bible (see *1 En.* 56:6–8; *Sib. Or.* 3:663–701; *4 Ezra* 13:33–35), and it is also incorporated into the NT (Rev. 20:7–9).

Because Antiochus has perpetrated such heinous crimes against the Jews in Jerusalem, the author of Daniel is convinced that Antiochus must come to his end in Israel ("Beautiful Land"; 11:16, 41): **yet he will come to his end, and no one will help him** (11:45). Similarly, chapter 8 anticipates that God will supernaturally overthrow the king: "Yet he will be destroyed, but not by human power" (8:25). As far as we can tell from historical records, Antiochus came to his end after trying to rob the Temple of Artemis in Elymais. After being repelled by the worshipers, he moved to Tabae in Persia, where he was stricken with an illness that resulted in his death. Polybius reports, "In Syria King Antiochus, wishing to provide himself with money, decided to make an expedition against the sanctuary of Artemis in Elymaïs. On reaching the spot he was foiled in his hopes, as the barbarian tribes who dwelt in the neighbourhood would not permit the outrage, and on his retreat he died at Tabae in Persia, smitten with madness as some people say, owing to certain manifestations of divine displeasure when he was attempting this outrage on the above sanctuary" (Polybius, *Hist*. 31.9 [Paton, LCL]). There are several variants of this in Jewish tradition as preserved in the books of Maccabees. After failing to plunder the Elymais temple, Antiochus heard news of military success by the Jews against his forces in Judah. They not only had defeated the Syrian army but had removed the abomination in their temple and had restored the holy altar. "When the king heard this news, he was astounded and badly shaken. He took to his bed and became sick from disappointment, because things had not turned out for him as he had planned" (1 Macc. 6:8 NRSV). Then "he realized that he was dying" (2 Macc. 6:9 NRSV). He remembered all the evil he had done to the Jews, and he came to see his misfortune as the consequence of his sins. Apparently he died of despair (1 Macc. 6:1–17). An alternate account begins similarly. After being forced to retreat from the temple he was attempting to rob, and after hearing of his army's defeat in Judah, he was struck with an extremely painful disease in his internal organs. On his deathbed he vowed to make Jerusalem free and to become a Jew himself (2 Macc. 9:1–29). According to yet another version, Antiochus was killed while plundering a temple rather than after it. The priests were hiding above: "Opening a secret door in the ceiling, they threw stones and struck down the leader and his men; they dismembered them and cut off their heads and threw them to the people outside" (2 Macc. 1:16 NRSV).

12:1–3 / The revelation of chapter 11 continues through Daniel 12:1–4, so there should not be a chapter break here. This is clear from the temporal phrase **At that time** at the beginning of Daniel 12:1, which links this verse with the previous one; it refers to the time of the death of Antiochus IV (11:45). However, "that time" (12:1) occurs three times in the verse for emphasis and serves to connect this verse not only with what precedes but also with what follows: the death of the oppressor is thus joined to the great time of distress (12:1) and to the rescue that follows, because at that time the faithful Jews will be saved (12:1). More than that, this phrase has eschatological overtones, for in the mind of the humanlike seer, the end of Epiphanes signifies the ultimate end (see 11:24, 27, 35, 36, 40, 45). Furthermore, "at that time" is akin to "in/on that day," both of which are used eschatologically by the prophets to indicate a future time when God will intervene in human history (e.g., Isa. 26:1; 27:1–2; Jer. 3:17; 4:11; Joel 3:1–2; Zeph. 1:12; 3:19–20; Zech. 12:3–4; 13:1–2).

Therefore, when the end comes, Antiochus will die and **Michael, the great prince . . . , will arise** (12:1). On the one hand, Michael's arising may be military, since his role earlier in this final section of Daniel was to fight against the spirit princes of Persia and Greece (10:13, 20–21). In this context, then, presumably he appears in order to rescue the Jews by fighting against their oppressors, whether construed as the demons in the celestial realm or as their ungodly human counterparts. Michael is a great warrior **who protects** Daniel's **people** with the result that they **will be delivered** (12:1). The NT supports the martial role by portraying Michael as commander of the heavenly army, engaging in battle with the devil and his angels (Rev. 12:7). On the other hand, the arising may be judicial, because what follows suggests a courtroom scene and a judgment based on who is listed in a book. As such, it calls to mind the judgment setting of Daniel 7 (see esp. 7:10–11, 22, 26). Michael's function may be to carry out the sentence of destruction on God's enemies (Dan. 7:9–11, 26; see also Zech. 3:1–5; 11QMelch 2.13; *1 En.* 2:11–13), or perhaps he is to act as defense attorney for the Jews by arguing for their vindication. The NT supports the juridical understanding too by recounting how Michael enters into a legal dispute with Satan over the body of Moses before the bar of heaven (Jude 9). The two roles are not contradictory but complementary, so it is possible that the biblical writer intends to project both of them—Michael as combatant and advocate.

The "time of distress" will be greater than any previous one, yet Daniel's "**people—everyone whose name is found written in the book—will be delivered**" (12:1). Perhaps the writer is reflecting on Jeremiah 30:7: "How awful that day will be! None will be like it. It will be a time of trouble for Jacob, but he will be saved out of it." The notion of a great tribulation that will precede the second coming of Jesus is incorporated into NT apocalyptic theology too (Matt. 24:21–31; Mark 13:19–27; Luke 21:20–28; Rev. 7:14). "The book" is the book of life (Exod. 32:32–33; Ps. 69:28; Isa. 4:3; Ezek. 13:9; Mal. 3:16–18). In most of the OT, where there was no clear teaching concerning a resurrection, the book would have been understood to contain the names of those who were part of God's covenant people. Here in Daniel, which does teach the resurrection of the dead, it might be a list of those chosen to be raised from the dead, or it might just record those destined for life instead of death, meaning those who will survive the persecution. The belief in a book of life continues in the NT (Phil. 4:3; Rev. 3:5; 13:8; 17:8; 20:12, 15). This book is different from two other types of documents the seer speaking with Daniel is aware of: the books of judgment, which are records of individuals' deeds (Dan. 7:10; cf. Rev. 20:12), and the book of truth, which is an account of future events as God has predetermined them (Dan. 10:21).

Following the deliverance of Daniel's people will be a resurrection of the dead: **Multitudes who sleep in the dust of the earth will awake: some to everlasting life, others to shame and everlasting contempt** (12:2). This verse is remarkable in the light of other passages in the Hebrew Bible. Ancient Israelite religion taught that when humans die, they go to Sheol, the grave—a dark place where there is no praise of God (Pss. 6:5; 88:10–11; 115:17; Isa. 38:18–19). If it can be called life after death, it is not a very desirable one, for in that place "there is neither working nor planning nor knowledge nor wisdom" (Eccl. 9:10). Humans are no better than animals, for "all have the same breath" (Eccl. 3:19) and all will return to dust (Eccl. 3:19–21). While it is true that Enoch (Gen. 5:24) and Elijah (2 Kgs. 2:9–12) did not die, there is no promise in those stories that anyone else would have eternal life. In fact, the opposite is implied: only those two merited being taken to heaven, while everyone else will die and go to the grave, whether they are righteous or wicked, good or evil, whether one sacrifices or not—everyone experiences the same fate (Eccl. 9:2–3). Sometimes humans are brought back to life (2 Kgs. 4:18–37; 13:20–21), but these are special miracles, and presumably the individuals who were raised ultimately had to die again.

Although we encounter the motif of the resurrection in the famous dry bones passage in Ezekiel, it is used symbolically for the restoration of the people of God, not for the resurrection of individuals from the dead. When Ezekiel sees the dead bones come alive, it is a metaphor anticipating the return of the Jews from exile in Babylon (Ezek. 37). Sometimes Hosea 6:1–2 is cited in support for the doctrine of the resurrection in the OT: "Come, let us return to the LORD. He has torn us to pieces but he will heal us; he has injured us but he will bind up our wounds. After two days he will revive us; on the third day he will restore us, that we may live in his presence." For two reasons this is not apropos: first, like Ezekiel 37 it is about the restoration of the community, and second, the context seems to be healing rather than resurrection. It is thus like those psalms (e.g., Pss. 30:3; 86:13) that seem to talk about being brought back from the dead, when they are probably only about someone recovering from a life-threatening illness, as when people say today, "the patient had one foot in the grave." There is one more passage that might teach bodily resurrection: "But your dead will live; their bodies will rise. You who dwell in the dust, wake up and shout for joy. Your dew is like the dew of the morning; the earth will give birth to her dead" (Isa. 26:19). This verse is disputed, though, because some scholars interpret it analogically for the Israelite community, similar to Ezekiel 37. However, this verse is part of the "Isaianic Apocalypse" and may, like Daniel, also be very late in the history of the Bible (postexilic). As such, it is quite possible that whoever wrote it intended to teach a literal, bodily resurrection from the dead. In fact, because of the similar imagery between this passage and Daniel—waking from the dust—it may be that this verse inspired and influenced the author of Daniel. Nevertheless, since there is no consensus on Isaiah 26:19, and most agree that the other two passages are communal and symbolic, Daniel 12:2 is the first undisputed, unambiguous teaching on the resurrection of individuals from the dead in the Bible (it is found in the Apocrypha: e.g., 2 Macc. 7:9–23; 12:43–45).

But what does Daniel 12:2 actually teach? Many questions swirl around this passage because the formulation is so terse. Does it refer to a universal or partial resurrection? If partial, who will be raised, and what becomes of those who stay dead? Is it a bodily resurrection? Will the ones who rise live on earth or in heaven? Will the wicked rise too, or does "everlasting shame and contempt" mean that they will stay dead? If the wicked are raised, what does it mean to suffer "everlasting shame and contempt"? What actually becomes of them? Do they go to hell (i.e., some place of torment)?

The text does not seem to affirm a universal resurrection, because it stipulates that "multitudes" or "many" will rise, but not all. Although in certain contexts "many" might mean "the many"—indicating "the group" or "the whole"—it cannot mean that here, because of the particular Hebrew construction. The writer uses a partitive *min* to communicate that those who awake are a part of the whole (Collins, *Daniel*, p. 392). In other words, the whole group comprises the dead; a portion of them will return to life. The NIV obscures this by leaving out the word "from" or "of" in its translation. Instead of "multitudes who sleep . . . will awake" (NIV), a better translation is "many from among those who sleep . . . will awake" or "many of those who sleep . . . will awake." At the time that the book of Daniel was composed, the doctrine was in its incipient stage. As it developed in Judaism and Christianity, it became universally inclusive: the righteous and the wicked will be raised from the dead (John 5:28–29; Acts 24:15).

Who the "many" are is a more difficult question. It is important for the interpreter to consider the context carefully. The apocalyptist was mainly concerned about how his people, the Jews, were responding to the Seleucid persecution. Some were maintaining their faith, refusing to participate in the pagan cult, and suffering martyrdom (1 Macc. 1:60–64). Others were assimilating, eating pork that had been sacrificed to Zeus, and worshiping the Greek gods, in order to save their lives (1 Macc. 1:41–52). Therefore, it seems reasonable to follow a number of modern scholars (e.g., Collins, *Daniel*, p. 392; Anderson, *Signs and Wonders*, p. 149; Seow, *Daniel*, p. 188; and Towner, *Daniel*, p. 167) who argue that the author of Daniel understood the ones raised from the dead to be only Jews and only those who died during the time of conflict during Antiochus IV's reign. Those who had been faithful unto death would be raised **to everlasting life,** while those who had turned apostate would be raised **to shame and everlasting contempt** (12:2). Some commentators hold that Daniel 12:2 only predicts the resurrection of the righteous Jews, the renegade Jews being left in the grave to be treated with "shame and everlasting contempt" by the survivors (e.g., Hartman and Di Lella, *Daniel*, p. 297; Lacocque, *Daniel*, pp. 243–44). An argument for this view is the use of the word "contempt," which is only found in one other place in the Hebrew Scriptures, where it refers to the contempt the living ones have for the corpses of the rebels (Isa. 66:24; NIV "loathsome"). Once again, though, the Hebrew grammar is decisive, laying out two groups who will be raised. The structure "some . . . some [NIV "others"]" suggests the following meaning: many from the dead will rise—*some* of those who rise will attain everlasting life, while *some* who rise will experience shame and everlasting contempt. This resurrection is qualitatively different from revivification in that life continues forever. As already noted above, others who were raised from the dead had to die again (2 Kgs. 4:18–37; 2 Kgs. 13:20–21; cf. Lazarus in John 11), but Daniel speaks of "everlasting life" and "everlasting contempt" (Dan. 12:2).

There is no rationale given for this radically new understanding of life after death, and of course, we would not expect one since the author is presenting this as a vision that comes to Daniel, not as a theology developed through careful thinking. Nevertheless, there is a context for this belief in resurrection, and even if we accept that it comes by divine revelation, we might want to ask why God chose to make it known at this time. It seems to be a matter of theodicy. We have only to look at the writings of Ecclesiastes to see that in the absence of resurrection truth, life seems empty and vain. If in this life the righteous suffer and the wicked prosper (Eccl. 8:14), and there is no hope for redress of grievances in the next life (Eccl. 3:9–13; 9:1–6), "everything is meaningless" (Eccl. 1:2). The apocalyptist was sure that God would invade history to put a stop to the decimation of his people. But what about the people who had already been murdered for their faith? There must be justice for them. And what about the Jews who had betrayed their faith and their God? After dying were they to sleep peacefully in the grave with impunity? The author of Daniel could not accept the old dogma that the same fate awaits all (Eccl. 9:2–3), so he embraced a vision for justice beyond the grave that included a limited resurrection of the dead.

Unfortunately, the other questions evoked by Daniel 12:2 are not answered clearly by the text. It does not specify a bodily resurrection, so conceivably they could return from the grave as spirit beings, like angels. Since the Hebrew concept of humanity includes corporeal existence, that does not make the most sense, but we do not know. Neither does Daniel tell us what the resurrected ones do, how or where they live, or in what sense life goes on. There is no teaching about the creation of a new heaven and earth (cf. Isa. 66:22) or of a place of torment, like hell. Nor is there any mention of those who died in previous eras.

Verse 3 exhibits synonymous parallelism: **those who are wise,** in the first line, corresponds to **those who lead many to righteousness,** in the second; following the verb **will shine,** the phrase **like the brightness of the heavens** is parallel to **like the stars for ever and ever.** The "wise" are not just any wise people; they are the *maskilim* of Daniel 11:33—the group to which Daniel belongs. In that earlier verse their calling was to "instruct many" (i.e., the other Jews). Here, their task is to "lead many to righteousness," which is probably another way of saying the same thing (Collins, *Daniel*, p. 393). In other words, by teaching their fellow Jews, the wise are leading them to righteousness. This expression is an allusion to Isaiah 53:11, which says that Yahweh's servant "will lead many to righteousness" (NIV "will justify many"). In that passage, the servant makes others righteous through vicarious suffering, whereas here in Daniel, it is done through education. However, suffering is not absent from this context. The wise "will fall by the sword or be burned or captured or plundered" (Dan. 11:33). Moreover, as a result of this persecution, they "will stumble, so that they may be refined, purified and made spotless" (Dan. 11:35; cf. 12:10).

By saying that the wise "will shine like the brightness of the heavens" and "like the stars," the humanlike seer talking with Daniel intends to connect them somehow with the heavenly hosts, or angels. In the Bible, stars often symbolize celestial beings: in Job 38:7, the term "angels" is parallel with "morning stars"; in Judges 5:20, the "stars" who fought from heaven against Israel's enemy were probably understood to be members of God's army (see also Rev. 12:4). Within Daniel, though, is an even better example, in the vision of chapter 8. The little horn, representing Antiochus IV, lifts himself to the level of the heavenly host, even making himself as great as the Prince of the host, and casts down "some of the starry host" (Dan. 8:10–11). Here in Daniel 11:2b–12:4, there is a vision for the end when everything will be set right: Antiochus is destroyed; Michael stands up; the faithful martyrs are resurrected; and the wise are exalted like the stars. This reversal of roles serves to vindicate the righteous Jews: the one who elevated himself in hubris (Dan. 8:10–11; 11:36–37) is debased, while the ones who were brought low by the evil king's oppression (Dan. 8:10; 11:33–35) are raised up to shine in the firmament. The text does not explicitly say that the wise humans will actually become stars or angels after the resurrection; it says only that their effulgence will resemble that of the heavenly host. Therefore, the connection between the ones who lead many to righteousness and the celestial bodies is symbolic, not literal.

12:4 / Daniel is instructed to close up and seal the words of the scroll until the time of the end (12:4). A better translation for the first verb is "to keep hidden" or "secret" rather than merely "to close up" as in the NIV. Similarly, Gabriel tells him earlier to "seal up the vision" of chapter 8, "for it concerns the distant future" (8:26). One wonders, then, whether this new command applies only to the last revelation, communicated in Daniel 10:2b–12:3, or whether it concerns the whole book. It seems to be the latter, since the epilogue, which concludes the book, makes an additional reference to the sealing: "Go your way, Daniel, because the words are closed up and sealed until the time of the end" (12:9). The secrecy is part and parcel of apocalyptic literature, with its pseudonymous authorship and *ex eventu* (after the event) form of prophecy, where the apocalyptist writes about happenings in his own time as if they were predicted in an earlier age. Although the book may be written in the second century, the writer takes on the guise of Daniel, a hero of faith from the days of the Babylonian exile in the sixth century. The author records visions and predictions for his own day (likely the Hellenistic era during the time when Antiochus IV is persecuting the Jews), utilizing the voice of an ancient revered prophet in order to encourage his oppressed coreligionists. One element that goes with the writing of this apocalyptic book is that the book was to be sealed and hidden away until the time of the end. Then it would be discovered, opened, and read, with the result that people in the last days would be amazed at how well it addressed their situation and also would be strengthened to be faithful unto death, knowing that there is hope of a resurrection. The author is telling his audience that the book has no relevance for the people in exile because it concerns what is in the distant future in relation to them. In fact, the Jews of Daniel's day would not even see the scroll, for it would be hidden away. It speaks to those living in the time just before the coming of the kingdom of God, which the biblical writer thought would be in his century. In contrast to Daniel, in the NT apocalypse John is told: "Do not seal up the words of the prophecy of this book, because the time is near" (Rev. 22:10; see also Rev. 5:1, 4–5; 10:4).

The fact that the book circulated in the time before Jesus supports the argument that its author was not attempting to predict the coming of the Antichrist or the second advent of Jesus. The idea is that the book would be opened when the events recorded in it were imminent. Yet the appearance of the Antichrist and the return of Christ would have been in the distant future from the perspective of Jews in the pre-Christian era, and they have still not transpired in our day over two thousand years later. Other events that the author of Daniel was trying to foretell, such as the resurrection and the complete manifestation of the kingdom of God, have also not been fulfilled yet. So, if the book was really written by Daniel in the exile and meant to presage those events, it should have remained hidden and sealed until just before the end, whenever that will be. Why was it opened and circulated so long before the actual apocalypse? Why does so much of the book seem to focus on the Hellenistic era and particularly the time of Antiochus IV? Why does it appear to announce that the end will come in that time? Many commentators arrive at this answer: the book was authored by an apocalyptic writer in the Hellenistic era who thought that he was living in the last days.

Those who prefer the traditional sixth-century date of Daniel have suggested that the reason the book of Daniel was known before the time of the end is that there were two copies made: a sealed original and a public copy that would have circulated. It is argued that the sealing was not to conceal it but to preserve the original from corruption (Miller, *Daniel*, p. 320). The evidence given to support this is a passage in Jeremiah where a real-estate document is prepared in this way (Jer. 32:9–12). However, since Daniel is an apocalyptic work, not a real-estate document, the goal of sealing appears to be really to hide it. If an open copy circulated, it would defeat the whole purpose of sealing and concealing the apocalyptic scroll, which was not supposed to become known until the end of time. Furthermore, no mention is made of such an open copy in the book of Daniel. It is clear from Jeremiah, the same book from which the above example comes, that biblical writers did not always make copies of scrolls, because Jeremiah had to dictate his words a second time to Baruch after the king burned the first scroll (Jer. 36:27–28). In addition, a sealed original would not necessarily preserve the text from tampering. If the purpose of sealing was to guard against errors entering into the text during the copying process, it would work only if the original was not lost and if it remained available (and unsealed) to compare against it any copies. As an example, we do not possess any original writings of Scripture—including Daniel—against which to compare our copies. All we have are copies of copies of copies, which have been subject to the imperfect process of scribal activity. Our copies, although quite accurate, do contain discrepancies and copy errors. Finally, it would have been disobedient for Daniel to produce an open copy for circulation after being expressly commanded to keep the scroll secret and sealed (12:4).

In the time of the end, **many will go here and there to increase knowledge** (12:4). The NIV translation is possible, but a more literal translation is "many will go here and there and knowledge will increase," or "many will go here and there that knowledge may increase" (author's translation; Montgomery, *Daniel*, p. 474). Scholars have puzzled over the meaning of this cryptic statement and its place in the chapter. It is helpful to consider a similar passage in Amos: "'The days are coming,' declares the Sovereign LORD, 'when I will send a famine through the land—not a famine of food or a thirst for water, but a famine of hearing the words of the LORD. Men will stagger from sea to sea and wander from north to east, searching for the word of the LORD, but they will not find it'" (Amos 8:11–12). The verb translated "wander" in Amos is the same verb rendered "go here and there" in Daniel. The NRSV has a better translation of Amos 8:12, because it more clearly shows that Daniel is alluding to it: "They shall wander from sea to sea, and from north to east; they shall run to and fro, seeking the word of the LORD, but they shall not find it." Daniel agrees with Amos that in the latter days, people will travel everywhere looking for God's word (Amos) or knowledge (in Daniel's terms), and although he does not go on to say it, as Amos does, the apocalyptist probably also concurs that they will not attain it. The reason for thinking this is the connection between the first half of Daniel 12:4 and the second half, which the Amos passage illuminates: because the revelations of Daniel are sealed up, people will seek information and understanding in vain. However, the implication is that once the book of Daniel is unsealed, then knowledge will be discovered and disseminated (Collins,

Daniel, p. 399). Another interpretation is that this verse refers to the time after Daniel's apocalypse is opened: many will go here and there and knowledge will indeed increase, because people will have access to this vital source of truth. This is a more upbeat point of view that actually clashes with the harsh judgment of Amos (Seow, *Daniel*, pp. 189–90). The above two explanations are based on the MT as it stands, and both make excellent sense. There is one final reading of the text, which involves a textual emendation: replacing "knowledge" with "evil" (see the Additional Note on 12:4). If this reading is correct, then the seer talking with Daniel is predicting a decline in society as things move toward the consummation of all things: "many will go here and there and evil will increase." It is difficult to choose among these interpretations, but the first is most compelling because it recognizes the allusion to Amos, which in turn accounts for the connection between the two parts of the verse.

So, what is Daniel 11–12 all about? Certainly, what is absolutely unique is the way these chapters, unlike other predictions in Scripture, include minute specifics. The author relentlessly pursues his purpose: simply to show that history has a *telos*—an end, a goal. He saw all of the secular events from the Persian era onward as leading up to his day in such a way that there was a crescendo of intensity. All of history was coming to a climax in the person of the arch-tyrant Antiochus IV and in the terrorizing of the Jewish people, with the result that the author anticipated an imminent divine intervention in human affairs. In his mind, God could not stand by idly and watch his covenant people continue to be slaughtered. The author fervently believed that heaven would destroy the oppressor, deliver the Jews under the aegis of the archangel Michael, raise many from the dead for the purpose of a judgment, and bring in the eternal reign of God. And we know he was correct about some things, for Antiochus did fall, and one day God will bring his kingdom with the concomitant resurrection and last judgment.

Additional Notes §11

Most of the historical details in Dan. 11:2–39, which chronicles Persian through Hellenistic times, can be corroborated from ancient sources; see esp. Polybius, Josephus, and 1 and 2 Maccabees. For histories of the period based on these and other writings from antiquity, see F. W. Walbank et al., eds., *The Hellenistic World* (vol. 7, pt. 1 of *The Cambridge Ancient History*; Cambridge: Cambridge University Press, 1984); V. Tcherikover, *Hellenistic Civilization and the Jews* (New York: Atheneum, 1975); and E. Schürer, *A History of the Jewish People in the Time of Jesus* (New York: Schocken, 1961).

11:2b / The trouble with this part of v. 2 comes at the end. The MT has *ya'ir hakkol 'et malkut yawan*. The particle *'et* usually introduces the definite direct object. Therefore, *malkut yawan*, **the kingdom of Greece**, should be the object of the verb *ya'ir*, **he will stir up**. The word *hakkol* ("all," "the whole"; NIV **everyone**) seems to be the subject. The result is "When he has gained power by his wealth, the whole will stir up the kingdom of Greece." What does "the whole" refer to? When it occurs, as here, with the definite article, its meaning generally comes from the context, that is, the "things (or persons) just mentioned" (BDB, p. 482). The thing referred to in the context is wealth. In other words, all the wealth of this king will stir up the kingdom of Greece. This means that the king of Greece will covet the wealth of Persia and go after it. It feels awkward, but it does make sense of the Hebrew and is the most natural way to read it. Most English translations are similar to the NIV, reading *'et* as "against" and taking *hakkol*, "the whole," as the object: "he shall stir up all against the kingdom of Greece" (RSV, NRSV). There is one instance where *'et* seems to mean "against" (Jer. 38:5), but this is rare. Furthermore, one would still expect an *'et* before *hakkol* if it is the object.

"The kingdom of Greece" may be a gloss, because it is surprising to have a nation identified here. This chapter tends to be enigmatic, mentioning "the king of the North" and "the king of the South," usually without naming them (Montgomery, *Daniel*, p. 424). Dan. 11:3–4 indubitably speaks of Alexander's kingdom, but in a cryptic manner, since these verses do not actually mention Greece. Perhaps the text originally said only, "he will stir up everyone," or "it [the wealth] will stir up everyone." Since that was elusive, a scribe added in "the kingdom of Greece" to make it clear.

11:5 / The Hebrew of this verse is peculiar. Nevertheless, it is possible to read *umin sarayw weyekhezaq 'alayw umashal mimshal rab memshalto* as **"but one of his commanders will become even stronger than he and will rule.** His dominion [is] a great dominion" (similarly, Collins, *Daniel*, p. 363). However, most read *umashal*, "and he will rule," with what follows rather than with what precedes. That seems more plausible except that *umashal mimshal rab memshalto* means "and he will rule a great dominion, his dominion," which is incomplete. A number of scholars emend *memshalto* to *mimmemshalto* (so also BHS n. 5d). Adding the comparative *min* on the front makes much more sense, yielding "and he will rule a dominion greater than his dominion," that is, Seleucus will rule a dominion greater than Ptolemy's dominion. With two *mem*s (the Hebrew letter *m*) in the text already, a third could easily have dropped out. This accords better with the history as well.

11:6 / The phrase translated **after some years**, *uleqets shanim*, is literally "and at the end of years." But the NIV is correct in translating as it does. The phrase is not eschatological here, pointing to the end of time; rather, it points to the end of an indefinite period of time (BDB, p. 893). For the eschatological 'et qets, "time of the end," see 8:17; 11:35, 40; 12:4, 9.

The Hebrew expression for **her power**, *koakh hazzeroa'*, literally means "the strength of the arm" (RSV adds "her," that is, "the strength of her arm"; NRSV and NIV also add "her" but correctly interpret the idiom to mean "power").

The MT has *uzero'o*, "and his arm," which the NIV translates as **and his power**. The word "arm" occurs appropriately a few words before in the idiom "the strength of the arm," which does indeed connote power. Here it is awkward. It is better to remove the conjunction and to repoint the noun as *zar'o*, "his seed," meaning "his offspring." This reading is supported by Theodotion and the Vulgate. We should not read "and he and his power will not last" with the NIV, nor "and he and his offspring will not last" with the NIV footnote, but simply "and his offspring will not last."

The NIV translates in the text **and her father** but offers an alternative reading in the footnote: **child** (citing the Vulgate and Syriac for support). The MT reads *wehayyoledah*, "and the one who fathered her," which is possible grammatically, but it does not fit the events, because her father died earlier. However, if we repoint the text to *weyaldah*, "and her child," it makes eminent sense, for the son was murdered along with Berenice. Therefore, the marginal reading is superior.

The phrase **in those days** is in v. 6, so the NIV translates: "In those days she will be handed over." However, the phrase comes at the end of the verse in Hebrew, and the verse division may be in the wrong place. It makes better sense to read it with what follows in v. 7, as in the RSV: "In those times a branch from her roots shall arise"; or NRSV: "In those times a branch from her roots shall rise up."

11:8 / Several ancient sources record how Ptolemy seized **their gods, their metal images and their valuable articles of silver and gold.** For example, in his commentary on Daniel, Jerome reports that the plunder Ptolemy brought back from Seleucid Syria totaled 40,000 talents of silver and 2,500 valuable vessels and images of the gods, including the very images which Cambyses had taken to Persia after conquering Egypt (Jerome, *Jerome's Commentary on Daniel* [trans. G. L. Archer Jr.; Grand Rapids: Baker, 1958], p. 123; see also the Canopus Decree [238 B.C.] and Josephus, *Against Apion*, 2.48; all three are cited in Montgomery, *Daniel*, p. 431).

It is unusual to have the explicit mention of **Egypt**, since the author normally uses the veiled expression "the king of the South." If it is a gloss, it shows that from very early times it was clear that "the king of the South" was a reference to Egypt. The LXX substitutes "the king of Egypt" for "the king of the South" in several places (e.g., 11:5, 6, 9). It may be original, as Egypt is mentioned later, in 11:42, 43.

11:13 / The Hebrew expression *uleqets ha'ittim shanim*, "and at the end of the times, years," is usually translated as the NIV has it: **and after several years.** Like the expression *uleqets shanim*, "and at the end of years," in v. 6, it is not eschatological but indicates the end of a period of time. See the Additional Note on 11:6.

11:17 / Where the NIV reads **and will make an alliance with the king of the South**, the MT has *wisharim 'immo we'asah*, "and upright ones with him and he will make/do," which is probably not original. Though it might be possible to read the first part with the opening clause ("He will determine to come with the might of his entire kingdom and upright ones with him"), it is awkward and it leaves the verb *we'asah*, "and he will make/do," dangling. Therefore, the NIV is justified in emending to *mesharim 'immo ya'aseh*, "he will make an alliance with him." The reading *mesharim*, "alliance," instead of *wisharim*, "and upright ones," is supported by the LXX. The reading *ya'aseh*, "he will make," instead of *we'asah*, "and he will make," is supported by 4QDan^c as well as by the LXX. Interestingly, v. 6 also has the idiom "to make an alliance" (*la'asot mesharim*), using the infinitive *la'asot* rather than the imperfect *ya'aseh*. The phrase "with the king of the South" in the NIV is not in the Hebrew. The MT has *'immo*, "with him." While the "him" probably does refer to Ptolemy, the text is ambiguous and should be translated that way: "and will make an alliance with him."

The statement referring to **a daughter** is interesting in the Hebrew: *ubat hannashim yitten-lo*, "and he will give him the daughter of women." Just as "son of man" (7:13) means "a human" or "a man," so "a daughter of woman" would be "a human woman." However, it is definite here and plural, which may indicate the superlative: "the greatest of women." This would show how highly regarded Cleopatra was (Montgomery, *Daniel*, p. 441; Collins, *Daniel*, p. 381). The variant "the daughter of men" is supported by 4QDan^c and the LXX. I favor this reading, although the meanings are very similar. The NIV's "a daughter" is infelicitous. If we prefer a more literal translation here, then we should choose "the daughter of women" (RSV) or "the daughter of men." If we want a translation that is less literal but carries the meaning, then we should select "a woman" (NRSV), or if we take the Hebrew to be superlative, "the woman."

In the statement **in order to overthrow the kingdom**, the words "the kingdom" are supplied. The Hebrew reads *lehashkhitah*, "to destroy her." It cannot refer to Cleopatra. Antiochus hardly gave his daughter in marriage in order to destroy her. On the one hand, it is possible to retain the feminine suffix, taking it to mean "the kingdom" (*malkut*) of Egypt (thus NIV, RSV, and NRSV) or taking it to be a reference to Egypt from the sense of the passage (Driver, *Daniel*, p. 175). On the other hand, 4QDan^c has "to destroy him" (*lehashkhito*) instead of "her," which improves the text. Antiochus married off his daughter "in order to destroy him," that is, Ptolemy.

Where the NIV has **but his plans will not succeed or help him**, the MT reads: *welo' ta'amod welo'-lo tihyeh*, "but it will not stand and it will not be for him." The NIV makes tolerable sense of this. It may be an allusion to Isa. 7:7, which reads: *lo' taqum welo' tihyeh*, "it shall not stand, and it shall not come to pass" (NRSV). This is more likely, considering that in late Hebrew *'amad* often takes the place of *qum* (R. Polzin, *Late Biblical Hebrew: Toward a Historical Typology of Biblical Hebrew Prose* [HSM 12; Missoula, Mont.: Scholars Press, 1976], p. 148). The *lo*, "for him," is questionable since it is not represented in the LXX translation. However, since it is in 4QDan^c, we should leave it in.

11:18 / The last part of the verse is a problem. In the statement *bilti kherpato yashib lo*, **and will turn his insolence back upon him,** the use of *bilti* is odd. It usually follows a negative particle and means "not" or "except." Since the clause before already mentions his insolence (*kherpato lo*), the second occurrence (*kherpato yashib lo*) may be an erroneous repetition, so perhaps it should be omitted. Another way to deal with it is to change *lo bilti* to *lebilti*, "so that not" or "in order that not" (Collins, *Daniel*, pp. 365–66). This is a very slight emendation. A possible translation might be "but a commander will put an end to his insolence so that he cannot return his insolence to him."

11:20 / Instead of the noun **his successor,** the Hebrew has a clause: *we'amad 'al-kanno*, "Then one will arise in his place" (see also vv. 7, 21, 38).

The Hebrew for **a tax collector to maintain the royal splendor** is a little awkward: *ma'abir nogas heder malkut*, literally, "he will cause to pass through an exactor of glory of a kingdom." The MT does not have the verb "to maintain," but this is one way to make sense of it in English. The NRSV has "who shall send an official for the glory of the kingdom." Another suggestion is "who will make a tribute collector of royal splendor pass through" (Collins, *Daniel*, p. 366). This seems closer to the target.

The Hebrew phrase *be'appayim* normally would mean **in anger,** but the cognate term in late Aramaic may mean "in public." This reading is supported by Theodotion in the Greek tradition.

11:21 / The NIV is interpreting when it translates, **he will invade the kingdom when its people feel secure.** The MT says simply *uba' beshalwah*, "he will come in quietness," probably meaning "without warning" (RSV, NRSV) or "in stealth" (Collins, *Daniel*, p. 366). The Hebrew has "kingdom," but not in this place; it is later in the verse. Nor does the Hebrew have the word "people." A better translation would be "He will come in quietness and seize the kingdom."

11:22 / As mentioned in the commentary, **then** should not be used to translate the conjunction *waw* here, as the events are not consecutive. Furthermore, **an overwhelming army** is not equivalent to *zero'ot hashetep*, better rendered "the forces of the flood," because the Hebrew has a plural noun, literally, "arms"; it signifies "forces" or "armies" (see also vv. 15, 31), not "an . . . army." However, the definite article in the Hebrew text seems awkward in this case, so it is preferable to follow BHS and repoint the noun *hashetep*, "the flood" (represented by the adjective "overwhelming" in the NIV), as *hishatop*, the infinitive absolute, which intensifies the finite verb *yishatepu*, "they will be swept away." This emendation does not change the received consonantal text, which was originally written without vowels, but only its vocalization. So far we have "forces will be utterly swept away before him" (similarly, RSV and NRSV). The next verb, *weyishaberu*, "and they will be broken," is plural like the first verb and the noun "arms" or "forces." Therefore, it should be read with what goes before, not with what follows, as in the NIV: **both it and a prince of the covenant will be destroyed** (translating "destroyed" instead of "broken," v. 22). The final result: "forces will be utterly swept away before him and broken."

11:23 / The Hebrew for **after coming to an agreement,** *umin hitkhab-berut 'elayw,* literally means "and from the agreement unto him." The preposition *min,* "from," is usually understood temporally: "and from the time that an alliance is made with him" (RSV); "and after an alliance is made with him" (NRSV; see also NIV). It is also possible to see a causative meaning: "from the alliance" means "because of the alliance," "on account of the alliance," or "by means of the alliance." Montgomery translates, "*And by confederacy* (of others) *with him he shall work deceit*" (italics original; Montgomery, *Daniel,* p. 450).

The word translated **people** is *goy,* which is usually rendered "nation." Here it may refer to a small group of supporters, or a military unit. Possibly it refers to the band of Hellenistic Jews who supported Antiochus IV (Lacocque, *Daniel,* p. 227, citing Schürer, *History of the Jewish People,* p. 20); if so, "a small nation" actually fits better as a translation.

11:24 / For the NIV's **when the richest provinces feel secure, he will invade them,** literally the MT reads, "In quietness and into riches of a province he will come." Presumably the "quietness" refers to the unsuspecting territories the king would attack. The NIV communicates the meaning. Compare NRSV: "Without warning he shall come into the richest parts of the province."

11:26 / The term for **the king's provisions** is *pat-bago,* meaning "rich food," "delicacies," or "royal food." It also occurs in 1:5, 8, 13, 15, 16 (see the Additional Note on 1:5).

11:30 / Whereas most translations transliterate the Hebrew word *kittim* as Kittim, the NIV renders it as **the western coastlands.** Initially it designated Kition, a place on the island of Cyprus. Apart from Daniel, in the Bible it refers to Cyprus and perhaps to other islands or coastlands in the Mediterranean (Isa. 23:1; Jer. 2:10; Ezek. 27:6). By late OT times, it clearly could refer to any people of the islands or coastlands of the Mediterranean. However, "Kittim" is often used in the literature of Qumran for the Romans, as it is here in Daniel. Since it is a cipher for the Romans rather than a general designation, "Kittim" is preferable to "the western coastlands."

11:32 / The *marshi'i berit,* "the ones who act wickedly against the covenant" (NIV **those who have violated the covenant**), are the people who have assimilated to Hellenistic culture. They are also mentioned at Qumran (1QM 1.2).

While the NIV reads **will firmly resist him,** the Hebrew, *yakhaziqu we'asu,* more literally reads "they will display strength and act." If we understand by "resist" that these Jews are refusing to eat from the pagan sacrifices, then the translation is acceptable. However, the NIV may be going too far, implying active resistance against the king. It is not clear that the verse is suggesting that these Jews participated in the Maccabean revolt. Therefore, the NRSV is better: they "shall stand firm and take action." This leaves the action more ambiguous.

11:33 / Two of the terms that appear in this verse, *maskil,* **"wise** one," and *rabbim,* **many,** are used in the *Community Rule* from Qumran for "master" and "members," respectively. The shared terminology with Daniel probably derives from the shared historical roots that the movements behind Daniel and Qumran had in common (see C. Hempel, "*Maskil(im)* and *Rabbim*: From Daniel to Qumran," in C. Hempel and J. M. Lieu, eds., *Biblical Traditions in Transmission* [JSJSup 111; Leiden: Brill, 2006], pp. 133–56).

11:36 / Several words in this verse are familiar from other texts: **He will be successful until the time of wrath** (*za'am*) **is completed** (*kalah*), **for what has been determined** (*nekheratsah*) **must take place** (*ne'esatah*). The language here is similar to Isaiah's: "For the Lord GOD of hosts will make a full end [*kalah*], as decreed [*wenekheratsah*], in all the earth" (Isa. 10:23 NRSV); "For in a very little while my indignation [*za'am*] will come to an end [*wekalah*], and my anger will be directed to their destruction" (Isa. 10:25 NRSV). Earlier Gabriel tells Daniel: "I am going to tell you what will happen later in the time of wrath [*za'am*], because the vision concerns the appointed time of the end" (Dan. 8:19). Likewise, Gabriel says that "desolations have been decreed [*nekheretset*]" (Dan. 9:26) and the king will "set up an abomination that causes desolation . . . until the end [*kalah*] that is decreed [*nekheratsah*] is poured out on him" (Dan. 9:27).

11:39 / Although the NIV translates **he will attack the mightiest fortresses with the help of a foreign god,** the Hebrew has no verb here meaning "attack." The MT has the more general verb *'asah*, "to do." Of course, with "fortresses" as the object, it is possible to understand what he is "doing" to the fortresses as "attacking." However, if the MT is followed, the verb should be translated "to deal with" as in the NRSV: "He shall deal with the strongest fortresses." This communicates the ambiguity of the Hebrew. "Dealing with fortresses" may mean building them, strengthening them, or placing troops in them; it does not have to mean attacking them. This is especially so if the fortifications are those of the Akra, or Jerusalem citadel, which Antiochus built up and held control of. But it may not be best to follow the MT. The expression *lemibtsere ma'uzzim*, "fortresses of strongholds," is usually understood as the superlative, "mightiest fortresses." If we repoint "mightiest" (*lemibtseru*) as a *piel* participle instead of a noun, it yields "those who enclose fortresses" or "those who fortify strongholds" (Collins, *Daniel*, pp. 368, 388). Then the word *'m* could be revocalized as the noun "people" (*'am*) instead of the preposition "with" (*'im*; "the help of" is supplied by the translator and is not in the Hebrew): "people of a foreign god." Putting this all together, we get "He will act for those who fortify strongholds, the people of a strange god" (Collins, *Daniel*, p. 388).

11:41 / In Hebrew, the text reads *rabbot*, **many,** but the text does not say what the "many" refers to. Since it is in the feminine plural form, the NIV takes it to be *'aratsot*, **"countries,"** a feminine plural noun that occurs in the previous verse. Most scholars repoint as *ribbot*, "myriads" or "tens of thousands" (so RSV, NRSV, and many commentators). In other words, it may be saying that "tens of thousands" of people "will fall" rather than "many countries." Compare also v. 12: "he shall cast down tens of thousands" (RSV; NIV "will slaughter many thousands").

11:45 / The word rendered **tents**, *'appeden*, only occurs here in the Hebrew Bible. It is actually a Persian loanword from *apadana*, meaning "palace" (BDB, p. 66). When used, as here, of a situation out in the field (as opposed to a city, where an actual palace building would be denoted), it would refer to the large complex of royal pavilions an important king might have for his quarters.

12:4 / The word for **knowledge** is *da'at*, but instead of the equivalent Greek word, the LXX has "evil," which translated back into Hebrew is *ra'ah*. Since the Hebrew *d* looks very much like an *r* and the *t* compares to the *h*, it is quite possible that the original text had "evil," which was accidentally changed to "knowledge" in what was handed down in the MT.

§12 The Final Revelation: Epilogue (Dan. 12:5–13)

In the body (Dan. 11:2b–12:4) of the Final Revelation, Daniel 12:3 is the last verse of the vision itself. Daniel 12:4 marks the conclusion of the vision narrative with the command to Daniel to seal it up. The body of the revelation, containing the main vision, was introduced by a prologue (10:1–11:2a). It is followed by an epilogue (12:5–13). Some scholars think that this section was added later, perhaps in several installments. However, if the larger unit, which began with Daniel 10:1, ended at 12:4, it would be too abrupt. For the sake of balance, some or all of the epilogue must have followed the vision in order to offset the prologue and provide a fitting conclusion.

The structure of the Final Revelation exhibits an A-B-A pattern. (A) It begins with Daniel at a river where a heavenly being encounters him and he reports in the first person. (B) The angel then speaks, informing the prophet what will transpire up to and including the end. (A) It ends as it begins, with Daniel at a river, meeting and dialoguing with celestial beings and reporting on it.

There are a number of parallels between the vision of chapter 8 and that of chapters 10–12. Both accounts are set by a canal (8:2) or river (10:4; 12:5–7). In both chapters Daniel is overwhelmed by the visions (8:18, 27; 10:9, 15), and angels strengthen him (8:18; 10:10–11, 16, 18) and instruct him about end times (8:19–26; 10:2–12:4). In both instances, the heavenly visitor affirms that the revelation given is true (8:26; 11:2). In both narratives a celestial being asks, "How long?" (8:13; 12:6). Both include a timetable of about three and a half years (8:14; 12:7, 11, 12). In both cases Daniel is told to seal up the vision (8:26; 12:4).

12:5–7 / After the instruction to seal up the scroll, Daniel speaks again. This last great section of the book begins the same way: **I, Daniel** (12:5; cf. 10:2). The earlier occurrence is followed by an account of Daniel's three-week fast. Here, Daniel looks and sees **two others**, that is, two other heavenly beings besides the one mentioned in Daniel 10:4–6 who has been talking to Daniel and giving him revelation. One stands on this bank of the river and one stands on the opposite bank (12:5). The scene description calls attention to the river, which is where the episode commenced in chapter 10. However, in the prologue, it is called "the great river" (10:4), which I argued was more likely the Euphrates than the Tigris (see also 8:2, where the Ulai Canal is the setting for a vision).

One of the angels addresses a question to the **man clothed in linen** (12:6), the same man who was depicted this way earlier (10:5). This man is **above the waters of the stream** (12:6). This may mean that he is up in the air above the river (Driver, *Daniel*, p. 203) or that he is further upstream (Goldingay, *Daniel*, p. 281; Collins, *Daniel*, p. 369). The question posed is: **How long will it be before these astonishing things are fulfilled?** (12:6). "Astonishing things" is one word in Hebrew, a plural noun from the root *pl'*, meaning "wonder" or "miracle." Since this root normally denotes the awesome works of God (e.g., Exod. 15:11; Pss. 77:11, 14 [77:12, 15 MT]; 78:12; 88:10, 12 [88:11, 13 MT]; 89:5 [89:6 MT]; Isa. 25:1), it might refer to the amazing events revealed in Daniel 11:2–12:3, especially the stand of Michael and the resurrection of the dead, announced toward the end. However, a word formed from the same root is used earlier in Daniel 8:24 and 11:36 for the astoundingly evil deeds of Antiochus IV, so it is better to understand the angel inquiring about the end of the tyrant and his oppression. This interpretation finds further support from the contexts of both chapters 8 and 12. In the parallel passage in chapter 8, a holy one asks a similar question: "How long will it take for the vision to be fulfilled?" (8:13). The text goes on to explain the vision, not in positive descriptions of the saving deeds of God, but in negative terms listing the vile acts of Antiochus: the taking away of "the daily sacrifice, the rebellion that causes desolation, and the surrender of the sanctuary and of the host that will be trampled underfoot" (8:13). Therefore, the question is asking when the persecutions will cease. Similarly, what follows the question in Daniel 12 concerns the demise of Epiphanes: when the one who shatters the power of the holy people will come to an end. As a result, it is better to attribute the "astonishing things" to Antiochus IV and understand the question to be about his destruction.

The response of **the man clothed in linen** is that he lifts **his right hand and his left hand toward heaven** and makes an oath (12:7). When making an oath, it was more usual to raise one hand (Gen. 14:22; Exod. 6:8; Deut. 32:40; Isa. 62:8; Rev. 10:5–6), but here, both hands are raised to stress the gravity of the situation. Otherwise, lifting the hands was a gesture of prayer or praise (Isa. 1:15; Pss. 28:2; 63:4; 134:2). The heavenly being swears **by him who lives forever** (Dan. 12:7; see also Dan. 4:34; Rev. 10:5–6). People would often swear, "As the LORD lives" (e.g., Judg. 8:19;

1 Sam. 14:39, 45; 19:6; 20:3, 21; 25:26, 34), while God swears, "As I live" (Num. 14:21, 28; Isa. 49:18; Jer. 22:24). The closest parallel to Daniel is when God says, "As I live forever" (Deut. 32:40). Perhaps the reason for the presence of two other celestial beings is for them to witness the oath, as the Torah seems to require (Deut. 19:15; cf. Deut. 4:26; 30:19; 31:28). The angel announces the time period: **It will be for a time, times and half a time** (Dan. 12:7). As in Daniel 7:25, this is the apocalyptist's cryptic way of saying three and a half years, that is, a year, two years, and half a year. Using the weeks-of-years scheme from chapter 9, a week of years is seven years, so half a week of years is three and a half years (Dan. 9:27). This might be worked out as 1,150 days (= 2,300 evenings and mornings; Dan. 8:14), 1,290 days (Dan. 12:11), or 1,335 days (Dan. 12:12).

The last part of verse 7 is difficult to translate. Literally, it says, "When the shattering of the power of the holy people accomplishes, all these things will be accomplished." If the verb "accomplishes" does not require an object, the sentence makes better sense: "When the shattering of the power of the holy people is accomplished [that is, "ended"], all these things will be accomplished" (see the Additional Note on 12:7). Similarly, the NRSV translates, "When the shattering of the power of the holy people comes to an end, all these things would be accomplished." The NIV translation (**When the power of the holy people has been finally broken, all these things will be completed** [12:7]) suggests that the holy people have power but that when they lose it, the end will come. This does not accord with the rest of the book or with history, for on the contrary, the holy people were being persecuted by Antiochus Epiphanes so that he was shattering their power. The promise that can engender hope in that situation is not the further breaking of their power but the breaking of the king, which will lead to the Jews' deliverance. The text therefore must point to the time "when the shattering of the power of the holy people comes to an end," that is, when all things will be accomplished.

12:8–10 / Daniel says, "I heard, but I did not understand" (12:8). So he asks the heavenly being, "What will the outcome of all this be?" (12:8). This is puzzling, since Daniel has just been given a very detailed revelation concerning future events. Furthermore, at the beginning of this large block that runs from Daniel 10 to 12, the author says that "the understanding of the message came to him in a vision" (10:1). So, what is it that he does not understand? One way to answer this is to explain that Daniel is being portrayed as a figure living in the sixth century B.C. by a second-century author who wishes to inject some verisimilitude here by recognizing that Daniel could only have a limited understanding of the future events he has just penned. From our vantage point (and from the author's), we can comprehend many more of the details of chapter 11 than Daniel could, since we have historical records, while he would no doubt have been baffled by some elements he recorded, because what he recounted still lay in front of him in time. So, this question reminds us that even when God gives revelation, it is limited, with the result that a measure of mystery still remains (Seow, *Daniel*, p. 193). Certainly, if the book originated close to the sixth century B.C. (i.e., prior to the events foreseen), the level of mystery in Daniel's understanding would have been all the greater. Another way to respond is to allow that the author portrays Daniel as understanding the vision of chapter 11 as he claimed (10:1), but in Daniel 12:8, Daniel is only asking about what the angel has just said in the oath, namely, the cryptic expression "a time, times and half a time" (12:7). In other words, he is presented as not fully grasping what that means or how it will actually be played out in history. Finally, it could be that the character Daniel simply wants to know what will happen next in God's eschatological timetable. He fathoms what is to come from the time of Persia up to "the end": the death of Antiochus IV, the victory of Michael, the resurrection, and the judgment. However, being portrayed as an intellectually curious individual, he now he wishes to learn what will transpire after that (Collins, *Daniel*, p. 400).

Sadly, Daniel's quest for additional insight is frustrated. Earlier, Daniel was instructed to "close up and seal the words of the scroll until the time of the end" (12:4). Apparently he obeyed, for the angel now says, **"Go your way, Daniel, because the words are closed up and sealed until the time of the end"** (12:9). This means that Daniel should carry on with his life and not concern himself with uncovering any more apocalyptic secrets. Whatever understanding Daniel has already been given will be concealed in his scroll until the end, but whatever he was inquiring about is not for him to know, as no new revelation is forthcoming.

What is for him to know is that at the time of the end, **many will be purified, made spotless and refined** (12:10). These same three verbs are used in Daniel 11:35, although with different verbal forms and in a different order. There it is the wise ones who will "be refined, purified and made spotless." But this is achieved through suffering as they stumble or fall victim to persecution (11:33–35). In that context the "wise" ones instruct the "many" (11:33), indicating two different groups. Here in chapter 12, it is not just the wise ones who are purified; the subject is the "many." Purification is open to all the righteous Jews, not just the teachers (Hartman and Di Lella, *Daniel*, p. 313). Another difference is that Daniel 12:10 does not mention suffering. In fact, it is possible to translate the first two verbs as reflexives rather than passives: "Many shall purify themselves, and make themselves white, and be refined" (12:10 RSV). If persecution is implicitly understood, though, then the verbs should all be translated as passives (Montgomery, *Daniel*, p. 477).

In contrast to the purified ones, **the wicked will continue to be wicked** (12:10); a better translation is "the wicked will continue to act wickedly." This may be an allusion to those "who have violated the covenant" (11:32), because both passages use the same verb. (In 11:32, the NIV translates the verb "to act wickedly" as "to violate" because of the object "covenant"; here the NIV has "to be wicked.") The author of Daniel identifies with **those who are wise** (12:10). He and his party see themselves as recipients of esoteric knowledge not available to the apostate Jews who have assimilated to Hellenistic culture and religion. The wise ones **will understand** where history is heading and will grasp the significance of the events that are occurring in their day, whereas the wicked will remain in the dark.

12:11–13 / Verses 11 and 12 contain numbers that hint at a future event or at two separate events. The first number is 1,290 days (12:11). The clock starts ticking when the daily sacrifice is abolished and the abomination that causes desolation is set up (12:11). We are not told what will happen at the end of that time. The next verse sets a time of 1,335 days (12:12). Again the text does not specify what will happen at the conclusion of that period, but everyone who waits for and reaches that point will be blessed (12:12). The term "waits" may be an allusion to Habakkuk: "For the revelation awaits an appointed time; it speaks of the end and will not prove false. Though it linger, wait for it; it will certainly come and will not delay" (Hab. 2:3; see also Dan. 8:17; 11:27, 35).

These time periods are close to three and a half years. It is clear, then, that what is anticipated is not the cleansing of the temple, because that took place after three years (1 Macc. 1:54; 4:52–54). It is possible that the author or authors of Daniel had specific historical events in mind that are now obscure to us. Alternatively, the numbers may have been understood symbolically, again, with symbols that elude us today (Hartman and Di Lella, *Daniel*, pp. 313–14). Another possibility is that there are different calendars involved, which would account for the different calculations of three and a half years (see the Additional Note on 12:11–12). By playing with different systems, trying different combinations of numbers, and adding in intercalary months, it might be possible to account for all three figures. However, this method of explaining the numbers seems forced. It appears more likely that these are attempts to predict the end, when God's kingdom and the resurrection would come, as announced in Daniel 12:1–3. If so, then verses 11–12 need to be read along with other passages in the book that set times.

First there is the general indication of three and a half years in the expression "a time, times and half a time," which is used earlier in this chapter (12:7) and elsewhere in the book (7:25; cf. 9:27). Then there are the "2,300 evenings and mornings" (= 1,150 days) of Daniel 8:14. As mentioned earlier, in the discussion of chapter 8, that passage does seem to predict a period of time between the desecration of the temple and its reconsecration. Once again note that that period was only three years in duration. Therefore, it is likely that the author of that passage was expecting something more than the restoration of sacrifice. Perhaps when Daniel 8:14 was written, the author expected the coming of God's kingdom to bring the restoration of the sacrifice. When the Maccabees drove out the Seleucids and cleansed the temple after three years, the community held on to the date with hopes of seeing the resurrection occur. When the 1,150 days passed uneventfully, they pushed the date ahead to 1,290 days (12:11). When nothing happened after that period, a final date was set: 1,335 days (12:12). When the end still did not come, they added the conclusion to the book: **As for you, go your way till the end. You will rest, and then at the end of the days you will rise to receive your allotted inheritance** (12:13). Daniel is directed to live his life normally until it is time for him to die. The end will eventually come, and Daniel is guaranteed a part in the resurrection of the dead along with all other faithful followers of the Lord.

Additional Notes §12

12:5 / The term for **river** is *ye'or* (see also 12:6 and 7). While this Hebrew word normally identifies the Nile in Egypt (e.g., Exod. 2:3, 5; 4:9; 7:15, 18), in this verse it just means "river."

12:6 / The Hebrew text does not contain a word for **fulfilled**, so a more accurate translation would be "How long will it be until the end of these wonders?" (NRSV; lit. "Until when is the end of the wonders?"). The NIV is interpreting the word *qets*, "end," as "fulfilled," but the word "end" is a significant term in this unit (11:6, 13, 27, 35, 40, 45; 12:4, 9, 13) and in apocalyptic literature, so it should not be omitted from the English translation.

12:7 / As it is pointed the MT says, "when the shattering of the power of the holy people accomplishes" (NIV **When the power of the holy people has**

been finally broken, all these things will be completed). There should be an object to the infinitive *kallot*, "accomplishes," but there is none. When this verb is repointed as *qal* instead of *piel*, it does not require an object, and it makes better sense: "when the shattering of the power of the holy people is accomplished."

Many commentators further emend the text by repointing the participle "shattering" (*nippets*) as *qal* rather than *piel* and then transposing it with the word for "power"; this yields the translation "when the power of the shatterer of the holy people ends" (BDB, p. 478; *BHS*; Collins, *Daniel*, p. 369). This improves the text by focusing more on the one who does the shattering, which is the emphasis of the biblical writer. However, caution is advised when emending the text, and the transposition is not necessary; it is also possible to read "shatterer" without rearranging the words: "when the shatterer of the power of the holy people comes to an end." This too would refer to the demise of the wicked despot who shattered the Jews (i.e., Antiochus Epiphanes), in agreement with the earlier prediction that his death would set in motion other end-time events (11:45), such as the appearance of Michael and the resurrection (12:1–2; Collins, *Daniel*, p. 399). In other words, the angel vows that when the persecutor dies, all will be accomplished.

12:10 / Collins takes the fact that in Dan. 12:10 purification is open to the **many**, whereas in 11:33–35 it is only available for the "wise," as evidence that the two passages may come from different authors (Collins, *Daniel*, p. 400).

12:11–12 / Different calendars yield different totals of days within three and a half years. A lunar calendar of 28 days times three and a half years is 1,176 days, which is close to the first figure of 1,150 (8:14). Using a 30-day lunar calendar yields 1,260, which is close to the second figure of **1,290 days** (12:11). A solar calendar of 365 days produces 1,278 days, which is even closer to 1,290. For an attempt to make sense of all three numbers, see Goldingay, *Daniel*, pp. 309–10. In 1895, H. Gunkel was the first to propose that these numbers are attempts to predict the end (see H. Gunkel, *Creation and Chaos in the Primeval Era and the Eschaton: Religio-Historical Study of Genesis 1 and Revelation 12* [trans. K. W. Whitney Jr.; Grand Rapids: Eerdmans, 2006], pp. 171–73). This interpretation is followed by most modern commentators (see Montgomery, *Daniel*, p. 477; Collins, *Daniel*, pp. 400–401).

For Further Reading

Alexander, J. B. "New Light on the Fiery Furnace." *JBL* 69 (1950), pp. 375–76.

Anderson, R. A. *Signs and Wonders: A Commentary on the Book of Daniel.* ITC. Grand Rapids: Eerdmans, 1984.

Archer, G. "Daniel." Pages 1–157 in vol. 7 of *The Expositor's Bible Commentary.* Edited by F. E. Gaebelein. Grand Rapids: Zondervan, 1985.

Baldwin, J. G. *Daniel: An Introduction and Commentary.* Downers Grove, Ill.: InterVarsity, 1978.

Barr, J. "Daniel." Pages 591–602 in *Peake's Commentary on the Bible.* Edited by M. Black and H. H. Rowley. London: Thomas Nelson, 1962.

Barthélemy, D., and J. T. Milik. *Discoveries in the Judaean Desert I: Qumran Cave I.* Oxford: Clarendon, 1956.

Berger, P.-R. "Der Kyros-Zylinder mit den Zusatzfragment BIN II Nr. 32 und die akkadischen Personennamen im Danielbuch." *ZA* 64 (1975), pp. 192–234.

Bertram, G. "*hypsistos.*" *TDNT.* Vol. 8, pp. 614–20.

Betz, O. "*phōnē.*" *TDNT.* Vol. 9, pp. 288–90, 298–99.

Bright, J. *A History of Israel.* 3rd ed. Philadelphia: Westminster, 1981.

Brown, R. E. *The Semitic Background of the Term "Mystery" in the New Testament.* Philadelphia: Fortress, 1968.

Charles, R. H. *A Critical and Exegetical Commentary on the Book of Daniel.* Oxford: Clarendon, 1929.

Charles, R. H., ed. *The Apocrypha and Pseudepigrapha of the Old Testament.* Oxford: Clarendon, 1913.

Clermont-Ganneau, C. S. "Mané, thécel, pharès et le festin de Balthasar." *Journal Asiatique* 8 (1886), pp. 36–67. Reprinted in *Recueil d'archéologie orientale,* vol. 1 (Paris: Leroux, 1888), pp. 136–59.

Collins, J. J. *Daniel: A Commentary on the Book of Daniel.* Hermeneia. Minneapolis: Fortress, 1993.

Cowley, A. E. *Aramaic Papyri of the Fifth Century B.C.* Oxford: Clarendon, 1923.

Coxon, P. W. "Another Look at Nebuchadnezzar's Madness." Pages 211–22 in *The Book of Daniel in the Light of New Findings.* Edited by A. S. Van der Woude. Leuven: Leuven University Press, 1993.

———. "Daniel III 17: A Linguistic and Theological Problem." *VT* 26 (1976), pp. 400–409.

Cross, F. M., Jr. *Canaanite Myth and Hebrew Epic: Essays in the History of the Religion of Israel.* Cambridge, Mass.: Harvard University Press, 1973.

———. "The Council of Yahweh in Second Isaiah." *JNES* 12 (1953), pp. 274–77.

Dahood, M. *Psalms I, 1–50.* AB 16. Garden City, N.Y.: Doubleday, 1965.

Davies, P. R. "Daniel Chapter Two." *JTS* 27 (1976), pp. 392–401.

Driver, S. R. *The Book of Daniel.* Cambridge: Cambridge University Press, 1936.

Eissfeldt, O. "Die Menetekel-Inschrift und ihre Deutung," *ZAW* 63 (1951), pp. 105–14.

Eliade, M. *Patterns in Comparative Religion.* New York: Sheed & Ward, 1958.

Frank, R. "The Description of the 'Bear' in Dn 7,5." *CBQ* 21 (1959), pp. 505–7.

Freedman, D. N. "The Prayer of Nabonidus." *BASOR* 145 (1957), pp. 31–32.

Gibson, M. D. "Belshazzar's Feast." *ExpTim* 23 (1911–12), p. 181.

Ginsberg, H. L. "The Oldest Interpretation of the Suffering Servant." *VT* 3 (1953), pp. 400–404.

———. *Studies in Daniel.* Texts and Studies of the Jewish Theological Seminary of America 14. New York: Jewish Theological Seminary of America, 1948.

Ginzberg, L. *Legends of the Jews.* 6 vols. 4th ed. Philadelphia: Jewish Publication Society of America, 1959.

Goldingay, J. E. *Daniel.* WBC 30. Dallas: Word, 1989.

Gowan, D. E. *Daniel.* AOTC. Nashville: Abingdon, 2001.

Gunkel, H. *Creation and Chaos in the Primeval Era and the Eschaton: Religio-Historical Study of Genesis 1 and Revelation 12.* Translated by K. W. Whitney Jr. Grand Rapids: Eerdmans, 2006.

Gurney, R. J. M. "The Four Kingdoms of Daniel 2 and 7." *Them* 2 (1977), pp. 39–45.

Hallo, W. W., and W. K. Simpson. *The Ancient Near East: A History.* 2nd ed. Belmont, Calif.: Wadsworth/Thomson, 1998.

Hartman, L. F., and A. Di Lella. *The Book of Daniel.* AB 23. Garden City, N.Y.: Doubleday, 1978.

Hayes, J. H., and J. M. Miller, eds. *Israelite and Judaean History.* London: SCM, 1977.

Hempel, C. "*Maskil(im)* and *Rabbim*: From Daniel to Qumran." Pages 133–56 in *Biblical Traditions in Transmission.* Edited by C. Hempel and J. Lieu. JSJSup. Leiden: Brill, 2006.

Herodotus. *Histories.* Translated by A. D. Godley. Vol. 1. LCL. London: William Heinemann, 1931.

Herrmann, S. *A History of Israel in Old Testament Times.* Philadelphia: Fortress, 1981.

Isbell, C. D. *Corpus of the Aramaic Incantation Bowls.* SBLDS 17. Missoula, Mont.: Scholars Press, 1975.

James, E. O. *The Tree of Life: An Archaeological Study.* Leiden: Brill, 1966.

Jeffery, A. "The Book of Daniel: Introduction and Exegesis." Pages 339–549 in vol. 6 of the *Interpreter's Bible.* Edited by G. Buttrick. New York: Abingdon-Cokesbury Press, 1956.

Jerome. *Jerome's Commentary on Daniel.* Translated by G. L. Archer Jr. Grand Rapids: Baker, 1958.

Koester, H. *Introduction to the New Testament.* 2 vols. Philadelphia: Fortress, 1982.

Lacocque, A. *Le Livre de Daniel.* Commentaire de l'Ancien Testament 15b. Neuchâtel/Paris: Delachaux et Niestlé, 1976.

Lipiński, E. Review of André Lacocque, *Le Livre de Daniel.* VT 28 (1978), pp. 233–39.

Longman, T., III. *Daniel.* NIVAC. Grand Rapids: Zondervan, 1999.

Lucas, E. *Decoding Daniel: Reclaiming the Visions of Daniel 7–11.* GBS 18. Cambridge: Grove Books, 2000.

Martens, A. *Das Buch Daniel im Lichte der Texte vom Toten Meer.* SBM 12. Würzburg: Echter, 1971.

Meyers, C. L., and E. M. Meyers. *Haggai, Zechariah 1–8.* AB 25B. Garden City, N.Y.: Doubleday, 1987.

Millard, A. R. "Daniel 1–6 and History." *EvQ* 49 (1977), pp. 67–73.

Miller, S. R. *Daniel*. NAC 18. Nashville: Broadman & Holman, 1994.

Montgomery, J. A. *The Book of Daniel*. Edinburgh: T&T Clark, 1927.

Myhrman, D. W. "An Aramaic Incantation Text." Pages 342–51 in *Hilprecht Anniversary Volume*. Leipzig: J. C. Hinrichs, 1909.

Oppenheim, A. L. *Ancient Mesopotamia: Portrait of a Dead Civilization*. Rev. ed. Chicago: University of Chicago Press, 1977.

———. *The Interpretation of Dreams in the Ancient Near East*. Philadelphia: American Philosophical Society, 1956.

Parpola, S. "The Assyrian Tree of Life: Tracing the Origins of Jewish Monotheism and Greek Philosophy." *JNES* 52 (1993), pp. 161–208.

Polybius. *The Histories*. Translated by W. R. Paton. Vol. 6. LCL. Cambridge, Mass.: Harvard University Press, 1927.

Polzin, R. *Late Biblical Hebrew: Toward a Historical Typology of Biblical Hebrew Prose*. HSM 12. Missoula, Mont.: Scholars Press, 1976.

Porteous, N. W. *Daniel: A Commentary*. OTL. Philadelphia: Westminster Press, 1965.

Porter, B. N. *Trees, Kings, and Politics: Studies in Assyrian Iconography*. Fribourg: Academic Press, 2003.

Robinson, H. W. "The Council of Yahweh." *JTS* 45 (1944), pp. 151–57.

Rowley, H. H. "The Unity of the Book of Daniel." Pages 249–80 in *The Servant of the Lord and Other Essays on the Old Testament*. 2nd ed. Oxford: Blackwell, 1965.

Schürer, E. *A History of the Jewish People in the Time of Jesus*. New York: Schocken, 1961.

Schwantes, S. J. *A Short History of the Ancient Near East*. Grand Rapids: Baker, 1965.

Seebass, H. "*'acharith*." *TDOT*. Vol. 1, pp. 207–12.

Seow, C. L. *Daniel*. Louisville: Westminster John Knox, 2003.

Smith-Christopher, D. L. "The Book of Daniel." Pages 19–152 in vol. 7 of *The New Interpreter's Bible*. Edited by L. Keck. Nashville: Abingdon, 1996.

Tadmor, H. "The Sin of Sargon" (Hebrew). *Eretz Israel* 5 (1958), pp. 150–63.

Tcherikover, V. *Hellenistic Civilization and the Jews*. New York: Atheneum, 1975.

Towner, W. S. *Daniel*. Interp. Atlanta: John Knox Press, 1984.

Walbank, F. W., E. A. Astin, M. W. Frederiksen, and R. M. Ogilvie, eds. *The Hellenistic World.* Vol. 7, pt. 1 of *The Cambridge Ancient History.* Cambridge: Cambridge University Press, 1984.

Walton, J. H. "The Four Kingdoms of Daniel." *JETS* 29 (1986), pp. 25–36.

Whitcomb, J. C. *Darius the Mede.* Grand Rapids: Eerdmans, 1959.

Widengren, G. *The King and the Tree of Life in Ancient Near Eastern Religion.* Uppsala: Lundequist, 1951.

Will, É. "The Succession to Alexander." Pages 23–61 in vol. 7, pt. 1 of *The Cambridge Ancient History.* Edited by F. W. Walbank et al. Cambridge: Cambridge University Press, 1984.

Williamson, H. G. M. *Ezra, Nehemiah.* WBC 16. Waco, Tex.: Word, 1985.

Wills, L. M. *The Jew in the Court of the Foreign King: Ancient Jewish Court Legends.* Minneapolis: Fortress, 1990.

Wise, M., M. Abegg Jr., and E. Cook. *The Dead Sea Scrolls; Revised Edition: A New Translation.* New York: HarperCollins, 2005.

Wiseman, D. J. *Chronicles of Chaldaean Kings [626–556 B.C.] in the British Museum.* London: Trustees of the British Museum, 1956.

Wolters, A. "Untying the King's Knots: Physiology and Wordplay in Daniel 5." *JBL* 110 (1991), pp. 117–22.

Xenophon. *Cyropaedia.* Translated by W. Miller. Vol. 7. LCL. London: William Heinemann, 1914.

Young, E. J. *The Prophecy of Daniel.* Grand Rapids: Eerdmans, 1949.

Zimmerli, W. *Ezekiel.* Vol. 2. Philadelphia: Fortress, 1983.

Subject Index

Abednego, 40, 42, 53, 62, 63, 98, 103, 108, 109, 112, 114, 115, 116, 117, 161, 285
Abiram, 172
Abraham, 62, 108, 230
abstaining, 71
Achan, 172
Adam, 62
Agathocles, 275–76
Ahab, 82, 108, 150, 152
Ahasuerus, 4, 183, 241, 270
Ahiqar, 138
Akitu Festival, 146
Akkadian language, 61, 62
Alexander IV Aegus, 186
Alexander the Great, 4–5, 37, 91, 111, 185, 186, 197, 201, 212, 269, 270, 271–72
Amel-Marduk, 3, 62, 101
Amos, 154
Ancient of Days, 187, 189
angels, 14, 42, 104, 111, 115, 128, 139, 170, 206, 207, 209, 210, 231, 232, 251–53, 256–59, 260, 261, 297–98, 309–10
annointed one, 9, 32, 234, 235, 236–38, 240, 244
Antichrist, 44, 288, 289, 299
Antigonus Monophthalmus, 201–2, 273
Antiochus (son of Seleucus IV), 186
Antiochus I Soter, 186
Antiochus II Theos, 91, 186, 273–74
Antiochus III the Great, 5, 91, 186, 199, 201, 272, 275–78
Antiochus IV Epiphanes, 5–7, 9, 34–35, 37, 39–40, 41, 49, 65, 66, 78, 83, 84, 88, 91, 105, 106, 109, 111, 112, 114, 115, 122, 131, 132, 147, 151, 162, 164, 165, 179, 184–85, 186, 191, 192, 197, 200, 201, 202–4, 205, 206, 209, 211, 213–14, 217, 219, 222, 238, 239–40, 259, 269, 272, 276, 277–83, 286–87, 289–92, 311

Apocalypse of Weeks, 233
apocalyptic genre, 10–11, 14–15, 301
Aramaic language, 20–21, 22, 23–25, 61, 76, 81, 150, 221
archangels, 256
Arioch, 77, 85, 99
Artaxerxes I Longimanus, 4, 123, 183, 235, 270
Artaxias of Armenia, 185
ashes, 225
Ashkelon, 72
Ashpenaz, 59, 66, 73, 75
assimilation, 105
Assyrian Empire, 2, 42, 91, 92, 111, 138, 211, 219
astrologers, 79, 80, 81, 98, 103, 108, 126, 141, 148
Astyages, 4
Azariah, 22, 53, 60, 62, 64, 76, 83, 98, 161

Baal, 69, 99, 181, 189, 258
Ba'al Shamem, 287
Babel, tower of, 57
Babylon, 53, 54, 57, 58, 60–62, 70, 154
Babylonian Empire, 2–4, 31, 56, 92, 211, 269; and Median Empire, 8
Babylonians, 73, 74
Balaam, 120
band, 129, 130
beasts, 43, 131, 132, 134, 142, 143, 144, 147, 170, 181–84, 187–88, 194, 195, 196, 197, 215–16
Bel and the Dragon, 19, 21
Belshazzar, 3, 7, 37, 39, 41, 47, 53, 122, 125, 143, 145, 146, 147, 148, 149, 150, 151, 155, 157, 158, 159, 179, 223
Belteshazzar, 53, 54, 62, 63, 74, 125, 247
Berenice, 91, 273–74
blessings, 167
Book of the Watchers, 233
Book of Truth, 262
burning, 108, 110, 112, 114, 115, 119

Subject Index

Cambyses, 4, 199, 271
Camping, Harold, 50
Carchemish, battle of, 56, 72
Cassander, 5, 202, 212
Catholic Church, 32
Chaldeans, 61, 79, 81, 82, 98, 103, 108, 115
Christ, 95
Chronicles, books of, 56, 58
chronological discrepancies, 11, 43, 53, 78, 79, 92, 160, 173, 223, 245, 246–47, 279, 288
Chrysolite, 252
circumcision, 6
Cleopatra I, 91, 277, 304
Clermont-Ganneau, C. S., 158
Collins, J. J., 51
concubines, 146, 147
confession, 221, 225, 226, 227, 228, 229, 249, 255
contest motif, 76, 121
Cornelius, 135
cosmic-tree motif, 127, 128
court officials, 59, 73, 107
covenant, 226
creation myths, 181, 258
Cross, F. M., 159
Cyprus, 306
Cyrus II (the Persian), 4, 37, 53, 69, 70, 92, 137, 155, 156, 157, 159, 162, 173, 179, 183, 200, 223, 224, 235, 236, 245, 246, 265, 270

Dagon, 57, 69, 274
Daniel, 17–18, 53, 59, 61, 62, 63, 64, 67, 68, 77, 78, 82, 83, 89, 97, 103, 106, 121, 125, 126, 148, 149, 150, 163, 180, 220, 247–62
Daniel, book of: audience, 91; authorship, 16, 17, 21–28, 76, 298–99; canonical arrangements, 18–20; chapters' historical and contextual background, 28–30; chiastic literary structure, 76; circulation of, 299–300, 312; dating of, 1, 15–17, 32–33, 298–301; genre, 9–10, 10–15, 301; historical background, 2–7; historical problems, 7–10, 15–16; history of interpretation of, 30–33; inspired and authoritative, 2; language issues, 20–21; literary development in stages, 21–28;
theology of, 33–50; timetable of, 8–9, 48–50; unity of, 27–28
Darius I Hystaspes, 4, 8, 36, 41, 84, 107, 123, 124, 156, 162, 183, 199, 241, 270, 271
Darius III Codomannus, 4, 270, 271
Darius the Mede, 8, 23, 37, 92, 155, 156, 159, 162, 166, 167, 179, 223, 264, 268
Dathan, 172
David, 57, 129, 150
Dead Sea Scrolls, 21–22
Deborah, 203
decrees, 134
defile/defilements, 63, 64, 65, 67, 71, 75
Demetrius (son of Seleucus IV), 5, 186, 273, 278
demons, 256
denunciation, 168, 176
determinism, 263
Deuteronomistic History, 33
Diadochi, 5, 90, 91, 195, 201–2, 212, 269, 272
dietary rules, 63, 64, 65, 71
Dionysus, 65
divine council, 187–88, 190, 257
diviners, 85, 96, 98, 126, 141, 148
dominion, 151, 170
Dorcas, 135
doxology, 84, 85, 123, 124
dream interpretation, 53, 54, 61, 67, 68, 76, 77, 79, 80, 81, 82, 86, 89–96, 125, 127, 134, 190–94, 212–14
dream narratives, Daniel's, 181–90, 198–208
dream narratives, Nebuchadnezzar's, 86–96, 100, 127–33
Dura, 97

Egypt, 69, 273, 281, 303, 304
Egyptian Empire, 2, 276–77
El, 18, 189
Eliakim, 62
Elijah, 69, 97, 150, 294
Elisha, 150
enchanters, 79, 98, 126, 141, 148
enemies, destruction of, 171–72
Enoch, 294
1 Enoch, 128
Epiphanes, 6, 29, 122, 131. *See also* Antiochus IV Epiphanes.

eschatology, 14–15, 42–43, 48–50, 209–12, 240–41
eschaton, 49
Esther, 63
Eulaeus, 281
eunuchs, 59, 60, 73
Euphrates River, 250, 265
evangelism, 40–42
evil, 33–35, 37
Evil-Merodach, 62, 155, 159
execution, 66, 82, 83, 99
exile/deportation, 53, 54, 55, 58, 59–62, 63, 107, 220, 224, 247, 248
exodus, 228
Ezekiel, 17–18, 182, 209, 210, 294
Ezekiel, book of, 56
Ezra, 4, 225

faith, 170
false witness, 171, 176
fasting, 249
food, 63, 64, 65, 66, 67, 71, 74, 75
foreign domination, 78
four kingdoms, 5, 91, 94–95, 101, 173, 269
fourth kingdom, 30–31, 32
four winds, 181, 202, 216
Freedman, D. N., 159
furnace, 104, 105, 108, 110, 111, 112, 114, 115, 119
future, 77

Gabriel, 34, 42, 188, 190, 208, 214, 219, 220, 221, 230, 231–32, 254, 256, 257, 260, 307
Gadatas, 155
Gaumâta, 271
Gedaliah, 3
Gehazi, 150
genre. *See* Daniel, genre
Ginsburg, H. L., 159
goat, 199, 200–201, 215, 216, 219
Gobryas, 155, 156
God, 56, 61, 69, 111, 116, 141; control of earthly powers by, 179; favor of, 66, 67, 126; hand of, 147–48, 152, 157; of heaven, 99, 134; intervention by, 112, 113, 115, 116, 117, 119, 169, 170, 230; kingdom of, 31, 38–39, 70, 71, 78, 94–95, 111, 124, 132, 135, 173, 198, 284, 289; kingship of, 36–38; living, 35,
173; manifestations of, 147–48; Most High, 35, 120, 123, 128, 132, 139, 140, 141, 150, 193; names for, 35–36; as Prince of host, 204; revelations of, 84, 85; reverence and fear of, 177; righteousness of, 229; wrath of, 210–11, 213, 219, 227
Gog, 291
Goldingay, J. E., 51
Goliath, 57
governors, 107
Great Commission, 41
Greece, kingdom of, 4–5, 30, 31, 91, 184, 195, 199, 200–201, 212, 264, 269, 302
Gubaru, 241
Gudea of Sumer, 100

Habakkuk, 180, 211
Hadassah, 63
Haggai, 138
Haman, 109, 115, 165, 167, 171
Hammurabi, 136, 166
Hananiah, 22, 53, 60, 62, 64, 76, 83, 98, 161
Hanukkah, 1, 7
harp, 118
Hasideans, 284
Hatti, 72
Heaven, 35, 135, 138, 139, 140
heavenly beings, 14, 34, 42, 43, 44, 96, 115, 128, 132, 187, 190, 191, 251–53, 256–59, 297–98, 309–10
Hebrew language, 20–21, 25–27, 197
Heliodorus, 278, 279, 280
Hellenistic period, 1, 105, 269
Hellenization, 185
henotheism, 256
Herakles, 272
herald, 107, 118
Hesiod, 87
Hezekiah, 111
Hippolytus, 105
historical genre, 10
hope, 15
horns, 9, 10, 24, 25, 27, 40, 47, 91, 92, 118, 151, 179, 184–86, 191, 192, 196, 197–202, 206, 212, 216–17, 272, 298
host of heaven, 203, 217
hubris, 131, 211, 286, 290

humanity, 132
humility, 39–40, 86, 88, 89, 128, 139, 140

idolatry, 88, 104, 106, 107, 109, 110, 113, 116, 147
illumination, 221, 224
image, 103, 110, 114
intercessory prayer, 230
interpret/interpretation, 77, 98
Isaac, 167
Isaiah, 180
Isaiah, book of, 68
Isaianic tradition, 88
Ishtar, 63
Islam, 32
Israelites, 60

Jacob, 62, 167
Jason, 5–6, 63, 282
Jehoahaz, 62
Jehoash, 136
Jehoiachin, 3, 55, 58, 60, 183
Jehoiakim, 3, 53, 54, 55, 56, 57, 58, 59, 60, 62, 69, 71, 72, 150, 152, 222
Jehoshaphat, 82
Jephthah, 167
Jeremiah, 150, 151, 152, 154, 171, 180, 220, 261
Jeremiah, book of, 56, 68, 147, 223–25, 235
Jeremiel, 256
Jericho, 172
Jerome, 105
Jerusalem, 55, 57, 218, 235, 236, 238, 276–77, 289
Jerusalem temple, 3, 4, 6, 57, 147, 205, 209, 239, 269, 281–82; second temple completed, 4
Jeshua, 237, 238, 240
Jesse, 129
Jesus, 31–32, 135, 174–75, 193, 232
Jewish leaders, 53
Jews/Judaism, 56, 57, 62, 65, 66, 67, 70, 88, 97, 164, 179, 185, 239, 293, 306; and Cyrus II, 4; persecution of, 5–7, 83, 105, 106, 109, 111, 112, 114, 115, 116, 122, 138, 162, 164, 165, 179, 185, 191, 192, 202–4, 209–10, 211, 239, 269, 281–85, 310
Jezebel, 150

Job, 115, 139, 140, 171
John the Baptist, 128, 232
Jonah, 136
Joseph, 54, 63, 66, 69, 75, 77, 85, 86, 126, 141
Josephus, 30–31
Joshua, 63, 108, 203, 237
Josiah, 150
Judah, 54, 56, 59, 60, 62, 71, 72, 111, 129, 138, 211, 276
Judah, end of, 43
Judah, revolt of, 3
Judas Maccabeus, 284
judgment, 33–34, 46–48, 138, 139, 211, 222, 225, 227, 228, 289
Judith, book of, 65

kasdim, 74
kings, 36–38, 111, 185–86
Kings, books of, 55, 147
kings and kingdoms, 94, 122, 123, 124, 129, 132, 138, 139, 140, 151, 178–79, 181–90, 196, 199–208, 258
king's guard, 99
kingship, 241
knowledge, 67, 68, 100, 300
Korah, 172

Labashi-Marduk, 3
Lagi/Lagide, 273
Lamentations, book of, 56
lamenting, 139
Laodice, 273, 274
law/laws, 166–67, 173, 175
learning, 69
Lee Jang Rim, 50
Lenaeus, 281
Leviathan, 182, 258
linen cloth, 251
lions / lions' den, 165–66, 169–70, 176, 182
literature, 61
Lotan, 181
lycanthropy, 130
lyre, 118
Lysimachus, 5, 202, 212

Maccabean revolt, 1, 7, 39, 65, 88, 214, 276, 283, 284, 289, 306
magicians, 54, 61, 69, 74, 75, 76, 77, 79, 82, 88, 97, 98, 126, 141
Malachi, 138

man, 188, 193, 219
Marduk, 57, 63, 74, 125, 155, 181, 258
martyrs/martyrdom, 105, 116, 117, 168–69, 171, 285
Mary, 232
maskilim, 73
Mattaniah, 63
Mattathias, 283
Media/Medes, 2, 3–4, 8, 31, 90, 91, 92, 154, 156, 183, 199, 212, 247, 269
Melchizedek, 120
mene, 152–54, 158
Menelaus, 6, 280, 282
Merneptah, 100
Meshach, 40, 42, 53, 62, 63, 74, 98, 103, 108, 109, 112, 114, 115, 116, 117, 161, 285
messenger, 127
Messiah, 95, 234, 240
metamorphosis, 131
Micaiah, 82, 152
Michael, 35, 42, 47, 193, 209, 256, 257, 258, 264, 267, 270, 293
Miller, William, 32, 49–50
miracle, 116, 117
Miriam, 230
Mishael, 22, 53, 60, 62, 64, 76, 83, 98, 161
mixtures, 93, 94
monotheism, 256
Mordecai, 63, 115, 171
Moses, 69, 97, 137, 230, 234
Mount Zion, 88, 95
musical instruments, 107, 108, 118
mystery, 84, 100, 127

Nabonidus, 3, 4, 23, 101, 122, 131, 132, 141, 142, 143, 145, 146, 147, 155, 159, 223; illness of, 8
Nabopolassar, 2
Nathan, 150
Nebuchadnezzar, 2–3, 23, 37, 40, 47, 53, 54, 55, 56, 57, 58, 59, 62, 63, 65, 68, 69, 70, 71, 72, 77, 78, 81, 82, 96, 97, 101, 103, 105, 106, 109, 110, 112, 115, 116, 121, 122, 123, 124, 125, 136, 142, 143, 145, 146, 150, 154, 155, 158, 159, 179, 183, 244
Neco, 62
Nehemiah, 4, 225, 226, 235, 236, 238
Neo-Babylonian Empire, 2

Neriglissar, 3, 101
Nineveh, 136
Nitocris, 149
nobility, 60, 73

officials, 107
Onias III, 5–6, 63, 204, 208, 237, 238, 239, 240, 278, 279, 280
Ophir, 265
Ovid, 87

pagan gods, 69, 88
Paneas, battle of, 276
parsin, 152, 153, 154, 158
peoples, nations and men of every language, 23, 104, 107, 118, 123, 172
peres, 154
Pergamum, 280
periodization of history, 14, 233
persecution. *See* Jews/Judaism, persecution of
Persian Empire, 4–5, 7, 31, 90, 91, 92, 111, 154, 156, 183, 195, 199, 247, 264, 269, 270–71
Persian language, 107
Peter, 253
Phanuel, 256
Pharaoh, 54, 69, 77, 85, 141
Philip V of Macedonia, 275
Philip Arrhidaeus, 185, 201, 272
Philistia, 55, 72
Philistines, 57
pipes, 118
polytheism, 257
Porphyry, 32
power, 111
prayer, 83, 164, 167, 168, 174, 230, 232; Daniel's, 221, 222, 225–30, 242
Prayer of Azariah, 19, 21, 115, 120
Prayer of Nabonidus, 85, 131, 141, 142, 147
predestination, 263, 285
prefects, 107
pride, 137, 140, 143
priests, 60, 251
Prince of the host, 204, 256, 286
prophecy after event, 14
prophetic genre, 10
pseudonymity, 14
pshr, 98

Subject Index

Ptolemies/Ptolemaic kingdom, 5, 91, 94, 269, 273
Ptolemy I Soter, 202, 212, 273
Ptolemy II Philadelphus, 91, 273
Ptolemy III Euergetes, 274
Ptolemy IV Philopater, 275
Ptolemy V Epiphanes, 5, 91, 275, 277, 303
Ptolemy VI Philometor, 185, 280, 281, 290
Ptolemy VII Euergetes, 185, 282
Ptolemy Lagus, 201–2
purity/impurity, 64, 65, 71, 75, 312

queen, 149
Qumran, 223

Raguel, 256
Rahab, 181, 258
ram, 199, 200, 215
Raphael, 209, 256
Reformation, 32
renunciation, 135, 144
repentence, 221
rescue, 174
resurrection, 9, 45–46, 293–98
retribution, 221
revelations, 14, 248–49, 251, 260
ribs, three, 195
righteousness, 135, 297
Roman Empire, 6, 30, 31, 92, 277
Roxane, 272
royal family, 60
royal rage, 110, 114

sabbath, 233
sackloth, 225
saints of the Most High, 191
salvation by faith, 136
Samuel, 136, 150
Sarah, 62
Saraqa'el, 256
sarisim, 59, 73
Satan, 258
satraps, 107, 117
Saul, 136, 150, 253
Scipio Asiaticus, 277
Scopus, 276
Scripture, 223–24
sea, the, 181, 194
Seleucia, 274, 275
Seleucid kingdom, 5, 91, 94, 269, 273

Seleucus, 201–2, 212
Seleucus I Nicator, 186, 273, 302
Seleucus II Callinicus, 186, 274–75
Seleucus III Ceraunos, 275
Seleucus III Soter, 186
Seleucus IV Philopator, 5, 186, 202, 278
Sennacherib, 82, 170, 290
Seventh-Day Adventist Church, 50
seven times (years), 104, 114, 127, 131, 135, 138
seventy weeks of years, 9, 220, 222, 232–37, 243–44
seventy years, 224
seven years, 239
Shadrach, 40, 42, 53, 62, 63, 98, 103, 108, 109, 112, 114, 115, 116, 117, 161, 285
Sheol, 45–46, 294
Sheshbazzar, 63
Shinar, 57, 72
Sibylline Oracles, 233
Sidon, 276
Simon, 278
sin, 53, 138, 142, 143, 211, 222, 225, 226, 229, 249; punishment for, 33–34
Sin, cult of (moon god), 3
sixty-two sevens, 237–38, 244
Sodom and Gomorrah, 230
Solomon, 66, 226
Song of the Three Young Men, 19, 21, 120
son of man, Jesus as, 31–32, 44–45, 193
sorcerers, 79
sovereignty, 151
statues, 87, 88, 90, 100, 103, 105, 106, 107, 114, 134
suffering, 33–35, 171, 312–13
Suffering Servant, 284
Surafel, 256
Suru'el, 256
Susa, 198–99, 215
Susanna, 18, 19, 21, 115
symbolism, 14

tabernacle, 235
Tammuz, 287
Tarshish, 252
tekel, 152, 154, 158
temple vessels, 146, 147, 157

Tent of Meeting, 235
terror and fear, 125, 148, 158, 253, 254, 255
Theodotion, 247
throne, 187
Tiamat, 181, 258
Tigris River, 250, 265
timetable, of Daniel, 8–9, 48–50
Torah, 206
touching of lips, 261
transgression, 233–34
treasure house of God, 73
tree imagery, 127, 128, 129, 130, 134. *See also* cosmic-tree imagery
trembling, 255
trials, 170, 171

understanding, 68, 69, 243, 259
Uriel, 209, 256

visions, 83, 84, 148, 248–49, 260
voice from heaven, 137–38, 144

War Scroll, The, 258
watchers, 127, 128
Whisenant, Edgar, 50

wicked, 313
wicked ruler, 43–44
wine, 63, 64, 65
wisdom, 67, 68, 69, 84
Wise, M., 51
wise men, 79, 81, 82, 83, 85, 98, 99, 111, 125, 126, 145, 148
wise ones, 283–84, 297, 313
witness, 40–42
works righteousness, 135, 136, 229
writing on wall, 147–48, 152, 157

Xerxes, 4, 109, 163, 183, 223, 241, 270, 271

Yahweh, 35, 57, 69, 72, 115, 124, 181, 189, 220, 241–42, 258; of hosts, 203
Yamm, 181, 189

Zaphenath-Paneah, 54, 63
Zechariah, 138, 232, 237
Zedekiah, 3, 63, 108
Zerubbabel, 63, 237
Zeus Olympios, 105, 106, 218, 239, 245, 286, 287
zoanthropy, 130

Scripture Index

Old Testament

Genesis 1:2, 181; 1:5, 208; 1:11–12, 194; 1:20–22, 181; 1:21, 194; 1:24, 194; 1:25, 194; 1:26, 89, 134, 257, 260; 1:26–27, 89–90, 189; 1:28, 89, 132, 134, 170; 2:14, 251; 2:19, 134; 2:20, 62; 2:21, 210, 254; 3:5, 138; 5:24, 46, 294; 6, 18; 6:2, 115; 6:4, 115; 7:1, 179; 7:11, 181; 8:1, 179; 8:2, 44; 8:16, 44; 8:22, 44; 9:1, 179; 9:1–17, 226; 9:4, 64; 10:10, 72; 11, 57; 11:2, 57, 72; 11:4, 129; 11:7, 257; 11:8–10, 57; 11:9, 57; 14:1, 99; 14:9, 72, 99; 14:18, 120; 14:19, 120; 14:20, 120; 14:22, 120, 310; 15, 226; 15:1, 18, 255; 15:12, 210, 254; 15:16, 213; 15:18, 250; 17, 226; 17:3, 209; 17:5, 62; 17:15, 62; 18:1–19:1, 189; 18:23–33, 230; 19:1–11, 170; 20:3, 18; 21:33, 187; 24:3, 99; 24:7, 99; 26:24, 255; 27:30–40, 167; 27:40, 135; 28:12, 18; 31:10, 18; 31:11, 18; 31:21, 250; 31:24, 18; 32:28, 62; 32:32–33, 189; 37:7, 100; 37:9, 100; 37:36, 77, 99; 38:24, 108; 39:1, 54, 77, 99; 39:1–4, 66; 39:4, 179; 39:6, 54; 39:7–20, 73; 39:21, 54, 179; 40–41, 13; 40:5, 98; 40:8, 77, 98; 40:12, 98; 40:16, 77, 98; 40:18, 98; 40:22, 98; 41:1, 249; 41:2, 67, 100; 41:3, 100; 41:8, 54, 69, 75, 77, 79, 98, 99, 190; 41:10, 77, 99; 41:11, 98; 41:12, 77, 98, 99; 41:13, 98; 41:15, 69, 98; 41:16, 77, 86; 41:17, 100; 41:24, 54, 69, 75, 77, 79; 41:25, 77; 41:25–32, 54; 41:28, 77; 41:37–44, 179; 41:38, 68, 77, 126, 141; 41:39, 54, 69; 41:39–41, 54; 41:40, 163; 41:40–41, 54; 41:40–42, 77; 41:42, 54, 77, 148; 41:45, 54, 63, 97; 46:23, 261; 49:1, 100, 259, 267

Exodus 1–13, 69; 2:3, 314; 2:5, 314; 3:2, 187; 4:6, 314; 5:6, 175; 5:10, 175; 6:8, 310; 7:3, 141, 263; 7:15, 314; 7:18, 314; 7:22, 69; 8:3, 75, 79; 8:7, 69; 8:14, 75, 79; 8:15, 75, 79, 263; 8:18, 69; 8:32, 263; 9:11, 69, 75, 79; 9:34, 263; 12:2, 250; 12:12, 36, 69; 14:7, 158; 14:19–20, 170; 15:11, 310; 16:7–8, 139; 17:6, 95; 18:1–2, 97; 19:16, 252; 19:18, 187; 20:18, 252; 20–35, 226; 22:18, 79; 23:15, 250; 23:16, 250; 23:31, 250; 25:18–20, 243; 26:33, 286; 26:34, 286; 28:5, 251; 28:6, 251; 28:20, 252; 29:38–42, 205; 30:26, 235; 31:18, 148; 32:1–14, 230; 32:2, 144; 32:14, 137; 32:32, 228; 32:32–33, 263, 293; 34:7, 172; 34:15, 64; 34:22, 250; 34:28, 225; 39:13, 252; 40:9, 235

Leviticus 6:10, 251; 11:1–47, 64; 16:4, 251; 16:29, 266; 16:31, 266; 16:32, 251; 17:10–13, 64; 21:9, 108; 21:17–23, 60; 22:18–25, 60; 23:5, 250; 23:23–25, 250; 23:27, 266; 23:32, 266; 25:2–7, 224; 26:19, 144; 26:27–45, 227; 26:40–45, 225

Numbers 4:15, 243; 5:11–31, 170; 6:25, 229; 12:13, 230; 14:21, 311; 14:27, 139; 14:36, 139; 16:11, 139; 16:23–33, 172; 17:5, 139; 20:11, 95; 22:5, 250; 23:19, 188, 196; 24:14, 100, 259, 267; 24:16, 120; 28:2–8, 205; 29:7, 266

Deuteronomy 1:7, 250; 1:15, 175; 4:12, 253; 4:19, 203, 258; 4:26, 311; 4:30, 100, 259, 267; 4:34, 141; 5:4, 187; 5:26, 169; 6:22, 141; 7:9, 226; 8:2–3, 144; 8:10–18, 137; 8:18, 137; 9:9, 225; 9:10, 148; 12:2, 141; 12:23–24, 64; 15:1–11, 224; 18:10, 79; 19:15, 311; 19:19, 171; 20:5, 175; 21–13, 249; 22:9–11, 194; 24:16, 172; 27:15–26, 227; 28, 33; 28:15–68, 227; 28:49–50, 212; 29:20, 227; 29:26, 258; 30:19, 311; 31:6, 261, 268; 31:7, 261, 268; 31:23, 261, 268; 31:28, 311; 31:29, 259, 267; 32:8, 115, 120; 32:8–9, 257; 32:38, 64; 32:39, 151; 32:40, 310, 311; 33:2, 191; 33:19, 291

Joshua **1:4**, 194, 250; **1:6**, 268; **1:7**, 268; **1:9**, 268; **3:10**, 169; **5:14**, 96, 203, 209, 254, 256; **5:15**, 256; 7, 172; **7:15**, 108; **7:25**, 108; **8:31**, 242; **9:1**, 194; **10:11**, 258; **15:47**, 194; **23:4**, 194; **24:2–3**, 250; **24:14–15**, 250; **24:19**, 141

Judges **4:21**, 210; **5:17**, 291; **5:19–20**, 258; **5:20**, 203, 298; **6:22–23**, 255; **6:23**, 261; **8:19**, 310; **8:23**, 36, 38; **11:29–40**, 167; **13:20**, 96, 209; **19:20**, 261

1 Samuel **1:3**, 203; **1:11**, 203; **2:3**, 154; **2:6–7**, 151; **2:7–8**, 143; **2:18**, 251; **3:2–21**, 249; **4:4**, 182, 203; **4:19**, 261; 5, 69; **5:1–2**, 57; **5:2**, 274; **5:3–7**, 57; **6:17**, 57; **8:6–7**, 36, 38; **10:9–13**, 249; 12, 150; **12:10**, 228; **12:24**, 200; **14:39**, 311; **14:45**, 311; **15:1–23**, 150; **15:24–31**, 136; **15:25**, 228; **16:7**, 60; **16:12**, 60; **16:13**, 60; **17:26**, 169; **19:6**, 311; **20:3**, 311; **20:21**, 311; **21:9**, 57; **22:18**, 251; **25:26**, 311; **25:34**, 311; **26:12**, 210, 254

2 Samuel **6:2**, 182; 7, 226; **7:14**, 38; **10:16**, 250; **12:20**, 250; **13:23**, 249; **14:2**, 250; **22:11**, 243; **22:14**, 120

1 Kings **1:31**, 170; **2:3**, 242; **3:12**, 69; **4:21**, 250; **4:24**, 250; **6:23–28**, 243; 8, 225; **8:30**, 230; **8:35**, 167; **8:46–51**, 225; **8:47**, 226; **8:50**, 66; **8:54**, 167; **9:28**, 265; **10:11**, 265; **11:5**, 74; **14:15**, 250; 18, 36; **18:1–40**, 69; **19:1–8**, 170; **21:20–26**, 150; 22, 82; **22:17–28**, 152; **22:19**, 115, 203; **22:19–22**, 187; **22:19–23**, 128, 134, 257; **22:48**, 265

2 Kings **2:9–12**, 294; **2:11**, 46; **3:15**, 249; **3:27**, 211; **4:18–37**, 294, 296; **5:21–27**, 150; **7:2**, 158; **7:19**, 158; **9:25**, 158; **13:14–19**, 167; **13:18–19**, 136; **13:20–21**, 294, 296; **14:1–6**, 172; 17, 33; **18:33–35**, 111; **19:7**, 291; **19:15**, 182; **19:34**, 111; **19:35**, 170; **23:34**, 62; **24:1**, 3, 55, 58, 71–72; **24:5**, 58; **24:6**, 55; **24:10**, 71; **24:10–15**, 58; **24:12**, 3, 60; **24:13**, 3; **24:14–15**, 3, 60; **24:17**, 63; **24–25**, 33; **25:8**, 99; **25:27**, 3; **25:29–30**, 62

1 Chronicles **3:1**, 17; **13:6**, 182; **19:16**, 250; **21:8**, 228; **22:19**, 266; **24:5**, 204; **29:11–12**, 89

2 Chronicles **9:26**, 250; **11:16**, 266; **12:7**, 227; **13:20**, 253, 261; **22:9**, 253, 261; **30:12**, 148; **34:25**, 227; **36:5–7**, 55; **36:6**, 55; **36:6–7**, 58; **36:9–10**, 58; **36:19–22**, 224; **36:19–23**, 59; **36:21**, 224; **36:22**, 265; **36:23**, 99, 265

Ezra **1:1**, 265; **1:1–4**, 4, 97, 183; **1:2**, 99, 265; **1:2–4**, 70; **1:7–8**, 183; **1:11**, 63; **2:62**, 64, 75; **3:2**, 63; **3:7**, 183, 265; **4:3**, 265; **4:5**, 8, 265, 270; **4:6**, 4, 183, 270; **4:7–8**, 183, 270; **4:11**, 183; **4:13**, 175; **4:13–16**, 163; **4:19–21**, 235; **4:21**, 118; **4:22**, 163, 175; **4:23**, 183; **4:24**, 8, 270; **5:5–7**, 270; **5:12**, 61; **5:13**, 118; **6:1**, 118, 270; **6:3**, 118; **6:3–5**, 4; **6:6–12**, 117; **6:9**, 99; **6:12–15**, 270; **6:14**, 270; **6:14–15**, 8; **7:1**, 270; **7:6**, 148; **7:7**, 270; **7:12**, 89, 99, 123, 175; **7:14**, 175; **7:21**, 99; **7:25**, 175; **7:26**, 175; **8:1**, 270; **8:2**, 17; **8:21**, 266; **8:24**, 204; **9:4**, 255; **9:6–15**, 225; **9:8**, 228; **9:10**, 228; 10, 255; **10:1**, 225, 255; **10:3**, 255; **10:6**, 255; **10:9**, 255

Nehemiah **1:1**, 199; **1:4**, 99; **1:5**, 99, 226; **1:5–11**, 225; **1:6–7**, 226; **2:1**, 250, 270; **2:3**, 170; **2:4**, 99; **2:20**, 99; 4, 238; **5:14**, 270; **7:6**, 143; **7:64**, 64, 75; **9:1–2**, 225; **9:5–37**, 225; **9:20**, 141; **9:26**, 217; **9:30**, 227; **9:32**, 226, 228; **9:34**, 226; **10:6**, 17; **12:22**, 8, 183, 270; **13:6**, 270

Esther **1:1**, 163, 199; **1:1–2**, 270; **1:1–3**, 183; **1:2**, 199; **1:5**, 199; **1:12**, 110; **1:14**, 199; **1:15–17**, 270; **1:19**, 167, 199, 270; **2:3**, 199; **2:5**, 63, 199; **2:7**, 63; **2:8**, 199; **3:8–9**, 109; **3:9**, 165; **3:15**, 199; **4:1–3**, 225; **7:7**, 110; **7:10**, 115, 171; **8:8**, 167; **8:9**, 163; **8:14**, 199; **9:6**, 199; **9:11**, 199; **9:12**, 199; **10:2**, 199

Scripture Index

Job 1–2, 128, 187; **1:1–2:13**, 21; **1:6**, 115, 257; **2:1**, 115, 257; **3:1–42:6**, 21; **4:13**, 210; **5:1**, 143; **7:1**, 248; **9:13**, 181; **14:7**, 129; **14:14**, 248; **15:15**, 191; **25:6**, 196; **26:12**, 258; **26:12–13**, 181; **28:16**, 265; **28:19**, 265; **31:6**, 154; **31:24**, 265; **35:15**, 254; **38:1**, 115; **38:2–39:30**, 140; **38:7**, 115, 298; **40:7–41:34**, 140; **40:11**, 144; **42:7–17**, 21

Psalms 2, 291; **2:8**, 38; **6:3**, 207; **6:5**, 46, 294; **7:11**, 219; **7:15–16**, 171; **7:17**, 120; **8:4**, 44, 188, 196; **8:5**, 196; **8:6–8**, 89; **9:2**, 120; **9:15**, 171; **13:1–2**, 207; **16:10**, 46; **18:2**, 95; **18:4–6**, 46; **18:12**, 252; **18:13**, 120; **18:14**, 252; **18:27**, 144; **18:31**, 95; **18:46**, 95; **19:14**, 95; **21:7**, 120; **21:9**, 108; **22**, 139; **22:13**, 166; **28:1**, 95; **28:2**, 310; **29:1**, 115; **29:7**, 252; **30:3**, 46, 295; **30:9**, 46; **31:2–3**, 95; **33:6**, 203; **34:9**, 191; **35:17**, 207; **35:26**, 200; **37:21**, 135; **37:35**, 141; **42:2**, 169; **42:9**, 95; **45:9**, 265; **46**, 291; **46:7**, 203; **46:11**, 203; **47:2**, 120; **48**, 291; **48:2**, 202; **50:2**, 202; **50:14**, 120; **52:8**, 141; **52:10**, 141; **55:12**, 200; **55:13**, 200; **55:14**, 175; **55:17**, 168; **57:2**, 120; **57:4**, 166; **57:6**, 171; **58:6–11**, 50; **59:4–5**, 50; **62:2**, 95; **62:6–7**, 95; **62:9**, 154; **63:4**, 310; **64:2**, 175; **65:7**, 181; **66:10**, 116; **66:12**, 116; **68:4**, 189; **69:22–29**, 50; **69:28**, 263, 293; **70:1–3**, 50; **72:1–2**, 136; **72:8**, 250; **73:23**, 46; **73:23–26**, 46; **73:26**, 46; **74:10**, 207; **74:13–14**, 182; **75:7**, 151; **75:7–8**, 50; **76**, 291; **77:11**, 310; **77:12**, 310; **77:14**, 310; **77:15**, 310; **77:16**, 181; **78**, 95; **78:12**, 310; **78:15**, 181; **78:16**, 95; **78:35**, 95; **78:56**, 120; **79:5**, 207; **79:6**, 227; **80:1**, 182; **80:4**, 207; **80:11**, 250; **80:17**, 196; **80:18**, 196; **82**, 128, 187; **82:1**, 136, 187, 257; **82:2–7**, 257; **82:3–4**, 136; **82:6**, 115, 136; **82:6–7**, 187; **82:8**, 187; **86:13**, 46, 295; **88:10**, 310; **88:10–11**, 294; **88:10–12**, 46; **88:11**, 310; **88:12**, 310; **88:13**, 310; **89:1–37**, 226; **89:5**, 191, 310; **89:6** LXX, 310; **89:6–8**, 128, 187; **89:6–10**, 257; **89:9–10**, 181–82; **89:10**, 258; **89:26**, 38; **89:46**, 207; **90:10**, 225; **90:13**, 207; **91:1**, 120; **92:12–14**, 141; **92:13–15**, 141; **93**, 36; **94:3**, 207; **94:22**, 88; **95**, 36; **95:1**, 88; **96**, 36; **96:13**, 47; **97**, 36; **97:3**, 187; **97:4**, 252; **97:7–9**, 257; **98:9**, 47; **99:1**, 182; **104:3**, 189; **104:6–9**, 181; **106:9**, 181; **106:24**, 202; **107:26**, 181; **109:6–31**, 50; **110:1**, 38; **113:7–8**, 143; **115:17**, 46, 294; **118:22**, 95; **121:4**, 128; **126:2–3**, 200; **132**, 226; **134:2**, 310; **135:9**, 141; **135:15–18**, 169; **136:24**, 135; **139:16**, 263; **144:1–2**, 88; **144:3**, 196; **145:13**, 124

Proverbs **3:34**, 144; **11:2**, 40; **16:18**, 40, 125; **19:5**, 171; **24:12**, 154; **26:27**, 171; **28:10**, 171; **29:23**, 40

Ecclesiastes **1:2**, 286, 297; **1:13**, 266; **1:17**, 266; **2:24**, 148; **3:9–13**, 297; **3:10–21**, 45; **3:19**, 294; **3:19–21**, 294; **7:21**, 266; **8:9**, 266; **8:14**, 297; **8:16**, 266; **9:1**, 148; **9:1–6**, 297; **9:2–3**, 45, 294, 297; **9:5–6**, 46; **9:10**, 46, 294

Song of Songs **1:1**, 286; **5:11**, 265

Isaiah **1:1**, 19; **1:9**, 203; **1:15**, 310; **1:24**, 203; **2:1–4**, 40; **2:2**, 100, 219, 267; **2:2–3**, 88, 95; **2:11–17**, 144; **4:3**, 293; **6**, 134, 180; **6:1–7**, 187; **6:1–8**, 128, 257; **6:2**, 243; **6:3**, 88; **6:6–7**, 261; **6:11**, 207; **6:11–12**, 207; **7:7**, 304; **7:20**, 250; **8:1**, 180; **8:7**, 250; **8:14**, 95; **9**, 38; **10:5**, 138, 211; **10:12–15**, 211; **10:12–19**, 138; **10:16–19**, 211; **10:23**, 286, 307; **10:24–26**, 211; **10:25**, 286, 307; **10:32**, 291; **10:33–34**, 291; **11**, 38; **11:1**, 129; **11:3–4**, 136; **11:6–9**, 170; **11:9**, 88, 170; **11:11**, 72; **13:12**, 265; **13:17**, 68, 91; **13:17–22**, 138, 156; **14**, 204, 286; **14:12**, 203; **14:13–15**, 151; **14:14**, 120, 203, 204; **14:15**, 203; **14:25**, 291; **21:1–4**, 261; **21:2**, 68, 91, 216; **21:5**, 156; **22:1–10**, 156; **23:1**, 306; **24:21**, 139, 204, 258; **24–27**, 13, 204, 257–58; **25:1**, 310; **25:8**, 95; **26:1**, 293; **26:19**, 46, 295; **27:1**, 182, 258; **27:1–2**, 293; **28:16**, 95;

29:1–8, 291; 29:11, 216; 30:8, 180; 30:25, 215; 37:7, 291; 37:16, 182; 37:36, 170; 38:18–19, 294; 39:7, 73; 40–55, 38, 40, 41, 95, 284; 40:1–2, 128, 248; 40:2, 217; 41:3, 200; 41:20, 148; 41:21–29, 96; 42:5–8, 40; 42:6, 173; 42:6–7, 124; 42:9, 96; 43:2, 115; 43:5, 115; 43:10–13, 40; 43:12, 124, 173; 44:4, 215; 44:6–19, 96; 44:8, 40; 44:18, 169; 44:25, 95; 44:26, 96; 44:28–45:4, 138, 183; 45:1, 4, 236; 45:1–7, 97; 45:3, 84; 45:14, 40, 96, 124; 45:14–15, 173; 45:22, 40, 124; 46:1, 125; 46:1–2, 274; 46:10, 96; 47:5–15, 96; 47:9, 79; 48:3, 96; 48:5–6, 96; 49:5–6, 41; 49:6, 40, 173; 49:7, 40, 124, 173; 49:18, 311; 49:22–23, 40, 124, 173; 49:23, 40, 96; 51:9, 182, 258; 51:10, 181; 51:12, 196; 52:13, 284; 52:14, 266; 53:11, 284, 297; 55–66, 40; 55:3, 39; 55:5, 39; 56–66, 13; 56:4–5, 73; 56:6–7, 173; 58:4–10, 225; 59:3, 64, 75; 60:1–12, 40; 60:3–12, 124; 60:14, 96, 124; 60:16, 124; 61:3, 250; 62:6, 128; 62:8, 310; 63:3, 64, 75; 63:12–13, 181; 65:17, 209; 65:25, 170; 66:2, 255; 66:5, 225; 66:22, 94, 209, 297; 66:24, 296

Jeremiah 1:1, 19; 1:4, 108; 1:8, 171; 1:9, 260; 1:11–12, 154; 1:12, 228; 1:20, 108; 2:2, 108; 2:10, 306; 2:12, 110; 2:18, 250; 2:48, 108; 3:5, 110; 3:8, 108; 3:10, 110; 3:12, 108, 109, 110; 3:14, 110; 3:17, 293; 3:19, 110, 202, 276; 4:11, 293; 4:21, 207; 5:11, 156; 6:24, 109; 7:10–11, 229; 7:20, 227; 10:9, 265; 10:10, 169, 219; 11:16, 141; 12:4, 207; 20:7–8, 171; 21:2, 72; 21:7, 72; 22:13–19, 150; 22:15–16, 136; 22:24, 311; 22:25, 72; 23:18, 187; 23:18–22, 128; 23:20, 219; 24:1, 100; 25:1, 55, 56, 235; 25:11, 224; 25:11–12, 59, 220, 224, 235; 27:2, 130; 27:5, 151; 27:5–7, 151; 27:6, 89, 134; 28:14, 89; 29:4–14, 224; 29:8–10, 224; 29:10, 59, 234; 29:10–14, 220; 29:22, 105, 108; 30:2, 180; 30:7, 293; 30:18–22, 235; 30:24, 219; 31:28, 227; 31:29–30, 172; 31:38–40, 235; 32:9–12, 299; 32:16–25, 225; 32:20, 141; 33:17–18, 237; 36:27–28, 300; 38:5, 302; 39:9, 99; 42:18, 227; 44:6, 227; 44:21, 226; 44:27, 228; 46:2, 56, 72; 46:6, 250; 46:10, 250; 47:6, 207; 48:7, 274; 48:26, 200; 48:42, 200; 49:3, 274; 49:16, 144; 49:18, 196; 49:36, 181; 50:2, 125; 50:40, 196; 51:11, 68, 91, 183; 51:13, 219; 51:27–29, 91; 51:28, 68, 183; 51:39, 156; 51:44, 125; 51:57, 156; 52:12, 99; 52:33–34, 62

Lamentations 3:35, 120; 4:18, 219; 5:8, 144

Ezekiel 1, 115; 1:1, 251; 1:1–3, 19; 1:4, 187; 1:5, 268; 1:7, 251; 1:11, 252; 1:13, 187, 251; 1:14, 251; 1:15–21, 187; 1:16, 251; 1:22–28, 182; 1:23, 252; 1:24, 251; 1:26, 189, 208, 260, 268; 1:28, 209, 254; 2:1, 44; 2:3, 44; 2:6, 44; 2:8, 44; 3:17, 188; 3:23, 209; 6:17, 216; 7:2, 219; 7:3, 219; 7:6, 219; 7:24, 144; 8:2, 268; 8:3, 198; 8:14, 287; 9:2, 251; 9:3, 251; 9:8, 209; 9:11, 251; 10:1, 268; 10:2, 251; 10:5, 243; 10:6, 251; 10:7, 251; 11:16, 115; 11:24, 198; 13:9, 293; 14:14, 17; 14:20, 17; 17:23, 88; 17:24, 129, 144; 18, 172; 19:4, 165; 19:8–9, 165; 20:6, 202; 20:15, 202; 20:40, 88; 22:31, 219; 26:7, 89; 27:6, 306; 28, 204, 286; 28:3, 18; 31:11, 129; 31:15, 129; 34:23–25, 237; 37, 46, 294, 295; 37:9, 181; 37:24–28, 237; 38:16, 100, 219, 267; 39:2, 291; 39:4, 291; 40:1, 148; 40:2, 88, 198; 40:3, 268; 42:11, 268; 43:3, 209; 44:4, 209; 44:9–16, 237; 46:13–15, 205; 47:10, 194; 47:15, 194; 47:19, 194; 47:20, 194

Daniel 1, 264; 1–6, 1, 11, 12–13, 14, 17, 20, 29, 53, 64, 178, 179, 247; 1:1, 1, 7, 15, 53, 55, 56, 58, 68, 71–72, 198, 246, 247; 1:1–2, 54–59, 138, 213, 224; 1:1–6, 17; 1:1–7, 54; 1:1–2:4a, 20, 23, 25–27, 197; 1:2, 35, 53, 56, 57, 72–73, 111, 145, 146, 184, 222, 282; 1:3, 59, 60, 62, 73; 1:3–5, 59–62; 1:4, 26, 53, 54, 60, 61, 73–74, 103, 227, 243; 1:5, 7, 56, 61, 62,

Scripture Index 333

68, 74, 78, 306; **1:6**, 60; **1:6–7**, 62–63; **1:7**, 54, 64, 74; **1:8**, 28, 62, 64, 66, 74–75, 249, 306; **1:8–10**, 63–66; **1:8–12**, 21; **1:8–15**, 285; **1:8–16**, 56; **1:9**, 35, 54, 56, 66, 75; **1:10**, 12, 66, 75, 103; **1:11–14**, 66–67; **1:12**, 249; **1:13**, 62, 74, 103, 306; **1:15**, 13, 62, 67, 74, 103, 306; **1:15–16**, 67, 249; **1:16**, 62, 67, 306; **1:17**, 26, 35, 53, 56, 61, 67–68, 103, 227, 243; **1:18**, 72, 78, 268; **1:18–20**, 27, 68–69, 126; **1:18–31**, 7; **1:19–20**, 56, 97; **1:20**, 13, 17, 54, 61, 69, 75, 76, 78, 79, 111; **1:21**, 1, 37, 53, 59, 69–71, 173, 246–47; **2**, 8, 39, 249, 263; **2:1**, 7, 8, 68, 69, 72, 77, 78–79, 125, 133, 190, 254; **2:1–2**, 148; **2:2**, 75, 77, 78, 79–80, 83, 98, 141; **2:2–11**, 79; **2:3**, 80, 125, 133, 254; **2:4**, 76, 77, 81, 98, 170, 182, 197; **2:4–10**, 98; **2:4–11**, 81; **2:4b**, 20, 25; **2:4b–6:28**, 27; **2:4b–7:28**, 20, 23, 27, 178, 197; **2:5**, 66, 77, 98, 117; **2:5–6**, 81; **2:5–9**, 81–82; **2:6**, 77, 98; **2:7**, 81, 98; **2:8**, 83, 99; **2:8–9**, 82; **2:9**, 82, 95, 98, 99, 175; **2:9–21**, 99; **2:10**, 98; **2:10–11**, 82, 85; **2:10–12**, 82; **2:11**, 37, 85, 95, 126; **2:12**, 77, 99; **2:12–13**, 66; **2:13**, 77, 175; **2:13–23**, 25, 26, 77, 83–85; **2:14**, 77, 99, 157; **2:15**, 77, 83, 175; **2:15–16**, 78; **2:16**, 78, 83, 85, 98; **2:17**, 63, 83, 98; **2:17–18**, 98; **2:18**, 35, 83, 99–100, 127, 220, 287; **2:19**, 11, 35, 36, 37, 83, 84, 99, 100, 127; **2:20**, 35, 84; **2:20–23**, 123; **2:21**, 37, 84, 192, 213; **2:22**, 84; **2:23**, 35, 84; **2:24**, 77, 83, 85, 88, 98; **2:24–25**, 83; **2:24–28**, 85–86; **2:25**, 77, 83, 85, 98, 149; **2:26**, 63, 98; **2:27**, 84, 85, 98, 100, 127, 141; **2:27–28**, 36, 82, 86, 89**2:28**, 35, 72, 77, 84, 85, 100, 194, 259, 267; **2:29**, 84, 100, 127; **2:29–30**, 86, 89; **2:30**, 77, 84, 88, 89, 98, 100, 127; **2:31**, 90, 100, 103; **2:31–33**, 100; **2:31–35**, 86–88; **2:32**, 182; **2:32–33**, 87; **2:33**, 90, 93, 184, 212, 272; 269; **2:34**, 16, 28, 32, 46, 87, 93, 102, 195, 214; **2:34–35**, 29, 31; **2:35**, 46, 87, 88, 95, 102; **2:36**, 88, 98, 101; **2:36–38**, 37, 88–90, 182; **2:36a**, 100; **2:37**, 35, 38, 89, 99; **2:37–38**, 89, 134; **2:38**, 89, 90, 101, 103, 105, 111, 127, 134; **2:39**, 90–92, 94, 183; **2:39–43**, 90; **2:40**, 90, 92, 93, 94, 101, 184, 188, 269; **2:40–42**, 90; **2:40–43**, 92–94, 184, 212, 272; **2:41**, 90, 93, 94; **2:41–43**, 269; **2:42**, 93, 94; **2:43**, 91, 94; **2:44**, 31, 35, 39, 46, 88, 93, 94, 99, 101, 124, 139, 173, 188; **2:44–45**, 29, 31, 46, 94–96, 140, 195; **2:45**, 15, 28, 93, 94, 95, 98, 101–2, 188, 214; **2:46**, 40, 72, 96; **2:46–47**, 172; **2:46–49**, 96–98; **2:47**, 36, 37, 40, 84, 96, 100, 103, 111, 123, 127; **2:48**, 17, 69, 77, 97, 98, 106, 126, 148, 149, 163; **2:48–49**, 7, 54, 117, 124; **2:49**, 97, 98, 103, 163; **3**, 264, 285; **3:1**, 103, 104, 105, 119; **3:1–7**, 105–8; **3:2**, 98, 104, 107, 117, 119; **3:2–3**, 107; **3:3**, 104, 107, 117, 119; **3:4**, 104, 107, 118; **3:5**, 104, 107–8, 118, 119; **3:6**, 104, 108; **3:7**, 104, 107, 118, 119; **3:8**, 103, 104; **3:8–12**, 108–10; **3:9**, 119, 170; **3:10**, 104, 157; **3:11**, 104; **3:12**, 103, 104, 106, 118–19, 157; **3:13**, 37, 103, 104; **3:14**, 104, 106; **3:15**, 103, 104, 111, 112, 113, 114, 119, 161; **3:16**, 112, 119; **3:17**, 35, 104, 110, 111, 112, 113, 114, 119–20, 169; **3:17–18**, 28, 50, 112; **3:18**, 37, 104, 105, 106, 113, 120; **3:19**, 104, 114; **3:19–20**, 37; **3:19–23**, 114–15; **3:20**, 104, 114; **3:21**, 103, 104, 114, 116; **3:22**, 13, 104, 114, 115, 162, 171; **3:23**, 103, 104, 120; **3:24**, 103, 104, 119; **3:24–25**, 115, 120; **3:24–30**, 115–17; **3:24–45** LXX, 120; **3:25**, 37, 42, 103, 104, 115, 208; **3:26**, 35, 104, 116, 120, 170; **3:27**, 104, 116, 171; **3:28**, 35, 37, 104, 115, 116, 128, 208; **3:28–29**, 37, 41; **3:28–30**, 123; **3:29**, 35, 36, 41, 104, 107, 117, 118, 157, 162, 172; **3:30**, 104, 117, 124, 163; **3:31**, 86, 104; **3:31–33**, 124; **3:32**, 120; **3:46–50** LXX, 120; **3:47–48** LXX, 115; **3:51–90** LXX, 120; **4**, 8, 249; **4:1**, 23, 107, 118, 123, 132; **4:1–3**, 121, 122–25, 139, 140–41, 143; **4:2**, 23, 35, 120, 140, 141, 194; **4:2–3**, 41, 123; **4:3**, 23, 84, 118, 122, 123, 124, 125, 157, 173; **4:3–4**, 310; **4:4**, 137, 141; **4:4–9**, 125–27; **4:4–18**, 178; **4:4–19**, 121; **4:5**, 133, 141–42, 148, 183, 190,

254; **4:6**, 100, 118, 125, 142, 157; **4:6–7**, 126; **4:7**, 98, 125, 141, 142; **4:7–9**, 36; **4:8**, 11, 63, 68, 77, 125, 126, 141–42, 163; **4:9**, 17, 63, 68, 77, 84, 97, 98, 100, 124, 126, 127, 142, 149, 163; **4:9–12**, 134; **4:10**, 100, 127, 142; **4:10–12**, 90, 122; **4:10–18**, 127–33; **4:11**, 125; **4:12**, 127, 134, 142; **4:13**, 127, 128, 191; **4:14**, 120, 128; **4:14–17**, 122; **4:15**, 129, 130, 135, 142; **4:16**, 130, 131, 138, 142–43, 183; **4:17**, 35, 37, 38, 39, 120, 122, 124, 127, 128, 129, 132, 134, 139, 140, 141, 143–44, 183, 184, 191, 213, 263; **4:18**, 64, 68, 77, 100, 126, 163; **4:19**, 125, 133, 134, 148, 150, 214, 215, 254; **4:19–27**, 121, 133–37; **4:19–33**, 133; **4:20**, 125; **4:20–21**, 134; **4:20–22**, 90; **4:21**, 120, 134; **4:22**, 120, 125, 130, 134; **4:23**, 127, 128, 131, 138, 142, 144; **4:24**, 35, 120, 134, 135, 140, 141, 144, 263; **4:25**, 35, 37, 39, 89, 120, 122, 124, 129, 130, 131, 132, 135, 138, 139, 140, 141, 142, 144, 183, 184, 213; **4:26**, 35, 99, 135; **4:27**, 135, 136, 140, 143, 144, 150; **4:28**, 137; **4:28–30**, 39; **4:28–33**, 121, 133, 137–38; **4:29**, 137; **4:30**, 47, 125, 137, 139; **4:30a**, 143; **4:31**, 120, 138, 144; **4:31–32**, 47; **4:32**, 35, 37, 39, 89, 120, 122, 124, 129, 130, 131, 135, 138, 139, 140, 141, 184, 213; **4:32–33**, 130, 142; **4:33**, 124, 131, 135, 138; **4:34**, 35, 39, 122, 124, 131, 132, 138, 139, 140, 141, 173, 183, 286; **4:34–35**, 39, 41, 84, 123, 140; **4:34–37**, 121, 138–40, 143, 172, 178, 260; **4:34b–35**, 122; **4:35**, 85, 124, 138, 139, 200, 213, 272, 286; **4:36**, 139, 140; **4:36–37**, 140; **4:37**, 35, 39, 40, 41, 84, 85, 99, 123, 129, 144; **4:37b**, 122; **5:1**, 7, 146, 157; **5:1–4**, 282; **5:1–7**, 145–48; **5:2**, 7, 118, 143, 146, 157; **5:2–3**, 149; **5:2–4**, 47; **5:3**, 7, 157; **5:4**, 28, 147; **5:5**, 47, 147, 148, 157, 282; **5:6**, 125, 133, 157–58, 254; **5:7**, 98, 148, 158, 163; **5:7–8**, 149; **5:8**, 148; **5:8–9**, 254; **5:8–16**, 148–49; **5:9**, 118, 125, 133, 149; **5:10**, 149, 170; **5:10–16**, 215; **5:11**, 7, 11, 68, 77, 98, 142, 143, 148, 149, 158, 163; **5:11–12**, 17, 158; **5:12**, 98, 149, 157, 158, 163, 247; **5:13**, 7, 143; **5:14**, 68, 77, 142, 149; **5:15**, 98, 149; **5:16**, 98, 149, 158, 163; **5:17**, 64, 150; **5:17–23**, 150; **5:17–29**, 150–55; **5:18**, 35, 38, 120, 143, 150, 151, 184; **5:18–21**, 143, 145; **5:18–24**, 122; **5:18–31**, 7; **5:19**, 107, 151; **5:20**, 47; **5:20–21**, 15, 129; **5:20–23**, 39; **5:21**, 35, 37, 47, 89, 111, 142, 151, 184; **5:22**, 47, 129, 150, 151; **5:22–30**, 282; **5:23**, 35, 47, 99, 151; **5:24**, 47, 147, 152; **5:25**, 152, 158–59; **5:25–28**, 28, 153; **5:26**, 35, 39, 152, 153; **5:27**, 154; **5:28**, 23, 92, 153, 154, 199; **5:29**, 54, 77, 124, 155, 163; **5:30**, 28, 39, 61, 146, 155, 157; **5:30–31**, 7, 8, 68, 155–56; **5:30–6:1**, 223; **5:31**, 8, 23, 37, 92, 154, 156, 159–60, 162, 223; **6**, 37, 264, 285; **6:1**, 8, 15, 156, 162, 175, 223; **6:1–2**, 176; **6:1–9**, 162–67; **6:2**, 148, 157, 163, 175; **6:2–3**, 176; **6:3**, 157, 163, 175, 176; **6:4**, 164, 173, 175, 176; **6:4–9**, 37; **6:5**, 164, 173, 175, 176; **6:6**, 170, 175–76; **6:6–7**, 168; **6:7**, 28, 106, 118, 174, 175, 176; **6:8**, 23, 92, 118, 164, 173, 175, 176, 199; **6:9**, 118, 175; **6:10**, 35, 118, 167, 168, 220, 225; **6:10–17**, 167–69; **6:11**, 118, 168, 174, 175; **6:12**, 23, 92, 106, 118, 164, 168, 173, 174, 175, 176, 199; **6:12–13**, 37; **6:13**, 104, 118, 157, 168, 174, 175, 176; **6:14**, 157, 168, 169, 174; **6:14–15**, 167, 174; **6:15**, 23, 92, 118, 164, 173, 175, 199; **6:16**, 35, 118, 161, 169, 174, 175; **6:17**, 166, 176; **6:18**, 169, 176; **6:18–20**, 169; **6:18–24**, 169–72; **6:19**, 169, 176; **6:20**, 35, 37, 169, 170, 174, 176; **6:21**, 170; **6:22**, 35, 42, 104, 170, 174; **6:23**, 165, 170, 171, 174, 176; **6:24**, 13, 103, 115, 162, 171, 176–77, 195; **6:25**, 23, 107, 118, 123, 172; **6:25–27**, 121; **6:25–28**, 172–75; **6:26**, 23, 35, 37, 41, 118, 123, 124, 139, 157, 162, 169, 172, 173, 177; **6:26–27**, 35, 41, 84, 124; **6:27**, 23, 35, 37, 85, 111, 118, 123, 141, 157, 173, 174, 177; **6:28**, 8, 37, 92, 117, 124, 159, 173; 7, 9, 39, 220, 231, 246, 249, 263, 264, 284; **7–12**, 1, 11,

12, 13–13, 17, 20, 24, 173, 178, 179, 190, 232, 285; **7:1,** 8, 11, 146, 157, 180, 194, 195, 265; **7:1–8,** 131, 180–86; **7:2,** 100, 180, 181, 194; **7:2–7,** 14, 179; **7:3,** 43, 181; **7:3–7,** 9, 181; **7:4,** 183, 189, 194–95; **7:4–6,** 43, 182; **7:5,** 189, 195; **7:6,** 183, 189, 195, 200, 270; **7:7,** 15, 31, 47, 182, 184, 201; **7:7d–8,** 184, 196; **7:8,** 24, 27, 34, 37, 40, 43, 47, 91, 131, 184, 185, 195–96, 197, 200, 216, 269, 279, 286; **7:9,** 47, 187; **7:9–10,** 18, 43, 48, 187; **7:9–11,** 293; **7:9–14,** 15, 187–90; **7:10,** 47, 48, 187, 263; **7:10–11,** 293; **7:11,** 40, 43, 47, 91, 188, 269, 279; **7:11a,** 184, 196; **7:12,** 84, 99, 188; **7:13,** 15, 31, 32, 39, 44, 45, 131, 188, 189, 190, 191, 196, 208, 209, 251, 252, 260, 304; **7:13–14,** 16, 43, 181; **7:14,** 31, 39, 94, 107, 118, 188, 189, 190, 191; **7:15,** 125, 133, 190; **7:15–16,** 42, 197, 230, 232; **7:15–18,** 190–91, 192; **7:16,** 14, 128, 190; **7:17,** 190, 196; **7:18,** 35, 39, 94, 120, 128, 132, 180, 191, 192; **7:19,** 192, 195; **7:19–27,** 192–93; **7:20,** 34, 43, 47, 192, 197, 200, 279; **7:20–22,** 91, 184, 196; **7:20–24,** 37; **7:20–26,** 269; **7:20b,** 27; **7:20b–22,** 24, 27; **7:21,** 9, 12, 27, 34, 37, 43, 114, 179, 191, 197, 231, 285; **7:21–22,** 192; **7:22,** 35, 37, 39, 47, 90, 94, 120, 132, 293; **7:23,** 192, 195, 232; **7:24,** 47, 184, 185, 192; **7:24–25,** 91, 184, 196; **7:24–26,** 37; **7:24b–25,** 24, 27; **7:25,** 9, 14, 29, 34, 35, 37, 40, 43, 48, 84, 90, 99, 111, 114, 120, 132, 179, 192, 197, 198, 218, 239, 279, 285, 286, 311, 314; **7:26,** 43, 47, 192, 293; **7:26–27,** 140; **7:27,** 9, 29, 31, 35, 37, 38, 39, 43, 48, 90, 94, 120, 124, 132, 139, 188, 192; **7:28,** 20, 35, 41, 148, 190, 193–94, 197, 214, 254, 266; **8,** 9, 220, 221, 231, 242–43, 246, 264, 269, 309, 310, 314; **8:1,** 146, 157, 195, 197, 198, 231, 265; **8:1–2,** 198–99; **8:1–4,** 4; **8:1–7,** 15; **8:2,** 198, 199, 215, 251, 309, 310; **8:3,** 92, 197, 199, 212, 215–16, 251; **8:3–7,** 92; **8:3–12,** 199–206; **8:4,** 111, 197, 199, 200, 216, 272, 276, 286; **8:5,** 197, 200, 212, 215–16, 219, 255; **8:5–7,** 4; **8:5–8,** 1, 27, 37; **8:6,** 201; **8:7,** 91, 111, 199, 201; **8:8,** 5, 15, 91, 181, 200, 201, 202, 216, 272; **8:9,** 197, 202, 216–17, 276; **8:9–11,** 114, 152; **8:9–12,** 43, 47, 91; **8:9–13,** 27; **8:10,** 201, 202, 203, 206, 217, 218, 231, 256; **8:10–11,** 197, 201, 298; **8:10–12,** 12, 34, 37, 191, 279; **8:10–13,** 202, 285; **8:10–14,** 179; **8:11,** 34, 131, 197, 204, 205, 206, 211, 217, 218, 256, 283, 286; **8:11–12,** 197, 206; **8:12,** 203, 205, 206, 217–18, 234; **8:12a,** 205; **8:12b,** 206; **8:13,** 16, 43, 105, 205, 206, 207, 209, 218, 219, 229, 234, 239, 246, 283, 287, 309, 310; **8:13–14,** 48, 206–8; **8:14,** 17, 29, 43, 49, 192, 198, 239, 246, 309, 311, 314, 315; **8:15,** 44, 189, 208, 219, 243, 260, 268; **8:15–16,** 197, 251; **8:15–17,** 42; **8:15–18,** 252; **8:15–19,** 14, 208, 232; **8:15–26,** 208–14; **8:16,** 42, 190, 197, 208, 209, 231, 243, 256; **8:17,** 14, 44, 96, 125, 133, 188, 198, 209, 210, 243, 260, 267, 285, 303, 313; **8:18,** 210, 231, 242, 253–54, 261, 309; **8:19,** 198, 210, 211, 212, 219, 260, 267, 285, 307; **8:19–26,** 309; **8:20,** 4, 198, 199, 208, 212; **8:21,** 27, 37, 212, 216, 219; **8:22,** 5, 212, 213, 272; **8:23,** 43, 212, 234; **8:23–24,** 279; **8:24,** 34, 43, 213, 310; **8:24–25a,** 203; **8:24–25,** 47, 114, 179; **8:25,** 15, 28, 34, 37, 40, 88, 131, 197, 204, 210, 212, 213, 214, 256, 279, 292; **8:25b,** 203; **8:26,** 95, 214, 248, 260, 298, 309; **8:27,** 133, 190, 197, 214–15, 220, 254, 266, 309; **8:45,** 285; **9,** 9, 225, 230, 234, 236, 238, 243, 244, 246, 255–56, 264, 266; **9:1,** 4, 8, 15, 37, 61, 195, 241, 264, 265; **9:1–2,** 222, 223–25; **9:1–20,** 33; **9:2,** 35, 220, 221; **9:3,** 225, 230, 242, 255; **9:3–4,** 221, 260; **9:3–14,** 225–28; **9:3–19,** 222; **9:3–21,** 221; **9:4,** 35, 220, 226, 230, 242; **9:4–19,** 53, 56; **9:4b–8,** 242; **9:4b–19,** 220, 221, 242; **9:5,** 226; **9:6,** 226, 227; **9:7,** 227, 242; **9:7–14,** 221; **9:8,** 35, 220, 226, 227, 242; **9:9,** 35, 227; **9:9–10,** 242; **9:10,** 22, 35, 220, 242; **9:11,** 43, 227, 242, 247; **9:12,** 43, 227, 242; **9:13,** 26, 35, 220,

226, 242; **9:13–15,** 242; **9:14,** 35, 220, 227, 228, 242; **9:15,** 35; **9:15–19,** 228–30; **9:16,** 242; **9:17,** 35, 229, 242; **9:18,** 242; **9:19,** 230, 242; **9:20,** 35, 225, 230, 242, 249, 255–56; **9:20–21,** 220, 221, 260; **9:20–23,** 252, 255; **9:20–27,** 222, 230–41, 269; **9:21,** 42, 128, 189, 190, 209, 210, 220, 230, 231, 242–43, 256, 260, 264; **9:21–22,** 14, 42; **9:21a,** 230; **9:22,** 26, 220, 228, 232, 243; **9:23,** 235, 236, 241–42, 243, 248, 249, 254, 255, 256, 261; **9:24,** 9, 14, 206, 234, 243–44; **9:24–27,** 32, 222; **9:25,** 9, 26, 32, 49, 70, 160, 228, 235, 236, 237, 238, 242, 243, 244, 269; **9:25–26,** 9, 32, 237; **9:26,** 6, 31, 32, 160, 204, 208, 210, 219, 229, 236, 237–38, 240, 244, 245, 275, 280, 307; **9:26–27,** 179, 285; **9:27,** 7, 9, 16, 29, 43, 47, 48, 105, 192, 205, 229, 239, 240, 242, 245, 280, 283, 287, 307, 311, 314; **10,** 231, 242–43, 246, 252–53, 266, 311; 264; **10–12,** 220, 221, 253, 264–65, 309; **10:1,** 11, 37, 59, 63, 159, 173, 195, 214, 246–49, 247–48, 249, 253, 265, 270, 309, 311, 312; **10:1–11:1,** 246; **10:1–11:2a,** 246–68, 309; **10:1–12:4,** 221; **10:2,** 255, 309; **10:2–3,** 225; **10:2–9,** 249–54; **10:2–12:4,** 309; **10:2b–12:3,** 298; **10:3,** 66, 249, 250, 254, 266; **10:4,** 250, 251, 265, 309; **10:4–6,** 309, 310; **10:4–11,** 14, 255; **10:4–20,** 232; **10:5,** 42, 189, 251, 254, 260, 265, 310; **10:5–6,** 252, 260, 266; **10:5–8,** 248; **10:6,** 251, 252, 254; **10:7,** 248, 249, 253; **10:7–11:1,** 266; **10:8,** 133, 248, 249, 253, 261, 266; **10:8–10,** 125; **10:9,** 96, 209, 210, 231, 253, 260, 309; **10:9–10,** 231; **10:10,** 42, 210, 242, 252, 254, 261, 266, 267; **10:10–11,** 309; **10:10–12,** 254–54; **10:11,** 243, 249, 254, 255, 261, 266; 260; **10:12,** 35, 225, 243, 249, 256, 259, 260, 261, 262; 255; **10:12–13,** 191, 231; **10:13,** 37, 42, 128, 139, 204, 209, 248, 252, 256, 257–59, 266, 293; **10:13–14,** 42; **10:14,** 86, 100, 211, 219, 243, 248–49, 253, 262, 267, 285; **10:14–15,** 258, 259–61, 260; **10:15,** 260, 309; **10:15–16,** 231; **10:16,** 42, 189, 208, 210, 243, 252, 260, 261, 267, 268, 309; **10:16–17,** 190; **10:16–19,** 261–62; **10:17,** 261, 267–68; **10:18,** 42, 208, 210, 231, 242, 260, 261, 268, 309; **10:19,** 249, 254, 255, 261, 262, 268; **10:20,** 27, 92, 159, 191, 195, 262, 264; **10:20–11:2a,** 262–65; **10:20–21,** 42, 139, 248, 257, 293; **10:21,** 42, 187, 204, 209, 248, 256, 262, 264, 268, 294; **10:21a,** 262; **10:21b,** 268; **11,** 5, 9, 248, 259, 262–63, 269, 273, 285, 288, 290, 292, 312; 249; **11–12,** 259–60, 301; **11:1,** 8, 264, 265, 268; **11:1–39,** 11, 14; **11:1a,** 264; **11:2,** 7, 15, 214, 249; **11:2–3,** 15, 269; **11:2–12:3,** 310; **11:2–12:4,** 246, 253; **11:2–39,** 288, 301, 309; **11:2a,** 262; **11:2b,** 270, 271, 302; **11:2b–12:4,** 269–308, 298, 309; **11:3,** 270, 271, 272, 276, 297; **11:3–4,** 271–72, 302; **11:4,** 15, 181, 272; **11:4–20,** 269; **11:5,** 273, 302, 303; **11:5–9,** 273–75; **11:5–20,** 16; **11:6,** 5, 91, 94, 210, 219, 253, 261, 273, 274, 302–3, 304, 314; **11:7,** 274, 305; **11:8,** 270, 274, 303; **11:9,** 274–75, 303; **11:10,** 275; **11:10–19,** 275–78; **11:11,** 111, 201, 202, 275; **11:12,** 275, 307; **11:13,** 200, 202, 210, 219, 275, 303, 314; **11:14,** 275, 276; **11:15,** 276, 305; **11:15–16,** 200; **11:16,** 111, 199, 201, 202, 272, 276, 286, 291; **11:17,** 91, 94, 277, 304; **11:18,** 277, 305; **11:19,** 277–78; **11:20,** 278, 305; **11:21,** 212, 278, 279, 288, 305; **11:21–24,** 278–81; **11:21–39,** 9, 16; **11:21–45,** 269; **11:22,** 6, 238, 275, 279, 305; **11:23,** 280, 306; **11:24,** 280, 281, 293, 306; **11:25–28,** 281–82; **11:26,** 62, 74, 275, 281, 306; **11:27,** 210, 211, 219, 267, 281, 285, 289, 293, 313, 314; **11:28,** 281–82; **11:29,** 211, 267; **11:29–30a,** 6; **11:29–35,** 282–85; **11:29–37,** 91; **11:30,** 219, 264, 282, 291, 306; **11:30–39,** 179; **11:30b–31,** 6; **11:31,** 7, 16, 43, 105, 205, 229, 239, 245, 282, 283, 287, 305; **11:32,** 283, 306, 313; **11:32–35,** 264; **11:33,** 26, 37, 41, 53, 68, 114, 227, 243, 283, 284, 297, 306–7; **11:33–34,** 276; **11:33–35,** 222, 298, 312, 315; **11:34,**

Scripture Index

15, 16, 88, 214, 276, 284; **11:35**, 14, 26, 53, 74, 210, 211, 219, 227, 243, 267, 281, 283, 285, 289, 293, 297, 303, 312, 313, 314; **11:36**, 36, 40, 43, 131, 152, 184, 200, 204, 210, 211, 272, 276, 286, 288, 289, 293, 307, 310; **11:36–37**, 298; **11:36–39**, 286–88; **11:37**, 131, 287; **11:37–39**, 40; **11:38**, 287, 305; **11:39**, 16, 287, 288, 307; **11:40**, 14, 210, 219, 275, 285, 289, 290, 293, 303, 314; **11:40–45**, 9, 10, 11, 16, 285, 288–92; **11:41**, 111, 202, 276, 290, 291, 307; **11:42**, 290, 303; **11:43**, 290, 303; **11:44**, 290, 291; **11:45**, 9, 202, 210, 213, 219, 240, 245, 289, 291, 293, 308, 314, 315; **12**, 252, 263, 310, 311, 312; **12:1**, 34, 37, 42, 43, 47, 48, 187, 193, 209, 248, 256, 263, 292, 293; **12:1–2**, 15, 315; **12:1–3**, 47, 264, 285, 292–98, 314; **12:1–4**, 9, 44, 259, 269–70, 292; **12:2**, 34, 43, 46, 47, 48, 68, 210, 263, 264, 294, 295, 296, 297; **12:3**, 26, 41, 53, 68, 74, 227, 243, 283, 284, 309; **12:4**, 14, 16, 210, 212, 219, 260, 267, 298–301, 300, 301, 303, 308, 309, 312, 314; **12:5**, 310, 314; **12:5–6**, 252–53; **12:5–7**, 251, 309–11; **12:5–13**, 14, 246, 284, 309–15; **12:6**, 49, 207, 210, 219, 246, 309, 310, 314; **12:7**, 14, 29, 35, 192, 214, 238, 309, 310, 311, 312, 314–15; **12:8**, 215; **12:8–9**, 42; **12:8–10**, 311–13; **12:9**, 210, 214, 219, 298, 303, 312, 314; **12:10**, 26, 53, 227, 243, 246, 283, 285, 297, 312, 313, 315; **12:11**, 7, 16, 17, 29, 43, 48, 205, 229, 238, 239, 245, 283, 287, 309, 311, 313, 314; **12:11–12**, 313, 315; **12:11–13**, 246, 313–14; **12:11–19**, 192; **12:12**, 17, 29, 49, 239, 309, 311, 313, 314; **12:13**, 14, 17, 29, 47, 49, 210, 219, 259, 314

Hosea **1:1**, 19; **1:10**, 169; **3:5**, 100, 219, 267; **6:1–2**, 294; **11:7**, 120; **13:7–8**, 182; **13:9**, 209; **14:4–7**, 209; **14:8**, 141

Joel, 13; **2:32**, 263; 3, 291; **3:1–2**, 293

Amos **7:1**, 100; **7:4**, 100, 181; **7:7**, 100; **8:1**, 100; **8:1–2**, 209, 219; **8:2**, 154; **8:11–12**, 300; **9:11–15**, 209

Jonah **1:5–6**, 210; **3:4**, 136; **3:6–9**, 225; **5:1–3**, 136

Micah **3:5**, 150; **4:1**, 100, 219, 267; **4:1–2**, 88, 95

Nahum **1:5**, 219

Habakkuk **1:2**, 207; **1:6**, 211; **1:6–11**, 219; **1:8**, 200; **2:2**, 180; **2:3**, 212, 219, 260, 267, 285, 313; **2:4**, 211; **2:6–19**, 211; **3:12**, 219

Zephaniah **1:12**, 293; **2:10**, 200; **3:19–20**, 293

Haggai **2:12**, 243

Zechariah 1–7, 190; **1:7–17**, 207; **1:8**, 100; **1:12**, 207, 211, 219; **1:12–17**, 224; **1:14–17**, 211; **2:6**, 181; **2:11**, 173; **3:1–5**, 293; **4:3**, 237; **4:7**, 88; **4:11–14**, 237; 5, 57; **5:11**, 72; **6:5**, 181; **7:14**, 202; **8:20–23**, 173; **8:23**, 96; **9–14**, 13; **9:10**, 250; **11:16**, 144; **12:3–4**, 293; **13:1–2**, 293; **14:2**, 291; **14:3–9**, 291; **14:10**, 88; **14:16–19**, 173

Malachi **1:4**, 219; **1:7**, 64, 75; **3:5**, 79; **3:12**, 202; **3:16**, 187; **3:16–18**, 293

New Testament

Matthew **2:13–15**, 170; **3:1–2**, 39; **3:2**, 31; **3:10**, 128; **3:27**, 144; **4:8–9**, 239; **4:17**, 39, 241; **5:20**, 135; **5:44–45**, 172; **6:1**, 135; **6:2–4**, 135; **6:5–6**, 168; **6:10**, 50, 193, 241; **6:16–18**, 250; **6:17**, 174; **6:28–30**, 70; **6:33**, 71; **8:20**, 44, 193; **9:6**, 44, 193; **9:14–15**, 250; **9:27–30**, 254; **10:7**, 241; **10:28**, 116, 169; **10:32–33**, 117; **11:11–12**, 241; **11:19**, 44, 193; **12:28**, 42, 241; **12:42**, 69; **13:31–32**, 129; **15:18–20**, 71; **16:13**, 276; **17:5**, 144; **17:6**, 209; **17:6–7**, 254, 255; **19:28**, 45, 47, 187, 193; **21:42**, 95; **21:44**, 95; **23:12**, 40, 144; **23:15**,

41; 24:1–2, 31; 24:3, 49; 24:3–31, 31; 24:4–21, 49; 24:5, 43; 24:9, 43; 24:15, 19, 43, 283; 24:15–16, 31, 239; 24:21, 43; 24:21–31, 293; 24:27, 45, 193; 24:30, 45, 133, 193; 24:31, 181; 24:36, 49, 263, 285; 25, 46; 25:21–46, 136; 25:31, 48; 25:31–46, 48; 25:32–33, 48; 25:34–36, 48; 25:41–43, 48; 25:46, 48, 172; 26:3–5, 174; 26:14–16, 174; 26:26–29, 226; 26:36–55, 174; 26:64, 45, 193; 27:18–24, 174; 27:60, 174; 27:66, 174; 28:3, 187; 28:4, 209; 28:5, 255; 28:18–20, 41

Mark 1:14–15, 31, 39, 42; 2:10–11, 31; 4:30–32, 129; 5:7, 120; 7:6, 242; 8:23, 254; 8:27, 276; 8:31, 31; 8:38, 31; 9:3, 187; 9:9, 31; 9:13, 242; 10:21, 135; 12:10–11, 95; 13:7, 238; 13:14, 239, 283; 13:19–27, 293; 13:22, 43, 141; 13:27, 181; 14:21, 242; 14:61–62, 31; 16:15, 41

Luke 1:11–20, 232; 1:13, 255; 1:19, 42, 209, 257; 1:20, 260; 1:26, 42, 209, 257; 1:26–38, 232; 1:30, 255; 1:32, 120; 1:51–53, 144; 2:10, 255; 2:46–47, 69; 3:22, 144; 4:40, 254; 4:43, 39; 6:27–28, 172; 6:35, 120; 6:35–36, 172; 8:28, 120; 10:5, 123; 10:9, 241; 10:18, 204; 10:20, 263; 11:20, 31, 148, 241; 12:19, 137; 12:20–21, 137; 13:18–19, 129; 14:11, 40, 144; 16:16, 241; 17:12–19, 84; 17:20–21, 241; 18:1–8, 171, 256; 18:9–14, 230; 18:14, 40; 20:17, 95; 20:18, 31, 95; 21:20–28, 293; 21:24, 218; 21:28, 42; 22:19–20, 226; 22:30, 47

John 1:3, 252; 2:7, 44; 3:13, 45; 3:34, 266; 4:34, 266; 4:48, 141; 5:23, 266; 5:24, 266; 5:28–29, 46, 48, 296; 5:30, 266; 5:36–38, 266; 6:16, 263; 6:18, 263; 6:44, 263; 6:62, 45; 6:64, 263; 7:21, 72; 11, 296; 12:28, 144; 12:28–29, 253; 13:34–35, 226; 14:15, 226; 14:21, 226; 14:23, 226; 15:10, 226; 15:12–14, 226; 15:17, 226; 19:10, 89

Acts 1:6–7, 49; 1:7, 84; 1:8, 41; 2:38, 226; 3:19, 226; 4:18–20, 171; 4:30, 141; 5:5, 156; 5:12, 141; 5:19–20, 171; 5:29, 164; 5:31, 226; 5:40–41, 171; 6:6, 165; 6:7, 165; 6:11, 165; 6:15, 165; 7:22, 97; 7:48, 120; 9:7, 253; 9:36, 135; 10:2, 135; 11:5–9, 71; 11:9, 144; 12:1–10, 171; 13:2, 250; 13:16, 41; 13:26, 41; 14:8–12, 96; 14:13, 96; 14:18, 96; 14:23, 250; 15:29, 64; 16:19–26, 171; 17:30, 226; 17:30–31, 48; 17:31, 171; 20:21, 226; 21:25, 64; 22:9, 253; 24:15, 46, 296; 27:24, 255; 28:28, 254

Romans 5:8–9, 226; 8:35–39, 259; 9:15–24, 263; 9:33, 95; 10:13, 263; 12:17–21, 172; 13:1–5, 89, 151, 172; 14:17, 71; 15:4, 224; 15:19, 141

1 Corinthians 1:1–13, 123; 1:18–2:16, 155; 1:26, 71, 155; 1:26–32, 144; 1:27–28, 71; 2:7–16, 71; 3:12–15, 48; 8, 65; 8–10, 64; 10:4, 95; 15:22–26, 42, 45, 193; 15:24–26, 241; 16:22, 193, 241

2 Corinthians 1:8–11, 83; 4:4, 239; 5:10, 48, 171; 6:14–7:1, 71; 7:9–10, 226; 11:23–29, 171; 12:12, 141

Galatians 4:4–5, 31

Ephesians 2:8–9, 136; 2:10, 136; 5:12, 42; 5:16, 99; 6:10–18, 258; 6:12, 139, 258; 6:18, 230

Philippians 2:8–9, 133; 2:9–11, 42; 4:3, 263, 294; 4:19, 83

Colossians 2:20–23, 71

1 Thessalonians 2:16, 213; 4:14–17, 45, 193; 5:1, 84

2 Thessalonians 2:3–4, 32, 43; 2:3–10, 43; 2:4, 43, 239, 286

1 Timothy 2:1–4, 230; 2:9–10, 71; 6:15, 89; 6:18, 136

2 Timothy 2:12, 42; 3:14–17, 224

Hebrews **2:4**, 141; **7:1**, 120; **13:5**, 117

James **1:9–10**, 144; **4:7**, 258; **4:10**, 40

1 Peter **1:1–2**, 123; **2:6**, 95; **2:7**, 95; **2:8**, 95; **5:6**, 40, 144; **5:8**, 166; **5:8–9**, 258

2 Peter **1:1–2**, 123; **3:9**, 226; **3:10**, 95

1 John **1:9**, 226; **2:22**, 44; **2:15–16**, 116; **2:16**, 71; **2:18**, 44, 288; **2:22**, 288; **4:3**, 44, 288; **4:4**, 258

2 John **7**, 288

Jude **9**, 209, 257, 293

Revelation **1:7**, 42, 45, 133, 193; **1:11**, 180; **1:13**, 45, 193, 251; **1:13–15**, 252; **1:17**, 125, 133, 209, 210, 254, 255, 261; **1:19**, 180; **3:5**, 263, 294; **3:18**, 285; **4:4**, 187; **5:1**, 299; **5:4–5**, 299; **5:10**, 42; **6:10**, 171; **6:16–17**, 42; **7:1**, 181; **7:14**, 293; **9:14**, 250; **10:4**, 144, 299; **10:5–6**, 310; **10:8**, 144; **11:12**, 144; **11:15**, 132; **12:4**, 204, 298; **12:6**, 192; **12:7**, 42, 209, 257, 258, 293; **12:7–8**, 204; **12:8–9**, 42, 258; **12:14**, 14, 192; **13:1**, 43, 182; **13:2**, 43; **13:5**, 43, 192; **13:5–6**, 43; **13:7**, 43; **13:8**, 263, 294; **13:12–15**, 43; **13:17**, 43; **13:18**, 14; **14:13**, 144, 180; **14:14**, 45, 193; **15:2**, 182; **15:6**, 251; **16:1**, 227; **16:12**, 250; **17:8**, 182, 263, 294; **17:14**, 89; **19:8**, 251; **19:9**, 180, 214; **19:14**, 251; **19:16**, 89; **20:4**, 48; **20:6**, 42; **20:7–9**, 291; **20:10**, 42; **20:11–15**, 48, 156, 171, 172; **20:11–23**, 48; **20:12**, 48, 263, 294; **20:12–15**, 46; **20:15**, 48, 263, 294; **21:1**, 182, 209; **21:4**, 95; **21:5**, 180, 214; **21:27**, 263; **22:6**, 214; **22:8–9**, 96; **22:10**, 299

APOCRYPHA OR SEPTUAGINT

Baruch **2:11**, 228

Add. Daniel, Prayer of Azariah **24–25**, 115; **1–22**, 120; **23–27**, 120

Add. Daniel, Song of the Three Young Men **28–68**, 120

Add. Daniel, Story of Susanna **62**, 115

2 Esdras **4:1**, 256; **4:36**, 256; **5:13**, 249; **5:20**, 250, 256; **5:22–31**, 250; **6:35–59**, 250; **7:1–44**, 250; **10:28**, 256; **14:37–48**, 180

Judith **1:6**, 99; **3:8**, 106; **5:8**, 99; **6:19**, 99; **11:17**, 99; **12:1–2**, 65

1 Maccabees **1:3**, 200; **1:10**, 279; **1:11–13**, 239; **1:11–15**, 185, 210; **1:15**, 6; **1:16–17**, 281; **1:18**, 281; **1:19**, 281; **1:20–23**, 185; **1:20–24**, 205; **1:20–35**, 238; **1:21–23**, 28, 282; **1:21–24**, 147; **1:24**, 184, 282; **1:29**, 213; **1:29–35**, 7; **1:30**, 213; **1:34**, 287; **1:39**, 205, 250; **1:41–50**, 192; **1:41–52**, 296; **1:41–61**, 7; **1:41–64**, 65; **1:43**, 210; **1:44**, 284; **1:44–46**, 250; **1:45**, 205; **1:45–48**, 283; **1:47**, 205; **1:52**, 283; **1:52–53**, 210; **1:54**, 7, 16, 105, 208, 239, 283, 313; **1:54–61**, 185; **1:56**, 206; **1:57**, 105, 116; **1:59**, 7, 205, 283; **1:60–63**, 105, 116; **1:60–64**, 296; **1:62–63**, 65, 283; **1:64**, 210; **2:17b–18**, 283; **2:20**, 283; **2:23–26**, 283; **2:42–44**, 284; **2:60**, 170; **3:5–8**, 284; **3:30**, 280; **3:45**, 205, 218; **3:51**, 218; **4:38**, 205; **4:47–48**, 205; **4:52**, 208; **4:52–53**, 208; **4:52–54**, 313; **4:60**, 218; **6:1–16**, 213; **6:8**, 292; **6:8–16**, 203, 240; **6:12–13**, 214; **6:18–21**, 287; **6:18–31**, 7; **7:13**, 284; **10:20**, 148; **10:62**, 148; **10:64**, 148; **14:36–37**, 288; **15:43–44**, 148

2 Maccabees **1:16**, 292; **3**, 278; **3:4**, 278; **4:7**, 63; **4:7–10**, 185, 238; **4:12**, 6; **4:23–34**, 238; **4:23–38**, 208; **4:24**, 238; **4:30–34**, 6; **4:32**, 238; **4:33–35**, 204; **4:34**, 238; **5:2–4**, 258; **5:5–11**, 282; **5:5–16**, 6; **5:11–21**, 238; **5:23–26**, 7; **6:1–5**, 147; **6:2**, 7, 16, 205, 283, 287; **6:4**, 287; **6:4–5**, 7, 205; **6:5**, 239, 283; **6:7**, 65; **6:8–11**, 116; **6:9**, 292; **6:9–11**, 105, 116; **6:14**, 213; **6:18**, 105; **6:18–31**, 116; **6:31**, 105; **7:1–42**, 105, 116; **7:3**, 110; **7:9–23**,

295; **9:1–29**, 292; **9:5**, 214; **9:5–28**, 203, 240; **9:5–29**, 213; **9:8**, 204; **9:10**, 203; **9:11**, 131; **9:11–12**, 122; **9:12**, 131, 204; **9:13–17**, 97; **9:13–29**, 132; **12:43–45**, 295; **14:6**, 284

3 Maccabees **3:1**, 110; **5:1**, 110; **5:30**, 110

4 Maccabees **4:15**, 279

Sirach **3:29–4:10**, 135; **17:17**, 257

Tobit **10:11**, 99; **12:7–10**, 135

Widsom of Solomon **19:1–4**, 213

OLD TESTAMENT PSEUDEPIGRAPHA

Ascension of Isaiah **2:10–11**, 250

2 Baruch **5:7**, 250; **9:1–2**, 250; **12:5**, 250; **20:5–6**, 250; **21:1**, 250; **47:2**, 250

1 Enoch **2:11–13**, 293; **6:1–17**, 292; **9:1**, 256; **20:1–7**, 256; **40:8–10**, 256; **54:6**, 256; **56:6–8**, 291; **60:4**, 210; **71:3**, 256; **81:1–2**, 263; **81:6**, 180; **82:1**, 180; **93:2–3**, 263; **103:2–3**, 263; **106:19–107:1**, 263

4 Ezra **5:15**, 210; **12:1–13**, 30; **13:33–35**, 291

Jubilees **4:20**, 18

Sibylline Oracles **3:663–701**, 18

Testament of Reuben **1:9–10**, 250

DEAD SEA SCROLLS AND RELATED TEXTS

1QH **1.11–12**, 100; **11.9–10**, 100; **12.11–13**, 100; **13.13–14**, 100

1QM **3.8–9**, 100; **14.14**, 100

1QpHab *(Pesher Habakkuk)* **1–5**, 144; **7.1–5**, 100; **7.3**, 144; **7.8**, 100; **7.13–14**, 100; **8.14–9.7**, 144

4Q242, 8, 147

4Q243–245, 22

4Q245, 22

4Q246, 22, 101, 194, 215, 216

4Q552–553, 22

4QFlor (4Q174), 19

4QPrNab, 22, 85, 131, 141, 142–43

4QPseudo-Daniel, 22

1QS, **3.20–23**, 100; **9.18–19**, 100; **11.3–4**, 100

MISHNAH

ʿ*Abod. Zar.* **2.3**, 65; **4.8–12**, 65; **5.1–12**, 65

OTHER ANCIENT AND CLASSICAL WORKS

anon., *Bahman Yasht* 87

Diodorus Siculus, *Lib.* **2.29**, 74; **17.30**, 166

Eusebius, *Preparation for the Gospel* **9.41.6**, 137

Hammurabi, *Code of Hammurabi* **25**, 108; **110**, 108; **157**, 108

Herodotus, *Hist.* **1.95**, 91; **1.130**, 91; **1.183**, 87; **1.191**, 157; **3.31**, 166; **3.89**, 162

Hesiod, *Works and Days* **1.109–201**, 87

Josephus, *Ant.* **10.10.4§209**, 92; **10.210**, 29; **10.268–269**, 19; **10.269**, 198; **10.276**, 31; **11.8.5**, 96; **12.3.3**, 277; *Against Apion* **2.48**, 303; *J.W.* **6.310–314**, 31

Polybius, *Hist.* **26.10**, 280; **30.25–26**, 287; **31.9**, 292

Xenophon, *Cyropaedia* **7.5.24–30**, 155; **7.15**, 157

www.ingramcontent.com/pod-product-compliance
Lightning Source LLC
Chambersburg PA
CBHW060107170426
43198CB00010B/807